EXPLORING SECOND LANGUAGE CLASSROOM RESEARCH

A COMPREHENSIVE GUIDE

David Nunan
University of Hong Kong/Anaheim University

Kathleen M. Bailey
Monterey Institute of International Studies

HEINLE
CENGAGE Learning

Australia • Brazil • Japan • Korea • Mexico • Singapore • Spain • United Kingdom • United States

HEINLE
CENGAGE Learning™

Exploring Second Language Classroom Research: A Comprehensive Guide

David Nunan and Kathleen M. Bailey

Publisher: Sherrise Roehr

Acquisitions Editor: Tom Jefferies

Editorial Assistant: Cécile Bruso

Director, US Marketing: Jim McDonough

Product Marketing Manager: Katie Kelley

Academic Marketing Manager: Caitlin Driscoll

Content Project Manager: John Sarantakis

Print Buyer: Susan Carroll

Cover Designer: Lisa Mezikofsky/Dawn Elwell

Compositor: ICC Macmillan Inc.

For permission to use material from this text or product, submit all requests online at **www.cengage.com/permissions**
Further permissions questions can be emailed to **permissionrequest@cengage.com**

Library of Congress Control Number: 2008935117

ISBN-13: 978-1-4240-2705-7

ISBN-10: 1-4240-2705-5

Heinle
20 Channel Center Street
Boston, MA 02210
USA

Cengage Learning is a leading provider of customized learning solutions with office locations around the globe, including Singapore, the United Kingdom, Australia, Mexico, Brazil, and Japan. Locate your local office at **www.cengage.com/global**

Cengage Learning products are represented in Canada by Nelson Education, Ltd.

Visit Heinle online at **elt.heinle.com**

Visit our corporate website at **www.cengage.com**

Printed in the United States of America
2 3 4 5 6 7 18 17 16 15 14

*For my research students, who helped me refine my thinking
by trying out these ideas and activities.*
David Nunan

*For Rob McMillan,
Sarah Springer,
Will Radecki,
Marie-Lise Bouscaren,
Analisa Bouscaren Radecki,
Noel Isaiah Cortez Radecki Bouscaren,
and Fady—
thanks for being here these past few years.*
Kathi Bailey

CONTENTS

PREFACE

We wrote this book with the intention of providing an introduction to research in second and foreign language classrooms. It grew out of courses and workshops on classroom research that we have developed and taught for teachers' conferences and graduate programs in applied linguistics. We aim to provide an introduction to language classroom research that is accessible to readers who do not necessarily have specialist training in research methods.

The book has two overriding objectives. The first is to provide an overview of and introduction to language classroom research. To this end, we look at both substantive issues (that is, the topics and questions that have been investigated by classroom researchers) and methodological issues (the techniques and methods that researchers have employed for collecting data, interpreting the data, and presenting the results). The second objective is to help readers develop practical skills for carrying out original empirical investigations. Although the context of the book is the second language classroom, our intention has been to cover concepts and techniques that will be broadly applicable to a wide range of applied linguistics contexts.

Our intended readership includes language teachers, researchers, teachers-in-training, and language teacher educators. When we wrote the book, we had in mind a worldwide audience of language teaching professionals, including language teachers, teacher trainees, teacher educators, and those who run courses on classroom observation and research. We believe that it will be particularly well suited for candidates in teaching credential, master's degree, and Ph.D. programs for language teachers. To this end, the examples and studies reviewed were designed to appeal to teachers of many languages—not just English.

The structure of the book is transparent and will support people learning about the research process. There are four major thematically organized sections to the book. The first of these provides an overview of second language classroom research. The second deals with research design issues, looking at approaches to planning and implementing classroom research. In the third section, we examine a range of procedures for collecting data. In the final section, we focus on data analysis and interpretation issues, providing tools and perspectives for making sense of the data that have been collected.

Each section is preceded by an introduction that maps out the territory and sets goals for the readers. At the end of each chapter, you will find questions and tasks to help you solidify your understanding of the concepts covered. Throughout the book we have critiqued our own studies, to show that language classroom research seldom proceeds as smoothly as published accounts may make it seem.

After reading the book, you should be well positioned to carry out your own classroom-based investigations, regardless of the research tradition in which you choose to work. You will also be familiar with the findings of several key studies and be well prepared as critical consumers of others' publications in language classroom research. We hope that reading this book will positive and productive for you.

David Nunan and Kathi Bailey

ACKNOWLEDGMENTS

L ike most authors, we are grateful for the support of the many people who helped us launch this book.

At the Monterey Institute of International Studies in California, Kathi Bailey's work was supported by a professional development grant from Joseph and Sheila Mark, long-term supporters of higher education at MIIS.

At the University of Hong Kong, we were aided in our file management by Sanny Kwok, who never grew impatient with the flood of e-mail traffic.

We appreciate the meticulous word processing done by Ryan Damerow, Jaala Thibault, and Mica Tucci. We also benefited greatly from the Internet research, bibliographic skills, and computer prowess of Lawrence Lawson, our "digital detective" and editorial assistant.

At Cengage (formerly Heinle & Heinle), we appreciate the encouragement of Eunice Yeats, who got the project started; Tom Jefferies and Cécile Bruso, who saw it to fruition; and Ian Martin, who believed in it from its inception.

Finally, we acknowledge the valuable input of our research students, who have worked with us to refine these ideas over the years. They have asked questions, raised concerns, and pushed us to new levels of awareness as they conducted their own language classroom research. In particular, we appreciate the contributions of Julie Choi, Kevin Jepson, Elaine Martyn, Will Radecki, Sarah Springer, and John Thorpe, who allowed us to print excerpts from their original research projects. We hope that more teachers and graduate students like them will be motivated to undertake language classroom research as a result of reading this book.

PART I

SECOND LANGUAGE CLASSROOM RESEARCH
An Overview

The three chapters in this section provide an introduction to and overview of the field of second language classroom research. The first chapter takes a historical stance and provides definitions of key terms, considers the quantitative and qualitative traditions, and serves as an advance organizer for the book as a whole. The second chapter jumps right into the research process itself, outlining some of the typical procedures that allow us to plan, implement, and evaluate classroom research projects, regardless of the traditions within which we are working. Chapter 3, which concludes this section, builds on the ideas discussed in Chapters 1 and 2 and introduces three important concepts: variables, validity, and reliability.

Chapter 1: Introducing Second Language Classroom Research

By the end of this chapter, readers will

- gain an understanding of *empirical research;*
- have a clear understanding of what is meant by *classrooms* and *classroom research;*
- understand some similarities and differences among the psychometric tradition, naturalistic inquiry, and action research;
- see some value in combining data collection and analyses procedures from these various traditions;
- understand the differences among *product studies, process studies,* and *process-product studies;*
- see multiple possible roles for teachers in language classroom research.

Chapter 2: Getting Started on Classroom Research

By the end of this chapter, readers will

- have some ideas about developing researchable questions of their own;
- understand the difference between an annotated bibliography and a literature review;
- understand the steps involved in writing a literature review of their own;
- know the differences among nominal, ordinal, and interval data and variables;
- understand the need for operationalizing constructs and be familiar with three procedures for writing operational definitions of key terms;
- recognize control and experimental groups in a experimental study and be able to explain the logic behind them;
- be aware of some basic design considerations in both experimental and nonexperimental research.

Chapter 3: Key Concepts in Planning Classroom Research

By the end of this chapter, readers will

- understand the logic of hypothesis testing and be able to pose their own research questions;
- understand the main types of variables that are used in language classroom research;
- be familiar with internal and external reliability measures for insuring quality control;
- have a clear understanding of internal and external validity as central quality control concepts in any approach to language classroom research;
- know the difference between *samples* and *populations* as these terms are used in research;
- be familiar with the correlation design and the criterion groups design as they are used in language classroom research;
- be able to explain the difference among several research designs that are frequently used in language classroom research.

1

Introducing Second Language Classroom Research

There are two kinds of people in this world—those that divide the world into two kinds of people and those that don't. (attributed to Robert Benchley, as cited in Sreedharan, 2006, p. 54).

INTRODUCTION AND OVERVIEW

The primary goal of this book is to provide an introduction to research in second and foreign language classrooms. Our interest in writing this book grew out of courses and workshops on classroom research that we have developed and taught for teachers' conferences and graduate programs in applied linguistics. The book is intended for people who want to do classroom research—specifically language teachers, teacher trainees, teacher educators, researchers, and those who run courses on classroom observation and research. We aim to provide an introduction to language classroom research that is accessible to readers who do not necessarily have specialist training in research methods.

Overriding Objectives

The book has two overriding objectives. The first of these is to provide an overview and introduction to language classroom research. To this end, we look at both substantive issues (the topics and questions that have been investigated by classroom researchers) and methodological issues (the techniques and methods that researchers have employed for collecting data, analyzing and interpreting their data, and presenting the results). The second objective is to help readers develop confidence and practical skills for carrying out their own empirical investigations. To this end, we will suggest topical foci and provide tasks to help readers identify their own areas of interest. We will also provide guidance and activities for developing research skills.

Many years ago, Long (1983a) advanced several reasons for the study of second language classrooms, particularly on the part of teachers in preparation. In the first place, Long argued that classroom-centered research can provide a great deal of useful information about how foreign language instruction is actually carried out (in contrast to what people imagine happens in classrooms). Secondly, classroom-centered research can promote self-monitoring by classroom practitioners. Third, the various observation schemes for classifying classroom interaction can be used by teachers to investigate their own classes and the classes of colleagues. Finally, involvement of teachers in classroom research can help them to resist the temptation to jump on the various methodological bandwagons that come rolling along from time to time. Descriptive studies of what actually goes on in classrooms can help teachers evaluate the competing claims of different syllabi, materials, and methods.

Our hope, then, is that having reached the end of this book, readers will have a clear idea of the state of the art in terms of what researchers (including teacher researchers) have looked at and how they have gone about their investigations. We also hope that teachers and future teachers who read this book will be encouraged to examine their own classroom contexts systematically. Having read the book and completed the questions and tasks set out in the various chapters, readers should understand key concepts and methods in classroom-based research. They should also be able to relate these concepts and issues to their own teaching situations.

Recurring Themes

This book has several recurring themes. The first is that empirical research matters. The second is that there are many roles for teachers in the research process. Even those teachers who do not plan to do research themselves should be knowledgeable, informed, and critical consumers of others' research. The third is that as classrooms are specifically constituted to facilitate language learning, we should develop skills for systematically finding out what goes on in them. Fourth, we argue that no single approach to language classroom research is inherently superior to others; instead, the choice of a research method should be determined by the purpose of the study—a point we will return to throughout this volume.

REFLECTION

What are your own personal goals in reading this book? What do you hope to get out of it?

When we began our own teaching careers (more years ago now than we wish to admit), there was a preoccupation with a search for the one best method, and a range of methods was presented to teachers for adoption. However, as it turned out, methodological prescriptions were rarely supported by research. As teachers, we were supposed to take such prescriptions on faith. Our view now is that research is unlikely ever to provide a packaged solution to the challenges of language teaching. However, empirical research does have an important place, alongside common sense and experience, in helping teachers to determine what they can and should do to facilitate language learning.

Our second theme is that there is a central place for teachers in the research process. In many instances, teachers are the people best positioned to conduct classroom investigations. We are not suggesting that teachers should replace academic researchers in all cases, but that it is often appropriate that they become partners in the research enterprise to find answers to questions of pedagogy. In other cases, teachers themselves should investigate their own teaching and their students' learning. The ability to do research is not a matter of one's appointed position, but rather of one's knowledge, skill, and attitude.

The third theme—developing skills for investigating classroom processes—is one we hope readers will take to heart. We believe our own teaching has improved through the systematic application of research procedures in our work. Whether we are taping and transcribing our learners' group work or making regular entries in our teaching journals, we have found answers to questions and solutions to puzzles by viewing our own classes through research lenses.

The fourth theme is that of questioning the alleged superiority of one research method over another. We are not willing to take sides in what has historically been the quantitative-versus-qualitative debate. Instead, we will argue that appropriateness should be the guiding principle. That is, as researchers we must be eclectic and choose data collection and analysis procedures that are appropriate for answering the research questions we pose.

We begin this first chapter by reviewing two broad traditions that have been important in language classroom research over the past fifty years. This orientation is followed by a section in which we trace the historical development of classroom research. Here we look at the evolution of the field from large-scale, highly expensive, and largely inconclusive methods comparison studies to more localized, naturalistic (and often teacher-driven) studies. This section provides a backdrop to the next, in which we define classroom research, starting with definitions of the two concepts that are central to this book, namely *classrooms* and *research*. We then introduce action research, which is emerging as the third main approach to language classroom research.

The final section of the chapter briefly considers the impact of technology on language education and, in particular, how technology is currently forcing a redefinition of what we mean when we refer to classrooms. To examine a technology-based context, we will summarize a sample study conducted about online language learning. The chapter concludes with questions and tasks designed to encourage the reader to contest the ideas presented in the chapter against the reality of their own context and situation. Suggestions for further reading and a Web site to explore are also provided.

We have used the term *empirical research* in the text above. What does this phrase mean to you? Is it the same as *experimental research*?

TWO MAIN CLASSROOM RESEARCH TRADITIONS

In general, two broad approaches or traditions to classroom research have been historically dominant in language education. These are the psychometric and the naturalistic traditions. (A third approach, action research, has become increasingly important in the past three decades and will be introduced below.) In later chapters, we will explore specific research methods and procedures situated within these broad traditions. Here we will provide a brief overview to orient you to these two main approaches.

The Psychometric Research Tradition

Early classroom research was dominated by the *psychometric* tradition. Psychometric studies are studies that seek to measure psychological properties—such as attitude—and psychological operations—such as language learning. In this approach, the aim is to test the influence of different variables on one another. It is sometimes called *experimental research* because it often involves setting up formal experiments to test hypotheses using psychometric data collection and analytic procedures. It is sometimes referred to as *quantitative research* because the data are typically numeric in nature. Such data consist of measurements, tabulations, ratings, or rankings.

In language classroom research, the psychometric tradition has often been used to investigate the mental mechanisms hypothesized to underpin second language acquisition. Assuming that the more interaction there is, the greater the language acquisition will be, researchers ask questions such as, "What kinds of classroom tasks maximize student-student interaction?" These sorts of questions are important because answering them can help us to understand how to guide students in improving their language proficiency.

Language classroom researchers working in the psychometric tradition typically investigate the effect of different methods, materials, teaching techniques, types of classroom delivery, and so on, on language learning. A typical question might be, "Does Method X result in more effective language learning than Method Y?" In this sort of study, different groups of students are taught using the two different methods. At the end of the process, the students are tested, and the groups' average test scores are analyzed statistically to determine whether any differences between the scores are powerful enough to be considered significant. Making this determination depends on the researchers controlling the variables involved in the study. If the research has been carefully designed and carried out, the researchers can determine whether observed differences in the groups' scores are due to the different teaching methods or are a matter of chance.

In order to make claims about the effectiveness of one method over another, or one set of materials over another, researchers working in the psychometric tradition must be sure that it is the particular method or the materials under investigation that are causing any observed differences in the students' test scores rather than some other variable(s). For this reason, working in the experimental mode requires researchers to exercise a great deal of control over the variables that might influence the outcome of a study. Such control is seldom possible in real classrooms, where teachers and students are going about the business of teaching and learning. For this reason, among others, classroom research has broadened its methodological scope to include more naturalistic approaches to data collection and analysis in recent years.

The Naturalistic Research Tradition

In *naturalistic research*, also called *naturalistic inquiry*, the aim is to obtain insights into the complexities of teaching and learning through uncontrolled observation and description rather than to support the claim that Method X works better than Method Y, or that Course Book A is better than Course Book B. In classroom research, therefore, this approach is centrally concerned with documenting and analyzing what goes on in naturally occurring classrooms that have been constituted for the purposes of teaching and learning rather than for the purposes of investigating teacher and learner behavior. Naturalistic research is sometimes called *qualitative research*, as opposed to *quantitative research*, because it is concerned with capturing the qualities and attributes of the phenomena being investigated rather than with measuring or counting.

Naturalistic inquiry is sometimes seen as subjective in nature while psychometric research values objectivity. Originally these terms, *subjective* and *objective*, referred to point of view. That is, objective information was information about an object that existed independent of the observer. In contrast, subjective information existed in the mind of the subject rather than external to that person. Over the years, however, these two terms, as they are used in research, have taken on slightly different meanings. Objective information has come to be seen as verifiable, factual, and, therefore, valuable, while subjective information is not usually verifiable by an external observer and, therefore, is sometimes considered less valuable in the psychometric tradition. However, in action research and in some realizations of the naturalistic inquiry tradition, the participants' viewpoints are indeed valued.

In his book on interpretive approaches to classroom research, van Lier (1988, p. 37) justifies a focus on the subjective, qualitative tradition on five grounds:

1. Our knowledge of what actually goes on in the classroom is extremely limited.

2. It is relevant and valuable to increase that knowledge.

3. This can only be done by going into the classroom for data.

4. All data must be interpreted in the classroom context, i.e., the context of their occurrence.

5. This context is not only a linguistic or cognitive one, but it is also essentially a social context.

Although van Lier's comments were written more than two decades ago, they remain true today.

Naturalistic research is actually a cover term for several different research methods. Two of the methods that have frequently been used in language classroom research are ethnographies and case studies. Both of these methods will be covered in detail in future chapters, but here we will briefly consider them to illustrate naturalistic inquiry.

Large-scale, long-term studies aimed at investigating classrooms as cultural systems are called *ethnographies*. The roots of the ethnographic tradition in language classroom research can be traced to anthropology:

> In anthropology, the ethnographer observes a little-known or 'exotic' group of people in their natural habitat and takes fieldnotes. In addition, working with one or more informants is often necessary, if only to describe the language. Increasingly, recording is used for description and analysis, not just as a mnemonic device, but more importantly as an estrangement device, which enables the ethnographer to look at phenomena (such as conversations, rituals, transactions, etc.) with detachment. The same ways of working are applied in classrooms. However, recording (and subsequent transcription) is of even greater importance here than in anthropological field work, since many more things go on at the same time and in rapid succession, and since the classroom is not an exotic setting for us but rather a very familiar one, laden with personal meaning. (van Lier, 1988, p. 37)

Thus, a classroom ethnography views the language classroom (or program or school) as a cultural system whose patterns can be discovered through longitudinal data collection and analysis.

Case studies are another prevalent form of naturalistic research in classrooms, but this term is a bit tricky to define. In a case study, we investigate a unit of something. That unit can be a learner or a teacher or a teacher-in-training. It can be a particular class or a program or a school. A case study is often characterized as being an in-depth analysis of one particular exemplar of the thing we wish to understand—one teacher-in-training, one disruptive learner, or one after-school program. However, there are also case studies that examine parallel cases—two learners, for example, or three classrooms—and yet still use the case study methodology.

Typically, case studies involve the researcher's long-term, or *longitudinal*, involvement in the research context, as well as detailed data collection about the person or entity being investigated. Case studies are not as broadly contextualized as ethnographies and will often not work at the levels of cultural description that characterize ethnographies. Instead, case studies focus on one case (or a few cases) to explore a research issue in depth.

There is increasing interest in applying naturalistic inquiry techniques to the investigation of language classrooms. In 1996, we published a collection of original classroom-oriented research studies. In our introduction to the volume, we wrote:

> Our hope was to bring together a series of rich descriptive and interpretive accounts, documenting the concerns of teachers and students as they teach, learn and use languages. . . . The book was born partly out of frustration as we sought in vain for appropriate qualitative studies as models for our own students, and partly out of respect for and fascination with teaching and learning. (Bailey and Nunan, 1996, p. 9)

In the years since that collection was published, many more classroom studies have been conducted in the naturalistic inquiry tradition, and there are now methodological resources available for researchers and teachers who wish to use the data collection and analysis procedures of naturalistic inquiry. (See, for instance, Henze, 1995; K. Richards, 2003.) We will deal with some of these procedures in detail in subsequent chapters of this book.

Combining Traditions in Language Classroom Research

The gap between the two dominant research traditions discussed above may seem impossibly wide. However, they represent the two ends of a continuum rather than two mutually exclusive domains. In fact, both the psychometric tradition and the naturalistic inquiry tradition represent different families, or cultures, of empirical research. That is, *empirical research* is the cover term, meaning research based on the collection and analysis of data.

REFLECTION

In an earlier reflection task, we asked you to think about the meaning of empirical research. How closely did your understanding of that term match the point of view presented here? If there were differences, what were they?

Both the more quantitatively oriented psychometric tradition and the more qualitatively oriented naturalistic inquiry tradition consist of a wide range of research methods and procedures that can be helpful in investigating language

	Quantitative Data Collection	Qualitative Data Collection
Quantitative Data Analysis	Computing statistical comparisons of learners' test scores to see if there are any statistically significant differences between groups taught with different methods (Test scores = data that have been quantitatively collected; computing statistical comparisons = a quantitative data analysis procedure)	Tabulating the observed frequency of certain errors in language students' writing samples (Samples of language students' writing = data that have been qualitatively collected; tabulating the occurrence of certain errors = a quantitative data analysis procedure)
Qualitative Data Analysis	Categorizing language students as advanced, upper intermediate, intermediate, or lower intermediate on the basis of the learners' test scores (Test scores = data that have been quantitatively collected; proficiency categorizations = a qualitative data analysis procedure)	Summarizing written field notes to yield prose profiles of various teachers' teaching styles in an observational study (Field notes = data that have been qualitatively collected; summarizing = a qualitative data analysis procedure)

FIGURE 1.1   Examples of combined qualitative and quantitative procedures in data collection and analysis

classrooms empirically. In fact, Allwright and Bailey (1991) argue against the oversimplistic contrast of quantitative-versus-qualitative research. They state that classroom data can be collected either quantitatively or qualitatively, and that it can also be analyzed quantitatively or qualitatively. **Figure 1.1** shows some examples from language classroom research.

REFLECTION

Based on what you already know about language classroom research and about yourself, do you have a predisposition for either quantitative or qualitative data collection? What about quantitative or qualitative data analysis? If you do favor one approach over another, explain your position to a colleague or classmate.

Skim through a recent issue of a professional journal that publishes research in our field. (Likely journals include *TESOL Quarterly, Modern Language Journal, Prospect, Language Learning, System, Language Teaching Research*, and the *Asian Journal of English Language Teaching*.) Do the data-based articles involve quantitative or qualitative data collection, or both? Do they entail quantitative or qualitative data analysis, or both?

Many published studies contain elements of psychometric research and elements of naturalistic research. In fact, Grotjahn (1987) argues that the quantitative/qualitative distinction can refer to three different aspects of research. These are (1) the design (whether the study is based on an experimental, quasi-experimental, or non-experimental design); (2) the form of data collected (whether the study yields quantitative or qualitative data); and (3) the type of analysis (whether the data are analyzed statistically or interpretively). Combinations of these three elements define the two *pure* research designs described above—the psychometric approach (experimental design, quantitative data, statistical analysis) and the naturalistic approach (non-experimental design, qualitative data, interpretive analysis). Grotjahn calls these the analytical-nomological paradigm and the exploratory-interpretive paradigm, respectively.

However, Grotjahn's framework also yields six mixed or 'hybrid' forms. For example, R. L. Allwright (1980) investigated the length of learners' speaking turns and how they got those turns in two lower-intermediate ESL classes. He tape recorded the classes and transcribed the audiotapes. There was also a classroom observer present to take notes during the taping. In this case, the design was non-experimental, the data were qualitative in nature (audiotapes and transcripts thereof), and the analysis was both interpretive and statistical. We will return to these issues in Chapter 15, when we consider mixed-methods research.

When we look at published research, we find Grotjahn's claims about research design possibilities are borne out. As Bailey (2005) notes, "When the experimental tradition was dominant, and alternative research paradigms were scorned for yielding 'soft' data, one seldom saw researchers combining procedures drawn from the different traditions" (p. 30). In recent years, however, language classroom research has employed a range of procedures to address research questions and test hypotheses.

In fact, the emerging trend has been to combine various means of data collection and analysis. For example, Donato, Antonek, and Tucker (1994) describe their study of a Japanese FLES (foreign language in the elementary school) program as a *multiple perspectives analysis* because it captured numerous points of view. These researchers collected a wide range of data derived from questionnaires completed by parents and learners, oral interviews, reflections from the Japanese teacher, questionnaires from other teachers at the school, and an observation system. The authors conducted statistical analyses with some of the data and did a descriptive analysis of the children's interviews. Donato et al. conclude, "To understand the complexity of FLES programs requires diverse sources of evidence anchored in the classroom and connected to the wider school community" (p. 376). In other words, the language learning and teaching these authors investigated was too complex to be treated satisfactorily with a single type of data or a single analytic method.

The multiple perspectives analysis described by Donato et al. (1994) typifies a methodological paradigm shift in language classroom research. Attempts to combine various types of data collection and analysis from different research traditions used to be rather uncommon. Nowadays, such efforts are frequently viewed as appropriate and helpful. The general trend in language classroom research has been to a broadened acceptance of varied research approaches. At this point, a brief historical overview of this transition will be helpful in terms of understanding the various data collection and analysis procedures we will explore in this book.

A BRIEF HISTORICAL BACKGROUND

In this section, we will take a historical approach and briefly review some illustrative investigations into language acquisition in classroom settings. These studies typify the development of second language classroom research and show how the different research traditions have been realized over the years.

An early example of classroom research in the psychometric tradition was conducted by Scherer and Wertheimer (1964). The project was a classic 'methods-comparison' study in which the researchers set out to compare the grammar-translation method of teaching with the then innovative audiolingual method. The research question guiding the study was as follows: Is audiolingualism a more effective method of learning a foreign language for college-level learners than grammar-translation?

The subjects in this study were two groups of college students learning German as a foreign language. One group was instructed in listening, speaking, reading, and writing using translation and grammar studies. The other group was taught by the innovative audiolingual method, in which the emphasis was on listening and speaking rather than on reading and writing. In audiolingualism, translation was avoided and grammatical rules were learned inductively rather than deductively. At the end of the two-year experimental period, both groups were tested, and the scores were analyzed to decide whether differences were statistically significant.

REFLECTION

What do you think these researchers found? Before reading further, try to predict the results of their study based on your own reading and experience, both as a teacher and as a language learner.

As it turned out, the study by Scherer and Wertheimer did not demonstrate conclusively that one method was superior to the other, as students' scores reflected the strengths of the respective methods. Students instructed according to the grammar-translation method did significantly better than the audiolingual students on tests of reading and translation, while the audiolingual students did significantly better at listening and speaking.

Numerous criticisms were leveled at the Scherer and Wertheimer study. One of these was that the researchers did not look at what actually went on in the classrooms themselves. (See Clark, 1969.) They simply assumed that the teachers were following the particular method under investigation. Nor did they collect data on the teachers' understanding of the principles underpinning the respective methods. This type of research is referred to by Long (1980) as *black box* research because we have no way of knowing what actually happened in the classroom itself. It is also called a *product study* because the researchers only looked at the outcomes—the products of the teaching methods investigated.

In contrast, there are many published classroom-based investigations that can be called *process studies*. That is, they focus on the classroom processes of teaching and/or learning, but they do not try to measure learning outcomes in any way. This type of research (e.g., the study of students' speaking turns by R. L. Allwright [1980], described above) attempts to understand what happens in classrooms without making causal claims as to one set of materials, a given teaching method, or a particular curriculum being better than another in promoting language learning.

One methods comparison study that did go inside the 'black box' is that by Swaffar, Arens, and Morgan (1982). These researchers set out to evaluate the relative efficacy of audiolingualism in comparison with cognitive code learning in the teaching of German as a foreign language. This research project had several similarities to Scherer and Wertheimer's in that both studies attempted to compare two competing instructional methods. However, it differed from the earlier study in that Swaffer et al. were aware of the need to look at what was actually happening in the classrooms rather than making assumptions about what was happening. In addition, before going into the classrooms, the researchers surveyed the teachers by getting them to indicate how often they used certain practices, such as the explicit teaching of grammar.

REFLECTION

Which conclusion below do you think Swaffer and her colleagues found?

- audiolingualism was superior to cognitive code learning
- cognitive code learning was superior to audiolingualism
- the two methods were equal in their effectiveness

What determined your choice?

In fact, Swaffar et al. (1982) found that at the level of classroom action, the concept of teaching 'method' was questionable because teachers used a range of techniques rather than adhering slavishly to either audiolingualism or the cognitive code method:

> Methodological labels assigned to teaching activities are, in themselves, not informative because they refer to a pool of classroom practices which are uniformly used. The differences among major methodologies are to be found in the ordered hierarchy, the priorities assigned to the tasks. Not *what* classroom activity is used, but *when* and *how* form the crux of the matter in distinguishing methodological practice. (p. 31)

Swaffer et al. went on to recommend a fundamental rethinking of the search for the best method because their investigation of actual classroom practices showed that the distinction between different teaching methods at the level of classroom activity was not a salient one.

In terms of research design, these authors were able to demonstrate the importance of collecting process data from inside the classroom as well as product data in the form of test scores. Thus, the report by Swaffar et al. is an example of what has come to be known as a *process-product study* (Long, 1984) because it combined observational data about what actually occurs in language classrooms with measures of learning outcomes.

Despite the emerging awareness that it was useful to incorporate both process and product data into the design of classroom research, the debate between proponents of quantitative and qualitative research remained heated. This opposition continued even though books were beginning to appear that attempted to demonstrate the mutual dependence of the two traditions. (See, for example, Chaudron, 1988.) It seemed that, for some, the psychometric approach and naturalistic inquiry represented fundamentally different and possibly incompatible ways of looking at the world.

The discussion of product studies, process studies, and process-product studies did lead to positive developments, however. Recognizing the importance of collecting data from inside the 'black box' stimulated the development of observation instruments of various levels of complexity. One of the most comprehensive instruments is the COLT (Communicative Orientation to Language Teaching), which was originally developed for investigating different kinds of second- and foreign-language programs in Canada. This scheme was theoretically motivated by communicative language teaching, as can be seen in the following quote (Allen, Fröhlich, and Spada, 1984):

> Our concept of *communication feature* has been derived from current theories of communicative competence, from the literature on communicative language teaching, and from a review of recent research into first and second language acquisition. The observational categories are designed (a) to capture significant features of verbal interaction in L2 classrooms and (b) to provide a means of comparing some aspects of classroom discourse with *natural* language as it is used outside the classroom. (p. 233)

By reducing classroom behavior to sets of quantifiable categories, the COLT observation system enabled researchers to make direct comparisons between disparate language classes (and even language programs), and then to link the behaviors to learning outcomes. Spada (1990), for example, used the scheme to compare the ways in which three different teachers interpreted theories of communicative language teaching in their classroom practice and "to determine whether differences in the implementation of communicative language teaching principles had any effect on learning outcomes" (p. 301).

As mentioned above, research like this is known as process-product research because it attempts to link classroom processes with learning outcomes. For instance, in Spada's (1990) study, significant differences were found between the listening test scores of students in the three different groups, and these were linked directly to the teachers' behavior:

> In interpreting the different performance of learners on the listening test, the investigator examined both quantitative and qualitative differences in the listening practice offered in the three classes. The quantitative results revealed that class A spent considerably more time in listening practice than the other two classes, yet class A improved the least. However, because the listening practice in this class did not prepare learners for the listening input as carefully as the listening comprehension instruction did in classes B and C, the investigator concluded that qualitative rather than quantitative differences in instruction seemed a more plausible explanation for significantly more improvement in listening comprehension in classes B and C. (p. 303)

Thus, Spada's study connected the process variables (what students and teachers actually did during lessons) with the product variable (the measurement of students' improvement in listening comprehension).

This section has provided a brief historical overview of trends in language classroom research. We will now turn to definitions of several key terms which will be used throughout the remainder of this book. These terms include *classroom*, *data*, and *classroom research*.

DEFINING CLASSROOM RESEARCH

In the foregoing sections we have repeatedly alluded to *classroom research* as if the term were totally transparent. Indeed, the concept of *classroom* is probably straightforward to most readers. A classroom is a place in which teachers and learners are gathered together for instructional purposes: "The L2 classroom can be defined as the gathering, for a given period of time, of two or more persons (one of whom generally assumes the role of instructor) for the purposes of language learning" (van Lier, 1988, p. 47). This definition encompasses everything from one-on-one tutorial sessions to a professor lecturing to hundreds of students. However, with the development of distance learning, and, in particular, the use of technology, the "gathering together" may happen in a virtual classroom rather than in a physical space. (We will look at the nature of the online classroom later in the chapter.)

The general term *research* has been defined as "the organized, systematic search for answers to the questions we ask" (Hatch and Lazaraton, 1991, p. 1). A somewhat more elaborated description says that *research* is a "systematic process of inquiry consisting of three elements or components: (1) a question, problem, or hypothesis; (2) data; and (3) analysis and interpretation" (Nunan, 1992, p. 3).

The term *data*, as it is used in this book and elsewhere, refers to records of events (Bateson, 1972). In language classroom research, data are not limited to test scores or other measurements. They can include audiotapes or videotapes of lessons, transcripts of interactions, entries from students' or teachers' journals, responses to interview questions, recordings of students' speech as they do tasks, responses to questionnaires, samples of students' written work, and so on.

To the three components of research discussed above, we would add that the results of the inquiry should be published (in the sense of being made public) so that they can be subjected to critical scrutiny and can inform the field. Sharing research results can also provide us with new ideas and alternative ways of analyzing and interpreting the data. Publication can be formal and written, in book chapters or in print or electronic journal articles. But it can also be less formal and unwritten, as in conference presentations or progress reports to colleagues. **Figure 1.2** illustrates various possible combinations of formal or informal, and written or unwritten dissemination of research projects.

Classroom research is sometimes called *classroom-based* or *classroom-centered research*. These terms refer to the procedures described above being conducted in classrooms:

> Classroom-centered research is just that—research centered on the classroom, as distinct from, for example, research that concentrates on the inputs to the classroom (the syllabus, the teaching materials) or the outputs from the classroom (learner achievement scores). It does not ignore in any way or try to devalue the importance of such inputs and outputs. It simply tries to investigate what happens inside the classroom when learners and teachers come together. (D. Allwright, 1983, p. 191)

	Formal	Informal
Written	Refereed or invited book chapters, journal articles (electronic or print medium)	Listserv postings about classroom research projects
Unwritten	Refereed or invited conference presentations	Discussions of research findings at in-house teachers' meetings

FIGURE 1.2 Possible types of publication of research results

You will also find references in the literature to *classroom-oriented research*. This research consists of studies conducted outside the classroom, in laboratory, simulated, or naturalistic settings, but which make claims for the relevance of the outcomes for classroom teaching and learning. In this book, we will typically use the cover term *classroom research*, which encompasses both classroom-based and classroom-oriented studies. While the great bulk of the work we look at is classroom-based, use of the slightly broader term enables us to refer to relevant studies conducted outside classrooms as well.

In 1991, Nunan carried out a detailed review of classroom-based and classroom-oriented studies. Of fifty studies reviewed, only fifteen were actually classroom-based (Nunan, 1991a). In the years since that review, however, many more classroom-based studies have been conducted, and we will summarize several of those research projects in the various chapters of this book. One particularly interesting development during the past two decades has been the advent of classroom action research, the topic of the next section.

REFLECTION

What does the term *action research* mean to you? Have you read any action research reports in the past? If so, what do you recall about this approach? If not, what can you predict?

ACTION RESEARCH

Action research is an emerging tradition in language classroom research. This method consists of the same elements as regular research, that is, questions, data, and interpretation. What makes classroom action research unique is that it is conducted by classroom practitioners investigating some aspect of their own practice. In other words, it is carried out principally by those who are best placed to change and, as a result, improve what goes on in the classroom.

This is not to say that research carried out by non-classroom-based researchers doesn't lead to change. Nor does it suggest that researchers and teachers might not collaborate in the research process. However, nonpractitioner-driven research is often motivated by a desire to identify relationships between variables that can be generalized beyond the specific sites where the data are collected. The primary motivation for action research is the more immediate one of bringing about change and improving teaching and learning in the classrooms where the research takes place.

Action research as a method involves systematic procedures for collecting data and understanding their meaning in a local context. Carr and Kemmis (1986) describe action research as "a form of self-reflective enquiry undertaken by participants in social situations in order to improve the rationality and justice of their own practices, their understanding of these practices, and the situations in which these practices are carried out" (p. 1). The name *action research* comes from the fact that planning and taking action are central components of the action research method.

Carr and Kemmis (1986) emphasize the ongoing cyclical nature of action research. The first step is to develop a plan for action to improve what is happening. The next steps are to implement the action plan and to gather data in order to observe the effects of the action taken in the context in which it occurs. The final steps in the cycle are to reflect critically on the process and then plan a second round of research, and so on. The cyclic investigation continues until the action researcher has accomplished his or her goals.

Another definition comes from Cohen and Manion (1985), who describe action research as small-scale interventions "in the functioning of the real world" (p. 208). Such research is intimately connected to the contexts in which it is conducted. It can involve the collaboration of teachers and other researchers. Cohen and Manion outline eight stages in the action research process:

1. Identify the problem.
2. Develop a draft proposal based on discussion and negotiation between interested parties, i.e., teachers, advisors, researchers, and sponsors.
3. Review what has already been written about the issue in question.
4. Restate the problem or formulate hypotheses; discuss the assumptions underlying the project.
5. Select research procedures, resources, materials, methods, etc.
6. Choose evaluation procedures.
7. Collect the data, analyze the data, and provide feedback to the research team.
8. Interpret the data, draw out inferences, and evaluate the project. (pp. 220–1)

While there are other models of action research, this list provides a helpful overview of the steps involved in conducting this sort of classroom research.

Bailey (2005) contrasts action research with both experimental and naturalistic research as follows:

> While experimental research is often directed at hypothesis testing and theory building, and naturalistic inquiry aims to understand and describe phenomena under investigation, action research has a more immediate and practical focus. Its results may contribute to emerging theory, and to the understanding of phenomena, but it does not necessarily have to be theory-driven. (p. 25)

To note that action research has a practical focus does not demean its value. As van Lier (1994a) has observed, "We must never forget that it is . . . important to do research on practical activities and for practical purposes, such as the improvement of aspects of language teaching and learning" (p. 31). (See also van Lier, 1994b.)

In this section, we have given a brief account of action research, a topic that is elaborated upon and described in greater detail later in this volume. To summarize, it is a method of conducting research that involves the participants (such as teachers and learners) in ongoing, cyclical investigations of their own contexts (in our case, classrooms). However, *action research* should not be confused with *classroom research* or *teacher research*.

As noted above, the term *classroom research* refers to research conducted in classrooms—regardless of who does it or what methods are used. *Action research*, in contrast, is an actual research method, in that it involves a codified sequence of steps. It can be effectively employed in language classrooms but has also been used in other settings—in neighborhoods, in community centers, etc. *Teacher research*, in contrast, is characterized by who conducts the investigation. Of course, teachers can conduct action research in classrooms (Bailey, 2001a), but they are not limited either by method or locale. For instance, a university-level EFL teacher might wish to investigate his students' use of English outside the classroom—talking to tourists, using the Internet, and so on. The similarities and differences between classroom research, teacher research, and action research are summarized in **Figure 1.3.**

Type of Research	What	Who	Why
Classroom Research	Investigations carried out in classrooms utilizing a range of qualitative and quantitative methods of data collection and analysis	University-based researchers, graduate students, and/or teachers	To generate insights and understanding, to test hypotheses, to generate theory, and/or to produce outcomes that can be generalized
Teacher Research	Investigations carried out in or out of classrooms, utilizing a range of qualitative and quantitative methods of data collection and analysis	Teachers	To improve practice, and/or to generate insights and understanding to related practice and theory
Action Research	A cyclical process of identifying practical problems or challenges, formulating a plan for addressing them, taking action, evaluating the results, and planning subsequent rounds of investigation	Participants in a setting, including teachers (sometimes in collaboration with others)	To improve one's own practice, to solve problems, and/or to satisfy curiosity

FIGURE 1.3 Comparing classroom research, teacher research, and action research

THE CLASSROOM REDEFINED—'VIRTUAL' CLASSROOMS

At the present time, technology is having a profound impact on all aspects of life. In education, the ease with which computers can bring people together across time and space is forcing a redefinition of the classroom. In the opening section, we discussed ideas from D. Allwright (1983) and van Lier (1988), who suggested that classrooms could be defined as places where individuals were gathered together for purposes of teaching and learning. However, through technology, this "gathering together" no longer requires the individuals to inhabit the same physical space.

The following vignettes illustrate some of the changes wrought by technology in language education and teacher preparation:

- A student in Toronto who was unable to attend class reviews a transcript of the lesson that is posted on the Web after the conclusion of the class.

- A teacher educator in Auckland conducts a graduate class on second language acquisition through a text chat site with students in San Diego, Bangkok, Istanbul, and Buenos Aires.

- A secondary school teacher in Hong Kong posts all of her assignments and class handouts onto the class Web site. Students can work with these materials online and download those that they want to keep in hard-copy form.

- Using voice chat, EFL students in Beijing, Seoul, and Tokyo take part in a conversation class with a teacher based in Bogotá.

- A school in Osaka has its students complete an online placement test which automatically assesses and places them into instructional groupings in a fraction of the time it used to take using a pencil-and-paper test.

- A student in an academic writing program on a field trip in Rio de Janeiro submits a draft of his assignment to his teacher in Los Angeles as an e-mail attachment. The teacher inserts comments and returns the assignment to the student via e-mail.

Changes brought about by technology "challenge our self-concept as foreign language teachers, because, much more than in the past, we are now called upon to redefine our roles as educators, since we need to mediate between the world of the classroom and the world of natural language acquisition" (Legutke, 2000, p. 1).

This redefinition of the classroom is also having an effect on language classroom researchers who now have to go beyond the four walls of the traditional classroom to conduct research. For example, a recent study into the discourse features of classroom interaction broadened its focus from face-to-face classrooms and included virtual classrooms. The researchers looked at similarities and differences in the two kinds of discourse as well as at the advantages and disadvantages of these two kinds of classrooms (Christison and Nunan, 2001). We will return to these issues and other ideas about online teaching and learning when we consider discourse analysis and other approaches to analyzing classroom interactions.

REFLECTION

Have you ever taken or taught a course online? If you have, what were the differences in the online interaction and what you might experience in a similar course taught in a face-to-face classroom context? If you haven't, what do you think the differences might be?

SAMPLE STUDY

Kevin Jepson was an experienced language teacher with a strong interest in technology. As he learned about research methods in our field and studied second language acquisition (SLA), he became intrigued with the research about conversational interaction promoting language learning. Jepson wanted to investigate what happened during conversations in online classes. He was particularly interested in *negotiated interactions*, since a great deal of SLA research suggests that negotiation processes are key factors in language learning. Negotiated interactions are those in which the interlocutors—the people who are speaking—must try to understand one another's meaning. Based on his review of the literature, Jepson (2005) defined negotiation of meaning as "a cognitive process that speakers use to better understand one another, that is, to increase the comprehensibility of language input" (p. 79).

Jepson (2005) compared the interaction in two kinds of online English chat rooms: those with spoken (voice) chats and those with typed (text) chats. The technology permitted the students in the voice chat rooms to actually talk to one another in real time. The text chat rooms allowed the students to communicate in real time but they had to type their ideas and comments on the computer and then post them to the chat. He posed two research questions about this context:

1. Which types of repair moves occur in text and voice chats?
2. What are the differences, if any, in the repair moves in text chats and the repair moves in voice chats when time is held constant?

The repair moves Jepson studied had been identified in previous research. They consisted of two main categories: negotiation of meaning and negative feedback. The negotiation of meaning category had five types: (1) clarification requests, (2) confirmation checks, (3) comprehension checks, (4) self-repetitions and paraphrases, and (5) incorporations. The negative feedback category also had five types: (1) recasts, (2) explicit correction, (3) questions, (4) incorporations, and (5) self-corrections.

The data for this study were recorded simultaneously in the voice chat rooms and the text chat rooms of an online English program using two computers. Jepson audio-recorded five minutes of voice chats at the same time he saved the texts generated by the participants in the typed chat rooms. He repeated this procedure five times, for a total of twenty-five minutes of typed chat and twenty-five minutes of voice chat. Jepson later transcribed the interaction in the voice chat rooms. He counted the number of times the participants engaged in negotiation of meaning and in negative feedback.

REFLECTION

Imagine being a language learner participating in an online chat conducted in a language other than your native language. What do think the differences would be for you as a participant if the chat were typed compared to a chat in which you were actually talking? What differences do you think Jepson found when he compared the repair moves in the voice chats and the typed chats?

The results of this study are interesting and complex and too numerous to list in detail here. The main findings can be summarized as follows: (1) There were more repair moves in general in the voice chats than in the text chats. (2) Likewise, there was more negotiation of meaning in the voice chats than in the text chats. (3) There were fewer negative feedback repairs than negotiation of meaning repairs. All of these differences were statistically significantly different.

PAYOFFS AND PITFALLS

There are a number of pitfalls in choosing to conduct research, perhaps particularly classroom research. It is time-consuming, and it can be quite challenging. In addition, the entire process can be frustrating if you don't have the proper tools, training, or guidance. You may work in a system that does not value teachers doing research, so you might wonder what the importance is of undertaking the effort.

Research can also be frustrating if you conduct a study and the results are not what you had hoped for. Or perhaps you complete your study and give a presentation about it at a conference, but the audience is unimpressed with your work, or even hostile. You might write a formal report on the research and submit it to a journal, only to have the paper rejected for publication and to receive harsh criticism from some unknown, anonymous reviewers. (Don't worry! This is part of the process. We have both had numerous papers rejected by reviewers.)

Nevertheless, there are many payoffs associated with conducting research—especially research in language classrooms. As teachers and teacher educators, we are constantly amazed and renewed by the interesting things we learn about teaching and learning through the research process. And on those occasions when a paper or conference presentation has been accepted, we have benefited from the processes of writing and delivering our ideas, and getting feedback from others.

We have also found that our research efforts influence our teaching, and vice versa. Particularly when we have conducted research, including action research, in our own classrooms, we have gained new insights that we might not have gained if we had simply gone on teaching day after day. Through the years, we have developed new skills, both as teachers and as researchers, and have made many new friends and acquaintances by getting involved in research.

CONCLUSION

The aim of this chapter has been to set the groundwork for the rest of the book. We have described the main characteristics of two predominant traditions—psychometric research and naturalistic inquiry. We have considered how those traditions have underpinned the evolution of classroom research. We have provided a brief historical overview, as well as a definition (and redefinition) of classrooms and of research. We have contrasted action research, teacher research, and classroom research as concepts, and have also explored the notion of teacher-initiated action research. We have suggested that teachers have many possible roles in the research process, including being active researchers themselves.

We will end the chapter with discussion questions and tasks that you can use to deepen your understanding of the issues presented here. We will also suggest some readings that should be helpful to you if you wish to pursue these topics further.

QUESTIONS AND TASKS

1. Identify a research question that would be most appropriately studied in the psychometric tradition and one that would be best investigated using naturalistic inquiry. Compare your ideas with a classmate or colleague.

2. What mental image does the term *teacher-researcher* evoke for you?

3. What is your attitude towards the idea of teachers doing research?

4. What skills would be needed by a teacher who wanted to do research? Make a list and compare it with the list of a classmate or colleague.

5. Given your current teaching situation, or a situation with which you are familiar, what do you see as the advantages and disadvantages of teacher involvement in language classroom research?

6. Think of a situation in a language class (whether you are the teacher or a learner) that you would like to change. What would be the action(s) you could take if you were going to conduct an action research project about that situation?

7. How have developments in technology caused you to redefine your own notion of 'the classroom'?

8. List three to five key issues that you'd like to see addressed by classroom researchers, or that you yourself would like to investigate in your classroom.

9. What is your view of *objectivity* and *subjectivity* in language classroom research? Can you see a place for subjective data and interpretations or should all research be objective in nature?

10. In your view, what is the relationship between teaching and research—specifically language classroom research as we have defined the term in this chapter?

SUGGESTIONS FOR FURTHER READING

If you would like to learn more about the early history of language classroom research, we recommend the articles by D. Allwright (1983), Brumfit and Mitchell (1990a), Gaies (1983), Long (1983a; 1984), Pica (1997), and Seliger (1983a). For book-length treatments of classroom research, see D. Allwright and Bailey (1991), Brumfit and Mitchell (1990b), Chaudron (1988), McKay (2006), Nunan (1992), and van Lier (1988).

For comparisons of the various traditions in language classroom research, see Bailey (1998a; 2005). For good introductions to action research, we recommend Burns (1998), Nunan (1990, 1993), van Lier (1994a), and Wallace (1998). A classic methods comparison study is by Smith's (1970) report on the Pennsylvania Project, which contrasted cognitive language teaching and audiolingual method. See also Otto (1969).

If you would like to read Jepson's (2005) paper comparing voice chat and typed chat, you can find it easily online. It is available at the Web site for the online journal *Language Learning and Technology*:

http://llt.msu.edu/vol9num3/jepson.

2

Getting Started on Classroom Research

Writing is easy. All you do is sit and stare at a blank sheet of paper until drops of blood form on your forehead. (Fowler, as cited in Applewhite, Evans, & Frothingham, 2003, p. 300)

INTRODUCTION AND OVERVIEW

Most books on classroom research eventually get around to the practical side of the business, usually culminating with a chapter on doing research. However, we decided to jump in and introduce some of the practicalities, along with the difficulties, of doing research from the very beginning of this book. There are several reasons for this decision. First, we want you to start thinking about the research process from your own perspective right at the outset. We also hope that you might "get your feet wet" by doing some relatively informal problem posing, data collection, and data analysis before you get to the end of the book. Thirdly, we hope that this chapter will provide a lens through which you can view the rest of the book. We want you to be able to read about data collection and analysis issues with a strong grounding in the practicalities of the research process.

In essence, this chapter outlines some of the typical procedures that underpin the planning and implementation of a classroom research project, regardless of the research tradition you choose. In any such project, whether it is carried out by experienced university researchers with large grants or classroom teachers who are simply interested in understanding and improving the quality of what goes on in their classrooms, researchers need to consider the following questions:

- What aspect of classroom teaching and learning am I interested in, and what specifically is it about this issue that I really want to know?

- Does anybody else have an answer to my question?
- How do I get started?
- What kinds of data will be relevant to my research interest and question?
- How will I gather those data?
- What techniques exist for analyzing my data?
- How can I make my research available to anyone else who might be interested?

These questions correspond to the following phases of a research project: (1) area identification, (2) question formation, (3) literature review, (4) planning and implementation, (5) data collection, (6) data analysis, and (7) reporting. In this chapter, we will deal with each of these areas although we will mainly focus on area identification, question formation, the literature review, and defining variables during the planning stages of research. Additional issues in data collection and analysis will be dealt with further in subsequent chapters about particular research methods.

We also want to introduce the idea that research is a kind of culture. It has its own values, norms, artifacts, rules, and procedures. Like others sorts of cultures, research has subcultures. If you keep this metaphor in mind as you read this book, you can imagine yourself as being an anthropologist, exploring the culture(s) of language classroom research. We will return to this theme from time to time as we cover the concepts of research design and research methods.

DEVELOPING A RESEARCH QUESTION

We said in Chapter 1 that a minimum requirement for an activity to qualify as research is that it needs to contain three key components: "(1) a question, problem, or hypothesis, (2) data, and (3) analysis and interpretation" (Nunan, 1992, p. 3). We also added a fourth element—that is, the activity should be published. We are using the term *publish* here in its original and broadest sense of 'to make public.' If we don't make our work public, then it is not available to others. And if it is not available to others, then it cannot be subjected to critical scrutiny. Without critical scrutiny, the activity is more like reflective teaching than research. (Of course, reflective teaching is a valuable undertaking in its own right, but that is not our focus in this book.)

As suggested by the components above, the first step is posing a research question. Getting the research question right is one of the most important things to do in beginning a research project. Unless you get the question right, the subsequent steps in the research process are often impossible to carry out. In this section, we look at some of the issues you need to consider in formulating a research question.

In some approaches to research (such as the experimental method in the psychometric tradition), the question is posed first, followed by the data collection and the analysis. The research question is typically written in question form, but it may be posed as a particular form of sentence called a *hypothesis*. A hypothesis is a carefully worded statement that the researcher sets out to test by collecting relevant data and analyzing those data. In the culture of the psychometric tradition—and especially the experimental method—the skills of hypothesis posing and testing are highly valued. (We will return to hypothesis testing in Chapters 3 and 4.)

In other kinds of research, such as ethnography, the researcher may start out with a research question that is somewhat general and broadly formulated. The researcher then collects some initial data that help to refine and shape the research. In other words, there is an interaction between the data and the research question. It's almost as if the data and the question are having a conversation.

For many teachers who wish to do classroom research, the research idea is initially prompted by a problem, puzzle, or challenge that arises in the course of their teaching. For example, a foreign language teacher may find that when the students get really involved in communicative group work tasks, they tend to switch to their first language. So, the teacher's initial questions might be, "What prompts students to switch from the target language to their first language, and how can I encourage them to work in the target language?" This view of the situation may then lead the teacher to exploring the complexities of code mixing and code switching.

REFLECTION

Take a few moments to reflect on your own classroom, or a classroom with which you are familiar. Brainstorm a list of issues that might provide the basis for classroom research.

If you are having difficulty coming up with ideas for research, you might follow Hatch and Lazaraton's (1991) suggestion that you keep a research journal. Such a journal can be a useful resource when it comes to defining what interests you and identifying a research area. Here is how such a journal might be developed:

> Each time that you think of a question for which there seems to be no ready answer, write the question down. Someone may write or talk about something that is fascinating, and you wonder if the same results would obtain with your students, or with bilingual children, or with a different genre of text. Write this in your journal. Perhaps you take notes as you read articles, observe classes, or listen to lectures. Place a star or other symbol at places where you have questions. These ideas will then be easy to find and transfer to the journal. Of course, not all these ideas will evolve into research topics. Like a writer's notebook, these bits and pieces of research ideas will reformulate themselves almost like magic. Ways to redefine, elaborate or reorganize the questions will occur as you reread the entries. (pp. 11–12)

TABLE 2.1 General areas of interest and more specific research topics

Area	Topic
Teacher questions	The relationship between teacher questions and learner responses
	Closed versus open questions
	Display versus referential questions
Direct instruction	Inductive versus deductive teaching
	Teacher input and learner output
	Wait time and learner output
	Teacher speech modifications
Error correction and feedback	What types of errors to correct
	When to correct errors
	How to correct errors
	Student self-correction
Classroom management	Departures from the lesson plan
	Managing mixed-ability groups
	Teaching large classes
Student interaction	L1 versus L2 talk
	Monitoring language use in group work
	Increasing the amount of student talk
Task analysis	The different demands that tasks make on learners
	Task type and difficulty
	The relationship between task types and learner language
Learning strategies	Strategy differences of good and poor learners
	The effect of consciously teaching strategies
	Strategy use by learners of various proficiency levels
Affective factors	Enhancing learners' motivation
	Managing learners' anxiety
	Learners' attitudes and achievement

Other sources of ideas can be found at the ends of articles, theses, or dissertations. These reports usually include a section called "Suggestions for Further Research."

Table 2.1 contains some general research areas and topics for classroom research. This list is very selective and is intended only to be illustrative since there are many other topics that could form the basis for classroom investigation.

As we have suggested, research questions can come from many different sources—a problem that arises in the classroom, an interesting article, discussions with colleagues, a journal of research ideas that we have kept over time, and so on. One advantage of reading about the topic in question is that we may well find a study that can help us take our research interests forward. For example, although we are particularly interested in listening comprehension, we may find a study on the effect of background knowledge on reading comprehension. This study might prompt us to ask whether the effects of background knowledge function in listening activities as well. As another example, we may read a study on the development of morphemes in German as a foreign language that suggests the acquisition order of these morphemes can't be changed by instruction. This idea may cause us to wonder whether there are certain grammatical forms in English that are also impervious to instruction.

After identifying a general area that is of interest to us, such as listening comprehension or grammatical development, the next step is to pose and refine the question, so that answering it is both doable and worthwhile. We may well have a worthy question such as, "Is there a list of grammar items in English that appear in a certain order that can't be changed by instruction?" However, when we reflect on the question, we may decide that it is beyond our ability to deal with at the moment, perhaps because of lack of time, expertise, and/or resources.

Having identified a general area and a topic within that area, the next task is to formulate a question or questions. This process is much more challenging than it might seem to someone who hasn't done it before. Researchers and graduate students sometimes take months to get their questions right. For example, recognizing the breadth of the morpheme acquisition issue described above, we may decide to work on a small part of the puzzle. After further thought and additional reading, we may decide to restrict our attention to the acquisition of question forms. Our new question might read, "What is the order of acquisition of *wh*-questions in English? Do learners acquire questions with *is* (such as, 'Where is your school?') before they acquire *do* questions (such as, 'Where do you live?')?"

ACTION

Select one of the topics in Table 2.1 that interests you and turn it into a researchable question.

Wiersma (1986) recommends a three-step procedure in developing a question: (1) general identification of area issue or problem, (2) restating the issue (almost like writing a title for your study), and (3) refining the issue in forming a specific question to be answered by the research. **Table 2.2** provides examples of area identification through to question formation.

In another treatment, Seliger and Shohamy (1989) suggest that the preparatory stage of a research project should involve four phases:

Phase 1: Formulating the general research question (which may emerge from the experience and interests of the researcher, other research in language acquisition, or sources outside of second language acquisition)

Phase 2: Focusing on the question (in which the researcher decides on the importance and feasibility of the question)

Phase 3: Deciding on an objective

Phase 4: Formulating the research plan or objective

As you can see, there is a great deal of thought and work involved in research before we even begin to collect data!

TABLE 2.2 Deriving questions from original issues (adapted from Weirsma, 1986)

Original Issue	Restatement	Refined Question
Achievement and teaching techniques	A study of the effects of three teaching techniques on reading achievement scores of junior high school students	Do three different teaching techniques have differing effects on the reading achievement scores of junior high school students?
Bilingual education	A study of the characteristics of bilingual education in the elementary schools of City A	What are the characteristics of bilingual education as it is implemented in the elementary school of City A?

ACTION

Think about the following important topics in language education. Try doing Phases 1 and 2 of Seliger and Shohamy's (1989) list above, using one of these topics.

Content-based instruction   Teacher questions

Having formulated a question or questions, the next step is to evaluate the question. Not all questions are researchable, and not all researchable questions are worthwhile. It is therefore important, as you begin to develop a research plan, to keep your motives in mind. Ask yourself *why* you propose to investigate a particular question. Coming up with a satisfactory justification before you invest a lot of intellectual, physical, and emotional energy in the research may save you a great deal of frustration once you actually embark on the research.

REFLECTION

Which of the following questions are researchable? Which, in your opinion, are worth researching? Are there any that, while being researchable, are not really feasible in practical terms?

1. Do learners of English as a foreign language acquire the ability to form *yes/no* questions by inverting the subject and the auxiliary verb before they acquire *wh*-questions formed through *do* insertion?
2. Should culture be part of the foreign language curriculum?
3. Are language teachers who wear formal dress more likely to work for private language schools or university language centers?

You probably decided that all of these questions are problematic for different reasons. The first is researchable, but probably only for someone who has a grant or is doing doctoral research in second language acquisition, since answering this question thoroughly would require considerable time and resources. (For example, it might entail testing learners over a period of time, perhaps tape-recording and transcribing their speech, or collecting and analyzing their writing samples, and so on.)

The second question is not really a research question because it primarily involves making a value judgment. It seeks an opinion rather than information based on data. In empirical research, answers to research questions come directly from the data that are collected and analyzed in the course of the research. Of course, some people (and we would include ourselves in this group) believe that it is impossible to learn a language without also learning the culture. Others, including some of our acquaintances who have developed multilingual competence themselves, believe that language and culture are separable. A more researchable question in this area would be, "What attitudes do teachers hold towards teaching culture as part of a foreign language curriculum?" However, this question is quite different from Question 2 in the Reflection box above.

The third question is certainly answerable, but one would have to ask whether doing so would be worthwhile. Sociologists may be able to read deep meaning into the proclivity for formal business clothing on the part of teachers who work in private schools, but for us the relationship is essentially meaningless.

Here are two important questions to ask yourself when you are formulating your research questions: What will I have learned if I answer this research question? What will the language-teaching field have gained when I have answered this research question? If the answer is "Nothing," then it's probably best not to proceed with your research question in its present form. It may require more refinement or elaboration, or you may want to focus on other topics instead.

We have seen that at the outset of classroom research projects, it is important to pose our research questions carefully. They should be researchable and important questions that lead to an improved understanding of language, language teaching, and/or language learning. We turn now to the literature review—an important part of the overall research process and one that can inform the posing of appropriate research questions.

REFLECTION

Here is a story that Kathi Bailey tells her research students. Read the story and see what it has to do with posing appropriate research questions.

My mom took a course in *ikebana*—Japanese flower arranging—at night school in California. The European and North American traditions of flower arranging often involve large bouquets of flowers, but the Japanese tradition uses fewer flowers and emphasizes the harmony and simplicity of the arrangement.

The students (all American women) were told to bring flowers to the first night of class. When the Japanese instructor entered the room, her eager pupils were sitting at the large tables with mountains of flowers piled in front of them. In true Anglo-American fashion, they had collected huge bouquets to bring to class.

The Japanese instructor looked at the flowers, looked at the women, and then said, "Ladies, this is a course on Japanese flower arranging. Please divide your stack of flowers in half and set one half aside." She waited while the students divided their flowers. Then she said, "Now look at the flowers that remain. Divide the flowers in half and set half aside." Again she waited while the students separated their flowers into two smaller groups and put half of them off to the side. When they had done so, the instructor said, "Now we are ready to being Japanese flower arranging."

WRITING THE LITERATURE REVIEW

Novice researchers often equate the process of doing a literature review with doing research. It is true that reviewing the literature is important, but locating and summarizing what others have written about a topic is often called *library research* or *secondary research* (J. D. Brown, 1988). In this book, we are concerned with *empirical research*—that is, investigations in which the researchers collect and analyze original data of their own in order to answer the research questions they have posed.

A literature review can be published as a stand-alone piece or as part of a report on empirical research. There are at least four main reasons for doing a literature review when conducting empirical studies. We will examine each in turn.

The first reason for doing a literature review is to obtain background information on the area that you have chosen to investigate. A systematic literature review will acquaint you with previous work in the field and should alert you to problems and potential pitfalls in your chosen area. It will also help you locate clear definitions of key terms.

The second reason is to help you to identify *research gaps* (Cooley and Lewkowicz, 2003), which involve work that hasn't yet been done. Having reviewed and summarized the work of others, you will be able to spell out a research space or gap in the research literature that you propose to fill. Finding and articulating such gaps is part of developing the rationale for your research.

The third reason is to discover tools that could help you answer your own research question. For example, you may find a questionnaire someone else has developed that is directly related to your interest, or you might learn about a classroom observation instrument that would be useful in your study. So, as long as you choose judiciously and cite your sources properly, it is acceptable to utilize research procedures and tools developed by others.

Finally, reading widely in the field can help to reassure you that your proposed research question has not already been answered by someone else. There are few things more disheartening than to invest time and energy into a research project, only to find that someone else has been there before you. However, there is a value to replicating studies in new contexts. By *replicating*, we mean repeating a study (whether your own or someone else's) with different participants, and perhaps with some improvement upon the earlier study.

The first step in developing the literature review is to create an annotated bibliography. This resource lists those studies you have consulted that have a bearing on your own research. These may range from brief reports to entire books. Each entry in the bibliography would be annotated with a concise summary of its contents as they relate to your proposed study. The annotated bibliography should contain a full reference in whichever style you favor. We prefer the American Psychological Association (APA) guidelines, which can be obtained from their Web site at www.apa.org. The APA format is relatively straightforward and is used by many of the leading journals in our field.

ACTION

Visit the APA Web site and note the format for citing books, articles in journals, and chapters in books.

An annotation is a brief summary of a book, article, or chapter that you can consult in planning and writing about your own research. Annotating a research report can help you analyze and synthesize what you have read, and it will help you understand and remember the information. Here is an example of an annotation based on Jepson's (2005) research comparing the interaction in voice and text chat rooms, which served as the sample study in Chapter 1:

Jepson, Kevin. (2005). Conversations—and negotiated interaction—in text and voice chat rooms. *Language Learning and Technology*, 9(3), 79–98.

Jepson wanted to investigate the "quality of interaction among English L2 speakers in conversational text or voice chat rooms" (p. 79). He compared the voice chats and text (typed) chats of non-native speakers interacting on the Internet. He investigated which types of repair moves occur in text and voice chats, and looked for any differences between the repair moves in the typed chats and the voice chats. Jepson recorded ten 5-minute, synchronous chat room sessions (five of text-chats and five of voice chats). "Significant differences were found between the higher number of total repair moves made in voice chats and the smaller number in text chats" (p. 79). The repairs in the voice chats were often related to students' pronunciation issues. He used chi-square to analyze the quantitative data.

Annotations like this can be entered into a computer database and filed alphabetically in a word-processed document. Your annotated bibliography is then ready to be drawn on when you create your literature review. You will see that we have put the full reference at the top of this annotation. It is very important to keep careful records of your sources, making sure your reference list is complete and accurate, so you don't have to spend valuable time searching for missing or incomplete references.

The difference between an annotated bibliography and a literature review is that the former consists of separate entries arranged alphabetically by author, while a literature review is thematically organized: It extracts, records, and synthesizes the main points, issues, findings, and research methods of previous studies. We like to use the analogy of a quilt to explain this relationship. The annotations are like bits of cloth, the raw materials, assembled and organized before you start quilting. An effective literature review, in contrast, is more like a well-designed and carefully executed quilt. It is a unified whole.

In ordering and arranging your literature review, Merriam (1988) suggests that it is a good idea to differentiate between *data-based research* and *conceptual* (or *non-data-based) research* (referred to above as *secondary research*). Data-based studies drawn on and report empirical information collected by the researcher. Non-data based writings, on the other hand, "reflect the writers' experiences or opinions and can range from the highly theoretical to popular opinions" (p. 61).

When writing literature reviews, some researchers distinguish between substantive and methodological issues, and discuss these ideas in separate sections of the review. Substantive issues refer to *what* researchers actually investigated, that is, the content of their research (e.g., teacher talking time, decision making, task types, etc.). Methodological issues refer to *how* the researchers did their research, that is, the data collection and analysis techniques they used (e.g., observation, checklists, transcript analysis, teaching journals, stimulated recall, etc.).

Weirsma (1986) listed the following useful steps for creating a literature review:

1. Select studies that relate most directly to the problem at hand.
2. Tie together the results of the studies so that their relevance is clear. Do not simply provide a compendium of seemingly unrelated references in paragraph form.
3. When conflicting findings are reported across studies—and this is quite common in educational research—carefully examine the variations in the findings and possible explanations for them. Ignoring variation and simply averaging effects loses information and fails to recognize the complexity of the problem.
4. Make the case that the research area reviewed is incomplete or requires extension. This establishes the need for research in this area. (Note: This does not make the case that the proposed research is going to meet the need or is of significance.)
5. Although the information from the literature must be properly referenced, do not make the review a series of quotations.

6. The review should be organized according to the major points relevant to the problem. Do not force the review into a chronological organization, for example, which may confuse the relevance and continuity among the studies reviewed.

7. Give the reader some indication of the relative importance of the results from studies reviewed. Some results have more bearing on the problem than others and this should be indicated.

8. Provide closure for the section. Do not terminate with comments from the final study reviewed. Provide a summary and pull together the most important results. (pp. 376–377)

In our experience, these guidelines can be very helpful, especially to novice writers. You can also use these guidelines as criteria in evaluating literature reviews written by other researchers.

ACTION

Find a journal article or a book chapter about classroom research. Skim the literature review. How have the authors organized the information in their literature review?

SOME KEY CONCEPTS IN STARTING RESEARCH PROJECTS

In this section, we will describe and define some important concepts related to research design. These concepts are fundamental to understanding research of all kinds, not just classroom research. They are central to designing research projects of your own. There are many concepts that you will need to master for an advanced knowledge of research, and we don't plan to cover all of these here. In this section, we will restrict our attention to the following: types of variables, types of data, and operational definitions.

In Chapter 1, we noted that the psychometric tradition and naturalistic inquiry have been the historically dominant approaches to conducting language classroom research. We also said that action research is gaining ground as a viable approach to doing classroom research. No matter which of these approaches you use, the concepts of *data* and *variables* will be very important in planning your research.

Types of Variables and Types of Data

The notion of a variable is intuitively straightforward although students new to the research process often find this concept tricky, particularly when they are required to identify different kinds of variables in a research report. Simply put, a variable is something that is free to vary. A moment's thought will therefore reveal that the number of variables in the world is infinite. Think of the possible variables that might be included under the category of "personal characteristics." These might include, but would not be restricted to height, weight, eye color, handedness, income, number of siblings, number of hobbies, first language, country of origin, and so on.

Turning to language classrooms, the number of variables is also great. This action box lists several teachers' comments that are about variables that may influence teaching and learning.

ACTION

Think about the following statements made by teachers and identify the variables implicated in the statements.

Teacher A: I always used to teach grammar inductively, but I've recently started experimenting with deductive techniques.

Teacher B: Your grades on the listening test I gave you Friday are much improved.

Teacher C: I used to teach in an all girls' school, but I now teach in a coed school.

Teacher D: I just can't get my reading group motivated.

Teacher E: I've been trying to wait longer between asking a question and repeating the question or giving students the answer.

Teacher F: I seem to have a class of holistic learners this semester.

Here are the variable labels we would apply to these teachers' comments:

Teacher	Variable
A	Instructional method
B	Listening test scores
C	Students' gender
D	Learners' motivation
E	Instructional wait time
F	Learning style

These variables are different in kind because the data that comprise them are different. The simplest kind of data is known as *nominal data*. The word *nominal* is an adjective formed from *noun*. A nominal variable is something that can be named. Nominal data are also called *categorical data* because they involve putting things into categories to create variables. With nominal variables, we can create a series of 'boxes' that can be given a label and to which instances of each variable can be assigned. Gender, for example, is a nominal variable because we can label the boxes to which individual learners will be assigned as either *male* or *female*. (Jack goes in the male box; Jill goes in the female box.). Instructional method is another nominal variable. In this case, the boxes could be labeled *inductive* and *deductive*. Usually there is an "either/or" quality to nominal variables—people or data fit in only one category or another. For instance, students often come from one first-language background—say, Spanish or Arabic or Swahili or Dutch. (Students raised in bilingual homes would be classified differently.)

REFLECTION

Think of three other examples of variables made up of nominal data.

Not all variables are nominal to begin with although they can be turned into nominal variables. Consider test scores. Such data will typically be a sequence of numbers: 26, 74, 33, 52, 88, 81, 45, 62, and 49. These data cannot be assigned to boxes in the way gender and instructional method can. We could, if we wished, turn them into nominal variables by creating two (or more) boxes, say "high achievers" and "low achievers," and deciding, somewhat arbitrarily, that all learners who scored 50 and above would be placed in the high achievers' box, and those scoring less than 50 would be placed into the low achievers' box. Notice that this data reduction exercise results in less detailed information than do the original scores. Saying that *Billy is a low achiever, while Nancy is a high achiever* gives us less precise information than providing the students' actual scores. If we knew, for instance, that Billy had scored 49 and Nancy had scored 51, our interpretation of the students' proficiency would be much different than if Billy had scored 24 and Nancy 89.

Test scores and other measurements are typically considered to be *interval data* because they are measured on what is called an *interval scale*. This concept is easy to understand in terms of measurements of length, such as kilometers or inches. An inch is an inch whether it is the difference between fourteen inches and fifteen inches or between sixty-five inches and sixty-six inches. A kilometer remains the same length whether we are talking about the distance between four and five kilometers, or between 320 and 321 kilometers. The unit of measure is a constant interval. In the psychometric tradition, researchers often try to collect interval data because there are powerful statistical analyses that can be done with interval (or interval-like) data.

A third concept that is important in our field is *ordinal data*—that is, data that are represented in an order. In the example above, we can say that Billy scored lower than Nancy, whether their scores were 49 and 51, respectively, or 24 and 89, respectively. Ordinal data lack the precision of interval data, but they are often useful.

Ordinal measures are sometimes used in classroom research when precise counts or measurements are not appropriate or are not available. For example, if we lack a clear means of measuring fluency, we might ask a teacher to rank four students from the most fluent to the least fluent in speaking the target language. Let us say the teacher tells us that Keiko's spoken English is more fluent that Juan's, but Juan's is more fluent than Ahmed's. The teacher feels that Lee is the least fluent of the four students. The rank ordering of these students' names by fluency—Keiko, Juan, Ahmed, and Lee—is a set of ordinal data. Note that we cannot tell from rank-ordered data how much more fluent Keiko is than Juan, or how much less fluent Lee is than Ahmed. We only know their *relative* ranks in terms of the teacher's view of their fluency.

REFLECTION

Think of three more examples of interval data and three more of ordinal data that might occur in studies of language learning and teaching.

A final type of scale for measuring variables is the ratio scale, which measures absolute values such as temperature. Ratio scales are very important in the physical sciences, but they are of little value in applied linguistics because constructs such as language proficiency do not exist in absolute quantities. (Someone who obtains a score of 50 on a grammar test does not necessarily know twice as much grammar as someone who obtains a score of 25.) As they are of little practical interest to us in classroom research, we will not deal with ratio scales any further in this book.

REFLECTION

Which of the following variables involve interval, ordinal, and nominal (or categorical) data?

- Test takers' being put into two groups on the basis of the initials of their first names: those from A to N and O to Z.
- A list of test takers' names from the highest to the lowest scores (but without the scores being listed)
- A list of students' actual scores on the Test of English as Foreign Language

---

An interesting property of interval, ordinal, and nominal data is that they can be appropriately altered in one direction, but not in the other. That is, interval data can be converted to ordinal data (with some loss of precision, of course) but not the opposite. For example, if we know that Chin is sixty-five inches tall and that Maria is sixty inches tall, we can say that Chin is taller than Maria. But, if we are simply told that Chin is taller than Maria, we cannot tell exactly how tall the two students are unless we see them and measure their height. Likewise, interval data can be converted into categorical data once the categories have been established—tall, medium, and short, for instance. But just knowing that someone has been classified as being tall or of medium height or short does not tell us exactly what that person's height is.

ACTION

Here is a list of scores on a 100-point French grammar test. Consider these scores to be interval data, measuring the construct of French grammar knowledge.

Fred: 82 points	George: 95 points
John: 67 points	Marilyn: 98 points
Andrew: 84 points	Paul: 72 points
Meredith: 78 points	Whitney: 58 points
Leslie: 100 points	Steven: 52 points

Rank the students in order from highest to lowest in terms of their grammar test scores.

Now divide the students into those whose names start with letters in the first half of the alphabet and those whose names start with letters in the second half of the alphabet.

REFLECTION

Answer the following questions and compare your answers with a colleague or classmate.

1. What type of data were the students' actual French grammar test scores?

2. What type of data did you get when you ranked the students' names according to their grammar test scores (but did not include the scores themselves)?

3. What type of data did you have when you divided the students into those whose names start with letters in the first half of the alphabet and those whose names start with letters in the second half of the alphabet?

We have spent a fair amount of time discussing variables and the sorts of data you might use in your research (or read about in other people's reports) because these concepts influence a great many decisions about how we will collect and analyze our data. Another related and important issue is that of constructs and how they are operationalized, the topic of our next section.

Operationalizing Constructs

Constructs are a bit trickier to define than variables. In this book, we will use the term *constructs* to refer to all human qualities such as motivation, proficiency, aptitude, intelligence, and acculturation. Constructs are typically qualities that cannot be seen directly, but that have to be inferred from behavior. They are called *constructs* because we construct or 'invent' the labels to account for the behavior. For example, we observe a certain student spending three afternoons a week studying in the self-access learning center and say, "Wow! He's really motivated." You may have noticed that all constructs are variables because they are qualities that vary from one learner to another. (However, not all variables are constructs because some variables—like height, for instance—are directly observable.)

Constructs such as attitude, motivation, and language proficiency are not directly observable, so they pose challenges for people who want to investigate them. How do you investigate something like learner motivation that can't be seen? You have to create a way of eliciting behavior and/or information from the learner that can be observed and use the resulting data to make inferences about the unobservable quality. Questionnaires, for example, have been created to measure attitude, motivation, anxiety, and so on. (We will examine questionnaires in Chapter 5.)

This process of creating or choosing an instrument for eliciting or otherwise recording behavior that is subsequently used for making inferences about psychological constructs is known as *construct operationalization*. In the examples we saw above, students' scores on the Test of English as a Foreign Language provide one way of operationalizing the construct of language proficiency. Likewise, a teacher's ranking of students' speaking fluency is one way to try to capture, or operationalize, the construct of spoken fluency. Another way would be to define speaking fluency in terms of speed of speech. For example, fluency could be determined by the average number of syllables uttered per minute. If we were to operationally define spoken fluency in this way, we would need to collect data by recording speech samples and counting the number of syllables uttered per minute.

Regardless of the approach to research we take, when we operationalize constructs that interest us, it is important to define key terms (both variables and constructs). In fact, researchers use a particular approach to defining key terms, which involves writing *operational definitions*. These definitions are based on the on particular (often observable) characteristics of the things being defined. Operational definitions must be clear enough that the study could be replicated by someone else.

Operational definitions are usually developed in one of three ways (Tuckman, 1999). First, operational definitions can be based on experimenter manipulation. That is, a researcher generates or creates the phenomenon under investigation: "*Individualized instruction* can be operationally defined as instruction that the researcher has designed to be delivered by a computer (or book) so that students can work on it by themselves at their own pace" (p. 114). Second, some operational definitions are based on what a thing or person does, or how it operates. So, for instance, a researcher might define a *directive teacher* as one who "gives instructions, personalizes criticism or blame, and establishes formal relationships with students" (p. 116). Third, operational definitions can be developed using the internal properties of an individual or entity (and these are often documented through self-report). For instance, course satisfaction "might be the perception—as reported by subjects on questionnaires—that a course has been an interesting and effective learning experience" (p. 117). When you operationally define key terms in your own research, choose the approach that best suits the term(s) you are trying to define.

ACTION

Look at a research article on a topic that interests you. What key terms have been defined? Which of the approaches described by Tuckman (1999) were used to write the operational definitions?

Here is an example of how one researcher operationalized the constructs he was investigating. You will recall that Jepson (2005) investigated repair moves in voice chat rooms and text chat rooms. Based on his review of the literature (particularly papers by Long [1983b and 1983c]; 1996] and Y. Lin and Hedgcock [1996]), Jepson operationalized repair moves in two categories: "Negotiation of Meaning (NOM)" and "Negative Feedback (NF)," as shown in **Table 2.3**.

Jepson used these categories in his data analysis. It was important to have clear definitions and examples of the various types of repair moves because he wanted to have a second researcher code the data from the chat rooms as a quality control check. Also, if someone wanted to replicate Jepson's study (either with similar or dissimilar participants), they could use this table to code their data. Doing so would allow other researchers to compare their results to Jepson's. Having clear operational definitions and examples is also helpful to readers of research reports.

As Table 2.3 reveals, doing your literature review can provide you with clear operational definitions of key terms and appropriate ways to operationalize constructs important in your study. Making sure you are clear and consistent in defining terms and operationalizing constructs improves the entire research process—from articulating the research question or stating the hypothesis, to designing the study, choosing or crafting the data collection procedures, and analyzing the data. We will now turn to considerations of research design.

TABLE 2.3	Codes and operationalizations for repair moves in text and voice chat sessions (from Jepson, 2005, pp. 88–89)	
	Negotiation of Meaning (NOM; Long, 1983c)	Negative Feedback (NF; Long 1996)
Interlocutors (responding to text or speech initiated by another speaker)	**CR:** clarification requests (e.g., *What do you mean by X?*)	**R:** recasts (The interlocutor corrects the speaker's word or utterance by repeating it in its correct form. e.g., *This city is beautiful* in response to the speaker's *This city beautiful.*)
	CC: confirmation checks (e.g., *Did you mean/say X?*)	**EC:** explicit correction (The interlocutor tells the speaker of his/her mistake. e.g., *You should say, "This city is beautiful."*)
		Q: questions (The interlocutor asks a question in order to prompt the speaker to make a correction. e.g., *Can you try that again?*)
Speakers (initiating text or speech)	**COMP C:** comprehension checks (e.g., *Do you understand?*) **SR/P:** self-repetition or paraphrase (e.g., *Which / pli:s / uh, / pli:s /, uh, which landmark can I visit?*) **I:** incorporations (Speaker repairs utterance based on interlocutor cues; Y. Lin and Hedgcock, 1996, e.g., in response to a confirmation check: *Yes, I mean X.*)	**I/F:** incorporations (Speaker repairs utterance based on interlocutor feedback; Y. Lin and Hedgcock, 1996), e.g., in response to an explicit correction: *Sorry, this city is beautiful.*) **SC:** self-corrections (The speaker initiates adjustments to her or his own previous errors without assistance from the interlocutor e.g., *This has beeb, I mean been, great.*)

INITIAL RESEARCH DESIGN CONSIDERATIONS

A research design is analogous to an architect's plan for building a house. It lays out, in advance, approximately what the end product should look like. It suggests measurements for the different components of the structure, materials to be used, and steps for accomplishing the desired goal. Fortunately, in research there are a number of existing research designs and methodological tools that we can draw upon in planning a study, so that we don't have to start totally from scratch. The design you choose and develop is directly related to the research question(s) you are posing, and it will be influenced by your literature review.

So, as a next step, we will sketch out some of the initial design considerations that follow on from the question identification and literature review. The issues foreshadowed here are taken up and elaborated in succeeding chapters, so this section is meant to provide only a brief overview of research design considerations.

Design Issues in Experimental Research

One of the first things researchers need to consider is whether the research question suggests an experimental or a non-experimental research design. If the research involves testing the strength of one variable's influence on another, then an experiment may be needed. If the research question is more exploratory in nature, then action research or some sort of naturalistic inquiry may be more appropriate.

You will recall that in the psychometric approach, researchers typically set out to measure psychological constructs in some way. Often they do so because they want to investigate issues of *causality*. That is, they want to determine whether a change in one variable can influence, or cause, a change in another variable. To do so, researchers look for significant differences between groups on some common measurement. Remember the large-scale methods comparisons described in Chapter 1? Those researchers were trying to determine whether one particular method caused better language learning than a competing method. That is, they were investigating the effect of one variable (method of instruction) on another (language learning).

There are many types of research designs, but in the experimental method, most of the designs for investigating causality share four characteristics. First, the researcher pre-specifies and defines the variables of interest. Secondly, the researcher intervenes in and manipulates the learning environment in some way to see if he or she can cause a change to occur. In experimental research, the researcher's intentional intervention is called the *treatment*. In the strongest experimental designs, a third characteristic is that the subjects who participate in the experiment are randomly selected from the population they represent and then randomly assigned to the sample groups. The fourth characteristic is that at least one group of subjects, called the *control group*, does not get the treatment. When these conditions are met, the researcher is using what is called a *true experimental design*.

There are reasons for randomly selecting participants, which are related to the logic of the experimental method. Suppose you teach Japanese in

New Zealand and you have about forty beginning students of Japanese. Two beginning classes of approximately twenty students each have been scheduled. One of the beginner classes meets at 8 A.M. and the other meets at 3 P.M. The curriculum for the two beginner classes is the same, but you have considerable freedom to deliver it however you think best. At a conference, you attended a workshop on vocabulary development through the use of Total Physical Response (TPR) (Asher, Kusudo, and de la Torre, 1993)—a language teaching procedure that involves the students in intensive listening practice in which they respond to commands through physical actions. You would like to see whether using TPR with your learners will help them to learn and retain Japanese vocabulary items better than your regular teaching method does. So, you decide to conduct a little experiment. For one full month, up until the first examination, you will use TPR with one class of beginning students but not with the other class.

ACTION

Write the research question for the study about using TPR with the beginning Japanese students. What terms would you need to operationally define in preparing to carry out this study?

You could, of course, use TPR with both beginner classes and then see how well they do on the examination, but that would give you no point of comparison. You could test all the students about their knowledge of Japanese vocabulary before the TPR lessons and again after the six weeks of TPR lessons, but there would be little reason to do so since you know the students are true beginners. So, you decide to use TPR techniques with one class of Japanese learners and to use your regular teaching method with the other group. That way you can compare the vocabulary test scores of the two groups of students—those with whom you used TPR and those with whom you did not. The purpose of withholding the experimental treatment from one group is to be able to compare the learners' test scores and see if those who receive the TPR lessons outperform those who do not. (In other words, you want to see if using TPR causes a difference in the learners' Japanese vocabulary test scores.)

REFLECTION

Imagine that as you are planning your research project about TPR lessons and Japanese vocabulary learning, you find out that athletic practice for school sports will be held at 3 P.M. every afternoon, so any beginning students of Japanese who wish to participate in sports will enroll in your 8 A.M. class. You also learn that orchestra, band, and choir practices are held every morning from 7 to 9, so any of the music students who wish to take beginning Japanese will be in your afternoon class.

What are the implications of these facts for interpreting the outcomes of your study?

As you can imagine, given the different sorts of students who will probably enroll, these two beginning Japanese classes may be different from the outset (i.e., the more musical students will be in the afternoon class and the more athletic students will be in the morning class). Remember that your purpose in setting up the comparison is to see if students who received TPR training would do better than those without such training in terms of their Japanese vocabulary learning. But you will not be able to make strong claims that any differences you observe in the two groups' test scores are due to the use of TPR. The students' preexisting differences may influence the outcome as much as—or even more than—the TPR treatment.

For this reason—to counteract the possibility of preexisting differences influencing the results of a study—in formal experiments, researchers randomly select people to be in the experiment (and they are called the *sample*). They are selected from the population they represent. The researchers then randomly assign subjects to the different experimental and control conditions. The logic here is that randomly assigning subjects to different conditions distributes any possible 'contaminating' learner factors to both the experimental and control groups. If you were able to use *random selection* (from the population to the sample) and *random assignment* (from the randomly selected sample to the two different class periods) in your TPR experiment, you would then be in a better position to argue that any differences on the Japanese vocabulary test are due to the experimental treatment because—thanks to randomization—the other variables that might have had an effect (such as intelligence and aptitude) presumably exist in equal quantities in both the experimental and control groups, and therefore cancel one another out.

In most real-world educational contexts, teachers typically don't have the resources or the power to randomly select subjects from the population and/or randomly assign them to groups. (In the Japanese class example above, you cannot choose secondary school students at random to study Japanese. The students themselves make this choice. Nor can you select at random who will attend the morning and afternoon classes due to the schedule of music and sports in the curriculum.) As a result, relatively little language classroom research has used the *true experimental designs*. Instead, researchers working with regularly occurring classes often use what is called the *intact groups design*. That is, the groups are preexisting, before the experiment was set up, or for some reason they cannot be randomly selected and/or randomly assigned. Comparing the vocabulary scores of the morning and the afternoon beginning Japanese classes (when one group receives TPR training and the other does not) is an example of an intact groups design.

We will return to the types of research designs used in experimental research in Chapter 4, where we will examine that method in more detail. Keep in mind that there are many, many variations on the types of research design used in psychometric research, and here we have just begun to explore the possibilities.

Design Issues in Nonexperimental Research

Nonexperimental research is often underpinned by *what-if* and *what's-going-on* questions rather than by questions aimed at investigating causal relationships between variables. Typical nonexperimental classroom research questions include the following:

1. What are the classroom experiences of trainee teachers in inner-city classrooms?
2. What do learners believe about the nature of language and learning?
3. What happens when teachers increase *wait time* (the time between asking a question and then either reformulating the question or answering it)?

The best way to address these questions may not entail conducting an experiment. For instance, answering the first question might involve observing and interviewing teacher trainees completing their practice teaching assignments in inner-city schools. The second question could be addressed by interviewing language learners about their beliefs. There are no issues of causality involved in these two research questions that would necessitate comparing one group of teachers or learners to another.

The third research question above is somewhat more complex in terms of design issues. We could, for instance, set up an experiment in which some language teachers (those teaching the experimental groups) would intentionally lengthen their wait time (by counting to ten before reformulating a question or answering it if students do not respond). Other teachers (those teaching the control groups in the experiment) would just continue with their usual wait time. We could then compare the two sets of students on some measure of language learning or satisfaction.

However, it could be just as valuable NOT to set up an experiment. This question could be explored with action research. For example, a teacher might read that increasing one's wait time enhances both the quantity and the quality of student responses. She might then try to see if this would be true in her own class. She could plan an action research project in which she systematically increased her wait time and tape-recorded her lessons to see if there was an apparent difference in how the students answered questions or responded to comments. In this case, action research would be an appropriate choice of how to address the research question.

In discussing design issues in experimental research, we introduced the concept of *sampling*. This term often means the selection of research subjects from the wider population to be in the sample (i.e., to be participants in the experiment). However, there are sampling considerations in nonexperimental research as well.

If you are conducting a case study in the naturalistic inquiry tradition, for instance, you may choose a particular class, teacher, or learner as the unit of analysis because that class or person is typical in some way. For instance, you may choose to investigate the experiences of trainee teachers in inner-city classrooms by choosing one trainee who typifies the others (e.g., a female teacher with less than one year of experience doing her student teaching in a junior high school in New York City). The wider group that interests you (here, teacher trainees working in inner-city contexts) is called the *population*. The typical teacher you select may be chosen on the grounds that she apparently represents the population.

Likewise, if you want to know what learners believe about the nature of language and learning, you would first have to decide what the population is that interests you. Do you want to find out about adult learners, adolescents, or children? Do you want to find out about learners in *second language contexts* (where the target language is used in the surrounding society as the general language of communication) or *foreign language contexts* (where the target language is not commonly used in that environment)? Answers to these questions will strongly influence the choice of what learners to interview.

REFLECTION

Think about some classroom research that you would like to do. What case or sample might you study? What population would be represented?

In other situations, you may choose a particular case as the object of your investigation because that entity is somehow unique or special. For example, in an early classroom investigation, R. L. Allwright (1980) wanted to investigate how ESL learners got speaking turns in class. In the process, he found that some learners got many more than the typical number of turns and others got far fewer. So, after discussing the quantitative analysis of the number and length of turns taken by all the students, Allwright investigated a particular learner who got far more than his "fair share" of speaking turns in class. The close analysis of that learner's conversation with the teacher allowed Allwright to discover how he got so many turns. In this case, the learner's uniqueness was what caused the researcher to focus on him.

Sometimes sampling decisions are influenced by practical issues such as the availability of subjects or of a research setting. If you are living and working in São Paulo, for instance, it will be much easier and cheaper to observe and interview teacher trainees working there than in New York City. If you are teaching adult EFL learners in Seoul, it will be much more practical to learn about their beliefs regarding language learning and teaching than about the beliefs of learners in Cairo. Making sampling decisions on the basis of availability is known as *opportunistic sampling*.

In the experimental tradition, opportunistic sampling is frowned upon because it is not as powerful as random sampling in controlling variables. However, in some naturalistic inquiry, opportunistic sampling can increase our access to subjects and add depth to the database. For example, many of the earliest case studies of children acquiring two languages simultaneously were done by those children's parents. The parents had broad exposure to the children's emerging speech and could record their utterances at any hour of the night or day. In those instances, opportunistic sampling was an effective way of choosing subjects for in-depth observations over time.

Another sampling concern has to do with time. If you are collecting data from students in a language program, when is the best time to do so? Is it reasonable, for instance, to ask beginning learners of Chinese as a foreign language about their beliefs regarding language learning and teaching before they have had any experience with foreign language learning? Or should you wait until they have been enrolled in the Chinese class for a month or a semester? In fact, the answer depends on your research question(s). Think about the following options for articulating the research question that embodies an interest in language learners' beliefs:

1. What do learners believe about the nature of language and learning?
2. What do beginning learners believe about the nature of language and learning before starting to study a foreign language?
3. What do beginning learners believe about the nature of language and learning after one semester of studying a foreign language?
4. What is the difference, if any, between learners' beliefs about the nature of language and learning before and after one semester of studying a foreign language?

The way you articulate your research question(s) will clearly influence your data collection (whether you do so through questionnaires, classroom observations, etc.).

To summarize, research design issues, such as sampling, are important in nonexperimental research as well as in experimental studies. The design you choose is directly related to how you word your research question(s). The design will also be influenced by the literature you review.

SAMPLE STUDY

In this chapter, rather than summarize an entire study, we will report on how one classroom researcher got started on an investigation. This study was by Sarah Springer, a teacher who had enrolled in a graduate program in TESOL (Teaching English to Speakers of Other Languages). Through her course readings, she became interested in what factors promoted second language acquisition. Here are Springer's (2003) comments about choosing a research focus:

> My own training and previous experience as an EFL teacher in Europe had involved courses organized around grammatical syllabi that presented discrete linguistic forms in a linear progression. The first opportunity I had to work with groups of students using content- and project-based syllabi was in the summer of 2002. The . . . summer program had been designed to provide both a cultural exchange and academic research experience for Japanese university students who over

the course of three short weeks investigated a socially relevant topic of their choice. The research methods employed by the students include library and Internet background research, participant observation, public opinion surveys and focused interviews. In addition to visiting their community placement sites and attending classes and workshops in support of their developing research and technology skills, the students were also enrolled in courses on American Life and Communication Skills, and spent a considerable amount of time with their American host families. At the end of the session, each student must synthesize the results of their research by preparing and delivering a six- to eight-minute PowerPoint presentation.

My experience as a teacher in this program was very rewarding. However, as the session came to a close and I was attempting to write the questions for an end-of-session student survey, I began to reflect on the extent to which my previous conceptions of 'the English language' as a subject of study and the language learning process itself were only marginally relevant to the complex and clearly quite engaging experience in which the students . . . had been involved. Without a list of grammatical items that had been 'covered' I was at a loss as to how, specifically, their experiences in the program might have contributed to their language development. I was confronted by the discrepancy between my conviction that it had been a valuable and productive experience for them and my inability to answer a question which I initially framed as, "What did they learn?"

In the following semester I encountered numerous concepts in my Sociolinguistics and Second Language Acquisition courses that provided me with names for what I had experienced and gave me new frameworks with which I could analyze my summer experiences. By the end of the semester my question had evolved into the following: What implications does a much broader view of language and the language learning process have for my role and responsibilities as a language teacher? What changes come about in my expectations concerns the roles and responsibilities of the students? What impact does the shift to content- or project-based syllabi have on these classroom roles and on the language produced by course participants—both teachers and learners?" (pp. 2–3)

REFLECTION

Have you ever had an experience like Springer's, where a job change or a new opportunity led you to reflect on what you were teaching and why? If so, what issues arose for you? If not, can you imagine a context in which you might face such issues? (If you are a new teacher with limited experience, it would be worthwhile to ask an experienced teacher these questions.)

We will return to Springer's study in future chapters. At this point, we will consider some of the payoffs and pitfalls of designing language classroom research.

PAYOFFS AND PITFALLS

There are many practical problems that occur in language classroom research. Our purpose here is not to intimidate or worry you about conducting your own research but rather to help you prepare to overcome such problems by anticipating them. Careful planning in the design stages will help you avoid difficulties and disappointments in the data collection and analysis stages.

In fact, once you get to the point of fleshing out your research ideas, it is a good practice to spend some time anticipating the practical problems likely to get in the way of successfully completing the project. Anticipating problems and thinking about solutions can help smooth the research path. Problems encountered by our own graduate students include the following:

1. Lack of time (a particular problem for students who are also working or taking several courses)

2. Lack of expertise, particularly at critical points in the research process such as formulating a researchable question, determining the appropriate research design, and, in the case of quantitative research, selecting the appropriate statistical tool

3. Identifying subjects willing to take part in the research

4. Negotiating access to research sites (Unless you are collecting data in your own classroom or your own school, getting permission to collect data can be both time-consuming and frustrating.)

5. Issues of confidentiality

6. Ethical questions relating to data collection, which become acute when you want to collect data without alerting your subjects beforehand

7. The sensitivity of reporting negative findings, particularly if these relate to individuals you work with or know well

8. The difficulty of actually writing up the research

The last problem can become acute, particularly for researchers who are not native speakers of the reporting language or who lack confidence (and sometimes skill) in producing an extended piece of writing. We recommend writing regularly from the very beginning of the research process. This writing could be summaries of the background reading you are doing that may eventually find its way into the literature review in some shape or form. Or it could be reflections on the research process. Even if you eventually discard much of your earlier writing, the process itself will be an important stimulus to thinking.

It has been our experience that carefully planning the study in advance can reduce frustration, save time, and generate better research. In particular, getting the research question focused and worded correctly is central to all other decisions. However, it is also important to be flexible and to adapt to new conditions that may arise during your investigation.

ACTION

Think of some research you would like to conduct. Make a list of the problems you think might arise in your own research situation.

There are numerous payoffs to doing classroom research and particularly to investing time in the planning stages. Taking an idea from an initial interest to a research focus and then to a refined research question is intellectually intriguing and helps to clarify our thinking about the issue. Making research design and sampling decisions based on our refined research questions leads to all sorts of intriguing possibilities about how to best to collect and analyze data to investigate our topic.

Doing a thorough literature review can be a form of professional development because there is so much to learn about the issues that interest us! Likewise, if we return to our research-as-culture metaphor, reading widely and writing a strong literature review is a means of beginning to understand and then enter a particular part of the culture. It can also help you get up-to-date on new developments that will have occurred since you last took a course or read about a topic of interest.

Finally, although we have not gotten to this part of the story yet, doing the research itself—collecting and analyzing the data—can be great fun and extremely rewarding. As we will see when we revisit Sarah Springer's and Kevin Jepson's studies, as well as encountering others in future chapters, doing original research can help us make connections to the vast body of theory and existing research in our field.

CONCLUSION

In this chapter, we have looked at some of the practicalities of doing research, focusing on posing important and doable research questions, reviewing the literature, and considering some of the basics of research design. We have also reviewed important concepts including types of variables, types of data, constructs and construct operationalization, and sampling decisions. Finally, we have looked at initial design issues in experimental and nonexperimental contexts. The chapter closes with the usual questions and tasks to help you internalize these concepts, as well as suggestions for additional readings in case you would like to pursue these topics in more depth.

QUESTIONS AND TASKS

1. Find a classroom research article on a topic that interests you. Did the researchers pose research questions, hypotheses, or both? What key terms and constructs did they operationalize?

2. Find a teacher who has conducted some kind of classroom research, whether or not that study has been published. Ask the teacher what his or her research questions were and how he or she arrived at them.

3. Read a published account of an experimental study. How were the participants in the study (i.e., the sample) selected? What population were they supposed to represent?

4. Read the published accounts of two or more case studies. How did the researchers in those situations locate their subjects?

5. Find a report about an experiment on language learning or teaching. Which characteristics of the so-called true experimental designs did the study involve?

   A. The researcher prespecified and defined the variables of interest.

   B. The researcher intervened and provided a treatment.

   C. The subjects in the experiment were randomly selected from the population they represented and randomly assigned to groups.

   D. At least one group of subjects (the control group) did not get the treatment.

6. Ask an experienced researcher to discuss some of the challenges he or she has encountered in trying to set up a study. Find out what research tradition(s) he or she was using and what solutions emerged as the study progressed.

SUGGESTIONS FOR FURTHER READING

Freeman's (1998) book *Doing Teacher Research: From Inquiry to Understanding* is a good starting point for novice researchers. It uses extended examples of teacher research to illustrate the issues involved in getting started.

A helpful guide for preparing a literature review is Galvan's (1999) book *Writing Literature Reviews: A Guide for Students of the Social and Behavioral Sciences*. We also recommend *Dissertation Writing in Practice: Turning Ideas into Text* by Cooley and Lewkowicz (2003).

Chaudron's (1988) book *Second Language Classrooms: Research on Teaching and Learning* provides good background reading about the state of the art in language classroom research in the late 1980s.

Sometimes our students get discouraged because the articles they read in professional journals seem to suggest that everything went smoothly during the research process. In fact, this is seldom the case. Schachter and Gass (1996) have edited a collection of papers by experienced language classroom researchers. Their purpose was to give readers "an honest, behind the scenes look at what happens from the beginning to the end of a research project within a classroom context" (p. vii). The authors provide a candid look at the problems that almost inevitably occur in conducting classroom research.

3

Key Concepts in Planning Classroom Research

The blacksmith cannot criticize the carpenter for not heating a piece of wood over a fire. However, the carpenter must demonstrate a principled control over the materials. (van Lier, 1988, p. 42)

INTRODUCTION AND OVERVIEW

In this, the final chapter of Section 1 of this book, we will continue to build on the ideas presented in Chapters 1 and 2, with a special focus on planning your research design so that you can make good decisions about your data collection and analysis procedures. Having posed a research question and done your literature review, you are well set to begin planning your study, but what you actually do depends on the research questions or hypotheses you have posed and what your goals are in conducting the investigation.

For instance, if you wanted to conduct an action research study, like the possible investigation of a teacher's wait time described in Chapter 2, your research questions and procedures would be different from those you would use if you developed an experiment on wait time in which one group of teachers increased their wait time and another group did not, and you subsequently assessed the quantity and quality of verbal turns taken by the students of those two sets of teachers. Likewise, if you wanted to do a case study of one particular teacher trainee's experiences while doing his or her practice teaching in an inner-city school, the procedures would be quite different than if you wished to contrast the questionnaire responses of 200 trainees in Manchester and another 200 in Johannesburg. This questionnaire study would be more like classroom-oriented research than actual classroom-based research (see Chapter 1), but it would still be relevant and important to teacher educators and trainees.

Based on what you've read so far and what you already knew about research, think of a classroom-based or classroom-oriented study that you would like to do. Keep that idea in mind as you read this chapter.

The key point here is that there is no perfect research design or research method. As van Lier (1988) notes, the tools you choose depend on the goals you wish to accomplish. So, as we proceed through the next sections, please keep in mind that we do not advocate any of the main research traditions over the others out of context. However, we will begin this chapter with concepts associated primarily with research design in the psychometric tradition for two reasons: (1) historically it has been (until recently) the dominant tradition in classroom research, and (2) some of the vocabulary associated with quantitative data collection and analysis are used in other approaches as well. So, the psychometric tradition serves as a useful point of departure for discussions about several approaches to classroom research. For this reason, we will begin with the concept of hypotheses and hypothesis testing. We will then consider the sorts of threats to research design that can invalidate a study. Finally, we will discuss the ex post facto class of designs. This class consists of two important research designs, one of which enables us to investigate correlations of two or more variables. The other leads to nonexperimental comparisons of different groups. These designs are useful in language classroom research, and there are several examples of both in the published literature of our field.

HYPOTHESIS TESTING

In Chapter 2, we discussed writing clear research questions and operational definitions. We noted that in some instances researchers use hypotheses in addition to or instead of research questions. Hypotheses are especially important in experiments conducted in the psychometric tradition, but the concept has valuable applications to other types of research as well.

A *hypothesis* is a precisely worded statement about the expected outcomes of a study. Hypotheses are most closely (but not exclusively) related to research in the psychometric tradition. You will recall that this approach to research gets its name from the fact that researchers seek to measure psychological constructs. They do so largely to determine if there are causal relationships between variables. As a result, hypotheses in the psychometric tradition are frequently statements about possible causal relationships between variables, which are identified by looking for substantial differences between groups of subjects who have undergone different experiences.

In the psychometric approach, there are three main ways that hypotheses are worded. Each choice of wording has a certain underlying logic that will help you understand why researchers choose to articulate hypotheses as they do. The first of these is called the *null hypothesis* because it predicts that there will be no significant difference between groups of subjects.

The logic of posing a null hypothesis can be confusing, so we will examine it in some detail before proceeding. The idea of the null hypothesis is based on the concepts of proof and disproof. As the logic goes, in empirical research, we can never actually *prove* anything: We can only disprove, or *falsify*, claims. This philosophy of *falsificationism* in science was advanced by the philosopher Popper (1968; 1972). Popper argued that we can never prove anything through observation; we can only disprove tentatively established hypotheses. His famous example is called the white swan argument. According to Popper, 1,000 sightings of white swans does not entitle us to claim "all swans are white" as a scientific fact. We can tentatively put forward the hypothesis "all swans are white," but we should then go in search of a single disconfirming black swan. If your experience of seeing swans is limited to North America or Europe, you might assume that all swans are white. But you could never prove that all swans are white because you could never possibly see all the swans in the world, nor could you see all the swans that have ever lived, are living now, or will live in the future. In fact, if you were to go to New Zealand and visit the lake at Rotorua, you would see thousands of black swans there, but the existence of even one black swan disproves, or falsifies, the hypothesis that all swans are white.

The null hypothesis in experimental research works with this same logic. Researchers pose a null hypothesis and then set out to reject it. For example, in designing the hypothetical study discussed in Chapter 2 (about using Total Physical Response with learners of Japanese), we might pose the following null hypothesis (symbolized by a capital H with the subscript zero, to represent "null"):

H_0: There will be no statistically significant difference in the Japanese vocabulary test scores of beginning students taught with Total Physical Response and those taught with traditional methods.

In setting out to test this hypothesis, researchers would actually collect data and conduct analyses that will allow them to reject (i.e., disprove) the null hypothesis.

There are two other ways to word hypotheses. The first is called the *alternative hypothesis* because it is an alternative to the null hypothesis. Such a statement is, in fact, the position that the researcher would probably like to support but can never really prove. (Remember the black swans!) The alternative hypothesis is simply an affirmatively worded restatement of the null hypothesis. If we can reject the null hypothesis, we can accept the alternative hypothesis. The alternative hypothesis wording is often symbolized by an H (for *hypothesis*) with the subscript A (for *alternative*), like this:

H_A: There will be a statistically significant difference in the Japanese vocabulary test scores of beginning students taught with Total Physical Response and those taught with traditional methods.

Posing a null hypothesis is a conservative approach to getting started on research design. It is typically used where there is no previous research or theory to suggest that there will be a significant difference between groups. The null hypothesis format is also used when there is existing research, but the results of that research have been mixed or contradictory. (You would discover that situation in reviewing the literature.)

In the case where we do have theory and/or research findings suggesting that there will be a significant difference between groups, researchers often use the third option and pose what is called an *alternative directional hypothesis*. In this context, researchers feel a bit more confident about the likely outcomes and therefore take the risk of making a specific prediction about the outcomes of the study. Here is an alternative directional hypothesis based on the example above. It is indicated with the symbols H_{A-1}:

> H_{A-1}: There will be a statistically significant difference in the Japanese vocabulary test scores of beginning students taught with Total Physical Response and those taught with traditional methods, with the students who had TPR instruction outscoring those who did not.

This wording is referred to as *directional* because the alternative directional hypothesis predicts the direction the difference will take (i.e., which group will perform better than the other in a two-group comparison).

ACTION

Compare the null hypothesis, alternative hypothesis, and alternative directional hypothesis discussed above. Circle or underline the specific differences in their wording.

How a researcher chooses to word the hypothesis in a study is important. The choice of the null hypothesis, the alternative hypothesis, or the alternative directional hypothesis is part of what influences the choice of statistical analyses of our data—a point we will return to later. In the meantime, just be aware that (1) sometimes researchers (especially those working in the psychometric tradition) pose hypotheses instead of (or in addition to) posing research questions, and that (2) such hypotheses can be worded in various ways. Whether the researcher poses a null hypothesis or an alternative hypothesis or an alternative directional hypothesis is largely a function of how much existing research and/or theory is available to guide the prediction.

ACTION

Skim a research report in a professional journal or anthology from our field. Did the author(s) use research questions, hypotheses, or both? If they used hypotheses, were the statements written as null hypotheses, alternative hypotheses, or alternative directional hypotheses? (It is not uncommon for researchers to pose the null hypothesis they wish to reject and also the alternative hypothesis they wish to accept.)

MORE ABOUT VARIABLES AND RESEARCH DESIGN

A great deal of research is aimed at establishing some kind of causal association between variables of the kinds we have just been discussing. For example, a teacher may be interested in seeing if there is a causal relationship between methods of grammatical instruction (inductive or deductive) and students' test scores. His or her research question might be, "Do students who receive inductive instruction do better on standardized grammar tests than those who receive deductive instruction?" Of course, both *inductive* and *deductive grammar instruction* would need to be operationally defined.

In this study, the method of instruction would be called the *independent variable*, while the students' test scores would be called the *dependent variable* because they presumably depend on, or are a result of, the independent variable. It is the independent variable (method of grammatical instruction, in this case) that is the focus of our attention in conducting an experiment because we want to know if manipulating that variable (by using either an inductive or a deductive method of grammar teaching) influences students' learning. If, for instance, one group of forty students outscores another group of forty students, and if the experiment has been carefully set up, the teacher-researcher can infer that the difference in scores "depended" on the two different teaching methods. For this reason, the difference we are looking for (by counting, rating, ranking, or measuring) is called the *dependent variable*.

The different subcategories, or *levels*, of the independent variable are what define the groups being compared. In this example the independent variable is the method of grammar instruction and it has two levels: inductive grammar teaching and deductive grammar teaching. To return to our earlier discussion about variables and data types, the independent variable here is *nominal* (or *categorical*) in nature: the teaching method is either deductive or inductive. The dependent variable, the standardized grammar test, yields interval data (the students' actual test scores). This design can be depicted by a simple box diagram, as shown in **Figure 3.1**.

Deductive Grammar Teaching (n = 40 students)	Inductive Grammar Teaching (n = 40 students)

FIGURE 3.1 A box diagram of a study with two levels of the independent variable

ACTION

Write the null hypothesis, the alternative hypothesis, and a directional alternative hypothesis for this example study about deductive and inductive grammar teaching. (Note: If you were really going to do this study, there would be two directions the directional alternative hypothesis could take. How you would state that alternative directional hypothesis would depend on your literature review.)

Of course, conducting research in real classrooms, which are full of lively language learners with all sorts of interesting human characteristics, is seldom as neat as conducting an experiment in a laboratory setting. Often the variable that interests us most is some kind of important but hidden construct, such as motivation, language learning experience, or aptitude. In any given class (as you know from your own history as a language learner and/or teacher), the students may have a wide range of aptitude, motivation, and experience with language learning. So, we want to be careful about making claims that the treatment (one of the *levels* of the independent variable in an experiment) is the thing that has caused any difference we may observe in the students' scores rather than some preexisting or uncontrolled factor.

Uncontrolled factors that influence the outcome of a study (in addition to or instead of the levels of the independent variable) are called *confounding variables* because they confuse or confound the interpretation of the results. In our comparison of deductive and inductive grammar teaching, for instance, if one group (say the treatment group) consists of more experienced language learners or students with higher aptitudes for language learning or students who are better test takers, those factors may cause them to excel on the grammar test rather than (or in addition to) the teaching method used.

Often you will be able to identify some factors that might become confounding variables in your study on the basis of your literature review. For example, suppose you read that left-handed learners do better with inductive teaching methods than with deductive teaching methods. If there were only a few left-handed people in the groups you were teaching and investigating, you might choose to eliminate their test results from the study. Doing so would make handedness a *control variable*—that is, a variable whose possible influence is controlled for by excluding it from the study. If researchers can anticipate possible problematic influences like these and control for them by planning them <u>out</u> of the research design, we say that those factors "have been controlled for."

Another way that researchers deal with possible influences on the relationship between the independent and dependent variables in a study is to use what are called *moderator variables*. These are factors that are identified at the outset of the study and are intentionally built *into* the data analysis to see if they have an influence on the outcome. Suppose you read some previous research on teaching methods that suggests that girls do better with inductive teaching and boys do better with deductive teaching. In that case, you might decide to build in gender as a moderator variable. To do so, you would make sure that there were roughly equal numbers of male and female students in the groups taught with the inductive and deductive methods, as shown in **Table 3.1**.

Note that the level numbers for the levels of the independent and moderator variables are often arbitrary. Inductive grammar teaching could just as easily be listed before deductive grammar teaching. Male students could be considered level 1 and female students level 2. In this situation, the numbers 1 and 2 are just labels—they are not data or scores of any kind.

When you add a moderator variable to your research plan and prepare to determine the effects of that moderator variable in your data analysis, you have

TABLE 3.1 A box diagram of a study with a moderator variable

| | Independent Variable: Teaching Method | |
	Level 1: Deductive Grammar Teaching (n = 40)	Level 2: Inductive Grammar Teaching (n = 40)
Moderator Variable: Gender		
Level 1: Female	(n = approximately 20 students)	(n = approximately 20 students)
Level 2: Male	(n = approximately 20 students)	(n = approximately 20 students)

created what is called a *factorial study* (i.e., one having a moderator variable). The word *factorial* here refers to the idea that another factor has been added to the research design. Some statistical procedures are equipped to handle *factorial designs* (i.e., those with both independent and moderator variables). Other statistics work only with designs that are limited to independent variables. (If you want to try doing some statistical analyses, there are several good resources that can help you do so, and we will list some later in this book. At this point, we are just focusing on variables and research designs.)

In any experiment, trying to determine causality—the relationships between the independent and the dependent variable—should be clear enough that we can say with confidence that the treatment caused any observed difference. For example, where substantial differences occur between the control and the experimental groups' performance on the dependent variable (the standardized grammar test in our grammar teaching example), we want to know those differences were the result of the type of instruction and were not caused by some other, unknown or unforeseen factors. In other words, researchers working in this tradition want to be able to say with great certainty that it was the treatment that *caused* the observed differences in the scores.

Why does this issue matter so much? It's because decisions are often based on research results—sometimes quite important decisions that affect the lives of teachers and learners. Suppose you conducted the study of deductive and inductive grammar teaching described above without imposing any control variables. If you found observed differences in the students' scores, and if the confounding variable(s) had influenced the outcome, you couldn't say with any degree of certainty that it was the teaching method that had led to those differences. This state of affairs could potentially lead to you claim that one teaching method is superior to the other, when in fact the teaching method is not what caused the observed differences. This problem leads us to the concept of *validity*, which is an issue in all sorts of research (not just those approaches associated with classroom research or the experimental method).

Validity means many different things in different contexts (and there are many different types of validity). In research design, validity has to do with the truth, or value, of our claims. Discussions of validity are linked to the concept of *reliability*. In fact, it is often said that there can be no validity without reliability. What these terms mean and why they are important in language classroom research is the topic of the next section. Validity and reliability are both concepts related to the quality (i.e., the value) of a study, particularly in the psychometric tradition.

ENSURING QUALITY CONTROL IN YOUR RESEARCH

Researchers take many steps to ensure that the outcomes of their investigations are useful. Two key concepts in this endeavor are reliability and validity. In fact, these concepts are so important that they are almost always discussed in research methods textbooks. Most researchers agree that data collection and interpretation must be reliable and valid in order for the activity to be considered viable research. So, what do these two terms mean?

Reliability as a Criterion of Quality

Reliability is a somewhat easier concept to grasp than validity, so we'll deal with it first. Reliability has to do with consistency. A familiar example is that of a scale used to measure one's own weight. If measurement on the scale changes each time you step on it, and you have not gained or lost any weight in the interim, the scale is not consistent. It is unreliable.

Similar problems can occur in language-related research. Suppose you and your teaching colleagues were administering placement tests to a group of new students entering your program, and you had agreed on a set of interview questions to ask each student as well as on a scoring system for rating their speaking skills. If one teacher was very strict in applying those standards and another was very lenient, the students could get quite different evaluations, depending on which teacher interviewed them. This issue is referred to as *inter-rater reliability* in the language assessment literature. A parallel problem that occurs is variability in one rater's application of a rating scale. Imagine that you began interviewing at 9 A.M. and interviewed thirty students during the day. By the time you got to the thirtieth student, you might be tired, bored, or rushed, and you might therefore be more stringent (or more lenient) with the rating scale than you had been with the first three or four students. The issue of a single rater's consistency over time is called *intra-rater reliability*. Both problems can be crucial in research projects that incorporate raters' assessments of students' skills.

ACTION

Skim a research report in our field. Did the author(s) take any steps to ensure the reliability of data collection instruments, of ratings, or of data coding processes?

A parallel problem can occur in classroom research. Suppose two different observers are analyzing the frequency of turn taking in language classrooms. If one observer chooses not to count utterances such as "Uh-huh" and "Okay" as turns but the other does, they will end up with very different counts of the turns taken in classroom discourse. In order to be reliable they need to start with the same clear operational definition of a speaking turn!

Whether we are doing action research, some kind of naturalistic inquiry (like a case study), or an experiment in the psychometric tradition, it is important to be consistent in recording and analyzing our data. In subsequent chapters, we will look in some detail at ways to enhance reliability in collecting and analyzing qualitative data (such as *inter-observer agreement* and *inter-coder agreement*). For now, let's just take an example. Look back at Table 2.3, Jepson's operational definitions and coding categories in his study of repair moves in voice and text chats. One reason for carefully operationally defining his terms and providing examples was so that another researcher could independently code a portion of his data. That process would allow Jepson to determine how sound his categories were.

In general, there are two types of reliability in research design: *internal reliability* and *external reliability*. Reliability is generally established through replication. If, in carrying out a study, you collect data twice (with the same students, who have not learned or forgotten anything in between the two data collection points and get the same results both times, then you can claim that your data are reliable, and your research has *internal reliability*. If, on the other hand, someone else replicates your study in similar circumstances and with similar subjects and gets similar results, then you can claim that your study has *external reliability*. In fact, *replicability* is a desirable quality in the psychometric tradition. It is defined as "the degree to which a study could be performed again on the basis of the information provided by the author" (J. D. Brown, 1988, p. 43).

There are three types of replicability as defined by Mitchell and Jolley (1988). The first is *direct replication*, or repeating the original study with virtually the same procedures and population. The second is *systematic replication* in which the subsequent study differs from the original in some intentional and systematic way. The third is *conceptual replication*, which intentionally uses different methods (e.g., a different treatment) in order to improve upon the original study. All three types of replicability are useful in language classroom research.

Validity as a Criterion of Quality

Validity is a little trickier than reliability to understand. There are two aspects to the concept that we will deal with here: internal validity and external validity. *Internal validity*, as described above, has to do with whether a study has been designed in such a way that the claims made by the researcher can be confidently upheld. In an experiment, for instance, the key question is, "Has the study been designed in such a way that the researcher can claim that the results are due to the causes manipulated by the researcher in administering the treatment?" That is, are differences in the dependent variable attributable to the treatment (i.e., are they internal to the design) and not to some other confounding variable(s)?

Let's put the issue of internal validity in the context of the study described above, which focused on the effect of inductive and deductive grammar teaching methods on students' standardized grammar test scores. If the students in the deductive classes get substantially higher scores than the students in the inductive grammar classes (or vice versa), we want to make sure those differences are due to the method of instruction and not due to other uncontrolled factors (such as the students' aptitude for language learning, gender, handedness, or test-taking skills). Saying that a study has *internal validity* means that the results on the dependent variable are directly and unambiguously attributable to the treatment.

ACTION

Read the following vignette and identify why the study has weak internal validity.

An ESL teacher in Australia wanted to see if using role plays would help improve the speaking fluency of his intermediate students in his adult evening class. So, he used role plays in class once a week for the second to fourteenth weeks of the semester. There were twenty-three students at the beginning of the term but only eighteen at the end of the semester, as two of the older students had to drop out due to health reasons and three of the younger ones had to stop, either because the class was too difficult for them or because they had work-related issues that prevented them from coming to class. At the end of the course, the teacher rated the students on their speaking fluency during the final role-play activities. He tape-recorded the role plays and asked another teacher to discuss with him her impressions of the students' fluency. Based on his success with role plays in that semester, he decided to incorporate role plays in his beginners' course the next term.

There is also a concern referred to as *external validity*, or *generalizability*. A study is said to have external validity if the findings can be extrapolated from the sample in the study to the broader population it represents. In classroom research, this question refers to whether the results of an experiment can be transferred to learning environments in the real world.

In order to deal with external validity, we must revisit two terms introduced in Chapter 2: *population* and *sample*. A population is simply a group of individuals who share a certain characteristic. We all belong simultaneously to multiple populations, the most inclusive of which is the human race. Other examples of populations would include Australian passport holders, billionaires, year-twelve students, people who are parents, and so on. These populations are all fairly easily operationalized.

Populations that are defined in terms of constructs are more abstract. For example, in classroom research, we might be interested in studying the population of "intermediate-level learners of Spanish" or the population of "highly motivated language learners" or "Chinese-English bilinguals." We would need to operationalize each of these constructs.

What does this idea of populations have to do with validity? When researchers want to investigate some aspect of the behavior of a given population, they need to work with a subset or sample rather than with an entire population. (Most populations are far too large to be studied directly.) However, when those researchers report their results, they usually want to make claims that are relevant to the entire population, not just to the sample of individuals who took part in the study. If the study has been set up in such a way that it is difficult or impossible to make such an extrapolation, then the research has weak *external validity*.

ACTION

Read the following vignette and identify at least three issues that contribute to the study's weak external validity.

A teacher of French as a foreign language at a prestigious secondary school in a wealthy neighborhood believed her use of dialog journals was helping the students in her two honors classes improve their spelling and grammatical accuracy in French. (Dialog journals are personal writings by the students in the target language, to which the teacher replies in an ongoing exchange. Typically, the teacher responds to the content and does not overtly correct the students' errors.) The students in the honors classes were selected because of their high achievement in French the previous year. To test her assumption, the teacher used dialog journals with the six students in her 9 A.M. class, but not with the eight students in her 10 A.M. class, for the entire fifteen-week semester. She read and responded to the six students' dialog journals three times each week. At the end of the semester, the students in both classes submitted twenty-page term papers written in French. Three of this teacher's colleagues each read and rated all the term papers without knowing about either the investigation or that only one of the two honors classes had engaged in the dialog journal project.

Making claims about a population on the basis of results from research on a sample drawn from that population is called *generalizing* the findings. To generalize the findings of an experiment is to say that the results of that experiment should hold up in the real world. For this reason, external validity is also called *generalizability*.

To summarize, we can think of internal and external reliability and internal and external validity as different issues in quality control. Each of these terms deals with a key question (Nunan, 1992). Internal reliability deals with the question, "Would an independent researcher, on reanalyzing the data, come to the same conclusions?" (p. 17). External reliability addresses the question, "Would an independent researcher, on replicating the study, come to the same conclusion?"

(ibid.). Next, internal validity is involved with the concern of whether, based on the research design, "we can confidently claim that the outcomes are a result of the experimental treatment" (ibid.). Finally, external validity addresses the question, "Is the research design such that we can generalize beyond the subjects under investigation to a wider population?" (ibid.).

In setting up a study, researchers must deal with a tension between internal and external validity. One of the interesting paradoxes of research design is that strengthening internal validity weakens external validity. Why is this so? It is because internal validity depends on carefully controlling all the variables that might influence the outcomes of an experiment. But exerting too much control over variables creates laboratory-like conditions that cannot be duplicated in classrooms in the real world, so the more pristine and carefully controlled an experiment is, the less it resembles actual classrooms. To the extent that the treatment in an experiment cannot be applied in the real world with the same results, the study is said to lack external validity. This tension, or trade-off, is represented in **Figure 3.2**.

Let's return to our hypothetical investigation of the effectiveness of inductive versus deductive approaches to grammar instruction. As a researcher working in the psychometric tradition, you might want to generalize your findings as widely as possible. However, based on your review of previous research it seems that girls often do better than boys in grammar learning, you might decide to only include boys in your study. By screening out the girls, you would strengthen the internal validity of the research because you would rule out gender as a possible confounding variable. However, you would also be weakening the

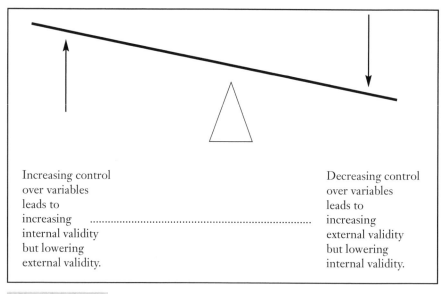

Increasing control over variables leads to increasing internal validity but lowering external validity.

Decreasing control over variables leads to increasing external validity but lowering internal validity.

FIGURE 3.2 The trade-off between internal and external validity.

external validity of the study because you could no longer extrapolate the results to all learners—only to boys. In fact, you could only make claims of relevance to boys in contexts that are similar to the one in which the study takes place. (This problem illustrates the importance of the moderator variable.)

The issue of generalizability (that is, extrapolating findings from samples to populations) is controversial. Some researchers working in the naturalistic inquiry or action research traditions, particularly those who are interested in capturing insights from authentic classrooms, argue that generalizability is not a criterion to which classroom researchers must aspire (Larsen-Freeman, 1996; van Lier, 1988). Such researchers argue that if we are to capture insights into the ways that real teachers and learners behave, then we need to study intact classrooms, not those that have been specially set up with randomly selected subjects for experimental purposes. For such researchers, *insight* rather than *proof* should be the standard for research. (We will explore these issues when we discuss data collection and analysis in the traditions of naturalistic inquiry and action research.)

THREATS TO VALIDITY

In the experimental tradition in psychometric research, the goals of internal and external validity are very important. This tradition is so well developed that over the years the kinds of problems that can occur have been described and cataloged. These problems are called *threats to validity*. This term encompasses any sort of difficulty that can cause problems in the interpretation of the results. Here we will consider a few of the threats that are especially prevalent in language classroom research. For the moment, we will continue discussing experimental research since experiments that try to determine causality provide many clear-cut cases where such threats can occur.

Threats to Internal Validity

You will recall that in an experiment, internal validity is the ability to claim that your findings are due to the treatment. That is, if there is a significant difference between the control and experimental groups, it should be unambiguously attributable to the treatment that the researchers planned and carried out. There should be no other possible explanation for the observed differences to have occurred.

In fact, this degree of confidence is rare. Let's go back to the study of deductive and inductive grammar teaching discussed above. We talked about *control variables* (those potential problems you recognize before beginning your research and therefore control by planning them out of the study) and *confounding variables*. Any confounding variable that you don't discover before conducting your research can influence the outcomes and therefore become a threat to validity in interpreting your findings. Imagine that you wish to conduct a study comparing inductive and deductive grammar teaching in the secondary school where you teach, but you must consider the following conditions:

1. You don't have the power to randomly select and randomly assign students to the deductive or inductive grammar teaching groups, so you choose your 8 A.M. intermediate class for the deductive teaching and your 2 P.M. intermediate class for the inductive teaching. When the term begins you learn that, due to the scheduling of the auto-shop class, there are no males in the 8 A.M. class, and, due to the schedule of the modern dance class, there are no females in the 2 P.M. class.

2. The textbooks are purchased by the school and you have no control over their selection. The required book for your intermediate classes is very heavily grammar-oriented with regular grammar rules and explanations in every chapter.

3. As the semester goes on, you get more and more enthusiastic about teaching grammar inductively. Likewise, teaching grammar deductively seems less interesting to you and less engaging to your students.

4. At the end of the semester, all the members of the 8 A.M. class ask if you will coach them and be their language club advisor. They have decided they like studying languages so much that they want to form a language club and they need a faculty advisor to do so.

5. At the fifth week of the term, you counsel four of the male students to drop out because they are doing so poorly they will certainly fail the course. As a result, you end up with ten males in the 2 P.M. class and twenty-four females in the 8 A.M. class.

Can you see how each of these conditions might influence the outcomes of any sort of grammar test you could give the two classes? All of these conditions represent threats to the internal validity of the study because each one could influence how well the two groups do on the test (the dependent variable). There may have been differences attributed to gender (1 above). All of the students got some inductively oriented input from the textbook (2 above). The quality of your own teaching may have differed in the two courses (3 above), and it appears that the students in the deductively taught class may be more motivated and enthusiastic than the others (4 above). Finally, the groups are of very unequal sizes, which might have influenced the type and frequency of participation during lessons, and some of the weaker male students have left one group (5 above).

In fact, this last condition—the unequal loss of research subjects from one group—is such an important issue that it has a special name: *mortality*. The term in this context doesn't mean that subjects actually die; it just means they disappear from the sample. Mortality is particularly problematic for longitudinal projects in which the passing of time can bring its own problems. For example, subjects (either teachers or students) can leave the school or change their mind about being involved in the project.

These and other kinds of problems can influence the performance of the control and experimental groups on the dependent variable(s) and, thus, damage the internal validity of a study. But there are also threats to the external validity, or generalizability, of classroom research. We will consider just a few such problems.

Threats to External Validity

You will recall that the issue of external validity has to do with whether the results of a study will apply to (generalize to) other people and other contexts besides the research sample and the research conditions. Sometimes experimental treatments are so specialized or so expensive that even if they were very effective, it is unlikely that they could be implemented in the "real world." At other times, the research subjects were unique in some way. Consider the following hypothetical research outcomes and think about why these studies might be weak in generalizability.

1. A kindergarten teacher finds that TPR is very effective with the bilingual five- and six-year-olds in her morning class. There are twelve pupils in the class and all twelve have tested quite high on a test of intelligence for children.

2. A pronunciation teacher works for a small company that handles the telephone service requests for an international computer manufacturer. The teacher conducts a study that shows that a particular software package used by the individual employees of the telephone service firm is highly effective in improving their English pronunciation. Each employee is required to use the software package ten hours per week for a period of three months as a condition of his or her employment.

3. A teacher at an international secondary school uses extended reading as a way of building her pupils' target language vocabulary and reading skills. The students are predominantly children of diplomats, and most of them have lived in four or five countries even though they are just teenagers.

Each of these situations includes interesting issues and for each we can imagine a viable research question that could be asked or a reasonable hypothesis that could be posed, but each situation is problematic in terms of its generalizability.

CORRELATIONS AND NONEXPERIMENTAL COMPARISONS

The comments above about experimental research design describe the strongest true experimental design. It has two or more groups, at least one of which gets the treatment and one of which serves as the control group. You will recall that to qualify as a true experimental design, the study must involve *random selection* (from the population to the sample) and *random assignment* (from the subject pool to the groups). The groups in the experiment are determined by the research question or hypothesis—and specifically by the levels of the independent variable. There may also be groups defined by the levels of one or more moderator variables.

But some very important types of research do not involve a treatment and cannot be called "experiments" in the strongest sense of the term. In some situations, rather than comparing groups, we want to determine the relationship, or correlation, between two or more variables as measured in one group of people. The research design for this situation is called a *correlation design*, and there are several statistical procedures that can be used to detect correlations across variables. Still other studies involve the use of statistical logic or other analytic procedures to look for differences among groups defined by preexisting conditions rather than by experimental treatments. Such studies are called *criterion groups designs* because they compare groups defined by some criterion.

Correlation designs and criterion groups designs are both part of the *ex post facto* class of designs. The phrase "ex post facto" is used because the researchers investigate the possible influence of conditions after the fact. In this section we will examine both of these designs, but we will begin with the criterion groups design because—like the other designs we have discussed so far—it allows us to compare two or more groups (even though there is no formal experiment going on).

Criterion Groups Designs

Think about the following researchable issues:

1. Two secondary school teachers share the opinion that their female students are naturally better at foreign languages than their male students. They plan a study to investigate this possibility systematically.

2. The members of an ESL faculty observe that students from some first language backgrounds seem to have less difficulty with English spelling than do students from other first languages. They decide to test this hypothesis.

3. Over the years, a language teacher notices that her left-handed students seem to have consistently better pronunciation than do most of her right-handed students. She wants to do a study to determine whether or not this is the case.

In the examples given above, the researchers did not make the students male or female; the researchers did not cause them to be native speakers of particular languages, nor did the researchers cause the subjects to be left-handed or right-handed. Instead, the researchers will study the possible influences of these conditions on some dependent variable(s) *after the fact*—that is after the conditions of interest in the comparison already exist. In other words, the students are already male or female (Situation 1), they already come from a particular L-1 background (Situation 2), and they are already left-handed or right-handed (Situation 3) before these studies begin. That is why we say that the criterion groups design is part of the *ex post facto class* of designs.

ACTION

Write the null hypotheses being tested in the three criterion groups designs described above.

You will recall one key characteristic of the *true experimental designs* is that they use *random selection* from the population to the sample and *random assignment* from the sample pool to the various groups in the sample (the control and experimental groups). In criterion groups designs, we may have random selection but we cannot have random assignment. Why? Think about it for a moment. In the study comparing the pronunciation of left-handed and right-handed language students (Situation 3 above), we might be able to randomly select left-handed and right-handed students from the entire population of foreign language learners. But we could not randomly assign them to groups in the study because the groups are defined by the subjects' handedness. This is, in fact, the defining characteristic of criterion groups designs: Subjects are grouped according to the criterion of interest, not according to random assignment.

When we use the ex post facto criterion groups design to test hypotheses or answer research questions with quantitatively collected data in the psychometric tradition, we often compare the average scores of the groups on the dependent variable. Statistical tools are used to make inferences that help us decide whether those differences are significant. In other words, statistics can be used to compare groups defined by preexisting conditions just as they can be used to identify significant differences between control and experimental groups in formal experiments. We will return to this point in subsequent chapters where we discuss quantitative data analysis.

Correlation Designs

Sometimes researchers are interested in seeing to what extent variables co-occur, or *correlate*. Correlation designs help us determine what sorts of factors seem to "go together" in a patterned, predictable way. For example, imagine yourself as a teacher of Spanish as a foreign language. Perhaps you notice that among your intermediate students, those who seem more confident and outgoing have better pronunciation. If you had a valid and reliable measure of confidence and extroversion as well as a valid and reliable way to measure Spanish pronunciation, you could administer both those measures to your students and then correlate the results. If you found a notable tendency of pronunciation scores to increase as extroversion scores increase, you could say there was a *positive correlation* between these two variables.

There are also instances where two variables seem not to correlate and even seem to be at odds. You might notice, for example, that the students who have better speaking German vocabularies seem to take less time finishing their reading assignments. You could investigate this apparent pattern with a correlation study by measuring the students' vocabulary and their reading speed. If you found a *negative correlation*, it would mean that as measures of one variable increase, measures of the other variable decrease. That is, the finding that as students' vocabulary increases, their reading speed decreases would be an example of a negative correlation.

Note that positive correlations are not inherently good, nor are negative correlations inherently bad. The words *positive* and *negative* just refer to the direction of the relationship between the two variables. In positive correlations, the measurements of the two variables increase/decrease together. In negative correlations, the measurements of one variable increase as the measurements of the other variable decrease.

Like the research designs that compare two or more groups, correlation designs can use either (or both) research questions or hypotheses. And, as we saw earlier, those formal statements can be worded (1) as null hypotheses, or (2) as non-directional, alternative hypotheses, or (3) as alternative-directional hypotheses. Here are the three types of hypotheses for the study described above regarding students' Spanish pronunciation and their tendency toward extroversion.

H_0: There will be no statistically significant correlation between students' extroversion scores and their scores on a Spanish pronunciation test.

H_A: There will be a statistically significant correlation between students' extroversion scores and their scores on a Spanish pronunciation test.

H_{A-1}: There will be a statistically significant positive correlation between students' extroversion scores and their scores on a Spanish pronunciation test.

As we saw in studies that compared groups, the choice of the null, the alternative, or the alternative directional hypothesis depends on your literature review. Where previous research and/or theory suggests a clear direction, you may pose the alternative directional hypothesis. Where the evidence for a direction is not strong, the culture of psychometric research requires a more conservative approach, so you would pose the null hypothesis.

REFLECTION

Look at the three hypotheses above. Notice the differences in their wording, compared to one another. Underline the key words that distinguish the three hypotheses.

ACTION

Write the null hypothesis, the alternative hypothesis, and the alternative directional hypothesis for the correlation design used to investigate the relationship between German reading speed and German vocabulary.

In summary, when using correlation designs, a researcher typically works with one group of people and measures two or more variables, collecting quantitative data. (There must be one group of subjects, each of whom is measured on at least two variables, in order to do the statistical analyses related to correlation.) The data are then analyzed to see if there is a statistically significant correlation between the two variables under investigation. That correlation could be either positive or negative, depending upon the relationship of the variables.

One very important point to understand is that correlation does not equate to causality. Determining that two variables co-occur is not the same as determining that manipulating one variable, the independent variable, causes a change in another, the dependent variable. In fact, in correlation studies, we don't really use those terms. Instead, we simply talk about the X variable (for example, good Spanish pronunciation) and the Y variable (e.g., confidence/extroversion). If we did indeed find a positive correlation between measures of good Spanish pronunciation and confidence/extroversion, we could not tell whether (1) good pronunciation causes learners to be confident and extroverted, or (2) being confident extroverted leads to good pronunciation. In this regard, correlation studies sometimes lay the groundwork for subsequent research to investigate causality. However, correlation studies are also valuable in and of themselves, as there are many variables in language learning and teaching whose relationships we need to understand.

So far, we have briefly discussed four different types of designs that are used in classroom research. These are the true experimental designs (actually, a class of designs), intact groups designs, criterion groups designs, and correlation designs. **Table 3.2** compares these designs on three categories.

TABLE 3.2 A comparison of true experimental, intact groups, criterion groups and correlation designs

	True Experimental Designs	Intact Groups Designs	Criterion Groups Designs	Correlation Design
Comparing two groups (or more)	+	+	+	−
Treatment for at least one group	+	+	−	−
Random assignment to groups	+	−	−	−

A CHECKLIST OF INITIAL DESIGN CONSIDERATIONS

In reading this chapter and the previous chapters, you have encountered a great deal of information and many new terms. Here we hope to pull some of that information together in a manageable way.

A checklist of questions for evaluating the design of a research project is presented in **Table 3.3**. Some of these questions have been covered in this chapter and previous chapters. Others will be dealt with in greater detail in the chapters to come.

You may use the questions in this checklist as you design your own research. You can also use them for reflecting on and analyzing research that you read.

SAMPLE STUDY

In this section, we will briefly summarize one of the earliest published classroom research studies conducted by a teacher in our field. Although this study was published many years ago, it dealt with an issue that still concerns language teachers today: language learners' classroom participation.

Hearing her colleagues discuss the difficulty of getting Asian students to talk in English classes at a university in the United States, a teacher decided to compare in-class participation patterns of Asian and non-Asian learners of English. (The researcher, Charlene Sato, was herself a Japanese-American ESL teacher and was very interested in ethnic styles in classroom discourse.) To investigate this perception, Sato (1982) decided to conduct some research to determine whether "ethnic patterns of participation were observable, as reflected in aspects of turn-taking" (p. 14).

To address these issues, Sato videotaped her own class during three fifty-minute lessons while she was teaching. (The students were told that the videotape process was a regular part of teacher training in that program, which

TABLE 3.3 A checklist for evaluating research designs in classroom research

Area	Evaluative Questions
Research Question	Is my question worth investigating? Is answering my question feasible? What are the constructs underlying my question? How can these constructs be operationalized?
Design	Does the research question imply a causal relationship between two or more variables, or does it suggest some other research focus? Does the question suggest an experimental or a nonexperimental design? (Am I after insight or evidence?)
Research Method	What methods are available for investigating my question? Which of these are feasible, given available resources and expertise? Is it desirable and possible to use more than one data collection method? What are the possible threats to the reliability and validity of my research? How can I deal with these threats?
Analysis	Will my data require me to do statistical analyses, interpretive analyses, or both? Will I have to quantify qualitatively collected research data? How might I do this? What skills do I have for doing the analyses? What skills do I need?
Presentation	What is the best way for me to 'publish' my research? Should I try to speak at a conference? Should I try to submit the study as an article?

was true.) In another teacher's class, three lessons were tape-recorded as Sato observed and took notes to record which students took speaking turns. In Sato's class, there were fifteen Asian students and eight non-Asian students, while in the other class, there were four Asians and four non-Asians. The two classes were at the same level of English proficiency in the ESL program.

ACTION

Using the description above, identify the following variables in Sato's study:

Independent variable:

Dependent variable:

Control variable:

Possible confounding variable(s):

To analyze the data, Sato (1982) coded the turn-taking behavior of the students in the six lessons. Her coding categories included general solicits (questions or tasks posed by the teacher to the whole class), the students' responses to general solicits, personal solicits (questions or tasks posed by the teacher to an individual), the students' responses to personal solicits, and self-selection by the students. She also coded whether the speaking turns were taken by Asian or non-Asian students.

REFLECTION

What do you think about the comparability of the data from the two classes in Sato's study? In her own class, the data consisted of the videotapes of three lessons. In the other teacher's class, Sato tape-recorded the lesson and took observational notes.

Sato's (1982) findings are interesting and complex. We will summarize only a few of them here. She found that, although the Asian students outnumbered the non-Asian students in the two classes combined (nineteen Asians versus twelve non-Asians), the non-Asian students took 63.5% of the total speaking turns. Further scrutiny revealed that the Asian students only self-selected a third of the time, while the non-Asian students self-selected two-thirds of the time. In terms of teacher-allocated turns, the Asian students were selected for turns by the teachers 40% of the time while the non-Asians were selected 60% of the time. (All these differences were statistically significant.) Sato's comment about her own turn distribution patterns is particularly insightful:

[T]he Asian American teacher behaved no differently than did the Caucasian American teacher on this measure (i.e., the teacher's nomination of students for turns). Whatever ethnic ties the former may have felt toward the Asian students, she nevertheless called upon them less often than she did the non-Asians. (p. 18)

We see this study as a very interesting effort by a teacher to investigate a commonly held view. Sato's study has influenced our thinking about turn taking in language classes, both as researchers and as teachers. Her work also influenced further research in our field.

PAYOFFS AND PITFALLS

In this chapter we have dealt with key concepts in planning language classroom research. By now, it is probably apparent that there are many payoffs and pitfalls involved in conducting classroom research, and your choice of research design can lead to both.

There are several payoffs involved in choosing a research design that is part of the psychometric tradition in language classroom research. These procedures are well codified: There are accessible training courses and numerous textbooks to help you learn about them. The threats to validity and reliability are well understood. In addition, research using these designs is often highly valued in academic contexts.

The pitfalls, of course, are the mirror image of the payoffs. In order to use the statistical analyses associated with the designs of the psychometric tradition, you may need special training (or at least guidance). There is a fair amount of jargon associated with this approach to language classroom research, so novice researchers sometimes feel overwhelmed by the amount of information to be learned. Just remember our research-as-culture metaphor. We often feel overwhelmed when we enter a new culture until we learn some basic vocabulary, the cultural norms and rules for behavior, and the important traditions and stories. But even though cultural adjustments take time, they do happen and they are worth doing. This is the case in learning these key concepts and mastering these design issues as well.

There are research design issues associated with naturalistic inquiry and action research as well, but there is considerable interplay among those two research traditions and the psychometric tradition at the level of design. In fact, Sato's (1982) study is a criterion groups design using observational methods of data collection and analysis. In the chapters to come, we will examine many such blendings. Our goal in doing so is to help you understand your choices as a well-informed researcher and consumer of research.

CONCLUSIONS

In this chapter, you read about hypotheses and hypothesis testing. We saw that there are specific wordings as well as reasons why researchers pose null, alternative, and alternative directional hypotheses. We noted the point that the research questions and/or hypotheses determine what sort of variables and research designs are involved in a study.

We looked at different sorts of threats to the validity and reliability of a study and discussed the ex post facto class of designs: the correlation design and the criterion groups design. These were then compared with the true experimental designs and the intact groups designs, which had been introduced earlier. The following questions and tasks, as well as the suggestions for further reading on these topics, should help you consolidate your understanding of these important issues in language classroom research.

QUESTIONS AND TASKS

1. It is often said that there can be no validity without reliability. What does this phrase mean? Do you agree?

2. Look back at the summary of Jepson's research, which was the sample study in Chapter 1. Based on the information provided, identify the following variables. (Hint: There can be more than one dependent variable in a study.)

   Independent Variable:

   Dependent Variable(s):

   Control Variable(s):

   Possible Confounding Variable(s):

3. Read the following description of a research context. Identify the possible threats to external validity in this study.

Teachers at a university in Hong Kong conduct research to determine the effectiveness of the school's new self-access English center. The teachers believe that using the self-access center will improve students' English as well as their attitudes toward using English. The self-access English center has a library of 1,500 recent movies in English, as well as computer packages that allow students to practice their pronunciation, build their vocabulary knowledge, and increase their reading speed in English. Every student who successfully completes a four-hour orientation program about the self-access center is issued his or her own laptop computer. In addition, as students leave the self-access center, they can enjoy free food and beverages at a snack bar connected to the center. After two semesters of collecting data, the researchers find that the students who used the self-access center have very positive attitudes toward using English.

---

4. Think of a way to replicate but improve upon Sato's (1982) research. You could compare the speaking turns of Asian and non-Asian students as she did. Or you could compare the speaking turns of male and female students. In fact, you could combine these two issues and use a *factorial criterion groups design*, using ethnicity as the independent variable and gender as the dependent variable. Draw the box diagram for a factorial criterion groups design study investigating the influence of ethnicity and gender on students' speaking turns in a language classroom.

5. In the replication of Sato's study that you envision, are you planning a direct replication, a systematic replication, or a conceptual replication? What do you see as the value of replicating a previous study?

6. Perhaps you have noticed the tendency of two variables to co-occur, or to run counter to each other. Brainstorm some research questions about these situations. This sort of research calls for a correlation design. Choose a research question you have posed and identify the X and Y variables.

SUGGESTIONS FOR FURTHER READING

D. Allwright and Bailey (1991) provide an introduction to language classroom research, including ideas about how to get started. The studies cited in that book are somewhat dated now, but the general approach to classroom research is still sound.

J. D. Brown (1988) wrote a book entitled *Understanding Research in Second Language Learning*. It is a good introduction to research design and basic statistics in the psychometric tradition.

Nunan's (1992) book *Research Methods in Language Learning* provides more detail on the concepts of internal and external reliability and validity.

PART II

RESEARCH DESIGN ISSUES

Approaches to Planning and Implementing Classroom Research

Although this section and the section that follows overlap somewhat, we see this particular section as a *big-picture treatment*. The section begins with a chapter on experimental methods, which is one of the two "pure" research paradigms (Grotjahn, 1987). The section also covers the other "pure" research paradigm—ethnography. Other approaches that are dealt with in this section include survey research, case studies research, and action research.

For many people, the experimental method is synonymous with *research*, and other approaches that draw on more naturalistic forms of inquiry are often seen as ground-clearing operations designed to yield preliminary data and to set the scene for experimental research. We don't see it that way. Case study research, surveys, and action research all have their value and—depending on the research questions and the overall intention of the research—can generate useful information where experiments may well be inappropriate.

Chapter 4: The Experimental Method

By the end of this chapter, readers will

- ▨ understand the main classes of research designs as well as the specific designs commonly used in this tradition;
- ▨ describe threats to internal and external validity;
- ▨ understand the basic assumptions underlying the logic of inferential statistics;
- ▨ differentiate between descriptive and inferential statistics;
- ▨ be familiar with some basic statistical tools (e.g., frequency distributions).

Chapter 5: Surveys

By the end of this chapter, readers will

- define survey research and explain its basic uses;
- differentiate between survey research and the experimental method;
- describe different kinds of sampling strategies for obtaining subjects;
- discuss the basic principles of questionnaire design;
- recognize potential problems in using various questionnaire item types;
- be familiar with various ethical issues in survey research.

Chapter 6: Case Study Research

By the end of this chapter, readers will

- discuss the characteristics of case studies;
- differentiate between case studies and experimental research;
- describe different types of case studies;
- state the advantages of case studies in language classroom research;
- discuss issues to consider in selecting a case;
- understand the factors that contribute to the quality of a case study.

Chapter 7: Ethnography

By the end of this chapter, readers will

- define ethnography and differentiate it from case study research;
- understand the distinction between emic and etic perspectives;
- articulate the principles that guide ethnography;
- describe four types of triangulation;
- discuss concerns about reliability and validity of ethnography.

Chapter 8: Action Research

By the end of this chapter, readers will

- define action research and differentiate among classroom research, action research, and teacher research;
- describe the steps in the action research cycle;
- articulate the value of action research for classroom practitioners;
- describe changes teachers have documented as a result of doing action research;
- discuss problems in action research and identify potential solutions.

4

The Experimental Method

Any time you use phrases like: "On average, I cycle about 100 miles a week" or "We can expect a lot of rain at this time of year" or "The earlier you start revising, the better you are likely to do in the exam," you are making a statistical statement, even though you may have performed no calculations. (Rowntree, 1981, p. 13)

INTRODUCTION AND OVERVIEW

In this chapter, we will look more closely at the *experimental method*, one of the two 'pure' research paradigms (Grotjahn, 1987). In Grotjahn's terms, this paradigm involves (1) experimental designs, (2) quantitative data, and (3) statistical analyses. The experimental method is basically a collection of research designs, guidelines for using them, principles and procedures for determining statistical significance, and criteria for determining the quality of a study. The experimental method is part of the psychometric tradition, and it is also referred to as the *scientific method*. For some researchers, the experimental method is the premier method, all others being 'ground clearing' operations, that is, preliminary data collection and interpretation exercises to prepare for a formal experiment.

We will begin this chapter by adding to our earlier discussion of possible confounding variables. Then we will add more research designs to those you have read about in earlier chapters. We will systematize this discussion by analyzing and exemplifying the research designs, dividing them into classes, and explaining their relationships to one another. Then we will use an extended example to look at the issue of extrapolating from samples to populations. This extrapolation is based on the logic of the normal distribution, which will be discussed as well.

As you read this material, keep in mind that different forms of research have different cultures. The experimental method has one of the most strictly codified sets of values and procedures of any of the main methods we will study. It also involves a fair amount of jargon, which can sometimes be a bit intimidating. But just imagine that you are learning new vocabulary, as you would when entering any new culture.

REFLECTION

What do you picture when you read the phrase *the experimental method*? What images does it evoke for you?

In this section, we will build on key concepts that were introduced earlier. These concepts included samples, populations, variables, reliability, and validity. As we saw earlier, experiments are generally conducted in order to test the strength of relationships between variables. We also saw that when the researcher is testing the influence of one variable on another, the variable doing the influencing is called the independent variable, while the one being influenced is called the dependent variable. For example, in a study of the effect of two different methods for teaching grammar, the teaching method would be the independent variable, and the students' performance on a test of grammar knowledge would be the dependent variable.

In Chapter 3, we discussed *confounding variables*—those factors that might negatively influence the interpretation of your results. In the experimental method, one of the researcher's key goals is to control and systematically manipulate variables in order to determine cause-and-effect relationships. This goal has such a high value in the culture of the experimental method that people have written extensively about the things that can go wrong. These types of confounding variables are also called *extraneous variables* or *threats to validity*.

QUALITY CONTROL ISSUES: THREATS TO INTERNAL VALIDITY

Quality control in the experimental method is largely a matter of understanding the many things that can go wrong and taking steps to prevent or minimize those threats. Many of these safeguards are embodied in the various research designs described here. As we saw in Chapter 3, there are threats to both internal and external validity. We will revisit these issues now in more detail.

The threats to internal validity can be divided into three categories (Tuckman, 1999). These are sources of bias based on experience, participants, and instrumentation. *Experience bias factors* are those "based on what occurs within a research study as it progresses" (p. 134). *Participant bias* is a result of the "characteristics of the people on whom the study is conducted" (ibid.). And *instrumentation bias* has to do with "the way the data are collected" (ibid.).

Threats to Internal Validity Based on Experience

There are three experience bias factors: history, testing, and expectancy. In this context, *history* refers to events—things that happen during an experiment, which may influence the results. For example, if classes in a study are disrupted due to natural disasters or political unrest, the research will be affected. History can also have an unintended influence on the outcomes of the treatment. Imagine you were teaching Japanese to secondary school students in an English-speaking country and running an experiment in which one group got to see films about Japan during class and one group did not. But if all the students go to see some popular new action film about Japanese samurai warriors outside of school, the treatment could be compromised by that event since both groups would have been exposed to the film.

Testing (also called the *practice effect*) refers to the fact that taking a pre-test may influence the subjects' performance on a post-test. That is, in addition to learning from the treatment, learners may do better on the post-test because the pre-test alerted them to what was being investigated in the study.

The third issue, *expectancy*, is an interesting psychological problem. Tuckman (1999) explains it this way:

A treatment may appear to increase learning effectiveness as compared to that of a control or comparison group, not because it really boosts effectiveness but because either the experimenter or the subjects believe that it does and behave according to this expectation. (p. 135)

These two threats are called *researcher expectancy* and *subject expectancy*, respectively.

There are steps researchers can take to overcome or minimize these problems. For example, if you use a design with a pre-test, it is important that the post-test be a different form of the test, instead of the same test the subjects encountered at the beginning of the study. (We will read about other safeguards later.)

Threats to Internal Validity Based on Participants

There are five participant bias factors, and you have already read about some of them. They are (1) selection, (2) maturation, (3) statistical regression, (4) experimental mortality, and (5) the interactive combinations of factors.

Selection as a threat to internal validity is the idea that somehow the groups to be compared turn out to be different before the treatment. Random selection and random assignment are used to combat this problem. The logic here is that randomly selecting subjects and then randomly assigning them to different conditions distributes 'contaminating' participant factors across both the experimental and the control group. You would thus be able to argue that any differences observed in terms of the dependent variable are due to the experimental treatment because the other variables that might have had an effect presumably exist in equal quantities in both the experimental and control groups, and therefore cancel one another out.

After randomly selecting your subjects from the population, you can use pre-test data elicited from all the subjects in the experiment before you assign them to groups. This step allows you to make sure, for instance, that the intermediate learners in two different groups are at roughly the same level of language development to begin with. Of course, using a pre-test introduces the possibility of the testing threat, so there are some trade-offs in the decisions you must make.

Maturation refers to the normal development people undergo whether or not they are receiving a treatment of some kind. This threat is particularly relevant in longitudinal studies involving children. If we see syntactic development in five-year-olds taught with a certain method for a school year, can we be sure that that development was due to the treatment, or was it due to the normal linguistic changes that small children experience in their first language, or both? This problem is addressed through the use of a control group, which is at the same developmental level as the treatment group and goes through the same experiences (except for the treatment itself) for the same period of time.

Statistical regression is the name of a tendency for people's test scores to change whether or not the knowledge, skill, or ability being measured truly changes. Tuckman (1999) gives as an example of the situation in which

> a group of students take an IQ test, and only the highest third and the lowest third are selected for the experiment, eliminating the middle third. Statistical processes would create a tendency for the scores on any post-test measurement of the high IQ students to decrease toward the mean, while the scores of the low IQ students would increase toward the mean. Thus, the groups would differ less in the post-test results, *even without experiencing any experimental treatment.* (p. 136)

Tuckman explains that this pattern happens because "chance factors are more likely to contribute to extreme scores than to average scores, and such factors are unlikely to reappear during a second testing" (ibid.). Using subjects who represent an entire range of ability levels in your design is one way to avoid this problem.

Experimental mortality (or just *mortality*) is the problem of losing subjects from the study. It can be especially worrisome if the groups end up being of quite different sizes because people dropped out. To deal with this threat, researchers often try to recruit more people for a study than they may actually need. Researchers must sometimes also try to locate subjects who took the pre-test and experienced the treatment (or were in the control group) but then moved away or were absent when the post-test was administered.

As the name suggests, the *interactive combination of factors* happens when more than one threat is present in a study. For example, if you conduct a study of reading readiness and choose two intact groups for a study—say, two classes of kindergartners at two different schools—you may end up with children from widely divergent socioeconomic backgrounds. It is possible that the more afflu-ent children have better nutrition and more opportunities to be read to than do the poorer children. This is, in part, a selection issue, but if those children are developing at different rates as a result of their nutrition, then you may also have a maturational issue. Careful planning is needed to avoid these sorts of problems.

Threats to Internal Validity Based on Instrumentation

The term *instrumentation* refers to the "measurement or observation proce-dures used during an experiment" (Tuckman, 1999, p. 137). Instrumentation includes tests, questionnaires, observation systems, elicitation devices, audio- and videotaping—in short, any means of collecting data. The threat of instru-mentation is also sometimes called *instability of measures* (Brown, 1988, p. 39), because it occurs if the measurement or recording processes change during the experiment.

Instrumentation is related to reliability since it involves consistency in data gathering. To minimize this threat, data collection procedures must "remain *constant across time* as well as *constant across groups* (or *conditions*)" (Tuckman, 1999, p. 138). The most likely instrumentation problem in classroom research involves studies with human observers taking notes or using coding systems during class-room interaction. If the observers are not consistent as they collect data, the data will not accurately represent the events being observed. Observer training, rater training, and the careful piloting of all questionnaires and data collection devices are the best safeguards against instrumentation problems.

REFLECTION

In Chapters 1, 2, and 3, find two examples of instruments used in research that might be subject to the instrumentation threat.

QUALITY CONTROL ISSUES: THREATS TO EXTERNAL VALIDITY

In Chapter 3, we saw that *external validity* (or *generalizability*) is the extent to which the findings of an experiment will generalize to nonexperimental contexts. There are four issues of concern about external validity: (1) the reactive effects of testing, (2) the reactive effects of experimental arrangements, (3) the interaction effects of selection bias, and (4) multiple-treatment interference (Tuckman, 1999).

The external validity threat called *reactive effects of testing* is related to the *testing threat* (or *practice effect*) to internal validity. In this situation, the presence of a pre-test may give the effects of the treatment a boost. Then, when the outcomes of the experiment are transferred to the real world where no pre-test is involved, that extra boost will be lacking. This problem is also applicable to attitude questionnaires (ibid.). If a researcher administers a questionnaire at the start of an experiment in order to see if the subjects' attitudes change as a result of the treatment, the questionnaire may sensitize the subjects to the fact that attitude is an issue in the study. As a result, they may respond more positively to the questionnaire when it is administered following the treatment, leading the researcher to conclude that the treatment improved students' attitudes. However, that improvement may not be present (or may not be as pronounced) in nonexperimental conditions where there is no pre-test attitude questionnaire.

The *reactive effects of experimental arrangements* threat is a very interesting problem. This idea refers to the fact that sometimes just knowing that one is in an experiment is enough to cause a difference that may be captured by the dependent variable, whether or not one is in the treatment group! You may come across the term *the Hawthorne effect* as a label for this threat because of a famous experiment carried out at the Western Electric Company in Hawthorne, Illinois, in the 1920s:

> The researchers wanted to determine the effects of changes in the physical characteristics of the work environment as well as in incentive rates and rest periods. They discovered, however, that production increased regardless of the conditions imposed, leading them to conclude that the workers were reacting to their role in the experiment and the importance placed on them by management. (ibid., p. 140)

In other words, simply being included in a study can influence subjects' behavior. If you conduct observational research in a class other than your own, the teacher may say to you, "The students were on their best behavior because you were here," or "The students were really rowdy because you were here." These are examples of the reactive effects of experimental arrangements in language classroom research.

REFLECTION

Think about the times that you have observed a class or have been observed when you were teaching a class. Did any reactive effects occur? What were they? Who was affected? What might be done to counteract such problems when an observer visits a language class?

The threat known as the *interaction effects of selection bias* occurs when the sample in an experiment is not really representative of the population from which it was drawn. This is a major issue for language classroom researchers because it hinges upon first defining the population we wish to study and then upon sampling from that population appropriately. For example, assume you are interested in cognitive style and you wish to investigate the effects of analytic versus holistic teaching styles on language learners. You conduct a study with a hundred students who are divided into two groups, one of which is taught analytically while the other group is taught holistically. Unfortunately, after you finish your study, you read a research report about left-handed people tending to be more holistically oriented and right-handed people tending to be more analytically oriented. When you check your records, you see that only one of the hundred subjects was left-handed. This is unfortunate because left-handed people make up about thirteen percent of the population. So, left-handed people have been underrepresented in your sample.

A way to cope with this threat is a process called *stratified random sampling*. This term means that before we select people from the population to be in the sample, we determine what the relevant characteristics of the population are (like handedness) and make sure the levels (strata) in the sample represent the population appropriately. In this case, we would make sure that the sample included about thirteen percent left-handed people. If there were enough left-handed people included in the sample, you could even build in handedness as a moderator variable to check its effects in your research on holistic and analytic teaching styles.

Finally, there is a threat known as *multiple-treatment interaction*. This threat is hard to manage in classroom research, especially in second language settings where students have access to the target language outside of class. It can be a problem in foreign language settings, too. Imagine that you are using an intact groups design, in which your 9 A.M. class of secondary school French students is taught with the traditional materials, but you supplement the lessons for your 1 P.M. class with recordings of French popular music. The students in the 1 P.M. class respond enthusiastically and even share the French music recordings with their friends in the 9 A.M. class. In effect, the comparison group has now gotten the treatment!

RESEARCH DESIGNS IN THE EXPERIMENTAL METHOD

In order to deal with these threats, the experimental method includes many different research designs to counteract the possible confounding variables that could influence the internal and external validity of a study. The various designs have different strengths and weaknesses. Anyone who chooses to do an experiment must balance the focus of the research question against the time and resources available for conducting the study in order to choose the best design.

In this section, we will review some research designs discussed in Chapters 1, 2, and 3 (the true experimental designs, the intact groups design, and two in the ex post facto class—correlation and criterion groups designs). We will also introduce some other designs that are used in the experimental method. To show you the differences among these designs, we will start with a research situation and develop it through a series of evolving scenarios. (There are many more research designs in the experimental method. We are just describing some of the most important ones here.)

Scenario 1: The One-Shot Case Study Design

Suppose you are an EFL program administrator. You want to determine whether or not the students taking the TOEFL preparation course in your program are benefiting from the course. You decide to conduct a study in which the twenty students in the course are tested on the TOEFL at the end of the fifteen-week term.

REFLECTION

When you have completed this study, what information will you have about the students? What information will you lack?

This research design is called a *one-shot case study*. (This phrase does not mean the same thing as the term *case study* does in naturalistic inquiry—a point we will explore in Chapter 6.) The one-shot case study is a weak design because of the problems inherent in the interpretation of the results. Since there is no pre-test, we don't know how proficient the students were in English at the beginning of the TOEFL preparation class. As a result, we can't really say, on solid empirical grounds, whether the course helped them (though the students and teacher may be sure that it did). And since only one set of data is available, no comparisons are possible.

Scenario 2: The One-Group Pre-Test Post-Test Design

You still want to determine whether or not the students taking the TOEFL preparation course are benefiting from the class, but you realize some things that could be done to improve the study. You decide to add a pre-test to your design, so the twenty students in the course are tested on the TOEFL at the beginning and at the end of the fifteen-week term.

REFLECTION

What information will you have at the end of this study that you wouldn't have had after conducting the one-shot case study described in Scenario 1?

This design is called a *one-group pre-test post-test design*. It is a weak design, but it is an improvement over the one-shot case study because you can at least tell if the students made progress by comparing their scores at the beginning of the class with their scores at the end. (Hence the name *pre-test post-test design*.) Comparing the pre-test and post-test scores allows you to determine whether they made progress *during* (but not necessarily *because of*) the TOEFL preparation course. (Perhaps they got extra tutoring outside of class or had some English-speaking friends.)

The difference between the pre-test scores and the post-test scores is called the *gain scores*. If the students' post-test scores are higher than their pre-test scores, then we can conclude that their English (as measured by the TOEFL) has improved. But be forewarned: There are also *negative gains scores*—when the post-test scores are lower than the pre-test scores. This situation can be discouraging for both teachers and students. It may mean the students have experienced some loss of proficiency, or that they didn't test as well the second time, or that there is just some flux in the measurement process. (We will return to this point later.)

REFLECTION

What steps could you take to refine this design so that you could confidently say that the students' measured improvement was in fact due to the TOEFL preparation course?

Scenario 3: The Intact Groups Design

Suppose you wonder whether or not the TOEFL preparation course helps the students increase their TOEFL scores. You conduct a study in which the twenty students in the course are tested on the TOEFL at the end of the fifteen-week term. You will compare their end-of-term TOEFL scores to those of twenty similar students in another class that meets at the same time of day and for the same number of hours every week. However, the students in that class are not studying specifically to prepare for the TOEFL.

ACTION

Answer these questions about the study described above.

1. What is the research question or hypothesis for this study?
2. What is the independent variable and how many levels does it have?
3. What is the dependent variable?
4. What are the two control variables?
5. Identify one problem inherent in this study.
6. What are two things that could be done to improve this study?

Compare your answers with those of a classmate or colleague.

As you will recall from Chapter 2, this research design is called an *intact groups design*. It is known as a weak design because of the problems inherent in the interpretation of the results, but it is stronger than the one-shot case study or the one-group pre-test post-test design.

REFLECTION

What are the weaknesses inherent in the intact groups design? (Think back to our discussions of randomization in Chapters 2 and 3.)

The main problems with the intact groups design stem from the fact that the subjects in the groups being compared were not randomly selected from the population, nor were they randomly assigned to groups. (Hence, the name "intact groups design.") Without randomization (and without a pre-test), we cannot be certain that the groups being compared were identical (or at least quite similar) to begin with. Perhaps the students in one group are more motivated than those in the other group, or have greater language aptitude or higher language proficiency to start with. As a result, we cannot be sure that any differences we find are truly due to the treatment (the TOEFL preparation course). Therefore, when we use an intact groups design we must be conservative when we report the results.

These three designs—the one-shot case study, the one-group pre-test post-test design, and the intact groups design—all belong to the *pre-experimental class* of designs. They are pre-experimental in that they lack some of the defining characteristics of the true experimental designs.

ACTION

Decide which of the three designs discussed above is being used in each of the following research situations.

1. An Arabic teacher wanted to know whether pronunciation exercises improved her students' pronunciation of difficult words. She gave the students a pronunciation test before doing the pronunciation exercises, and then she tested them again after the class.

2. A teacher used two different methods to teach vocabulary with her two intermediate French classes. One group got a list of randomly ordered, unrelated words to memorize. The second group got the same vocabulary lists, but in addition, the teacher created jazz chants using the words. At the end of the term, both classes were tested over the vocabulary presented in the course.

3. A teacher wanted to see if listening to Spanish radio programs would help the pronunciation of his beginning Spanish students. He consistently assigned three hours per week of listening to Spanish radio for homework. At the end of the course, the teacher asked a native Spanish speaker to judge the students' pronunciation.

Compare your ideas with those of a classmate or colleague.

Scenario 4: The Nonequivalent Control (Comparison) Groups Design

Suppose you are an EFL program administrator who wants to determine whether or not the students taking the TOEFL preparation course in your program are benefiting from the course. You conduct a study in which the twenty students in the course are tested on the TOEFL at the beginning and at the end of the fifteen-week term. You will compare their TOEFL scores to those of twenty similar students in another class that meets at the same time and for the same number of hours each week. These students are not studying for the TOEFL, but they are also tested at the beginning and end of the fifteen-week term with the same pre-test and post-test that the TOEFL preparation students take.

REFLECTION

What element has been added to this scenario that was not present in Scenario 3, which described the intact groups design?

ACTION

Reread the paragraph above and answer these questions.

1. What is the research question or hypothesis for this study?
2. What is the independent variable and how many levels does it have?
3. What is the dependent variable?
4. What are the two control variables?
5. Identify one problem inherent in this study.
6. What are two things that could be done to improve this study?

Compare your answers with those of a classmate or colleague.

This research design is called a *nonequivalent control groups design*, or—more properly— a *nonequivalent comparison groups design*. (The name comes from the fact that the groups were not randomly sampled so we cannot claim they are conceptually equal.) This design is not as strong as the true experimental designs because it lacks randomization, but it is stronger than the one-shot case study, the one-group pre-test post-test design, or the intact groups design.

The benefit of the nonequivalent comparison groups design over the intact groups design is the data from the pre-test. Those data allow you to say whether or not the groups were identical (or quite similar) at the beginning of the term. You can also compare the groups' gain scores instead of just their post-test scores.

However, because the groups being compared were intact (i.e., they were not randomly sampled or randomly assigned), there are still limitations on the claims you can make. In fact, that is why we prefer the term *comparison groups* in the design's name rather than *control groups*. By definition, a *control group* is one made up of people randomly selected from the population and randomly assigned to the groups in the study. In addition, in the strongest designs—those in the true experimental class—which group serves as the control group is often randomly determined, perhaps by the flip of a coin. This step is a further safeguard to ensure that there are no known preexisting differences that might influence the outcome of the study.

Scenario 5: The Time Series Design

At this point, in order to introduce two different research designs, we want to change our focus a bit. Let's look at the TOEFL preparation course from the point of view of the teacher. In this situation, there is only one group of students—a very familiar situation in language classroom research.

Imagine that you are the teacher for this course and that there are twenty students. You want to help the students prepare for the TOEFL. Given the importance of academic vocabulary on the TOEFL, at the end of every week you give the students a twenty-item quiz that tests the vocabulary for that week. The average scores on the quizzes tend to be around 13 or 14 points each week.

During the eighth week of the semester, you administer a practice TOEFL. Several students are unhappily surprised by their low scores. The experience of taking the practice TOEFL seems to motivate them, and, thereafter, they exert more effort in studying for the weekly vocabulary quizzes. In the weeks after the practice TOEFL, you notice that the quiz scores are higher than they were before the practice exam, with the average ranging between 16 and 18 points. The average scores on the weekly vocabulary quiz are indicated by the asterisks (*) in **Figure 4.1.** The vertical gray bar indicates the administration of the practice TOEFL.

This scenario is an example of the *time series design*. In this design there is only one group, so comparison with another group is not possible. However, it is possible to compare the group's average scores before the practice TOEFL, which we can think of as a treatment, with their average scores after the practice TOEFL. We can use this design, for instance, to help answer the question of whether or not administering the practice TOEFL motivated the students to

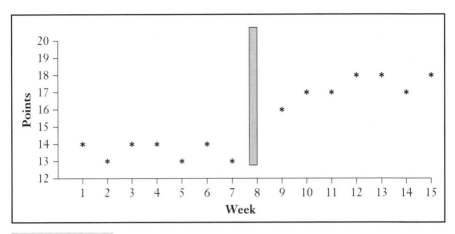

FIGURE 4.1 Average scores on weekly twenty-point vocabulary quizzes before and after the administration of the practice TOEFL

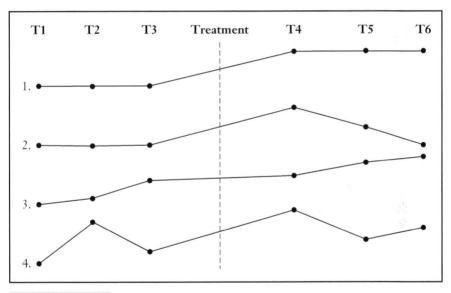

FIGURE 4.2 Possible outcomes in a time series design (Tuckman, 1999, p. 169)

study harder. From the data above, it appears that that effort resulted in higher vocabulary quiz scores.

In the time series design, the group under investigation serves as its own control. That is, before the treatment, the students are functioning as a control group, but after the treatment, they are analogous to an experimental group. This situation is far from ideal, but it can be informative. We need to be careful, though, about interpreting the results, as shown in **Figure 4.2.** In this figure, *T* stands for time.

The inference that the treatment caused an effect is most justified in cases 1 and 2 above. It is least justified in cases 3 and 4 (Tuckman, 1999).

REFLECTION

Why does Tuckman (1999) assert that cases 3 and 4 suggest that the treatment has not caused an effect?

These four sets of data all provide different information about the possible effects of the treatment. The first line in Figure 4.2 tells us that the scores were higher after the treatment than they were before, and that they remained consistently high. The second line tells us that the scores improved after the treatment but that the improvement tapered off later. The third line indicates that the scores were higher after the treatment and continued to increase, but we cannot say that the treatment caused this improvement because the scores had already begun to increase before the treatment. It appears that this developmental trend might have continued with or without the treatment being administered. Finally, in the fourth line, the scores are somewhat erratic. They improve immediately after the treatment and then drop back down again, but the scores were relatively high at one point before the treatment as well.

Scenario 6: The Equivalent Time Samples Design

Another design that is used in contexts where there is no comparison group or control group is called the *equivalent time samples design.* It is related to the time series design. To see how this design works, we will use another scenario related to the TOEFL preparation course.

Once again, please imagine that you are the teacher for the course. You have implemented the practice of giving weekly vocabulary quizzes to encourage the students to study the academic vocabulary covered in class. You read a research article about the importance of providing a meaningful context for the study of vocabulary and you decide to test the author's ideas. For every other week of the fifteen-week term, starting with the first week, you provide a story at the beginning of the week that offers a clear, memorable context for the vocabulary the class will study that week. On alternate weeks, you simply provide the week's vocabulary list without contextualizing the vocabulary items in a story. At the end of every week you administer a twenty-point quiz. The results are depicted as a bar graph in **Figure 4.3.**

REFLECTION

What can you infer from the results depicted in Figure 4.3?

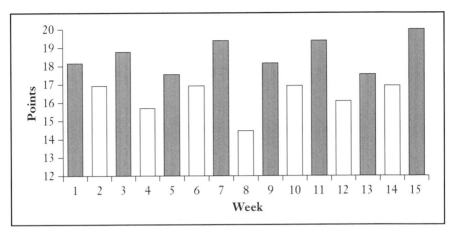

FIGURE 4.3 Average scores on weekly twenty-point vocabulary quizzes for weeks with contextualization (gray bars) and weeks without contextualization (white bars)

Once again, when we work with the equivalent time samples design, we say that the group serves as its own control. There is no separate control or comparison group, but we are able to compare the scores on the dependent variable (the twenty-point vocabulary quiz) for the weeks when contextualization was provided with the vocabulary scores for the weeks when it was not. In effect, the contextualization is the treatment, and it is alternately provided and withheld from the same group of students. This design is stronger than the time series design because multiple comparisons are possible. That is, since the treatment has been given and withheld several times, we have a better chance of detecting its effect (if any).

These three designs (the nonequivalent comparison group design, the time series design, and the equivalent time samples design) all belong to a class called the *quasi-experimental designs*. This class is characterized by (1) the possibility of making comparisons on the dependent variable, but also by (2) the lack of a randomly sampled and randomly assigned control group.

REFLECTION

Think of a research question that you could address with a time series design and one that could be addressed using the equivalent time samples design. Remember that these are designs that can be used when no control group (or even a comparison group) is available. Given that fact, what could you confidently say about the possible outcomes of your two studies?

Identify the particular quasi-experimental design involved in each of the following situations. Compare your ideas with those of a colleague or classmate.

1. An EFL teacher in Turkey wanted to see if having a party where only English was spoken would have an impact on the conversational fluency of her students. The party was arranged for the middle of the semester. Every week before the party, she recorded a brief conversation with each student. After the party, she continued to record the weekly conversations to try to determine whether the party had had an impact on the students' conversational fluency.

2. A teacher of Swedish as a second language wondered whether implementing drama techniques would improve her students' pronunciation. The teacher tested the pronunciation of her three intermediate speaking classes at the beginning of the term. With the 9 A.M. group, she used just regular conversation practice. With the 11 A.M. class, she used role plays in addition to conversation practice. And with the 2 P.M. class, she used role plays and conversation practice, but she also had the students perform scripted plays in Swedish. At the end of the term, she tested all the students again to see whether their pronunciation had improved and, if so, whether those gains differed across the three groups.

3. An EFL teacher in Shanghai wanted to determine the effect of translating new vocabulary items into Chinese for the students (instead of just talking about their meanings in English). She gave vocabulary quizzes every week and tried the translation approach to vocabulary teaching every other week. At the end of the semester, she compared the student' quiz averages for the weeks following the translation approach with those from the weeks in which only English explanations were used.

Scenario 7: Post-Test Only Control Group Design

We are now moving into a different class of designs—the *true experimental designs*. These are characterized by (1) random selection of subjects from the population, (2) random assignment of subjects to groups, and (3) the presence of an actual control group.

Let's return to the situation about the TOEFL preparation class. Please imagine once more that you are an EFL program administrator who wants to determine whether taking the popular TOEFL preparation course in your program helps the students. You conduct a study in which the twenty students in the course are tested on the TOEFL at the end of the semester. You will compare their TOEFL scores to those of twenty similar students who are tested at the same time but who are not studying for the TOEFL.

In order to make sure the two groups of students are as similar as possible, you randomly draw forty names from the list of over a hundred students who wish to take the TOEFL preparation course. Then you randomly assign twenty of those names to one group and twenty to another group. Finally, you flip a coin to see which group will enroll in the TOEFL preparation class this term and which group will wait until next term. This second group is placed in a grammar review course, which meets at the same time and for the same number of hours as the TOEFL preparation course.

ACTION

Answer the following questions about this study.

1. What is the research question or hypothesis for this study?
2. What is the independent variable and how many levels does it have?
3. What is the dependent variable?
4. Name a problem inherent in this study.
5. What is one thing that could be done to improve this study?

Compare your ideas with those of a classmate or colleague.

This research design is called the *post-test only control group design*. It is one of the true experimental designs because of the presence of a control group and the random selection and random assignment of subjects.

Scenario 8: Pre-Test Post-Test Control Group Design

You have probably already realized from the name of this design what additional change could be made. If we simply add a pre-test to the study in Scenario 7, we will have a pre-test post-test control group design. The independent variable and its levels remain the same.

REFLECTION

Now what is the dependent variable? What is one possible threat to validity inherent in this design?

The *pre-test post-test control group design* is one of the true experimental designs because of the presence of a control group and the random selection and random assignment of subjects. In one sense, it is stronger than the post-test only control group design because you can measure improvement (through the gain scores). However, it is also susceptible to the testing threat.

COMPARISON OF MAIN RESEARCH DESIGNS
IN THE EXPERIMENTAL METHOD

So far in this chapter, we have studied eight research designs. In Chapter 3, we discussed the criterion groups design and the correlation design, which are the two members of the ex post facto class. The four main classes of designs and the various specific designs that comprise them are depicted in **Table 4.1.**

If you start with the upper left box in Table 4.1 and draw a large Z through the four boxes, you will have a way of remembering the increasing power of these designs. That is, the pre-experimental designs are the weakest, followed by the quasi-experimental designs and then the ex post facto designs. The true experimental designs are the strongest. Within the culture of experimental research, this relative strength is a function of increasing control over variables. The stronger designs are those with the greatest internal and external validity.

Three designs are marked with asterisks in Table 4.1. The addition of one or more moderator variables in these designs makes them *factorial*. For example, a *factorial post-test only control group design* is one in which there are one or more moderator variables in the study. Theoretically, it would also be possible to add a moderator variable to an intact groups design or a nonequivalent comparison groups design, but this is rarely done because adding a moderator variable adds complexity to the statistical analysis. Since these designs are relatively weak, it's hardly worth the extra effort to add a moderator variable.

Another way to contrast these designs is to list their defining characteristics. **Table 4.2** does so by answering the following *yes/no* questions:

Column 1: Does the design involve more than one group of subjects?

Column 2: Does the design involve administering a treatment?

Column 3: Does the design involve a randomly selected, randomly assigned control group to compare with the experimental group(s)?

TABLE 4.1 Major designs and classes of research designs in experimental research (after Shavelson, 1981, pp. 30–44)

Pre-Experimental Class	Quasi-Experimental Class
1. One-Shot Case Study	1. Nonequivalent Control (or Comparison) Groups Design
2. One-Group Pre-Test Post-Test Design	2. Time Series Design
3. Intact Groups Design	3. Equivalent Time Samples Design

Ex Post Facto Class	True Experimental Class
1. Criterion Groups Design*	1. Post-test Only Control Group Design*
2. Correlation Design	2. Pre-test Post-test Control Group Design*

TABLE 4.2   Comparison of ten experimental research designs

Design	1	2	3	4	5	6	7
One-shot case study	No	Yes	No	No	No	No	No
One-group pre-test post-test	No	Yes	No	No	Yes	No	No
Intact groups	Yes	Yes	No	Yes	No	No	No
Nonequivalent comparison groups	Yes	Yes	No	Yes	Yes	No	No
Time series	No	Yes	No	No	Yes	No	No
Equivalent time samples	No	Yes	No	No	Yes	No	No
Criterion groups	Yes	No	No	Yes	No	Yes	No
Correlation	No	No	No	No	No	Yes	No
Post-test only control group	Yes	Yes	Yes	No	No	Yes	Yes
Pre-test post-test control group	Yes	Yes	Yes	No	Yes	Yes	Yes

Column 4: Does the design involve some other kind of comparison group?

Column 5: Is a pre-test given?

Column 6: Is random selection used to constitute the sample?

Column 7: Is random assignment used to constitute the groups?

There are some caveats to remember when interpreting this table. First, it is important to distinguish between the presence of an actual control group (Column 3) and some other sort of comparison group (Column 4). Secondly, in correlation studies, the statistics used to perform the correlation analyses are always based on two (or more) sets of data from one group of people. However, some studies include different sets of correlation statistics if correlations are sought in more than one group. (We will deal more with the statistics used in correlation designs in Chapter 13.)

ACTION

With a classmate or colleague, talk through the *yes/no* responses in Table 4.2. Make sure you understand how these seven defining characteristics can help you identify these research designs in the experimental method.

RESEARCH DESIGN ISSUES AND INFERENTIAL STATISTICS

To review these concepts, let's consider a situation in which an experiment might be an appropriate way of gathering data. Imagine that you have developed some innovative listening materials based on authentic radio and television programs. You have used these materials with good results in your secondary school EFL classes. Although you feel strongly that your innovative materials are superior to the school's traditional listening program, your colleagues are skeptical. Your challenge is to test the possible superiority of your materials. You have several options here. You could obtain the opinions of the students through surveys and questionnaires. Alternatively (or additionally), you could ask a sympathetic colleague to observe your classes and make an observational record of the teaching and learning that goes on. However, you may feel that these steps are unlikely to sway your more skeptical colleagues, who are only likely to be convinced by superior test scores.

Your first thought is to test your students' listening comprehension at the end of the semester, and, assuming that the results are favorable, present these findings to your colleagues. However, you come across the following criticism of such an approach (which you now recognize as the one-shot case study design):

> Much research in education today conforms to a design in which a single group is studied only once, subsequent to some agent or treatment presented to cause change. Such studies might be diagrammed as follows:
>
> XO
>
> [X = the treatment administered to the subjects, and O = the observation.] [Unfortunately] . . . such studies have such a total absence of control as to be of almost no scientific value . . . It seems well-nigh unethical . . . to allow as theses or dissertations in education, case studies of this nature (i.e., involving a single group observed at one time only). (Campbell and Stanley, 1963, pp. 176–177)

If you are convinced by this argument, your next inclination might be to test two of your classes—one taught with the innovative materials and one taught with the traditional approach. (Doing so would involve using the intact groups design.)

However, you quickly realize that it is no good simply testing the students at the end of the semester and comparing their scores because the groups might not have been at the same level to begin with. The solution would seem to be to test both groups at the beginning and at the end of the semester. Then, if the group that has been taught through the innovative materials makes greater gains in listening comprehension than the traditional group, you can presumably ascribe the superior results to the innovation. (Here you will recognize the nonequivalent comparison groups design.)

Your research design is becoming more rigorous, but it is not yet rigorous enough to allow you to make claims that there is a causal relationship between the independent variable (the innovative materials) and the dependent variable (the students' listening comprehension test results). There is always the possibility that factors other than the innovative materials are responsible for any observed differences in the scores.

REFLECTION

Make a list of possible issues that might be responsible for differences in the groups' scores in the study described above. Do these issues affect the internal validity or the external validity of the study?

There are many possible influences that can affect the outcome of a study such as this one. If different teachers are involved in teaching the different groups, then it could be the teachers rather than the materials that make a difference. If one teacher works with both groups, you will have controlled for teacher style as a factor, but the teacher's enthusiasm for (or boredom with) one type of materials could influence the results. Even the time of day at which a class is held can affect learning outcomes. These issues weaken the internal validity of the study because it is not possible to state categorically that the treatment brought about any differences observed in the students' test scores.

While factors such as those mentioned above may impinge on research outcomes, participant factors (such as the selection threat) are the most pervasive. For example, you may have happened to select a group of fast-track or high-aptitude students as the recipients of the experimental authentic materials, and a group of slow learners that used the traditional materials. In order to guard against the possibility that factors such as age, motivation, or aptitude might influence the research outcomes, sound experimental design in the psychometric tradition suggests that you assign subjects randomly to the control and experimental conditions.

Using randomization puts you in a better position to argue that any observed differences on the end-of-course test are due to the innovative materials because possible confounding variables that might have had an effect (such as intelligence and aptitude) are presumably evenly distributed in the experimental and control groups. You can also test both groups of students before the experiment just to make sure that the groups really are the same, though this step introduces the possibility of the testing threat. (Doing so would entail the use of the pre-test post-test control group design.)

Unfortunately, in ongoing programs, it is not always practical to rearrange students and randomly assign them into different groups or classes. In many schools, if an experiment is to be conducted, it will have to be with classes to which students have been preassigned. That is why the intact groups design and the nonequivalent comparison groups design are so often used in language classroom research—because they involve groups that were already established (by means other than randomization) without the researcher's control. In these circumstances, while the internal validity of the experiment is weakened, the study may still be worthwhile.

Imagine that you are able to carry out the experiment described above. You randomly assign ten final-year secondary school students to the control group and ten to the experimental group. A 100-point listening pre-test indicates that the groups are at the same level of proficiency. You teach both groups for a semester, using the innovative authentic materials with the experimental group and the traditional materials with the control group. At the end of the semester, the groups are retested with an alternate form of the 100-point listening test. You calculate the averages:

	Control Group:	Experimental Group:
Post-test average:	80	85

The experimental group has thus outscored the control group.

Are you entitled to claim that the innovative materials are superior to the traditional materials? If so, why? If not, why not?

The answer to the question is "Not yet!" You have selected a sample, or subset, of all the possible students in the final year of secondary school as your experimental subjects. If you retested them again tomorrow, or if you selected a different group of subjects and tested them, it's highly unlikely that you would get exactly the same scores. The students might be more tired (or more energetic), or the weather could affect their performance. In short, a whole range of factors could be responsible for test score variation. What you need to decide is whether the variation in scores between the control and experimental groups might have happened by chance, or whether the differences were a result of the experimental treatment. In order to do this, you must make inferences based on statistical procedures.

FROM SAMPLES TO POPULATIONS: THE LOGIC OF INFERENTIAL STATISTICS

The aim of this section is to introduce you to the logic of statistical inference. The information presented here will probably not equip you to carry out your own statistical analyses, but it should help you to understand and appreciate the logic behind the statistical procedures that enable researchers to make claims about an entire population based on a sample or subset of subjects from that population.

In most research, it is not possible to collect data from the entire population in which we are interested. Consider your investigation of the authentic materials in secondary school EFL classes. Although not impossible, it would be extremely time-consuming and cumbersome to obtain data on all the secondary school EFL students in your country, state, province, county, or prefecture. (In fact, that's what national examination boards and international testing companies try to do.) Normally, someone who wanted to carry out such an investigation would select a sample of students (say 20, 100, or 2,000 or more) from the wider population and test them.

However, a problem immediately arises. The problem has to do with deciding the extent to which the data obtained from the sample are representative of the population as a whole and, in fact, what that population is. In everyday life, overgeneralizations are common (witness the prevalence of "dumb blond" jokes). But overgeneralizations also occur in research when investigators fail to recognize that their subjects are not fully representative of the population being investigated.

Here is an anecdote from Rowntree (1981) that illustrates the complicated issue of matching samples and populations:

> During the Second World War, gunners in bombers returning from raids were asked from which direction they were most frequently attacked by enemy fighters. The majority answer was "from above and behind." (p. 23)

REFLECTION

Why might it have been unwise to assume, supposing you were a gunner, that this claim would be true of attacks on gunners in general?

Rowntree provides the following answer to the question:

> The risk of a false generalization lay in the fact that the researcher was able to interview only the *survivors* of attacks. It could well be that attacks from below and behind were no less frequent, but did not get represented in the sample because (from the enemy's point of view) they were successful. (ibid.)

He goes on to say that this issue of matching samples and populations is a paradox of sampling:

> A sample is misleading unless it is representative of the population; but how can we tell it is representative unless we already know what we need to know about the population and therefore have no need of samples! The paradox cannot be completely resolved; some uncertainty must remain. Nevertheless, our statistical methodology enables us to collect samples that are likely to be as representative as possible. This allows us to exercise proper caution and avoid over-generalization. (ibid.)

To help protect against overgeneralization, researchers use several procedures based on descriptive and inferential statistics. (Explaining all these procedures is beyond the scope of this book, but we will deal with some in Chapter 13.)

TABLE 4.3 EFL students' scores on a listening comprehension test (n = 20)

Student ID	Control Group Scores	Student ID	Experimental Group Scores
C-1	80	E-1	85
C-2	82	E-2	87
C-3	78	E-3	83
C-4	77	E-4	82
C-5	83	E-5	88
C-6	80	E-6	85
C-7	76	E-7	81
C-8	84	E-8	89
C-9	75	E-9	84
C-10	85	E-10	86
Mean	**80**		**85**

Descriptive Statistics

To understand the logic behind the procedures that enable extrapolation from samples to populations, you need to be familiar with a number of statistical concepts. The two most important of these are the *mean* and *standard deviation*. These are two of the *descriptive statistics*—so labeled because they describe the sample.

For experimental researchers, two particularly interesting features of numerical data sets are the extent to which individual items in the data set are similar and the extent to which they differ or are dispersed. The most important measure of similarity is the numerical average, or *mean* (symbolized by a capital X with a horizontal bar above it and called *X-bar*). The average is obtained by adding the individual scores together and dividing the sum by the total number of scores. To illustrate, let's look at the post-test scores from the students in the control and experimental groups in the (hypothetical) study about innovative listening materials.

The scores presented in **Table 4.3** are simply listed in order of the students' identification codes. They are not organized in any particular fashion. It can be quite useful to rank order these scores, in order to see existing patterns more clearly. When we rank order these scores, we find the data in **Table 4.4**.

The lowest score in this entire data set is 75 and the highest score is 89. The difference between the highest score and the lowest score is the *range*. This is one of the descriptive statistics. (Ranking the scores in this way is useful because it allows us to see the range quickly.) The range in the control group was 75 to 85 and the range in the experimental group was 81 to 89. So, just by looking at

TABLE 4.4 Ranking of EFL students' scores on a listening comprehension test (n = 20)

Ranking of Control Group Scores	Control Group Scores	Ranking of Experimental Group Scores	Experimental Group Scores
1	85	1	89
2	84	2	88
3	83	3	87
4	82	4	86
5.5	80	5.5	85
5.5	80	5.5	85
7	78	7	84
8	77	8	83
9	76	9	82
10	75	10	81
Average	80		85

the difference in the ranges, we can see that the experimental group did better. However, range is also reported in terms of its absolute value. That is, we sometimes subtract the lowest score from the highest score. Using this procedure, we can say that the range for the control group is ten, and the range for the experimental group is eight. We cannot tell which group did better—we can only tell that there was more variability in the control group's scores than in the experimental group's scores.

REFLECTION

In Table 4.4, in the columns that provide the ranking of the two groups' scores, there are two places where the rank is given as 5.5—one for the control group and one for the experimental group. Why do you think these ranks are given as 5.5 instead of 5 and 6?

The answer to the question in the reflection box above has to do with principles of decision making. Let's use the prize money in a golf tournament as a metaphor. One golfer is the first place winner, and he receives a check for $100,000. Two golfers are tied for second place. The prize money for second place is $50,000, and the prize money for third place is $30,000. What is a fair way to decide which golfer was second and which was third, since their scores were tied? The answer is to add the prize money for second place and third place and divide that total amount by two (for the two tied golfers). So, instead of flipping a coin to decide who gets $50,000 and who gets $30,000, we add these two sums and get $80,000. We then divide that amount by two and the two second place contestants each receive $40,000.

The same logic applies in a set of ordinal data when you have tied ranks. Look at the ranks that the scores would have covered, had they not been tied. In Table 4.4, these are the fifth and sixth ranks. Since the tied scores are identical, instead of calling one "fifth" and the other "sixth" they are both assigned the rank of 5.5—halfway between the fifth and sixth ranks.

Frequency Polygons

Another way to look at these test data is to see how many students obtained each particular score. Let's start with the scores of all twenty students combined. We can list the score values across the bottom axis of a chart and the number of people who obtained each particular score on the vertical axis. The term *frequency* here refers to how often each score was obtained. In **Figure 4.4,** each asterisk shows how many people out of the twenty subjects in the study received each possible score value.

If you were to draw bars down from each of these asterisks to the horizontal axis, you would have a bar graph, or *histogram*. If you were to draw a line connecting these asterisks, you would have what is called a *frequency polygon*—a chart of the frequency with which each score value was obtained. Notice that no one got a score of 79. At this point the line connecting the asterisks would drop down to the horizontal axis, to indicate that no one received that score.

The frequency polygon is a very important conceptual tool as well as an informative visual aid. In fact, the frequency polygon is the basis for many of the most important statistical procedures that we use in language classroom research.

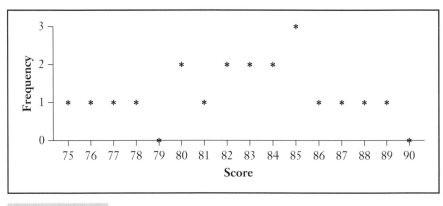

FIGURE 4.4   Frequency of 20 EFL students' scores on a listening comprehension test

In Figure 4.4, we combined the scores of the control and experimental group, but you can also draw a frequency polygon that contrasts two or more sets of data. Using the chart framework below, plot the scores for the control and experimental groups separately. Remember that for any score that did not appear in the data, the frequency is zero.

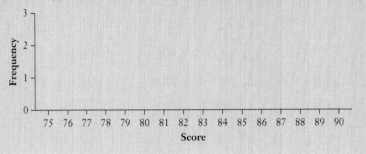

With very small samples like this, frequency polygons can be nearly flat. But an interesting thing happens when large data sets are plotted on a frequency polygon. Imagine for a moment that ninety-five students actually took this 100-point test. If we had that many scores to enter in the frequency polygon, it might look something like this:

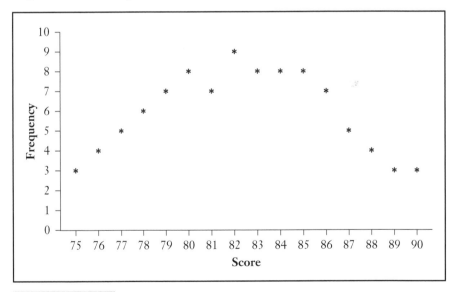

FIGURE 4.5 Frequency of EFL students' scores on a listening comprehension test (n = 95)

If you connect the asterisks in **Figure 4.5,** you can see the rough shape of a bell emerging. In fact, a frequency polygon with this shape is called a *bell curve* or a *bell-shaped curve* because it is typically high in the middle with sloping sides tapering off to tails on the left and right. It is also called the *normal distribution* because it is such a common pattern when variables are measured in large groups of people. That is to say, the characteristic being measured (whether it is height, intelligence, language aptitude, etc.) is distributed normally throughout the population. Relatively few people score very low on the measurement and relatively few people score very high. Most people score somewhere in the middle of the range.

Keep in mind that "we never get a completely normal data distribution. The normal distribution is an idealized concept" (Hatch and Lazaraton, 1991, p. 194). But with large samples, the pattern does appear, and this fact leads to some interesting opportunities for analyzing data. In very large data sets, the normal distribution is predictable. The shape of the bell is smooth and regular, and its sides are very symmetrical, like this:

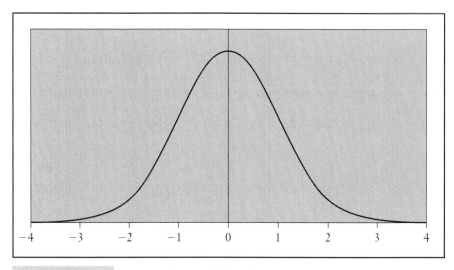

FIGURE 4.6 Standard normal distribution (downloaded from http://www.tushar-mehta.com on August 14, 2006)

The vertical line drawn straight down from the apex of the bell in **Figure 4.6** represents the midpoint or *median*—defined as the middle score in a data set. In the normal distribution, it also represents the *mean*—the average—and the *mode*—the most frequently obtained score in that data set. That the line represents the median makes sense because the bell is symmetrical. The fact that it represents the mode also makes sense because the bell's apex (the high point) shows the most frequent score. These three descriptive statistics are collectively referred to as the *measures of central tendency* because they all provide information about the tendency of scores to cluster in the middle range of the curve.

The three other descriptive statistics are the *range* and *standard deviation* discussed above, and also *variance*. (We will discuss variance in Chapter 13.) Together these make up the *measures of dispersion* because they provide information about the variability in a set of scores—how dispersed the scores in the data set are. The standard deviation is the most important measure of dispersion. It tells us the average amount by which scores in the data set vary from the mean. In other words, it tells us how spread out the scores are. In Figure 4.6, the numbers running along the horizontal axis (from negative four to four) represent standard deviations.

REFLECTION

Why is the number zero directly under the line that represents the mean, the median, and the mode in Figure 4.6? (This issue is a matter of logic and definition rather than of mathematics.)

Calculating the standard deviations for the scores in Table 4.3 gives us the values reported in the last row of **Table 4.5**. (We won't go into the formula for calculating the standard deviation here. We will work with it in Chapter 13.)

We said earlier that the ranges for the scores of the control and experimental groups were ten and eight, respectively. Can you see how the range is reflected in the standard deviations reported in Table 4.5? Since standard deviation is an index of how spread out the scores are in a given data set, it makes sense that where there is a wider range there will be a bigger standard deviation.

TABLE 4.5 Scores, means, and standard deviations of two groups of EFL students on a listening comprehension test (n = 20)

Student ID	Control Group Scores	Student ID	Experimental Group Scores
C-1	80	E-1	85
C-2	82	E-2	87
C-3	78	E-3	83
C-4	77	E-4	82
C-5	83	E-5	88
C-6	80	E-6	85
C-7	76	E-7	81
C-8	84	E-8	89
C-9	75	E-9	84
C-10	85	E-10	86
Mean	**80**		**85**
Range	**10**		**8**
	(75–85)		(81–89)
Standard deviation	3.25		2.58

To put the concept of standard deviation in a practical context, think about the situation where you are about to start teaching three different classes of intermediate English students. For all three classes, the mean score on the program's 100-point placement exam was 70 points. But the standard deviations for the three classes were 15, 10 and 5 points. What do these values tell you about the composition of the three classes? As a teacher, what can you expect as a result of this variability?

Inferential Statistics

At this point, we want to remind you of some things that you already know about percentages. We want to build on your existing knowledge and confidence to introduce a new concept.

ACTION

Look at the pie charts below and decide what percentage of the area of each circle is indicated by the various sections.

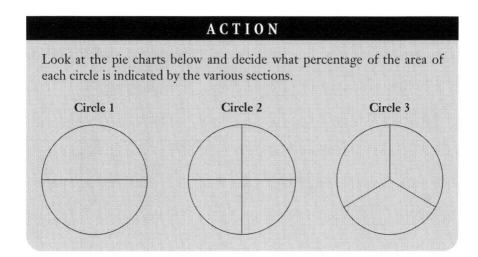

We are quite sure that you recognize the percentages represented by these divisions. In Circle 1, the sections of the bisected pie chart represent 50% and 50%. In Circle 2, the pie chart is divided into four equal portions. Each segment represents 25% of the whole circle. And in Circle 3, we have three equal sections, each of which represents 33⅓% of the whole circle. You recognize these percentage values because you have seen charts like this ever since you started school.

We can use the image of the normal distribution to indicate percentages, too. As noted above, when the bell curve is bisected by the vertical line representing the mean, the median, and the mode, 50% of the scores fall above that line and 50% fall below it. (Remember the frequency polygons where you connected the asterisks. A *bell curve* is just a symmetrical frequency polygon.)

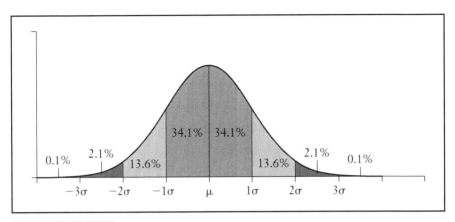

FIGURE 4.7 The areas under the normal curve, as indicated by standard deviations (downloaded on August 13, 2006 from Wikipedia)

The image of the bell curve can also be divided in predictable, recognizable ways.

When you see a chart of the normal distribution, it usually has numbers written on the horizontal axis. These numbers range from negative four to positive four, as mentioned above, to indicate the location of the standard deviations in the diagram. But, for ease of interpretation, such diagrams also often have vertical lines drawn that represent the standard deviations. These lines help us see percentage divisions, as shown in **Figure 4.7**. (Just think of this as a different shaped pie chart—one with which you may not be very familiar at this time.) Here and elsewhere the Greek symbol σ (the lower-case sigma) stands for standard deviation. The symbol μ (the Greek letter *mu*) represents the population mean.

Means and standards deviations are important when it comes to comparing different sets of interval data, such as test scores from a control group and an experimental group. We can also think about the standard deviation and the mean of a population. Imagine you are reviewing reading test scores for nine-year-olds in 100 different primary schools. Those scores are likely to be reported as schoolwide averages because looking at individual scores for all the nine-year-old pupils at 100 schools would be a daunting task. Even looking at the individual class means for every school would be very time-consuming, since there could be five to ten classes of nine-year-olds at every school. Seeing the scores reported as schoolwide averages is economical and it also allows us to make comparisons across the various schools.

If we were to draw a frequency polygon using the 100 schools' reading averages as the data to be entered in the polygon, we would once again get a bell-shaped curve. This time the data points in the frequency polygon would not represent individual students' scores but rather the mean reading scores of the 100 schools.

We have already discussed the concept of a population. Statistically, a population is defined in terms of means and standard deviations. If the means and standards deviations for two sets of test scores are quite similar, then the subjects can be said to be drawn from the same population. If they are very different, then they are drawn from different populations. The key question here is, "How different do they have to be for us to be confident in claiming that they come from different populations?" The phrase *statistically significant* has to do with this question of how different a set of scores must be (or how strong a correlation must be) in order to consider the difference (or the correlation) important and trustworthy.

Over time, researchers using the experimental method have agreed that results can be considered statistically significant if there is a less than 5% chance that they are wrong—that is, if the results are due to chance rather than to an actual relationship between the variables being investigated. (There are some situations where more stringency is required and the level is set at a 1% chance instead.) Another way to say this is that researchers generally want to have 95% (or 99%) confidence that their results are trustworthy before they reject the null hypothesis and accept the alternative hypothesis. So, when you read that a difference or a correlation was statistically significant, it means that the values obtained met the statistical requirements for having confidence that the results were not due to chance.

REFLECTION

The mean, median, mode, standard deviation, range, and variance are the descriptive statistics. What do you think is meant by *inferential statistics*?

Let's return to our hypothetical investigation into the relative effectiveness of the innovative versus traditional listening materials. On the end-of-the-semester test, we discovered that the mean score for the traditional (control) group was 80, and the mean score for the innovative (experimental) group was 85. The control group continues to represent the population from which it was drawn. What we want to know now is whether, through our experimental treatment, we have 'created' a different population—roughly defined as "listeners taught through innovative materials based on authentic input." In order to answer this question, we need to know not only the mean for each group, but also the standard deviation. The reason is that the further an individual score is from the group mean, the less likely it is to occur by chance, and statistical tools can tell us fairly precisely how likely or unlikely this is.

How likely? Here's where the standard deviation comes in. Please take our word for this temporarily (or read ahead in Chapter 13). As shown in Figure 4.7, for any given set of normally distributed scores, 68% of all scores will be within one standard deviation of the mean, 95% of scores will be within two standard deviations, and 99% will be within three standard deviations.

When there is a large difference between the means for the control and experimental groups, we can say that the difference is statistically significant. How large a difference is determined by the standard deviations in the bell-shaped curve. For instance, if the mean for the control group falls between two and three standard deviations below the mean for the experimental group, we can say that there is less than a 5% possibility that this difference would occur by chance. If our level of confidence is set at 5%, then we can say that the difference is *statistically significant*. Therefore, we can conclude that the innovative materials were significantly superior to the traditional materials in enhancing listening skills. Keep in mind, however, that there is still a 5% possibility that the difference could have occurred by chance.

Given that the control group remains 'untreated,' it represents the population of interest. The experimental group represents a changed version of that original population—a group that benefited (we hope!) from the treatment. And this is what is meant by *inferential statistics*: We use the data from the sample to make inferences about what would happen to the population if the treatment were implemented there (i.e., if it were generalized). We do that, quite often, by comparing the means and standard deviations of the sample groups to one another, using particular statistical formulae.

Now let's go back to our data in which the control group mean was 80 and the experimental group mean was 85. We can use an inferential statistic called a t-test (the *t* here always being printed in lower case) to see if these differences are statistically significant. The t-test is specially designed for comparing two means of small groups where the means are based on interval data. (We will learn more about t-tests and other inferential statistics in Chapter 13.) And in fact, when we conduct the t-test on these data, we find that there was a statistically significant difference between the control and experimental groups. Using the innovative listening materials did improve the students' scores on the listening comprehension test. Now you can confidently show your skeptical colleagues your results!

In this section, we have oversimplified things somewhat. (If you are really curious about these issues, you can read ahead in Chapter 13.) Our purpose here is simply to provide a very basic introduction to the logic behind statistical inferences and to show you the basis upon which researchers working in the experimental tradition make their claims for significance.

We will use these statistical concepts in future chapters to illustrate the ways classroom researchers have analyzed their data. At this point, we will summarize a study that illustrates many issues related to research design and threats to validity.

A SAMPLE STUDY

Many years ago, Kathi Bailey was involved as an observer in a process-product study, the results of which were never published. We will describe it here because it is a beautiful example of a formal experiment in language teaching and because there is much to be learned from the way the project evolved.

The research project was conducted at a large military school in the United States, which had a program in Russian as a foreign language. The students were young adults. The study was designed to determine whether the school's regular method of teaching Russian was more effective, or whether *Suggestopedia* was more effective.

Suggestopedia is a language teaching method that was originally developed by Lozanov (1979; 1982). It uses music to relax the students, who are given new target culture identities in the class. There is little or no formal error correction and students learn by hearing and seeing lengthy dialogs in the target language. The method develops speaking fluency, reading skills, and vocabulary. Suggestopedia normally requires extensive teacher training, and there is a Suggestopedia institute that provides that training.

The military school's usual teaching method, in contrast, emphasized grammatical accuracy. There were frequent tests, and error treatment was regularly used to help the students improve their grammar, pronunciation, word knowledge, etc.

The researcher set up a classic textbook experiment. He was able to randomly select a group of forty people from the incoming Russian students. All forty were true beginners in Russian. He then randomly assigned these students to two groups, each of which comprised two Russian classes. There were ten students in each class. Two classes were taught with Suggestopedia and two with the regular teaching method. (See **Figure 4.8.**) The two Suggestopedia classes were taught by certified instructors who had been trained in the method. The other classes were taught by regular employees at the school—all experienced Russian teachers.

The students were all true beginners of the Russian language, so no pre-test was necessary. But the researcher did administer an attitude questionnaire to all forty students before the classes began, so that he could compare their attitudes before and after the Russian course. At the end of the course, all forty students were given the attitude questionnaire again, and their Russian ability was also tested.

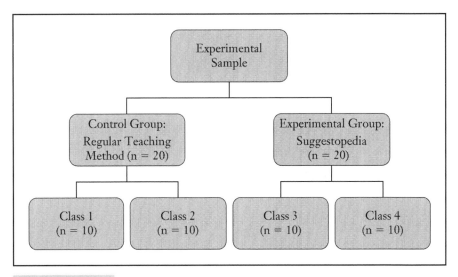

FIGURE 4.8 The control and experimental groups in the sample study

---

ACTION

Answer the following questions based on what you know about this study.

1. What were the likely research questions in this study?

2. What is the independent variable and how many levels does it have?

3. What are the dependent variables? (Hint: There are two.)

4. What is one control variable?

5. What is the design of this study? (Hint: This is a trick question. Think about the dependent variables.)

6. Can you anticipate any possible threats to validity in this situation?

Compare your ideas with those of a classmate or colleague.

The researcher clearly understood the differences among process studies, product studies, and process-product studies. (See Chapter 1.) For this reason, he arranged for trained classroom observers to be present (one at a time) in some of the Suggestopedia classes and some of the regular classes. The observers were to take notes on the sessions so that if any significant differences were found between the results yielded by the two teaching methods, those outcomes could be linked to the actual teaching and learning processes documented by the observers.

Several interesting problems arose as the study progressed. We report these problems with great respect for the researcher, who had set up a well-designed experiment.

First, the Suggestopedia teachers—who were visitors from out of town—looked at the fifteen-week curriculum and said that they could cover that amount of material in ten weeks instead of the fifteen weeks the regular classes would take. Therefore, the Suggestopedia classes ended five weeks before the regular classes, even though they had covered the same curriculum. At that point, the students who had been in the Suggestopedia classes were tested and then integrated into the regular classes.

Secondly, due to the normal scheduling patterns at the school, the students taught with the regular method had many different teachers during a typical day. The two Suggestopedia classes each stayed with one teacher for the entire day. There were never substitutes in the Suggestopedia classes, but due to administrative requirements of meetings and testing, substitute teachers were frequent in the regular classes. (In fact, one day when Kathi Bailey entered a classroom quite early, before the regular teacher had arrived, a student said, "Oh, no! Not another one!" When the observer introduced herself and asked him what he meant, he said he had thought she was another substitute teacher.) In addition, one of the teachers using the regular method found it too stressful to be observed so often and chose to drop out of the study.

On a different occasion, when Bailey was observing a Suggestopedia class, another visitor was present. That person was introduced as a representative of the Suggestopedia training program. When it was time for a break, the students all left the classroom. That observer approached the teacher and said, "What are you doing? This isn't Suggestopedia!" The teacher replied, "I know, but what can I do? The students want grammar rules and error correction."

The students in both the control and experimental groups were young military personnel, who lived together in large dormitories. They had been assured at the outset of the experiment that their performance on the post-test would in no way influence their subsequent job postings. But the students in the Suggestopedia classes apparently doubted this promise, and—knowing that they would face the school's regular accuracy-oriented testing at the end of the experiment—several of them began to study at night in the dormitories with their friends who were in the regular classes. In fact, the two groups of students regularly exchanged their Russian class materials.

REFLECTION

What threats to validity can you identify in the description above?

PAYOFFS AND PITFALLS

As the sample study illustrates, there are many pitfalls in using the experimental method to conduct language classroom research. Many of these problems stem from the difficulty of controlling all the possible confounding variables associated with research on human subjects. Human beings have agency, desires, anxieties, and goals that are often far beyond the ability of the researcher to manage in any comprehensive way. As a result, even in the strongest research designs, threats to validity sometimes arise that compromise the interpretation of the results. In classroom research,

> the security of isolating variables and defining them operationally, a security obtained by laboratory-like experiments and statistical inferences, is largely lost, as the researcher is forced to look for determinants of learning in the fluid dynamics of real-time contexts. (van Lier, 1998, p. 157)

Indeed, classroom research "entails a very large number of human and institutional factors that can affect research design and outcomes in many unforeseen and unforeseeable ways. It is not for the timid" (Rounds and Schachter, 1996, p. 108).

There is also a more philosophical problem with the experimental method. For some people, if a phenomenon is not measurable, it is not worth studying. For them, the psychometric tradition, and the experimental method in particular, may be the only valuable ways of conducting research. However, in an effort to quantify phenomena of interest we may miss important issues. We may not investigate key variables because they are not easily quantified, or we may focus on trivial issues that are easy to quantify. Furthermore, the data collected in language classroom research are often collected from people, but the need to quantify and the widespread use of group averages sometimes make it seem that individual learners are represented only by test scores. And the seeming dehumanization of participants is also noticeable when researchers talk about the sample in a study as "experimental subjects."

Another problem relates to the issue of objectivity and subjectivity. The experimental method emphasizes objectivity in hopes of counteracting the threats of researcher and subject expectancy. As a result, teachers (and learners) have typically not been seen as potential collaborators in language classroom research conducted with the experimental method. Teachers have had important roles, but often primarily as deliverers of a particular treatment in an experiment. However, for teachers, it is sometimes very difficult to be simply a treatment deliverer when students' needs and desires run counter to the prescribed treatment. (Remember the Suggestopedia teacher's comment, "I know, but what can I do? The students want grammar rules and error correction.")

There are also several payoffs associated with the experimental method. First, it is a well-documented, highly codified approach to conducting educational research with well-developed quality control procedures. There are many textbooks available and it is relatively easy to locate courses if you wish to get further training.

Secondly, the experimental method is an internationally recognized way of conducting research. If you conduct an experiment in Jakarta and publish your findings in *Prospect*, the TESOL journal of Australia, readers in Germany, Iran, India, Canada, and Brazil will all understand the report (provided they have been trained in the language and culture of the experimental method).

Third, there are clear criteria for interpreting the outcomes in such research. The concept of statistical significance provides the field with ways to understand whether a correlation is powerful enough or whether a difference in scores is big enough to warrant generalizing the results of the study.

Fourth, because of the emphasis on operational definitions and controlling variables, it is sometimes possible to make comparisons across studies conducted at different sites. The widely understood research designs and numerous statistical procedures allow researchers to replicate studies conducted by other people.

Finally, because it has high prestige in many contexts, using the experimental method may enable researchers to obtain grant money or get their reports published in venues that are not as accessible to those trying to publish action research reports or the findings of naturalistic inquiry. (Of course, the research has to be done well in order to be published. Simply using a prestigious research method is no guarantee that your report will be accepted.)

CONCLUSIONS

The experimental method has been very important, historically, in all sorts of research, in both the physical and social sciences. It has often been used in language classroom research, but with varied success, since it is so difficult to control all the possible confounding variables that can arise in research with real people. It is, however, a valuable approach to understanding teaching and learning, and it has influenced many other approaches, as we will see in future chapters.

QUESTIONS AND TASKS

1. Identify the specific design in each of the following research situations.

   A. At the beginning of an advanced composition course for international college students, the instructor had each student write an in-class essay about the differences between the educational systems of their host country and their home countries. After ten weeks, the teacher had the students write on the same topic. Then the two sets of essays were mixed together at random and rated by another teacher who did not know about the experiment.

   B. A Greek teacher in Australia wanted to test the hypothesis that exposing his students to the cultural setting of the target language would enhance their language learning. The first three weeks of the class he tested them every week on basic grammar points from the lessons discussed in class. The fourth week, he took them to a Greek festival, complete with food, music, dancing, and traditional Greek clothing. The following three weeks, he gave them weekly tests on the grammar lessons.

   C. A French teacher in a secondary school wanted to know if using new vocabulary words in a hands-on experience would help students remember them. So, she performed an experiment using her two beginning French classes as the groups to be compared. One group met in the home economics classroom kitchen and made crêpes while learning the words for the ingredients. The other group met in class as usual, read about crêpes, and made vocabulary lists of the ingredients. After this experiment, the teacher tested both classes with a vocabulary quiz to see which group did better.

D. The teacher of an elementary Spanish class wanted to know how well the students would perform at the end of the course since he had changed to a new textbook. He used the students' final exam scores at the end of the semester as an indication of the success of the new textbook.

E. A language teacher wanted to determine the relationship between oral proficiency and grammatical accuracy of his students. (He knew that his teaching method stressed speaking skills but that his students would be faced with standardized tests of grammatical accuracy.) He designed a study in which he could plot the students' scores on an oral proficiency interview against their scores on a 100-point grammar test.

F. An ESL teacher in Scotland wanted to compare the listening comprehension of his students from Asia, Latin America, Europe, and Africa. He administered a test of English listening comprehension and then computed the mean scores for the students from these four regions.

G. The ESL teacher in Scotland wondered whether those students who had traveled in the United Kingdom had better listening comprehension than those who hadn't. For this reason, he added U.K. travel experience as a moderator variable in his study comparing the listening comprehension scores of students from Asia, Latin America, Europe, and Africa.

H. A German language teacher wanted to know if viewing videotapes about various aspects of German culture would increase her students' vocabulary acquisition. So, she taught her German course for sixteen weeks with the curriculum divided into four four-week modules. She gave the students a vocabulary test at the end of every second week. In the third week of each module, she showed a German film about art, theatre, music, sports, etc. At the end of the semester, she compared the four average scores from the weeks with films and the four average scores from the weeks without films.

2. What is/are the research questions for each of the situations described above? Can you state the hypothesis (or hypotheses) for each situation?

3. Not all the designs we have studied are represented in the paragraphs above. Which ones are not represented here? Choose one of those missing designs and write a brief scenario that provides sufficient detail for your colleagues or classmates to be able to identify which specific design you are describing. Exchange your paper with a classmate or colleague.

4. Turn back to Chapter 3 and reread the summary of Sato's (1982) investigation of the turn-taking behaviors of the Asian and non-Asian students in two ESL classes. How might the different data collection procedures used in those two classes lead to the instrumentation threat in her study?

5. Look back at the vignettes of the sample studies in Chapters 2 and 3. Identify the threats to validity in those studies, using the vocabulary introduced here.

6. The increasing strengths of the research designs enable researchers to cope with the threats to validity, but such threats are often present. For each design discussed above, identify the specific threat(s) that may influence your interpretation of the findings.

7. Read the following situation and decide how you could design a study to address your friend's request.

> You have a friend who has been teaching English in Japan for many years. Your friend noticed that those of her students who often sang English songs at karaoke clubs seemed to have better pronunciation, better listening skills, better speaking fluency, and better English vocabulary skills than those students who did not participate in karaoke singing.
>
> Your friend began to use karaoke singing regularly as an activity in her English conversation classes for adult students. This experience was so successful that she created a Web site, called "Karaoke Corner." The Web site provides music and lyrics so students can sing along with English songs in the privacy of their own homes. The Web site also offers follow-up activities with the English song lyrics—cloze passages, vocabulary quizzes, and reviews of grammar structures used in the songs. The Web site has been running for over three years, and your friend now has about four thousand clients (both adults and teenagers) who visit the site regularly and pay to sing along in English. Your friend also has two employees who request formal copyright permission to use the songs and who regularly update the Web site with new songs and activities.
>
> Now your friend wants to expand the market for "Karaoke Corner" by showing how successful its regular users are in improving their English skills. She wants you to collect some data that would encourage companies to pay for "Karaoke Corner" subscriptions for their employees. Since she knows you are learning about conducting research, she asks you to design a study that would provide evidence that would show potential corporate clients the effectiveness of the products and services offered by the "Karaoke Corner" Web site.

A. Pose the research question(s) you wish to ask. You could write a formal hypothesis if you wish.

B. Identify the independent variable in this context. How many levels of the independent variable will you use in your investigation? Why?

C. Determine what the dependent variable would be.

D. Do you want to incorporate a moderator variable? If so, what is it?

E. What are some possible confounding variables you should be aware of in carrying out this research?

F. What are some possible control variables you would like to impose?

G. Think about how you could operationally define all those variables.

H. Select a research design from among those that we have discussed.

I. Identify the strengths and weaknesses of the study as planned.

J. Identify the practical difficulties in carrying out this study as planned.

8. We noted at the beginning of this chapter that sometimes the jargon associated with the experimental method can be a bit confusing. This is partly the case because there are many synonyms. Look at the two columns of words below. Draw a line matching each item in the left column with its synonym in the right column.

Average	Experimental method
Bar graph	Practice effect
Normal distribution	Generalizability
Testing threat	Threats to validity
External validity	Histogram
Confounding variables	Mean
Scientific method	Bell (shaped) curve
Hawthorne effect	Reactive effects of experimental arrangements

SUGGESTED READINGS

For more information on research designs, see Mitchell and Jolley (1988), Shavelson (1981, 1996), and Tuckman (1999).

J. D. Brown (1988) provides a very good description of the normal distribution. He also provides a clear introduction to the descriptive statistics (1988; 2001).

CHAPTER

5

Surveys

You can't catch an elephant with a butterfly net. Then again, you can't catch a butterfly with an elephant net. (K. M. Bailey on questionnaire design to her research students)

INTRODUCTION AND OVERVIEW

This chapter is devoted to surveys and, more specifically, to questionnaires. Here we will define surveys and questionnaires and then expand on the concepts of populations and samples introduced earlier. Next, we will look at designing and piloting questionnaires, both in paper format and online. We will consider several quality control issues, including the wording of items, the translation and back-translation of questionnaire items, and ethical issues in questionnaire design. The chapter ends with a summary of a study in which EFL learners responded to an online survey, followed by a discussion of the payoffs and pitfalls of survey research utilizing questionnaires.

Surveys belong to a disparate assortment of data collection techniques under the rubric of *elicitation devices*. In this context, *to elicit* means to cause people to do or say something, so an elicitation device in second language research is a procedure for getting research subjects to do or say something in response to a stimulus.

Studies using elicitation are extremely common in language teaching research. In fact, all research techniques can be classified as either *elicitation*, or *nonelicitation*. In a survey of the research literature reported in 1991, Nunan found that around half of the studies analyzed used elicitation techniques. Such techniques have been common in second language acquisition research, as far back as the original morpheme order studies of the 1970s. Not surprisingly, elicitation techniques vary enormously in scope, aim, and purpose. They include the use of artifacts designed to stimulate language production, such as pictures, diagrams, and even standardized tests, as well as surveys, which collect data through questionnaires and interviews. (Interview procedures are sometimes classified under the rubric of survey research, but we will treat interview procedures in a separate chapter.)

In this chapter, we will look specifically at survey research using questionnaires—written data elicitation devices. Questionnaires have often been used in classroom research, but perhaps more in classroom-oriented studies than in classroom-based studies. Questionnaires administered to teachers, parents, and/or students can amplify and improve upon a classroom-based study.

For example, a very early and important published example of language classroom research was a study by Seliger (1977). He wanted to investigate an element of turn taking in the target language. He believed that some learners could be characterized as "high input generators"—that is, language learners who participated in conversations in ways that generated input from their *interlocutors* (the people they were talking with). He hypothesized that the high input generators would outscore "low input generators" on a test of language achievement. However, since he was studying a group of ESL learners in the United States, he realized that they had opportunities for English input outside of class as well. So, he included a questionnaire in his study called the "Language Contact Profile." It asked students about their use of English outside the classroom. When Seliger analyzed his results, he found that the high input generators outscored the low input generators on both the measure of English achievement and also on the Language Contact Profile. The data from this questionnaire provided an added dimension to the research in terms of understanding how interaction in the target language can improve students' learning.

Defining Survey Research

Surveys are widely used for collecting data in most areas of social inquiry, from politics to sociology, from education to linguistics. In general education, their use ranges from large-scale demographic studies of community attitudes and expectations to small-scale studies carried out by a single researcher (Cohen and Manion, 1985). The overall purpose of a survey is to obtain a snapshot of conditions, attitudes, and/or events of an entire population at a single point in time by collecting data from a sample drawn from that population.

Surveys have also been used frequently in applied linguistics to gather data on a range of issues (D. Johnson, 1992):

> Survey methods have been used by second language, bilingual education, and foreign language researchers to study a wide variety of issues that impinge on language learning. These include the changing demographic context, the institutional settings in which L2 professionals function, the policies that affect learning and teaching, program administration, teacher preparation, attitudes of teachers and professors toward language varieties, classroom practices, target language norms, and student language use and growth. (p. 105)

According to Dörnyei (2003), surveys are especially well suited for asking factual questions, behavior questions, and attitudinal questions. The overriding consideration, however, is matching the data collection procedure to the research question you are posing or the hypothesis you are testing.

Questionnaires and Experimental Research

Questionnaires are defined as "any written instruments that present respondents with a series of questions or statements to which they are to react, either by writing out their answers or selecting from among existing answers" (J. D. Brown, 2001, p. 6). (*Respondents* are the people who complete and return the questionnaires to the researchers.) Many kinds of questionnaires elicit numeric responses, so surveys are sometimes grouped in quantitative approaches to research. They are part of the psychometric tradition in that they try to measure psychological constructs.

However, the term *survey research* is not identical to *experimental research* even though questionnaires are often used as dependent variables in experiments. For instance, researchers sometimes try to determine whether a particular experimental treatment causes a change of attitude among the research subjects, so an attitude questionnaire may be administered at the beginning and the end of the experiment, and the two sets of responses compared. (This was what the researcher did in the sample study at the end of Chapter 4 to ascertain the students' attitudes before and after their first Russian course.)

REFLECTION

Survey research is distinguished from experimental research in several respects. Think of at least one way that a survey might differ from an experiment.

The main difference between conducting an experiment and conducting a survey is that, while the experimental researcher intervenes and manipulates variables to test relationships, the survey researcher typically does not.

> The researcher doesn't "do" anything to the objects or subjects of research, except observe them or ask them to provide data. The research consists of collecting data on things or people as they are, without trying to alter anything. A survey researcher might want to know about teachers' honest attitudes towards their school principals, unaltered by the act of asking. The more intrusive a survey, the lower the chances that it will accurately reflect real conditions. (Jaeger, 1988, p. 307)

So, the broad goal of survey research is to elicit subjects' ideas, attitudes, opinions, and so on without influencing those data in any way. The challenge for survey researchers is to design questionnaires that capture the information they wish to elicit without unduly shaping that information.

TABLE 5.1	Steps in carrying out a survey
Step	**Key Question**
1. Define objectives	What do we want to find out?
2. Identify target population	Who do we want to know about?
3. Carry out a literature review	What have others said/discovered about the issue?
4. Determine sample	How many subjects should we survey and how will we identify them?
5. Identify survey instruments	Will the data be collected through questionnaires, interviews, or both?
6. Design survey procedures	How will the data collection actually be carried out?
7. Identify analytical procedures	How will the data be assembled and analyzed?
8. Determine reporting procedure	How will the results be presented?

Whether you use a questionnaire as part of an experiment, in naturalistic inquiry, or in action research, there are eight key steps that need to be carried out in conducting a survey. These are set out in **Table 5.1**.

In the remainder of this chapter, we will focus on questionnaire research. (Readers should see J. D. Brown [2001] and Dörnyei [2003] for more detailed discussions of these steps.) We begin with further information about populations and samples.

POPULATIONS AND SAMPLES

One of the most important questions a survey researcher must confront is the following: What is the population I wish to learn about by way of the survey? Political surveys, particularly those carried out in the run up to an election, generally purport to reflect the entire population of eligible voters (although they also report a margin of error—usually between 2 and 5%). It would not, of course, be practical to obtain data from the entire population. In fact, that's what the election itself is meant to do. A major task for the survey researcher, therefore, is to select a representative sample from the population as a whole. The idea that the sample represents the population is important if the predictions based on the opinion poll are to be accurate.

REFLECTION

If you wished to study voting intentions, one way to collect data for a large-scale survey, which claims to represent the entire population of a voting district, would simply be to go into the street and question people at random. Why do you think this may not be a sound way of collecting the data?

TABLE 5.2 Strategies for survey sampling (adapted from Cohen and Manion, 1985)

Strategy	Procedure
1. Simple random samples	Select subjects at random from a list of the population.
2. Systematic sampling	Select subjects in a systematic rather than random fashion (e.g., select every twentieth person).
3. Stratified sampling	Subdivide population into subgroups (e.g., male/female) and randomly sample from subgroups.
4. Cluster sampling	Restrict one's selection to a particular subgroup from within the population (e.g., randomly selecting a school from within a particular school district rather than the entire state or country).
5. Convenience sampling	Choose the nearest individuals and continue the process until the requisite number has been obtained.
6. Purposive sampling	Subjects are handpicked by the researcher on the basis of his/her own estimate of their typicality.

Sampling Strategies

In large-scale surveys, the major problem with *simple random sampling* is that it may mask differences between underlying subgroups within the population. For example, men and women often have different voting patterns and preferences in elections. Therefore, it is important to be sure that men and women are represented in the sample in proportion to the ratio of men and women in the voting population. **Table 5.2** shows some of the different sampling strategies available to the researcher.

REFLECTION

A researcher at a college wished to gather students' opinions about a proposed change from the fifteen-week semester system to the ten-week quarter system. To gather data, she stood outside the library and asked every fifth student who left the building whether they were for or against the proposed change.

1. What kind of sampling strategy was she using? (See Table 5.2.)
2. What kind of data was she gathering—nominal, ordinal or interval?
3. What threat(s) to validity may be present in using this procedure? (Remember the gunners discussed in Chapter 4.)

Sample Size

Sample size is an ongoing issue in any research in which the investigator wants to make inferences from samples to populations. Common sense suggests that the larger the sample size, the more accurate the inferences that can be made about the population. In addition, for reasons explained in Chapter 4, where we discussed the normal distribution, when researchers work with quantitative data analyses, larger numbers are desirable because of the properties of the bell-shaped curve. Most statistical procedures based on the normal distribution work better with larger data sets. That is why researchers working in the experimental method and/or with questionnaire data often conduct "large N studies."

However, accurate estimates can be obtained from relatively small numbers of subjects. Fowler, who produced one of the standard textbooks on survey design, dismisses the common misperception that the adequacy of a sample depends on the fraction of the population included in that sample, arguing that "a sample of 150 people will describe a population of 15,000 or 15 million with virtually the same degree of accuracy assuming all other aspects of the sample design and sampling procedure were the same" (Fowler, 1988, p. 41).

A moment's thought will show why this is so. You will recall from Chapter 4 that the further a score or measurement is from the overall population mean, the less likely it is that that particular score or measurement would have been obtained by chance. (Really high scores are usually due to ability or proficiency, and really low scores are usually due to a lack thereof.) If we were to tell you that Subject A scored 72 on a test, and then asked you to predict the mean for the whole class of twenty students, this would clearly be impossible. The best you could do would be to say, "Around 72." However, if we said that Subjects B and C scored 69, and 73, you could then begin to make predictions. It is unlikely, for example, that the mean would be 36.

A general rule of thumb for survey research is to get as many people as possible to complete the questionnaire if you are working with quantitative data that you plan to analyze quantitatively. Most of the inferential statistics work better with more than thirty subjects in the sample, and their results become more trustworthy with much larger numbers. Also, if you are working with qualitative data, you will be able to see patterns more clearly if you have a larger data set.

On the other hand, if you are a teacher conducting research with your own class and you have twenty students, surveying them is just fine, depending on your research question(s). In future sections we will read about an action research project in which a teacher gathered some very interesting data by using a questionnaire with a class of only five learners.

REFLECTION

Do you see a role for a questionnaire in any of the research topics that interest you?

QUESTIONNAIRE DESIGN

In Table 5.2, we noted that the first step in survey research is deciding what we want to find out in the process of administering our questionnaire and analyzing the results. Doing so hinges on posing clear and appropriate research questions and operationally defining all constructs and key terms.

The idea of operationalizing constructs (discussed in Chapter 2) is extremely important in any discussion of questionnaire design. This is because the questionnaire embodies the attitudes, beliefs, and practices that you wish to document by administering it to your respondents. The questionnaire becomes your main research instrument. In effect, it operationalizes the constructs you wish to measure.

Getting questionnaires 'right' can be notoriously difficult, and constructing an instrument that will actually give you the data you need for your research requires considerable skill. In this section, we will consider some of the fundamentals of questionnaire design, looking first at question types and question wording, then at organizing questionnaires. (In later chapters, we will consider ways of quantifying qualitative data.)

Closed Items on Questionnaires

Questionnaire items can be either closed or open-ended. A closed item is one in which the range of possible responses is determined by the researcher and the respondents select from or evaluate the options provided. For example: "Foreign languages should be compulsory in secondary school. Agree/neutral/disagree." An open-ended item is one in which the subject can decide what to say and how to say it. For example: "What do you think about the proposal that foreign language should be compulsory in secondary school?" Questionnaires can use only closed questions, only open-ended questions, or a mixture of closed and open-ended questions. One frequently used format is to have closed items followed by a space for open-ended comments.

For example, Springer and Bailey (2006) conducted research about teachers' experience with and attitudes regarding nineteen reflective teaching practices (e.g., discussing teaching with trusted colleagues, keeping a teaching journal, observing colleagues, being observed, and so on). They constructed and distributed their questionnaire using SurveyMonkey®—an Internet-based program that allowed them to build the items, collect the data, and do preliminary analyses electronically. Each reflective teaching practice was addressed in two closed items—one asking about their respondents' experience with the practice and one asking them about how appealing the practice is. The statements on the closed items were rated on a nine-point scale. After each pair of items, a space was provided for optional open-ended comments. **Figure 5.1** below shows an example of the questionnaire layout. The two paired items for each reflective practice address teachers' experience and attitudes. The paired sequential closed items are followed by a space for optional open-ended comments.

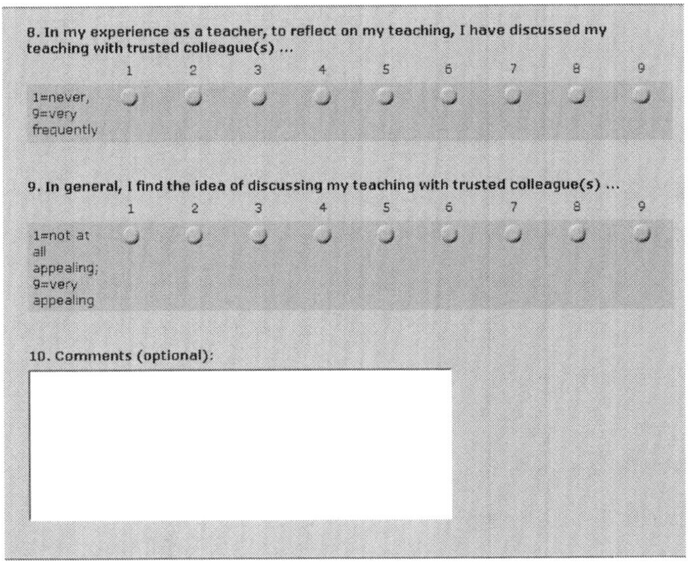

FIGURE 5.1 Sample items using a computer-delivered Likert scale

REFLECTION

Make a list of the pros and cons of using closed and open-ended questions. Compare your list with that of a classmate or colleague.

There are several advantages of using closed items. These include practicality in terms of the ease and speed with which people can respond to the questionnaire. Also, providing the options for respondents to select or evaluate provides the great benefit of comparability because it constrains the variation you can get in the responses. This factor enhances the data analysis process greatly. All in all, the benefits of questionnaires have made them very important tools in survey research in psychology, sociology, sociolinguistics, general applied linguistics research, and, to some extent, language classroom research.

A wide range of closed item formats can be used. Some of the question types used in closed question surveys are presented in **Table 5.3.**

It is important to remember that the question format you choose will constrain the type of data that you get. For example, in the grid format shown in Table 5.3, a program director completing this grid would indicate in each cell the number of people in that age range (e.g., there may be twelve students in Level 1 who are between the ages of eighteen and twenty-four). But we cannot tell, from that datum alone, how many of those twelve students are eighteen years old, how many are nineteen years old, and so on. Likewise, this particular

TABLE 5.3 Closed question types in survey questionnaires (adapted from Youngman [1986], as cited in Bell [1987])

Question Type	Example
1. List	Indicate your qualifications by circling any of the following that apply to you: Certificate, Diploma, B.A., M.A., Ph.D.
2. Category	Indicate the grade you achieved on the Use of English Examination A, B, C, D, E, F
3. Ranking	Rank the following from 1 to 4 in order of preference. "In class, I like to learn best by studying . . ." ____ with the whole class. ____ in small groups. ____ in pairs. ____ by myself.
4. Scale	Circle one of the following phrases to indicate your attitude to the following statement: "In class, I like to learn by having the teacher explain everything to me." Strongly Agree, Agree, Disagree, Strongly Disagree
5. Quantity/frequency	Circle one of the following answers. How many hours did you spend practicing English outside of class last week? 1, 2, 3, 4, 5, 6, 7, 8, 9, 10 or more
6. Grid	How many students of the following age groups are enrolled in the four levels of the Intensive English Program?

Level/ Number	18–24 years old	25–30 years old	31–40 years old	41–50 years old
Level 1				
Level 2				
Level 3				
Level 4				

grid does not permit the possibility that there are any students younger than eighteen or older than fifty enrolled in the program.

For these reasons, you should think carefully about your research question in designing your questionnaire. The research question determines the analysis you wish to do with your data, and that will influence the decisions you make about the format of the questions. Remember the elephant and the butterfly: you can hunt for either one, but you have to have the proper net to capture your quarry.

Look at the item types in Table 5.3. Decide what sort of data—nominal, ordinal, or interval—each question type will elicit from respondents.

There are two very important closed-item formats that have been used in applied linguistics research. One is called the *semantic differential scale* and the other is called a *Likert scale* (pronounced like "LICK-ert"). Both have important potential applications in second language classroom research.

Likert scales are named after their originator, a psychologist named Rensis Likert (1932), who developed the technique for measuring people's attitudes about various social concerns (Busch, 1993). Likert scales are often used in applied linguistics research (including language classroom research) "to investigate how respondents feel about a series of statements" J. D. Brown, 2001, p. 40). In this format, "the respondents' attitudes are registered by having them circle or check numbered categories (for instance, *1, 2, 3, 4*, or *5*), which have descriptors above them" (ibid.).

Let us take as an example an issue that was introduced earlier in this chapter. A Likert scale could be used to investigate people's attitudes about the desirability of foreign languages being required subjects in secondary school. To gather information about this issue, a researcher could ask the following question:

Should foreign languages be compulsory in secondary school?
___ Yes   ___ No

Or, if more precise information were needed about the respondents' attitudes, the researcher could word the item as follows:

Foreign languages should be compulsory in secondary school.
___ Agree   ___ Neutral   ___ Disagree

You may also see this format, in which *SA* represents "strongly agree," *A* stands for "agree," and *N* represents "neutral." *D* and *SD* represent "disagree" and "strongly disagree," respectively. Respondents circle their choice:

Foreign languages should be
compulsory in secondary school.   SA   A   N   D   SD

The benefit of the Likert scale item is that it allows researchers to gather more fine-grained information about attitudes in the form of numerical data. In a Likert scale, the issue would be presented like this and respondents would circle a number:

	Strongly Agree . . . . Strongly Disagree				
Foreign languages should be compulsory in secondary school.	1	2	3	4	5

REFLECTION

What types of data—nominal, ordinal, or interval—are elicited by these four response formats about the issue of whether or not foreign languages should be compulsory in secondary school?

1. Should foreign languages be compulsory in secondary school?   Yes   No

2. Foreign languages should be compulsory in secondary school.   Agree   Neutral   Disagree.

3. Foreign languages should be compulsory in secondary school.   SA   A   N   D   SD

Strongly Agree . . . . Strongly Disagree

4. Foreign languages should be compulsory in secondary school.   1   2   3   4

The *semantic differential* format is a variation on the Likert scale format in which pairs of opposite adjectives are place at the two ends of a continuum. An item using a semantic differential scale might look something like this:

Intelligent __ : __ : __ : __ : __ Unintelligent	
Impolite __ : __ : __ : __ : __ Polite	
Educated __ : __ : __ : __ : __ Uneducated	

Respondents see or hear some sort of stimulus material and react to it by placing an *X* or a check mark between these polar opposites at a point that indicates their opinion of the stimulus material. This format has been used frequently in sociolinguistic research to assess people's reactions to accented speech using recorded speech samples as the stimulus material. Students' writing samples can also be used as the stimulus material.

Teachers can use this format in conducting needs assessments with their students or getting feedback on lessons. Dörnyei (2003, p. 41) gives the following example:

Listening comprehension tasks are

       Difficult __:__:__:__:__:__:__ Easy

       Useless __:__:__:__:__:__:__ Useful

The semantic differently concept was used by Thorpe (2004) in an action research project on the use of authentic news broadcasts. He wanted feedback from the Korean learners of English in his class about the various kinds of news broadcasts and teaching activities he used. Here are just two examples from a simple questionnaire he gave the students at the end of each lesson:

Please draw a single straight line (|) on the horizontal continuum (—) to indicate your opinion.

The news story was

  Very Easy _____ Very Difficult

I found the teaching activity

  Not At All Helpful _____ Very Helpful

Thorpe made sure that all the lines were of equal length, both on all the items for the questionnaire after a particular lesson and on the questionnaires he gave the students after all the lessons. This strategy allowed him to measure the distance where the students' marks were placed on each line. He was therefore able to compare students' opinions, both to one another and over time. (We will return to Thorpe's data in Chapter 8 when we study action research.)

Perhaps you noticed that in both examples above, sometimes the more positive adjective is on the left and sometimes it is on the right. This placement is intentional. Researchers use it to avoid what is called a *response set*— a habitual or patterned way of responding to items that is independent of the items (Mitchell and Jolley, 1988). For instance, a respondent may rush through a questionnaire and simply mark all the positive options without really thinking about their content. Switching the positive and negative adjectives breaks up this tendency to some extent.

You will recall from Chapter 3 that we distinguished among nominal, ordinal, and interval data. The differences among these types of data are important, partly because the type of data you work with determines the types of analyses you may use.

There is a great deal of discussion about whether Likert scale items provide us with interval data or ordinal data. Some researchers feel that Likert scale items with numbers, as shown above, "are assumed to yield interval data" (Mitchell and Jolley, 1988, p. 403). Tuckman (1999) says,

> A Likert scale lays out five points separated by intervals assumed to be equal distances. It is formally termed an equal-appearing interval scale. . . . Because analyses of data from Likert scales are usually based on summated scores over multiple items, the equal-interval assumption is a workable one. (p. 216)

Tuckman makes this point because of the value and nature of true interval scales. We said in Chapter 2 that interval scales are those on which the unit of measure is a constant interval.

However, there is another important feature of true interval scales and that is that their properties are known and widely used. For instance, an inch is an inch whether you are using a ruler in Australia, Canada, Egypt, Kenya, or Brazil. A kilometer is the same distance whether you are riding a bike in France, Thailand, or China. The same cannot be said of Likert scales since we do not know if "agree" means the same thing to each person using the scale. If two students "strongly disagree" with a statement on a Likert scale, does that mean that they are equal in the vehemence with which they disagree? We cannot know because there is no standardized measure of agreement as there is with inches and kilometers. (See Busch [1993] and Turner [1993] for further discussion of this position.)

You may have noticed that in the example screen shot from Springer and Bailey (2006) above, the Likert scale was nine points long. The researchers used a nine-point scale in order to provide respondents with more choices since the computer-delivered questionnaire would not allow them to mark pluses or minuses, or to circle two numbers. In addition, "from a statistical viewpoint, longer scale lengths of seven or more categories are more desirable because of the grain in score variability" (Busch, 1993, p. 735). Hatch and Lazarton (1991) state that Likert scales become interval-like when the length of the scale is increased.

Whether Likert scale data should be treated as interval data or ordinal data hinges on many factors. If you are a graduate student trying to complete a research project or meet graduation requirements, you should consult your professor or research advisor. In any case, you need to show that you understand the issue of interval versus ordinal data when you choose the statistical procedures to use in your data analysis. (See Chapter 13.)

Open-Ended Items on Questionnaires

Open-ended questions are "items where the actual question is not followed by response options for the respondent to choose from but rather by some blank space (e.g., dotted lines) for the respondent to fill" (Dörnyei, 2003, p. 47). As

Mackey and Gass (2005) note, there is a trade-off between the control and convenience of closed items and the depth of response in open-ended items:

> Closed-item questions typically involve a greater uniformity of measurement and therefore greater reliability. They also lead to answers that can be easily quantified and analyzed. Open-ended items, on the other hand, allow respondents to express their own thoughts and ideas in their own manner, and thus may result in more unexpected and insightful data. (p. 93)

While responses to closed questions are easier to collate and analyze, researchers often obtain more useful information from open-ended questions.

It is also likely that responses to open-ended questions will more accurately reflect what the respondent wants to say. It is not uncommon on paper-delivered questionnaires to find that respondents have circled both 3 and 4 on a five-point scale, or that they have written in "3 +" instead of simply circling 3 or 4. (Electronically delivered questionnaires avoid this problem by forcing the respondent to indicate click on particular numeral.) Open-ended items also allow respondents to express mixed feelings and shades of meaning.

J. D. Brown (2001) says that open-ended items come in two basic formats: fill-in questions and short-answer questions. Fill-in questions require very specific information, such as the following questions intended for the adult children of immigrant parents in England:

Please provide the following background information:

Country where you were born: _____

Language(s) spoken in your home by your family: _____

Your age upon arrival in England: _____

Short-answer questions are more open-ended and "usually require a few words or phrases" (ibid., p. 39). Some examples are printed in the box below:

What are your earliest memories of living in England? _____

_____.

What are your earliest memories of speaking English in England? _____

_____.

Sometimes open-ended questions are posed in a *yes/no* format, but if you use this approach, it is important to pose an explicit follow-up question as well:

Did you ever translate documents or interpret English for your parents?
___ Yes ___ No

If you checked "Yes," please give an example: _____

_____.

Do you feel that English is easy to learn? Why or why not? _____

_____.

Notice that when you use these item formats, the space you provide indicates to the respondents how long a response you are hoping to receive.

Dörnyei adds a third type of open-ended question—sentence completion. In this format, the questionnaire designer provides the opening clause of a sentence and then provides space for the respondent to complete the idea. In this format, the item is usually worded from the perspective of the respondent (i.e., it uses *I, my,* and *mine* instead of *you, your,* and *yours*).

Please complete the following sentences:

As a child, one thing I **liked** about attending school in England was __

_____.

As a child, one thing I **disliked** about attending school in England was

_____.

A particular kind of completion item that has been used in second language acquisition research is called a *discourse completion task*. In a discourse completion task, part of a conversation is provided in written form and the respondents are asked to write what they would say if they were actually in this conversation. This format is especially useful if you wish to "investigate speech acts such as apologies, invitations, refusals, and so forth" (Mackey and Gass, 2005, p. 89). Discourse completion tasks frequently specify potentially important factors, such as the age and status of the interlocutors. Here is an example that involves making a request to a person of higher status:

You are a student in a linguistics course. Your backpack is stolen and your linguistics textbook was in it. You cannot afford to buy a new copy, but you need a copy of the book over the weekend to prepare for the midterm exam, which will be given on Monday. You decide to ask your professor if you may borrow her copy. You go to her office and say to her,

_____

_____

_____

For addressing some research questions, it can be useful to constrain the response by providing more of the conversation.

You ask your linguistics professor if you can borrow her copy of the textbook. Yours has been stolen and the library copy is checked out. You want to use her textbook over the weekend because the linguistics midterm exam is scheduled for Monday.

_____

_____

The professor says, "Very well, but I'll need it back Monday morning at nine o'clock. Oh, and please don't mark in it."

Using discourse completion tasks can save substantial time compared to waiting for people to use particular speech acts, such as the request above, in natural speech and hoping that you will be around to record the data when such requests do occur. Sometimes discourse completion tasks are posed in a multiple-choice format, but this makes them closed items that show something about the learners' ability to recognize appropriate speech acts but that do not show the learners' actual productive abilities. For example:

You ask your linguistics professor if you can borrow her copy of the textbook. Yours has been stolen and the library copy is checked out. You want to use her textbook over the weekend because the linguistics midterm exam is scheduled for Monday. You go to the professors office and say,

A. "Hey, can I borrow your text book?"
B. "Excuse me, Professor, may I borrow your textbook over the weekend?"
C. "My textbook was stolen. Can I use yours over the weekend?"
D. "Excuse me, Professor, but unfortunately my textbook was stolen and the library copy has been checked out. May I please borrow your copy?"

We are now back to the trade-off between closed items and open-ended items on questionnaires. Whether you use one or the other or a combination of the two, open-ended questions should be easy to answer. Alreck and Settle (1985) advise that open-ended items should be direct, brief, and clear. They provide the following questions for evaluating the effectiveness of survey questions:

1. Does the question focus directly on the issue or topic to be measured? If not, rewrite the item to deal with the issue as directly as possible.

2. Is the question stated as briefly as it can be? If the item is more than a few words, it may be too long and should be restated more briefly.

3. Is the question expressed as clearly and simply as it can be? If the meaning will not be clear to virtually every respondent, the item should be reformed. (p. 101)

Bailey (1992) conducted research with a very short, simple questionnaire consisting of only three open-ended items. She wanted to investigate the issue of innovation at the level of the individual teacher rather than at the level of departmental or programmatic innovations, or large-scale systemic change. She asked teachers to respond in writing to the following prompt:

Think of a positive change you have made in your own teaching. It could be a change in content, in philosophy, or procedure. The important thing is that it be a change for the better which you have made and which has remained with you. I am interested in learning about changes that last in your work as a language teacher—that is, I am trying to understand how teachers bring about their own professional development. (p. 263)

Bailey then asked the respondents to describe what they changed, to explain why they had made the change, and how they had made it. As it turned out, the open-ended questions about what and why teachers had changed were relatively straightforward to analyze. But the *how* question had not been specific enough. Bailey had meant to gather information about the actual processes teachers had used to bring about the changes they desired. Unfortunately, in addition to (or in some cases, instead of) that information, she got comments about the difficulty and speed of the process. For instance, in response to the *how* question, teachers wrote things about the process being very slow, or being very demanding of their time and energy, without really explaining what steps enabled them to carry out the change.

This problem did not arise in the piloting of the questionnaire. It was only in the process of struggling to analyze the data that Bailey realized she should have been more specific in posing the question. The sort of responses she anticipated receiving would have been more about actual strategies and processes. For instance, one teacher talked about the innovation of providing authentic materials (what she changed) because the required textbook (which had been written by a senior member of the department) was dry, boring, and out-of-date. In response to the question of how she brought about the use of authentic materials, the teacher wrote that she and her students agreed that the authentic materials were more helpful and more interesting, so they agreed to keep secret from the administration the fact that they were not using the required text. This detailed answer to the *how* question contrasted sharply with comments such as "very slowly" or "with great difficulty."

It can often be helpful to provide respondents with examples as guidance. If you do this, you must be careful to provide examples that will counteract (or at least not trigger) subject expectancy.

The real power of open-ended items is explained by Dörnyei (2003), who says that in spite of questionnaires' limitations,

> open-ended items still have merits. Although we cannot expect any soul-searching self-disclosure from the responses, by permitting greater freedom of expression, open-format items can provide a far greater "richness" than fully quantitative data. The open responses can offer graphic examples, illustrative quotes, and can also lead us to identify issues not previously anticipated. (p. 47)

An additional issue is that researchers sometimes "need open-ended items for the simple reason that we do not know the range of possible answers and therefore cannot provide pre-prepared response categories" (ibid.).

Organizing Your Questionnaire

Once you have settled on the questions that you want to ask, and you have decided how you want to frame them, the next step is to organize the questionnaire. The ordering of the questions should make sense to the respondents, and there should be an ordered progression from one question to the next. **Table 5.4** provides guidelines for organizing a questionnaire.

QUALITY CONTROL ISSUES IN QUESTIONNAIRE RESEARCH

As we have seen in previous chapters, quality control is a major concern no matter what approach to research we espouse. In this section we will review some important advice about crafting questionnaire items. (We use the word *crafting* intentionally because there is a fair amount of skill involved and practice is needed to produce questionnaire items that actually measure what you want them to measure.) We then discuss the importance of piloting questionnaires and of using translation as needed. Finally, we will consider some of the ethical issues associated with the collection and analysis of questionnaire data.

TABLE 5.4	Steps in organizing a questionnaire (adapted from Alreck and Settle, 1985, p. 160)
Step 1	Picture the questionnaire in three major parts: initiation, body, and conclusion.
Step 2	Begin with the most general questions and avoid those that might be threatening or difficult to answer.
Step 3	Remember the initial portion sets the stage and influences the respondents' expectations about what is to come.
Step 4	Be sure the body of the questionnaire flows smoothly from one issue to the next.
Step 5	List items in the body in a sequence that is logical and meaningful to respondents.
Step 6	Save the most sensitive issues and threatening questions for the concluding portion when rapport is greatest.
Step 7	List demographic or biographical questions last so that if some respondents decline, most of the data will still be usable.

Crafting Questionnaire Items

Getting the wording of the questions right is crucial in questionnaire design. One of the potential problems with any type of elicitation device is that the responses we get may well be artifacts of the elicitation devices themselves. To guard against this problem, the researcher should not ask 'leading' questions that reveal his or her own biases, such as, "Do you think that the concept of learner-centeredness is impractical and unrealistic?" Dörnyei (2003) gives examples of leading questions that start with phrases such as, "Isn't it reasonable to suppose that . . . ?" or "Don't you believe that . . ." (p. 54).

Furthermore, questions should not be complex and confusing, nor should they ask more than one question at a time. Here is an example that fails on both counts:

> Would you prefer face-to-face, online, or 'blended' instruction in intensive full-time or part-time mode with a single instructor or multiple instructors?

Such a question is likely to be highly confusing to respondents, and the answers are almost certain to be uninterpretable by the researcher.

ACTION

Look at the question quoted in the box above. How many constructs is it attempting to measure? How could you rewrite this question so that it is clearer?

This question should be rewritten as three separate items because it is trying to capture three different constructs: (1) the delivery mode, (2) the time devoted to study, and (3) the preferred number of teachers. Here is one possible rewording:

As a language learner, which do you prefer? Use an X to choose only one option for each line:

1. ___Face-to-face classes **OR** ___ Online classes **OR** ___ Blended classes

2. ___Intensive full-time study **OR** ___ Part-time study

3. ___Having a single teacher **OR** ___ Having more than one teacher

---

It is also important to use vocabulary that is familiar to the respondents. In the revision above, *teacher* has been substituted for *instructor* and the phrase *more than one* has been substituted for *multiple*. In addition, you should also make sure that the respondents understand key terms you are using. For instance, it might be important to indicate that *blended* in this context means a combination of face-to-face and online classes.

In research into language teaching and learning, another danger to avoid is culturally biased questions. Specialists on questionnaire research have pointed out that there is considerable intercultural variation concerning the type of information that can legitimately be sought by a stranger. (When Kathi Bailey first started teaching EFL in Hong Kong, she was very surprised by some of the questions she was asked by her students. After she explained the syllabus on the first day of class, she invited questions. In both of her speaking/listening classes, students asked her how much money she made as a teacher and what kind of man she liked.)

Major differences may exist between the culture of the researcher and that of the respondents, and these differences may affect the responses given. If you are planning to survey people from cultures other than your own, it is important to check with a native of that culture to make sure the items on your survey are appropriately worded and not offensive to the respondents.

REFLECTION

Can you think of any examples of cultural bias in questionnaire design in studies you have read or in questionnaires you have seen?

When you are constructing a questionnaire, it is important to take factors such as the following into consideration: the willingness of the respondents to make critical statements or to criticize, for example, their teacher or teaching institution; and the willingness of the respondents to discuss certain personal topics, such as age, salary, or opinions on political and social issues. Another concern is the extent to which shared values can be assumed, such as the concept of freedom of the press or free access to the Internet. There may also be differences in attitudes that can influence how people respond to questionnaire items. For example, the commonly held belief among many Western educators that classroom learning should be an enjoyable experience is not necessarily a universally held view. (In many contexts, *fun* and *enjoyment* are associated with entertainment, not education.)

Yet another trap to avoid is asking too many questions. Our own personal rule of thumb is to restrict the questionnaire to between thirty and thirty-five questions although this will depend on the types of questions being asked, that is, whether they are closed or open-ended. If you are using a paper questionnaire, you may get a better rate of return if you limit its length to the front and back of one sheet of paper. (If you do use the back of the page, it is important to add a note at the bottom of page 1 asking the respondents to turn the page over and continue on the back.)

It is also important to determine in advance how the data to be gathered will be analyzed. A trap for the inexperienced researcher is to collect the data and then realize that the question was asked in a way in which yielded data that cannot be analyzed to answer the question. Because of these and other pitfalls, it is imperative that questionnaires be piloted before the main study is carried out.

Sometimes researchers want to ask parallel questions of two populations involved in the same activity. In the context of second language classroom research, this pairing is most often teachers and students. As an example, Radecki (2002) conducted a study in the United Arab Emirates to "identify and compare student and teacher preferences in a laptop environment" (p. 2). The study used interviews and parallel questionnaires to "determine (1) student and teacher preferences in the areas of materials, grouping and activities in high-tech environment; (2) how these preferences differ for a high-tech and a low-tech environment; and (3) how teacher and student preferences differ" (ibid.).

To address these issues, parallel questionnaires were devised for the students and teachers in the study. The questions were reworded to elicit the perspectives of the two groups of respondents. For example, Question 21 on the *student* questionnaire said

Complete this sentence: "In classes with laptops, I usually like to _____."

a. listen to the teacher and take notes

b. work on exercises or homework

c. discuss issues in groups or with the whole class

d. work on a research paper or a project

e. do many different things, like listen to lectures, do exercises, have discussions, and do projects

Question # 21 on the *teacher* questionnaire read:

> Complete this sentence: "In classes with laptops, I usually like to _____."
> a. lecture while the students take notes
> b. have students work on exercises or homework
> c. discuss issues in groups or with the whole class
> d. have students work on a research paper or a project
> e. do many different things, like lecture, do exercises, have discussions, and do projects

Finally, as we have already indicated, constructing a reliable questionnaire that will tell you what you want to know is challenging and time-consuming. Before beginning the process, it is important to be clear about the objectives of the study, and each item should be referenced against one or more of the research objectives. There is no point in including items that don't elicit data addressing your research question(s). Likewise, you must make sure that there are no 'holes' in the questionnaire that lead to gaps in the data. So, as a final step before you pilot your questionnaire, cross-reference the items against the research questions and objectives of the study. Make sure the draft instrument satisfies the purposes of the research you have planned.

Piloting Your Questionnaire

The concept of *piloting* a questionnaire (or any other data collection procedure) is like a dress rehearsal in the theater. By administering the questionnaire before the actual data collection, you can locate any unclear items, misnumbered items, confusing instructions, and so on.

Piloting a questionnaire is at least a two-stage process. First, after you have carefully organized and proofread your questionnaire, you should pre-pilot it with a few colleagues, especially those who are familiar with the population you wish to sample. You may need to revise the questionnaire somewhat based on their feedback. Then you pilot the questionnaire by administering it to a small number of people who are part of the population you wish to sample but who will not be in the sample themselves. You should be physically present when you pilot the questionnaire with this group so that you can ask them for feedback and answer their questions. Doing so will give you valuable input about possible problems in the questionnaire before you actually administer it to the sample from whom you wish to collect the data.

Translation Issues

If your questionnaire is going to be completed by people who are not native-speakers of the questionnaire language, you need to take special steps to make sure it does not become a reading test. For instance, if your questionnaire is going to be administered to ESL or EFL students enrolled in an English program, you should show the questionnaire to some teachers and/or administrators before you pilot it with a small group of the students. The teachers and administrators are likely to be familiar enough with the students' proficiency so they can tell you immediately if the language of the questionnaire is too difficult for the intended respondents. Keep in mind that syntactic, vocabulary, and discourse-level factors in the questionnaire can all introduce difficulties for the non-native reader. If your respondents do not fully understand the language of the items, then you cannot be sure that they have responded truthfully or completely to the questionnaire.

REFLECTION

Have you ever completed (or been asked to complete) a questionnaire in a language other than your first language? How did you respond? Was your proficiency sufficient to allow you to understand the questionnaire and express yourself well? Or did your proficiency constrain your understanding and/or your output in some way? If you have never been in this situation, try to imagine what it would be like.

One solution that is sometimes used if the respondents are language learners is to translate the questionnaire into the learners' native language. This solution can work well if you are sampling from one or a few first-language groups, but it becomes very unwieldy if many different first languages are represented in your sample.

If you do decide to translate your questionnaire, there is an important procedure for checking on the accuracy of the translation. This procedure is called *back translation* and it works like this: First, the original questionnaire is drafted, piloted, and revised. When the questionnaire is in its final form, it is translated into the respondents' first language by a competent bilingual translator. Next, another bilingual translator, working from the translation and without seeing the original version of the questionnaire or speaking to the first translator, puts the questionnaire back into the language it was originally written in. Then you and the two translators (if you are not one of them) compare the original version of the questionnaire with the back-translated version. If there are any differences in wording, the translators try to resolve the ambiguity in the translated version and help you clarify your intended meaning before you administer the questionnaire. At this point, you are ready to pilot your questionnaire.

Doing a back translation is time-consuming and can be costly. However, making sure you have a proper translation of your questionnaire from the outset is an important professional step in enhancing the reliable and valid measurement of the constructs you wish to capture. In the long run, back translation may save you time, money, and work because you will get interpretable results from more people if the questionnaire is fully understandable.

ACTION

Look at a questionnaire that was used in a published research article in our field. Was it translated into the learners' first language? If not, do you think the questionnaire was appropriate for the subjects' level of proficiency as described in the article? Cite specific examples to support your opinion.

Ethical Issues

Questionnaires elicit a kind of self-report data—that is, data in which the *respondents* are providing information about themselves. As a result, in order to get truthful data, it is important to promise your subjects confidentiality whenever you can. Usually confidentiality is accomplished by treating the questionnaire data anonymously. That is, the respondents are not identified in any way that will indicate who gave what opinions, ideas, information, etc., in responding to the questionnaire. Here is an example of how one group of researchers promised confidentiality to the students who completed their questionnaire:

> Your answers to any or all questions will be treated with the strictest confidence. Although we ask for your name on the cover page, we do so only because we must be able to associate your answers to this question-naire with those of other questionnaires which you will be asked to answer. It is important for you to know, however, that before the ques-tionnaires are examined, your questionnaire will be numbered, the same number will be put on the section containing your name, and then that section will be removed. By following a similar procedure with the other questionnaires, we will be able to match the questionnaires through matching numbers and avoid having to associate your name directly with the questionnaire. (Gliksman, Gardner, and Smythe, 1982, p. 637, as cited in Dörnyei, 2003, p. 23.)

The main points here are (1) you are likely to get better data if you promise your respondents anonymity, but (2) if you can't promise complete anonymity, you must guarantee confidentiality in the handling and reporting of the data.

ACTION

How could the comments about confidentiality quoted above (from Gliksman et al., 1982) be rewritten in a simpler fashion? Produce a version of these comments that would be appropriate for lower-intermediate English learners.

Based on his review of the literature on questionnaire design, Dörnyei (2003) has synthesized five ethical principles of data collection. We agree that these principles are valuable, so we have excerpted from them here.

> Principle 1. No harm should come to the respondents as a result of their participation in the research. . . .
>
> Principle 2. The respondent's right to privacy should always be respected and no undue pressure should be brought to bear. . . .
>
> Principle 3. Respondents should be provided with sufficient initial information about the survey to be able to give their informed consent concerning participation and the use of data. . . .
>
> Principle 4. In the case of children, permission to conduct the survey should always be sought from some person who has sufficient authority. . . .
>
> Principle 5. It is the researcher's moral and professional (and, in some contexts, legal) obligation to maintain the level of confidentiality that was promised to the respondents at the outset. (pp. 91–92)

We believe these principles offer sound advice, no matter what constructs you are trying to measure with your questionnaire. (For the full discussion of these principles, see Dörnyei, 2003, pp. 91–92.)

A SAMPLE STUDY

In this section, we present a sample study based on a survey. While surveys are widely used in applied linguistics, they are less common in classroom research. The study we have selected is classroom-oriented rather than classroom-based in that the data were collected outside of the classroom although the study was carried out in order to inform classroom action.

The survey was conducted by Nunan and Wong (2006) to investigate the learning styles and strategies of good and poor language learners. The study was carried out among undergraduate students who were native speakers of Cantonese. The subjects were 110 undergraduate students drawn from all the faculties at the University of Hong Kong.

The aim of the study was to explore whether there are identifiable differences between good and poor learners. Language proficiency was defined in terms of grades obtained on the Hong Kong Examinations Authority Use of English Examination—a high-stakes English language examination that all students have to take in order to graduate from high school. The aim of the research was to investigate whether there were any common practices among language learners who did well in English within the Hong Kong education system as compared with those who did not. Ultimately, the research was intended to provide practical guidelines for teachers to add a learning-how-to-learn dimension to their teaching.

Research Questions

Seven aspects of language learning and use were investigated in the study. The following research questions were posed about the two groups of learners (those who did well on the Use of English Examination and those who did not):

1. Are there any differences between the good and poor language learners in terms of their overall learning style?

2. Are there any differences between the good and poor language learners in terms of their individual learning strategy preferences?

3. Are there any differences between the good and poor language learners in terms of their target language practice outside of class?

4. Are there any differences between the good and poor language learners in terms of their areas of academic specialization?

5. Are there any differences between the good and poor language learners in terms of their perceptions of the importance of English?

6. Are there any differences between the good and poor language learners in terms of their perception of language ability?

7. Are there any differences between the good and poor language learners in terms of their enjoyment of learning English?

Research Procedures

The independent variable was whether the students could be characterized as being good or poor English learners. This construct was operationalized using the grades the students obtained on the Hong Kong Exams Authority Use of English Exam. There were two levels of the independent variable. 'Good' learners were defined as those who obtained an A on the examination. 'Poor' learners were those who obtained an E or F. The dependent variable consisted of the students' responses to a questionnaire on strategy preferences, learning practices, and attitudes.

A thirty-item questionnaire developed by Willing (1988; 1990) was adapted for the purposes of the research. This questionnaire was selected because it has been a robust instrument in numerous studies over the years (see, for example, Nunan, 1999, and Nunan and Wong, 2003). In addition to identifying individual learning strategy preferences, this questionnaire also enables the identification of four overall learning style orientations: (1) communicative, (2) concrete, (3) authority-oriented, and (4) analytical.

In addition to the thirty items in the original questionnaire, which asked learners to indicate their preferred ways of learning in and out of class, the questionnaire collected the following data:

Home faculty (academic specialization)

Grade on the Use of English Exam

Number of hours per week using English out of class

Importance of English to the student personally

The student's self-rating of English level

Extent to which the student enjoys learning English

The questionnaire was placed on a Web site, and a message was posted to the students' list inviting them to take part in the study.

There were two main advantages to distributing the survey electronically. In the first place, it saved an enormous amount of time and paper. More importantly, the Web program was set up to provide detailed analyses and collation of student responses. This procedure also eliminated costly and time-consuming effort by the researchers in having to tabulate paper-and-pencil responses and then having to enter those data for computer analysis.

REFLECTION

From a research perspective, do you see any disadvantages of distributing the survey electronically?

Subjects in the Sample

One of the major problems with the study from a research perspective has to do with sampling and defining the population for the research. As the researchers did not actively recruit subjects, there is no way of knowing whether those who chose to respond were representative of the student population as a whole.

In all, 674 students responded to the survey. Of these, 77 reported that they had received an A on the Use of English Exam. Another 33 reported that they had received an E or F on that exam. Thus, the two groups being compared in this criterion groups design consisted of the "good learners" (n = 77) and the "poor learners" (n = 33), in terms of their self-reported grades on the Use of English Exam. So, these 110 students made up the two comparison groups used in this ex post facto criterion groups design.

Results

The results relating to the seven research questions are summarized below.

1. Overall learning style
   The majority of the good learners (53%) were labeled as 'communicative' learners. The dominant orientation on the part of poor learners was 'authority-oriented' (36%).

2. Learning strategy preferences
   There was a marked difference in the learning strategy preference between the two groups. The five most popular preferences for each group were as follows:

   The good language learners
   "I like to learn by watching/listening to native speakers."
   "I like to learn English words by seeing them."
   "At home, I like to learn by watching TV in English."
   "In class, I like to learn by conversation."
   "I like to learn many new words."

   The poor language learners
   "I like the teacher to tell me all my mistakes."
   "I like to learn English words by seeing them."
   "I like the teacher to help me talk about my interests."
   "I like to have my own textbook."
   "I like to learn new English words by doing something."

3. Amount of time spent using English out of class
   Forty percent of good learners reported spending between one and five hours a week on English outside of class. Twenty-nine percent spent more than ten hours a week on English outside of class. In contrast, no poor learners spent more than ten hours a week outside of class, and 70 percent spent less than an hour a week on English outside of class.

4. Faculty
   The majority of the good learners were studying in the faculties of Arts, Law, and Medicine. Poor language learners tended to come from Engineering and Science.

5. Perceptions of the important of English
   On this question, responses were identical between good and poor learners. Ninety-seven percent of respondents in both groups rated English as either 'important' or 'very important.'

6. Self-rating of English level
   This was an interesting finding. Subjects self-rated themselves on a five-band proficiency rating scale, and the results were tabulated against their

reported Use of English Exam scores. Fifty-six percent of good learners rated themselves in the two top levels of the scale, while only six percent of poor learners rated themselves at this level.

7. Enjoyment of learning English

There was also a statistically significant difference between higher and lower proficiency students in terms of their enjoyment of learning English. Forty percent of higher proficiency students reported enjoying English a great deal, while only six percent of the lower proficiency did. In contrast (sadly and not surprisingly), twenty-four percent of lower proficiency students reported that they did not like learning English at all.

Implications

Nunan and Wong (2006) identified a number of implications, particularly for teachers working with poorer language learners. The main implication was to encourage such learners to see language as a tool for communicating rather than as a body of content to be memorized. Developing independent learning strategies and reducing students' dependence on the teacher were also recommended. Learners should also be encouraged to develop a greater range of strategies and to activate their language outside of the classroom. Following Christison (2003), the researchers suggested that teachers audit their own classroom practices to identify the strategies that they themselves favor.

Limitations of the Study

As these authors acknowledge, the greatest single weakness of the study is in identifying the population from which the sample is drawn. The researchers did not actively draw the sample from the undergraduate population but rather invited all students to take part. As is often the case in questionnaire research, it is by no means certain that those who volunteered are representative of the undergraduate population as a whole. This issue is an example of a very common *threat to external validity* in survey research. That is, if we don't know the characteristics of the population represented by the survey sample, we won't know how generalizable the results of the survey may be.

We can see by the numbers of subjects that more than twice as many good students completed the questionnaire as did poor students (seventy-seven versus thirty-three). Fortunately, there are inferential statistical procedures that work well with unequal numbers of subjects in the groups being compared. But, here again, we do not know the parameters of the population in this case. That is, of all the students who take the Use of English Examination (the population), we do not know what proportion of those students get As and what proportion get Es and Fs. It may be that students who did not do well on that exam were reluctant to complete the questionnaire.

PAYOFFS AND PITFALLS

Written surveys are powerful tools for collecting specific information, potentially from a large group of people. Carefully designed questionnaires allow researchers to gather data about people's attitudes, beliefs, and practices. They can consist of any combination of open-ended and closed questions. The structure provided by closed questions gives researchers a certain amount of control over the type of information they wish to elicit, while open-ended questions allow for more creativity and variety on the part of the informants.

One benefit of questionnaires is that collecting data with them is more efficient than with interviews, and they "elicit comparable information from a number of respondents" (Mackey and Gass, 2005, p. 94). In addition, surveys can be administered orally (face-to-face, by telephone) or in writing (via e-mail, through the mail, or in person; ibid.). Respondents can complete questionnaires individually or in groups, with or without the researcher present.

The payoffs of questionnaire research include the possibility of getting a wide range of data from many different people. Those data can be analyzed quantitatively to provide percentages, means, and standard deviations about different respondents' views. Open-ended comments can also be analyzed qualitatively to identify key themes and unique responses.

The pitfalls of survey research using questionnaires cannot be ignored, however. One was alluded to above: Typically, people who complete questionnaires are those who wish to complete surveys. Such volunteers may or may not be representative of the population they are supposed to represent. They may be more confident, for instance, or more proficient in the language of the questionnaire, or perhaps they simply have more time on their hands or care more about the topic than do those who choose not to respond.

Another potential problem is that of *self-report*. This term applies in any context where the research subjects are reporting on their own behavior or attitudes. It is a natural human tendency to represent oneself in a good light, so sometimes people leave out or downplay negative factors, and increase or emphasize positive factors. For example, in a questionnaire about how many hours per week students use the target language outside of class, if the respondents feel it is desirable to use the target language outside of class, they may inflate their estimates of the hours they spend in such activities. Another issue related to self-reporting is that people may simply be unaware of their practices and, thus, report them from an uninformed position.

A related problem is *subject expectancy* (introduced in Chapter 4). In this context, the term refers to the idea that survey respondents may think they know what the researcher is expecting and, therefore, respond accordingly. This problem arises from the natural urge to please. It can be particularly important if you are a teacher surveying your own students or a program administrator asking students in your program to respond to a questionnaire.

With open-ended items, another difficulty is that respondents may be uncomfortable expressing themselves in writing—and probably even more so if they are writing in a second or foreign language. As Mackey and Gass (2005) point out that people may "provide abbreviated, rather than elaborative, responses" (p. 96). These authors suggest providing sufficient response time, letting people respond in their first language, and letting people respond orally (especially if they have limited literacy skills) as ways to counteract this problem.

Having drafted, organized, constructed, edited, pre-piloted, piloted, and administered a questionnaire, the next task is to collate and interpret the responses. As we have indicated, the great advantage of closed questions is that they yield responses that can be readily collated, particularly if you are using a computerized statistical package. Or, if—as in the sample study for this chapter—the data are collected through the Internet, in which case much of the tabulation and analysis can be done electronically. Free-form responses from open-ended questions, which may result in more useful and insightful data, are much more difficult to analyze (although there are ways of doing this, as we will see in later chapters).

The sample study presented here (Nunan and Wong, 2006) as well as the study by Springer and Bailey (2006) mentioned above, both used electronically delivered questionnaires to gather data. There are great advantages to using computer-delivered questionnaires (e.g., speed of distribution and return, savings in terms of postage and photocopying, ease of tabulating results, etc.). But one disadvantage that cannot be overlooked is that of the digital divide. If you are administering a questionnaire via the Internet, you can only distribute it to and expect responses from people who have cheap and easy Internet access. For example, Springer and Bailey (2006) wished to get a wide international sample of respondents and asked a colleague in Vietnam to encourage her colleagues to complete the questionnaire. However, the colleague responded that they really could not do so because none of them had personal computers, the school's computer was reserved for administrative and instructional purposes, and using an Internet café to respond to a lengthy questionnaire would have been prohibitively expensive. This situation may change gradually in the future as Internet access becomes more widespread, but for now it is an issue to be aware of.

One of the limitations inherent in questionnaire research is "the relatively short and superficial engagement of the respondents" (Dörnyei, 2003, p. 47). Because questionnaires typically provide a 'snapshot' they "cannot aim at more than obtaining a superficial, 'thin' description" (ibid.) of the issue under investigation. However, there are situations when getting a good clear snapshot by eliciting data from a number of people in a uniform format can be a very useful accomplishment.

CONCLUSIONS

In this chapter, we have looked at survey research. The bulk of the chapter is devoted to the issue of questionnaire design and issues of quality control. While there are limitations to questionnaires, they can be very useful in language classroom research, whether we are working in the psychometric tradition, doing naturalistic inquiry, or conducting naturalistic research.

QUESTIONS AND TASKS

1. Brainstorm a list of research question relating to classroom-based or classroom-oriented research that could be investigated through some type of questionnaire.

2. Use one of the research questions you've brainstormed to create a draft research plan using the eight-step procedure set out in Table 5.1.

3. Locate an empirical study in our field that used a questionnaire as (part of) its data collection procedure. (Questionnaires are typically printed in the appendix of a published research report.)

   A. What construct(s) was the questionnaire designed to capture?

   B. What kinds of item format(s) does the questionnaire use? (Refer to Table 5.3 above.)

   C. In that same questionnaire, does it appear that the researcher(s) followed the advice of Alreck and Settle (1985) about organizing a questionnaire? (See Table 5.4 above.)

   D. Were the instructions clear and appropriate?

   E. If the questionnaire was to be completed by language learners, were the instructions and items written appropriately for the respondents' proficiency level?

   F. What sampling procedures did the researcher(s) use to identify the respondents?

   G. Did the questionnaire utilize open-ended items, closed items, or both?

   H. What sort of data did the questionnaire items elicit? (If the items were closed, were the data nominal, ordinal, interval, or some combination of these)?

   I. Based on your reading of the article, can you identify any possible threats to validity?

   J. Take the questionnaire yourself, imagining you were a member of the intended sample. What insights do you gain by completing the questionnaire.

4. If you were to replicate the study you read, what improvements would you make to the research design? What changes, if any, would you want to make to the questionnaire itself?

SUGGESTIONS FOR FURTHER READING

If you are going to work with questionnaires, we recommend Dörnyei's (2003) book *Questionnaires in Second Language Research*. It has many clear examples and suggestions for formatting questionnaires. It is written in a "user-friendly" style.

Likewise, J. D. Brown's (2001) book *Using Surveys in Language Programs* was written specifically for people in our field. It includes chapters on planning a survey project, designing a survey instrument, gathering and compiling survey data, analyzing survey data statistically, analyzing survey data qualitatively, and reporting on a survey project. The appendices also contain helpful examples of several entire questionnaires. Consulting this volume will certainly help you design better questionnaires.

For interesting discussions about the issue of whether Likert scales yield interval or ordinal data, see Busch (1993), Davidson (1998), Hatch and Lazaraton (1991), and Turner (1993). See also Gu and Wen (2005).

Reid (1990) has written about the problems of conducting survey research with second language learners as the respondents.

6

Case Study Research

If you study grains of sand, you will find each is different. Even by handling one, it becomes different. But through studying it and others like it, you begin to learn about a beach. (Larsen-Freeman, 1996, p. 165)

INTRODUCTION AND OVERVIEW

The focus of this chapter is the case study in second language research and its applicability to classroom research. Methodologically speaking, the case study is a 'hybrid' in that almost any data collection and analytical methods can be used. In this chapter, we define case studies and explore issues and problems associated with case study research. We will see that, while there are potential problems, especially with the traditional concept of external validity, case studies have considerable value.

The case study has played an important role in applied linguistics research, especially in studying first and second language acquisition. In fact, case studies have a long history in research on language learning, so we will review some of the early work that influenced the development of this research method in our field. However, in spite of their importance, defining case studies is not particularly easy as we will see in the next section.

REFLECTION

In Chapter 4, we talked about one-shot case studies as a weak research design in the experimental tradition. You may have already guessed that we are using the term *case study* somewhat differently in this chapter. What do you expect the differences will be?

A *case study* is a detailed, often longitudinal, investigation of a single individual or entity (or a few individuals or entities). In applied linguistics research, case studies can best be classified as a type of naturalistic inquiry in that they typically do not involve any sort of treatment. Instead, researchers working in the case study tradition set out to learn what is happening—whether it is with a child learning his first language, an adult developing literacy skills, a particular class of preschool children, a novice teacher, or any other entity of interest.

In experimental research, case studies (or "one-shot case studies" as they are often called) have traditionally been seen has having limited value. This is because their lack of control over variables prohibits researchers from making strong causal claims—a problem of internal validity. With only one or a few subjects, the argument goes, we can never be sure the population is well represented, so generalizing the findings of a case study to a population is a dubious undertaking—a problem of external validity. Given these concerns, the perceived value of case studies in the experimental research tradition is that they may generate hypotheses that can later be tested in experiments. However, from the perspective of naturalistic inquiry, the case study method is very important in other ways and in its own right.

In the one-shot case study design of the experimental tradition, the researcher applies a treatment and observes its apparent effects in a post-test or some other form of after-treatment measurement. There is no pre-test, nor is there any comparison group. In naturalistic inquiry, however, "the researcher usually does not provide experimental *treatments* or interventions that might modify the process of change" (Duff, 2008, p. 41). Nor does the researcher exert control over variables in a naturalistic case study:

> rather, the data reflect natural changes in the learner's behavior and knowledge, influenced by numerous possible factors, such as the environment, physical maturation, cognitive development, and schooling, which the researcher must also take into account in order to arrive at valid conclusions concerning learning processes and outcomes. (p. 41)

Indeed, when we compare case study research in naturalistic inquiry with the experimental research tradition, we see that "the strengths of one approach tend to be the weaknesses of the other" (ibid., p. 42).

Case study research assumed a great deal of importance in education in the 1970s, when it was embraced by a group of researchers and evaluators in Cambridge, England. Three members of the Cambridge Action Research Network (CARN), Adelman, Jenkins, and Kemmis (1976), produced an important position paper in which they argued that case studies are not merely pre-experimental and that *case study* is not a term for a standard methodological package. The issue of whether or not case studies are 'pre-experimental'—mere ground-clearing operations for more 'rigorous' experimental research—was challenged by Adelman et al.

> Although case studies have often been used to sensitize researchers to significant variables subsequently manipulated and controlled in an experimental design, that is not their only role. The understandings

generated by a case study are significant in their own right. It is tempting to argue that the accumulation of case studies allows theory-building via tentative hypotheses culled from the accumulation of single instances. But the generalizations produced in a case study are no less legitimate when about the instance, rather than the class from which the instance is drawn (i.e., generalizing about the case rather than from it). (Adelman et al., 1976, p. 140)

In this extract, the authors assert that the investigation of a single instance is a legitimate form of inquiry and that the case study researcher need not feel bound to report the instance as an exemplar of a class of objects, entities, or events.

Having determined what a case study is not, Adelman et al. go on to suggest that it is the study of an "instance in action" (1976, pp. 2–3). In other words, the researcher selects a single entity from a class of objects or phenomena, which could be 'bilingual speakers', 'second language classrooms,' etc., and investigates the way that the entity functions in context.

To give you a feel for this "single instance" idea and why it's important to see how an "entity functions in context," here is an example of a description of a few minutes of classroom time. The focus is largely on a single child. The description below (quoted from Carrasco, 1981, p. 168) is based on a videotape of children in a bilingual classroom. The "case" here is a Hispanic girl called "Lupita," or perhaps it is a brief series of interactions that she engages in—a classroom episode. Her teacher had thought Lupita was not a very capable student. The excerpt describes what the observers saw when they watched the videotape, focusing on Lupita's interactions with her classmates.

The Taped Scene: Briefly, what they saw was Lupita performing and interacting outside of teacher awareness during free time. After having finished the Spanish Tables instructional event task—she was the first to finish the task—Lupita decided to work on a puzzle in the rug area. She was soon joined by two other bilingual girls, each successful in placing a few pieces back on the puzzle template. Then Marta, a bilingual child assessed by the teacher as a very competent student, asked Lupita for help in placing her first piece on the template. Lupita not only helped her but also taught her how to work with it by taking Marta's hand and showing her where and how it should be placed. Lupita continued to help her for a short while and then returned to her own puzzle. A few moments later, Lupita disengaged herself from her puzzle work and became interested in what a boy, who had just entered the scene, was doing with a box of toys. Lupita asked him if she could play with him when, suddenly, the boy was interrupted by the classroom aide who asked him if he had finished his work at the Spanish Tables, trying to convey to him that he shouldn't be there. The boy did not quite understand, perhaps, what was being asked of him. Lupita turned around and told him that he should go back to finish his work. He left and Lupita continued working on her puzzle, which was almost completed. Marta again asked for help after not having accomplished very much since the last bit of assistance from Lupita. Lupita helped Marta for a short time, then returned to her own task. The teacher then entered the scene, moved past them toward the piano, and played a few notes to cue the children that the event would be over in two minutes and to begin to prepare for the next event. Lupita sped up her effort while Marta continued to have trouble. Lupita finished her puzzle, then helped Marta with hers, while the third child in the scene, who was sitting next to Marta, approached Lupita's side with the puzzle and nonverbally indicated that she also needed help. Lupita told Marta to continue to work on hers alone while she helped the third child and asked if she could help her finish the puzzle. Lupita, working quickly with the third child's puzzle, directed Graciela to go help Marta since she needed help. After Lupita and the third child put away their finished puzzles, Lupita looked around and noticed that Graciela and Marta were still at theirs. She quickly approached them, knelt down in front of them, took command, and helped them finish in time for the next lesson. This taped scene clearly showed Lupita's competence as a leader and teacher as well as her ability to work puzzles. Moreover, it seemed to reveal how Lupita's peers perceived her as compared to how the teacher perceived her.

REFLECTION

If you were a classroom observer who watched Lupita and later described her interactions during this lesson to a colleague who hadn't been there, what could you say about her? What can you infer about Lupita from this description?

Defining Case Studies

Different authors have defined cases studies in different ways. Those who come from a background of naturalistic inquiry see this method much differently from those who come from the experimental tradition. Because it is so difficult (and some would argue, not helpful) to try to control variables in naturally occurring classroom settings, in this book, we will consider case studies from the perspective of the naturalistic inquiry tradition. The definitions printed below reflect this orientation.

ACTION

Study the following definitions, identify commonalities, and then come up with your own definition of a case study.

1. A case study is an empirical inquiry that investigates a contemporary phenomenon within its real-life context; when the boundaries between the phenomenon and the context are not clearly evident; and in which multiple sources of evidence are used (Yin, 1984, p. 23).

2. A case study is defined in terms of the unit of analysis. That is, a case study is a study of one case. A case-study researcher focuses attention on a single entity, usually as it exists in its naturally occurring environment (D. Johnson, 1992, p. 75).

3. [A case study] is a phenomenon of some sort occurring in a bounded context (Miles and Huberman, 1994, p. 24).

4. The qualitative case study can be defined as an intensive, holistic description and analysis of a single entity, phenomenon, or social unit. Case studies are particularistic, descriptive, and heuristic and rely heavily on inductive reasoning in handling multiple data sources (Merriam, 1988, p. 16).

5. A case is a single instance of a class of objects or entities, and a case study is the investigation of that single instance in the context in which it occurs (Nunan, 1992, p. 79).

6. The most common type of . . . [case study] involves the detailed description and analysis of an individual subject, from whom observations, interviews, and (family) histories provide the database. . . . [Case study methodology] may involve more than one subject. . . . It may be based on particular groups (e.g., group dynamics within a classroom); organizations (e.g., a summer intensive language learning program at a university); or events (e.g., a Japanese language tutorial . . . where one could examine the amount of time a teacher speaks in either Japanese or English for class management purposes) (Duff, 1990, p. 35).

7. "A case study is what you call a case, in case, in case you don't have anything else to call it" (unidentified student cited in Jaeger, 1988, p. 74).

Commonalities Across Definitions

Despite their differences, these definitions have two main commonalities. The most important of these is the notion that a case is a 'bounded instance.' By *bounded* we mean "defined" or "having boundaries"—whether those boundaries are physical (a certain school site, a child), or temporal (as in a lesson, which has a beginning and an end). You can think of the metaphor of a fenced-in area as being bounded. In classroom research, the bounded instance can be a single learner or teacher, one classroom, a school, or even a particular school district. The second commonality is that the phenomenon is studied in context. Unlike formal experiments, which control and manipulate variables and look for causality, case studies are centered on description, inference, and interpretation. They also contrast with surveys, in which the researcher asks standardized questions of large representative samples of individuals. The case study researcher typically observes the characteristics of an individual entity—a child, a clique, a class, an educational program, or a community—in that entity's naturally occurring situation. As a result, "case studies clearly have the potential for rich contextualization that can shed light on the complexities of the second language learning process" (Mackey and Gass, 2005, p. 172).

This issue of contextualization is very important, because "each human case is complex, operating within a constellation of linguistic, sociolinguistic, sociological and other systems, and the whole may be greater than—or different from—the sum of its parts" (Duff, 2008, p. 37). Experimental research typically attempts to neutralize contextual differences through the use of control variables. (See Chapter 3.) Case studies, in contrast, explore and describe the context as an essential part of understanding the phenomenon under investigation.

An example of language classroom research that illustrates both the bounded instance and the contextualized nature of case studies is found in Donato and Adair-Hauck (1992). They reported on two secondary school French teachers' lessons about the future tense. The two teachers are called Elizabeth and Claire in the report. They used different but clearly patterned strategies for teaching the future tense. Elizabeth took eight lessons to cover this structure and Claire took ten. The researchers videotaped and then transcribed these lessons, and analyzed the transcripts in order to document the two teachers' styles. Elizabeth's orientation was more monologic and Claire's was more dialogic.

These authors used a unit of analysis called the *instructional episode*: "a detachable piece of instructional material having a recognizable beginning and end point for both teacher and students. . . . In this study, the instructional episode for analysis consisted of a unit containing the target structure the future tense" (ibid., p. 77). The classroom data about the two teachers' styles are very convincing. Part of what makes this study compelling reading for teachers is that as readers we can relate to the choices Elizabeth and Claire make about how to teach the future tense.

REFLECTION

Based on what you have read so far, and on your previous reading, what do you see as the advantages of case study research? What might be some disadvantages?

OTHER CHARACTERISTICS OF CASE STUDIES

There are some other key characteristics that many case studies have in common. In addition to boundedness and contextualization, according to Duff (2008), these characteristics include multiple perspectives or triangulation, particularity, and interpretation. In addition, longitudinality is a characteristic of many, but not all, case studies.

Longitudinality, Multiple Perspectives, and Triangulation

One tremendous value of case studies is that a researcher normally studies the case for a long period of time. A *longitudinal case study* "examines development and performance over time" (Duff, 2008, p. 40). Longitudinal case studies provide "multiple observations or datasets, as information is collected at regular intervals, over the course of a year or longer" (ibid.). For example, Leopold's (1978) research on his daughter's language acquisition covered three years. Not all case studies are longitudinal in nature, but this characteristic is one of the main strengths of the approach.

One key characteristic of case studies is the detailed nature of the data. As you can see from the description of Lupita, the observational record derived from the videotape shows us exactly how the child behaves. We come away from the description with a clear understanding of her interactions with other children. This clear understanding occurs in reading well-written case studies because

> by concentrating on the behavior of one individual or a small number of individuals (or sites) it is possible to conduct a very thorough analysis ("thick" or "rich" description) of the case and to include triangulated perspectives from other participants or observers. (Duff, 2008, p. 43)

A related characteristic of case study reports is that they often include detailed presentations of primary data, including transcript excerpts, speech and/or writing samples, journal entries, and so on (ibid.).

The concept of multiple perspectives relates to the idea that many points of view can be brought to the analysis of case study data. Usually, this is accomplished through a process called *triangulation*. This term is a metaphor borrowed from navigation, surveying, and astronomy. Hammersley and Atkinson (1983) explain triangulation using the analogy of people wanting to locate their position:

> A single landmark can only provide the information that they are situated somewhere along a line in a particular direction from that landmark. With two landmarks, however, their exact position can be pinpointed by taking bearings on both landmarks; they are at the point where the two lines cross. (p. 198)

In qualitative data collection, the metaphor refers to a quality control strategy. In social research, if "diverse kinds of data lead to the same conclusion, one can be a little more confident in that conclusion" (ibid.). (This concept is widely used in naturalistic inquiry, and we will revisit it in more detail in Chapter 7 when we discuss ethnography.)

An example arose in Chapter 1 where we cited the study by Donato, Antonek, and Tucker (1994). Their investigation of a Japanese FLES (foreign language in the elementary school) program captured numerous perspectives in data from questionnaires completed by parents and learners, reflections from the Japanese teacher, questionnaires from other teachers at the school, interviews, and an observation system.

Particularity

The concept of particularity as a characteristic of case studies is related to the boundedness of the case. In other words, "a single case or nonrandom sample is selected precisely *because* the researcher wishes to understand the particular in depth, not to find out what is generally true of the many" (Merriam, 1998, p. 208).

Here, the analogy of a camera that uses different lenses will be helpful. Survey research, as described in Chapter 5, takes a wide angle view. It captures the landscape—a panorama of mountains, streams, and trees. Case study research, in contrast, uses a close-up lens. It examines the individual wildflower or provides a detailed study of a leaf. Although the flower and the leaf are part of the landscape, looking at the photo shot with the wide-angle lens will not allow us to see the petals of the flower or the delicate veins of the leaf.

In second language classroom research, we may choose to focus on a particular student, or a particular teacher, or perhaps one particular conversational exchange among three pupils doing group work. It is the close examination of the particular phenomenon that allows case study researchers to go into great detail in terms of data collection and analysis.

Interpretation

To interpret something is to construe or attach meaning to it, that is, to understand it. When we look at case study data, we analyze those data and that analysis can be either qualitative or quantitative or both. Interpreting results in data has to do with explaining what they mean. This comment is true of statistical analyses as well of more qualitative analyses, and case study research employs interpretation in both contexts.

An example interpretation in language classroom research is found in Ulichny's (1996) investigation of an interaction in an intermediate adult ESL conversation class. Ulichny documented a particular classroom speech event, which contained three different discourse activities. One student, Katherine, is talking about why she decided not to continue with her volunteer work—a role she undertook in order to practice her English. So, one discourse activity consisted of the actual *conversation* among Katherine, another student, and the teacher, with the rest of the class listening. But, as Katherine's story goes on, the teacher soon "exits from the conversation to work on specific elements of the language" (p. 756). The teacher exits her role as a listener to the story for a "*correction* move or a *conversational replay*" (p. 756). She also offers "*instruction, in* which [the teacher] involves the whole class in language work" (p. 754). Through a detailed interpretation of the transcript, Ulichny shows how the conversation is subjugated to correction and instruction. In the process, Katherine is gradually rendered "silent in the telling of her story" (p. 754).

TYPES OF CASE STUDIES

Deciding whether any given investigation is or is not a case study is not always easy or straightforward. As noted above, the term *case study* has been defined in various ways, and it is probably easier to say what a case is not than what it is. While it seems reasonably clear that the study of an individual learner or an individual classroom is a case, what about an investigation of an entire school or even a whole school district? Any of these could be the focus of a case study.

In addition to focusing on a variety of topics for possible investigation, case studies can serve a range of purposes and display various characteristics. Stenhouse (1983), one of the 'fathers' of case study research in education, developed a typology of case studies. The first type he identified as the *neo-ethnographic*, which is the in-depth investigation of a single case by a participant observer. Next, is the *evaluative*, which is a "single case or group of cases studied at such depth as the evaluation of policy or practice will allow (usually condensed fieldwork)" (p. 21). In contrast with these first two, the *multi-site case study* consists of "condensed fieldwork undertaken by a team of workers on a number of sites and possibly offering an alternative approach to research to that based on sampling and statistical inference" (ibid.). Such research probably approaches ethnography (see Chapter 7), particularly if it attempts to capture a wide range of issues and questions. The final type consists of *action case studies*. These are school case studies undertaken by teachers who use their participant status as a basis on which to build skills of observation and analysis.' (ibid.). A typology based on Stenhouse is set out in **Table 6.1**.

TABLE 6.1 The case study: A typology (following Stenhouse, 1983)

Type	Description
Neo-ethnographic	The in-depth investigation of a single case by a participant observer
Evaluative	An investigation carried out in order to evaluate policy or practice
Multi-site	A study carried out by several researchers on more than one site
Action	An investigation carried out by a classroom practitioner in his or her professional context

Other researchers have categorized case studies in different ways. For instance, Yin (2003, as cited in Duff, 2008, pp. 31–32) discusses exploratory, descriptive, and explanatory case studies. He sees defining questions and hypotheses as the main purpose of exploratory case studies. A descriptive case study, as the name suggests, provides a contextualized and detailed description of the entity under investigation. An explanatory case study is intended to reveal causal relationships.

REFLECTION

What do you see as the advantages of these different types of case studies? What might be some disadvantages?

THE VALUE OF CASE STUDIES

Adelman et al. (1976) argue that there are six principal advantages of case study research in educational settings. In the first place, in contrast with some other research methods, case studies are 'strong in reality,' and therefore likely to appeal to classroom teachers who will be able to identify with the issues and concerns raised. Secondly, they claim that one can generalize from an instance to a class. (For example, you may recognize in R. L. Allwright's (1980) case study of a conversation between Igor and his teacher a number of garrulous students you have known.) A third strength of the case study is that it can represent a multiplicity of viewpoints and can offer support to alternative interpretations. Fourth, if they are properly presented, case studies can also provide a database of materials that may be reinterpreted by future researchers. Fifth, insights yielded by case studies can be put to immediate use for a variety of purposes, including staff development, within-institution feedback, formative evaluation, and educational policy making. Finally, case study reports are often written in a more accessible style than are conventional experimental research reports, and are, therefore, capable of serving multiple audiences. Because they are 'user-friendly,' case studies can contribute to the democratization of decision making in ways that studies based solely on quantitative data and statistical analyses may not.

REFLECTION

Look back to the brief description of Lupita's interactions with her classmates. Which of the six advantages of case studies identified by Adelman et al. (1976) are discernable if we consider that excerpt to be a "mini" case study, or some data from a longitudinal case study?

Case studies have played an important role in applied linguistics, where they have principally been employed as a tool to trace the linguistic development of first and second language learners. A classic in the field of first language acquisition is R. Brown's (1973) longitudinal investigation of the semantic and grammatical development of three children acquiring their first language. Another case study that has had considerable influence is Halliday's (1975) research on the language development of his own son. Studies such as these have played an important part in enhancing the status of the case study in applied linguistics.

In second language acquisition, case studies "have generated very detailed accounts of the processes and/or outcomes of language learning for a variety of subjects" (Duff, 1990, p. 34). The types of subjects studied, according to Duff, range "from young children in bilingual home environments, to adolescent immigrants, adult migrant workers, and university-level foreign language learners" (ibid.). Case study methodology can also embrace a wide variety of research questions. Duff discusses this point with regard to the field of second language acquisition (SLA):

> Recent questions addressed in [case studies] in SLA research have included . . . How do children manage to function with two linguistic systems at a time when most children are attempting to master one? Why do some learners fossilize in their acquisition of a second language (in some or all domains), while some continue to progress? In what ways do the forms and functions of constructions in a learner's interlanguage (IL) differ? What features characterize the prototypical "good language learner"? How do learners react to and/or benefit from different methods of instruction? Is there a critical period for SLA? (ibid.)

Thus, case studies can be used to address a range of research questions about both instructed and uninstructed language acquisition.

We concur with Duff, who says that case studies are attractive for a number of reasons:

> When done well, they have a high degree of completeness, depth of analysis and readability. In addition, the cases may generate new hypotheses, models and understandings about the nature of language learning or other processes. . . . In addition, longitudinal case study research helps to confirm stages or transformations proposed on the basis of larger (e.g., cross-sectional) studies and provides developmental evidence that can otherwise only be inferred. (Duff, 2008, p. 43)

Thus, among researchers in the naturalistic inquiry tradition, there is wide recognition of the value of case studies. We turn now to the practical issue of how to select a case.

SELECTING THE CASE

As noted above, the case selected for investigation may be one person or a few people. For instance, Carless (1999) conducted a case study of three primary school teachers in Hong Kong, and Harklau (2000) studied three ESL community college students. Case studies have also been conducted about single or multiple classrooms, one or a group of schools (see, e.g., Wang's [2003] case study of English language teaching in China).

Reasons for selecting the particular case(s) to be studied are varied. Ideally, a case can be chosen that embodies the phenomenon the researcher wishes to investigate:

> The individual case is usually selected for study on the basis of specific psychological, biological, sociocultural, institutional, or linguistic attributes, representing a particular age group, a combination of first and second languages, ability level (e.g., basic or advanced), or a skill area such as writing, a linguistic domain such as morphology and syntax, or a mode or medium of learning, such as an online computer-mediated environment. (Duff, 2008, pp. 32–33)

In some of the early literature on second language acquisition, cases were chosen because the individuals were especially interesting or unusual. For instance, one of the classic early studies in the second language acquisition literature is J. Schumann's (1978a, 1978b) investigation of acquisition and acculturation. Schumann was part of a team that carried out a ten-month study of two adults, two teenagers, and two children who were all Spanish speakers acquiring English. One of the adults, Alberto, a thirty-three-year-old Costa Rican, made very little progress in learning English in comparison to the others despite a period of intensive instruction. Schumann studied Alberto and concluded that his lack of linguistic development could be attributed to his social and psychological distance from the target culture and the fact that the limited amount of English he had managed to acquire was sufficient for him to fulfill his communicative needs. In fact, this point of view became a testable hypothesis that other researchers later investigated.

In other instances, an inviting, accessible context has prompted the choice of the case. For instance, Peck (1980) looked at the role of language play in the English development of two Mexican boys whose parents were graduate students in the United States. The family lived in their university's married-students' housing complex, which meant that Peck had ample opportunities to record the boys' developing language in the context of them playing with other children in English. Thus, the situation provided an ideal opportunity and a compelling context for studying language play in second language acquisition.

Other people have selected cases because of the ease of access to the individual(s) the researcher wished to study. Many parents have studied their own children's language acquisition. For example, Celce-Murcia (1978) investigated her daughter's bilingual acquisition of English and French over a period of years, in both California and France. Burling (1978) documented his son's acquisition of Garo and English. The opportunity to investigate child bilingualism in this way arose when the family went to live in India when the boy was a year and four months old. In conducting this case study, the researcher had ready access to his son in a very interesting situation—total immersion in a new language and culture.

Sometimes, a case seems to jump out of the data for a different sort of study. For example, in an early and influential classroom research project, R. L. Allwright (1980) investigated the turns, topics, and tasks in two lower-level ESL classes in California. For a period of ten weeks, both classes were tape-recorded for two of their twenty instructional hours per week, while an observer took notes. Allwright analyzed the data by transcribing the audiotapes and counting the number and types of turns taken by the various students and the two teachers. One student, whose pseudonym was "Igor," got many more turns than did his classmates. This numerical discrepancy caused Allwright to look more closely at Igor's interactions with the teacher, to see how he got so many turns. One conversation was analyzed in great detail because it showed how Igor's discourse moves caused the teacher to give him more turns through her repeated attempts to understand his message.

In another classroom study, Block (1996; 1998) investigated the perceptions of six adult English learners and their teacher in Spain. They all kept oral diaries (i.e., they made tape-recorded diary entries) on a daily basis. Block wanted to compare the teacher's and the students' views of salient activities during the lessons. He himself observed some of the lessons. In the data analysis, it became clear that one student, whose pseudonym was "Alex," provided detailed comments in which he "questioned and criticized what was going on in class" (Block, 1996, p. 183). Block chose to focus part of his report on Alex's perspectives because "if we are to understand classroom culture better, we must examine not only harmony but conflict" (ibid.). The case study of Alex is embedded in Block's larger discussion of the classroom research as a whole. In discussing this choice, Block cites D. Allwright's (1988) comment in deciding to focus on Igor: "This is the starting point for the case-study approach, where one learner stands out as of particular interest" (p. 178).

REFLECTION

Think about the reasons given above for selecting a particular entity as a "case" for investigation. Given the research topics that interest you, what would be a case that you could study? For what reason(s) would you select that entity?

QUALITY CONTROL ISSUES IN CASE STUDIES

As case studies are concerned with the observation, documentation, and analysis of a single instance, many of the quality control issues we looked at in earlier chapters of the book will be revisited here from the perspective of case study. However, since we are viewing case studies from the perspective of naturalistic inquiry, we will also introduce other issues that do not typically arise in discussions of the experimental approach to language classroom research.

External and Internal Validity in Case Studies

In relation to validity, there are two points of view. On the one hand, there are the researchers who feel that internal validity is important in any kind of research, but external validity may be irrelevant (see, e.g., Larsen-Freeman, 1996; van Lier, 2005). In fact, Larsen-Freeman (1996) questions "whether generalizability has ever been attainable in classroom research" in general—not just case studies (p. 164). For many qualitatively oriented researchers, according to Duff (2008), "the term *generalizability* itself is considered a throw-back to another era, paradigm, ethos, and discourse in research" (p. 50).

On the other hand, some researchers believe that the purpose of such observation is to make generalizations from the entity to the wider population to which it belongs (see, for example, Cohen and Manion, 1985, p. 120). People working in this perspective argue that tests of validity ought to be as stringently applied to the case study as to any other type of research. Yin (1984), for example, believes that reliability and validity are just as important for case study research as they are for other kinds of research. He suggests that four critical tests confront the case study researcher:

- reliability (demonstrating that the study can be replicated with similar results)
- construct validity (establishing correct operational measures for the concepts being studied)
- internal validity (establishing a causal relationship, whereby certain conditions are shown to lead to other conditions, as distinguished from spurious relationships)
- external validity (establishing the domain or population to which a study's findings can be generalized)

In relation to the internal validity of case study research, Yin (1984) claims that this is a matter of concern only in

> causal or explanatory studies, where an investigator is trying to determine whether an event x led to event y. If the investigator incorrectly concludes that there is a causal relationship between x and y without knowing that some third factor—z—may actually have caused y, the research design has failed to deal with some threat to internal validity. (p. 38)

Another problem relating to internal validity is the frequent necessity for case study researchers to make inferences (which they have to do every time they deal with an event that cannot be directly observed). Thus, an investigator will 'infer' that a particular event resulted from some earlier occurrence, based on interview and documentary evidence collected as part of the study. Other researchers argue that this is not just a concern in case studies: Internal validity is a matter of concern in all types of research because it deals with the question of whether investigators are really observing what they think they are observing.

Particularization and Transferability

Some researchers argue that internal validity has to take precedence over external validity on the grounds that without internal validity, the study is meaningless, and it makes no sense to attempt to apply meaningless outcomes to broader populations. This is a matter of logic: If a researcher claims that a certain variable caused learning or improved teaching but is wrong about that conclusion, then it is problematic to try to generalize that finding to a wider context.

A major concern for some researchers has to do with the extent to which one can extrapolate from a given case to the class of entities from which it is drawn.

Generalization has been a serious stumbling block for case study researchers who see the need to argue from the single instance to the general. However, Stake (1988) argues for the particularity of the case and rejects the need for generalizability:

> The principal difference between case studies and other research studies is that the focus of attention is the case, not the whole population of cases. In most other studies, researchers search for an understanding that ignores the uniqueness of individual cases and generalizes beyond particular instances. They search for what is common, pervasive, and lawful. In the case study, there may or may not be an ultimate interest in the generalizable. For the time being, the search is for an understanding of the particular case, in its idiosyncrasy, in its complexity. (p. 256)

A similar position is taken by van Lier (2005). He contrasts case studies with experimental research and process-product studies. (See Chapter 1.)

> In the past, case studies have often been accorded less status than more rigorously controlled experimental or process-product studies because, as the argument often goes, case studies are not generalizable. However, this criticism is unwarranted. It is probably true that it is difficult to generalize from an individual (or a group) to an entire population without the presence of strict controls to account for environmental variables. However, there is also a form of generalization that proceeds not from an individual case to a population, but from lower-level constructs to higher-level ones. Furthermore, in the practical world in which case studies are conducted, *particularization* may be just as important—if not more so—than *generalization*. (p. 198)

According to van Lier, *particularization* means that "insights from a case study can inform, be adapted to, and provide comparative information to a wide variety of other cases" (ibid.). However, readers and researchers must take contextual differences into account when doing so.

This idea has also been discussed by Larsen-Freeman (1996, citing Clarke, 1995). She says that *particularizability* involves helping teachers find connections between research results and the particulars of their own classroom realities. In her view, those sorts of connections are more valuable than the statistical concept of generalizing findings from studies using samples randomly drawn from a defined population.

A related concept is the *transferability* (also called *comparability*) of hypotheses, principles, and/or findings (Duff, 2008; Lincoln and Guba, 1985). In this idea, it is up to the readers of case studies to decide for themselves "whether there is a congruence, fit, or connection between one study context, in all its complexity, and their own context, rather than have the original researchers make that assumption for them" (p. 51).

REFLECTION

Have you ever read a case study about a learner that reminded you strongly about someone you had known? What is your opinion of particularizability and transferability?

Yin also argues that construct validity is especially problematic in case study research. This problem is due to the frequent failure of case study researchers to develop a sufficiently operational set of measures and because 'subjective' judgments are used to collect their data. This point leads us to the issues of subjectivity and objectivity.

Subjectivity and Objectivity

A subjective stance is not automatically considered to be negative in naturalistic inquiry even though objectivity is a hallmark of (or at least a desideratum in) experimental research. Various naturalistic inquiry methods have their own means of establishing quality control in the objectivity-subjectivity dichotomy. (We will revisit this point in some detail in Chapter 7, where we discuss ethnography.)

What is sometimes seen as subjectivity may be a by-product of involvement. Well-documented case studies are valuable because of the illuminating insights and vivid exemplars they provide. For example, Schmidt (1983) conducted a longitudinal case study of Wes, an adult learner of English in Hawaii. Wes and Schmidt were close personal friends. As a result, Schmidt could observe and record Wes's speech frequently and in a wide range of contexts, and the data collection was sustained over a period of time. Regarding his interpretation of the data, Schmidt notes, "The judgments given here, as in most case studies, are . . . ultimately subjective, deriving their validity only from close personal friendship and familiarity with the subject, observations of his behavior, and discussions with him and others who know him well" (p. 142). (See also Schmidt, 1984.) While experimental researchers would see this intense involvement as posing a threat to objectivity, well-written case studies are valuable precisely because this familiarity and involvement enables the author to convincingly portray the individual or site under investigation.

For the most part, qualitative researchers "do not see subjectivity as a major issue, as something that can or should be eliminated. Rather, they see it as an inevitable engagement with the world in which meanings and realities are constructed (not just discovered) and in which the researcher is very much present" (Duff, 2008, p. 56). In fact, Duff quotes Stake (1995) as saying that subjectivity is "an essential element of understanding" (p. 45).

REFLECTION

How do you feel about the subjectivity issue in case study research? Can you find research results convincing if they are not totally objective?

Case Studies and Hypothesis Testing

Yin (1984) makes an interesting defense of the case study from the perspective of external validity. He argues against drawing an analogy between case study and survey research, suggesting, in fact, that it is a false one. (See Chapter 5 for an introduction to survey research.) He says that critics of case study research

> are implicitly contrasting the situation to survey research, where a 'sample' (if selected correctly) readily generalizes to a larger universe. This analogy to samples and universes is incorrect when dealing with case studies. This is because survey research relies on statistical generalization, whereas case studies . . . rely on analytical generalization. (p. 39)

Yin's argument here is somewhat obscure. He seems to be arguing that a single case can be deployed to falsify an assertion or hypothesis rather than to support it. In fact, that has happened in second language acquisition research.

Here is the logic. You will recall from Chapter 3, where we discussed hypothesis testing, that the philosopher Popper (1968; 1972) argued that we can never 'prove' anything through observation; we can only disprove tentatively established hypotheses. His famous example is the 'white swan' argument—that is, a thousand sightings of white swans do not entitle us to claim all swans are white as a scientific fact. We can tentatively put forward the hypothesis that all swans are white, but this hypothesis can be falsified, or disproved, by a single disconfirming black swan.

To exemplify this issue, let's return to J. Schumann's (1978a; 1978b) study of Alberto, the Spanish speaker who made very little progress with his English over the tenth-month period of the study. Alberto was able to get along and fulfill his communicative needs with very limited English. Schumann concluded that Alberto's lack of linguistic development was due to his high social and psychological distance from the target culture. This point of view became a testable hypothesis, which suggested that low social distance and psychological distance are required for language acquisition to occur.

Later, Schmidt (1983; 1984) challenged this hypothesis through his case study of Wes, which we summarized above. Although Wes's English was very limited (like Alberto's), he had very low social and psychological distance from English speakers. Schmidt thus refuted Schumann's hypothesis about low social and psychological distance being the keys to successful language acquisition. In effect, Wes was the black swan.

In summary then, we can see three positions that may be taken with regard to case studies and the issue of generalizability:

> Position 1: Case studies can achieve the status of generalizability when findings from many studies are aggregated.

> Position 2: Generalizability is not necessarily the only end of research. The particular and the unique might be just as worthwhile to document.

> Position 3: Generalizability is unnecessary in those case studies that set out to falsify a hypothesis.

Which of the three positions listed above could be used to justify the following study?

Janet Allbright is investigating the different stages of acquisition that learners go through as they acquire English. She uses a six-stage model of acquisition that she has come across in the literature. This model argues that all the grammatical structures of English can be placed into six groups, or stages, and that learners must pass through each of these stages in turn. Her chosen methodology is case study. She records and analyzes the conversations of an immigrant learner of English over a two-year period and compares the learner's stages of language development from beginner- to intermediate-level of proficiency.

This study could be justified by Position 1 above. Janet could argue that she is adding one more case to the growing number of cases in the second language acquisition literature. On the other hand, if she were able to document evidence of her learner 'skipping' one of the six hypothesized stages of acquisition, which would disconfirm the hypothesis, she could justify her case study in terms of Position 3.

A SAMPLE STUDY

Sometimes, case study research is criticized for being atheoretical, and it is true that case studies are sometimes more data-driven than theory-driven (Duff, 2008). Nevertheless, "much case study research is embedded within a relevant theoretical literature and is motivated by the researcher's interest in the case and how it addresses existing knowledge or contributes new knowledge to current debates or issues" (p. 57). In this section, we will summarize a case study that has a very strong tie to theory.

Nassaji and Cumming (2000) analyzed the interactions of an ESL teacher and young Farsi speaker learning English in Canada. The child, whose pseudonym was Ali, was six years old and had moved to Canada from Iran. The researchers examined dialog journal exchanges between Ali and his teacher, Ellen (also a pseudonym), over a period of ten months. It might be argued that this study is more an example of classroom-oriented research rather than classroombased research (see Chapter 1) since it did not investigate classroom interaction per se. However, the interactions between Ali and Ellen were part of their natural ongoing relationship as learner and teacher; it's just that the interactions under investigation were written instead of spoken.

The authors quote Peyton's (1990) definition of a *dialog journal* as "a written ongoing interaction between individual students and their teacher in a bound notebook" (p. 100). Ellen told her students to write about things that interested them personally. The authors say, "The journals were written every few days as part of routine classroom activities, forming a continuous flow of exchanges in single notebooks (comprising four notebooks in total)" (p. 101).

Data Collection and Analysis

The article is richly illustrated with excerpts from the dialog journal exchanges. Ali's earliest dialog journal entries were his first attempts at writing English. Here is an example that consists of Ali's entry, Ellen's response, and Ali's reply to her. These data are reproduced (from Nassaji and Cumming, 2000, p. 109) with Ali's own spelling, punctuation, and capitalization:

> Ali: Today is Tuesday.Dec.19th 1995. The Temperature is 11 A.M. It is a Cold Day. I very very miss kathryn.
>
> Ellen: Kathryn was a very kind student. We will all miss her very much. Do you think she will miss us?
>
> Ali: yes

One key point is that all of these dialog entries were written before either the teacher or the student were aware that they would be used for research. For this reason, the dialog journal data "represent naturalistic classroom data" (Nassaji and Cumming, 2000, p. 101).

REFLECTION

Have you ever used the dialog journal procedure, either as a teacher or a language learner? What do you think about this idea for encouraging learners to communicate their ideas in writing in the target language? What do you think about using dialog journal entries as data in language classroom research?

To analyze the data, the researchers employed a coding scheme of fourteen language functions. These categories were first developed by Shuy (1993), who also studied dialog journal interactions. The fourteen categories are listed below (from Nassaji and Cumming, 2000, p. 102):

1. Reporting personal facts
2. Reporting general facts
3. Reporting opinions
4. Requesting personal information
5. Request academic information
6. Requesting general information
7. Requesting opinions

8. Requesting clarification
9. Thanking
10. Evaluating
11. Predicting
12. Complaining
13. Apologizing
14. Giving directives

As it turned out, only eleven of these categories were used in this study because neither the teacher nor the student requested academic information (5) or complained (12), and thanking (9) happened very rarely or was embedded as part of other functions.

In addition to the function coding described above, the researchers divided the dialog journal entries into *T-units*. This is a unit of syntactic complexity defined by Hunt (1970) as an independent clause and any attached subordinate clause(s). So, a subordinate clause alone is not a T-unit. A full sentence is a T-unit, whether it is a simple sentence or a complex sentence. A compound sentence is categorized as two (or more) T-units, as shown below:

1. It's raining. (One T-unit)
2. It's raining, which is unfortunte. (One T-Unit)
3. It's raining and there is lots of lightning. (Two T-units)
4. It's raining, there is lots of lightning, and I hear thunder. (Three T-units)

For both the function coding and the T-unit analysis, Nassaji and Cumming (2000) checked their inter-coder agreement. They reported strong inter-coder indices:

> Our inter-coder agreement on a sample of 20 per cent of the data selected from every 5th journal entry (101 T-units over 10 exchanges), was 100 per cent (i.e., full agreement) for the segmentation of the data into T-units and 92 per cent for the coding of the language functions. The few discrepancies in coding were resolved through discussion. (p. 103)

REFLECTION

Based on what you have read so far, what do you think were the research questions that Nassaji and Cumming wished to address?

Sociocultural Theory

The first paragraph of Nassaji and Cumming's (2000) report begins with the following questions (which, at first glance, may seem more like attention getters and topic nominators than explicit research questions): "What does a ZPD (zone of proximal development) look like? How might we recognize one? How do we know whether it is happening or not?" (p. 95). They say that "answers to these questions are fundamental to guide—indeed should form a rationale for—the practices of language learning and teaching" (ibid.).

The *zone of proximal development* (often called the ZPD) is a feature of socio-cultural theory, which originated with Vygotsky (1978, 1986). This theory holds that all learning is socially constructed and that learning occurs in the ZPD. But what exactly is this concept? Vygotsky (1978) defined the zone of proximal development as "the distance between a child's actual development level as determined by independent problem solving and the level of potential development as determined through problem solving under guidance or in collaboration with more capable peers" (p. 86).

Another important concept in sociocultural theory is *scaffolding*, which is "generally understood in cognitive psychology as progressive help provided by the more knowledgeable to the less knowledgeable" (Nassaji and Cumming, 2000, p. 98). Scaffolding is not just providing an answer—it is helping someone arrive at an answer. Think of the term in its metaphoric sense: A scaffold is erected around a building that is either being renovated or being built. The scaffold is there to help the workers reach the problem areas or unfinished areas that need attention. When those areas have been dealt with, the scaffolding is removed. It is an intentionally temporary structure. Through scaffolded interaction with others, learners move from what they can currently do independently to another level of capability, and this process happens within the ZPD.

Nassaji and Cumming (2000) say, "At the heart of the sociocultural perspective is defining the dialogic nature of teaching and learning processes within the ZPD as well as designing research that exemplifies its nature" (p. 97). They decided that "in order to study the ZPD in detail, [they] needed to look to dialogue journals—a situation where language teaching and learning are organized so that communication is systematically dialogic" (p. 99). They identified their 'research gap' (see Chapter 2) in this way:

> Little of the previous inquiry into dialogue journals with second language learners, however, despite its taking a functional approach to the analysis of communication, has adopted an explicitly Vygotskian theoretical framework. . . . Likewise, previous research about the ZPD in second language education has mostly focused on spoken, rather than written, interactions." (ibid.)

These authors set out to examine in detail the dialog journal exchanges between Ali and Ellen in terms of what the entries could reveal about the ZPD. The longitudinal data collection process allowed the researchers to see how the systematic written interactions between the teacher and the child changed over time. Nassaji and Cumming used the T-unit analysis and the function coding to analyze any possible changes. In terms of the quantitative and qualitative dimension discussed in Chapter 1 (see Table 1.1), this case study involves qualitative data collection—the dialog journal entries. These data were then analyzed both qualitatively (through categorization) and quantitatively.

The findings of this study are interesting and varied. We will note just a few of them here, starting with the quantitative results. These were discussed in terms of the frequency of the eleven different functions that appeared in these data as percentages of the total T-unit the authors identified in the journal entries.

Quantitative Results

The majority of Ali's entries (58%) involved reporting general facts. Twenty percent were reporting personal facts, and 18% were reporting opinions. The other eight functions coded were requesting personal information (0.2%), requesting general information (2%), requesting opinions (0.2%), requesting clarification (0.2%), evaluating (0.7%), predicting (0.7%), and apologizing (0.7%).

The functions coded in Ellen's entries were reporting general facts (13%), personal information (23%), requesting general information (4%), requesting opinions (10%), requesting clarification (2%), evaluating (10%), predicting (9%), apologizing (0.7%), and giving directions (2%).

Regarding these quantitative findings, Nassaji and Cumming (2000) say that

the variety and value of Ellen's language functions have to be recognized, not simply as proportional frequencies, but for the ways in which she pitched her discourse to match Ali's basic 'reporting' mode. We assume Ellen was striving to scaffold their written interactions to prompt Ali's potential for learning English in this context. (p. 104)

The numerous examples of dialog journal entries that the researchers provide help the reader interpret and verify this interpretation.

Qualitative Results

In repeatedly reviewing the dialog journal exchanges, the researchers found five patterns that "display salient aspects of their mutual process of constructing a ZPD" (Nassaji and Cumming, 2000, p. 106). These five patterns "of complementary asymmetry" (p. 111) are discussed and some will be exemplified below:

1. Questioning: "In the early weeks of the journals, Ellen posed simple routine questions seemingly to engage Ali in the discourse and to show Ali how to interact" (ibid.).

Example:
Ali: Today is +14 A.M. May 1995 is 23th. Yestoday is my borday. I am 7 yors old. I love my Mom and my Dad. Today is Teusday. I love my Teacher. I love Appl TREE.
Ellen: Did you have a birthday cake?
Ali: Yes.

2. Give and Take: "At times when Ali increased the frequency of language functions he used, Ellen correspondingly decreased hers, seemingly to allow

Ali greater 'voice.' . . . Conversely, every few weeks, Ellen increased her frequency of language functions, possibly to prompt Ali to increase his. In many cases when Ali wrote shorter journal entries with fewer language functions, Ellen tended to produce comparatively lengthier responses and more language functions" (ibid., pp. 108–109). Here are examples of both types of exchanges:

Example (ibid., p. 108):

Ali: Today is Mounday.June 1995 5th. Yestoday is god Day. YesToday I aM going To park. Today is teperature is +19 A.M. I love grass. I love park. I Love My scool. I Love My Teacher. I am seven yors old. I love you Mr. [Ellen]. I Love baby dish and tadpole. I love my clas RooM. Do you laik me. I love frog. I love sole dog. I love my mom and my Dad.

Ellen: Yes, I like you Ali.

Example (ibid., p. 109):

Ali: Today is Thursday.Nov.the 2nd 1995. The temperature is +15 A.M. today is a raning Day. Halloween is ower. I Go checo or churet last Night. and I saw tisha and Mayer and bengeneh. the End.

Ellen: What did you get for Trick-or-Treat? What was your costume? Dear [Ali], I am glad you listened to and obeyed your mother at 12:00. She is trying to help you learn. We will see you tomorrow with a big smile! From Mrs [Ellen].

Ali: Notheng.

3. Reporting and Requesting: The data showed that reporting and requesting were the two language functions that Ali and Ellen used the most frequently. Nassaji and Cumming felt that over the course of the journal entries, Ellen pitched her journal entries to match both Ali's comments and his language proficiency. They report that "by the final weeks of the journal exchanges, the two had reached a relatively harmonious balance in terms of their communicating" (ibid., p. 110). They make the point that, initially, Ellen frequently requested Ali's opinions, but "as the journals progressed, Ali came to produce more opinions and Ellen gradually refrained from requesting them" (ibid., p. 111). This interpretation would not have been possible if the researchers had not collected longitudinal data.

4. Evaluations: Over time, as Ali used more language functions, "Ellen provided more evaluative functions, mostly as praise to Ali for his accomplished output" (ibid., p. 111). Conversely, she produced fewer evaluative remarks when Ali wrote less.

5. Appropriating Spoken into Written Forms: In analyzing the journal entries, Nassaji and Cumming (2000) found that "Ali often spontaneously added a third, closing response to the written interactions, forming the triadic structure of 'request for information-answer-acknowledgment' common to classroom and conversational spoken discourse" (p. 112). Ali added a reacting move after Ellen's comment in forty-seven out of the ninety-five journal exchanges, thus making them triadic. This pattern occurred even in the first week of Ali's journal:

Example:
Ali: Today is Manday, May is 8th. The Yestoday is 6th. I lave Mrs.[Ellen] My frand shawN. May 1995. Today +6.

Ellen: Shawn and I love you too, Ali.

Ali: Me too.

The authors say the use of this typically spoken triadic speech structure in Ali's writing may suggest that "Ali was learning new mediational means from a variety of sources around him, such as classroom or conversational discourse" (ibid., p. 113). His English abilities were developing through the process of "extending what is appropriate in one domain to another" (ibid.).

Earlier in this chapter, we cited Duff's (2008) characterization of case studies as being interpretive. The comments from Nassaji and Cumming (2000), as they discussed these five patterns in the qualitative analysis, illustrate the interpretive nature of case studies.

Implications for Understanding the ZPD

Nassaji and Cumming (2000) show how the patterns in Ellen's and Ali's dialog journal exchanges "sustained—in a complementary, dynamic, and evolving manner over nearly a year—conditions for an ESL student's learning English literacy, scaffolded by his teacher" (p. 113). They note that although Ali's spelling, vocabulary, grammar, and penmanship were faulty, they were emerging gradually and Ali and Ellen were able to communicate in the dialog journal exchanges. Writing English in this way "seemed to help Ali perform in his second language, while Ellen demonstrated an ongoing sensitivity to his doing that" (p. 114).

One charge that is sometimes leveled at case studies is that they are data-driven rather than theory-driven, but this is not always the case (Duff, 2008). In fact, one of the strengths of the case study by Nassaji and Cumming is this strong connection to sociocultural theory. Duff (2008) states, "It is up to the researcher to articulate the theoretical framework guiding the study, the relationship between the study and other published research, the chain of reasoning underlying the study, and the theoretical contribution the study makes" (p. 49). Nassaji and Cumming have both conducted their research and reported their findings in such a way that readers new to sociocultural theory can understand the concept of the ZPD through their discussion and the many examples of dialog journal entries that they include.

As a teacher, how do you scaffold learners' language development? Think of three clear instances where you feel you were able to help a learner move ahead in the ZPD. Share them with a colleague or classmate. (If you don't yet have language teaching experience, think of some sort of scaffolding you have done in another context.) The purpose of this task is to help you check your understanding of scaffolding.

PAYOFFS AND PITFALLS

You will recall from Chapter 3 that one threat to validity in experimental research is *mortality*—the loss of subjects from the sample. In case study research, this issue is usually called *attrition* (Duff, 2008). This is one of the biggest pitfalls of conducting a case study on an individual. If you lose access to that person, you can no longer collect data—a problem reminiscent of the familiar warning not to put all your eggs in one basket. This problem has occurred when the family of a child being studied has moved or when new job opportunities have taken adult learners out of the researcher's reach. Sometimes, individuals decide they do not want to be the subjects of an investigation and remove themselves from the study entirely.

Another pitfall, perhaps especially for novice researchers, is that to conduct a longitudinal case study takes time, commitment, and being systematic. Months or years may be needed to track changes and answer particular research questions. Embarking on a longitudinal case study also requires the researcher to be disciplined and dedicated in recording and managing the data. For instance, if you choose to examine the development of English speaking fluency among seven-year-old pupils over the course of a school year, you must observe these children regularly. You will also need to carefully and consistently label and store any audiotapes or field notes documenting the children's interactions for an entire year. Finally, you will also have to do a substantial amount of transcription.

In spite of these pitfalls, there are considerable payoffs in carrying out a well-conducted case study. For example, for novice researchers, working with one subject or one site may be much more manageable than trying to implement "large N" research or to collect data at several sites. Looking closely at one learner or a few learners may allow the researcher to notice and appreciate small changes occurring over time that might not be noticeable in a cross-sectional study of many subjects. Likewise, the varied types of data collection used in case studies, including close and prolonged observation, may reveal important changes that are not captured by language tests and other sorts of measurements used in experimental research.

CONCLUSION

In this chapter, we have reviewed the role of the case study approach as a viable and important research method in applied linguistics, and especially in investigations of first and second language acquisition. We have contrasted the strengths of case studies in the naturalistic inquiry tradition with the relative weakness and low status of the one-shot case study in experimental research. We also discussed quality control issues and the value of case studies in our field, and we summarized some classroom-based case studies. In general, we find the case study approach to be extremely valuable, provided the data are collected and analyzed with sufficient care. We believe the case study by Nassaji and Cumming illustrates this sort of careful investigation. The following questions and tasks are intended to help you review and solidify the concepts presented here.

QUESTIONS AND TASKS

1. In Chapter 2, we talked about the importance of posing research questions and choosing appropriate means to answer them. Write three to five research questions that could be addressed using case studies. Think of the kinds of cases that would be appropriate to investigate these research questions. Share you list with your classmates or colleagues.

2. Does the following discussion (Stake, 1988) revolve around the issue of internal reliability, external reliability, internal validity, or external validity? How convincing do you find the arguments made?

> Many people criticize case study research because there is too little indication of the degree to which the case is representative of other cases. Usually it is left to the reader to decide. Of course it is easy to argue that a sample of 'size one' is never typical of anything, except itself.
>
> For some research purposes, it will be essential that the 'case examined' be representative of some population of cases. Presumably, the case could be so unique that it might be unwise to consider any finding as true of other cases. However, . . . the unique case helps us to understand the more typical cases. Whether or not a case should be representative of other cases depends on the purpose of the research. It would be presumptuous to dismiss all findings as invalid because the case was not demonstratively representative. Some findings—for the purposes some readers have—do not depend on generalizing to a population of cases.
>
> A case study is valid to the reader to whom it gives an accurate and useful representation of the bounded system. Accuracy of observing and reporting is not a matter of everyone seeing and reporting the same thing. Observers have different vantage points. . . . Readers have different uses for research reports. One

reader expects an exact facsimile of the 'real thing'. Another reader is attending to a new type of problem that had not previously been apparent. The validity of the report is different for each, according to the meaning the reader gives to it. (p. 261)

3. Can you think of any studies in which generalizability might be unimportant? Under what circumstances would you find particularity and transferability to be sufficient criteria for quality control?

4. Look back at the description of Lupita. Try to find some examples of Lupita scaffolding other children's learning or performance of tasks.

5. If you could look at all the dialog journal entries between Ali and Ellen, what would you want to look for? What do you think you would find?

6. In our summary of Nassaji and Cumming's (2000) study of dialog journal exchanges, we have reported the percentages from the function coding in a prose paragraph. The original authors used a bar graph to report these findings. Using the data provided above about the quantitative results, draw a bar graph comparing the functions that appeared Ali's and in Ellen's dialog journal entries. What are the advantages and disadvantages of reporting these data in a graph or in a paragraph?

7. We have included five excerpts from Ali's and Ellen's dialog journal exchanges in this chapter. In each excerpt, Ali provided the date. If you arrange these excerpts in chronological order, can you find any evidence of Ali's developing English language proficiency? What data would you consider to be evidence of such development?

8. Which characteristics of case studies are apparent in our brief summary of the study by Nassaji and Cumming (2000)?

9. Read one of the case studies cited in this chapter or in the suggestions for further reading below. Then see which of the following advantages discussed by Adelman et al. (1976) are present in the study you chose. For example, in describing Donato and Adair-Hauck's (1992) study of two secondary school French teachers' lessons, we said that teachers can relate to the choices Elizabeth and Claire made about teaching the future tense—an example of *A* below.

A. Case studies are 'strong in reality,' and, therefore, likely to appeal to classroom teachers who will be able to identify with the issues and concerns raised.

B. One can generalize from a case, from an instance, to a class.

C. Case studies can represent a multiplicity of viewpoints and can offer support to alternative interpretations.

D. Case studies can also provide a database of materials that may be reinterpreted by future researchers.

E. Insights yielded by case studies can be put to immediate use for a variety of purposes, including staff development, within-institution feedback, formative evaluation, and educational policy making.

F. Case study data are usually more accessible than conventional research reports and, therefore, capable of serving multiple audiences.

10. Look at three of four published case studies from our field. Would you characterize them as data-driven or theory-driven? For those you consider to be theory-driven, what theory or theories do they address? Which of the six principle advantages identified by Adelman et al. (1976) apply to these case studies?

SUGGESTIONS FOR FURTHER READING

We recommend Duff's (2008) book *Case Study Research in Applied Linguistics* as well as van Lier's (2005) chapter on case studies.

An early collection of second language acquisition case studies can be found in the volume edited by Hatch (1978). The chapters are not technically classroom research studies, but they are interesting to teachers and researchers nevertheless. We also recommend all the case studies cited in this chapter.

Recently, case studies have been done about teachers or teachers-in-training. For good examples, see K. E. Johnson's (1996) study of a student teacher completing her ESL practicum and Tsui's (2003) case study of four teachers in Hong Kong.

7

Ethnography

Stories told well and compellingly can have an unparalleled power to create and make a difference to the world. And that is what our job is, to make a difference. (Christiane Amanpour, 2005, CNN Commentary).

INTRODUCTION AND OVERVIEW

Ethnography is a very important research method in the naturalistic inquiry tradition. It is considered a form of qualitative research; however, not all qualitative research is ethnography. In Grotjahn's (1987) terms, ethnography represents the second of the 'pure' forms of research in that (1) the data are collected nonexperimentally, (2) the data themselves are usually qualitative in nature, and (3) they are typically subjected to interpretive analysis. (See Chapter 1 above.) In other words, in terms of Grotjahn's framework, ethnography contrasts with experimental research on all three points.

Ethnography is "the study of a people's behavior in naturally occurring, ongoing settings, with a focus on the cultural interpretation of behavior" (Watson-Gegeo, 1988, p. 576). Its goal is to provide "a description and an interpretive explanatory account of what people do in a setting (such as a classroom, neighborhood or community), the outcome of their interactions, and the way they understand what they are doing" (ibid.).

Ethnography is a particularly valuable research method, but the term also refers to the results of such research. Watson-Gegeo (1988) explains that "as *product*, ethnography is a detailed description and analysis of a social setting and the interaction that goes on within it" (p. 582). In addition,

as *method*, ethnography includes the techniques of observation, participant observation, . . . informal and formal interviewing of the participants observed in situations, audio- or videotaping of interactions for close analysis, collection of relevant or available documents and other materials from the setting, and other techniques as required to answer researcher questions posed by a given study. (p. 583)

In this chapter, we will first summarize the background and some key characteristics of ethnography. Then we will consider four principles of ethnography and the typical stages of an ethnographic study. Next, we will focus on the role of the researcher within the research process, including participant and nonparticipant observation, and developing emic and etic perspectives. We will then grapple with several thorny issues related to quality control in ethnography, first by examining ethnography in terms of the traditional criteria of reliability and validity. However, we will see that ethnography can be more appropriately evaluated by its own criteria.

As you read this chapter, keep in mind our metaphor about research cultures. If your main background in research is the experimental method, you will find that ethnography has a very different culture. Its values, goals, norms, and vocabulary are not the same as those of the experimental method in the psychometric approach.

REFLECTION

Based on your earlier readings, both in this book and elsewhere, what do you already know about ethnography? If you see a book or article whose title begins, "An Ethnography of . . . ," what do you expect to read about the topic?

Background to Ethnography

Like many other research methods, ethnography entered applied linguistics from another field, in this instance, *anthropology*. In fact, anthropology is one of the parent disciplines of linguistics, and many eminent early linguists were trained as anthropologists.

Anthropology is the study of cultures and societies. Anthropologists typically spend long periods of time living and working among the people they are studying. Originally, this immersion was among little known and so-called 'primitive' groups, such as the indigenous peoples of New Guinea, Africa, and North and South America.

However, researchers came to see that they could apply anthropological research techniques to the investigation of groups and subgroups within their own cultures. For example, in a classic study carried out in the 1930s, Whyte (1981) portrayed the street corner societies of the urban poor. Smith and Geoffrey (1968) conducted a yearlong study of a secondary school classroom in the United States using ethnographic procedures. In the field of applied linguistics, Heath

(1983) spent almost ten years documenting the lives and patterns of interaction among people in two rural communities in the southern United States.

Because it stems from anthropology, ethnography is understandably different—in both philosophy and practice—from research based on the scientific method. In fact, ethnography contrasts markedly with experiments in its assumptions, procedures, and attitudes toward evidence. In principle, there is no reason why a research program should not combine experimental and ethnographic procedures, and, in fact, there are increasing calls for 'hybrid' research. However, a tension between ethnography and the experimental method persists. This tension reflects the fact that the two traditions are underpinned by different beliefs about what counts as evidence, how that evidence should be interpreted, and what the role of the researcher is within the research process. In short, these two research cultures reflect two different ways of looking at the world.

This tension is apparent in the following quote from Heath (1983), who wrote a classic ethnographic account of the role that language plays in the educational process. In the introduction to her book, she writes,

> Educators should not look here for experiments, controlled conditions, and systematic score-keeping on the academic gains and losses of specific children. Nor should psycholinguists look here for data taped at periodic intervals under similar conditions over a predesignated period of time. What this book does do is record the natural flow of community and classroom life over nearly a decade. The descriptions here [are] of the actual processes, activities, and attitudes involved in the enculturation of children. (pp. 7–8)

Heath's stance is one that appeals to many applied linguists, including language classroom researchers. The growing interest in finding alternatives to formal experiments has been fuelled by skepticism on the part of some leading researchers over the ability of controlled experiments to "produce the definitive answers that some researchers expect" (Ellis, 1990a, p. 67). As a result, in the past three decades, more researchers have turned to the naturalistic inquiry tradition—ethnography in particular—in order to understand language use, as well as the practices and beliefs of people involved in language teaching and language learning.

Language classroom ethnographies include van Lier's (1996a) report of a bilingual (Quechua and Spanish) program in Peru; Duff's (1995; 1996) research on dual-language secondary school programs in Hungary; Harklau's (1994) three-and-a-half-year study of Chinese immigrant children in California; Canagarajah's (1993) account of university EFL students in Sri Lanka; Cleghorn and Genesee's (1984) report of a French immersion project in Canada; Shaw's (1996; 1997) investigation of graduate-level, content-based language instruction in the United States; Lin's (1999) comparison of four English classrooms in Hong Kong whose students came from different socioeconomic environments; and Crago's (1992) contrast of Inuit family communication styles and school communication patterns in Northern Quebec. Two early collections of articles based on ethnography were edited by Green and Wallat (1981) and Trueba, Guthrie, and Au (1981).

Characteristics of Ethnography

Ethnographies fall in the naturalistic inquiry tradition, but they differ from other forms of qualitative research in three main ways: they are longitudinal, they are comprehensive, and they view people's behaviors in cultural terms.

REFLECTION

If you have already read an ethnography, were these three characteristics evident in that study? Try to provide an example of each way from your reading.

In order for ethnographers to capture a society in all of its complexity, ethnography must of necessity be long-term. In ethnography, data are collected through "intensive detailed observation over a long period of time" (Watson-Gegeo, 1988, p. 583). As noted above, Heath spent nearly ten years conducting her research, and Canagarajah's research on his own EFL students in Sri Lanka took a full year. Duff, the author of the sample study we summarize at the end of this chapter, made several different extended trips to Hungary to collect her data, and she also lived there for a period of time.

Secondly, the aim of ethnography is to provide a descriptive and interpretive account of all aspects of the society, from language and communication to kinship patterns, from mating rituals to festivals. This type of research is by definition comprehensive because everything that is observed has to be accounted for.

Third, the rules and norms of interaction are described in cultural terms. Cultures are characterized by (often largely implicit) rules and norms of interaction. Ethnographers try to identify these rules and norms, describe them, and use them to calibrate the behavior they are describing. For example, when we were younger, there was an implicit rule that when a second-generation elder (e.g., a grandparent) was present in a social situation children "didn't speak until they were spoken to." This rule was never spelled out, but an ethnographer could have identified this particular aspect of behavior and described it. The ethnographer could probably also explain why the cultural rule evolved and describe its effect on the discourse and the interactional behavior of the group.

TABLE 7.1 A comparison of case studies and ethnographies

Characteristic	Case Studies	Ethnographies
Person(s) studied	One or a few individuals	Groups of people
Main goal of research	To document and describe in detail one case (or a few cases) that may (or may not) be representative of a larger class of cases	To document and describe in detail the behaviors, speech patterns, and cultural values of a group
Focus of the study	Specific focus on the bounded case	Broad focus on a group as a whole
Duration of study	Can be lengthy (e.g., in a case study of language acquisition) or brief (e.g., where an interaction alone is the case)	Longitudinal by definition—often lasting for years of intense immersion in the culture
Types of data collected	Often qualitative (audio or video recordings, observational notes, interview data); sometimes quantitative	Often qualitative (observational field notes, interview data, documents, life histories); sometimes quantitative
Types of data analysis	Often qualitative; also quantitative	Often qualitative; sometimes quantitative

It is these three dimensions that distinguish ethnographies from other forms of naturalistic inquiry, particularly case studies. While it is typical to have longitudinal case studies, it is not so common to find case studies that extend over many years. Case study researchers also deal with one or a few cases rather than with culturally defined groups. They are usually selective in what they want to document. They do not attempt to describe all aspects of behavior comprehensively. Finally, they rarely attempt to frame their accounts in cultural terms. However, case studies are sometimes embedded in ethnographies to illustrate and vivify aspects of observed behavior. **Table 7.1** contrasts case studies and ethnographies.

PRINCIPLES OF ETHNOGRAPHY

There are certain principles that guide ethnographic research, whether it is carried out by anthropologists documenting little-known cultures or by applied linguists trying to understand the very familiar culture of language classrooms. Watson-Gegeo (1988) has discussed four key principles of ethnographic research. These four key principles can apply to classroom ethnographies as well as to wider ranging studies.

Focus on Cultural Patterns in Groups

First, "ethnography focuses on people's behavior in groups and on cultural patterns in that behavior" (Watson-Gegeo, 1988, p. 577). An example is Cleghorn and Genesee's (1984) report on a French immersion program in Canada. One of the findings was that

> interaction among the staff was conflictual and that the underlying tension could be related to societally based group conflict. . . . [T]he teachers used two main interaction strategies to minimize interpersonal conflict and to maintain a semblance of professional harmony: (1) avoidance of social interaction and (2) the predominant use of English in cross-group communication. (p. 595)

In other words, although a goal of the French immersion program was to promote bilingualism and intergroup communication, the teachers themselves frequently did not communicate across groups, and when they did, the code was usually English.

Ethnography is Holistic

The second principle is that "ethnography is holistic; that is, any aspect of a culture or behavior has to be described and explained in relation to the whole system of which it is a part" (Watson-Gegeo, 1988, p. 577). Duff's comment about the Cleghorn and Genesee (1984) ethnography of the immersion program in Canada illustrates this principle. In summarizing their interpretation, Duff (1995)—herself a Canadian—says that their study

> focused on interactions among anglophone and francophone teachers in a Montreal school with both early French-immersion and regular English-stream programs at a time of rather acute provincial political/linguistic tensions and misgivings. Participant observation revealed that, ironically—and indeed contrary to the publicized objective of immersion to foster harmony, understanding and bilingualism across Canada's largest linguistic communities—the teachers from the two ethnolinguistic groups avoided contact with one another, resented each other's presence and resorted to English, the dominant language of the country but not of that province, in cross-group discussions. (pp. 507–508)

Thus, the findings were couched in the context of the much broader political and linguistic issues affecting the whole country at the time.

Theoretical Frameworks as Starting Points

Third, "ethnographic data collection begins with a theoretical framework directing the researcher's attention to certain aspects of a situation or certain research questions" (Watson-Gegeo, 1988, p. 578). For instance, Canagarajah's (1993) study of his students' motivation for studying English in postcolonial Sri Lanka utilized Giroux's (1983) theory about pedagogies of resistance and the ideological properties of social institutions to help investigate and explain the ambiguities of his students' (sometimes conflicting) attitudes toward learning English.

Ethnography is Comparative

Fourth, "ethnographic research is comparative" (Watson-Gegeo, 1988, p. 581). That is, it allows for comparisons across cultures and across settings. An apt example of this principle is found in Watson-Gegeo's own work. Based on her research in Hawaii, she wrote the following:

> First-grade Hawaiian children's reading scores on nationally normed tests improved dramatically after the introduction of reading lessons based on "talk-story" speech events in the Hawaiian community. A key characteristic of talk story is co-narration, the joint presentation of personal experiences, information, and interpretations of events by two or more storytellers.

When Watson-Gegeo later studied rural communities in the Solomon Islands, she was hoping to find an analog in that culture that could be used in elementary schools there because there was a very high failure rate of children in English immersion classrooms. She wrote,

> As an ethnographer, my expectation had not been that I would find an exact equivalent to talk story (part of a Hawaiian emic framework) in the Solomons but rather that I might discover a corresponding speech event that, like talk story, could be adapted for classroom use. It now appears that a Solomon Islands speech event called "shaping the mind" may be the right candidate. As a speech event, shaping the mind involves the intensive teaching of language, proper behavior, forms of reasoning and cultural knowledge in special sessions characterized by a serious tone, a formal register of speech, and tightly argued discussion. (p. 582)

Clearly "shaping the mind is based on an emic teaching framework different from both Hawaiian talk story and from American/Western models of education" (pp. 581–582). It is Watson-Gegeo's comparison of the two teaching speaking events and their potential as teaching strategies that illustrate the comparative principle.

STAGES OF THE RESEARCH PROCESS

Three stages of ethnography have been described by Watson-Gegeo (1988). In the *comprehensive stage*, the researcher studies "all theoretically salient aspects of a setting" (p. 584) by conducting broad observations, interviewing members of the culture, taking a census, and so on. Next is the *topic-oriented stage*, which involves clarifying and narrowing the topic. This stage generates focused research

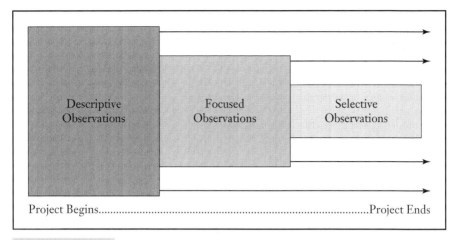

Project Begins...Project Ends

FIGURE 7.1 Changes in the scope of observation in ethnographic research (adapted from Spradley, 1980, p. 34)

questions. Finally, the *hypothesis-oriented stage* entails testing hypotheses and answering research questions. Further focused observations and in-depth interviews occur at this stage, and some quantification may be used.

The emergent nature of ethnographic research affects the type of observational focus ethnographers use. Spradley (1980) has discussed how the focus of the researcher's observations changes during the various stages of ethnographic research:

> Participant observation begins with wide-focused *descriptive observations*. Although these continue until the end of the field project . . . , the emphasis shifts first to *focused observations* and later to *selective observations*. (p. 34)

Figure 7.1 depicts the stages of observations Spradley describes.

These stages are well documented in an ethnographic study by Shaw (1983), who investigated the communication patterns in engineering classes at a university in California. He did so, first, by actually enrolling in one course for an entire semester. This choice allowed him to be a participant observer in that course. In addition, Shaw also regularly observed seventeen other engineering courses in which he was a nonparticipant observer.

Shaw identified several stages in his study. He began by establishing the conditions and limitations of the study and choosing the research sites (in this case, the engineering courses). During this phase, he conducted a pilot study and then started his longitudinal data collection. Next, he selected a particular engineering class to tape-record and began interviewing professors. After that, a general picture emerged as Shaw observed and began to transcribe his audiotapes. Thereafter, hypotheses were generated by reviewing the transcribed engineering lessons. Then the transcripts were completed, reviewed and analyzed, and the data were compared to the hypotheses that had been generated. Finally, a model of engineering discourse emerged. (See Chaudron [1988, p. 48] for the reproduction of a helpful table from Shaw's doctoral dissertation, which summarizes this sequence in more detail.)

If you think back to the earlier chapters of this book, you will see that the order of stages in ethnography is very different from the way experiments are planned and carried out. In formal experiments, the researchers first review the literature and pose research questions and/or testable (i.e., falsifiable) hypotheses. Experimental researchers attempt to identify all the relevant variables in advance so that they can control and manipulate those variables in order to determine what causes certain observed effects. The data collection and analyses are clearly and carefully planned in advance in order to test the hypotheses with optimal internal validity.

However, ethnographers often take what's called *grounded theory* as their orientation. Grounded theory is "the practice of deriving theory from data rather than the other way around" (Nunan, 1992, p. 57). Grounded theories are those "based in and derived from data and arrived at through a systematic process of induction" (Watson-Gegeo, 1988, p. 583). This sequence leads to the hypothesis posing happening later in an ethnographic study than it does in an experimental study, as illustrated by Shaw's (1983) research. Richards (2003) reminds us, however, that "while the [grounded theory] tradition does insist that the research process works from data to theory, rather than vice versa, it also insists that the aim of the process is to generate a theory" (p. 16). He adds that "this process is open to every researcher and not limited to a tiny group of influential thinkers who develop 'grand' theory" (ibid.).

REFLECTION

Do you have a personal preference? Would you rather pose a hypothesis first and then collect the data against which to test it? Or would you prefer to start with a more general idea and let the specific hypothesis emerge from the data?

ETHNOGRAPHERS' ROLES

Ethnographers can take a variety of roles within the given research context. Originally, anthropologists were outsiders who went into a culture to study it. They were clearly not members of the culture. As a result, two of their challenges were to gain the trust of the members of that culture and to learn how to participate in that society so that they could collect valid and reliable data. As they gained entry into the field, anthropologists conducted observations along a continuum of involvement. They were often engaged in the activities of the group they were studying as *participant observers.* In other instances, they would observe but not be actively engaged, in which case they were functioning as *nonparticipant observers.*

Later, when ethnographers began to study social groups that were more accessible, there were situations where researchers investigated groups of which they were already a part. In these cases, there was no need to gain entry into the field or to gain the trust of the members of an exotic culture: Under these circumstances, the ethnographer was already a member of the culture and could therefore readily function as a participant observer.

REFLECTION

What do you think would be the advantages and disadvantages of conducting an ethnography of a group of which you were a member? Try to imagine yourself collecting data on a sports team, a teaching staff, a community network, a religious organization, or any other kind of club or organization (official or unofficial) to which you may belong.

Participant and Nonparticipant Observation

Participant observation, one of the hallmarks of ethnography, is defined as "observing while interacting with those under study" (Watson-Gegeo, 1988, p. 583). The following statement by Fox (2004) captures the essence of the approach and illustrates the delicate balancing act that an ethnographer must manage between objectivity and subjectivity, as well as the tensions, dilemmas, and contradictions that result:

> Anthropologists are trained to use a research method known as "participant observation," which essentially means participating in the life and culture of the people one is studying to gain a true insider's perspective on their customs and behavior, while simultaneously observing them as a detached, objective scientist. Well, that's the theory. In practice it often feels like that children's game where you try to pat your head and rub your tummy at the same time. It is perhaps not surprising that anthropologists are notorious for their frequent bouts of 'field-blindness'—becoming so involved and enmeshed in the native culture that they fail to maintain the necessary scientific detachment. (p. 4)

As Richards (2003) notes, "Adopting this perspective enables the researcher to move from outsider to insider status" (p. 14). However, he adds that it is not the ethnographer's goal "to become a complete insider, because this would mean taking for granted the sorts of beliefs, attitudes, and routines that the researcher needs to remain detached from in order to observe and describe" (pp. 14–15).

What Fox (2004) calls "field-blindness" is also referred to as "going native." It can be a problem even for researchers working in familiar cultures, and even when they are in the role of nonparticipant observers. For example, Bailey

(1982; 1984) did an observational study of international teaching assistants (TAs), who were non-native speakers of English, teaching in an English-medium university in California. The research question was, "What are the classroom communication problems of non-native speaking teaching assistants?" The question had been spurred by numerous complaints from American undergraduate students who claimed their TAs did not speak English well enough to be teaching at the university. After conducting a ten-week pilot study, Bailey observed twenty-four physics and mathematics classes (taught by both native and non-native teaching assistants) three times each over the course of a ten-week term. As the term was drawing to a close, she began to relate more and more to the non-native speaking TAs and to feel that the American undergraduate students in those TAs' classes were largely unsophisticated, xenophobic, spoiled children who were not taking responsibility for their own educations. She had to remind herself regularly that her purpose was to gather data and to understand the viewpoints of both the students and the TAs in addressing the research question.

REFLECTION

If you were a researcher trying to collect data and you found yourself identifying too strongly with a subset of your research population, what steps could you take to overcome this problem in your data collection phase? What could you do in the data analysis phase?

Another interesting issue has to do with the covertness or overtness of data collection. That is, when the ethnographer is already a member of the culture under investigation, it is not necessarily obvious to others that he or she is conducting research. In this context, data are sometimes collected covertly as a way of overcoming the *observer's paradox* (Labov, 1972). This is the interesting problem that by observing, we may change the very thing we wished to observe in its natural occurrence. (In Chapter 4, we saw two parallel problems in experimental research—the reactive effects of testing and the reactive effects of experimental arrangements.) The observer's paradox is likely to be triggered if the ethnographer is an outsider to the culture. Over time, an ethnographer may gain some degree of acceptance as people get used to his or her presence. You will recall that Heath (1983) spent nearly ten years in the community she studied, visiting families, engaging in chores, going to church services, and attending community events. This long-term, diverse involvement helped her overcome the observer's paradox.

Figure 7.2 shows that there are different possible stances to take on the continuum of overt-versus-covert data collection as well as participant versus nonparticipant observation. The stance chosen depends on the ethnographer's purpose in studying a culture and how sensitive the behavior is that he or she is observing.

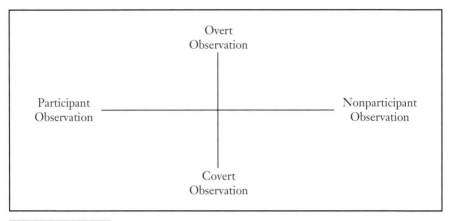

FIGURE 7.2   Overtness and participation in conducting observations (adapted from Bailey, Curtis, and Nunan, 2001, p. 161)

REFLECTION

Imagine a research situation for each of the four quadrants in Figure 7.2. When would it be appropriate to conduct covert observations? How to you feel about the ethics of observing people when they are unaware that data collection is going on?

Developing and Documenting Emic and Etic Perspectives

Ethnographers' deep and long-term involvement in the culture under study allows them to develop two main perspectives on the behavior they document, called the "emic" and the "etic" perspectives. These terms are borrowed from the distinction between phonemic and phonetic characteristics of speech sounds developed by Pike (1964). The contrast is explained by Watson-Gegeo (1988) as follows. In using an *emic perspective*, the ethnographer discovers the "culturally specific frameworks used by the members of a society/culture for interpreting and assigning meaning to experiences" (p. 579). The emic perspective captures the culture members' point of view. Emic analyses incorporate the participants' perspectives and interpretations in the descriptive language they themselves use.

In developing an *etic perspective*, on the other hand, the "researcher's ontological or interpretive (external) framework" (Watson-Gegeo, 1988, p. 579) comes into play. This is the outsider's perspective, and it can be informed by academic theories. We do not mean to suggest that an emic view is right and an etic view is wrong, or vice versa. They are simply two points of view that may differ and should both be documented.

Sometimes the emic view and the etic view are parallel, but at other times they contrast. As an example, you will recall that Bailey was a nonparticipant observer in the Russian teaching methods experiment that served as the sample study in Chapter 4. One of the teachers in that research had a very consistent pattern of treating the learners' oral errors immediately and explicitly. As a teacher, teacher educator, and language learner, Bailey felt that the teacher's approach to error treatment was somewhat heavy-handed. But, as a classroom observer collecting research data, she had to document her own personal reaction simply as an opinion and then set it aside in her mind while she observed the classes. Most of the young military students clearly had a different attitude toward this teacher. They often responded gratefully and enthusiastically to the teacher's correcting moves. In fact, one day after class, a student told Bailey that he really appreciated the way the teacher corrected their errors because it helped him and his classmates prepare for an important accuracy-oriented test they would be facing soon.

This anecdote illustrates the importance of the researcher being aware of and documenting differences between the emic perspective and the etic perspective. Doing ethnography requires that researchers actively seek out and understand the participants' explanations of the world. As van Lier (1990a) notes,

> Working with both emic and etic categories, the ethnographer continually walks a fine line between naïve observation and externally imposed interpretation. However, this is perfectly acceptable, so long as the researcher remains aware of and committed to the requirement to analyze all observations and scrutinize all interpretations and inferences rigorously. (p.43)

The connection between the longitudinal nature of ethnography and developing the emic perspective is that gaining entry into the field, developing the trust of the participants, and documenting their point of view often takes a tremendous amount of time (Richards, 2003).

QUALITY CONTROL IN ETHNOGRAPHY

Ethnography is no less rigorous in its quality control procedures than other kinds of research, but the criteria for quality may differ somewhat. For heuristic purposes, we will first consider quality control in ethnography through the traditional psychometric criteria of reliability and validity. We will then turn to more appropriate criteria for writing and judging ethnographies. This discussion necessarily leads us to a reconsideration of causality as a motivating concern in conducting research.

As with case studies, major questions have been raised over the reliability and validity of ethnographic research. Most of these criticisms stem, either explicitly or implicitly, from the fact that ethnographies involve the detailed, longitudinal investigation of a particular situation or context. In contrast to the control over variables exerted by experimental researchers, ethnographers try *not* to alter the naturally occurring contexts they study. Also, historically, the qualitative collection and analyses of data have been paramount in ethnographies.

As a result, the usual criticisms about reliability and validity of all sorts of qualitative data collection and analysis procedures are often raised about ethnographic research.

REFLECTION

List other criticisms that you think might be leveled against ethnographic research in terms of reliability and validity. How might an ethnographer respond to these criticisms?

Challenges Specific to Ethnography

Challenges to the reliability and validity of ethnographic research include the quantity of data involved, the descriptive nature of the research, the uniqueness of much ethnographic research, and the role of the researcher. We will address each of these points in turn.

Ethnographies produce huge quantities of data. For example, a relatively focused study into the lifelong learning experiences of sixty learners of English as a second language yielded many hundreds of pages of interview data transcripts (Benson and Nunan, 2005). For practical reasons, it is only possible to include a small quantity of the original data in any published account of the research, even in a booklength manuscript. This constraint makes it impossible for outsiders to either reanalyze the data themselves or to replicate the study.

Because ethnographies involve the detailed description and interpretations of the behavior of particular people in specific contexts, each ethnography is, in a sense, unique. Ethnographers are careful about selecting the sites and the groups for their research, but they would seldom, if ever, be concerned about randomization. For many ethnographers, these facts render irrelevant the issue of external validity (i.e., there is no attempt to generalize the results of the study to a broader population).

ACTION

Turn back to Table 5.2, which refers to sampling strategies. Which of the strategies listed there do you think ethnographers might use to identify their observation sites and the people they wish to study?

One key feature of ethnographies and, indeed, of much naturalistic research, is the presence of the researcher as an active participant in the research site. Because the researcher is interacting with his or her informants over a prolonged period of time, he or she will establish a relationship with the informants that will be unique and, therefore, nonreplicable by another researcher. Likewise, as we saw in Chapter 6 with regard to case studies, there is often a worry about subjectivity in situations where researchers have close relationships with people involved in the study.

The active involvement of the ethnographer with the research site and his or her possible influence on the behavior of the informants in the study is captured by Heath (1983) in the following vignette. It also shows how careful she was to minimize her impact on the community she was studying.

> I spent many hours cooking, chopping wood, gardening, sewing and minding children by the rules of the community. For example, in the early years of interaction in the communities, audio and video recordings were unfamiliar to community residents; therefore I did no taping of any kind then. By the mid-1970s, cassette players were becoming popular gifts and community members used them to record music, church services, and sometimes special performances in the community. When such recordings became a common community-initiated practice, I audiotaped, but only in accordance with community practices. Often I was able to write in a field notebook while minding children, tending food, or watching television with families; otherwise, I wrote fieldnotes as soon as possible afterwards when I left the community on an errand or to go to school. In the classrooms, I often audiotaped; we sometimes videotaped; and both the teachers and I took fieldnotes as a matter of course on many days of each year. (pp. 8–9)

This purposeful, prolonged involvement with the participants is a very different stance from the intentionally detached objectivity of experimental researchers.

Concerns about Traditional Reliability in Ethnographic Research

Reliability in the experimental sense has to do with the consistency of measurement. There are parallel concerns about consistency in ethnographic research as well. In Chapter 3, we distinguished between internal reliability and external reliability (replicability). That distinction will guide this discussion as well.

A detailed and considered analysis of problems associated with the traditional notions of reliability and validity in ethnographic research was provided in an influential paper by LeCompte and Goetz (1982). Although they use the term *ethnography* rather loosely to cover a range of qualitative methods, their analysis is helpful and we will summarize it here.

LeCompte and Goetz define external reliability in terms of replication. They point out that at first sight, ethnography may seem beyond replication in comparison with laboratory experiments. Given the naturalistic setting, the fact that the researcher may be attempting to record processes of change over time, and the possible uniqueness of the situation and setting, the use of standardized controls may be impossible. In reporting the research, constraints of time and space may preclude the presentation of data in a way that would enable other researchers to reanalyze those same data and come to similar conclusions.

LeCompte and Goetz's study finds that replicability can be enhanced if researchers are explicit about five key aspects of the research (as cited in Nunan, 1992). They should provide details on the following: (1) the status of the researcher(s) within the research site; (2) who the informants are and how they were selected; (3) the social situations and conditions in place when the research was carried out; (4) the analytic constructs and premises underlying the research, and (5) the methods of data collection and analysis. Let us examine these five points in more detail.

First, attending to their own status in the research context requires researchers to be explicit about the social position they hold within the group being investigated. LeCompte and Goetz (1982) say that no ethnographer can exactly replicate the findings of another because even if an exactly parallel context could be found, the second researcher would be unlikely to hold the same status in the second social situation.

A related problem is finding parallel informants in the second research context. This issue emerges as a major concern when we consider that the knowledge to be gathered will be largely shaped by those who provide it. It is therefore imperative for researchers to describe their informants very carefully and to explain the criteria they used in selecting particular informants for interviews, detailed observation, embedded case studies, and so on.

Third, the social situation and conditions in which the data are obtained also need to be described explicitly. These contextual issues include both the physical conditions and the economic and sociopolitical conditions that affect the group being studied. Having access to this information is central to the readers' ability to understand and the context and to evaluate the ethnography appropriately.

Fourth, precise definitions of constructs and premises are also crucial. As LeCompte and Goetz (1982) note,

Even if a researcher reconstructs the relationships and duplicates the informants and social contexts of a prior study, replication may remain impossible if the constructs, definitions, or units of analysis which informed the original research are idiosyncratic or poorly delineated. Replication requires explicit identification of the assumptions and meta-theories that underlie choice of terminology and methods of analysis. (p. 39)

Ethnographers may define the constructs themselves and/or cite definitions found in relevant literature. They may also define constructs in terms of the emic uses of the participants in the study. The key point is to be explicit and precise.

Finally, the methods of data collection and analysis must be clearly explained—as much for the credibility of the results as for concerns about reliability. For example, readers should be told if field notes were made during or after the events that were observed. If the notes were made afterwards, how much time had elapsed between the event and recording the notes? How often were the field notes written? Such questions will affect readers' confidence in the data.

Internal reliability (often just called *reliability*) is a tricky concept in ethnography and other types of qualitative research. In quantitative psychometric research, it refers to the consistency with which constructs are measured. In experiments, internal consistency has to do with the certainty with which the results can be attributed to the treatment. But in ethnography it has more to do with how well things are described. We will consider four issues related to internal reliability in ethnography: (1) using low-inference descriptors, (2) involving more than one researcher or collaborator, (3) utilizing peer examination or cross-site corroboration, and (4) recording data mechanically.

A *low-inference descriptor* describes behavior that can be readily identified by an independent observer. For example, *wait time* (the length of time that a teacher pauses after asking a question) is a low-inference descriptor because it can be verified; that is, it can be independently observed and quantified. A *high-inference descriptor*, on the other hand, requires the observer to make inferences about what is going on. Comments such as "student lacks interest in activity," or "students were on task during the activity" are examples of high-inference descriptors. While it might be tempting to document only low-inference descriptors in order to increase reliability, the most interesting phenomena in classrooms are likely to be highly inferential in nature.

R. L. Allwright (1980) has described high-inference descriptors as "only a very weak representation of some underlying criteria that cannot yet be satisfactorily described" (p. 169). He adds that "the main defense of the use of such high-inference categories must be that, if they are tolerably workable, they capture things that are interesting; whereas low-inference categories, though easy to use and talk about, are liable to capture only uninteresting trivia" (ibid.).

REFLECTION

In all forms of naturalistic research—ethnographies included—one very effective means of guarding against threats to internal reliability is to use more than one researcher. (See the discussion of *triangulation* below.) However, for long-term studies, this approach can be extremely expensive. One way of getting around this problem is to enlist the aid of local informants to validate the interpretations of the ethnographer. For example, Canagarajah (1983) conducted a yearlong ethnographic study in Sri Lanka of students' motivation for studying

English in college. He was the teacher in that context. As such, he involved his students by soliciting their written impressions of English in the first week of class, administering a questionnaire about the students' social and linguistic backgrounds, and conducting oral interviews in Tamil, the students' home language. He also made field notes about the course as a participant observer. Canagarajah (1993) wrote the following about his own role as a teacher researcher:

> My daily interaction with the students in negotiating meanings through English and participating in the students' successes and failures, with the attendant need to revise my own teaching strategy, provided a vantage point to their perspectives. Moreover, I enjoyed natural access to the daily exercises and notes of the students and the record of their attendance without having to foreground my role as researcher. As the teaching progressed, I stumbled into other naturalistic data that provided insights into students' own point of view of the course, such as the comments students had scribbled during class time in the margins of the textbook (which, due to frequent losses, was distributed before each class and collected at the end). (p. 606).

REFLECTION

What do you think would be the advantages and disadvantages of conducting a classroom ethnography as a teacher researching your own class, program, or school?

According to van Lier (1990a), "scientists in all walks of life need to conform to certain standards by which the peer group evaluates them. This is no different in ethnographic research" (p. 44). Peer examination involves the corroboration by other researchers who have had experience in similar settings. LeCompte and Goetz (1982) say this corroboration can proceed in three ways. First, the researchers may utilize outcomes and findings from other field workers in their report. Secondly, findings from studies carried out concurrently may be integrated into the report. (This step provides a form of cross-validation.) Third, if sufficient primary data are included in the published report, these data may be reanalyzed by other researchers.

The final strategy that researchers can use to increase internal reliability is to have available mechanically recorded data in the form of audio- and or video-recordings. The strategy allows others to analyze the primary database for the research. Electronically recorded data also allow researchers to check and augment their field notes. (The corollary is equally important: Having good field notes helps readers to interpret and contextualize their electronically recorded data.)

While these four strategies are valuable ways of increasing the internal reliability of a study, they may not all be practical for someone who has limited

TABLE 7.2	Guarding against threats to the reliability of ethnographic research (adapted from Nunan [1992], following LeCompte and Goetz [1982])
Type	**Questions**
External Reliability (Replicability)	Is the status of the researcher made explicit?
	Does the researcher provide a detailed description of the subjects?
	Does the researcher provide a detailed description of the context and conditions under which the research was carried out?
	Are constructs and premises explicitly defined?
	Are data collection and analysis methods presented in detail?
Internal Reliability	Does the research utilize low-inference descriptors?
	Does it involve more than one researcher/collaborator?
	Does the researcher invite peer examination or cross-site corroboration?
	Are data mechanically recorded?

resources. The use of multiple sites and additional researchers will almost certainly be very expensive. As we have already indicated, the predominant use of low-inference descriptors is also problematic because behaviors that are not directly observable are often very interesting. For example, some of the most important studies in classroom research have looked at learner characteristics such as motivation, interest, power, anxiety, authority, and control. (See, for example, Canagarajah's (1993) study of students' motivation for English learning in Sri Lanka.) These are all high-inference phenomena.

Table 7.2 summarizes some important questions about internal and external reliability in ethnographic research. The strategies embodied in these questions can be used to guide ethnographers in conducting research and writing their reports. They can also be used by readers of ethnography to evaluate such reports.

Concerns about Traditional Validity in Ethnographic Research

As we have seen, validity is a more challenging concept than reliability since it is underpinned by that most intangible of constructs—truth. We will divide this discussion into two parts, focusing first on internal validity and then on external validity.

Internal validity in experimental research is the extent to which a researcher could attribute the outcomes of an experiment to the treatment. In ethnography, internal validity involves the question of whether the researcher's conclusions were justified by the data collected and the analyses thereof.

LeCompte and Goetz (1982) argue that ethnographies are strong on internal validity. They base this claim on four characteristics of ethnographic research:

First, the ethnographer's common practice of living among participants and collecting data for long periods provides opportunities for continual data analysis and comparison to refine constructs and to ensure the match between scientific categories and participant reality. Second, informant interviewing, a major ethnographic data source, necessarily is phrased more closely to the empirical categories of participants and is formed less abstractly than instruments used in other research designs. Third, participant observation, the ethnographer's second key source of data, is conducted in natural settings that reflect the reality of the life experiences of participants more accurately than do contrived settings. Finally, ethnographic analysis incorporates a process of researcher self-monitoring . . . that exposes all phases of the research activity to continual questioning and reevaluation. (p. 43)

(In this context, LeCompte and Goetz are using the term *internal validity* somewhat more broadly than it is normally used in experimental research.)

Some of the concerns about internal validity in experimental research arise in doing ethnography. Because the ethnographer typically studies a group for a long period of time, maturational changes or the attrition of informants occurring during the course of the research might affect the outcomes. Normally, both these concerns are addressed by the very nature of ethnographic inquiry. That is, the longitudinal data collection procedures capture change as the daily life of the group is documented. In addition, movement in and out of groups (through birth, death, relocation, and so on) is a normal part of the cultural existence that ethnographers strive to document.

Threats to internal validity in experimental research are sometimes related to bias in the selection of subjects in a study—a threat that is normally dealt with through randomization. In ethnographic research, informants are often chosen precisely because they meet a certain criterion. For instance, if you wish to study the identity construction of recent immigrants in secondary schools, you would choose a group of recently arrived teenagers to observe. In writing an ethnography, it is important to explain exactly why and how an observation site and group were chosen, but it is not a requirement that they be randomly selected.

We saw in experimental research that the reactive effects of the testing and the reactive effects of experimental arrangements can be matters of concern. The parallel question in ethnography is whether the outcomes are due in part to the presence of the researcher in the context. This issue, which we have already labeled *the observer's paradox*, is also called *reactivity*. It can be dealt with by building the trust of the participants, by prolonged immersion in the research context, and by behaving ethically and appropriately in that context.

Because ethnography intentionally does not impose artificial controls, people who come from the culture of experimental research often wonder whether alternative explanations for phenomena might not be posed. In fact, ethnographers work rigorously to examine alternative explanations for phenomena as they develop the emic and etic perspectives in their research. When sufficient data from different sources rule out alternative explanations, they can be excluded.

REFLECTION

You have now seen several contrasts between experimental research and ethnography in terms of internal validity. Which of these differences did you predict? Which, if any, do you find troublesome? In which situation described above (if any) do you prefer the ethnographic stance over the experimental stance, or vice versa?

Concerns arise about external validity as well. The results of a study cannot be generalized if the phenomena being investigated are unique to a particular group or site. Someone who wishes to generalize the findings of an ethnography must ask if the historical experiences of a particular group make it so unique that findings about that group cannot be legitimately extended to other groups. There may also be a worry that constructs and terminology are not common to different cultures and research sites. These concerns are summarized in **Table 7.3.**

TABLE 7.3 Guarding against threats to the validity of ethnographic research (adapted from Nunan [1992, p. 63], following LeCompte and Goetz [1982])

Type	Questions
Internal Validity	Is it likely that maturational changes occurring during the course of the research will affect the outcomes?
	Is there bias in the selection of informants?
	Is the increase or attrition of informants over time likely to affect outcomes?
	Have alternative explanations for phenomena been rigorously examined and excluded?
	Are outcomes due in part to the presence of the researcher?
External Validity	Are some phenomena unique to a particular group or site and therefore noncomparable?
	Are cross-group comparisons invalidated by unique historical experiences of particular groups?
	To what extent are abstract terms and constructs shared across different groups and research sites?

If ethnography is judged from the experimental perspective, external validity can sometimes be seen as a major weakness. Some would argue that it is impossible to generalize interpretations from the particular site in which the data were collected to other sites. For this reason, some researchers (e.g., Watson-Gegeo, 1988) suggest that comparison rather than generalization is a more appropriate goal for ethnographies. By aggregating and comparing the insights from a series of ethnographies, generalizations may ultimately emerge, but it is comparisons and contrasts across cultures that are illuminating.

Other researchers argue that external validity is not something that ethnographic researchers need to be concerned with (see, for example, Richards, 2003; van Lier, 1990a). They say that generalizability is an important ground rule of experimental research because the experimental method was devised specifically to allow generalizations to be made from samples to populations. They argue, however, that this is not a rule to which other research paradigms need subscribe. In effect, requiring an ethnographer to adhere to the rules of experimental research is like asking a basketball player to obey the rules of volleyball or vice versa—it simply does not make sense.

REFLECTION

What is your stance on this issue? Do you think that ethnographies should strive to meet the 'rules' of external validity?

Alternative Criteria for Evaluating Ethnography

In a sense, we can think of traditional reliability and validity as comprising an etic framework—one borrowed from experimental research. A more emic perspective would be to judge ethnographies through the criteria developed by the members of that particular culture—the ethnographers themselves.

Quality control in ethnography goes beyond debates about the traditional criteria of reliability and validity. Indeed, much has changed since LeCompte and Goetz (1982) wrote their landmark treatise on validity and reliability in ethnographic research. These days some qualitatively oriented researchers argue quite convincingly that there are other standards by which ethnography should be judged. Ethnography is subject to its own quality control mechanisms, and van Lier describes four of these (1990a, p. 45; italics in the original):

1. Every study needs to be scrutinized for its adherence to the *emic* and *holistic principles*.

2. The notion of *context* needs to be examined in great detail and the role of context in interpretation must be made explicit.

3. Ethnographic research must be *open*, that is, it must examine and report its own processes of inferencing and reasoning, so that its procedures can be profitably discussed.

4. Ethnography must be either *broad* (longitudinal) or *deep* (micro-ethnographic). . . . Ethnography requires intensive immersion in the data, whether this is the daily language use of an entire culture, or one small story told by a child.

Micro-ethnography is the in-depth study of interaction following emic principles. That is, an ethnographer might record a story about an adventure and do a detailed analysis of the discourse, relating it to the culture from which it comes. This is what Watson-Gegeo was referring to when she wrote about "audio- or videotaping of interactions for close analysis" (1988, p. 583).

In terms of evaluating ethnographic research, van Lier states that the notion "of quality as a superordinate concept is crucial. It encompasses both reliability and validity. However, since these latter terms are associated with experimental and statistical norms, I prefer to use the terms adequacy (of argumentation and evidence) and value (within a theory, i.e., internal, and to human affairs in general, i.e., external)" (1990a, p. 35). **Figure 7.3** depicts the relationship among these terms.

Qualitative research in general comes under fire from people who are committed to experimental research as the only appropriate way to discover truth. Writing about what he calls "qualitative inquiry," Richards (2003) says that the key issue in evaluating qualitative inquiry is trustworthiness—a concept

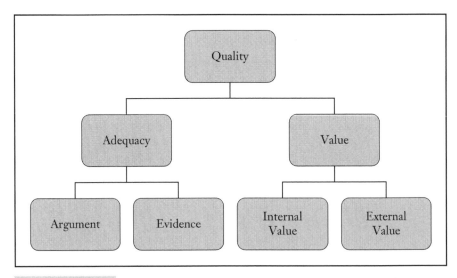

FIGURE 7.3   Concepts for determining quality in ethnography (adapted from van Lier, 1990a, p. 35)

developed by Lincoln and Guba (1985). Following these authors, Richards (2003) discusses three criteria for evaluating qualitative inquiry, including ethnography. In the quotes below, he juxtaposes these concepts with their experimental cousins in brackets:

- *Credibility* [internal validity] depends on evidence of long-tem exposure to the context being studied and the adequacy of data collected (use of different methods, etc.).

- *Transferability* [external validity] depends on a richness of description and interpretation that makes a particular case interesting and relevant to those in other situations.

- *Dependability* [reliability] and *confirmability* [objectivity] are to be assessed in terms of the documentation of research design, data, analysis, reflection and so on, so that the researcher's decisions are open to others. (p. 286)

(You will recall that *transferability* and other similar issues arose in Chapter 6 when we discussed quality control in case studies.)

In fact, research of all kinds raises quality control issues, and each tradition demands that researchers show that they have taken the appropriate steps to insure both reliability and validity. As van Lier (1988) has noted, "The blacksmith cannot criticize the carpenter for not heating a piece of wood over a fire. However, the carpenter must demonstrate a principled control over the materials" (p. 42).

ACTION

Fill in each blank below with one of these three sets of criteria for judging ethnography. Each criterion is followed by its experimental analog in brackets.)

Dependability [reliability]
Transferability [external validity]
Credibility [internal validity] and *Confirmability* [objectivity]

1. _____depends on evidence of long-tem exposure to the context being studied and the adequacy of data collected (use of different methods, etc.).

2. _____depends on a richness of description and interpretation that makes a particular case interesting and relevant to those in other situations.

3. _____ should be assessed in terms of the documentation of research design, data, analysis, reflection, and so on, so that the researcher's decisions are open to others.

A central part of this argument hinges on whether a study is seeking to establish causal relationships or not and whether, in fact, causal relationships can be identified in areas as complex as social behaviors, such as language learning and teaching. The problem is this: "If it is assumed *a priori* that L2 learning is caused by certain *sufficient* conditions, the researcher's job is to circumscribe those conditions so that, whenever they obtain, the occurrence of L2 learning can be accurately *predicted*" (van Lier, 1990a, p. 36). This point is nicely illustrated by considering the event of a tree blowing down in a storm:

It is clear that not every time the wind blows against a tree, that tree will fall down. When we study the phenomenon, we must add qualifications and amendments which are endless: the wind must blow hard enough, the tree must be fragile enough, the roots must grip the soil insufficiently, the soil must be loose enough, etc. In addition, we must take into account the position of the tree among buildings, other trees, and so on. It would probably be impossible to lay down all the conditions which would ensure a guaranteed tree-falling-down event. So even if we are able to say: "The wind caused that tree to fall down," we are still not able to specify exactly what it will take for another tree, say the orange tree in the back yard, to fall down. (p. 37)

This comparison concludes with the important caveat that "it is obvious that L2 learning is an event which is vastly more complex than a tree blowing down" (ibid.).

How does the tree-falling-down analogy relate to this discussion? In experimental research, internal validity has to do with creating a research situation (by controlling and manipulating variables) in which the researcher can confidently claim a causal relationship between the independent and dependent variable. However, establishing causal relationships is not an issue if the researcher is primarily concerned with providing a detailed description, analysis, and interpretation of the chosen context and situation (as is the case with ethnography) rather than with applying treatments and establishing causality. In fact, van Lier (1990a) argues that

a simple causal view is inappropriate in classroom research for one very uncontroversial reason, namely that teaching does not cause learning. Many times learning takes place without teaching, and, perhaps equally often, the teaching event is not followed by a learning event. (p. 38)

He concludes that "most of our efforts at doing experiments or quasi-experiments, with all the attempted controls of variables and randomizations of treatment may be doomed to failure (especially given the complexity of language learning processes)" (ibid.).

In classroom ethnographies, van Lier (1990a) says that taking a causal view is not necessary: "It is sufficient to say that the people involved can make an effort to create optimum conditions so that learners can get on with the business of learning in the best way that they see fit, and can help each other in the process" (p. 40). He calls this approach to research *interpretive*, while causally oriented experimental research is often called *normative*.

REFLECTION

Now that you have read about quality control issues in both ethnography and experimental research, do you have a preference for one or the other? These are the two "pure" research paradigms in Grotjahn's (1987) framework. They are apparently juxtaposed to each other in (1) the research design, (2) the nature of the data, and (3) the type of analysis used. Do you feel more comfortable with one research culture or the other?

TRIANGULATION IN ETHNOGRAPHIC RESEARCH

Ethnographies are strengthened and can be judged in part by the extent to which they use a number of procedures that fall under the general heading of *triangulation*. This concept is best known in ethnography, but in all forms of qualitative research it provides a way for researchers working with nonquantified data to check on their interpretations of those data. By incorporating multiple points of view, researchers can check one perspective against another. If more than one type or source of data leads to the same conclusion, researchers have more confidence in those conclusions. (See van Lier, 1988, for further discussion of these points.)

Triangulation is a geometric concept borrowed from navigation, astronomy, and surveying. Hammersley and Atkinson (1983) state that if people wish to locate their position on a map,

> a single landmark can only provide the information that they are situated somewhere along a line in a particular direction from that landmark. With two landmarks, however, their exact position can be pinpointed by taking bearings on both landmarks; they are at the point where the two lines cross. (p. 198)

In qualitative data collection, the triangulation metaphor refers to a quality control strategy. In social research, if "diverse kinds of data lead to the same conclusion, one can be a little more confident in that conclusion" (ibid.).

In anthropology, triangulation is used as a process of verification that gives researchers confidence in their observations. Denzin (1978) described four types of triangulation. The first is *data triangulation*, in which different sources of data (teachers, students, parents, etc.) contribute to an investigation. Secondly, *theory triangulation* is used when various theories are brought to bear in a study. (Theory triangulation is probably the least commonly used in our field.) The third form is *researcher triangulation*, in which more than one researcher contributes to the investigation. Finally, *methods triangulation* involves the use of multiple methods (e.g., interviews, questionnaires, observation schedules, test scores, field notes, etc.) to collect data.

These concepts come to us from anthropology, but they can be applied to classroom research conducted with a range of methods. Here is an example from Springer (2003). As you may recall from the sample study at the end of Chapter 2, she was interested in what factors promoted second language acquisition in language classrooms. After having taught a project-based course and experienced the students' learning in that context, she began to reconsider her earlier teaching experiences using grammar-based syllabi. Her evolving research focus led to these questions:

> What implications does a much broader view of language and the language learning process have for my role and responsibilities as a language teacher? What changes come about in my expectations concerning the roles and responsibilities of the students? What impact does the shift to content- or project-based syllabi have on these classroom roles and on the language produced by course participants—both teachers and learners? (pp. 2–3)

To address these questions, Springer arranged to observe another project-based course, taught by a different teacher, for academically oriented ESL students in California. The course revolved around the students carrying out a series of four photojournalism projects. Springer took the role of an observer in the course, switching from a nonparticipant stance to a participant stance as needed, with the full cooperation of the teacher. In describing the context, she wrote,

> In addition to being project-based, this course also entailed some measure of student contact with the target language community (both in person or via newspapers or the Internet) and involved the use of computer technology for the completion of tasks and presentation of the final product. (p. 3)

The final project for the course consisted of a magazine that the students produced through site visits, interviews, and a variety of computer tools.

In conducting this study, Springer became interested in scaffolding and contingent language use. In Chapter 6, we defined *scaffolding* as "progressive help provided by the more knowledgeable to the less knowledgeable" (Nassaji and Cumming, 2000, p. 98). In naturally occurring conversations, *contingency* is the tendency of one speaker's turn to be influenced by a preceding speaker's turn. That is, a subsequent utterance is contingent upon one or more preceding utterances. (See van Lier, 1989.) Springer's (2003) literature review led her to the following descriptions of these concepts:

> For Aljaafreh and Lantolf (1994), three significant characteristics of *scaffolding* [italics added] are that it be graduated, dialogic and contingent.

TABLE 7.4	Sources of triangulation in Springer's (2003) study of a project-based ESL course on photojournalism (p. 46)
Methods Triangulation *entails the use of multiple methods to collect data*	**running field notes** during the photojournalism class (researcher in the role of an overt nonparticipant observer and participant observer)
	journal entries by the researcher based on immediate and delayed retrospection on photojournalism class observations (as well as thoughts on research questions and notes on discussions with the classroom teachers)
	audio recordings of the photojournalism class (digital minidisc [MD] recordings using a stereo microphone, which was normally placed in the center of the table; also some recordings from an additional recorder placed near individual groups during group/pair work)
	copies of student-generated coursework: four major assignments (biography of a peer, photo manipulation & commentary, restaurant review, news story)
	copies of materials used in class: (1) T-generated worksheets; (2) T-collected authentic materials; (3) T-led group-generated lists and brainstorms; (4) S-collected authentic materials and homework assignments; (5) S-generated pair-work tasks
	group interviews with the students (documented using field notes and digital audio recording): (1) background biographical information on each student; (2) prior study of English; (3) reactions to statement: "The photojournalism course looks like fun, but some teachers would be skeptical that it's not really related to learning English."
	interviews with the classroom teachers (most are optional and would be documented using field notes and digital audio recording; retrospective journal entries on three preliminary meetings): (1) reactions to the class, general +/− impressions; (2) discussion of student requests to have less or no core next session; (3) discussion of actual course schedule—flexibility/ changes/retrospective changes; (4) reactions to ideas about themes and recurring elements
Data Triangulation *different sources of data are used*	**students** **classroom teachers** **observer/researcher** **program administrator**
Theory Triangulation *various theories are brought to bear in a study*	**project-based learning** **pedagogical scaffolding** **contingent language use**
Researcher Triangulation	**none**—only one researcher contributed to the study

This means that assistance should be offered along a scale from least to most explicit only to the extent to which it is needed—no more and no less—and that the only way to determine this point is through dialogue with the other person. (p. 18)

Contingency [italics added] is the quality of language use that can most directly be associated with engagement and learning (van Lier, 1996b, p. 171). Contingencies draw upon what we know and connect this to what is new. It is thus part of the essence of learning. (p. 74)

To understand the roles of scaffolding and contingent language use in the photojournalism class, Springer used a range of data collection and analysis procedures. The combination of these procedures made her research very strong in terms of triangulation. The types of triangulation she used are documented in **Table 7.4.**

A SAMPLE STUDY

We have chosen Duff's ethnography of dual immersion programs in secondary schools in Hungary as the sample study for this chapter for three main reasons. First, it illustrates many of the principles and practices of ethnography described above. Secondly, it provides a fine example of a classroom ethnography that is embedded in a wider sociolinguistic and sociopolitical context. Third, it is accessible to interested readers in various publications.

One of the published papers is entitled "Different languages, different practices: Socialization of discourse competence in dual-language school classrooms in Hungary" (Duff, 1996). It is that publication from which we will draw the bulk of this summary. The study investigates

the socialization of discourse competence in these two types of instructional environment—the traditional and the non-traditional, the monolingual and the bilingual—and explores the impact of educational reform on school life and the ways in which students are inducted into academic discourse practices in the two contexts through different kinds of performance tasks. (p. 407)

This study evolved from Duff's participation in an earlier project that investigated the efficacy of having dual-language education in Hungary. (See Duff, 1991a; 1991b.)

The Context of the Study

The context Duff (1996) investigated consisted of dual-language programs—late immersion programs in Hungarian secondary schools—and comparison schools with more traditional curricula. In the dual-language schools, English was the medium of instruction in the majority of courses, including mathematics, history, biology, physics, and geography. However, chemistry courses and Hungarian language and literature courses were taught in Hungarian.

The research was conducted from 1989 to 1990, and the effects of Hungary's transformation from a highly controlled country to an independent republic greatly influenced the social and political climate in which the study was done. Of the historical context, Duff (1995) writes,

> In the mid-1980s, educational reforms in Hungary granted schools more autonomy from the state and within just a few years, up to 30 dual-language programs with an assortment of Western languages had been established with support from the Ministry of Education. . . . In the same period, EFL programs mushroomed in schools, universities, and other institutions. (p. 509)

Duff (1996) chose history lessons for her data collection because history "is a compulsory subject in the Hungarian curriculum, is enjoyed by most students, and is rich in both interaction and in linguistic and cognitive structures (e.g., narrative, description, cause-effect)" (p. 413). She observed history lessons in both dual-language and traditional schools to allow for comparison across the two types of programs.

Focus of the Investigation

Duff provides a fascinating account of how the wider sociopolitical context played out in secondary school classrooms. In particular, she focuses on a speech event that is called the *felelés* in Hungarian. This is a form of daily oral recitation in which the teacher calls on a student to come to the front of the room and report on the previous lesson, responding to questions from the teacher in the process. The students do not know in advance whether or not they will be called upon to recite. Their performance is graded on a scale of one to five (with one being the low mark), and the teacher announces the student's grade aloud to the class immediately following the recitation. Duff (1996) says, "In my fieldwork, it was apparent that *felelés* evoked a strong and often visible emotional response from those familiar with it—which was practically every Hungarian I met" (p. 411). She writes,

> Students may be quite critical of the chronic stress associated with the anticipation of numerous possible recitations every day as well as the formality and rigidity of the structured interaction. Once exposed to instruction in which the traditional *felelés* is no longer practiced, students were especially vocal about its perceived abuses. (p. 421)

The *felelés* was a sort of educational ritual in traditional Hungarian class-rooms. This recitation was standard practice for assessing students' knowledge and motivating them to study in traditional classes. Duff (1996) connects this activity to traditional Prussian educational practices. She notes, "The system creates the ritual, but the ritual also creates the system; hence, change in one is bound to effect change in the other" (p. 409). As the broader sociopolitical context in Hungary began to change, so did educational practices. In the newly established dual-language programs, this change extended to the types of opportunities for students to speak in class.

Duff (1995) noticed that while the *felelés* was being used in the traditional programs, in the dual-language classes it was being replaced with other forms of in-class oral communication, such as open-ended discussions and brief lectures by students. She posed two research questions about this situation:

1. Was instructional discourse in English-medium history classes different from Hungarian medium non-dual-language classrooms and, if so, what might account for this?
2. What parallels exist between microlevel discursive changes (or differences) in these lessons and changes taking place countrywide? (p. 505)

Data Collection

In order to answer these questions, Duff videotaped approximately fifty history lessons, which were taught by three teachers working at four different secondary schools located in different parts of Hungary. She usually observed a given teacher's class for a period of two weeks in order to see the development and review of themes across a unit of instruction.

The videotaped data were transcribed. Any data that originally occurred in Hungarian were translated into English. In addition to making her observational field notes, Duff also interviewed students, teachers, and administrators. She included discussions with consultants and copies of students' essays in her database. The reports of her research are replete with excerpts from the transcripts so readers can get a strong sense of the interaction among students and teachers, both in dual-language and traditional classrooms.

The processes of transcription and translation were facilitated by the students themselves. Duff (1995) says, "Nearly a dozen . . . students volunteered to be my part-time research assistants, helping with transcription, translation, verification, and interpretation, especially during their summer vacation; in this way, we became quite familiar over time" (p. 513). Involving the students in this way helped her to counteract the observer's paradox to some extent.

Key Findings

One of the differences between the traditional programs and the dual-language programs was the less frequent use of the *felelés* in the dual-language programs. In fact, Duff (1995) observed that, to a large extent, "the daily recitation period had been rejected by most of the history teachers in the dual-language programs" (p. 517).

The speech events that replaced the *felelés* consisted of brief prepared lectures by students, often delivered from written notes, as well as question-and-answer sessions, pair work, and group work. Duff contrasts the traditional *felelés* with the students' prepared presentations:

> Despite some similarities with the recitation (i.e., extended oral discourse produced by a student on an academic topic), the English lectures did not appear to be as taxing or as frequent an activity for students. . . . But as a relatively new activity, the procedures, students' roles, and responsibilities were still being negotiated, and this revealed some of the ambiguities of the changing discourse practices at schools. (ibid., p. 519)

In addition, unlike in the *felelés*, the students were able to select their speech topics themselves and prepare in advance. Duff provides a case study of one particular teacher and class from the broader study that illustrates this change in daily classroom practice.

The changes in these speech events in the dual-language schools are connected to the broader social and political changes within Hungary:

> Schools, generally thought to be conservative institutions, have not been immune from many of the restructurings and ambiguities that have resulted from decentralization. . . . Dual-language schools in Hungary represent an especially vital system in which many of these changes have occurred at an accelerated and magnified rate, perhaps because they had a head start before 1989 and perhaps also because the interface of Western (or non-Hungarian) and Hungarian systems and the languages they promote takes place day by day in classrooms, corridors, and teachers' offices. In those spaces, teachers, visitors and students, often with different ideological, linguistic, and sociocultural backgrounds, come together in the name of a progressive new model of education. (ibid., p. 529)

In making this rather positive comment about a "progressive new model of education," Duff is not imposing her own point of view on the data. Rather, these ideas and opinions represent the emic perspective of the teachers, students, and administrators in the dual-language schools.

Duff's report is richly textured and highly contextualized. We have provided only a very brief summary here. Her research provides a clear example of a language classroom ethnography as well as guidance for other researchers (e.g., in terms of the transcription conventions used; see Duff, 1996).

PAYOFFS AND PITFALLS

Ethnography is by definition longitudinal (with the exception perhaps of micro-ethnography). Therefore, conducting ethnographic research and writing about such investigations can be very time-consuming processes. Many ethnographers have spent years in a site, learning about the culture, gaining the trust of the informants, and often even learning the language of that culture in order to communicate with the people being studied. The depth required by good ethnographic analyses means they do not fit easily into what van Lier (1990a) calls "the cycle of conference presentations" (p. 45)—that is, "a brief treatment period, a testing session, a twenty-page write up, all probably wrapped up in three to six months from start to finish." He counsels that "ethnography is not conducted that quickly" (ibid.).

In fact, Richards (2003) identifies the longitudinal nature of ethnography as its main drawback because

> it requires extended exposure to the field, which makes it very difficult for the researcher to stay in work during the period of investigation. It is methodologically unacceptable to settle for quick forays into the field in order to scoop up data and retreat. (p. 16)

Richards notes that even though it may be "legitimate to use methods characteristic of ethnography, these do not in themselves mean that you are working within this tradition" (ibid.). For this reason, it is important to distinguish between true ethnographies and research that might more properly be called qualitative.

Because of the prolonged immersion of ethnographers in the field, the sheer quantity of data can be overwhelming. For novice researchers in particular, it is important to take care in organizing, labeling, dating, and storing all field notes, audio tapes, videotapes, archival documents, photographs, and maps. We will return to these issues in Chapter 14 when we discuss the analysis of qualitative data.

Another concern is that ethnography as a research method and grounded theory as an orientation may not suit some researchers' personalities and cognitive styles. As van Lier (1990a) points out, "the heuristic quality of ethnography makes it an inherently insecure pursuit, since there are no firm external rules and guidelines for proper scientific conduct" (p. 41). For this reason, it seems essential to have a high tolerance for ambiguity before undertaking ethnographic fieldwork. In addition, "the worker in the field is essentially alone, and inevitably learns as much from opportunities missed, false leads too strenuously pursued, and insights by-passed in inexplicable ways, as from routine description and categorization" (ibid.). For these reasons, doing ethnography requires a substantial commitment of time and personal fortitude.

Finally, researchers interested in learning more about ethnography may encounter difficulty in finding training courses. As van Lier (1990a) notes, without such training it is difficult to have a clear idea as to what constitutes 'good' or 'bad' ethnography. He adds that

> although this problem also exists in normative types of research, workers in the latter tradition have the advantage that most graduate degree programs have substantial components of quantitative research design and statistics training, whereas training in ethnography is rarely available. (p. 44)

However, there is some progress being made in this regard as more and more university faculties recognize the value of qualitative research and begin to offer courses in its procedures. (See Levine, Gallimore, Weisner, and Turner, 1980, for an early report on this effort.)

In spite of these numerous pitfalls, there are also several important (but perhaps less tangible) benefits of ethnography. We have already alluded to one that is specific to classroom research—involving teachers and learners while documenting their (emic) point of view. As Canagarajah's (1993) study in Sri Lanka illustrates, teachers themselves are sometimes in an ideal position to do classroom ethnography because they are naturally placed participant observers. They must, of course, strive to develop the etic point of view and to be aware of their own biases if they do conduct ethnographic research in their own classrooms, but we see no a priori reason why this concern cannot be addressed.

Another profound benefit of ethnographies is that the information they provide is different from that provided with the experimental method. This information, says van Lier (1990a), "may either be compatible or contradictory. Whichever way things turn out, a diversity of research programmes is essential to promote an enrichment of theoretical and professional knowledge" (p. 50).

Likewise, ethnographies—like case studies—are often more accessible to reading audiences without statistical training. As a result, they may have more impact or reach a wider public than will purely quantitative experimental reports.

We began this chapter with a quote from Christiane Amanpour of CNN. She said, "Stories told well and compellingly can have an unparalleled power to create and make a difference to the world. And that is what our job is, to make a difference." This journalist's credo can also serve well as guidance for ethnographers. One of the most crucial payoffs of a really good ethnography is the compelling story that it brings to readers. To illustrate this point, we close this chapter with an extended quote from van Lier (1996a), who conducted research in rural schools in Peru. His brilliant description of "the daily grind" provides readers with a clear and vivid understanding of students' and teachers' classroom lives.

The project in Peru was the initiation and monitoring of a bilingual Spanish-Quechua program. Spanish is the dominant national language and Quechua is the local language and, therefore, the home language of the children. His portrait of a typical day begins as he leaves his base in the town of Puno and spends weeks at a time in the rural, isolated *altiplano*, where subsistence farming is the main industry. As you read the following paragraphs, imagine yourself as an ethnographer in this context. The story begins with van Lier telling us that "the trip takes about four hours, depending on road conditions" (p. 368).

We arrive in Tiyaña just after eight in the morning. The school, consisting of three classrooms (adobe walls and corrugated tin roof) and a storeroom (*almacen*), which the *director* (the principal) has converted into his living quarters, is still locked. There is no community center as such (apart from the school itself), just a scattering of low adobe houses strewn across the pampa, with tilled fields in between the houses and further out, against the low foothills of the *Cordillera*. Gradually the children and the teachers (three in total) begin to arrive from various directions. Meanwhile, the *awicha*, or grandmother, a tiny old woman living in a small house next to the school, comes over for a chat in Quechua, from which I cannot gather much more than that the teachers are good-for-nothing layabouts and drunks, the children are a nuisance, and the weather continues to be awful.

When the teachers arrive, one by one, we greet, exchange news, and discuss plans for the week. Around nine o'clock the *profesor de turno* (teacher-on-duty; this week it's Gerardo's turn) whistles for the *formación*. The children line up, grade by grade, facing the school. The students receive a pep talk, general announcements about meetings or various community activities, sing a couple of songs (including the national anthem), perhaps do a bit of marching in place. All this is in Spanish, with a few comments repeated in Quechua for the benefit of the smallest ones (*los más chiquitos*).

Students continue to arrive in dribs and drabs through the *formación* (many of them having to walk up to an hour from their widely dispersed homes across the pampa). Around 9:30 the students are marched into their classrooms. In Tiyaña there are three teachers, which means that every teacher has two grades. The director, Luis, has the first and sixth grades, which is unusual (adjacent grades being the rule in combination classes). I begin by observing a couple of classes and plan to start the oral entry test for the first grade after lunch.

The classroom is fairly spacious, with barely adequate light from two rows of small windows in opposite walls. About half of the window panes are broken. There is no electricity (or running water or other amenities) in the school or in Tiyaña as a whole, for that matter, and the room is quite cold early in the morning. The sixth grade students (ten children) sit at one end of the room, facing the back wall, the first grade students (seventeen children) at the other, facing the front.

At 10:30 there is recess, and Luis and I stand outside against the wall which is now warmed by the sun to warm ourselves for a while. Then the teachers, several of the biggest kids, and I play volleyball after putting up the net. It is almost 11:30 before the director declares that it is time to go in again. Another lesson follows and at 12:15 it is lunchtime.

The children take their plate or mug and go to the back of the school where the kitchen is. Several sixth graders and a few *madres de familia* (mothers who do this voluntarily) have prepared *el quaker* (oatmeal), which they dole out to the children.

At about 1:30 Gerardo blows the whistle for *formación*. At that moment the *Teniente Gobernador* (the elected leader of Tiyaña), Don Anselmo, arrives on his bicycle. We talk a bit, and he makes some announcements to the assembled children about vaccinations for cattle, the importance of hygiene, and the need to study hard in school. He speaks in a mixture of Spanish and Quechua, with Quechua predominating.

Around two o'clock the children march into their classrooms again. Assisted by an older student, I start the oral Quechua test (about five to ten minutes per child), using a structured interview format. At three o'clock there is another recess which lasts 'til four, and then the children are sent home. One teacher, Ignacio, rides home on his little motorbike. The other teacher, Gerardo, walks across the pampa to a house where he rents a room.

Later on Luis fetches a bucket of water from an open water hole behind the school, and I help him cook dinner (the inevitable *sopita*, or soup, made with potato, tomato, noodles, and a few other bits and pieces that happen to be available) on a primus stove, sharing some ingredients. Gerardo comes over to join us.

The other days proceed very much like the first one. On Wednesday I go to Qotokancha (Ignacio gives me a ride over on his motorbike), where there are only two teachers, each one taking care of three grades—but otherwise a similar routine is followed. On Friday afternoon I wait for the car to take me back to Puno. (pp. 368–369)

This level of detailed description continues throughout the rest of the report, in which van Lier documents the instructional practices and learning challenges facing the teachers and pupils.

The paper includes a fascinating micro-ethnographic analysis of the children's efforts to follow instructions and copy what the teacher has written on the chalkboard. But because the text is apparently meaningless to them, the children copy individual letters vertically down the page, instead of writing words and sentences horizontally. A particularly poignant observation has to do with their copying of the Spanish word *campo* (field), when van Lier (1996a) notes:

Many students have written *canipu* or *canipo* instead of *campo*, every time they have copied the word. This is a very puzzling error, until I take a good look at the blackboard and notice a small spot on it, just above the third leg of the letter *m* in *campo*. Since *canipu/-o* is not a word in Spanish, this is clear evidence of how mechanical the students' copying activities are. (p. 372)

Given the depth and detail of van Lier's writing, the reader is left with a vivid picture of the educational context as well as sense of compassion and clarity about his understanding of the teachers and children in the *altiplano* of Peru.

CONCLUSION

In this chapter, we have considered the background and some key characteristics of ethnography, which came into applied linguistics from the parent discipline of anthropology. We summarized four principles of ethnography and the typical stages of ethnographic research, exemplifying each point with excerpts from classroom ethnographies. We looked at two of the important roles and responsibilities ethnographers take on, including participant and nonparticipant observation, and the goal of developing both emic and etic perspectives. Several important issues were raised regarding quality control in ethnography, but we found that, rather than focusing narrowly on the traditional criteria of reliability and validity, ethnography can be more appropriately evaluated by its own criteria.

Ethnography represents a very different research culture from experiments and surveys. A rigorously researched, well-written ethnography can be a powerful tool for informing readers about a particular cultural group (whether it is a remote tribal culture, a neighborhood street gang, the weekend bowling league, or a language class), and for relating the daily life of that group to the broader cultural context within which it is situated.

QUESTIONS AND TASKS

1. Look at the following topics from language classroom research. First, list two or three behaviors associated with each topic. Then categorize the nature of each behavior as being either low-inference (clearly definable in operational terms; easy to verify) or high-inference (less easily defined or verified).

   Error treatment
   Fluent speech
   Teaching the past tense
   Self-initiated turns
   Social climate
   Teacher praise for students
   Teaching style
   Use of the first language

2. From the list above, choose one of the high-inference topics and/or behaviors that interests you. Try to write a clear, operational definition for the term. Check some key references on the topic to see how other researchers have defined the construct. Do you see any ways that some elements could be more low-inference in nature?

3. Read an ethnographic study you have located or one cited in this chapter or listed below in "Suggestions for Further Reading." Does the study utilize high-inference or low-inference categories or both in its data collection and/or data analysis procedures? Were the categories clearly defined and explicitly stated so that you could replicate the study if you wished?

4. In the ethnography you read, did the researcher function as a participant observer or a nonparticipant observer? Were the data collection procedures overt or covert?

5. What kinds of triangulation are utilized in the ethnography you read—data triangulation, researcher triangulation, methods triangulation, and/or theory triangulation? If one or more of these strategies was *not* used, can you think of a way that the researcher(s) could have improved the study through additional triangulation?

6. LeCompte and Goetz (1982) say ethnographic researchers should be explicit about the following five key aspects of the research:

   A. the status of the researcher(s) in the research site,

   B. who the informants are and how they were chosen,

   C. the social situations and conditions when the research was carried out,

   D. the analytic constructs and premises underlying the research, and

   E. the data collection methods and analytic methods.

   Analyze the ethnography you have read. Did the author(s) report on all five of these key points? If not, which are missing from the report?

7. LeCompte and Goetz (1982) also claim that ethnographies are strong on internal validity on the basis of four characteristics of ethnographic research:

   A. The ethnographer's common practice of living among participants and collecting data from long periods provides opportunities for continual data analysis and comparison to refine constructs and to ensure the match between scientific categories and participant reality.

   B. Informant interviewing, a major ethnographic data source, necessarily is phrased more closely to the empirical categories of participants and is formed less abstractly than instruments used in other research designs.

   C. Third, participant observation, the ethnographer's second key source of data, is conducted in natural settings that reflect the reality of the life experiences of participants more accurately than do contrived settings.

   D. Fourth, ethnographic analysis incorporates a process of researcher self-monitoring . . . that exposes all phases of the research activity to continual questioning and reevaluation. (p. 43)

   Which of these characteristics were present (and convincing) in the ethnography you read? Which were weak or absent? What could the researcher(s) have done to improve upon any gap(s) you have noted?

8. A link between teaching and learning, on the one hand, and classroom ethnographies, on the other, is that if ethnography is "done right, it actively encourages the participation of teachers and learners" (van Lier, 1990a, p. 49). How does Duff's ethnography measure up in this regard?

9. What quality control issues were addressed in the ethnography you read? Did the study address reliability and validity or did it talk in more qualitative terms about trustworthiness? If the latter, were credibility, transferability, and dependability discussed?

10. Four quality control mechanisms specific to ethnography were described by van Lier (1990a):

    A. Every study needs to be scrutinized for its adherence to the *emic* and *holistic principles*.

    B. The notion of *context* needs to be examined in great detail and the role of context in interpretation must be made explicit.

    C. Ethnographic research must be *open*, that is, it must examine and report its own processes of inferencing and reasoning, so that its procedures can be profitably discussed.

    D. Ethnography must be either *broad* (longitudinal) or *deep* (micro-ethnographic). . . . Ethnography requires intensive immersion in the data, whether this is the daily language use of an entire culture, or one small story told by a child. (p. 45)

    Did any of these criteria emerge in the ethnography you read? If not, can you see ways that one or more of these might have helped to improve that study?

11. Think of three to five research questions that you might be able to address by conducting an ethnography. What group would you wish to study? What kind of data would you want to collect? Would you be a participant observer, a nonparticipant observer, or both at different times? Would the data be collected overtly or covertly?

SUGGESTIONS FOR FURTHER READING

We recommend all the ethnographies cited in this chapter. If you would like to read more about the bilingual Spanish-Quechua program in Peru, please see van Lier's (1996a) article. There is also a booklength account of this context by Hornberger (1988). For further information about the classroom ethnography in Sri Lanka, you can read Canagarajah's (1993) original article and an interesting response to it by Braine (1994), who is from Sri Lanka himself.

We have cited Watson-Gegeo's (1988) paper extensively. A slightly different treatment of ethnographic principles is provided by van Lier (1990a), who stresses that two main principles of ethnography are (1) an emic point of view, and (2) a holistic concern for context. See also van Lier's (1988) book.

Freeman (1992) investigated the construction of shared understandings in a high school French class. This report provides an excellent example of a researcher developing the emic perspective, and of the way research questions emerge and evolve as an ethnographic study progresses.

If you wish to develop a research proposal in the general culture of qualitative research, we recommend Marshall and Rossman's (2006) *Designing Qualitative Research*. It provides clear guidance in reader-friendly prose.

Methodological guidance for people who want to do qualitative work in our field is gradually becoming more available. We recommend Richards (2003), the special issue of *TESOL Quarterly* edited by Davis and Lazaraton (1995), and a review by Henze (1995).

8

Action Research

For teachers "to fully embrace the principles and philosophy of action research, they need to begin by reinventing themselves.... We can only create alternatives to the existing method and structures after we have restructured ourselves" (Mingucci, 1999, p. 16).

INTRODUCTION AND OVERVIEW

In this chapter, we look at action research—an approach that is particularly well-suited for teachers conducting classroom research. First, we will define the approach and then provide an example of the action research cycle. We will talk about getting started with a plan for an action research study and about collecting data. Then we will consider quality control issues in action research before summarizing a sample study. We will close with the usual "payoffs and pitfalls," but we will also make a case for the use of action research as a powerful tool that can empower teachers to take control of their own professional development.

Defining Action Research

Action research is becoming increasingly prominent in the research methodology literature in our field. (See, for example, Burns, 1999; 2004; Edge, 2001; Nunan, 1990; 1993; Wallace, 1998; van Lier, 1994a.) As an approach to research, it has been around since the 1940s, when it first appeared in the social science literature (Lewin, 1946; 1948). In the 1980s, it was adapted by educators such as Carr and Kemmis (1986), who described it as follows:

> Action research is simply a form of self-reflective enquiry undertaken by participants in order to improve the rationality and justice of their own

practices, their understanding of those practices and the situations in which the practices are carried out. (p. 162)

This description is widely cited and it highlights the practitioner-driven nature of action research as well as the social justice bias bequeathed to the concept by Lewin, a left-wing sociologist. However, it is rather too broad to work as a definition for a form of research, being basically a statement about reflective teaching. (See Richards and Lockhart, 1994.)

For us, there are key differences between reflective teaching and action research. One is that reflective teaching can be a solitary and private practice, but in action research, the results of the process—the outcomes or products—should be published. We are using *publish* here in its original sense: to make publicly available to others for critical scrutiny. Another difference is that reflective teaching could conceivably occur at one point in time, after a particular lesson, whereas action research is cyclic and iterative.

We define action research as a systematic, iterative process of (1) identifying an issue, problem, or puzzle we wish to investigate in our own context; (2) thinking and planning an appropriate action to address that concern; (3) carrying out the action, (4) observing the apparent outcomes of the action; (5) reflecting on the outcomes and on other possibilities; and (6) repeating these steps again. To our minds, the cycle described above must be carried out at least twice (and typically more often) for the investigation to qualify as action research.

A more philosophical definition of action research is provided by Kemmis and McTaggart (1982), who suggest that

[t]he linking of the terms 'action' and 'research' highlights the essential feature of the method: trying out ideas in practice as a means of improvement and as a means of increasing knowledge about the curriculum, teaching and learning. The result is improvement in what happens in the classroom and school, and better articulation and justification of the educational rationale of what goes on. Action research provides a way of working which links theory and practice into the one whole: ideas-in-action. (p. 5)

In this quote, the authors highlight connections between theory and practice. They also point out that action research entails more than simply providing descriptive and interpretive accounts of the classroom, no matter how rich these might be. Action research is meant to lead to change and improvement in what happens in the classroom. But, in contrast to experimental research, as Kemmis and McTaggert (1988) note,

[a] distinctive feature of action research is that those affected by planned changes have the primary responsibility for deciding on courses of critically informed action which seems likely to lead to improvement, and for evaluating the results of strategies tried out in practice. *Action research is a group activity.* (p. 6)

Thus, action research is not simply some form of investigation grafted onto classroom practice. Rather, it represents a particular stance on the part of the practitioner—a stance in which the practitioner is engaged in critical reflection on ideas, the informed application and experimentation of ideas in practice, and the critical evaluation of the outcomes.

REFLECTION

Based on your previous knowledge and what you have read so far, what would you say are the key characteristics of action research that distinguish it from both naturalistic inquiry and experimental research in the psychometric paradigm?

Characteristics of Action Research

To characterize action research in language classrooms, Nunan (1992) emphasizes the centrality of the teacher. He notes that this approach will have components similar to other types of research—that is, posing questions, collecting data, and then analyzing and/or interpreting those data. However, it is differentiated by the fact that it will be carried out by practitioners investigating their own professional context.

Similarly, Kemmis and McTaggart identify three defining characteristics of the approach. Educational action research, according to these authors, (1) is carried out by classroom practitioners; (2) is collaborative in nature; and (3) is aimed at bringing about change. Given this view, a teacher's descriptive observational research that was aimed at increasing understanding rather than bringing about change would not be considered action research by Kemmis and McTaggart—particularly if the study was conducted without the involvement of others. For these authors, collaboration and change are defining characteristics of the approach.

Cohen and Manion (1985) offer similar characteristics. They argue that action research is first and foremost situational, being concerned with the identification and solution of problems in a specific context. They also identify collaboration as an important feature of this type of research, and they state that the aim of action research is to improve the current state of affairs within the educational context in which the research is being carried out. If this educational context involves an entire school or program (as opposed to simply a single class), certainly teachers collaborating are in a better position to achieve this goal than are individuals working alone.

REFLECTION

Do you believe that collaboration should be a defining characteristic of action research? Why or why not?

We believe that action research has all of the characteristics of 'regular' research—that is, it requires research questions, data that are relevant to those questions, analysis and interpretation of the data, and some form of publication. We agree that it is the centrality of the classroom practitioner as a prime mover in the action research process that defines the approach and differentiates it from other forms of research. We also agree that action research should be aimed at bringing about change rather than simply documenting what is going on. However, we feel that Kemmis and McTaggart go too far in their assertion that in order to qualify as action research, the process must be collaborative. Certainly, collaboration is highly desirable. But to assert that such a process without collaboration cannot be called action research is unrealistic. Many practitioners would dearly love to collaborate, but they are simply not in a position to do so.

REFLECTION

Based on what you have read so far, how would you explain action research to a colleague who wanted to know more about it?

THE ACTION RESEARCH CYCLE

Most writers on action research agree that it is an iterative, cyclical process rather than a onetime event. In other words, unlike the "one-shot case study" design in experimental research, at least two action research cycles are required in order to resolve the problem or puzzle that initiated the research.

There are many visual frameworks that depict the action research cycle. We like the following image from van Lier (1994a), which is simple and clear. (See **Figure 8.1.**) It also depicts the fact that a researcher's goals may change over the course of an investigation. In addition, van Lier's model explicitly includes the step of reporting on the outcomes of the study.

In action research, the practitioner first identifies a problem or puzzle and conducts a preliminary investigation to gather baseline data. She then forms a hypothesis (though not necessarily in formal hypothesis testing language) and plans the intervention. Next, she takes action and observes the outcomes (a step analogous to data collection.) Then the researcher reflects on the outcomes (analyzes and interprets the data) and identifies a follow-up issue (or continues with the same issue), which informs a new cycle. **Table 8.1** provides an example (p. 231).

The sequence depicted in Table 8.1 would not necessarily stop at the end of the second cycle. The process could continue indefinitely, as long as new puzzles or problems suggest new goals. In the sample study at the end of this chapter, we will summarize an action research project that continued through two phases and included several cycles.

What Action Research Is Not

Sometimes it is helpful in trying to understand the characteristics of something as abstract as a research approach to determine what that entity is not, or what it

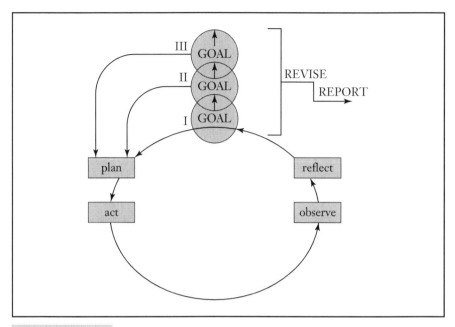

FIGURE 8.1 Cycles of action research (from van Lier, 1994a, p. 34)

does not do. Kemmis and Henry (1989) made these statements about what action research is *not*:

1. It is <u>NOT</u> the usual thing teachers do when they think about their teaching. It is systematic and involves collecting evidence on which to base rigorous reflection.

2. It is <u>NOT</u> (just) problem solving: it involves problem posing, too. . . . It is motivated by a quest to improve and understand the world by changing it and learning how to improve it from the effects of the changes being made.

3. It is <u>NOT</u> research on other people. Action research is research by particular people on their own work, to help them improve what they do, including how they work with and for others.

4. It is <u>NOT</u> the "scientific method" applied to teaching. . . . It adopts a view of social science which is distinct from a view based on the natural sciences (in which the objects of research may legitimately be treated as "things"); action research also concerns the "subject" (the action researcher) him- or herself.

Given these statements, we can see that action research is unlike both experimental research and naturalistic inquiry. Action research differs from experimental research in that the former—like naturalistic inquiry—works with naturally occurring groups and does not impose artificial control over variables. However, unlike researchers in the naturalistic inquiry tradition, action researchers do seek to intervene and bring about change (as do psychometric researchers conducting experiments). In fact, the "action" in action research is

TABLE 8.1 The action research cycle (adapted from Nunan, 1992, p. 19)

Cycle and Step	Example
Cycle 1	
Step 1: Problem/puzzle identification	"Student motivation is declining over the course of the semester."
Step 2: Preliminary investigation	"Interviews with students confirm my suspicion."
Step 3: Hypothesis formation	"Students do not feel they are making progress from their efforts. Learning logs will provide evidence of their progress."
Step 4: Plan intervention	"Have students complete weekly learning logs."
Step 5: Take action and observe outcomes	"Reading the learning logs suggests that learners are not really aware of their own progress."
Step 6: Reflect on outcomes	"Motivation is improving, but not as rapidly as desired."
Cycle 2	
Step 7: Identify follow-up puzzle	"How can I ensure more involvement and commitment by learners to their own learning process?"
Step 8: Second hypothesis	"Developing a reflective learning attitude on the part of learners will enhance involvement and motivation to learn."
Step 9: Take action and observe outcomes	"At the end of each unit of work, learners complete a self-evaluation of learning progress and attainment of goals."
Step 10: Reflect on outcomes	"Self-evaluations show not all learners feel they are improving, even though I think they are."

parallel to the treatment in experimental studies, but external researchers are not applying the treatment to subjects. Instead, in action research, the participants themselves decide what to do to bring about positive change.

Like naturalistic inquiry but unlike experimental research, the research questions may evolve as action research proceeds. And, because it is concerned with a particular situation, action research "tends to be rather messy and unpredictable" (van Lier, 1994b, p. 7), so the data collection and analysis procedures may also change. We turn now to discussion of the action research cycle with an example of how this evolution may come about.

Involving Our Students in Action Research

As teachers, to solve problems in our classrooms, we often need to understand the students' perspectives. There are several simple ways to collect data from students in an action research project, including many that are used in other approaches. Depending on the students' level of proficiency, you can collect data either in their home language or in the language they are studying. What matters most in this context may be their ideas (rather than or in addition to their target language proficiency). For this reason, you should consider the research question(s) you are addressing and choose the language that will allow the learners to understand the data collection processes and express themselves best.

Here are two examples of tools for collecting data from language learners. These are from a research report by Quirke (2001), who wanted to systematically elicit feedback from his students. He wrote, "The purpose of the investigation was to give students a voice in my teaching and thus help me adapt it to accommodate those students" (p. 82). Quirke carried out his action research for eight months in his reading classes at a women's college in Abu Dhabi. At the end of the lesson, he gave students time to complete the form in **Figure 8.2.**

At the beginning of the term, Quirke's students often left the *why* questions unanswered, but they began to provide responses around the third week of the term. By the end of the course, the students were providing answers to every question on the form.

Nine approaches to teaching reading were used over the next nine weeks. (See **Figure 8.3.**) At the end of the term, Quirke gave his students a form that listed the approaches they had used and asked for their ratings on the criteria of usefulness, difficulty, interest, and enjoyment. (His article does not explain the individual teaching approaches).

Please complete the following honestly.
   I will use your responses to plan our approach to reading classes next semester.

Week _____ Title of text _____

Approach _____

What was the aim of this class? _____

What did you learn during this class? _____

What did you enjoy most about the class?_____

Why? _____

What did you find most difficult? _____

Why? _____

Other comments: _____

FIGURE 8.2   A form for eliciting feedback on a reading lesson (from Quirk, 2001 p. 86)

Please complete the following table with numbers

1 = the most (e.g., the most enjoyable, the most useful)
9 = the least (e.g., the least enjoyable, the least useful)

Week	Approach	Useful	Difficult	Interesting	Enjoyable
1	Jigsaw reading				
2	Question cards				
3	Silent reading				
4	Group reading				
5	Analysis				
6	Clap				
7	Prediction				
8	Question writing				
9	Paragraph matching				

FIGURE 8.3   A form for eliciting students' feedback on reading approaches (adapted from Quirke, 2001, p. 86)

Another technique Quirke used is called a *graffiti board*—the use of a large sheet of paper or a chalkboard to gather students' feedback. The teacher would then leave the room during the regularly scheduled breaks and invite the students to add their comments on the graffiti board. After experimenting with various strategies for getting students' critical input, Quirke found that the graffiti board idea worked well if he started the process by posing just two questions inviting negative feedback, as shown in **Figure 8.4.** (The spelling and vocabulary reproduced here are the students' own work.)

What I DIDN'T like about the lesson	What I found MOST difficult
I don't like your lines.	The different with the 3 consepts
You give me sentence but I don't give you one	The draws for the lines because they are not clear.
The sentences and examples are not clear	I cant see the connection to now which you always say.
I get confused wit the past and perfect together—why do you do this???	
Why your line so confussing?	
What concept?	

FIGURE 8.4   A sample of a graffiti board (from Quirke, 2001, p. 88)

Quirke found that the students provided useful feedback that helped him to rethink and revise his lesson plans. He notes, "As far as my students are concerned, I am satisfied that these experiences of having their opinions sought and seeing them respected, did indeed help students developing their critical thinking skills" (ibid., p. 90).

REFLECTION

If you are currently teaching, think about an action research study you could conduct to address an issue in your own classes. What data collection tools and procedures could you use to elicit the students' input in that context?

QUALITY CONTROL ISSUES IN ACTION RESEARCH

Quality control in action research is largely a matter of being systematic and committed to engaging in the process over a period of time. Careful records must be kept regularly (e.g., by dating all diary entries, photocopying students' assignments, etc.), and the process of data collection must be religiously conducted. For instance, it is not acceptable for a teacher to skip writing in his teaching journal for a week because he is too busy. If the journal is a data collection procedure, it must be kept regularly and conscientiously over time. Creating and protecting the time to do so is part of the research process.

The discussion of triangulation in Chapters 6 and 7 is pertinent to action research as well. You will recall that Denzin (1978) described four types of triangulation. These are (1) *data triangulation*, which draws on different sources of data (teachers, students, parents, etc.); (2) *theory triangulation*, in which various theories are brought to bear; (3) *researcher triangulation*, when more than one researcher contributes to the investigation; and (4) *methods triangulation*, which involves the use of multiple methods (e.g., interviews, questionnaires, observation schedules, test scores, journal entries, etc.) to collect data.

As with case studies and ethnographies, all these types of triangulation can be usefully employed in action research. In particular, because of the participatory nature of action research, data triangulation can be used in most such studies. In our field, this goal usually involves gathering data from teachers and students. Administrators, young learners' parents, adult students' employers, and teachers' aides may also contribute data, depending on the focus of the study. The procedures discussed above (Quirke, 2001) provide some options for eliciting data from students.

Methods triangulation is also a natural fit with action research, which uses any data that can address the research questions posed when problems and/or puzzles are identified. Researcher triangulation can be developed by collaborating with colleagues or by inviting an external researcher to help with an action research project. Finally, to the extent that an action research project draws on theory, it is also possible to implement theory triangulation.

SAMPLE STUDY

The sample study presented here incorporates many of these quality control issues and illustrates a process for eliciting students' ideas. The teacher, John Thorpe, conducted this action research project in his own ESL class, but he collaborated with a colleague who was teaching the same group of students in a different class. The colleague focused on vocabulary learning in his action research project while Thorpe wanted to explore options in teaching listening comprehension through the use of television news broadcasts.

This focus came about because Thorpe was working with three Korean adult learners of English who were enrolled in a two-semester program sponsored by their government. Upon their return to Korea, the students would be facing a battery of English proficiency examinations. These students were worried about a listening comprehension test which consisted almost entirely of news broadcasts, so Thorpe decided to include television news broadcasts as part of their regular biweekly two-hour lessons. Thorpe (2004) described his study as a "two-phase, eight-cycle action research project" (p. 1). He gathered data by videotaping lessons, keeping a teaching journal, and having his students complete a questionnaire each week. He also discussed the videotaped lessons with his colleague.

REFLECTION

Based on the information given so far, what type(s) of triangulation did Thorpe use in his action research project?

Thorpe began his action research project with a literature review that informed his teaching as well as his research focus. Thorpe was an experienced teacher, but he was open to learning new things. He wrote,

Although I have over twelve years of classroom experience, I have only used TV news broadcasts sparingly. A review of the relevant literature . . . uncovered only scant information pertaining specifically to the pedagogical use of TV news broadcasts. . . . Although more recent resource books (e.g., Larimer & Schleicher, 1999) do include some useful ideas, in light of the popularity of TV news, I feel additional research using TV news broadcasts in the second or foreign language classroom is needed. This project aimed, then, to seek possible answers . . . to the following research question: *How can I best teach listening comprehension using TV news broadcasts?* (pp. 1–2)

The study also addressed another question: *Will participants and the teacher agree or disagree on the effectiveness of instruction?* This question stemmed from Kumaravadivelu's (1994; 2003) thinking on *perceptual mismatches* between teachers and students. Thorpe was curious about whether his interpretation of lesson activities matched those of his students.

In his graduate courses, Thorpe had read about action research, but this was the first time he actually carried out an action research study of his own. He knew this was the right approach to use, however, since he wanted to investigate and improve his own teaching while simultaneously helping his students to improve their listening comprehension. He notes that action projects typically do not follow the experimental tradition:

> My participants, for example, were not randomly selected nor were they necessarily typical of other language learners. I did not administer a pre- or post-test specifically designed to quantitatively measure their competence or achievement before or after a specified treatment. . . . In contrast, action research breaks down "the dichotomy between researcher and researched" (Auerbach, 1994, p. 695) and recognizes the value of intangibles. As van Lier (1996b) has keenly observed, "Intangibles are often more influential than tangibles. If you can't see it, that doesn't mean it isn't there. If you can't count it, that doesn't mean it doesn't count" (p. 2). (Thorpe, 2004, p. 7)

REFLECTION

Imagine yourself in Thorpe's position. How could you collect baseline data about your students' listening comprehension? What actions might you want to implement to address the questions would you pose?

Given this grounding, Thorpe initially planned the project as five research cycles to be conducted over five weeks during one term of instruction, but the project continued into a second phase the following semester. The interventions that he tried as the course progressed included giving the students their choice of which news story to listen to, providing transcripts of the story, letting the students choose when to view the transcript, providing written comprehension questions about the broadcast, having the students themselves write the questions, and varying whether the topic of the news story was familiar or unfamiliar to the learners. The two phases consisted of eight cycles, which are summarized in **Table 8.2**.

The data collection processes Thorpe used were varied and systematic. They gave him a clear picture of the students' responses to these interventions. To collect data, he videotaped all the listening activities in his class for a month. These included brief broadcasts from *CNN Student News*, which had not been simplified for language learners. Thorpe also used the transcripts of these broadcasts, which were available on CNN's Web site.

TABLE 8.2 Two phases of action research cycles (adapted from Thorpe, 2004, p. 40)

Cycle	Story Selection	Topic Familiarity	Control of Task	Transcript	Interventions
PHASE 1					
1	Teacher	Unfamiliar	Teacher	Not used	Participants choose story. Assumed they had background knowledge.
2	Participant	Familiar	Participant	Not used	
3	Participant	Unfamiliar	Teacher	Used before listening	Use of transcript prior to listening.
4	CNN	Unfamiliar	Teacher	Not used	CNN "chooses" story. Teacher prepares comprehension questions. Participants choose when to view questions.
5	Participant	Familiar	Participant	Used after listening	Participants choose story, participants write questions. Transcript used at the end.
PHASE 2					
1	Teacher	Familiar	Teacher	Not used	Parody instead of "straight" news.
2	Teacher	Familiar	Teacher	Optional use after initial listening	*The News Hour* replaced *CNN Student News*. Longer news story; grid format.
3	Teacher	Familiar	Teacher	Optional use after listening	Task given after initial listening; no pre-task schema activation.

Thorpe had two lessons per week with these students, so he planned each week to comprise one action research cycle. During the Tuesday class, he would implement the actions he had planned. Then each Thursday, after they had completed the listening activity, the students filled out a short questionnaire eliciting their ideas about both the news story and the classroom procedures used with it. The teacher himself also completed this questionnaire. The questionnaire format was based on an idea from Christison and Bassano (1995) in which the learners simply placed a vertical mark on a nine-centimeter line to indicate their opinion. This procedure allowed Thorpe to compare the

Directions: Please draw a single, straight line (|) on the horizontal continuum (___) to indicate your opinion. For example:

Compared to the United States, Japan is

very big └─────────────────────────────────────┼─────┘ very small

- -

The news story was

very easy └───┘ **very difficult**

I found the teaching activity

not at all └───┘ **very helpful**
helpful

I would recommend that John use the activity again.

strongly └───┘ **strongly**
disagree **agree**

Compared to the activity we did last week, I liked this one

a lot less └───┘ **a lot more**

In general, I feel my aural understanding of TV news has

not └───┘ **increased**
increased **significantly**
at all

Other comments (optional):

FIGURE 8.5 Student questionnaire about lessons used (adapted from Thorpe, 2004, p. 39)

participants' responses—both to each other's ideas and to their own subsequent responses over time. The student questionnaire is reprinted as **Figure 8.5.**

Before having the students complete the questionnaire, Thorpe explained to them how he was changing the teaching procedure. He also showed them their earlier questionnaires so they could compare their current reactions to those of the previous week. It was simple and quick for the students to fill out the form, and the data it yielded gave Thorpe information he would not have otherwise had.

Thorpe also recorded his own impressions of the lessons in his teaching journal, noting any particular problems or insights. He gave his colleague a videotape of the lesson, and they discussed it before he planned the next cycle. This process continued for five weeks—the five cycles of the first phase. Then

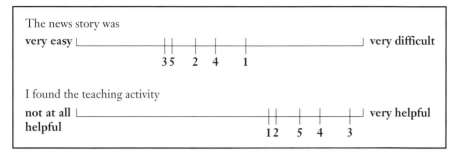

FIGURE 8.6 Students' cumulative responses to five cycles of the action research project

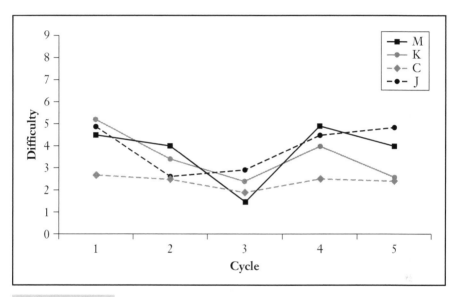

FIGURE 8.7 Individual student's ratings of the story difficulty

Thorpe compiled all the students' responses, as shown in **Figure 8.6.** The numbers refer to the five research cycles.

Thorpe (2004) measured how far from the left end each mark was and created line graphs using these data. This procedure allowed Thorpe to compare the students' various responses to the questions and to find patterns occurring over the five-week investigation. He could also compare his reactions to those of the participants.

Figures 8.7 and **8.8,** respectively, show the data from the teacher (J) and the students regarding the difficulty of the news stories and the helpfulness of the teaching activities. The nine-point scale derives from the fact that the students marked their impressions on the nine-centimeter line. This process gave Thorpe a clear visual way to represent and compare his students' opinions.

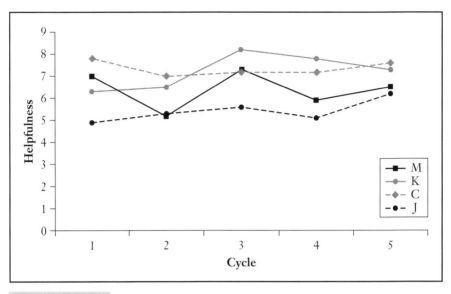

FIGURE 8.8 Individual students' ratings of the teaching activity

REFLECTION

What patterns do you notice in Figures 8.7 and 8.8? If you were the teacher, how would you interpret these data?

These data were compiled after the fifth cycle (at the end of the first course Thorpe [2004] had with these students and at the end of the first phase of the action research project). Here's part of what the teacher had to say about his interpretation of these data:

The line charts depicting the participants' collective responses are both enlightening and puzzling. On the one hand, a clear pattern can be seen between how participants rated the difficulty of a story and the teaching activity used: as perception of difficulty goes down, approval of the activity goes up. . . . The participants also appeared to link ease of understanding to the activity itself. In other words, if they found the story easy, it was in part due to the teaching procedure; if they found it difficult, this was at least partially due to the procedure as well. (p. 20)

Throughout the report, Thorpe uses initials to refer to the students, thereby protecting their confidentiality. They are known to readers as *C*, *K*, and *M*. In one case where the students had trouble understanding a news broadcast, Thorpe wrote,

> I was unsure if their difficulties were due to language, rate of speech, context, or subject matter. The situation was clarified upon reading the questionnaires. M wrote, "I found a big gap of understanding between international news and domestic news. It could be helpful to balance both of them." (p. 12)

Thorpe wondered if interest in the news stories might also be a factor in the students' listening comprehension. He and his colleague discussed this issue and decided he should let the students themselves choose the particular news story based on the brief "teasers" that CNN uses at the start of the broadcast to tell the listeners what stories will be covered. Of this decision he wrote,

> The primary drawback—that it would be more difficult for me to plan because I would have to prepare all the stories, not just one—led to a personal insight that had eluded me over my 12-year teaching career: I like to be in complete control. The realization brought to mind a series of nightmares I had had several years ago in which I entered my classroom only to realize that I had completely forgotten to prepare for the lesson! Despite being a very vocal advocate of student-centered classes, my actions showed that I prefer to control the classroom situation, exemplified by my use of carefully created and planned classroom material. What is particularly odd about this revelation is that I encourage students to take risks . . . and to be fearless in testing their hypotheses about language. Yet I did not appear willing to take my own risks by sharing control with the students. Thus the action research process of collaborative investigation transcended my original intentions. . . . I became aware of something previously unknown to me. As I would now consciously cede this absolute control I wondered: How would it go? (p. 12)

On Tuesday, the first day of the new cycle, Thorpe played the preview of the news broadcast and let the students choose the story they would listen to. They chose one about household germs. The teacher wrote,

> Although I had viewed the story before, my knowledge was not as thorough or complete as last week's news stories because my preparation time had been evenly spread across all four stories. However, since the participants would play a more active role in the process, I did not feel my knowledge of the story was insufficient. I felt the power distribution was more in balance because I, too, was seeking information from the news story. (p. 13)

At the Thursday class, continuing with this particular intervention, Thorpe had the students select a story from the news broadcast. They chose a report about a

Burger King restaurant in Baghdad. Of this experience, Thorpe said,

> Although there were parts I thought might give them problems I suppressed my desire to control the activity. My assumption was that, unless they specifically asked me, I would assume they understood the story. Of course, such reliance on the students is not always advisable. I could think of past situations where it would not be appropriate, but I believe these particular learners were capable of taking responsibility for their own learning. (p. 15)

Because the students took a more active role, Thorpe and his colleague felt that this cycle was better than the previous week's cycle, but only one student (K) thought so. The teachers wondered about the students' evaluations as the two of them were trying to promote a more learner-centered approach. They decided that culturally based expectations might be influencing the students' evaluations. Perhaps these learners were accustomed to a more traditional view of teachers' and students' roles (i.e., a knowledge-transmission model of education). To address this issue, Thorpe decided on a different action step. He would assign a particular task, but the students would still choose the news story they wanted to listen to. They selected a report on a serious wildfire in California. Before the class, Thorpe had cut the transcript of the story into strips that represented the turns of the various speakers in the broadcast.

> Each participant was given a packet of the strips and asked to arrange them in order. In reviewing their results, I was pleased not only with their ability to accomplish the task but in their reasoning as well. For example, C explained his arrangement by saying that he realized that the newscaster would probably speak first and last and that the reporter's speech would be interspersed with eyewitness testimony or some other corroborative statement. (p. 16)

After the students predicted the structure of the news story and possible alternatives, the teacher played the videotape for them. When he played it the second time, he stopped at the end of each segment so the students could ask questions. At the next class meeting, on Thursday, he repeated this process. He wrote,

> This time, the participants chose a story about a mine rescue in Russia. One additional insight participants gained from this activity was the use—very common in TV news—of word plays and puns. In this case, the newscaster referred to the rescue as a "miner miracle." What the participants realized was that the outcome of the story dictated the use of these plays on words. If, for example, all or most of the miners had died, the pun would not have been appropriate. This insight would be helpful in anticipating the outcomes of subsequent TV news stories and potential reasons why, for example, the newscaster smiled without apparent reason. I have found that these word plays and puns are often very difficult for learners to understand, even at advanced levels. (p. 16)

Thorpe read the questionnaires and found that the students viewed the story as relatively easy. He thought this perception was due to the fact that they had read the transcript before listening to the story. He wrote,

K and M both marked the *recommendation of activity* very highly as well. C, however, marked the activity as the lowest to date. What was most surprising about the results was that Stuart and I both thought that C was clearly the most involved in the task as he asked more questions and volunteered more comments than M or K. What could account for our misinterpretation of his classroom behavior? (pp. 16–17)

[Teachers'] subjective interpretations of participants' cues—e.g., involvement, participation, and success in completing tasks—cannot be assumed to be signs of pedagogical approval. These are components of our self-defined criteria of a successful lesson. Students, however, have different goals and different ways of evaluating the effectiveness of pedagogical procedures. I could not tell whether it was the task itself—the unscrambling of the transcript—that he did not like or doing it prior to viewing the story. Perhaps the procedure conflicted with his own preferred metacognitive strategy, which Oxford (2002) notes includes an individual's learning style preferences and how they plan a learning task. It could also be the result of a pedagogic mismatch (Kumaravadivelu, 2003), or a gap between what C felt were the learning objectives of the task and what I was trying to accomplish. (p. 17)

When Thorpe read C's comment to see what he had not liked, he found that the student had written, "We can listen first, and then answer about the story, then take a look at the transcript" (p. 17). Thorpe decided to use this student's suggestion during the next action research cycle. He also decided to address another student request—namely, that the class review the previous lesson's news story. After a discussion with his colleague, Thorpe decided to use CNN's lead story and write six questions in advance that required specific information about the story. He would give the students their choice of either hearing the questions before or after he played the tape.

For the fifth and final cycle, Thorpe decided to have the students themselves write comprehension questions about the news story. He reasoned that this process would

require them to construct a base meaning . . . from the scant input provided by the news tease. To put the control of the activity in their hands even more, I would allow them to again choose the news story. I would also give them a copy of the transcript, this time after playing the clip. The final change would be the elimination of the previous lesson's replay as my journal entries for this week expressed displeasure over the inordinate amount of time devoted to listening. (p. 19)

In my journal I noted that these lessons were among the best. The questions the participants generated were logical and well-planned and they controlled more of the lesson. Their reactions, however, were mixed. None liked the activity more than when I wrote the questions. (p. 20)

REFLECTION

At this point, Thorpe had finished the five-cycle action research project he had originally planned to conduct. What might he do next, if he decided to continue the project through further action research? Brainstorm a list of possible options for further investigation.

These procedures continued for five weeks. After completing these five cycles, Thorpe decided to extend the project for an additional three cycles. During this second phase, the data collection procedures were similar but not identical to those of the first phase. In the data collection for the second phase, Thorpe continued to videotape his classes, write in his teaching journal, and have his students complete the questionnaire about each lesson's activities. However, a schedule change meant that Thorpe and his colleague could now observe each other's teaching instead of being limited to viewing videotapes of one another's classes. Thorpe also made a change in his source materials from the minute-long *CNN Student News* reports:

In an effort to accommodate the participants' request and also to collect data on the use of longer video news segments, I decided to seek alternative news sources. I subsequently selected *The News Hour with Jim Lehrer* for several reasons. First, the stories are much longer—some as long as 20 minutes—and have a mix of straight news reporting and panel-like discussions often consisting of two people with opposing views. (pp. 22–23)

Thorpe posted a link to *The News Hour's* Web site on his course Web site since it contained complete transcripts of the broadcasts as well as links to the audio and video clips. This resource enabled the students to review the news stories if they wished.

Prior to beginning the second phase, I showed the participants a story from *The News Hour* to ensure their approval of the change. They told me that the style of reporting was similar to a Korean news broadcast and that, although the story they viewed was much longer, it was fairly easy to understand because both Jim Lehrer and *The News Hour* reporters spoke slowly and pronounced their words carefully. All three also indicated that they liked the change from *CNN Student News* because of the longer, more in-depth news stories the program offered. (p. 23)

As he had done after the first phase, Thorpe plotted the students' and his own data from phase two on line graphs. Even though there were only three action research cycles in this phase, the data yielded information that was helpful to the teacher. About the second phase, Thorpe wrote,

> An interesting and noteworthy pattern involved the similarities between my questionnaire responses and those of the participants. Unlike in phase one, where there were noticeable differences, in this phase our evaluations were more closely aligned. In particular, M's scores and mine were far more similar in phase two than in phase one. I think one possible explanation could be that by including the participants in the data collection process I was able to "align" my perceptions with theirs. (p. 30)

It seemed that the regular feedback Thorpe got from the students helped him to predict their needs and select materials and tasks they would find useful as well as judging the kinds of news broadcasts that would be appropriate. He wrote,

> The project had the added benefit of fostering awareness-raising skills, which Freeman (1989:28) believes trigger a "process of decision making based on the constituents of knowledge, skills, attitude, and awareness." In other words, it is through awareness that one's professional development—his or her knowledge, skills, and attitudes about teaching—will grow. My realization that I am, to be blunt, a control freak, is one example of my heightened awareness. The results of phase one also showed me that it is a good tactic to give participants the power to choose teaching material and to give them a say in deciding pedagogical procedures. However, I also found that these participants do not want complete control and prefer that I ask specific "answerable" questions derived from the story to gage their comprehension. (pp. 30–31)

Thorpe found that the perceptual mismatches between his view and the students' were less pronounced in phase two than in phase one. He attributed this difference to the systematic practice of collecting their feedback regularly in each cycle. He wrote,

> I think that including the participants in the project also increased the likelihood they would get involved in their own learning as well. . . . Involvement in action research—both in this study and my collaborative role in [my colleague's] project as well—can "make our work more purposeful, interesting, and valuable, and as such it tends to have an energizing and revitalizing effect" (van Lier, 1994a, p. 33). Although action research does not aim at generalizability, I have discovered both personal and professional insights that definitely can be applied to many other teaching situations. (pp. 31–32)

This summary shows how Thorpe used the action research cycles to systematically vary the changes he made in his teaching. He collaborated with a colleague and linked his own thinking to some related professional literature. After he finished this project, Thorpe wrote,

> One of the things I like best about doing action research is it motivates me to try something new and different and not to fret if the lesson tanks. In short, I think that the process of recording data in a systematic way by videotaping lessons, creating and then analyzing the results of student questionnaires, being observed by colleagues, and writing a journal can, in van Lier's (1994a) words, "make our work more purposeful, interesting, and valuable, and as such it tends to have an energizing and revitalizing effect." (p. 33)

PAYOFFS AND PITFALLS

There are both advantages and disadvantages of conducting action research. In this section, we will address likely pitfalls first and comment on possible solutions. We will then discuss the payoffs of doing action research.

Challenges in Doing Action Research

Nunan once worked as an advisor to a network of high school language teachers who were conducting action research. These teachers taught a variety of languages (e.g., Spanish, Italian, Vietnamese, Indonesian, Polish, and Greek) in Australia. The idea of setting up a support network with Nunan as the facilitator was to assist teachers in developing the basic skills of research design. These included (1) identifying a problem and turning it into a researchable question; (2) deciding on appropriate data and data collection methods; (3) determining the best way of collecting and analyzing the data; and (4) evaluating the research plan and reducing it to manageable proportions.

This group kept journals of their experiences during the semester-long project. Nunan asked them to document the challenges and difficulties they encountered. A content analysis of their records at the end of the semester revealed five major areas of concern as follows: (1) lack of time, (2) lack of expertise, (3) lack of ongoing support, (4) fear of being revealed as an incompetent teacher, and (5) fear of producing a public account of their research for a wider (unknown) audience.

Lack of time was the single biggest impediment for these teachers to carry out their action research. It was mentioned by every teacher in the network, and some teachers mentioned it virtually every time they made comments in their journals. Teachers are busy people, and involvement in the action research network, without release time from any of their other duties, added considerably to the burden of their daily professional life.

Not surprisingly, the second most frequently nominated roadblock on the road to success was lack of expertise. The word *research* raises all sorts of fears and uncertainties in the minds of teachers. It conjures up images of scientists in white coats with measuring instruments and mysterious methods of carrying out statistical analyses. In fact, one of the benefits of engaging in action research is to demystify the notion of research and the idea that one needs a license to practice. We believe most teachers have the potential to do classroom research, and they should be encouraged to add a reflective teaching and/or action research dimension to their professional armory.

The third most frequently nominated challenge was lack of support 'on the ground.' This lack of support most often came from the individual to whom the teacher reported (most typically the department chair or panel head) or the school principal. In some cases, the principal refused to sign the release allowing the research to go ahead. In other instances, permission was granted reluctantly—the attitude being, "Well, this is a lot of nonsense, but if you want to go ahead and waste your time, feel free. However, don't let it interfere with your proper job—which is to teach."

Interestingly, resistance sometimes came from colleagues. This negativity took the form of an attitude that to do research indicated that one had ideas above one's station. Lurking behind these negative attitudes was the notion that the appropriate job for a teacher is to teach, not to do research, and that this 'make-believe' role as researcher was not a legitimate thing for a teacher to be doing. To be fair, the opposite reaction was also encountered. A number of teachers reported that their status and esteem had risen among their peers as a result of having taken part in the action research network.

Some participants worried that by conducting action research, they might be revealed as incompetent teachers. Indeed, any form of research carries within it the possibility of a negative result—or no result at all. This view is reinforced to a certain extent by mainstream published research, which rarely reports that research outcomes were inconclusive. These teachers were investigating aspects of their own practice. Some felt that an inconclusive or negative outcome could be interpreted as a sign of failure, an indication that the person was an incompetent teacher. The fact that the results would be made public added to this particular anxiety.

Indeed, the fear of having to produce a public report on their research—particularly for a wide, unknown audience—was the final most frequently nominated problem area. Teachers who had no trouble developing a sensible and coherent plan and putting it into action baulked when it came to writing up and making their research public. A number wanted to stop at this point, asking "Why do we have to make it public?" and "I find writing so difficult." The answer, of course, is that without a public account, other teachers cannot benefit from your insights, and you cannot benefit from their feedback. The publication need not be an article in an international refereed journal, or even a formal written report. It might take the form of a presentation at a local teachers' conference or a discussion among colleagues at a brown-bag lunch.

Possible Solutions

We have experimented with a number of solutions to these problems. Chances of success for any given project will be maximized if there is someone to 'own' the project. Likewise, it is advisable that one or more advisors with training in research methods and experience in doing research are available as needed to provide assistance and support to teachers. In addition, teachers should be given some release time from face-to-face teaching during the course of their action research. Collaborative teams can be formed, desirably across schools or teaching sites, so that teachers involved in similar areas of inquiry can support one another. Finally, it is important that teachers are given adequate training in methods and techniques for identifying issues, collecting data, analyzing and interpreting data, and presenting the outcomes of their research. We will address each of these issues in turn.

First, completing an action research project is a little like completing a marathon at the same time as you carry out a wide range of other tasks. In order to succeed, teachers have to be in it for the long haul. After an initial burst of enthusiasm, some teachers 'hit the wall' (as marathon runners say). Energy and enthusiasm can begin to wane, and many teachers are tempted to put off essential data collection or analysis tasks, or even abandon the project completely.

Having an enthusiastic partner or team member can go a long way towards maintaining enthusiasm about the project. In the two action research networks Nunan advised, local facilitators filled this role. Both were senior teachers who had considerable experience as educational administrators. One of the local facilitators was completing a doctorate and was able to answer many teachers' queries directly. The other facilitator had recently completed a master's degree and was able to get help from his former professors. Importantly, these two facilitators had also successfully carried out action research projects of their own. This experience gave them credibility among the teachers and enabled them to act as a bridge between teachers and administrators.

These local facilitators were proactive as well as reactive. They maintained frequent contact with the teachers involved in the network through telephone conversations, e-mail correspondence, and occasional face-to-face meetings, and they were able to identify those teachers who were at risk of dropping out. When teachers contacted them with practical problems and blockages, the facilitators were able to offer advice from their own perspectives.

Secondly, even with the support of a collaborative network of fellow teachers, doing action reach can be lonely and isolating. The chances of long-term success will be enhanced if someone is available at reasonably short notice to provide technical advice. This support is important at all stages of the action research cycle.

Third, in order for teachers to succeed at conducting action research, it is important that they get some relief from their normal duties while they are doing action research. As an alternative, participating in an action research project could be counted as meeting professional development hours required by many school systems.

Fourth, establishing collaborative teams of action researchers, preferably across schools or teaching sites, can be very helpful. Such teams provide a structure whereby teachers involved in similar areas of inquiry can support one another. In addition, it is harder to abandon a project if your colleagues are counting on you to support them in their action research endeavors.

Another challenge is to convince teachers that qualitative data collection and analysis are, in fact, legitimate approaches to research. Many who have had minimal contact with research hold the mistaken idea that research must necessarily always involve statistical analyses. Ironically, it is this notion that lies behind much of the trepidation that teachers feel about doing research.

Finally, teachers should receive adequate training in procedures for identifying issues, for collecting, analyzing and interpreting data, and for presenting the outcomes of their research. Like any other form of classroom research, successful action research demands adequate planning and preparation. Providing teachers with training in research methods and adequate planning time *before* they embark on the project will enhance the chances of success. At the beginning of the process, once teachers have identified an issue, problem, or puzzle, it is important for them to think small. Many teachers, in the first enthusiastic flush of the project, begin sketching out a proposal that would require substantial doctoral-level research. (Remember the story about Japanese flower arranging!)

Benefits of Action Research

There are several significant payoffs for teachers who carry out action research investigations in their classrooms. In the first place, the research is centered on real problems, puzzles, or challenges teachers face in their daily work. It can therefore carry immediate benefits and tangible improvements to practice. Secondly, it can lead teachers to see connections between 'mainstream' theory and research and their own practice. Third, by increasing the teacher's control over and active involvement in his or her immediate professional context, it can empower the teacher.

One of the strong claims of proponents of action research is that it leads to improvements in practice. In our experience, teachers have been able to change their lesson plans and curricula, build collegial relations, and increase their confidence by conducting action research. Nunan (1993) documented changes made to classroom practice by the teachers as a result of being involved in the action research network described above. Although several teachers collaboratively investigated a particular issue (for example, implementing task-based teaching in their classrooms), most teachers worked on individual projects. However, once a month, they all met together for a half-day workshop to exchange ideas, share problems, and generally support each other. These teachers reported on the changes they had made in their classroom practice as a result of being involved in action research. (See **Table 8.3.**)

Table 8.3 illustrates a positive 'ripple effect.' These teachers felt that engagement in action research not only helped them solve specific problems in their classrooms, but it also led them to improve their classroom management and interaction skills.

If we think back to the issues of control over variables in experimental research leading to internal validity, we can see that the lack of control in action research means there can be no strong internal validity in the classical psychometric sense. As action researchers, we do not try to exert control over variables

TABLE 8.3 Changes made to classroom practice as a result of taking part in action research (adapted from Nunan, 1993, p. 47)

Action	More	About the Same	Less
tend to be directive	1	14	10
try to use a greater variety of behaviors	16	6	0
praise students	15	10	0
criticize students	0	11	13
am aware of students' feelings	18	6	0
give directions	4	16	5
am conscious of my nonverbal behavior	11	14	0
use the target language in class	19	6	0
am conscious of nonverbal cues of students	12	12	0
try to incorporate student ideas into my teaching	20	5	0
spend more class time talking myself	1	9	15
try to get my students working in groups	15	8	0
try to get divergent open-ended student responses	14	10	0
distinguish between enthusiasm and lack of order	9	15	0
try to get students to participate	18	7	0

that might influence the outcomes, so we cannot unequivocally say that the planned interventions *caused* the observed results. Instead, in conducting action research, teachers seek out options that seem to them to be convincing solutions to problems or classroom puzzles.

Likewise, there can be no external validity in action research because the conditions in any given setting could never be duplicated in another. Indeed, generalizability is not a goal of action research. Rather, action researchers seek local understanding and wish to improve their own practice.

However, like case studies and ethnographies, action research reports are often thought-provoking and comparable. We will cite just one example here. In Chapter 3, we reported on Sato's (1982) observational research on turn taking by Asian students in English classes. This concern is one that many teachers have faced. In fact, Tsui (1996) wrote a report on action research projects conducted by thirty-eight teachers in Hong Kong about this very issue.

In Tsui's report, the teachers first collected baseline data on the interaction in their classrooms. The teachers themselves identified five possible reasons to account for the students' apparent reluctance to speak in class. These were (1) the students' low English proficiency, (2) their fear of making mistakes and being derided for doing so, (3) the teachers' intolerance of silence, (4) the teachers' uneven allocation of turns, and (5) the incomprehensible input the students experienced in class—often in the teachers' speech.

As a result of their analyses, the teachers came up with several strategies for encouraging their students to speak during their English classes. The teachers chose various ways to document these strategies, which included lengthening their wait time, improving their questioning techniques, and accepting a variety of answers. Some teachers created more opportunities for peer support and group work and for establishing good relationships with the learners. Some chose to focus more on the content of students' contributions rather than the form.

Tsui (1996) did not make any claims about the generalizability of these findings, but the fact of the matter is that getting students to speak the target language in language classes is a concern for teachers in many parts of the world. It may be that some of the strategies these teachers used will be directly helpful to others, or indirectly helpful in suggesting alternative strategies.

CONCLUSION

We end this chapter where it began, with a quote from Mingucci (1999), who wrote about the role of action research in professional development. She said that for teachers

> to fully embrace the principles and philosophy of action research, they need to begin by reinventing themselves. Practitioners must look at themselves and their practices, as if for the first time, and try to see themselves as the central object of their research if true change is to occur. We can only address the outside world after we have addressed our individual internal ones. We can only create alternatives to the existing method and structures after we have restructured ourselves. (p. 16)

Thorpe's experience of learning to yield some control in his lessons illustrates this point.

In our view, action research can contribute to both the knowledge base of the field and the ongoing professional development of the teachers who use it to investigate important issues in their own classrooms. As van Lier (1994a) has noted, "Action research is hardly ever short-term, but . . . a way of working in which every answer raises new questions, and one can thus never quite say, 'I've finished.' " (p. 34)

QUESTIONS AND TASKS

1. Look back at the summary of Thorpe's (2004) action research project. Which of the "payoffs" described above were present in his case?

2. There are now several Web sites devoted to educational action research. Here are five that we believe are useful:

   1. A Web site of the Madison Metropolitan School District, Research Abstracts, is geared specifically to elementary and secondary school

contexts. The address is

http://www.madison.k12.wi.us

2. The Action Learning Project Web site provides reports and a description of a large project in Hong Kong. The address is

http://www.acad.polyu.edu.hk/~etwalp/

3. A Web site at Southern Cross University, Australia, while not specifically about language teaching research, is very helpful. It can be found at

http://www.scu.edu.au/schools/gcm/ar/arhome.html

4. A good Web site for a useful list of action research URLs that demonstrate lessons learned from other researchers can be found at

http://www.cudenver.edu/~mryder/itc/act_res.htm

5. An extensive database of articles and links to other resources can be found at

http://carbon.cudenver.edu/~mryder/itc/act_res.html

Visit one or more of these Web sites and see what sort of information and support are provided that could be helpful to you.

3. Read one or more of the action research reports described in the "Suggestions for Further Reading" below. What problems or puzzles were investigated? What data collection procedures were used?

4. If you are currently teaching, identify a problem or puzzle in your work that could be investigated by using the action research cycle. The first step, as illustrated by the teachers in Tsui's (1996) report, is to gather baseline data to help you understand the situation better. How could you gather such data? What sorts of data collection procedures are appropriate, given your context and your focus?

5. After you have collected some baseline data, determine your first action step. What exactly do you want to do in hopes of improving your situation?

6. Determine how you will gather data while and after your implement the first action step. Would videotaping or tape-recording be appropriate? Or could you invite a colleague to observe your lessons? Is there some sort of information that your students will produce which you could legitimately use in your study?

7. Turn back to Chapter 5 and review the various types of questionnaire items. What sort of questionnaire might be helpful in the action research project you are envisioning?

8. Think about how you could analyze the data that you do collect. What sorts of data analyses might be involved in your action research project?

9. Imagine a debate between a committed action researcher and a committed experimental researcher. What would they disagree about in terms of (1) permissible research questions, (2) ideal data collection procedures, and (3) appropriate data analysis procedures? What would they probably agree about?

SUGGESTIONS FOR FURTHER READING

Two booklength treatments about action research in language education are *Collaborative Action Research for English Language Teachers* by Burns (1999) and *Action Research for Language Teachers* by Wallace (1998). A collection of action research studies by language teachers was edited by Edge (2001). Michonska-Stadnik and Szulc-Kurpaska (1997) produced a volume of action research reports done by teachers in Poland.

Some early influential writing about action research in general education was done at Deakin University in Australia. Resulting publications include Carr and Kemmis, (1986), Kemmis and Henry (1989), and Kemmis and McTaggart (1982; 1988).

A number of publications from the National Center for English Language Teaching and Research (NCELTR) in Australia report teachers' investigations using action research. See, for example, the volumes edited by Burns, de Silva Joyce, and Hood (1995; 1997; 1999a; 1999b; 1999c; and 2000).

Other publications on action research in contexts of second or foreign language education include Burns (1995; 1997; 2000), Chamot (1995), Chan (1996), Crookes (1993; 1998; 2005), Curtis (1998; 1999), Duterte (2000), Kebir (1994), Knezedvic (2001), Knowles (1990), Kwan (1993), McPherson (1997), Mingucci (1999), Mok (1997), Nunan (1990; 1993), Ruiz de Gauna, Diaz, Gonzales, & Garaizer (1995), Szostek (1994), Tinker Sachs (2000), and van Lier (1992).

D. Allwright (1997; 2003; 2005) describes an alternative to action research that he calls *exploratory practice* (Allwright & Lenzuen, 1997). It emphasizes understanding over bringing about improvement. See also Fanselow and Barnard (2006).

If you would like to know more about perceptual mismatches between students' and teachers' views of language lessons, see Block (1996) and Kumaravadivelu (1994; 2003).

PART III

DATA COLLECTION ISSUES
Getting the Information You Need

In this section, we look at three families of procedures for obtaining language classroom data. The first of these is classroom observation, the second is the use of introspective methods, and the third is elicitation procedures. Although they have some natural alignments with some traditions rather than others, all of these procedures can be useful in any of the research traditions discussed in earlier chapters.

Chapter 9: Classroom Observation

By the end of this chapter, readers will

- describe five options for collecting data during classroom observations;
- evaluate, discuss, and critique two widely used observation schemes for coding classroom data;
- discuss the advantages and disadvantages of observation schemes as opposed to ethnographic narratives;
- articulate the issues involved in transcribing classroom interaction;
- use diagrammatic schemes such as maps and seating charts for capturing classroom interaction.

Chapter 10: Introspective Methods of Data Collection

By the end of this chapter, readers will

- define introspective data collection and differentiate between introspection and retrospection;
- define and exemplify the following introspective methods: think-aloud protocols, stimulated recall, diary studies, and [auto]biographical research;
- discuss quality control issues in introspective data collection.

Chapter 11: Elicitation Procedures

By the end of this chapter, readers will

- describe and exemplify a range of elicitation procedures, including interviews, production tasks, role plays, questionnaires, and tests;
- identify five different types of interviews and explain the differences among them;
- describe the relationship between production tasks and learner discourse;
- discuss the advantages and disadvantages of using elicitation procedures to gather data.

9

Classroom Observation

Observation is always selective. It needs a chosen object, a definite task, an interest, a point of view, a problem. . . . It presupposes interests, points of view and problems (as cited in Cohen and Cohen, 1980, p. 266).

INTRODUCTION AND OVERVIEW

In this chapter, we look at methods for directly documenting life inside the classroom. As language classrooms are specifically constituted in order to facilitate learning, it makes eminent sense to observe what goes on there.

In early classroom research, when product studies were dominant, there were relatively few investigations that involved a solid observational component. Since process studies have become more widely accepted in classroom research, the use of observation procedures in data collection has increased. In fact, with the recent emphasis on process studies and process-product studies, observational data collection procedures have become widely accepted and, in some cases, are seen as essential.

The Contexts of Classroom Observation

In Chapter 1, we quoted van Lier's (1988) definition of a classroom: "The L2 classroom can be defined as the gathering, for a given period of time, of two or more persons (one of whom generally assumes the role of instructor) for the purposes of language learning" (p. 47). We also noted that now, with the advent of online learning, the concept of a classroom has been expanded to include "virtual" classrooms, in which lesson participants may be separated by miles—even by continents! Nevertheless, D. Allwright's (1988) characterization of classroom research still holds true, whether teachers and learners are interacting in a physical space or an electronic lesson:

> Classroom-centered research is just that—research centered on the classroom, as distinct from . . . research that concentrates on the inputs to the classroom (the syllabus, the teaching materials) or the outputs from the classroom (learner achievement scores). It does not ignore in any way or try to devalue the importance of such inputs and outputs. It simply tries to investigate what happens inside the classroom when learners and teachers come together. (p. 191)

That is, indeed, a key purpose of observation: "to investigate what happens inside the classroom when learners and teachers come together" (ibid.).

REFLECTION

Given the information above about classrooms, how would you define *classroom observation?*

Defining Classroom Observation

For our purposes in discussing language classroom research, we will define *classroom observation* as a family of related procedures for gathering data during actual language lessons or tutorial sessions, primarily by watching, listening, and recording (rather than by asking). These procedures are both electronic and manual in nature, as shown in **Figure 9.1.**

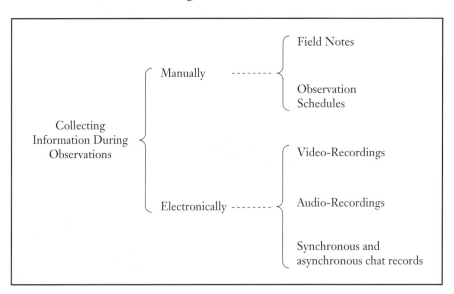

FIGURE 9.1   Options for collecting data during classroom observations (adapted from Bailey, 2006, p. 95)

Manual data collection can be either open-ended, as in the case of field notes that lead to ethnographic narratives, or they can be constrained by an observation schedule. This term may seem like it refers to a calendar of appointments for visiting classes, but actually an *observation schedule* is a codified system of observation categories. (People also say *observation scheme* or *observation system.*)

Historically, electronic data collection has been done with audiotape and videotape recorders, but recent technological developments are influencing our electronic data collection options. For example, online classes involve synchronous chats and asynchronous discussions, both of which yield records of the interaction.

APPROACHES TO CLASSROOM OBSERVATION

There are many ways of documenting classroom life, whether you are working as a participant or a nonparticipant observer. (See Chapter 7.) For example, you can use a range of manual data collection procedures, including field notes, observation systems, maps, and seating charts. If you have made electronic recordings of a lesson, you can code the data, but you can also transcribe the actual student and teacher utterances that occurred during the lesson. For many forms of online learning, the actual synchronous or asynchronous records of written turn taking provide natural transcripts that can be analyzed for some purposes. The various tools that researchers use to document what goes on in the classroom will have an impact on what they see and how they interpret what they see.

With strong records (transcripts, audiotape or videotape recordings, or high quality field notes) you can also use stimulated recall (Gass and Mackey, 2000). *Stimulated recall,* as the name suggests, is a procedure by which a researcher stimulates the recollection of a participant in an event by having that person review data collected during the event. The data used in stimulated recall usually consist of videotape or audiotape recordings, or transcripts made from such recordings, though some researchers have also used field notes. The benefit of using stimulated recall in classroom research is that you can document the perspective of lesson participants without interrupting them while the lesson is in progress. Also, by prompting their memories with data from the event, you can get better information than simply by asking them to remember the lesson without supporting data. We will return to stimulated recall in Chapter 10, when we discuss introspective methods.

Three basic approaches to documenting classroom interaction are (1) through the use of observation systems to code data (either in real time or using recorded data), (2) by recording and transcribing classroom interactions, and, less commonly, (3) by producing ethnographic narratives. In this section, we will look briefly at each of these approaches to show you how they provide very different perspectives on the lessons they document.

Using Observation Systems to Code Classroom Data

Some of the earliest classroom research in general education involved training observers to use category systems to document students' and teachers' behaviors and speech during lessons. Most observation systems can also be used to code interaction captured with videotape or audiotape recordings. Observation systems can be useful in focusing the observers' attention and in addressing some research questions.

REFLECTION

Study the data in **Table 9.1.** This record was produced by a classroom observer who used an observation scheme and made a tally mark every time a particular behavior occurred. How much can you tell about the lesson in which the observation took place? Can you make inferences about the following, for example?

● what the size of the class is
● whether the students are children or adults
● whether it is an EFL or ESL class
● what the focus or objective of the lesson is
● how long the interaction lasts
● when the interaction took place (at the beginning, middle, or end of the lesson)

REFLECTION

Given the tallies in Table 9.1, try to imagine the discussion that produced these data. As a hint, we will tell you that the interaction takes place in a classroom at the beginning of a lesson after lunch.

A coding system like the one depicted in Table 9.1 can either be used while the lesson is proceeding (in "real time") or later with videotapes or audiotapes of the lesson. If the system is used by an observer during the actual lesson, the tally marks are either made at regular time intervals (e.g., every three seconds) or every time a category change. Long (1980) describes and names these two approaches:

When each event is coded each time it occurs, we are dealing with a true *category system*. When each event is recorded only once during a fixed period of time, regardless of how frequently it occurs during that period, we have a *sign system*. (p. 6)

For instance, with some sign systems, observers code the activities every three seconds. Over time, the cumulative data provide a picture of predominant behaviors.

REFLECTION

What would be the advantages and disadvantages of using a category system or a sign system to record classroom interaction?

Producing Ethnographic Narratives

In Chapter 7, we discussed ethnography. Many of the procedures of ethnographic research have been adopted by classroom researchers. **Figure 9.2** presents an ethnographic narrative of the same interaction that was analyzed in **Table 9.1**. You will get a very different perspective on the interaction from this data set. Here the actual language used by the teacher and students is brought out, along with the interpersonal dynamics and the affective climate of the classroom.

TABLE 9.1 Use of an observation scheme for analyzing classroom interaction

Category	Tallies	Total
1. Teacher asks a display question (i.e., a question to which he or she knows the answer)	///	3
2. Teacher asks a referential question (i.e., a question to which he or she does not know the answer)	////	4
3. Teacher explains a grammatical point		0
4. Teacher explains the meaning of a vocabulary item		0
5. Teacher explains a functional point		0
6. Teacher explains point relating to the content (theme/topic) of the lesson	/	1
7. Teacher gives instructions/directions	//// /	6
8. Teacher praises	/	1
9. Teacher criticizes		0
10. Learner asks a question	///	3
11. Learner answers a question	////	4
12. Learner talks to another learner		0
13. Period of silence or confusion		0

The teacher enters the classroom in conversation with one of the students. "Of course I had lunch," he says. "Not enough. Why? Why?"

The student gives an inaudible response and joins the rest of the students who are sitting in a semicircle. There are eighteen students in all. They are a mixed group in both age and ethnicity.

The teacher deposits three portable cassette players on his table and slumps in his chair. "Well, like I say, I want to give you something to read—so what you do is, you have to imagine what comes in between, that's all . . ." He breaks off rather abruptly and beckons with his hand, ". . . Bring, er, bring your chairs a little closer, you're too far away."

There is some shuffling as most of the students bring their chairs closer. The teacher halts them by putting his hand up, policemanlike, "Er, ha, not that close." There is some muffled laughter. The teacher is about to speak again when a young male student breaks in with a single utterance, "Quiss?" The teacher gives him a puzzled look. "Pardon?"

The student mutters inaudibly to himself and then says, "It will be quiss? It will be quiss? Quiss?" Several other students echo, "Quiss. Quiss."

The teacher grins and shakes his head, "Ahm, sorry. Try again." The student frowns in concentration and says, "I ask you . . ." "Yes?" interjects the teacher. ". . . You give us another quiss?"

Slowly the light dawns on the teacher's face. "Oh quiz, oh! No, no, not today. It's not going to be a quiss today. Sorry . . . But, um, what's today, Tuesday, is it?"

"Yes," says the student.

The teacher frowns and flicks through a notebook on his desk. "I think on Thursday, if you like. Same one as before. Only I'll think up some new questions—the other ones were too easy."

The students laugh, then the teacher, holding up the daily newspaper, continues, "Um, Okay, er I'll take some questions from, er, from the newspaper over the last few weeks, right? So—means you've got to watch the news and read the newspaper and remember what's going on. If you do, you'll win. If not, well, that's life."

One of the students, a Polish woman in her early thirties says, "Will be better from TV." There is laughter from several of the students.

"From the TV?" echoes the teacher. "What, er, what programs?"

"News, news," interject several of the students.

There is an audible comment from one of the students. The teacher turns sharply and begins, "Did you say . . . ?" He breaks off abruptly. "Oh, okay. We'll have, er, it'll be the s . . . , it'll be the same." He pauses and then adopts an instructional tone as he attempts to elicit a response from the students. "There'll be different . . . ? Er, there'll be different . . . ? Different? Different? The questions will be on different . . . what? Different?"

"Talks," ventures one of the students near the front.

"Tasks? What?" says the teacher, giving a slight frown.

"Subject?" suggests another student rather tentatively.

The teacher gives her an encouraging look and says, "Different sub . . ." He extends his hand and narrows his fingers as if to say, "You've nearly got it."

"Subjects," says the student, beaming.

The teacher beams back, "Subjects, subjects, thank you. Right, yes."

FIGURE 9.2 Ethnographic narrative of a segment of classroom interaction

As you can see, the ethnographic narrative provides a more complete picture of the interaction than do the coded tally data. The actual language used by the participants is documented, along with comments about the social climate of the classroom. The major disadvantages of this particular method of carrying out classroom observations are the extremely time-consuming nature of the task and the biases inherent in the authorial comments that are woven into the narrative itself.

In a workshop on classroom interaction and research, a group of teacher researchers came up with the points in **Table 9.2** in response to the prompt above.

Transcribing Classroom Interaction

The third main way of presenting the interaction is through transcription. Making a transcript of classroom interaction can be very time-consuming. In fact, based on their experience, Allwright and Bailey (1991) estimate that it takes up to twenty hours to produce a high quality transcript of one hour of classroom interaction, depending on how detailed the transcript needs to be. (Good recordings of pair work or small group work take less time to transcribe, since the audiotape recorder can be closer to the individual speakers, and there are typically fewer overlapping turns or extraneous noises to complicate the transcription process.)

Transcripts can be analyzed through varied means, including coding. This procedure involves identifying selected bits of data as belonging to a certain class or category of behaviors. Here is a transcript that has been coded using a scheme devised by Bowers (1980), whose interaction categories are listed in **Table 9.3**.

TABLE 9.2 Advantages and disadvantages of observation schemes and ethnographic narratives for recording classroom interaction

	Advantages	Disadvantages
Observation System	May seem objective	Likely to distort actuality
	Good for observer to use while watching class	Does not show the human element
	Good for self-analysis by teacher	Very abstract
		Focuses on quantity not quality
	Easy to compare different interactional categories	Does not indicate success or failure
	Easy to focus on specific elements	Does not indicate sequences of interaction
	Orients one's mind set as observer	Open to misinterpretation
		Categories create straitjacket
	Visual presentation—easy to overview	Categories may be biased toward teacher
		Does not indicate length of interaction
Ethnographic Narrative	Displays significant paralanguage	Difficult to use for clinical purposes
	Reflects rapport between teacher and students	Time-consuming to write
	Gives overall effect of interaction	Allows distraction by focusing on unimportant details
		Open to emotive reporting
	Can be used to carry out subsequent tally-sheet analysis	Inadequate on its own
		Cannot be done in real time
	Shows real nature of questions asked	Requires high-quality recording equipment and/or note-taking skills
	Context given to support the language	

The data reported in the ethnographic narrative in Figure 9.2 are presented below as a transcript (adapted from Nunan, 1989, pp. 80–81). It has been analyzed using Bowers' (1980) categories.

T   Of course I had lunch . . . not enough . . . why? Why? (*sociating*)
     Well, like I say, I want to give you something to read (*organizing*)
     —so what you do is, you have to imagine what comes in between, that's all . . . (*organizing*)
     . . . Bring, er, bring your chairs a little closer, you're too far away er, ha, not that close (*organizing*)
S   Quiss? (*eliciting*)

TABLE 9.3 Bowers' (1980) categories for analyzing classroom interaction

Category	Description
Responding	Any act directly sought by the utterance of another speaker, such as answering a question.
Sociating	Any act not contributing directly to the teaching/learning task, but rather to the establishment or maintenance of interpersonal relationships.
Organizing	Any act that serves to structure the learning task or environment without contributing to the teaching/learning task itself.
Directing	Any act encouraging nonverbal activity as an integral part of the teaching/learning process.
Presenting	Any act presenting information of direct relevance to the learning task.
Evaluating	Any act that rates another verbal act positively or negatively.
Eliciting	Any act designed to produce a verbal response from another person.

T   Pardon? (*responding*)

S   It will be quiss? It will be quiss? Quiss? (*eliciting*)

Ss   Quiss . . . quiss (*eliciting*)

T   Ahm, sorry . . . try again (*eliciting*)

S   I ask you . . . (*eliciting*)

T   Yes?

S   You give us another quiss? (*eliciting*)

T   Oh, quiz, oh! No, no, not today . . . It's not going to be a quiss today . . . sorry . . . but, um, what's today, Tuesday, is it? (*eliciting*)

S   Yes (*responding*)

T   I think on Thursday, if you like . . . same as before . . . only I'll think up some new questions—the other ones were too easy . . . um, okay, er I'll take some questions from, er, from newspapers over the last few weeks, right? so—means you've got to watch the news and read the newspaper and remember what's going on . . . if you do, you'll win . . . if not, well, that's life (*organizing*)

S   Will be better from TV (*sociating*)
    [laughter]

T   From the TV? . . . What, er, what programmes . . . (*eliciting*)

Ss   News, news (*responding*)

T   Did you say . . . ? Oh, oh, we'll have, er, it'll be the s . . . , it'll be the same . . . there'll be different . . . ? er, there'll be different . . . ? Different? Different? The questions will be on different . . . what? Different? (*eliciting*)

S   Talks (*responding*)

T	Tasks? (*evaluating*)
	What? (*eliciting*)
S	Subject? (*responding*)
T	Different sub . . . (*eliciting*)
S	Subjects (*responding*)
T	Subjects, subjects, thank you . . . right, yes (*evaluating*)

ACTION

Check your own analysis against the categorizations above.

SYSTEMS FOR OBSERVING LANGUAGE CLASSROOM INTERACTION

In the history of language classroom studies, researchers have developed numerous observation schemes for documenting the life of language classroom. (Such systems are also called *observation schedules*, but in this book we will use the terms *observation schemes* or *observation systems* to avoid the possible confusion with a time schedule.) This proliferation has from time to time been criticized on the grounds that studies employing different schemes are difficult to compare. The reason for the proliferation is that different research questions and issues demand different data collection tools.

The earliest systems for observing language lessons were heavily influenced by research in general education. For instance, Moskowitz (1971; 1976) adapted Flanders' (1970) Interaction Analysis system to produce an instrument called Foreign Language Interaction Analysis, or "FLint." This instrument used the basic categories for coding teacher talk and student talk that Flanders had developed, but it also allowed for coding the interaction in two languages as needed for L2 educational research.

Observation systems can focus on many different facets of interaction: verbal, paralinguistic, nonlinguistic, cognitive, affective, pedagogical content, aspects of discourse, etc. (For an elaboration on these and other aspects of observation schemes, see Chaudron, 1988.) Copies of several different observation systems can be found in the appendices of Allwright and Bailey (1991).

In evaluating and selecting an observation scheme, the following questions need to be taken into consideration.

1. Does the scheme require the observer to check a behavior (such as the teacher asking a question) every time the behavior occurs, or is it necessary to make a check at regular intervals?

2. Does the scheme deploy high- or low-inference categories? (A high-inference category requires the observers to interpret the behavior they observe: For example: "Students are on task," or "Students are interested in the lesson.")

3. Does the scheme allow a particular event or utterance to be assigned to more than one category?
4. Is the instrument intended to be used in real time or with videotape or audiotape recordings?
5. Is the scheme intended principally for research or teacher education?
6. What is the focus of the instrument?

ACTION

Evaluate the observation system in Table 9.3 against these six questions.

Keep these questions in mind as your read the next sections of this chapter. We will discuss two observation systems that have been influential in second language classroom research and teacher education.

Foci for Observing Communications Used in Settings (FOCUS)

Some of the observation systems that have been used in language classroom research have been influential in teacher education and teacher supervision as well. An example is Fanselow's FOCUS system. *FOCUS* stands for Foci for Observing Communications Used in Settings. According to Fanselow (1977),

> In this system, communications both inside and outside of the classroom are seen as a series of patterned events in which two or more people use mediums such as speech, gestures, noise or writing, to evaluate, interpret and in other ways communicate separate areas of content, such as the meaning of words, personal feelings, or classroom procedure. (p. 19)

Each of these areas of content could be categorized as serving "one of four pedagogical purposes: structuring, soliciting, responding and reacting" (ibid.).

ACTION

Compare these four pedagogical purposes with the seven categories in Bowers (1980) system shown in Table 9.3 above. Summarize the differences and overlaps with a classmate or colleague.

Fanselow's FOCUS system is visually depicted as categories in five columns, each of which answers a question. The five column headings and the possible subcategories are listed below:

1. Who communicates? (teacher, individual student, groups, whole class)
2. What is the pedagogical purpose of the communication? (to structure, to solicit, to respond, to react)

3. What mediums are used to communicate content? (linguistic, non-linguistic, paralinguistic)
4. How are the mediums used to communicate areas of content? (attend, characterize, present, relate, re-present)
5. What areas of content are communicated? (language, life, procedure, subject matter). (Fanselow, 1977, p. 29)

The FOCUS system can be used to code live lessons in real time or videotaped lessons. Learning to use FOCUS involves studying the category descriptors and working with videotaped excerpts of classroom data to gain speed and confidence in coding. The value of the system is that it provides a way of characterizing teaching and learning activities that is meant to be descriptive rather than prescriptive.

Communicative Orientation to Language Teaching (COLT)

Over the years, observation schemes have become more elaborate. One of the most sophisticated is the Communicative Orientation to Language Teaching (COLT) Scheme, which we discussed briefly in Chapter 1. COLT was developed to enable researchers to evaluate intact classes (that is, existing classes that have been constituted for teaching and learning, not for research purposes). Like all observation systems, the COLT is ideologically loaded, and the various observation categories reflect assumptions about what makes an effective classroom. The ideology behind COLT is explained as follows by its designers:

[the aim of the scheme is to describe] some of the features of communication which occur in second language classrooms. Our concept of *communicative features* has been derived from current theories of communicative competence, from the literature on communicative language teaching, and from a review of recent research into first and second language acquisition. The observational categories are designed (a) to capture significant features of verbal interaction in L2 classrooms, and (b) to provide a means of comparing some aspects of classroom discourse with *natural* language as it is used outside the classroom. (Allen, Fröhlich, and Spada, 1984, p. 233)

Ten years later, Spada and Fröhlich (1995), in their booklength manual on the COLT system, stated that three major 'themes' in the L2 teaching and learning literature influenced the design of the COLT scheme. These were (1) the widespread introduction and acceptance of communicative approaches to L2 learning; (2) the need for more and better research on the relationship between teaching and learning; and (3) the need to develop psycholinguistically valid categories for classroom observation schemes.

The COLT consists of two parts. Part A focuses on the description of classroom activities and contains five subsections: the activity type, the participant organization, the content, the student modality, and the materials. Part B is

TABLE 9.4	Questions relating to the principal features of the COLT scheme (after Nunan, 1992, p. 99)

Feature	Questions
Part A: Classroom Activities	
1a. Activity type	What is the activity type—e.g., drill, role play, dictation?
2a. Participant organization	Is the teacher working with the whole class or not?
	Are students working in groups or individually?
	If there is group work, how is it organized?
3a. Content	Is the focus on classroom management, language, (form, function, discourse, sociolinguistics), or other?
	Is the range of topics broad or narrow?
	Who selects the topic—teacher, students, or both?
4a. Student modality	Are students involved in listening, speaking, reading, writing, or a combination of these?
5. Material	What types of materials are used?
	How long is the text?
	What is the source/purpose of the materials?
Part B. Classroom Language	
1b. Use of target language	To what extent is the target language used?
2b. Information gap	To what extent is requested information predictable in advance?
3b. Sustained speech	Is the discourse extended or restricted to a single sentence, clause, or word?
4b. Reaction or code or message	Does the interlocutor react to code or message?
5b. Incorporation of preceding utterance	Does the speaker incorporate the preceding utterance into his or her contribution?
6b. Discourse initiation	Do learners have opportunities to initiate discourse?
7b. Relative restriction of linguistic form	Does the teacher expect a specific form or is there no expectation of a particular linguistic form?

intended to capture the communicative features of the classroom. Seven features are identified: the extent to which the target language is used, whether there is an information gap, the extent to which sustained speech is encouraged, whether the teacher responds to code or message (that is, to form or meaning), incorporation of preceding utterance, discourse initiation, and relative restriction to linguistic form. Some of the key questions relating to each of these aspects and features are set out in **Table 9.4.**

In Table 9.4, we have presented the key categories of COLT in simplified form, to give you some idea of the scope and orientation of the system. It is worth noting that, while the authors of COLT have tried to devise a set of procedures that enable trained users to obtain reliable data, the categories and communicative features are subjective, and, as we noted above, ideological. The COLT scheme, for example, is predicated on the assumption that the existence of an information gap, the deployment of sustained speech, the opportunity for learners to initiate discourse and so on, will facilitate language development. At the time the scheme was devised, research lent support to these features. However, if such a scheme were to be developed today by a different group of researchers, then the chances are that the categories would be somewhat different.

This comment underlines the point that there is no such thing as totally 'objective' observation—that what we see will be conditioned by what we expect to see. Our vision will also be colored by the instruments we adopt, adapt, or develop to assist us in our observations. While the use of observation schemes can provide a sharper focus for our research than the use of unstructured observation, it can also blind us to aspects of interaction and discourse that are not captured by the scheme but that are important to an understanding of the lesson we are observing.

OBSERVATIONAL DATA AND DISCOURSE ANALYSIS

We will address discourse analysis more fully in Chapter 12. Here we just wish to raise some issues related to the use of observation to collect data that can be subjected to some discourse analytic process. Some forms of observation result in records of classroom data that can be analyzed using the varied procedures of discourse analysis, while others do not.

The advantage of observation schemes is that they serve to condense data and facilitate the process of identifying patterns. However, unless such schemes include the collection of actual direct quotes, they typically obscure or lose the very thing that is of most interest to language teachers and researchers—the language itself. Observation systems in which the observer codes (i.e., interprets and assigns to categories) interaction as it occurs result in data for which readers only see the tallies—not the interaction that led to those tallies. For this reason, transcripts that can be subjected to discourse analysis are extremely valuable sources of information about classroom interaction.

Two of the first linguists to develop a system for the analysis of classroom discourse were Sinclair and Coulthard (1975). They showed that much classroom interaction consisted of a recurring pattern of teacher initiation, student response, and teacher feedback evaluating the response (the so-called "IRF pattern"). Here is an example of such a pattern:

> **Teacher:** The questions will be on different subjects, so, er, well, one will be about, er, well, some of the questions will be about politics, and some of them will be about, er . . . what? (Initiation)
>
> **Student:** History. (Response)
>
> **Teacher:** History. Yes, politics and history. (Feedback/evaluation)

Transaction		Transaction		Transaction	
Exchange	Exchange	Exchange	Exchange	Exchange	Exchange
move move	move move	move move	move move	move move	move move
act act act act	act act act act	act act act act	act act act act	act act act act	act act act act

FIGURE 9.3   Acts, moves, exchanges and transactions (after Sinclair and Coulthard, 1975)

Teacher: And, um, and . . . ? (Initiation)

Student: Grammar. (Response)

Teacher: Grammar's good, yes. (Feedback/evaluation)

The three-part IRF pattern was called an *exchange*. A series of exchanges made up a *transaction*, and transactions made up lessons. Exchanges consisted of finer-grained moves and acts. A transaction could consist of several different exchanges, which could include many moves and acts, as shown in **Figure 9.3**.

Each of these categories was further defined and exemplified in Sinclair and Coulthard's (1975) original description. For instance, moves included opening moves, answering moves, follow-up moves, framing moves, and focusing moves. This system was meant to be used for coding transcripts based on videotape or audiotape recordings rather than as a real-time data collection procedure.

REFLECTION

Based on your experience and what you have read so far, as well as your particular research interests, do you have a preference for real-time coding, or would you prefer to categorize behavior using videotapes, audiotapes, or transcriptions?

OBSERVING SOCIAL ASPECTS OF CLASSROOM INTERACTION

In addition to the actual utterances of learners and teachers, broader social aspects of classroom interaction are important. With the emergence of sociocultural theory (see, e.g., Lantolf, 2000), the social life of the classroom has come to be viewed as an important dimension of classroom research. By using the term *social life* in this context, we are referring to the interpersonal relationships, friendships, personality clashes, etc., that develop as students and teachers get to know each other and begin to relate to each other on a personal level. In traditional second language acquisition research, these aspects of classroom interaction are typically not included in the analysis. They can, however, have an

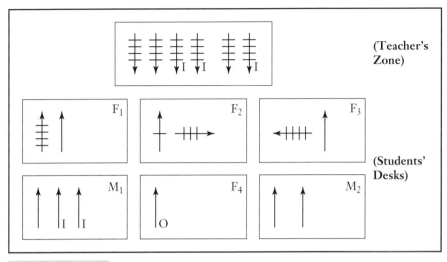

FIGURE 9.4   Sample SCORE data for a twenty-minute grammar review lesson with six students (from Bailey, 2006, p. 107)

important influence on the learning that goes on in the classroom and the kind of language that is generated.

SCORE Data

Capturing this aspect of the classroom can be challenging because it often requires us to make inferences about the mental and emotional states of teachers and learners. The process can be aided by seating charts (often called Seating Chart Observation Records, or SCORE data). One advantage of SCORE data is that teachers are very familiar with seating charts so they can easily interpret such records. SCORE data can also provide information about individual students, small groups, or an entire class (depending on the number of students present and the observer's vantage point). Acheson and Gall (1997) discuss using SCORE procedures for studying students' time on task, verbal flow, and movement patterns within the classroom. **Figure 9.4** shows a simplified example based on the data for a teacher and just six students.

REFLECTION

Using this key, write a description of the interaction shown in the SCORE chart in Figure 9.4. Or, with a colleague or classmate, describe the interaction orally.

The key to interpreting these SCORE data is shown in **Figure 9.5:**

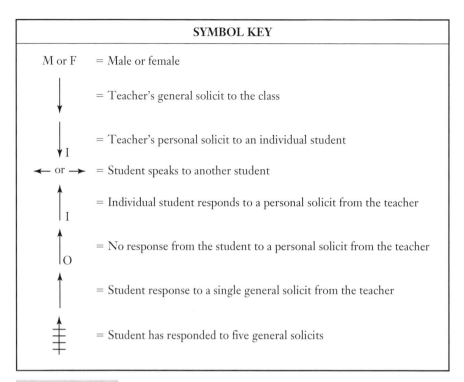

	SYMBOL KEY
M or F	= Male or female
↓	= Teacher's general solicit to the class
↓ I	= Teacher's personal solicit to an individual student
← or →	= Student speaks to another student
↑ I	= Individual student responds to a personal solicit from the teacher
↑ O	= No response from the student to a personal solicit from the teacher
↑	= Student response to a single general solicit from the teacher
↑≣	= Student has responded to five general solicits

FIGURE 9.5 Key to SCORE Data Symbols (from Bailey, 2006, p. 108)

The SCORE data depicted in Figure 9.4 give information about who initiates verbal turns and who responds to them. This simple system provides fast records of who speaks to whom and how often. Of course, these data tell us nothing about the length or content of the turns. Nor do these data convey any information about the participants' target language use, their accuracy, or their fluency. A SCORE chart like this one simply provides a frequency count of turns taken. Nevertheless, for some purposes and contexts, SCORE data are quite helpful and informative.

Classroom Maps

While visual representations like seating charts and maps do not preserve the actual discourse that occurred in the classroom, they do enable researchers to record the extent to which interactions occur. They also often allow patterns to emerge that are not immediately apparent in transcripts or other forms of documentation. For example, Bailey (2006) drew a map of a class taught by a non-native speaking teaching assistant in mathematics, whose class she observed on three different occasions. The map shows that there are forty-two desks in the classroom, but at the three different observations, eighteen, three, and seven students were present. At the scheduled time for one observation, no students attended the class. Bailey was puzzled as to why such a small class had been scheduled in such a large room, but when she checked with the mathematics department, she learned that thirty-five students were actually enrolled in the class. The number of empty desks might not have jumped out at her if she had only recorded the number of students present without drawing the map.

This particular teaching assistant had a very passive teaching style. His classes were characterized by long periods of silence as he wrote complex math problems on the board with his back to the students. When he finished writing on the board, he would turn to the class and ask them, "Any questions?" Later, when the observational field notes were analyzed, this particular teaching assistant was categorized in a type of TAs called the *mechanical problem solvers*. It seemed his English proficiency was not sufficient to allow him to write the problems on the board and talk about them at the same time. The way this issue connects to the observational maps of this classroom is that in revisiting the maps in the three sets of field notes, Bailey found that there had been an overhead projector in the classroom at all three lessons, but the TA had not used it. One possible implication to help him communicate better with his students would be that he could write the problems on a transparency before the lesson so he could discuss them more easily with the class. This realization was possible because every set of field notes documented the presence of the unused overhead projector.

Visual representations of movements through space can also "track and trace" students and teachers as they move about the classroom (Freeman, 1998, p. 203). Records such as these are excellent for revealing 'action zones' in the classroom (Shamim, 1996), and for determining whether particular students are singled out for the teacher's attention. They not only show the physical arrangement of the classroom, but they also allow the observer to record a range of behaviors, including the amount and type of interaction between participants.

ACTION

If you can observe a class, compile a SCORE chart such as the one in Figure 9.4 for a lesson or part of a lesson. As an alternative, you could complete the following procedure adapted from Freeman (1998, pp. 203–204).

1. Outline a bird's eye view of the classroom space that shows the walls and other structures as if you were looking at them from above.

2. Identify everything you can see; be as detailed as you reasonably can. Include yourself in the picture. Scale is less important than accurately including as much as possible.

3. Use the same symbol for a category (e.g., circles for students and squares for desks). You can create ways of showing differences within a category (e.g., green circle is a bilingual student; red square is a teacher's desk).

4. To record students' movements, draw a line from where the student starts to where he or she ends the movement. If the student makes the same movement more than once—perhaps he or she goes back and forth to the teacher's desk for help—you can put a check on the basic trace line to keep track of the number of steps.

Advice: The focus is on what you see as opposed to what you hear or think. To get students' views of the classroom, the teacher can ask students to create their own maps. This procedure also allows people to compare their own special perceptions. Now review what you have and brainstorm a list of research questions that are stimulated by the data.

THE CENTRAL ROLE OF OBSERVATION IN LANGUAGE CLASSROOM RESEARCH

As noted in Chapter 1, some classroom research carried out in the 1960s through to the 1980s involved experimental comparisons of different methods, materials, and teaching techniques. For example, Scherer and Wertheimer (1964) compared the use of grammar-translation and the audiolingual method with two groups of college students learning German as a foreign language in the United States. The grammar-translation group focused on reading and writing, while the other group received instruction principally in listening and speaking. At the end of the extensive and expensive two-year study, subjects were tested to see whether one group was superior to the other. The results were disappointing since the study was unable to demonstrate the superiority of one group over the other. The grammar-translation students did slightly better on reading and writing than the audiolingual students, while the latter did somewhat better on listening and speaking. However, as there had been no observation of actual lessons during the investigation, it was difficult to say what was really going on "inside the 'black box'" (Long, 1980, p. 1).

In his overview of observation in language research, D. Allwright (1988) suggested that perhaps the wrong question was being asked:

> [This research was conducted] on the assumption that it made sense to ask "Which is the best method for modern language teaching?", and that presumably on the additional assumption that once the answer was determined, it would then make sense to simply prescribe the 'winning' method for general adoption. (p. 10)

Since then, the value of observation has been demonstrated in process studies (those based primarily on observational data) and process-product studies (those based on classroom observational data and the examination of outcome measures). As a result, the product-only focus has largely been replaced in language classroom research.

Ellis (1990b) suggests that there are three broad approaches to classroom research. These approaches have different goals and methods, as shown in **Table 9.5,** but all can involve observation as an important approach to data collection.

In an important and influential review, Ellis (1988) synthesized the results of a large number of classroom observation studies and identified eight key factors

TABLE 9.5 Empirical research on L2 classrooms (from Nunan, 1992, p. 93, after Ellis, 1990b)

Category	Goal	Principal Research Methods
1. Classroom process research	The understanding of how the 'social events' of the language classroom are enacted.	The detailed, ethnographic observation of classroom behaviors
2. The study of classroom interaction and L2 acquisition	To test a number of hypotheses relating to how interaction in the classroom contributes to L2 acquisition and to explore which types of interaction best facilitate acquisition	Controlled experimental studies; ethnographic studies of interaction
3. The study of instruction and L2 acquisition	To discover whether formal instruction results in the acquisition of new L2 knowledge and the constraints that govern whether formal instruction is successful	Linguistic comparisons of L2 acquisition by classroom and naturalistic learners; experimental studies of the effects of formal instruction

that were associated with successful second language classroom acquisition. The following key factors are adapted and summarized from Ellis:

1. **Quantity of 'intake':** The amount of the target language that learners attend to is significant—quantity alone is insufficient (i.e., the quantity of language produced by the teacher as input).

2. **A need to communicate:** This need can be provided if the target language serves as the medium as well as the target of instruction.

3. **Independent control of the propositional content:** Learners have a choice over what is said, and part of this should be content known to the learner but not the teacher.

4. **Adherence to the 'here and now' principle:** In the early stages at least, encoding and decoding are facilitated if the things being talked about are present in the learning environment.

5. **The performance of a range of speech acts:** The learner should be encouraged to use a range of language functions and to perform a variety of roles with the classroom discourse (for example, initiating as well as responding to discourse).

6. **An input rich in directives:** Particularly in the early stages of learning, directives occur in familiar and frequently occurring contexts, they refer to the 'here and now,' they are morphosyntactically simple, and, as they require a nonverbal result, they are more likely to count as successful communication than interactions requiring a verbal response.

7. **An input rich in 'extending' utterances:** These are teacher utterances which pick up, elaborate, or in other ways extend the learner's contribution.

8. **Uninhibited 'practice':** This concept refers to the right of the learners to practice the target language without intending to communicate and to repeat utterances that are meaningful to the learners themselves.

ACTION

Using these eight categories from Ellis (1988), analyze the transcript above, in which the students ask about the possible "quiss."

QUALITY CONTROL ISSUES

As in other forms of data collection, reliability and validity are concerns in observational studies. You will recall that reliability embodies the concept of consistency. Likewise, in studies that collect data through observational procedures, a validity concern is whether the data collected represent the reality of the classroom.

In studies where data are recorded electronically, the issue is often one of coverage: How adequately does the audiotape or videotape recording capture what is going on? Audiotape recordings, of course, lack the visual mode, but they are often easier to make since small recorders can be placed on students' desks or in the middle of a table during group work. Video recordings capture the visual channel, but cameras can be more intrusive than audiotape recorders and may influence teachers' and students' behavior, especially if a camera person is present. However, in our experience, if you take time to acclimate the participants to the presence of the camera, and if they trust you, you can overcome much of the possible interference.

When a researcher takes field notes or codes data in real time, the human observer is the data collection instrument. In these cases, it is important to establish the viability of the observations. One procedure for doing so is to calculate inter-observer (or inter-coder) agreement. This process involves having two observers in the classroom at the same time or two observers working with the same video recording or audio recordings. Normally, observers are trained together with video recordings before they begin gathering "live" data in classrooms. By convention, an agreement level of at least 85% is required for the observers to be considered reliable. (See Chapter 14 for more information.)

Based on her experience with things that went wrong in her own observations, Bailey (1983a) wrote a brief article about Murphy's Law in language classroom research. (Murphy's Law is the belief that if anything can go wrong, it will.) The result was ten "lessons" for classroom observers:

1. If you are going to take notes, *always* carry paper and pens or pencils and something firm to write on, like a clipboard. (p. 4)

2. If you are going to tape record, make sure you have access to a good tape recorder and that you know how to operate it correctly. (p. 4)

3. *Always* investigate the classroom where you will be observing before the actual observation begins. (p. 4)

4. If you are observing regularly scheduled classes, *always* leave room in your plan to reschedule an observation as needed, in case a class is cancelled, or the teacher gets sick, or you miss your bus. (p. 5)

5. *Always* plan free time immediately after an observation so you can write your field notes if you aren't able to record them during the actual observation for any reason. (p. 22)

6. *Always* arrange a big enough subject pool that you can re-sample from among the possible subjects if your presence seems to affect someone's behavior noticeably, and *always* allow time for your subjects to become comfortable with your presence before you try to collect data on their behavior. (p. 22)

7. *Always* carry extra batteries (if you are using a battery-powered recording device). (p. 22)

8. *Never* allow yourself to be entrapped in an unwanted discourse act with a subject during an observation. (p. 22)

9. *Always* use, or consider using, multiple data collection procedures. (p. 22)

10. *Always* do a pilot study. (p. 22)

Some of the points made above may seem obvious, but we know of many projects—including our own and those of our graduate students—that have been negatively affected by breakdowns caused by very simple problems that had huge consequences.

Our advice, based on years of both successes and frustrations, is that if possible, you should collect data that are detailed and in-depth rather than relying entirely on data coded live in "real time," that is, during the observations. Data that are audio- or videotaped can later be coded or transcribed, as needed. But data that are simply coded cannot be reconverted to direct quotes or descriptions.

We also strongly encourage you to carry out a pilot study to try out and refine your observational procedures before you attempt to collect the data you wish to analyze. Doing a brief pilot study can reveal problems in coding categories, thoroughly familiarize observers with data collection procedures, and acquaint observers with the local conditions if they are not insiders to the school or program.

Observation can be used with other data collection procedures to provide methods triangulation. You will recall from Chapter 7 that methods triangulation involves the use of multiple data collection procedures (e.g., interviews, test scores, questionnaires, observation schedules, field notes, etc.) to collect data (Denzin, 1978; van Lier, 1988). For example, the team that worked on R. L. Allwright's (1980) study of turns, topics, and tasks in ESL classrooms included a participant observer who took notes during the lessons which were also tape-recorded. The recordings were later transcribed and the observer's notes were invaluable in interpreting ambiguous utterances and understanding the context of various comments. Block's (1996) investigation of an English course in Spain incorporated the teacher's and students' diaries and audio-cassette recordings, in addition to Block's own observational notes.

A SAMPLE STUDY

As the sample study in this chapter, we will discuss just a brief segment from an interesting article by Lynch and Maclean (2000), two teachers in a course entitled English for Medical Conferences, which "caters for health professionals who want to improve their ability to present papers in English at international meetings and conferences" (p. 226). These authors wanted to study the outcomes of building repetition into a task in which the learners explained a poster based on a research article to people who visited the poster exhibit (their classmates).

By *repetition* Lynch and Maclean do not mean the sorts of pattern drills where students repeat after a teacher. Rather they are referring to what they call recycling or retrials, "where the basic communication goal remains the same, but with variations of content and emphasis depending on the visitor's questions" (p. 227). The procedure that was used—both for teaching and for data collection—was this:

1. Participants are paired up and each pair is given a different research article. They have one hour to make a poster based on that article.

2. The posters are displayed around a large room. From each pair, one participant (A)—the 'host'—stands beside their poster, waiting to receive 'visitors' asking questions. The B participants visit the posters, one by one, clockwise. Their task is to ask questions about each poster. The host is instructed not to present, but to respond to questions. They are allowed only limited time (approximately 3 minutes) at each poster.

3. When the B participants arrive back at base, they stay by their poster and the A participants go visiting.

4. Once the second round is completed, there is plenary discussion of the merits of the posters (by the participants) and the teachers provide feedback on general language points. (p. 227)

So the "poster carousel," as these authors call this teaching-learning activity, provides built-in opportunities for reiterating and rephrasing core content repeatedly in a brief period of time to a series of interlocutors.

Two research questions were posed in this study: (1) "Do learners gain from repetition in the poster carousel—and do they think they gain?" And (2) "In what ways do they gain from repetition—and in what ways do they think they gain?" (p. 228). To address these questions, the researchers tape-recorded the poster session participation by fourteen students (radiologists and oncologists) and had the learners complete a self-report questionnaire. In terms of the focus of this chapter, their audio-recording process was a particularly interesting data collection strategy:

> We recorded all six interactions between each host and visitor by plac-
> ing an audiocassette recorder near each of the seven posters. This sort
> of recording is a routine part of the course and so the participants were
> used to being recorded by the time they did the poster carousel. All 14
> sets of six interactions were transcribed. (p. 229)

Thus the participants were familiar with tape-recording as an instructional tool, so we may assume that the observer's paradox (Labov, 1972) was minimized.

For the preliminary analysis, the authors focused on two particular learners, whose pseudonyms are Alicia and Daniela. These learners were chosen because of the extreme differences in their language proficiency. Alicia was from Spain and her English was the weakest in the class. She had a 4.0 on the IELTS (the International English Language Testing System) and a 400 on the TOEFL (the Test of English as a Foreign Language). In addition, she had scored only 5% on a dictation administered at the start of the course. Daniela was from Germany and had a score of 7.0 on the IELTS and a 600 on the TOEFL. Her dictation score had been 97% at the beginning of the course.

The authors provide a close analysis of the transcripts and show that both learners improved, though in different ways. However, their self-report data differed. Alicia said that she had not consciously changed her language during the carousel activity and that she hadn't been aware of any unplanned changes. In contrast, Daniela reported that she had intentionally changed the way she expressed her ideas as she talked with the various visitors to her poster. Specifically, she said,

> I wanted to use phrases I have learned during the course and I worked
> at it. . . . I tried to find out if different explanations were accepted [by the
> visitors]. I felt I was quite relaxed all the time. I got to know the vocab-
> ulary better during the time. (p. 231)

The article provides further data from the two learners' self-report statements as well as numerous illustrations from their transcribed conversations with the visitors to their posters. These data provide a good example of methods triangulation. What we find particularly compelling about this study is how the two teachers conducted practical research about a teaching activity and incorporated viable observations that did not detract from the students' normal focus on English language learning and use.

PAYOFFS AND PITFALLS

There are certainly some pitfalls to be avoided when you collect data through observational processes, and several of these have been alluded to above. To recap the main points, having an observer in the classroom, perhaps especially one with a video camera, can be disruptive. Students and teachers may act in ways that are not typical of their usual classroom behavior—an example of the Observer's Paradox (Labov, 1972). To counteract this problem, it is important that observers spend enough time in a site so that the participants in that context become familiar with the visitors and accept their presence in the classroom. It also helps if the students are familiar with the data collection devices, as they were in the study by Lynch and Maclean (2000).

Another major pitfall is the worry that what is observed can be influenced very strongly by the observer's own experiences and preconceptions. If a database consists solely of observational field notes or real-time coding done by a single observer, it is difficult to demonstrate the reliability of the coding or the validity of the observations. For these reasons, we recommend methods triangulation, particularly those combining observational field notes with electronic records. Video- or audio-recordings permit the researcher to transcribe interactions, and the resulting transcripts provide opportunities for more precise analyses than does real-time coding.

In addition, having electronically recorded data, such as audiotapes, video-recordings, or chat transcripts, is very useful in studies employing stimulated recall to get the participants' interpretations of events. Having been an observer in the lessons where such data were collected can give the researcher a first-hand vantage point for asking key questions about the interactions that occurred.

Transcription itself, while valuable and informative, can be a daunting process. Unless you have good quality recordings, transcribing language learners' speech can be terribly time-consuming and frustrating. This problem is substantially reduced in studies involving typed chats or online forum discussions, in which a transcript of the interaction is automatically produced by the program.

In spite of these problems, the benefits of using an observation component in classroom research are too numerous to overlook. Without observational data, we are limited almost entirely to product studies—and even if their outcomes are interesting and provocative, we cannot say with much confidence what elements of classroom interaction and instruction led to any significant gains or differences that may emerge. Some form of observation is essential in any process study or process-product study.

CONCLUSION

This chapter has focused on observation as an essential tool in conducting language classroom research. We defined language classroom observation as a family of related procedures for gathering data during actual language lessons or tutorial sessions, primarily by watching, listening, and recording (rather than by asking). Such procedures include audio- and video-recording, coding, making maps and seating charts, and writing ethnographic records.

The observational procedure(s) you choose depend on the research question(s) you address in your study. In general, we recommend collecting more detailed data (rather than just doing live coding during a lesson) and using methods triangulation so you can verify your data and establish the reliability of your observations.

QUESTIONS AND TASKS

1. If you are currently teaching a class, tape-record or videotape a lesson. After class, make a detailed journal entry for yourself about things that interested you or puzzled you during class. Then use the recording to investigate your questions.

2. If you have a colleague who can observe your teaching, carry out the task above with an observer in the room taking field notes or gathering SCORE data. Compare your journal entry with the observer's data and with the electronic recording.

3. If you are not currently teaching, ask a language teacher if you could observe a class for nonevaluative purposes. Use a procedure described in this chapter to gather data. Discuss those data with the teacher.

4. Think of a research question that interests you. What role might be played in answering that question by any of the approaches to observation described in this chapter?

5. Look back at van Lier's (1996a) description of a typical day in the bilingual Quechua-Spanish school in Peru, which was reprinted at the end of Chapter 7. Based on just this description, draw a bird's eye view of the classroom depicted in that account.

6. Look back at the description of the child called Lupita, which appeared near the beginning of Chapter 6. Draw a map or make a SCORE record of her movement through the action zone and the people she interacted with.

7. Here is a SCORE chart (Nunan, 1989, p. 93) which records the number of times the teacher asked display questions (D) and referential questions (R) to various students, as well as the students' responses and the times they initiated turns. Student-student interaction is also recorded. Write a summary of the interactions in depicted in these SCORE data. (Note: It may help if you number the students in this chart.) Compare your interpretation with that of a classmate or colleague.

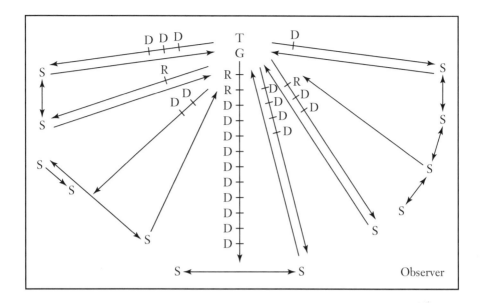

8. Transcribe a brief recording of some classroom interaction—five or ten minutes should be sufficient. What problems do you encounter as you transcribe? What benefits are gained by the transcription process?

9. Think of an activity that you use (or would like to use) in your language classes. What research question(s) could you ask about its efficacy? How could you address your research question(s)? What role would observational procedures play in your study?

SUGGESTIONS FOR FURTHER READING

For a history of the role of observation in language classrooms, see D. Allwright's (1988) book. If you would like to learn more about the FOCUS system for observation, see Fanselow (1977; 1987).

There are several sources available in case you would like to learn more about the COLT system for observing teaching. These include Allen, Fröhlich, and Spada (1984) and Spada and Fröhlich (1995).

If you would like to get started learning about observational processes, or training teachers about observational processes, we recommend Wajnryb's (1992) book *Classroom Observation Tasks: A Resource Book for Language Teachers and Trainers.*

K. E. Johnson's (1995) book on understanding communication in second language classrooms looks at how patterns of communication are established and maintained and how these affect learning.

10

Introspective Methods
of Data Collection

"A moment's insight is sometimes worth a life's experience"
(Oliver Wendell Holmes, 1981, p. 225)

"The universe is transformation: Our life is what our thoughts make it."
(Marcus Aurelius Antonius, *Meditations, IV,* as cited in Cohen and Cohen, 1980, p. 3).

INTRODUCTION AND OVERVIEW

One of the challenges confronting language researchers is that a great deal of the hard work involved in language learning is invisible. It goes on in the heads of language learners. During the days when behaviorist psychology dominated language research, it was considered both futile and irrelevant to investigate this invisible work since researchers were only interested in the observable characteristics of human behavior. Those days are long gone, and the focus is more and more on the cognitive processes underlying human performance and ability (see, e.g., Freeman, 1996a). It is widely accepted that if we want to understand what people do, we need to know what they think. Researchers often go to considerable lengths to derive insights into the mental processes underlying observable behavior.

This chapter discusses procedures for collecting or generating data through introspective means. First, we will consider two important data collection procedures during which research subjects talk about their thought processes and/or feelings. These are (1) the creation of think-aloud protocols, and (2) the use of stimulated recall. Then we will look at diary studies of language teaching and learning, which typically involve written data derived largely from introspection and retrospection. We will also briefly consider biographical and autobiographical research.

Defining Introspective Data Collection

As a research procedure, *introspection* is the process of observing and reporting on one's own thoughts, feelings, motives, reasoning processes, and mental states, often with a view to determining the ways in which these processes and states shape behavior. The tradition has been imported into applied linguistics from cognitive psychology, where it has aroused considerable controversy (Ericcson and Simon, 1987). Particularly contentious is the assumption that the verbal reports resulting from introspection accurately reflect the underlying cognitive processes giving rise to behavior. Critics of the approach argue that there might be a discontinuity between what the subjects believed they were doing and could articulate, and what they were actually doing.

In this chapter, we use the term *introspection* to cover techniques in which data collection happens at the same time as or very shortly after the events being investigated. We will also use it as a general rubric to cover research contexts in which the data are collected retrospectively, that is, some time after the events themselves have taken place. One challenge with this approach is the fact that the length of time elapsing between the mental event and the reporting of that event may distort what is actually reported. (In a sense, all the techniques reported here are retrospective because there will always be a gap, however fleeting, between the event and the report.)

Cohen and Hosenfeld (1981) distinguished three types of introspective data collection. The types are defined by the timing of the introspecting relative to the timing of the event being investigated. First, *concurrent introspection* (during the event) represents a particular point in time. Concurrent introspection occurs simultaneously with the event being investigated. In contrast, *immediate retrospection* occurs right after the event, and *delayed retrospection* occurs hours or more following the event. Thus, immediate retrospection and delayed retrospection

---

REFLECTION

In which of the following situations would concurrent introspection be advisable or acceptable? In which situations would immediate or delayed retrospection be preferable?

- While a student is taking a high-stakes entrance examination
- During a class discussion of vocabulary
- While a student is revising a composition using the teacher's and a peer's feedback
- During a group work activity in which three students are reaching a consensus
- While a student is reading a story in his second language as homework

Explain your choices to a classmate or colleague.

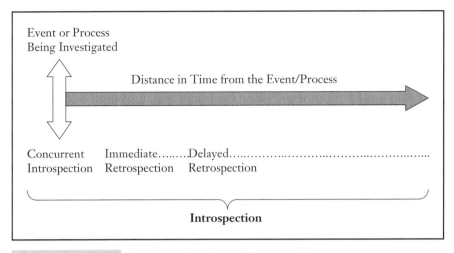

Event or Process
Being Investigated

Distance in Time from the Event/Process

Concurrent   Immediate........Delayed...
Introspection Retrospection Retrospection

Introspection

FIGURE 10.1   Introspection immediacy continuum

represent spans of time instead of particular moments. The more general cover term, *introspection*, entails all three zones, as depicted in **Figure 10.1** (adapted from Bailey, 1991, p. 64).

ACTION

Try engaging in all three of these introspective processes.

1. For concurrent introspection, say aloud what you are doing and thinking as you're reading this sentence.
2. For immediate retrospection, try to verbalize what you were doing just before you began reading this chapter.
3. For delayed retrospection, verbalize what you were doing exactly one week ago.

What are the internal mental differences you experience as you try each of these tasks?

Think-Aloud Protocols

In think-aloud techniques, subjects complete a task or solve a problem and verbalize their thought processes as they do so. The researcher records the verbalization and then analyzes the thought processes the subjects report. In this procedure, the gap between the mental process and the reporting is closer than with other techniques, such as stimulated recall and diaries. However, we may still question whether the verbalization accurately reflects the mental processes that accompany problem solving. It may be that the act of verbalizing the thought processes alters them in some way. (This concern is not peculiar to introspection. All researchers need to be aware of the possibility that their results may in some ways be artifacts of the data collection procedures they have used.)

Think-aloud protocols are the results of a data collection technique that involves verbal concurrent introspection. That is, a research subject talks about the process under investigation while he or she is engaged in doing that process—whether it is taking a language test, revising a composition, or reading a text in a foreign language. As the person thinks aloud (i.e., talks about his current thought processes), his self-report is audiotape- or videotape recorded. It is then transcribed and the written result is the "protocol."

In verbalizing their thoughts while performing a task, according to Ericcson and Simon (1993), research subjects "do *not* describe or explain what they are doing—they simply verbalize the information they attend to while generating the answer" (p. xiii). These authors maintain that if subjects verbalize only the thoughts they have as part of performing the research task, their thought sequence will not be changed by the process of thinking aloud. However, if people are told they must explain their thoughts, "additional thoughts and information have to be accessed to produce the auxiliary descriptions and explanations. As a result, the sequence of thoughts is changed, because the subjects must attend to information not normally needed to perform the task" (ibid., xiii).

Ericcson and Simon (1993) describe what they call "three levels of verbalization" elicited from research subjects:

1. The first level is simply reporting—that is, "the vocalization of covert articulatory or oral encodings, as required in the tasks" [being done]. "At this level, there are no intermediate processes and the subject needs expend no special effort to communicate his thoughts" (p. 79).

2. The second level involves some description and "explication of the thought content" (ibid.).

3. The third level "requires the subject to explain his thought processes or thoughts" (ibid.).

Ericcson and Simon caution that at the third level "an explanation of thoughts, ideas, or hypotheses or their motives is not simply a recoding of information already present in short-term memory, but requires linking this information to earlier thoughts and information attended to previously" (ibid.). They stress that verbalization at the second level "does not encompass such additional interpretative processes" (ibid.).

It is important to be aware of the sorts of mental processing we are asking participants in a research project to do for two reasons. First, we want to be sure to obtain the type of data that will address our research questions or hypotheses. Secondly, we don't want to impose additional mental tasks on the participants that would unduly influence the actual mental processes or emotional states that we are investigating.

Here is an example of instructions to experimental subjects (reprinted from Ericcson and Simon, 1993):

"In this experiment we are interested in what you think about when you find answers to some questions that I am going to ask you to answer. In order to do this I am going to ask you to THINK ALOUD as you work on the problem given. What I mean by think aloud is that I want you to tell me EVERYTHING you are thinking from the time you first see the question until you give an answer. I would like you to talk aloud CONSTANTLY from the time I present each problem until you have given your final answer to the questions. I don't want you to try to plan out what you say or try to explain to me what you are saying. Just act as if you are alone in the room speaking to yourself. It is most important that you keep talking. If you are silent for any long period of time, I will ask you to talk. Do you understand what I want you to do?" (p. 378)

How would you change this text to make it more easily understood by someone for whom English is a second language? Think about an intermediate ESL/EFL learner as the person who would be getting the instructions. You can either translate some version of this text into the learner's mother tongue or modify the English instructions above.

In addition to getting clear instructions, it is important for research subjects to understand that the think-aloud session is not a social event. In fact, Ericcson and Simon recommend that the researcher actually sit behind the subject who is introspecting and stay completely out of his or her field of vision (ibid., p. xiv).

Stimulated Recall in Second Language Research

The greatest limitation of the think-aloud technique in classroom research is that it cannot be used to collect data directly from real classes, as this would seriously disrupt the flow of the ongoing lessons. In such situations, researchers can use techniques such as retrospection and stimulated recall.

Retrospective data are collected some time after the events being investigated have taken place. Retrospection is quite controversial. For example, Nisbett and Wilson (1977) argue that the gap between the event and the reporting of the event will lead to unreliable data. It has also been claimed that if subjects know they will be required to provide a retrospective account, this knowledge will influence their performance on the task. Ericsson and Simon (1984) argue that the reliability of the data can be enhanced by ensuring that the data are collected as soon as possible after the task or event has taken place. In the case of collecting retrospective data on a lesson, ideally it should happen immediately after the lesson.

Like think-aloud protocols, *stimulated recall* is a procedure for generating introspective data, but it is used after the event under investigation instead of concurrently. The researcher uses data that were collected during the event (e.g., a videotape, audiotape, field notes, etc.) to stimulate the recollection of the people who participated in the event. In this way, the participants will not be distracted by having to introspect during a task, but it is hoped that the record of the original event will stimulate their memories sufficiently to produce good introspective data after the fact.

In our own research, for example, we have used stimulated recall to investigate teachers' decision making during language lessons. Nunan (1996) collected lesson plans and then tape-recorded language lessons taught by nine ESL teachers in Australia. He made notes while observing the lessons. Immediately after the lesson, he asked the teachers to focus on those points where they had departed from their lesson plans. Then he transcribed the recordings and asked the teachers to annotate the transcripts.

In a parallel study, Bailey (1996) observed and tape-recorded ESL lessons in California and made running field notes as the lessons proceeded. The audiotapes were transcribed and the teachers reviewed the transcripts and read the field notes. In the process, Bailey asked them to explain their decision making at the points where they had chosen to depart from their lesson plans. Those conversations were also tape-recorded. In both these studies, the teachers' recollections of their thought processes as they taught were stimulated by the data that had been collected during the actual lessons.

In classroom research using stimulated recall, the researcher records a lesson and then gets the teacher and, when feasible, the students to comment on what was happening at the time that the teaching and learning took place. The informants can look at a video or listen to a tape of the lesson, pausing at particular points of interest. Alternatively, field notes or transcripts of the lesson can be used as a memory aid.

Stimulated recall can yield insights into teaching and learning processes that would be difficult to obtain by other means. It is particularly useful in collaborative research because it enables teachers and students as well as the researcher to present their various interpretations of what happened in the moment-by-moment interactions that define a given lesson or classroom event. The interpretations can be directly linked to the classroom events that gave rise to them.

One of the most comprehensive investigations to use stimulated recall is reported by Woods (1989). The focus of the investigation was teachers' decision making. Woods used three data collection techniques—ethnographic interviews, ethnographic observation over time, and stimulated recall—to collect data on the decision making of eight ESL teachers. He describes the procedure as follows:

> [Stimulated] recall elicited teachers' comments about the options considered, decisions made, and actions taken in the classroom. . . . A lesson

was videotaped and subsequently viewed and commented on by the teacher. By pressing a remote pause button to freeze the video and then making a comment [captured on a composite videotape as a voice-over], the teacher provided a commentary about the lesson, the students or about what s/he was trying to do as the lesson transpired. The composite videotape containing the lesson and the superimposed comments was analyzed to determine the processes and bases of decisions made during the lesson. (p. 110)

The stimulated recall technique, along with follow-up interviews, enabled Woods to draw some interesting conclusions about processes of classroom decision making, including the following:

1. The overall process of decision making within the classroom context is incredibly complex, not only in terms of the number and types of decisions to be made, but also because of the multiplicity of factors impinging on them.

2. In terms of procedures for course planning, the most surprising finding was the tentativeness of teachers' advance planning. "Lessons were sketched out only in very vague terms and detailed planning occurred at most a couple of lessons in advance even by the most organized of the teachers" (ibid., p. 116)

3. Based on an analysis of the teacher interviews, Woods concluded that each teacher's course was internally coherent. He cites as an example one of the teachers whose decision making was driven by her desire to develop the independence of the students as learners.

4. The final major point to emerge was the fact that different teachers had quite different approaches, criteria for success, and so on, and that different teachers could take identical materials and use them in class in very different ways.

The aim of this study was to investigate teachers' interactive decision making, that is, the decisions they made 'online' as they taught. (In the context of research on teacher cognition *online* means during a lesson—a decision in real time.) As it was clearly not feasible for the researcher to interrupt the teachers in the middle of their lessons, he recorded the lessons and replayed the recordings for the teachers immediately afterwards.

REFLECTION

Given what you know so far, think of a research question that you'd like to address that could incorporate the stimulated recall procedure. What sort(s) of data would you use to prompt your participants' memories of the events being investigated?

Here are some data from Nunan's (1996) investigation into language teachers' interactive decision making. The researcher observed and taped a series of lessons and then used the tapes as a stimulated recall device. The following transcript is from a lesson based on a piece of authentic listening in which an interviewer questions people about their lifestyles. After the students listened to the tape, the following classroom interaction occurred:

T: What question does the interviewer ask? The interviewer? What question does the interviewer ask? What's the question in here?

S: You smoke?

T: You smoke? You smoke? That's not a proper question, is it really? Proper question is do you smoke? So he says "you smoke?" We know it's a question, because . . . why? You smoke? . . .

S: The tone.

T: The tone . . . the . . . the . . . what did we call it before? You smoke? What do we call this?

S: Intonation.

T: Intonation. You know by his intonation—it's a question. (p. 51)

REFLECTION

What would you have asked the teacher about what was going on in this piece of interaction if you were using this transcript to stimulate the teacher's recall?

The researcher was interested in why the teacher had in effect 'deauthenticated' the piece of authentic data by asserting that the interviewer was not asking 'proper' questions. The teacher reflected on the interaction and said that the issue of questions had not been part of the lesson plan.

T: . . . and also the on-the-spot decision like when it said "drink"

I: So you hadn't actually planned to teach that?

T: No I hadn't. I mean, really, that would be an excellent thing to do in a follow-up lesson—you know, focus on questions.

I: In fact, what you're asking them to do in their work is focus on the full question forms, and yet in the tape they're using a . . .

T: . . . wasn't, yeah. So, I suppose it's recognizing one question form by the intonation, then being able to transfer it into the proper question "Do you drink?" rather than "Drink?" I mean, that would be good to spend a lot more time on at another point. But it seemed like it was good to bring up there. Just to transfer the information. (ibid., pp. 50–51)

Introspecting on the lesson segment led the teacher to make the following comment:

> When I first looked at the material, I thought it was quite a straightforward listening so therefore if I give them a split listening it'll make it more challenging for them. I took the decision to do that [switch the focus to question forms] and I don't regret that. I mean, question forms are always difficult to do, they're always difficult to slot in unless you do a whole lesson on question forms, so to throw them in now and again like that is quite valid. (ibid.)

The stimulated recall session thus gave the teacher an opportunity to reflect on an online decision she had made. In this case, it reaffirmed the decision she had make in the heat of the teaching moment.

Diary Studies

Since the late 1970s, entries recorded in teachers' and learners' journals, or diaries, have been used as data in studies of second language acquisition and teaching. Language learning diaries have been kept in both formal and informal learning contexts, in foreign language and second language situations. Teaching journals have been kept by both novice and experienced teachers.

What is a *diary study* and how does it differ from a *diary* or *journal?* (We will use these two terms interchangeably, as they have been used in the existing literature for the past three decades.) According to Bailey and Ochsner (1983),

> A diary study in second language learning, acquisition, or teaching is an account of a second language experience as recorded in a first-person journal. The diarist may be a language teacher or a language learner— but the central characteristic of the diary studies is that they are introspective: The diarist studies his own teaching or learning. Thus he can report on affective factors, language learning strategies, and his own perceptions—facets of the language learning experience which are normally hidden or largely inaccessible to an external observer. (p. 189)

The learner's or teacher's experiences are "documented through regular, candid entries in a personal journal and then analyzed for recurring patterns or salient events" (Bailey, 1990, p. 215).

You will recall from Chapter 1 that Grotjahn (1987) characterized research paradigms in terms of (1) research design (nonexperimental, pre-experimental, quasi-experimental, and experimental designs); (2) the type of data collected (qualitative or quantitative); and (3) the type of analysis conducted (interpretive or statistical—i.e., qualitative or quantitative). In Grotjahn's terms, diary studies are typically pre-experimental or nonexperimental. They are based primarily on qualitative data (the written or tape-recorded diary entries), and they are usually analyzed interpretively (though some have been analyzed quantitatively as well).

Diaries can be kept by teachers or by learners. However, undertaking a diary study requires discipline and application because if the entries are not made consistently over time, patterns are unlikely to emerge. When keeping a diary for research purposes, a five-step procedure is recommended:

Step 1: Provide a context for the study by giving an account of your personal language teaching and/or language learning history (depending on whether the focus of the diary is on teaching or learning).

Step 2: Keep regular, uncensored accounts of the teaching or learning experience, trying to be as candid as possible

Step 3: Analyze the account for patterns and significant events. (See Chapter 14 for a discussion of techniques for qualitative data analysis.)

Step 4: Revise the 'raw' account for public consumption. For instance, students' names may be changed to pseudonyms, local abbreviations will be spelled out, and so on.

Step 5: Document and discuss the factors that appear to be important in language teaching/learning.

When keeping a diary, it is a good idea not to embark on the analysis too prematurely. If Steps 3, 4, and 5 are delayed until a substantial amount of data have been collected, then you will avoid coming to premature conclusions. Also, in the early stages, the accounts may appear to be rather inchoate and random. In our experience, many patterns only emerge in the longer term.

Since their appearance in the late 1970s, diary studies have gained viability as a data collection procedure in studies on language learning and teaching. Originally, the journal entries were analyzed by the diarists themselves, but later studies involved analyses by someone other than the diarist. The same pattern occurred in teachers' diary studies: At first, the data were analyzed by the diarists themselves, but later, researchers other than the diarists did the analyses. When the diarists themselves were also the analysts, the analytic processes were referred to as "primary" or "direct" or "introspective." When the analyses were done by someone other than the diarists, the process was called "secondary" or "indirect" or "non-introspective" (Curtis and Bailey, in press).

REFLECTION

In your viewpoint, what are the advantages and disadvantages of having language learners analyze their diary entries as opposed to an independent researcher? What about language teachers who keep journals about their own teaching? Should they analyze the data, or is that task better left to a researcher who was not teaching the class under investigation?

Table 10.1 lists a number of published diary studies on language learning. In some cases, the data were analyzed by the diarists, while, in some studies, other researchers analyzed the data. Some studies involved both primary and secondary analyses. Some of the diarists were teachers, but the diary studies listed in Table 10.1 are about language learning rather than teaching.

TABLE 10.1 Selected published research based on language learners' journals

Research Using Language Learners' Journals as Data	Language(s) Involved	Agent(s) of Analysis
Allison (1998)	English	Other
Bailey (1981)	French	Diarist
Bailey (1983b)	Various Languages	Diarist & Other
Birch (1992)	Thai & Mandarin	Other
Brown, C. (1985a; 1985b)	Spanish	Other
Campbell (1996)	Spanish	Diarist
Carroll (1994)	English	Other
Carson & Longhini (2002)	Spanish	Diarist & Other
Danielson (1981)	Italian	Diarist
Ellis (1989)	German	Other
Grandcolas & Soulé-Susbielles (1986)	French	Others
Halbach (2000)	English	Other
Hilleson (1996)	English	Other
Huang (2005)	English	Other
Jones (1994; 1995)	Hungarian	Diarist
Krishnan & Hoon (2002)	English	Others
Lowe (1987)	Mandarin	Other
Matsumoto (1989)	English	Other
Moore (1977)	Danish	Diarist
Parkinson & Howell-Richardson (1999)	French, Spanish, & English	Others
Peck (1996)	Spanish	Other
Porto (2007)	English	Other
Richards (1992)	Various Languages	Other
Rowsell & Libben (1994)	Various Languages	Others
Rubin & Henze (1981)	Arabic	Diarist & Other
Ruso (2007)	English	Other
Schmidt & Frota (1986)	Portuguese	Diarist & Other
Schumann (1980)	Arabic & Farsi	Diarists
Schumann & Schumann (1977)	Arabic & Farsi	Diarists
Simard (2004)	English	Other
Tinker Sachs (2002)	Cantonese	Diarist
Tyacke & Mendelsohn (1986)	English	Others
Warden, Lapkin, Swain, & Hart (1995)	French	Others
Woodfield & Lazarus (1998)	Swedish	Diarists & Others

A paper by Rivers (1979; 1983) is not listed in Table 10.1 because we don't consider it to be a diary study since no explicit analysis was provided. The publication consists solely of the author's diary entries about learning Spanish.

Both pre-service and in-service language teachers have kept journals about their teaching practice (e.g., Appel, 1995; Bailey, 2001b; Verity, 2000), or about their experiences in training programs (C. H. Palmer, 1992; G. M. Palmer, 1992; Polio and Wilson-Duffy, 1998). Like the language learning diary studies, in some cases, the teaching journals were analyzed by the diarists themselves, but, in others, the analysis was done by someone else—researchers or instructors in the training programs. Several of these studies are listed in **Table 10.2.**

The division of these two tables into diary studies about language learning and language teaching is not as neat as it appears. Many of the language learning diarists have been language teachers and/or applied linguists (see, e.g., Bailey, 1980, 1983b; Birch, 1992; Campbell, 1996; Carson and Longhini, 2002; Danielson, 1981; Grandcolas and Soulé-Susbielles, 1986; Jones, 1994; 1995; Lowe, 1987; Rubin and Henze, 1981; Tinker Sachs, 2002; Schmidt and Frota, 1986; Schumann, 1980; Schumann and Schumann, 1977). And, as noted above, some of the diaries kept by teachers have focused on their language learning (see, e.g., Lowe, 1987; Porto, 2007; Richards, 1992).

ACTION

If you are taking or teaching a language class, or can put yourself in a context to use your second language for a period of time, try making daily journal entries for at least a week. What challenges arise? What insights do you gain?

REFLECTION

After you have tried making entries in a learning or teaching diary, consider the following issues:

1. Should a diarist read other language learning or teaching diary studies while keeping a diary, or does this lead to "contamination" of the reported experience?

2. Should a diarist read about and comment on language learning theories while keeping a diary, or does this mold the diarist's recollections and insights to fit the theories?

3. Should a diarist try to take notes during the actual language learning or teaching experience (e.g., during an ongoing language lesson), so the impressions are more concurrent with the event? Or would that process be so distracting that it would interfere with language learning or teaching?

4. To what extent does the process of keeping a diary (for instance, of examining one's own language learning experience) influence the experience?

Compare your responses to those of your classmates or colleagues.

TABLE 10.2 Selected published research based on language teachers' journals

Authors(s) and Date	Language (to Be) Taught	Pre-/In-service Teacher(s)	Analysis
Appel (1995)	English	In-service	Diarist
Bailey (1990)	Various Languages	Pre-service	Others
Bailey (2001b)	English	In-service	Diarist
Block (1996)	English	In-service	Other
Brinton & Holten (1989)	English	Pre-service	
Brock, Yu, & Wong (1992)	English	In-service	Diarists
Cole, Raffier, Rogan, & Schleicher (1998)	English	Pre-service	Diarists
Delaney & Bailey (2000)	English	Pre-service	Diarist & Other
Grandcolas & Soulé-Susbielles (1986)	French	Pre-service	Diarists
Ho & Richards (1993)	English	In-service	Others
Jarvis (1992)	English	In-service	Other
Lee & Lew (2001)	English	Pre-service	Others
Matsuda & Matsuda (2001)	English	In-service	Diarists
McDonough (1994)	English	In-service	Diarist & Other
Numrich (1996)	English	Pre-service	Other
Palmer, C.H. (1992)	English	In-service	Other
Palmer, G.M. (1992)	English	In-service	Other
Polio & Wilson-Duffy (1998)	English	Pre-service	Others
Pennington & Richards (1997)	English	In-service	Others
Porter, Goldstein, Leatherman, & Conrad (1990)	Various Languages	Pre-service & In-service	Diarists & Others
Ruso (2007)	English	In-service	Diarist
Santana-Williamson (2001)	English	Pre-service & In-service	Other
Tsang (2003)	English	Pre-service	Other
Verity (2000)	English	In-service	Diarist
Winer (1992)	English	Pre-service	Other
Yahya (2000)	English	In-service	Diarist

(Auto)biographical Research

(Auto)biographical research has been a long-standing tradition in anthropology and sociology (see, e.g., Lieblich, Tuval-Mashiach, and Zilber, 1998; Plummer, 1983). However, it is a relatively recent arrival on the language research scene. The term is used to describe a broad narrative approach that "focuses on the analysis and description of social phenomena as they are experienced within the context of individual lives" (Benson and Nunan, 2005, p. 4). In *autobiographical research*, the researchers draw on their own experiences in generating data for the study. In *biographical research*, they draw on the introspective and retrospective accounts of others.

The studies reported in Benson and Nunan (2005) are wide ranging in terms of their research foci, the educational and geographical contexts, and the stories the language learners document. Substantively, the theme that holds the collection together is 'difference and diversity.' In contrast with experimental research and survey research, which attempt to connect learner differences to differences in proficiency and/or attitude, autobiographical studies examine a life story more holistically.

Methodologically, this body of research consists of retrospective case studies of individual learning experiences. Central to these case studies are the individual learners' narrative accounts of their experiences. Benson and Nunan (2005) make the following observation about this approach to research on language learning:

> One of the distinguishing features of (auto)biographical research is that it offers a longitudinal portrait of the phenomena under investigation. This enables us to generate insights that are beyond the reach of 'snapshot' research which captures a single reality, or a limited number of realities, at a single point in time. A common thread running through most of the accounts in this volume is that language learning practices and attitudes are unstable and change over time. In other words, difference and diversity exist not just between learners, but within learners at different stages of their language learning experience. (pp. 155–156)

In other words, autobiographical and biographical research provide in-depth case studies using retrospective narration as a primary method to generate data. Benson and Nunan note that mainstream second language acquisition research often tries to "isolate psychological and social variables such as motivation, affect, age, beliefs and strategies, identity and setting from each other" (ibid.). However, for learners it seems that often "these factors are intimately entwined, not just with each other, but with the learners' larger life circumstances and goals" (ibid.).

One of our graduate students, Julie Choi (2006) kept a diary account of her language learning experiences over a period of years. She used these records as the basis for a graduate dissertation documenting how she developed native-speaker competence in four languages: English, Korean, Chinese, and Japanese. Here is a description of the process she used:

> I began keeping a diary when I was 10. It was a way of expressing difficulties I experienced moving to different countries and learning new languages while constantly trying to fit in. Understandably, my diary became my best friend and a haven where my truest feelings could run free. I wrote daily—sometimes even four or five short entries during lunch, in class (half doodling), on the bus or at home. Predictably, most entries during my adolescent years dealt with friendships, relationships and feelings of "not belonging." I habitually transcribed daily events. They usually involved friends, teachers, family members or myself. I also noted things I saw on TV, overheard on the bus or in other contexts. In retrospect, I realize these observations also contained the seeds of many potential research questions. For example, "What does Silvia mean when she says, "We're not 'real Koreans' because we're Korean-American?" or why did the clerk speak to me slowly using his hands when it was clear I spoke fluent Japanese? Questions wandering through my diary somehow always found their way back to issues of language and culture.
>
> In my teaching career and graduate studies, I worked closely with language learners and intensified my curiosity with language, culture and identity. I became increasingly curious about certain aspects of language and how it affected my personal identity as I moved across geographical and cultural borders. Then I began to see a distinct pattern emerge in my writings. When it came time to choose a topic for my dissertation, my diary came to the rescue. With a bit of direction and research, I was able to open my eyes to the possibility of using the data from my diary for my thesis on language and identity. Embarking on this journey—traveling back to my past to figure out who I was in the present motivated me deeply and fervently (which helps when one is writing a thesis!).
>
> From hundreds of diary entries, letters, emails from friends, pictures and other data from my past, I carefully chose items on the themes of language learning, acceptance and how my identity transformed in the course of my life. Each segment of my narrative was based on one of the major stages in my life—childhood, adolescent and adult years. Once the relevant entries were found, I entered an interactive process with my own narrative and analyzed the data as honestly as possible. I read the collected material and generated a heading for each section. I reached a general hypothesis and changed and revised my interpretative conclusion as necessary by reading current theories within the literature on identity and language learning. (Choi, personal communication)

Choi's diary entries encompass many years of experience and her dissertation provides a detailed portrayal of a multilingual, multicultural person. She comments about possible connections between narrative data and second language acquisition theories:

> What attracts me about research using diary studies is when one looks carefully into the entries, patterns start to emerge and the stories shape and construct the narrator's personality and reality. By reading, analyzing and linking the stories to theories within SLA, I am able to find explanations to questions I have been asking throughout my life, the most noteworthy question being, "Who am I?"—a question I could not have answered without looking at my history. Even the most minor details can offer insights into important questions. By writing about my experiences, I have offered myself some sense of closure and assuaged my feelings of anger and sadness. My diary was a storehouse of authentic data. The insights I gathered from analyzing it make me realize how grateful I must be to the languages I own because they have given me prestige, self-confidence, a deeper understanding of myself, jobs and friends. Besides these gains, they taught me that I am more than just a Korean-American. I can be who I want to be depending on the language I speak and make my home from my own will and my imagination. These realizations empower me. They also humble me to a small, worn journal—my diary—that I wrote my life into and that then shone it back for me to understand and appreciate. (Choi, personal communication)

REFLECTION

Write three insights or observations that you get from Choi's account (*e.g., learning a language can have a powerful impact on personal identity*). If possible, share these insights with other people. Did you and your colleagues find similar or different issues in her comments?

An autobiographical approach to examining teachers' language learning histories was taken by Bailey, Bergthold, Braunstein, Fleischman, Holbrook, Tuman, Waissbluth, and Zambo (1996). As a seminar assignment, seven pre-service teachers wrote retrospective accounts of their language learning experiences addressing the following questions:

1. What language learning experiences have you had and how successful have they been? What are your criteria for judging success?

2. If you were clearly representative of all language learners, what would we have learned about language learning from reading your autobiography? What can be learned about effective (and ineffective) language teaching by reading your autobiography?

3. How has your experience as a language learner influenced you as a language teacher?

By reading, discussing, and comparing one another's language learning histories, these teachers found some common themes running through the documents. These included the importance of their own teachers' personalities and teaching styles (as opposed to methods and materials), the authors' concepts of good and bad teaching, their teachers' attitudes and expectations for students' success, and reciprocal respect between students and teachers. The authors also discussed students' and teachers' respective responsibilities for maintaining and supporting motivation to learn, as well as comparing the learning atmosphere in naturalistic versus formal instructional settings.

The motivation for this collaborative autobiographical research was the idea that "teachers acquire seeming indelible imprints from their own experiences as students and these imprints are tremendously difficult to shake" (Kennedy, 1990, p. 4). Writing their language learning histories enabled these pre-service teachers to bring those past experiences to the level of awareness in order to examine the possible influence of those experiences on their own teaching philosophies and practices.

QUALITY CONTROL ISSUES IN INTROSPECTIVE DATA COLLECTION

One difficulty with having language learners report on their learning is that not all learning processes may be available for introspection. Some processes may happen outside awareness. There are also conscious learning processes of which we are aware, and those are available for introspection. Some subset of those learning processes will be written about by the second language learner, as shown in **Figure 10.2** below:

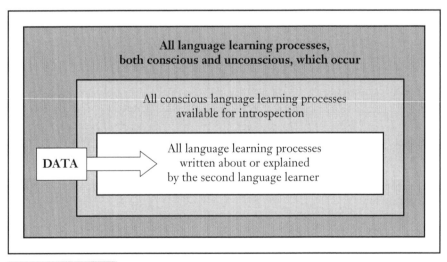

FIGURE 10.2   Subsets of language learning processes reported in introspective data collection (adapted from Bailey, 1991, p. 80)

Giving Clear Instructions

In cases where the diarist is not the data analyst, it is important to give the teachers or language learners clear instructions about making journal entries. The following instructions for keeping a diary are from Matsumoto (1989). The language learner was a native speaker of Japanese studying English:

> Please make daily entries in Japanese describing your classroom learning experience in the ESL program you are participating in this summer. You are asked to write about the content of your class or learning activities, and what you thought or felt about the class and any other things which are involved in your language learning experience. Please write your comments and feelings in as much detail as possible, honestly and openly, as if you were keeping your own personal, confidential diary. Try to write your entry before you have forgotten about the class content—as soon as possible after the class. (p. 170)

Here is another example of instructions to language learners keeping journals. The researcher (C. Brown, 1985b) compared the requests for language input of older (fifty-five to seventy-five years old) and younger (eighteen to twenty-five years old) adult learners of Spanish:

> This journal has two purposes. The first is to help you with your language learning. As you write about what you think and feel as a language learner, you will understand yourself and your experience better.
>
> The second purpose is to increase the overall knowledge about language learning so that learning can be increased. You will be asked to leave your language learning journal when you leave the [training program]. However, your journal will not be read by the teachers at the [training program]. It will be read by researchers interested in language learning.
>
> Your identity and the identity of others you may write about will be unknown (unless you wish it otherwise) to anyone except the researchers.
>
> You will be given 15 minutes a day to write. Please write as if this were your personal journal about your language learning experience. (pp. 283–284)

The learners in Brown's study also made their journal entries in English, their native language.

REFLECTION

What are the advantages and disadvantages of having language learners make diary entries in their first language as opposed to the target language?

Introspective Data Collection Methods and Triangulation

Introspective procedures are sometimes the only data collection processes involved in a study. For example, some diary studies have been based entirely on journal entries (see, e.g., Bailey, 1980, 1983b; Campbell, 1996; F. Schumann, 1980; Schumann and Schumann, 1977). In other cases, they have been used in connection with other types of data, which have permitted the researcher(s) to compare the outcomes of various kinds of data collection. (See, for instance, Block, 1996; Hilleson, 1996; and Schmidt and Frota, 1986.)

A strong example of data triangulation comes from a study by Ellis (1989), who used questionnaires, a cognitive style test, a language aptitude test, attendance and participation records, a word-order acquisition score, measures of speech rate, and the results of two proficiency tests, in combination with two learners' diaries. The learners—called Monique and Simon in the report—kept journals of "their reactions to the course, their teachers, their fellow students, and any other factors which they considered were having an effect on their language learning" (pp. 252–253). The diaries were collected regularly, photocopied, returned immediately, and treated confidentially.

The diary data show that Monique was "obsessively concerned with linguistic accuracy" (p. 254) and that she worried about making mistakes. The diary data contrast markedly with Monique's self-report on a questionnaire in which she characterized herself as confident and adventurous. In contrast, Simon showed "little concern for making errors" (p. 255) and his diary had no references to wanting the teacher to correct his mistakes. Thus in this report, the diary data not only helped to highlight the differences between these two learners but also to verify or challenge other forms of data collected in the research.

Some language classroom research has involved learners keeping spoken diaries to lessen the burden of having to write the entries. For instance, Block (1996) had learners of English in Barcelona, Spain, make oral entries in their journals, using their first language. The difficulty with learners or teachers making spoken entries as research data is that you will probably have to transcribe the audio-recordings, or portions thereof, at some point in your analysis. For this reason, we recommend written journal—and word-processed journal entries in particular—whenever possible.

Tips for Keeping a Language Learning Diary

Over the years, we have worked with many teachers and language learners who have kept diaries about their experiences. One of the most difficult things about undertaking a diary study is sticking with it over time. Based on our experience, we offer the suggestions below to help make writing your diary entries a systematic but easy experience. Try to set up the conditions for writing so that the diary keeping does not require a great deal of effort. The actual process of writing should be (or should become) almost effortless.

Here are some tips for language learners keeping diaries, but these ideas are applicable to teachers keeping journals as well. (See also Curtis and Bailey, in press).

1. If you are taking (or teaching) a regularly scheduled language class, set aside time each day immediately following the class to write in your diary. If you are not taking a class but are immersed in a target language situation, set aside a regular time and place each day in which to write your diary entries. Write daily and as soon as possible after class or after your attempts to use the target language.

2. Write your diary entries in a place you like (your favorite desk, outside with a pleasant view, in a sunny kitchen) where you won't be disturbed by friends or ringing telephones. If you are writing your diary by hand, use paper or a notebook that you like and a pen that is easy and comfortable to use. If you are word processing your diary, make sure you are familiar with the program and that you save and back up your entries regularly and religiously, in order to avoid the frustration of losing data.

3. Carry a small pocket notebook or personal digital assistant (PDA) with you so that you can make notes about your language experiences as they occur even if you don't have your actual diary with you. Some diarists have suggested keeping the notebook or PDA near your bedside so you can record any late-night or early morning thoughts.

4. If you are conducting a diary study about learning a foreign language, we believe the time devoted to writing about your language learning experience should at least be equal to the time spent in class. If you are immersed in the target culture, you will find you probably cannot record everything that happens in a day, so you may want to focus your diary on some particular aspect of your experience that interests you.

5. Keep your diary in a safe, secure place—a locked drawer, file cabinet, or briefcase. If you are word processing your data, make sure your files are password protected. The idea is for you to be able to write anything you want without feeling uneasy about other people reading and reacting to your ideas.

6. When you record entries in the original uncensored version of your diary, don't worry about style, grammar, and organization—especially if you are writing in your second language. The idea is to get complete and accurate data at a time when the information is still fresh in your mind. You can polish your presentation of the data at a later time when you edit the journal for public consumption. Thus, the original diary entries sometimes read like "stream of consciousness" writing.

7. Each time you write an assertion, ask yourself, "Why?" Why did you write that? What evidence do you have for the statement you just made? Some of the language learning journals that have been kept to date are full of fascinating but unsubstantiated insights. Try to support your insights and interpretations with examples from your class sessions, your daily interactions in the target culture, or actual language data.

8. At the end of each diary entry, note thoughts or questions that have occurred to you to consider later. Many anthropologists conducting field research keep an ideas file—brief notes on topics to explore further. This procedure is one way to refine your focus somewhat during the diary-keeping process and to guide future entries.

We strongly recommend word processing your diary entries rather than recording them by hand since having an electronic record greatly facilitates data analysis.

A SAMPLE STUDY

The sample study we have selected for this chapter is based on an EFL teacher's journal that was kept for two academic semesters (Bailey, 2001b). The author had many years of experience teaching ESL and working as a teacher educator in the United States, but then she taught at a university in Hong Kong for a year. (See Verity, 2000, for an account of a similar situation in Japan.) Upon returning to her regular graduate teacher training position a year later, Bailey noticed that her teaching (e.g., in statistics courses, language assessment seminars, and so on) had changed. She then decided to read through her Hong Kong diary entries to see if she could determine how those changes had come about.

The database for this report consisted of fifty-two single-spaced pages for fall semester and fifty-eight single-spaced pages for spring semester. These entries were word processed and saved electronically. Paper printouts of the diary entries were filed along with copies of the class handouts and lesson plans. The data were qualitatively analyzed and in the process, a number of teaching strategies related to scaffolding emerged. *Scaffolding* was defined by Bruner (1983, p. 60) as "a process of 'setting up' the situation to make the child's entry easy and successful, and then gradually pulling back and handing the role to the child as he becomes skilled enough to manage it." (Here the learners were young adults rather than children, but the concept is still useful.) The following scaffolding procedures were identified in the teaching diary (Bailey, 2001b):

1. the teacher's use of multiple channels for presenting information or instructions to the learners;

2. having the students "feed me back the task" (i.e., paraphrasing the instructions to check their understanding of the assignment);

3. having the students compare their ideas with a classmate privately before giving a public response to a solicit;

4. the teacher building in a recognition step (so the learners could identify the linguistic item of focus in the input prior to having to produce it themselves); and

5. the teacher using schema activators to prepare the learners for reading and listening tasks. (pp. 15–25)

These five techniques emerged from the diary entries, but the journal was not kept in order to document scaffolding concepts. Bailey kept the diary to document adjustments to her new teaching context in Hong Kong, but it later provided a rich database for examining how working with those EFL students had influenced her subsequent graduate level teaching upon her return to the United States. The five patterns listed above are illustrated in the report with dated excerpts from the diary to illustrate teacher learning over time.

PAYOFFS AND PITFALLS

As noted above, the use of think-aloud protocols came into applied linguistics from psychology. Ericcson and Simon (1993) explain the psychology research context as follows:

> From the beginnings of psychology as a science, investigators, impelled by the difficulties of relying wholly on external observation in studying mental processes, have questioned subjects about their experiences, thought processes and strategies. Claims for the validity of such verbal accounts were based primarily on the notion that individuals had privileged access to their experiences; as long as they were truthful, their reports could be trusted. (p. xii)

The legitimacy of introspective and retrospective data hinges on the concept of memory. As Ericcson and Simon explain, a subset of

> thoughts occurring during performance of a task is stored in long-term memory. Immediately after the task is completed, there remain retrieval cues in short-term memory that allow effective retrieval of the sequence of thoughts. Hence for tasks that can be completed in 0.5 to 10 seconds we would expect subjects to be able to recall the actual sequence of their thoughts with high accuracy and completeness. With long durations, recall will be increasingly difficult and incomplete. (ibid., p. xvi)

These authors acknowledge that self-report may be flawed: "Even where subjects are asked to report on their cognitive processes used during many trials of an experiment, we cannot rule out the possibility that the information they retrieve at the time of the verbal report is different from the information they retrieve while actually performing the experimental task" (ibid., p. xii). For this reason, they recommend that "whenever possible, concurrent verbal reports should be collected so that processing and verbal report would coincide in time" (ibid., p. xiii).

The reliability of the data will be enhanced if informants are given adequate contextual information about the study. According to Ericsson and Simon, steps should also be taken to ensure that informants do not make inferences that go beyond the task, although there may well be aspects of classroom interaction where the informant's inferences and interpretations are of central interest. Regardless of the focus, steps should be taken to eliminate researcher bias. (In retrospective data collection sessions, the researcher may fall into the trap of 'leading the witness.') Finally, where possible, subjects should not be informed that they will be required to retrospect until after they have completed the task.

The major pitfall of introspection is its potentially questionable reliability and internal validity. If we get people to engage in an introspective task on two different occasions, we may get different responses. If we do, then questions of reliability arise. More serious is the issue of internal validity. When subjects report on some inner state or thought process, how do we know they are telling the truth? They might not be lying. Rather, they may simply be unaware of the true nature of those processes.

The same goes for the interpretation of introspective diary entries. In her study of herself as a learner of French, Bailey (1980) analyzed the diary data and identified three key themes. However, she was completely unaware of the theme of competitiveness and anxiety that ran through the data until these issues were pointed out to her by her professor. She then reanalyzed her own data as well as the journals or reports of ten other learners and found a connection between competitiveness and anxiety (Bailey, 1983b).

There are many potential pitfalls in collecting introspective data, and these problems vary depending on whether you are using think-aloud protocols, stimulated recall, or diary studies. The main concern with the think-aloud protocols is that verbalizing one's thoughts may interfere with the process under investigation. In other words, collecting think-aloud data may trigger the observer's paradox (Labov, 1972).

Stimulated recall doesn't overburden the participants' thought processes or distract them during the event or process under investigation, and, in this sense, it is less intrusive than gathering the data for think-aloud protocols. If the stimulated recall procedure is used, however, it should be done as soon as possible after the event so the person's memories don't degrade too much. Think-aloud protocols, on the other hand, have the advantage of being generated concurrently with the event under investigation, but there is a worry that the data collection process itself might in some way influence or impede the normal mental processing about which the subjects are introspecting.

Stimulated recall helps overcome the danger of the possible interference caused by concurrent introspection but also distances the subject from the actual event. The possibility also exists that using stimulated recall may introduce thoughts or perceptions that were not present during the original event. If electronic recordings are used as the stimulating data, research subjects may be "put off" by the sound of their own voices on audiotapes or their images on videotape.

If transcripts are used as the data in stimulated recall, there is the added burden of transcribing data, which is very time-consuming. The transcription process thus inserts even more time between the event under investigation and the description of that event by the person doing the stimulated recall.

Finally, in cases where learners or teachers are making diary entries that will be analyzed by someone else, they may come up with responses that they think the researcher wants to hear. This problem can also occur with think-aloud protocols and stimulated recall.

Given the problems associated with retrospection, one may question whether the technique should be used at all. However, there are occasions when it is neither feasible nor desirable to collect data from informants as they are performing a task. This is particularly true of research conducted in actual classrooms.

The single greatest advantage of the introspective methods reviewed in this chapter is that they take us to a place that no other data collection method can reach—into the mind of the learner or the teacher. The inner cognitive and affective states of learners and teachers can only be indirectly plumbed by other methods such as elicitation and interviews. Thoughts, feelings, motives, reasoning processes, and mental states can really only be gotten at in any direct sense through introspection.

CONCLUSION

Introspective data collection procedures can be characterized in terms of when the data are generated relative to the event being investigated—concurrently with the event, immediately afterwards, some time afterwards, or long afterwards. In addition, the data collection can be very brief, as with think-aloud protocols and some stimulated recall procedures, or much longer as in the diary studies. Some autobiographical and biographical research spans years of data collection—or recollection.

While there are potential problems with these data collection procedures, introspective procedures help us identify and understand issues that are not readily accessible through other means. When used with other data collection procedures over time in studies that employ careful triangulation, they can provide helpful insights in research on language teaching and learning.

QUESTIONS AND TASKS

1. Think of a research question that interests you and that could be addressed with think-aloud protocols from language learners. First, determine what task(s) the learners will do as they think aloud. Then write the instructions to the learners about how they are to verbalize as they do the task(s).

2. Think of a research question you'd like to investigate using stimulated recall. What is the research question? What sorts of data would you use to stimulate your informants' recollection of the event(s) you wish to study?

3. Think of a research question that interests you and that could be addressed through data from language learners' or teachers' diaries. Write the instructions to the diarists about the journal entries you'd like them to make.

4. Complete the following table. Identify the pros and cons of the different techniques discussed in the chapter, and then suggest a possible research question that could be investigated using each technique.

Technique	Pros	Cons	Question
Think aloud			
Stimulated recall			
Diary entries			
Biographical research			
Autobiographical research			

5. In recent years, language classroom research has produced reports in which diary entries served as part of the data, along with data from other elicitation procedures. Think of a research question you would like to address in which learners' or teachers' diary entries could form a part of the database. What additional types of data would you use to address your question?

6. The diary extracts that follow have been taken from an unpublished diary kept by David Nunan. Study the extracts and complete the tasks that follow.

December 8
I've been living in Hong Kong now, and speak very little Cantonese. This is something I'm embarrassed and ashamed of, being a language teacher myself. Not that it's unusual. I have colleagues who have lived here twice as long as I have who speak even less Cantonese than I do.

So, what are the reasons? Firstly, it's a very difficult language. The commitment of time to make a decent fist of learning the language is enormous. Like most expats in Hong Kong, I lead a very busy life. In fact, I spend approximately half of my life traveling out of Hong Kong. Outside Hong Kong, the language is of little utility. If I'm going to learn a Chinese language it might as well be Putonghua.

Secondly, despite constant laments about the poor standard of English, most of the local Chinese that I interact with have a reasonable level of English. I would have to study Cantonese for many years for my Cantonese to be comparable to or superior to their English. From a practical, communicative perspective, there is therefore no need to learn the language. Shortly after I moved to Hong Kong, and had learned a few phrases, I tried to use it in public. The person I was attempting to communicate with said to me, in perfect English, "If you're going to speak Cantonese–speak Cantonese!" That kind of put-down was not encouraging.

Finally, I suffered foreign language interference. I speak Thai to a lower-intermediate level of proficiency, and there is a surprising number of cognates and false-cognates between Cantonese and Thai. Often a word will have the same pronunciation but a different tone.

December 9

I've set myself the goal of learning 1,000 words and phrases by June— only around five a day, but I'm having trouble remembering even that. The CD that L. got me is much better than tapes I have, but there's not enough repetition, and the phrases are presented out of context.

'Maai' rhymes with 'buy' so that should be easy enough to remember. I'm confused by the particles 'ma' and 'ah'. As far as I can figure out, 'ma' is a question particle, and 'ah' functions more like a question tag in English. So 'Mohng ma?' = 'Are you busy?' and 'Mohng ah?' = 'You're busy, are you?' the 'ah' form seems much more prevalent than the 'ma' form.

I tried creating little dialogues from the phrases I was trying to learn in order to give them some context, but didn't get very far. I don't even know how to say 'yes'. From what I know of other Asian languages, I guess there won't be a single word as there is in English.

Really frustrating! I have no idea how to give affirmative responses. The book I'm working with teaches 'Gei hou ma?' (How are you?) but not how to respond. To respond in the affirmative, I did what I'd do if speaking Thai—repeat the phrase. I have no idea if it's right or wrong. In response to 'mohng ma?' 'Are you busy?' I made up 'Hai la' because it's what I hear people in the office saying all the time. I'm sure it's wrong, but I have no other resources to use.

I checked with L. who suggested Gei hou (quite good) or simple 'hou' and 'hou mohng ah!' (very busy) or simply 'hou mohng' for answers.

At lunch, I was really pleased when I called for the check "Maaihdaan, mgoi" and the woman understood instantly.

December 15

Opportunities to get out and actually practice the language are close to zero. My Chinese friends and acquaintances are all totally bilingual, and even most of the cab drivers on Hongkongside are much better at English than I'll ever be at Cantonese. This is MUCH more like learning as a foreign than a second language. It it very demotivating.

December 22
Only one or two of the words that I worked on yesterday seem to have stuck. The 'organic' principle seems to be working here. I'm not learning one word perfectly one at a time. Rather, I seem to partially learn words and expressions, and then suddenly, several of them will seem to 'come together'. The more vocabulary you learn, the easier new vocabulary is to learn through a kind of 'lexical synergy'. For example, knowing 'jousahn' (good morning) made it relatively easy to learn 'good night' ('joutau').

December 28
Conversation practice with L. (40 minutes). We started practicing more freely today, and I tried to use whatever resources I had to communicate. It was hard work, but fun, and motivating when L. understood what I was trying to say. It's so motivating to have a sympathetic native speaker to reassure me that I AM making progress.

At one point I wanted to ask L. if she liked tea, so I said, "Nei jungyi yum cha." She corrected me to the like/not like form "Nei jung-mh-jungyi yum cha a?" I asked her why she didn't use the full form of the verb to like 'jungyi', but just part of it 'jung' in the first part of the negative/positive, i.e., why she didn't say "Nei jungyi-mh-jungyi yum cha a?" She looked mystified for a minute, not understanding what I was trying to say, then laughed, because she'd never noticed that the full form of the verb isn't used with this question form.

January 7
It's time to push ahead. I am constantly tempted to 'consolidate' rather than to work on new language.

This morning, L. asked me, "Nei yau mou tung nei go leiu gong dinwa a?" I knew instantly what she had asked, "Did you talk to your daughter (who just went back to England) on the phone?" I did this by recognizing the phrase "leiu gong dinwa" ("daughter speak phone"), although I wasn't able to respond appropriately. Eventually I came up with 'yau' (yes). L. then asked "Geisi a?" Using the context, I guessed that this must mean 'when'—also drew on the fact that 'Geido' means 'how much/how many' and made the assumption that 'Gei' combines with other particles to form 'wh-' questions. L. confirmed this 'Si' means 'hour'.

Use the diary entries above to answer the following questions:

* What are the factors that facilitated language learning?
* What factors inhibited the process?
* What research questions suggest themselves?
* What learning strategies does the diarist use?

7. Write a brief account of you own experiences as a language learner using the extract from Choi's retrospections above as a model.

- Did you find the introspective process easy or difficult?
- Did ideas and incidents that you had forgotten about come back to you during the writing process?
- How would you go about analyzing the data?
- If possible, share your account with someone who has completed the same task. What similarities and differences are there in the accounts?
- What insights did you gain about introspection as a data collection technique from doing this task?

SUGGESTED READINGS

Ericcson and Simon (1993) provide a thorough overview of the use of verbal reports and protocol analysis in psychology research. If you plan to work with think-aloud protocols, this book may be useful. For a chapter on the use of the think-aloud procedure in second language research, see Jourdenais (2001).

Færch and Kasper (1987) edited a collection of articles about introspection in second language research. This volume is the source of Grotjahn's (1987) category system, which we have cited throughout this book, as well as Ericcson and Simon (1987).

Gass and Mackey's (2000) book is an excellent source of information about stimulated recall in second language acquisition research.

Any of the diary studies listed in Tables 10.1 and 10.2 above will give you samples of how this introspective method has been used. Many are illustrations of classroom research, while others document language acquisition in naturalistic contexts.

For interesting critiques of the diary studies, see Fry (1988), Matsumoto (1987), and Seliger (1983b).

11

Elicitation Procedures

Field researchers would do well to study the efforts of their peers and predecessors not *because they expect to find ready guidelines and recipes—the knowledge involved in craft production is inherently tacit and noncodifiable—but to immerse themselves in the cultures and customs of their communities; that is,* to understand a complicated ethos rather than to find a simple formula. (Schrank, 2006, pp. 217–218)

INTRODUCTION AND OVERVIEW

The focus of this chapter is on elicitation procedures. These include interviews, production tasks, role plays, questionnaires, tests, and so on. Elicitation procedures vary enormously in terms of their scope and purpose as you can see from the preceding list. In the field of second language acquisition, studies using elicitation are extremely common. They are not quite so common in classroom research although they are widely used in classroom-oriented (as opposed to classroom-based) research.

In second language research, *elicitation* refers to all of the ways in which the researcher tries to obtain data directly from informants (rather than, for example, simply by observing them). In second language classroom research, the focus of interest could be the teacher, the students, or some aspect of teacher-student interaction. An unstructured interview with a teacher about his or her decisions made during a lesson would be an example of a teacher-focused elicitation study. A questionnaire administered to students to obtain their attitudes and feelings about studying a foreign language would be an example of a student-focused elicitation study.

Think of a study that you would be interested in doing. Based on what you know so far, would some sort of elicitation procedure be useful in your research?

INTERVIEWS

In this section, we will consider the interview as a family of elicitation procedures. We will look at structured, semi-structured, and unstructured interviews, as well as ethnographic interviews and focus group interviews. While most interviews are conducted face-to-face, they can also be carried out electronically—by telephone, via e-mail, or even through a chat room. Like other elicitation devices, interviews can be used to collect samples of learner language for analysis, the views and attitudes of informants, or their language learning histories.

Interview types can be placed on a continuum in terms of their formality. This continuum can range from unstructured through semi-structured to structured. The data that we obtain by interviewing must be recorded—either in writing, electronically, or both. Typically interview responses, or a subset of such responses, must be transcribed. However, an advantage of interviewing is that, unlike written questionnaires, interviews can be used with non-literate research respondents. In addition, even though interviewing is very time-consuming, it does not suffer from the same problems of low return rates that plague survey research.

Structured Interviews

The structured interview is like a questionnaire that is administered orally rather than in writing. The researcher normally works with one person at a time, asking him or her questions and recording the person's answers. The interview follows a pre-set list of questions, and the researcher is careful to elicit answers to the same questions from all of the respondents. Conducting a structured interview demands training and discipline on the part of the researcher to stick closely to the predetermined agenda. The advantage of using structured interviews is that they provide detailed data that is comparable across informants.

Semi-Structured Interviews

In a semi-structured interview, the researcher will have a general idea of how he or she wants the interview to unfold and may even have a set of prepared questions. However, he or she will use these questions as a point of departure for the interview and will not be constrained by them. As the interview unfolds, topics and issues rather than pre-set questions will determine the direction that the interview takes. The main difference between a semi-structured interview and an unstructured interview is that the former will adhere more closely to the researcher's agenda than the latter. Because of its flexibility, the semi-structured interview is preferred by many field researchers. Dowsett (1986), for example, writes that the semi-structured interview

> is quite extraordinary—the interactions are incredibly rich and the data indicate that you can produce extraordinary evidence about life that you don't get in structured interviews or questionnaire methodology—no matter how open ended and qualitative you think your questionnaires are attempting to be. It's not the only qualitative research technique that will produce rich information about social relationships but it does give you access to social relationships in a quite profound way. (p. 53)

Unstructured Interviews

An unstructured interview will develop according to the agenda of the interviewee rather than the agenda of the interviewer. While there will be a general theme underpinning the interview, it can take off in unexpected directions, which the interviewer will follow, picking up on issues and themes suggested by the interviewee. For example, the interviewer might begin by asking a teacher about how he or she modifies and adapts course books and other commercial materials into her lessons but then segue into the role of technology in language teaching.

Ethnographic Interviews

As we saw in Chapter 7, ethnography seeks to document both the emic (insider's) and the etic (outsider's) point of view. Ethnographers doing field research often use interviews to discover and develop the emic perspective. According to Spradley (1979), these interviews are like "a series of friendly conversations" between the researcher and the members of a culture (p. 58). Ethnographic interviews occur in the natural course of the longitudinal, ongoing relationships the ethnographer builds with the cohort in the study. They are characterized by (1) "a specific request to hold the interview (resulting from the research question)" (Flick, 1998, p. 93); (2) ethnographic explanations given in everyday language, in which the ethnographer tells the informant explicitly what he is seeking and why; and (3) specific question types that elicit information about how the participants construct meaning and organize their society.

Focus Group Interviews

We tend to think of interviews as one-on-one events involving an interviewer and an interviewee. However, focus group interviews involving several informants and a moderator are becoming increasingly popular (Stewart and Shamdasani, 1990). *Focus groups* are defined as "a research technique that collects data through group interaction on a topic determined by the researcher"

(Morgan, 1997, p. 6). Getting a group of students to view a video of one of their lessons and then eliciting their reactions to the lesson would be an example of a focus group interview. The term *focus* highlights that the fact that the researcher guides and focuses the discussion rather than letting informants take the interview in any direction that they wish. The advantage of a focus group rather than an individual interview is that the informants can stimulate and be stimulated by each other. The researcher may thereby elicit a richer data set than if he or she is conducting individual interviews.

REFLECTION

Can you think of any disadvantages of using focus group interviews when second language learners are the interviewees?

The choice to interview (and of the type of interview you might use) is directly related to your research question(s). Clearly, if you wish to investigate the perspectives of participants in a course or members of a culture, interviews are one way to gather in-depth data. The types of interviews described above are summarized in **Table 11.1**.

REFLECTION

Based on your previous reading and experience, as well as what you have read so far in this book, what do you see as the advantages of interviews? Do you have a preference for any of the types of interviews described above? If so, why?

As an example of classroom-oriented research using interviews, we have chosen an excerpt from a study by Galda (in press), an ESL teacher in a U.S. community college. She studied the English needs and the English language use of three elderly refugees who had been her students at one time. Part of her data collection involved interviewing them. The interviews were conducted in English. Here is Galda's description of her work with these three learners:

I was fortunate to work with three very special students, Falina, Luda, and Misha, in compiling the research data. Although I had worked with each of these students prior to the study, they were not enrolled in my classes during the research period. All three participants were from the former Soviet Union and had emigrated to the United States due to religious persecution. (All are heritage Jews.) They vary in their level of English proficiency, with Falina performing at a high-intermediate level, Luda at a basic level, and Misha at a beginning level of proficiency

TABLE 11.1 Types of Interviews

Type	Description
Structured	Structured interviews are similar to questionnaires that are completed orally rather than in writing. The researcher has a well-planned and clearly defined agenda and a set of questions that are adhered to fairly closely.
Semi-structured	Semi-structured interviews are less rigid than structured interviews but more systematic than unstructured interviews. The interviewer uses predetermined questions to elicit comparable data across interviewees, but also allows for expansion and elaboration in the responses.
Unstructured	In an unstructured interview, the interviewer knows, in a general way, where he or she wants to go with the interview but is happy to let the interviewer take the lead and follow themes and issues as they emerge in the course of an interview
Ethnographic	Ethnographic interviews occur in the researcher's longitudinal, ongoing relationships with the cohort. They include (1) a specific request for the interview, (2) understandable explanations about what information is being sought and why; and (3) specific question types to get information about how the participants construct meaning and organize their society.
Focus group	Focus group interviews involve a group of individuals rather than a single informant. Focus group interviews are popular with market researchers who want to obtain collective insights into a new product that they are placing on the market. In English language teaching, commercial publishers often use focus groups to get data on how new course materials and textbooks are working in the classroom.

(no previous knowledge of English). These students were enrolled in a computer skills course for ESL students when they volunteered to help with this project.

Galda explains how the data collection changed slightly as she got to know the three students better and they became more familiar with the interview process:

Over the course of the two semesters, I interacted with the student participants individually several times a week, chatting informally, helping each with their computer class assignments, and conducting interviews. Each of the participants took part in open-ended interviews for two hours each week for 20 weeks. These interviews focused on three or four major questions or themes. Many of these questions were "orientation" types of inquiries, ice-breakers chosen to help us all relax and to get to know each other better. Some centered on the participants' life experiences before coming to the U.S., in particular, their early memories of their own literacy development during childhood.

To maintain a natural, conversational interaction in the interview sessions, I initially hand-recorded field notes during these conversations. As the participants grew increasingly comfortable with me and the research being conducted, the conversations were audio-recorded and subsequently transcribed within hours of the interviews. In addition, I maintained a research journal that was updated after each interview session to help in the identification and recording of insights and impressions. I utilized the journal to process the conversations and to reflect upon my own thoughts, ideas, and further questions as the project progressed.

Galda used the interview data to build a cumulative picture of the three respondents' lives, prior to their emigration to the United States, and in particular to learn about their education and experiences of literacy:

Through the open-ended interview sessions, I learned a great deal about the life and literacy experiences that the participants had amassed before coming to the U.S. In addition, I gained insights into their perceptions of themselves as learners, as well as some of the personal learning goals identified by each individual. Finally, I managed to uncover self-perceptions held by each and detected some of the social identities constructed by these students as they negotiated their new social, linguistic, and academic environments.

Although the interviews were Galda's main data elicitation procedure, she also collected data by other means. This process allowed her to triangulate her findings.

In addition to the interview sessions, I spent one hour per week working with participants in tutoring sessions, helping them with their emerging language skills in computer, writing, and reading applications. The participants eventually consented to being recorded during the tutoring sessions, and these interactions were transcribed within hours of each session. Through the tutoring sessions, I gained insights into the learning strategies, learning styles, literacies, and learning experiences exhibited by the participants. I also gathered data concerning the construction of personal identity by each individual in this semi-social, semi-academic context.

In order to obtain a more rounded impression of each participant, I attended two full ESL class sessions with the participants each semester. During these visits, I recorded field notes using a divided page technique, which allowed for the recording of observed interactions on one side of the field note page. The other side of the field note page was then available to add additional comments and insights collected from course instructors discussing the observed interactions following the class visits.

Finally, I collected copies of student work and assignments, then examined these materials, mining them for additional data during the course of the semester. Through the examination of student-generated documents, I learned a great deal about the life and learning experiences of the participants. In addition, I was afforded some very personal insights into the perceptions these student participants held of themselves as both learners and as social beings. Finally, through their own carefully considered, self-generated words, I was able to identify additional personal learning goals articulated by the participants.

REFLECTION

Think of a research question that interests you. How might Galda's experience and ideas about interviewing be useful to you if you were to interview second language learners to collect (some of) your data?

ACTION

Galda's primary data collection procedure was the ongoing interview process, but she also achieved methods triangulation. Reread the paragraphs above and identify all the methods of data collection she used.

QUESTIONNAIRES

In Chapter 5, we saw that questionnaires are a popular elicitation device. They can be widely disseminated, particularly in this electronic age, and quantitative or categorical responses to closed questions can also be readily collated and analyzed with the aid of technology. Questionnaires bear a close family resemblance to interviews, particularly structured interviews, and many of the comments that we made about interviews in the preceding section are pertinent to questionnaires as well. In particular, the closed-ended items in a structured interview resemble a questionnaire administered to informants orally rather than in writing.

Questionnaires are very popular data collection devices with graduate students, who often have the idea that the ease of disseminating and collating data means that administering questionnaire is an 'easy' data collection option. However, constructing a sound questionnaire, one that is unambiguous and yields the data the researcher wants to collect, is notoriously difficult, as we saw in Chapter 5. This is especially so when the questionnaire is administered in the second language of the respondents.

COMBINING QUESTIONNAIRE AND INTERVIEW DATA

Interviews and questionnaires work well together. With questionnaires, which are typically completed in a noninteractive fashion, it is possible to get a range of responses from many people on a limited number of items. So, once they are developed, piloted, and validated, questionnaires are practical and convenient. In contrast, interactive interviews are less practical to administer, but they permit researchers to delve into people's ideas and ask them to expand upon their comments. In this sense, questionnaires permit us to sample broadly while interviews permit us to explore more deeply.

You may sometimes wish to employ a research design in which you first use questionnaires to get a broad cross section of information or opinions. You could subsequently use interviews to get more detailed data from a subgroup of your sample. Or you might use questionnaire data from a large number of teachers and students and then observe a smaller cohort selected from that larger group.

Here's an example. Imagine you are interested in the interactive decision making of language teachers—and, in particular, you want to know why and when teachers depart from their lesson plans. You design, pilot, and revise a questionnaire addressing this issue and distribute it to 100 language teachers. You send questionnaires to both native speakers (NSs) and non-native speakers (NNSs) of the languages they teach because you wish to compare the responses of these two groups. Thus, native speaking and non-native speaking teachers become the two levels of the independent variable.

Let's say that forty of the teachers return the completed questionnaire. You could first divide the responses into those of the NS and NNS teachers of their target languages. If you had included appropriate questions about the teachers' experience in the background section of the questionnaire, you could also identify them as more experienced and less experienced teachers, treating experience as a moderator variable. You now have a factorial criterion groups design.

The questionnaire responses—the dependent variable in this study—would certainly be informative, but you might wish to gather more detailed data from some of the teachers, so you could resample from among those who had returned the questionnaire. Suppose the original return rate had looked something like **Figure 11.1.**

So, perhaps you decide to interview two of the teachers from each cell in the design. We call this process the "sample-resample procedure." It allows you to obtain more detailed information from a subset of your respondents by

	Native Speaking Teachers (NS Ts) (N = 19)	Non-Native Speaking Teachers (NNS Ts) (N = 21)
More Experienced Teachers (N = 20)	N = 12	N = 8
Less Experienced Teachers (N = 20)	N = 7	N = 13

FIGURE 11.1 Questionnaire return in a hypothetical study of teachers' decisions to depart from their lesson plans

	Native Speaking Teachers (NS Ts) (N = 19)	Non-Native Speaking Teachers (NNS Ts) (N = 21)
More Experienced Teachers (N = 20)	N = 12	N = 8
	N = 2	N = 2
Less Experienced Teachers (N = 20)	N = 2	N = 2
	N = 7	N = 13

FIGURE 11.2 The "two-phase" or "raised" design

interviewing them. It results in a "raised design" or "two-phase design," as depicted in **Figure 11.2.**

Carrying out this sort of intensified data elicitation process in the second phase allows you to get more detailed information from a few people who represent the larger sample. You need to be careful to define your selection criteria clearly, but eliciting detailed information from a subset of your respondents provides more in-depth data in a practical way.

This sort of two-phase design can be used in various forms of methods triangulation. For instance, you could get questionnaire data first from teachers and then observe classes taught by some of those teachers. Or you could use archival data to locate certain groups of learners (highly successful versus less successful learners, as determined by an achievement test) and interview subsets of those groups.

PRODUCTION TASKS

Production tasks are techniques used to obtain samples of learner language, typically in order to study processes and stages of development that learners pass through as they develop their second language proficiency. Production tasks are therefore quite popular with second language acquisition specialists. The alternative—observation and recording of learner language in naturalistic situations—has a number of drawbacks. In the first place, it is very time-consuming, and learners may not produce sufficient quantities of the language structures, lexical items, or speech acts in question in order for you to detect patterns or come to conclusions about language development. Secondly, learners may simply not produce a particular language structure, lexical item, or speech act at all. It is impossible to conclude that a learner has not acquired an item simply because he or she has not used it in your presence.

Discourse Completion Tasks

One way that researchers try to elicit language samples from learners is through a procedure called *discourse completion*. In this situation, the researcher sets up a context and provides part of the discourse. The learner must then complete the interaction by expressing what he or she would say if he or she were actually in such a context.

For example, suppose you wish to gather data on how language learners complain in their target language. It may be very difficult to obtain complaint samples naturalistically unless you can find a situation where complaints are normally voiced, such as an ombudsman's office or the returns section of a department store. Even if you can find such a place, you would need to get permission to record people's speech, and you would still have to wait for non-native speakers of the target language to appear and voice their complaints.

Discourse completion tasks have been used to deal with this sort of impractical situation. An example would be something like this:

> **Instructions:** You receive your test back from your professor. You see that he has added the points incorrectly and that you should actually have ten more points than he gave you. What do you say to your professor?

The learner then writes (in a questionnaire) or says (in an interview context) what he or she thinks his or her response would be in this situation.

REFLECTION

What problems might occur in using this kind of prompt as a discourse completion task to collect data from language learners?

Sometimes a discourse completion task is framed as a brief conversation and the students are asked to complete the conversation. For instance, if you were trying to find out how language learners deal with denials of requests, you might use a discourse completion task like this one:

> You discover your library book must be returned today and you will have to pay a fine if you don't return it immediately. You say to your friend, "May I please borrow your bicycle to go to the library?"
> Your friend says, "No, I need it myself."
> You say, "_____"

REFLECTION

What problems might occur in using this kind of prompt as a discourse completion task to collect data from language learners?

Role Plays

Some researchers have used role play scenarios to elicit language learners' speech samples and ideas. For instance, as early as 1980, Fraser, Rintell, and Walters used two roles plays about awkward situations. In one, they asked respondents to imagine themselves at a parking meter with no change, having to borrow some coins from an older stranger as the meter maid draws closer and closer. In the second situation, they asked the respondents to put themselves in a situation where they were late to a lunch appointment with an older business acquaintance whom they do not know well. Here are the instructions that they gave:

> We are asking you to participate with us in a series of role playing exercises in which I will describe in some detail to you a situation and then ask you to tell me exactly what you would say or do. You should talk to me as if I were actually the person with whom you are speaking in the situation I will describe, even though I will not usually resemble that person. Sometimes you will indicate that an answer is unnecessary, or that you would be unwilling to say anything at all. Other times, you might want to go on at some length in expressing your views. Some people like to move around during these exercises; please feel free to do so.
>
> It is important for you to understand that we are in no way giving you a "mark" on your responses. There are no right or wrong answers. Sometimes more than one answer might be appropriate; if you think this is the case, please feel free to offer the alternatives. Also, if you want to talk about the situation after you respond or raise other topics you might feel to be relevant, please do so. (pp. 81–82)

The respondents were university students living in the United States. They were native speakers of Spanish and did these tasks in both Spanish and English.

Role plays have been used in language assessment as well as in data collection, but some researchers have voiced concerns about whether personality or acting ability may influence the outcomes (see, e.g., van Lier, 1989). Others have noted that students' abilities to play a role may be related to their experience. Bailey (1998b) gives an example of a native speaker of English doing two different role plays—one in English and one in Spanish, her second language. The speaker reported that the English role play was much more difficult because she couldn't imagine the situation, while the Spanish role play was fun and plausible.

Tests Used as Elicitation Procedures

In the instructions quoted above from Fraser et al. (1980), the authors are careful to point out that the role play responses will not be marked or graded at all. They do this because often research subjects—like students—feel like they are being tested and get anxious about performing a task correctly. Indeed, tests have often been used to elicit language samples from learners.

What do we mean by a test in this context? According to Wesche (1983), all tests consist of four components:

1. the stimulus material (whether this is an essay prompt, a listening passage, a reading text, etc.);
2. the task posed to the learner (the mental operations the learners must do);
3. the learner's response (e.g., choosing *A*, *B*, *C*, or *D*; writing an essay) and
4. the scoring criteria (whether they are objective or subjective).

Some familiar forms of tests are dictations, cloze passages, multiple-choice items, matching items, essays, and so on. All of these can be used to elicit samples of learner language, but the test chosen must be appropriate for the research and for the age and proficiency level of the people involved.

There are many kinds of tests, and it is beyond this scope of this chapter to review them all thoroughly. (Fortunately, there are many textbooks available to introduce language teachers to testing procedures.) Here we will briefly discuss two forms of tests that are commonly used in language classroom research for one purpose or another.

First, oral proficiency interviews are often used to elicit speech samples from learners. In this situation, it is not the learners' ideas per se that interest the researchers. Rather, it is the language used to express those ideas. Some familiar interview formats are the ILR (Inter-agency Language Roundtable) and the ACTFL (American Council of Teachers of Foreign Languages) Oral Proficiency Interview procedures. These are both conducted by trained interviewers to elicit speech samples from language learners (in a wide range of languages). The speech samples are typically recorded and rated by trained raters (who are usually the interviewers). The ILR system uses ratings of zero to five, with plus factors (e.g., 0, 0+, 1, 1+, 2, 2+, and so on) that indicate that a speaker has nearly reached the next level but cannot sustain performance there. The ACTFL rating system uses category labels (novice low, novice mid, novice high, intermediate low, intermediate mid, intermediate high, and so on) to characterize students' oral proficiency.

There are also numerous standardized language tests, particularly of English proficiency. A standardized test is one that is administered under uniform conditions, no matter when or where it is given. The scores are also reported on a standardized scale that does not vary from one administration and reporting period to another. Common standardized tests in language teaching include the IELTS, the TOEFL, the TOEIC, the SLEP, etc.

Tests are used in several ways in language classroom research. Sometimes they constitute the dependent variable in a study. For example, in a methods comparison, you may wish to see which group of beginning language learners scored highest on a test after a particular course of study. If the learners are not true beginners, a form of the test might be given before the course of study, so you could use a pre-test post-test control groups design and calculate the students' gains to see which group improved the most.

In other situations, tests determine what groups of learners are involved in a study. For instance, you might wish to compare learners who are very fluent, moderately fluent, and not fluent speakers of the target language as they undertake some curriculum in order to see if the curriculum works better for one sort of learner than another. In this case, the test of fluency would not be the dependent variable in the study; rather, it would be the instrument by which you define the types of learners that comprise the levels of the independent variable in a criterion groups design. Test results can also be used to classify people into different levels of the moderator variable.

Tests have a long and important history as tools in research, including language classroom research. However, there are many problems associated with tests, and it is not sufficient to simply construct a quick-and-dirty measure of student learning to use in a study. Nor should we select a commercially available test if it is not appropriate for the study.

The traditional criteria for evaluating tests include reliability, validity, practicality, and washback. *Reliability* is the idea that a test must be consistent across administrations. This concern is especially important when ratings are involved. *Validity* is largely a matter of whether a test is actually assessing what it was designed to measure. *Practicality* is the question of how many resources are used in developing, administering, and scoring a test in order to get the needed information. And, finally, *washback* is the effect of a test on teaching and learning. (Washback can be positive or negative, as well as intentional or unintentional.)

To these traditional criteria, Bachman and Palmer (1996) have added two more: authenticity and interactiveness. They define *authenticity* as "the degree of correspondence of the characteristics of a given language test task to the features of a target language use task" (p. 23). And *interactiveness* is defined as "the extent and type of involvement of the test taker's individual characteristics in accomplishing the task" (p. 25). Such characteristics include the students' language ability and background knowledge.

Picture Description Tasks

As noted above, researchers often attempt to overcome the shortcomings of naturalistic observation by setting up situations that are designed to force production of target language items. Some of the earliest studies of this type were the so-called morpheme acquisition studies (e.g., Dulay and Burt, 1973). These studies were designed to investigate the order in which certain grammatical morphemes (such as the copula verb *to be*, third person -*s*, past tense markers, and articles) were acquired by speakers of different first languages. The researchers wanted to know whether first language speakers of Spanish, for instance, would acquire the morphemes in an order that differed from that of first language speakers of Chinese. The classroom-oriented dimension to the study came in when researchers, having established that the acquisition orders were virtually identical regardless of the learners' first language, tried to change the 'natural order' of acquisition through a series of classroom interventions.

One common way of stimulating production was to ask the informant questions about a series of pictures. The morpheme order studies used a test known as the Bilingual Syntax Measure (BSM). The BSM consisted of a series of simple, colorful, cartoon-like drawings. The informant was shown the pictures one at a time and asked questions meant to elicit the target language items being investigated. For example, a picture designed to elicit the -*ing* form of the verb might show someone eating a meal while a little dog looks on hungrily. The BSM's scoring system determined how advanced a speaker's syntactic development was, based on the oral picture descriptions.

REFLECTION

Can you see any problems with this kind of picture elicitation device?

One challenge in using picture description tasks to elicit data is to come up with a *prompt* (what the researchers asks the informant in order to elicit a language sample) that does not include the target structure. For example, if the researcher asks, "What's the boy doing?", the -*ing* form of the verb in the question may act as a cue to the informant, which would have implications for the internal validity of the study. The researcher would have to say something like, "Tell me about the boy," instead.

Another problem is that the nonappearance of a target item does not necessarily mean that the informant has not acquired that item. In the example just cited, in response to the question, "Tell me about the boy," the informant might say, "He is happy." We cannot infer from this response that the informant has not acquired the *-ing* form of the verb simply because he or she has not used it. The researcher would need to pose a follow-up question, such as, "Why do you think he is happy?"

Another problem is that the language that is stimulated by the elicitation instrument might be an artifact of the instrument itself. This was a criticism leveled at the morpheme acquisition studies that used the BSM. Apparently, the present progressive (verb + *-ing*) form appeared with great regularity, partly because the BSM cartoons showed people doing things. As a result, the picture description task itself was partly responsible for the high number of present progressive instances in the data.

Using Tasks to Investigate Negotiation of Meaning

A considerable body of research has used production tasks to investigate *interactional modifications*, otherwise known as the *negotiation of meaning*. Such modifications include comprehension checks, clarification requests, incorporations, and so on. (If you turn back to Figure 2.3, you can find operational definitions and examples of these concepts as they were used in Jepson's [2005] study comparing language learners' interactions in voiced chats and text chats.) Such interactional modifications have been hypothesized to facilitate second language acquisition because they are triggered by signals of incomprehension from the learner's interlocutor that force the learner to restructure his or her utterance.

Drawing on the work of Long (1985), Nunan (2004) explains the relationship between interactional modifications and acquisition in the following way.

Long argues that linguistic conversational adjustments . . . promote comprehensible input because such adjustments are usually triggered by an indication of non-comprehension, requiring the speaker to reformulate his or her utterance to make it more comprehensible. If comprehensible input promotes acquisition, then it follows that linguistic/conversational adjustments promote acquisition. (p. 80)

REFLECTION

Which is the trigger and which the modified utterance in the following piece of interaction (Martyn, 2001, p. 33)?

A: She's a loner.

B: Sorry?

A: She stay away from others.

Much of the research stimulated by theoretical claims about relationships between the negotiation of meaning and acquisition sought to identify the characteristics of production tasks that maximize opportunities for students to negotiate meaning. In his own research, Long found that two-way tasks generated more interactional modification than did one-way tasks. (In a *two-way task*, all the students involved have unique information that has to be shared for the task to be successfully completed. In a *one-way task*, one participant holds all of the information that must be shared.) Similarly, Doughty and Pica (1986) found that there was more interactional modification when the information was required by the task rather than when it was optional. (Also see the studies by Pica and Doughty, 1985a; 1985b.)

Early studies were carried out in non-classroom 'laboratory' settings, and are therefore what we have called classroom-oriented rather than classroom-based research. Martyn (1996; 2001), however, conducted her research in intact classrooms.

REFLECTION

Why do you think that Martyn chose to carry out her investigations in intact classrooms?

Martyn used five production tasks: (1) jigsaw, (2) information exchange, (3) problem solving, (4) decision making, and (5) opinion exchange. From her literature review, she also isolated the following four cognitive demand features of tasks:

1. contextual support: whether embedded, reduced, or remote within the task (e.g., in the form of visuals)
2. reasoning demand: whether high or low
3. degree of task structure: whether high or low
4. availability of knowledge schema: provided or assumed through prior knowledge

Martyn then mapped these cognitive demand features onto the five production task types. This procedure resulted in the following matrix (see **Table 11.2**), which she used to investigate interactional modifications. Martyn found that tasks with the highest cognitive demand, such as the opinion exchange task, generated the most interactional modifications, while jigsaw tasks, with relatively low cognitive demand, generated the fewest modifications.

Martyn's study is valuable, not only because she worked in actual classrooms, but also because the kinds of tasks she chose to investigate are those which language teachers often use.

TABLE 11.2 Cognitive demand features used in Martyn's study of interactional modifications (from Nunan, 2004, p. 89, adapted from Martyn, 2001).

Task Type	Contextual Support	Reasoning Required	Degree of Task Structure	Available Knowledge
Jigsaw	embedded	not required	high	given
Information Exchange	embedded (for one learner)	not required	high	given
Problem Solving	some embedded	required	varies	given
Decision Making	context-reduced	required	low	given or available
Opinion Exchange	remote	required	low	variable/not required

A SAMPLE STUDY

For the sample study in this chapter, we decided to focus on some research by Snow, Hyland, Kamhi-Stein, and Yu (1996). They investigated the ideas of language minority junior high school students in Los Angeles, using oral interviews in both Spanish and English. Their research questions were the following:

1. What instructional practices do language minority students view as effective?
2. What is the role that they see themselves playing in the transmission of school values?
3. How can the school environment help language minority students to socialize into the new school culture?
4. In what ways can language minority students help their peers become successful in the new school system? (p. 306)

To address these questions, Snow et al. (1996) interviewed sixty-six students drawn from six different junior high schools about "student role efficacy—how they viewed their roles as students" (p. 307). Individual students were interviewed and the interviews were tape-recorded. Here is how the authors described the interviews:

> Each interview commenced with a warm-up activity in which the students were asked to fill in the captions of two cartoons. The interview

consisted of two different activities. The first was a card sort activity, conducted in English, in which the students were asked to create a "recipe" for the ideal class by selecting among a set of "ingredients." The following pairs of descriptors were printed on the opposite sides of index cards.

1. A class where I write journals in English or in Spanish.
   A class where I do not write in journals.
2. A class where I can speak English if I want to.
   A class where only English is spoken.
3. A class where the teacher is the center of attention.
   A class where I participate a lot.
4. A class where the teacher uses cooperative learning.
   A class where I work by myself.
5. A class where I learn only from the teacher.
   A class where I learn from my classmates.
6. A class where I have to take notes.
   A class where I am not expected to take notes.
7. A class where I help my classmates edit what they write before they write a final version of an assignment.
   A class where I am the only person who reads what I write before having my teacher read my assignment.

As students chose between the two descriptors on each card, they explained why they had selected these ingredients. By having students discuss their choices, we could see whether or not they understood the instructional technique in question, and we could gain more insight into the students' needs and preferences. Students then added two ingredients of their own, again explaining why they added these items while the interviewer wrote the student-generated items on new cards. In the final step, the students arranged all the cards (including their own two ingredients) in order, from the most to the least important ingredient for the ideal class. (pp. 307–308)

Thus, the forced-choice activity provided comparable data across all the students while the original ideas they contributed were open-ended and creative. The ranking of both the selected and the constructed "ingredients" provided the researchers with information they could not have gotten from either the provided categories or the students' own ideas alone.

The second part of the interview was conducted in Spanish. This was a problem-posing task involving a role play in which students were asked to explain how they would orient a new student in their school. The students were supposed to say how they would tell the new arrival what he or she would need to do to be successful. The instructions were given in Spanish and are reprinted below, along with the English translation:

> En tu clase hay un alumno nuevo que habla muy poco inglés. Tú eres el consejero de ese alumno y debes ayudarlo. ¿Qué es lo que ese alumno tiene que hacer para convertise en un buen alumno? ¿Cómo tiene que estudiar para un examen? Recuerda que tú debes aconsejar a tú nuevo compañero. ¡Su éxito depende de ti!
>
> [In your class there is a new student who speaks very little English. You are his advisor and you have to help him. What does the student have to do to become a good student? How does the student have to prepare for an exam? Remember that you have to help your new classmate. His success depends on you!] (Snow et al., 1996, p. 308)

Snow et al. (1996) provide the following commentary about this data elicitation procedure:

> The students, in general, responded readily to the task. They quickly assumed the role of the experienced student, offering advice to the newcomer. In some cases, the interviewers had to repeat parts of the question and prompt the students to respond to all parts of the situation. Five of the sixty-six students said that they could not perform the task in Spanish. They responded in English; however, their responses were not included in the analysis, since one objective of the task was to see if the students could communicate their meta-notions of student role efficacy in Spanish. (p. 308)

In addition to the qualitative analysis, the students' preferences in the card sort activity were analyzed quantitatively using a statistic called the chi-square analysis (see Chapter 13). Statistically significant preferences for the students' views of the ideal class emerged for the following descriptors in the card sort activity:

A class where the teacher uses cooperative learning.

A class where I write journals in English or Spanish.

A class where I participate a lot.

A class where I am expected to take notes.

A class where I help my classmates edit what they write before they write the final version of the assignment.

A class where I learn from my classmates. (pp. 308–309)

There were no statistically significant differences in the students' choices for the paired statements "A class where I can speak English if I want to," and "A class where only English is spoken." Their views about speaking English in class were varied:

> Some students indicated that they could learn English better if they had to use it. Others said that it would be rude or unfair to speak Spanish since some of their classmates did not understand Spanish. Some also said that it would be impolite to speak Spanish in a class where the teacher did not know what they were saying. One student indicated that he would speak Spanish only if he wanted to say something he did not want the teacher to hear. (p. 309)

The students' views about what constitutes an ideal class were also diverse. The greatest number of student-generated responses had to do with the teacher's role. Students offered the following ideas about their ideal class:

> A class where the teacher could help you more often—the teacher can give you more quality time and work with you until you get it.
>
> A class where the teacher can be your friend.
>
> A class where the teacher is nice.
>
> A class where teachers have positive attitudes.
>
> A class where the teacher is patient.
>
> A class where the teacher cares—where the teacher is on your back whenever you fool around.
>
> A class where the teachers are more open and more fun.
>
> A class where the teacher makes the class fun.
>
> A class where the teacher helps students when they need help.
>
> A class where I can get extra help on something I may find difficult.
>
> A class where the shy people are encouraged to participate.
>
> A class where everyone is encouraged to try.
>
> A class where teachers explain the assignments well.
>
> A class where the teacher is clear about assignments and deadlines.
>
> A class where the teacher doesn't give too much work but gives it correctly with enough information.
>
> A class where the teachers don't have to refer to the textbook so much.
>
> A disciplined class where the teacher teaches well and understands.
>
> A class where things work well; teachers help students improve their education.
>
> A class where the teacher assigns a lot of work.
>
> A class where teachers show you tests ahead of time to help you get a good grade.
>
> A class where the teacher asks questions before a test so that everybody is forced to study.

A class where the teacher gives homework three times a week.

A class where teachers want you to help them when they make errors. (pp. 309–310)

In their conclusion, these authors comment about their data elicitation procedures. They say the interviews reveal the students' "insights into effective instruction and their perceptions of strategies for successful academic behavior" (p. 316). The problem-posing role play task about helping the new student showed the researchers that the students were "developing metacognitive awareness of appropriate learning strategies . . . which contribute to academic success" (ibid.).

PAYOFFS AND PITFALLS

This chapter has focused on a range of elicitation procedures that have been used in classroom-based and classroom-oriented research. As always, there are both advantages and disadvantages in using these procedures.

REFLECTION

Brainstorm and list the possible payoffs that researchers might expect from using one or more of the elicitation devices discussed in this chapter.

The data collection techniques we have grouped together under the rubric of 'elicitation' have some obvious advantages. Because the techniques are so diverse, they can result in data that are incredibly rich, as Dowsett (1986), among others, has pointed out. Most can also be used in combination. For example, Benson and Nunan (2005) used both questionnaires and interviews in their investigations into language learning histories. This mixing and matching helps in methods triangulation. (See Chapter 7 for a detailed discussion of triangulation.)

Another advantage of eliciting data, and one that has already been touched on, is that elicitation can be a great time-saver, providing the researcher with large amounts of data in a much shorter time than would be required to collect such data through naturalistic observation. In fact, desired data may never be forthcoming if we simply sit and wait for it.

A third advantage of elicitation (which we will see when we discuss pitfalls below) is that elicitation enables the researcher to collect data that could simply not be obtained in any other way. For instance, the classroom researcher who wants to obtain insights into why the teacher made certain spontaneous decisions to depart from his or her lesson plan while the class was in progress could make certain inferences by sitting in on the teacher's class, or by viewing a video, but will never really know for sure without interviewing the teacher.

There are, of course, also pitfalls involved in using the various elicitation devices described in this chapter. Use of elicitation devices rather than naturalistic observation has been criticized on a number of grounds. In the first place, the researcher determines in advance what is to be investigated. There are at least two possible threats to the validity of such investigations:

> The first is that by determining in advance what is going to be considered relevant, other potentially relevant phenomena might be overlooked. The other danger, and one which needs to be considered when evaluating research utilizing such [elicitation] devices, is the extent to which the results obtained are an artifact of the elicitation devices employed (see, e.g., Nunan [1987] for a discussion on the dangers of deriving implications for second language acquisition from standardized test data). One needs to be particularly cautious in making claims about acquisition orders based on elicited data, as Ellis (1985) has pointed out. [In at least one study] it seems clear that the so-called order of acquisition is the creation of the elicitation device and the statistical procedures used to analyze the data. (Nunan, 1992, pp.138–139)

Regardless of these kinds of problems, however, elicitation procedures provide effective ways of gathering data that might otherwise be unobtainable.

CONCLUSION

This chapter has introduced a wide range of elicitation procedures, including five types of interviews. We also briefly revisited questionnaires and talked about how questionnaire data and interview data (or other kinds of data) can be combined in a two-phase design. We considered several production tasks—activities designed to get the participants in a study to provide language samples, their viewpoints, their language learning histories, and so on. The sample study summarized here used interviews with a card sort activity and a role play task to elicit ideas from junior high school language minority students.

QUESTIONS AND TASKS

1. Think of a research question that interests you in which the use of discourse completion tasks would be an appropriate form of data collection. Write three to five discourse completion tasks designed to elicit the target

language structures, lexical items, or speech acts you wish to investigate. Pilot them with two or more native speakers or highly proficient non-native speakers of the target language to see if the tasks actually elicit the forms you wish to investigate.

2. Think of a research question that interests you in which the use of a picture description task would be an appropriate form of data collection. Find three to five pictures that you could use. Write the instructions carefully, either in the native language of your intended subjects or in a clear and simple form of the target language. Try out the picture description task with two or more native speakers or highly proficient non-native speakers of the target language to see if the tasks actually elicit the forms you wish to investigate.

3. What do you think about using role play to elicit speech samples from language learners? Try writing a role play prompt that would elicit some data you would like to collect. Have one or more language learners try to do the role play you create.

4. Read a study that uses interview procedures to elicit data from informants. What type of interview was used? Were the researchers seeking language samples, the learners' ideas and views, information about their history, or some combination of these issues?

5. Think of a classroom-based research project in which you could first sample widely (e.g., through questionnaires) and then collect more detailed data from a subgroup of your sample using the raised design concept.

    A. What would be the research question(s) you'd want to address?

    B. How would you collect data from the larger original sample?

    C. How would you collect data from the small subset of the sample (e.g., interviews, classroom observations)?

    D. By what criteria would you select participants from the larger original sample to be re-sampled into the smaller group?

SUGGESTIONS FOR FURTHER READING

Elicited imitation is a research procedure which has been used widely in second language acquisition studies. For an interesting treatment of this topic, see Bley-Vroman and Chaudron (1994).

The volume edited by Perecman and Curran (2006), while not directed to language educators, offers a great deal of practical wisdom and personal advice on techniques and procedures for using elicitation techniques in field research.

The naturalistic inquiry tradition makes use of interviews extensively to get informants' perspectives. See, e.g., Flick (1998), Fetterman (1989), and Mason (1996). The classic treatment of the ethnographic interview is by Spradley (1979).

If you do not have a background in language assessment but would like to read some user-friendly books for teachers on this topic, we recommend Bachman and Palmer (1996), Bailey (1998b), H.D. Brown (2004), J.D. Brown (2005), and Hughes (1989). If you work with primary and secondary school children, a good resource about language assessment is Law and Eckes (1995), *Assessment and ESL: A Handbook for K-12 Teachers*.

Data Elicitation for Second and Foreign Language Research by Gass and Mackey (2007) is a fine resource about the elicitation procedures discussed here, as well as many others. It includes a chapter on classroom-based research.

PART IV

DATA ANALYSIS AND INTERPRETATION ISSUES

Figuring Out What the Information Means

In this final section, we do two things. First, we revisit and extend into the realm of data analysis several discussions that were initiated earlier in the book. Secondly, we draw together the themes that have emerged in the course of the book thus far. Because this volume contextualized the research process in terms of the classroom, the initial chapter in this section takes a somewhat detailed look at the analysis of classroom interaction. The chapters that follow deal, respectively, with methods for quantitative and qualitative data analysis. The section ends with the final chapter in the book, which pulls together themes and issues and revisits practical suggestions for getting started on designing and conducting your own studies as well as ways to publish them.

Chapter 12: Analyzing Classroom Interaction

By the end of this chapter, readers will

- be able to interpret transcripts of language classroom interaction;

- analyze transcripts of classroom interaction both quantitatively and qualitatively;

- demonstrate familiarity with a range of approaches to analyzing classroom interaction;

- state the main substantive issues that have been investigated in terms of teacher talk and learner talk;

- discuss the advantages and disadvantages of this approach to analyzing classroom data.

Chapter 13: Quantitative Data Analysis

By the end of this chapter, readers will

- be able to explain the measures of central tendency and measures of dispersion;
- understand the concept of degrees of freedom;
- understand the concept of statistical significance;
- know how to calculate and interpret the chi-square test;
- know how to interpret correlation coefficients, t-tests, and analysis of variance;
- identify several concerns about statistical analyses.

Chapter 14: Qualitative Data Analysis

By the end of this chapter, readers will

- describe qualitative data and give examples;
- identify different sources of data and suggest a range of methods for analyzing those data;
- discuss techniques for identifying patterns in qualitative data;
- describe the process of meaning condensation;
- define a grounded approach to data analysis;
- discuss technology-supported tools and techniques for qualitative data analysis.

Chapter 15: Putting it All Together

By the end of this chapter readers will

- be able to articulate the steps in the research process;
- be able to combine quantitative and qualitative approaches to data collection and analysis;
- create an original research plan based on the procedures described here;
- discuss ethical concerns in conducting language classroom research;
- evaluate research plans and prepare an effective research proposal;
- critique completed studies;
- be familiar with procedures for submitting abstracts for conferences and manuscripts for publication.

12

Analyzing Classroom Interaction

"The classroom is the crucible." (Gaies, 1980)

INTRODUCTION AND OVERVIEW

In this chapter, we examine ways of analyzing classroom interaction. In the first section of the chapter, we look at the nature of classroom discourse. We then consider transcribing and coding classroom interaction, followed by a section on analyzing learner language. Following a brief introduction to conversational analysis, we review some of the substantive issues that classroom researchers have investigated, including teacher talk and student-student interaction. The chapter ends with the usual discussion of quality control issues and a sample study.

Influenced by first-language classroom research, the earliest studies of language classroom interaction involved using live coding as the interaction occurred. These studies were said to employ "real-time coding" (as opposed to audio- or video-recordings, which could be stopped and replayed as many times as needed). Real-time coding could produce the sorts of SCORE data we saw in Chapter 9 or yield tallies of specific behaviors or utterance types.

For instance, Moskowitz (1971) adapted Flanders' (1970) interaction analysis system from first-language education research. She added categories to accommodate the use of the target language and the learners' native language to study effective teaching in foreign language classes. The resulting instrument, called FLint (for "foreign language interaction"), was used largely for teacher education purposes (see, e.g., Moskowitz, 1968; 1971). Moskowitz (1968) found that "teachers felt studying observational systems had influenced them to make numerous desirable changes in their teaching" (p. 218).

In another study that involved FLint for real-time coding, trained observers watched eleven foreign language teachers who had been identified as outstanding by their former students, as well as eleven typical foreign language teachers. The observers did not know that some teachers had been identified as outstanding and others as typical. Each teacher was observed teaching four different lessons: (1) grammar, (2) reading skills, (3) some sort of new material, and (4) a lesson based entirely on the teacher's choice.

When Moskowitz (1976) compared the results, she found eighty-five statistically significant differences in the coded behavior of the outstanding and typical teachers. Several contrasts were observed in three out of the four lessons coded. These included the fact that the outstanding teachers and their students used more of the target language than did the typical teachers and their students. There was also less off-task talk in the lessons taught by the outstanding foreign language teachers. There were more personalized questions as well as more praise and joking in the outstanding teachers' classes. In addition, the coding of nonverbal behaviors showed that the teachers identified as outstanding walked around more and looked at most of their students more often than did the typical teachers.

These findings were intriguing and the research methods Moskowitz used were appropriate at the time. But while these sorts of investigations were informative, they were problematic in the sense that the results of real-time coding could never be checked against the original classroom interaction data, nor could the actual utterances be analyzed. And unless there were two observers present during the lessons, it was not possible to compute inter-coder agreement.

Recently, with the advent of accessible, transportable, and affordable recording devices, as well as advances in discourse analysis, we have focused more on the analysis of tape- and video-recorded data. Such electronic recordings have many advantages over real-time coding since they can be replayed as often as necessary for transcription and/or coding. As a result of advances in both technology and research methodology in the past two decades, we have come to understand a great deal about classroom discourse and how it shapes students' opportunities to learn.

CLASSROOM DISCOURSE

Classroom discourse is the distinctive type of interaction that occurs between teachers and students, and also among students during lessons. It has a privileged place in the discourse analysis literature because it was one of the first genres to be exhaustively researched by linguists. You will recall from Chapter 9 that Sinclair and Coulthard (1975) found a consistently recurring pattern of teacher initiation, student response, and teacher feedback evaluating the response (the so-called IRF pattern) in classroom discourse. (In some reports, you will see this pattern referred to as IRE for initiation, response, and evaluation [Johnson, 1995], or QAC for question, answer, and comment [Markee, 2005].) It is our familiarity with the IRF pattern as a characteristic of classroom discourse that lets us recognize Extract 2 below as the teacher-student exchange.

Compare the following extracts. It is not difficult to identify which is an example of classroom discourse.

Extract 1:

A: What's the last day of the month?

B: Friday.

A: Friday. We'll invoice you on Friday.

B: That would be great.

A: And fax it over to you.

B: Er, well, I'll come and get it.

A: Okay. (McCarthy and Walsh, 2003, p. 176)

Extract 2:

A: What's the last day of the month?

B: Friday.

A: Friday. Very good.

Other classroom researchers have been influenced by Sinclair and Coulthard's work. For instance, Bowers (1980) expanded on their categories and developed a seven-category system for analyzing classroom discourse. It was given in Chapter 9 as Table 9.3 but is reprinted here as **Table 12.1:**

TABLE 12.1 Bowers' (1980) categories for analyzing classroom interaction

Category	Description
Responding	Any act directly sought by the utterance of another speaker, such as answering a question.
Sociating	Any act not contributing directly to the teaching/learning task, but rather to the establishment or maintenance of interpersonal relationships.
Organizing	Any act that serves to structure the learning task or environment without contributing to the teaching/learning task itself.
Directing	Any act encouraging nonverbal activity as an integral part of the teaching/learning process.
Presenting	Any act presenting information of direct relevance to the learning task.
Evaluating	Any act that rates another verbal act positively or negatively.
Eliciting	Any act designed to produce a verbal response from another person.

Analyze these two extracts using Bowers' categories. What patterns or regularities can you see?

Extract 3:

T: (Holding up a picture.) What's the name of this? What's the name? Not in Chinese.

S: Van. Van.

T: Van. What's in the back of the van?

Ss: Milk, milk.

T: A milk van.

S: Milk van.

T: What's this man?

S: Drier?

T: The driver.

S: The driver.

T: The milkman.

S: Millman.

T: Milkman.

Ss: Milkman.

T: Where are they?

Ss: Where are they?

T: Where are they? Inside? Outside?

S: Department.

T: Department?

S: Department store.

T: Mmm. Supermarket. (Nunan, 1988, pp. 84–85)

Extract 4:

T: The questions will be on different subjects, so, er, well, one will be about, er, well, some of the questions will be about politics, and some of them will be about, er . . . what?

S: History.

T: History. Yes, politics and history, and, um, and . . . ?

S: Grammar.

T: Grammar's good, yes, . . . but the grammar questions were too easy.

Ss: No!

S: Yes, ha, like before.

S: You can use . . . (inaudible)

T: Why? The hardest grammar questions I could think up—the hardest one, I wasn't even sure about the answer, and you got it.

S: Yes.

T: Really. I'm going to have to go to a professor and ask him to make questions for this class. Grammar questions that Azzam can't answer. [laughter] Anyway, that's um, Thursday, . . . yeah, Thursday. Ah, but today we're going to do something different . . .

Ss: Yes.

T: . . . today, er, we're going to do something where we, er, listen to a conversation—er, in fact, we're not going to listen to one conversation. How many conversations're we going to listen to?

S: Three. (Nunan, 1989, pp. 41–42)

Thus, Bowers added the categories of sociating, organizing, directing, and presenting to Sinclair and Coulthard's work. His other categories roughly paralleled theirs.

Drawing on Sinclair and Coulthard's (1975) exchange structure analysis (see Chapter 9), McCarthy and Walsh (2003) developed their own approach to analyzing classroom discourse. These authors say there are three key questions for researchers interested in studying classroom discourse:

1. What is the relationship between the speakers and how is this reflected in their language?

2. What are the goals of the communication (e.g., to tell a story, to teach something, to buy something)?

3. How do speakers manage topics and signal to one another their perception of the way the interaction is developing? How do they open and close conversations? How do they make sure they get a turn to speak? (p. 174)

According to McCarthy and Walsh, all these questions are relevant to language teaching. From their research, they have identified four basic discourse patterns, or modes as they call them, in classroom interaction. These are managerial mode, materials mode, skills and systems mode, and classroom context mode.

Managerial mode occurs when the teacher is setting up a lesson or lesson phase, or transitioning from one phase to another. Not surprisingly, it occurs most often at the beginning of a lesson. In *materials mode*, the discourse is driven by and flows from the materials being used. In *skills and systems mode*, the focus is on either one or more of the four skills (listening, speaking, reading, or writing) or on one of the three systems of language (phonology, lexis, or grammar). Finally, *classroom context mode* involves more conversational, real-world discourse opportunities.

REFLECTION

Look at two extracts below and decide if they represent managerial, materials, skills and systems, or classroom context mode. In many transcripts, *XXX* stands for unintelligible speech, but here it means that the teacher is reading out a blank filling exercise, so the *XXX*s represent the blank spaces that the students have to fill in the text. The equal signs (=) indicate latching, when one turn follows another without a pause, and brackets ([]) indicate overlapping turns.

Extract 5:

(The teacher is doing a blank-filling exercise with the students.)

Teacher:	ok . . . now . . . see if you can find the words that are suitable in these phrases (reading) in the World Cup final of 1994 Brazil XXX Italy 2 3 2 and in a XXX shoot-out . . . what words would you put in there?
Student A:	beat
Teacher:	what beat Italy 3 2 yeah in?
Student A:	in a penalty shoot-out
Teacher:	a what?
Student A:	in a penalty shoot-out
Teacher:	in a penalty shoot-out, very good, in a penalty shoot-out . . . (reading) after 90 minutes THE?
Students:	the goals goals goals (mispronounced)
Teacher:	the match was . . . what?
Student B:	match
Students:	nil nil
Teacher:	nil nil (reading) and it remained the same after 30 minutes OF?
Student C:	extra time
Teacher:	extra time, very good, Emerson. (McCarthy and Walsh, 2003, p. 180)

Extract 6:

Teacher:	he went to what do we call these things the shoes with wheels=
Student 1:	=ah skates=

Student 2:	=roller skates=
Teacher:	=ROLLer skates roller skates so [he went]
Student 1:	[he went] to=
Student 3:	=roller SKATing=
Teacher:	=SKATing=
Student 1:	=he went to=
Teacher:	=not to just he went [roller skating he went roller skating]
Student 1:	[roller skating he went roller skating]= (ibid., p. 181)

Extract 5 is an example of materials mode. Here the learners are completing a blank-filling exercise on sports vocabulary and the teacher directs the students' contributions; the talk is almost entirely determined by the materials. The sequence is classic IRF, the most economical way to manage the interaction, where each turn by the teacher is an evaluation of a learner's contribution and an initiation of another exchange. The discourse evolves from the material, which determines turn taking and topic (McCarthy and Walsh, 2003).

In Extract 6, an example of skills and systems mode, the teacher's goal is to get the learners to use irregular simple past forms (e.g., *went*). In this mode, the focus is the language system or a skill. Learning is typically achieved through controlled turn taking and topic selection, which are usually determined by the teacher. Learners respond to teacher prompts in an endeavor to produce accurate utterances (McCarthy and Walsh, 2003).

REFLECTION

Let's try categorizing two more extracts. Which modes are exemplified by Extracts 7 and 8?

Extract 7:

| Teacher: | Ok, we're going to look today at ways to improve your writing and at ways which can be more effective for you and if you look at the writing which I gave you back you will see that I've marked any little mistakes and eh I've also marked places where I think the writing is good and I haven't corrected your mistakes because the best way in writing is for you to correct your mistakes so what I have done I have put little circles and inside the circles there is something which tells you what kind of mistake it is so Miguel would you like to tell me one of the mistakes that you made? (McCarthy and Walsh, 2003, p. 179) |

> **Extract 8:**
>
> Student 1: =ahh nah the one thing that happens when a person dies my mother used to work with old people and when they died . . . the last thing that went out was the hearing about this person=
>
> Teacher: =aha
>
> Student 1: so I mean even if you are unconscious or on drugs or something I mean it's probably still perhaps can hear what's happened
>
> Student 2: but it gets=
>
> Students: but it gets/there are=
>
> Student 1: =I mean you have seen so many operation and so you can imagine and when you are hearing the sounds of what happens I think you can get a pretty clear picture of what's really going on there=
>
> Student 3: =yeah= (ibid., pp. 181–182)

In Extract 7, an example of managerial mode, we see an extended teacher turn and no learner turns. Here the focus is on the business side of the lesson (how mistakes are marked on the students' papers). There is repetition and the teacher hands over the exchange to a learner at the end of the monologue. The teacher uses the discourse markers *okay* and *so* as signals that help the learners to follow the talk.

Extract 8 illustrates classroom context mode, in which opportunities for genuine, real-world-type discourse are frequent and the teacher plays a less prominent role, allowing learners all the space they need. The teacher listens and supports the interaction, which often takes on the appearance of a casual conversation outside the classroom. In this bit of data, the teacher was working with six advanced adult learners. The teacher's aim was to generate discussion before doing a cloze exercise on the subject of poltergeists. Here the turn taking is almost entirely managed by the learners, with competition for the floor and turn gaining, holding, and passing—typical features of natural conversation. Topic shifts are also managed by the learners, with the teacher responding as an equal partner. Teacher feedback shifts from form-focused to content-focused and error treatment is minimal. This transcript seems to show genuine communication rather than a display or test of knowledge.

As you can see, interpreting and categorizing transcripts like these yields more specific information than does real-time coding. We turn now to a discussion focusing on transcribing and the use of transcripts in language classroom research.

GENERATING AND CODING TRANSCRIPTS

Once you have tape- or video-recorded some classroom interaction, you must decide whether to transcribe some or all of the interaction. This decision should be guided by your research question. In some cases, it may not be necessary to do any transcribing at all. Sometimes it is possible to count instances of a particular structure or speech act by simply listening to your recordings. Since it can take up to thirty minutes to transcribe one minute of interaction, you do not want to transcribe data unless it is strictly necessary. However, in our experience, transcription is extremely valuable—and well worth the time involved to generate good transcripts.

To be useful as research tools, transcripts must be accurate and detailed enough to represent the speech event under investigation:

> An authentic representation of the oral data—as close to the original as possible—is of crucial importance for linguistic analysis. . . . Oral data in themselves are evanescent. Preserving them is a first and primary objective for all further steps of analysis. (Ehlich, 1993, p. 124)

The more detailed the transcription process, the longer it takes to produce an accurate transcript. There are different schools of thought about the ideal level of detail, with some researchers (e.g., those that work in a tradition called conversational analysis) saying that an extremely fine-grained approach is necessary. Others feel that standard orthography (simply writing down what you hear) is acceptable. Our position varies, depending on what we are investigating and why.

Assuming that you decide to transcribe, the next decision is what transcription conventions to follow. Again, this decision will be tempered by the kind of research you are conducting and just what it is that you want to capture. If the research is looking at learners' pronunciation, it will probably be necessary to use phonetic symbols, such as those of the International Phonetic Alphabet (IPA). This system requires considerable training and skill, and its use exponentially increases the time taken to render speech into visual form. In IPA and other phonetic systems, each symbol represents one and only one sound of the language, so the IPA symbols convey details about pronunciation that cannot be recorded with simple orthography.

We generally favor using regular orthography, unless there is a compelling reason for using the IPA or some other form of phonetic transcription. For instance, if learners' pronunciation is part of your research focus, you will need to transcribe learners' speech phonetically. Extract 9 exemplifies regular orthography.

Extract 9:

Teacher: Let's check exercise four. How do you feel about exercise four, was that strange? Number four, ah, page one hundred fifty-four. Was it difficult? How did you feel?

Student 1:   It was easy! We did that!

Teacher: Ah, no, people, Pat turned off the tape recorder by pushing the stop button. We didn't do that. No, we didn't.

Student 1:	No?
Teacher:	No.
Student 1:	Ah!
Teacher:	How about that kind of pattern, how do you feel about that? Have you used that one before?
Students:	No.
Teacher:	Does it look easy?
Student 2:	I use the wrong way. I . . .
Teacher:	You used the wrong way? How was it?
Student 2:	I—how is it? I got the meaning. With reading, I get the meaning of this word with reading the dictionary, I got the meaning of this word. (Nunan & Lamb, 1996, p. 277)

Ellis (1984) provides the following classroom transcription system:

1. The teacher's or researcher's utterances are given on the left-hand side of the page.

2. The pupils' utterances are given on the right-hand side.

3. T = teacher; R = researcher; pupils are designated by their initials.

4. Each utterance is numbered for ease of reference. An 'utterance' consists of a single tone unit except where two tone units are syntactically joined by means of a subordinator or other linking word or contrastive stress has been used to make what would 'normally' be a single tone unit into more than one. (A *tone unit* is part of an utterance, usually consisting of more than one syllable, in which there is one major change in tone. The following utterance consists of two tone units. "It was **Kathi**, who decided not to **go**.")

5. Pauses are indicated in parentheses with one or more periods. For instance, (.) indicates a pause of a second or shorter, while a numeral with periods indicates the length of a pause beyond a second in duration. For example, (.3.) indicates a pause of three seconds.

6. XXX is often used to indicate speech that could not be deciphered.

7. Phonetic transcription (IPA) is used when the pupil's pronunciation is markedly different from the teacher's pronunciation and also when it was not possible to identify the English word the pupils were using.

8. . . . indicates an incomplete utterance

9. Words are underlined to show overlapping speech between two speakers or a very heavily stressed word. (p. 230)

10. A limited amount of contextual information is given in brackets.

This transcription system is simple enough to use with minimal training, and yet comprehensive enough to pick up most interactional features of interest.

There are many variations on the transcription conventions classroom researchers use. Here is the key to the transcription conventions from Duff (1996, pp. 431–432) in the sample study at the end of Chapter 7 on ethnography.

Transcription Conventions

1. **Participants:** T = teacher; S = student; Ss = two students; SSS = many students. Initials are used for students identifiable by name (e.g., M, SZ, J) rather than S.

2. **Left bracket** [: Indicates the beginning of overlapping speech, shown for both speakers; second speaker's bracket occurs at the beginning of the line of the next turn rather than in alignment with previous speaker's bracket.

3. **Equal sign** =: Indicates speech which comes immediately after another person's, shown for both speakers (i.e., latched utterances).

4. **(#):** Marks the length of a pause in seconds.

5. **(Words):** The words in parenthesis ( ) were not clearly heard; (x) = unclear word; (xx) = two unclear words; (xxx) = three or more unclear words.

6. **Underlined words:** Words spoken with emphasis.

7. **CAPITAL LETTERS:** Loud speech.

8. **((Double parenthesis)):** Comments and relevant details pertaining to interaction

9. **Colon:** Sound or syllable is unusually lengthened (e.g., rea::lly lo:ng)

10. **Period:** Terminal falling intonation.

11. **Comma:** Rising, continuing intonation.

12. **Question mark:** High rising intonation, not necessarily at the end of a sentence.

13. **Unattached dash:** A short, untimed pause.

14. **One-sided attached dash-:** A cutoff often accompanied by a glottal stop (e.g., a self-correction); a dash attached on both sides reflects spelling conventions.

15. *Italics:* Used to distinguish L1 and L2 utterances.

ANALYZING LEARNER LANGUAGE

In their book on analyzing learner language, Ellis and Barkhuizen (2005) identify three research paradigms in second language acquisition. These are the *normative*, the *interpretive*, and the *critical*. These paradigms approach the analysis of

TABLE 12.2 Three research paradigms in SLA (adapted from Ellis and Barkhuizen, 2005, pp. 10–11)

Normative	Interpretive	Critical
Quantitative methods supported by inferential statistics to test the strength of relationships between variables and differences between social groups.	Qualitative methods involving 'thick description' of the aspect of L2 learning under investigation from multiple perspectives (triangulation)	Qualitative methods identifying the 'discourses' learners participate in and how these position them socially.

learner language in very different ways that reflect the assumptions and purposes behind the paradigms. The purpose of normative approaches is to test a theoretically motivated hypothesis. The purpose of the interpretive paradigm is to describe and understand L2 acquisition through the intensive, and usually longitudinal, study of a limited number of cases. The critical paradigm investigates language acquisition in its sociocultural context. Table 12.2 sets out the kinds of analysis of learner language carried out within the three paradigms.

Classroom data come in many shapes and forms. Learner data can be classified into three different types: nonlinguistic performance data, samples of learner language, and verbal reports from learners about their own learning (Ellis and Barkhuizen, 2005). Nonlinguistic performance data include reaction times to linguistic stimuli, nonverbal measures of comprehension, and grammaticality judgments. Learner language samples can be elicited or naturally occurring. Verbal reports include self-reports, interview data, questionnaire responses, stimulated recall, think-aloud protocols, and self-assessments.

REFLECTION

Study the following extract. To what extent does it follow the IRF pattern identified by Sinclair and Coulthard? What variations are evident? What other comments would you make on the teacher talk?

Extract 10:

T: OK, let's try number one. Bin, why don't you start and Tomo will follow. Go ahead try it . . . Number one.

Bin: It warm this evening.

Tomo: Yes, the evenings are getting warmer.

Bin: I think it get warmer this evening.

T: OK . . . How could we change that a little bit?

Bin: Getting warmest?

Tomo:	The warmest?
T:	Let's take out "getting." Let's not use the verb "get," all right?
Bin:	It get warmest.
T:	Let's just say . . . let's take out "getting," let's say, "It's the warmest it's ever been." . . . "It's the warmest spring." How does that sound?
Bin:	OK.
T:	Let me write that down . . . (T writes on board: The evenings are getting warmer.) Well, let's see what you get.
Bin:	Getting warmer.
T:	Now, maybe we can look at this sentence and see how we can change it to make it better . . . OK, because remember because in the second sentence of our dialogue we use "getting" with the comparative, so for example . . .
Bin:	Getting warmest.
T:	The evenings are getting warmer.
Bin:	Getting warmer.
T:	OK, warmer . . . Is that the comparative or the superlative?
Ss:	Comparative.
T:	Comparative. OK? All right. "Getting" is the verb, what does that "getting" mean?
Bin:	Getting warmer.
T:	What does getting mean?
Tomo:	Starting.
T:	Starting, maybe becoming.
Vinny:	Becoming to.
T:	Beginning to, all right, so they are in the process of becoming, they're changing to the point of being warmer . . . they are becoming warmer.
Bin:	Evenings getting warmer.
T:	OK, evenings, all right . . . now, let's put in the superlative here . . . We'll go from this one "The evenings are getting warmer . . . to this one, "It's the warmest it's ever been."
Bin:	Evenings getting warmer.
Tomo:	It's the warmest it's ever been.
Bin:	It the warmest.
T:	Right, here we get the superlative, right? So what is the meaning of this sentence with the superlative?
Bin:	Warm.

> T: What does "it's" stand for? Or, "it has"?
>
> Bin: Warmest.
>
> Tomo: Evening.
>
> T: OK the evening, this particular evening, that we are talking about is the warmest ever, it's ever been before, it's one hundred ten degrees, so it's the warmest it has ever been.
>
> Tomo: It's the warmest it's ever been.
>
> Bin: Wow! One hundred ten? No, here, one hundred ten! Too hot!
>
> T: Bin?
>
> Bin: It the warmest, warmest it ever been.
>
> T: All right, good . . . let's go on . . . look at number two. (adapted from Johnson, 1995, pp. 19–20)

Extract 10 is taken from a book by Johnson (1995) on understanding communication in second language classrooms. The researcher used a form of discursive and interpretive analysis for making sense of the classroom interactions that she recorded. Here is what she had to say about the IRE (initiation-response-evaluation) pattern in this particular extract.

> Clearly the teacher-student exchanges . . . follow the IRE sequence. In almost every exchange the teacher provides an initiation, a student responds, and the teacher evaluates the response. However, embedded in these interactional sequences are options, usually signaled by the teacher, for altering the IRE pattern. For example, in several instances Bin's responses, which were incorrect, were not evaluated but were instead followed by a second initiation. Ignoring Bin's incorrect response, . . . the teacher repeats his question. This behavior, on the part of the teacher, seems to indicate to the other students that they are free to respond. . . . Thus this appears to be one acceptable alteration of the IRE sequence. (p. 21)

This extract and other bits of transcribed data above clearly display the amount of information we can get by transcribing classroom interaction. We turn now to a brief discussion of conversational analysis—an approach to research that requires extremely detailed transcripts.

CONVERSATIONAL ANALYSIS

Conversational analysis is a method for investigating talk, including classroom interaction data. It is an important ethnomethodological approach to analyzing spoken data beyond the classroom as well (see, e.g., Markee, 2000; 2003). However, here we will focus only on its use with classroom data, in which it allows researchers "to explicate how learning activity is organized on a moment-by-moment basis" (Markee, 2005, p. 355). *Conversational analysis* is defined as "a methodology for analyzing talk-in-interaction that seeks to develop empirically based accounts of the observable conversational behaviors of participants that are both minutely detailed and unmotivated by a priori, etic theories of social action" (ibid.).

Conversational analysis examines two main types of talk-in-interaction: ordinary mundane conversation and institutional talk. *Ordinary conversation* "may be thought of as the kind of everyday chitchat that occurs between friends and acquaintances" (ibid., p. 356). Within cultural subgroups, such talk has identifiable patterns and signals of turn taking, repair, leave taking, and so on. In ordinary conversation, "talk is locally managed, meaning that turn size, content and type are all free to vary, as is turn taking" (ibid.).

Institutional talk, in contrast, involves "various structural modifications to the sequential, turn-taking and repair practices of ordinary conversation" (ibid.). Markee notes that examples of institutional talk include debates, job interviews, press conferences, courtroom interactions, emergency calls, and so on. Classroom interaction, especially teacher-fronted classroom speech, can be considered to be a form of institutional talk because it "is characterized by the preallocation of turns and turn types in favor of teachers . . . who also typically initiate repairs" (ibid.). In fact, "teachers prototypically do being teachers by asserting in and through their talk the right to select the next speaker, to nominate topics, to ask questions, and to evaluate learners" (ibid.).

Markee (ibid.) lists five key characteristics of conversational analysis in second language acquisition research, including classroom research. He says it should be

1. Based on empirically motivated emic accounts of members' interactional competence in different speech exchange systems.
2. Based on collections of relevant data that are themselves excerpted from complete transcriptions of communicative events.
3. Capable of exploiting the analytical potential of fine-grained transcripts.
4. Capable of identifying both successful and unsuccessful learning behaviors, at least in the short term.
5. Capable of showing how meaning is constructed as a socially distributed phenomenon, thereby critiquing and recasting cognitive notions of comprehension and learning. (pp. 357–358; see also Markee, 2000)

These points are nicely illustrated in two transcripts of the same classroom event, one of which is much more detailed than the other. Three English students are discussing an article they have read about the greenhouse effect, and one learner does not understand the word *coral*. Here, for illustrative purposes, we will reproduce only a small bit of the two transcripts to show you the difference between a detailed regular transcript and a fine-grained transcript prepared for conversational analysis. Extracts 11 and 12 are based on a videotape of the group work. *L* stands for *learner*.

Given what you have read so far, what do you think some of the differences might be between a transcript prepared for conversational analysis and one for a less detailed form of interpretation?

Extract 11:

001   (L10 is reading her article to herself.)

002   L10: coral. what is corals

003   (4.0)

004   L9: hh do you know the under the sea, under the sea

005   L10: un-

006   L9: there's uh::

007   (2.0)

008   L9: [how do we call it]

009   L10: [have uh some coral]

010   L9: ah yeah (0.2) coral sometimes

011   (0.2)

012   L10: eh include /e̠/ s (0.2) un includes some uh: somethings uh-

013   (1.0)

014   L10: [the corals], is means uh: (0.2) s somethings at bottom of

015   L9: [(((unintelligible)))]

016   L10: [the] sea

017   L9: [yeah,]

018   L9: at the bottom of the sea,

019   L10: ok, uh:m also is a food for is a food for fish uh and uh

020   (4.0)

021   L9: food?

022   (0.3)

023   L10: foo-

024   L9: no it is not a food it is (.) like a stone you know?

025   L10: oh I see I see I see I see I see I know I know hh I see h a whit- (0.4) a

026   kind of a (0.2) white stone h [very beautiful]

027   L9: [yeah yeah] very big yeah

028   [sometimes very beautiful and] sometimes when the ship moves

029   L10: [I see I see ok] (Markee, 2005, pp. 359–360)

After this exchange, L10 confirms her understanding of coral by offering the Mandarin translation for that word to her group mates.

These same twenty-nine lines of transcript take up 107 lines in the parallel transcript prepared for conversational analysis, as shown in Extract 12. Here the actual speech is given in boldface while nonverbal behaviors are depicted in italics:

Extract 12:

((L9, L10, and L11 are all looking down at their class materials, reading an article on global warming. L9, who is facing the camera, is leaning her head on her left hand. L10 has her back turned to the camera and is facing L9. L11 is in profile but her hair hides her face))

001   L10: **coral. what is corals**

002   (1.3)

003   L9: ((*L9 moves her head slightly to her right to*

004   *look at the right-hand page of her materials.*))

005   (1.3)

006   L?: **hshhh**

007   (1.3)

008   L9: **[X_** ((*L9 looks up at L10, holding*

009   [hh *her chin in her left hand in*

010   *a thinking pose*))

011   (1.3)

012   L9: _____

013   L9: **do you know the under the sea::,** ((*L9 leans*

014   *forward and*

015   *drops her left*

016   *hand to her lap*))

017   L9: **........**((*L9 looks down at L10's article*))

018   L9: **under the sea::,**

      (Markee, 2005, p. 362)

This fine-grained transcription is a hallmark of conversational analysis. As you can see, the eighteen lines reproduced as Extract 12 account for only four lines of Extract 11. According to Markee (2005), inherent to conversational analysis is the idea that

> no detail of interaction, however small or seemingly insignificant, may be discounted a priori by analysts as not pertinent or meaningful to the

participants who produce this interaction. . . . A natural consequence of this position is that . . . transcripts do not just set down the words that are said during a speech event. Rather, they are extremely detailed qualitative records of how talk is co-constructed by members on a moment-by-moment basis. (p. 358)

So, to prepare a transcript for conversational analysis, it is important to document fillers, hesitations, in-breaths, pauses, silences, volume, lengthening of sounds, speakers speeding up or slowing down, and how turns overlap, as well as gestures, eye gaze, and facial expressions. This approach to transcription and interpretation of speech is sometimes referred to as *microanalysis* (see, e.g., Lazaraton, 2004).

It is important to state that for conversational analysts, "transcription cannot be viewed merely as a laborious chore that has to be completed before the real business of analysis can begin" (Markee, 2005, p. 358). Instead, "it is a crucially important, substantive first attempt at describing talk and co-occurring gestures, embodied actions and eye gaze phenomena as a unified, socially constituted context for second language learning activity" (ibid.).

An example of conversational analysis used in language classroom research is found in Ulichny's (1996) study of an interaction that took place in an ESL conversation class. The students were adult learners at the intermediate level. Two students and the teacher are having a conversation in which one learner, Katherine, talks about a decision to discontinue her volunteer work. (She had originally started volunteering for a chance to use English more often.) Ulichny's (1996) detailed analysis shows how the teacher "exits from the conversation to work on specific elements of the language" (p. 756). The discourse shifts from conversation to instruction, "which involves the whole class in language work" (ibid., p. 754), and to a *correction* move or a *conversational replay* (ibid., p. 756) for Katherine. The analysis clearly shows how the student is soon made "silent in the telling of her story" (ibid.).

SUBSTANTIVE CLASSROOM INTERACTION ISSUES

In this section, we look at substantive issues in classroom interaction. By *substantive issues*, we mean the 'what' rather than the 'how' of classroom interaction. The first subsection focuses on teacher talk, followed by a subsection on learner talk. In the final subsection, we look at teacher-learner interaction.

Teacher Talk

Teacher talk is a crucial element in the classroom. In second language contexts, researchers have investigated how teachers speak to minority language children (Strong, 1986). In many EFL contexts, teacher talk represents the only 'live' target language input that learners receive. Some of the questions that have been investigated in classroom research include the following: How much talking do teachers do, and how much of this is in the target language? What is the nature of teacher explanations? How and when do teachers correct learner errors? What kinds of errors receive attention?

A great deal of classroom research, in content classes as well as language classrooms, shows that when it comes to talking, teachers dominate. On average, it seems that teachers tend to talk around two-thirds of the time. Whether or not this is a good thing will depend on what one believes about the role of comprehensible input for acquisition. In the early stages of acquisition, extensive teacher input may be a good thing. It goes without saying, however, that this talk must be in the target language if it is to function as input for language acquisition. In some foreign language classrooms that we have observed, virtually all of the teacher talk has been in the students' first language. Use of the first language is usually ascribed to the fact that low proficiency students simply do not understand the target language. Another factor is the teachers' lack of confidence about their own language competence.

A major pedagogical function of teacher talk is to provide explanations. In fact, the naïve layperson probably believes that this is the central function of the teacher. There is some evidence, however, that teacher explanations may not be particularly effective, as you will see in the following reflection task.

REFLECTION

In the course of the following interaction, a student interrupts the teacher to ask why, in English, we say a *three-bedroom house* not a *three bedrooms house*. What do you think of the following teacher explanation? Is it adequate and or appropriate?

Extract 13:

T: OK, he's looking for a house with three bedrooms and what do we say? We don't in English we don't usually say house with three bedrooms . . . What do we usually say?

S: Three-bedroom house.

T: A three-bedroom house, a three-bedroom house, a three-bedroom house. So, what's he looking for?

S: For three-bedroom house.

T: What's he looking for?

S: House.

T: What's he looking for?

S: Three-bedroom house?

T: All right.

S: Why three bed, or three-bedroom? Why we don't say three bedrooms?

> T: Ahh... oh ... I don't know, um.
>
> S: Is not right.
>
> T: We don't say it. We don't say it. There's no explanation. But we often do that in English. Three-bedroom house.
>
> S: Don't ask for it.
>
> S: Yes.
>
> T: Well, do ask why. Ask why, and ninety-nine percent of the time I know the answer. One percent of the time nobody knows the answer. If I don't know the answer, nobody knows. [laughter] Ah, no, I don't know the answer, sorry.

In Extract 13, the teacher claims that there is no explanation for the grammatical issue that the student raises. This statement, of course, is incorrect, and the teacher quickly (and wisely) admits that he does not know the answer.

REFLECTION

How would you answer the question above? Why don't we say "three bedrooms house"? Have you ever told your students (or been told by a teacher), "There is no reason—that's just the way we say it"?

Explanations can focus on any aspect of language, be it grammatical, lexical, phonological, or pragmatic. These kinds of explanations can be identified and tabulated in various ways according to the focus of the research. For example, a study of the explanations given by novice and experienced teachers might look at the issue of whether there is any difference in the types of explanations given by teachers with varying degrees of experience. (Of course, you would need to operationally define what you mean by both "experienced" and "inexperienced" teachers, as well as define the categories for the focus of the explanation.) In addition, you would need an equal number of hours of instruction for the two types of teachers, and you should probably control for the foci of the lessons as well. You could tabulate and exemplify the instances of such explanations in a table like this one:

	Phonology Explanation	Grammar Explanations	Lexical Explanation	Pragmatics Explanations
Experienced Teachers				
Inexperienced Teachers				

Teacher questions have also received substantial attention by classroom researchers. Research has focused on the types of questions that teachers ask and the kinds of learner responses that they elicit.

Some years ago, researchers paid a great deal of attention to the use of display versus referential questions. A display question is one to which the questioner (often a teacher or a parent) knows the answer. Its purpose is to get learners to display their knowledge. In contrast, a referential question is one to which the person asking the question does not know the answer. In classrooms, in contrast with the outside world, there are very few referential questions. In one widely cited study, Brock (1986) investigated the effects of referential questions on ESL classroom discourse. The study was carried out with four experienced ESL teachers and twenty-four non-native speakers. Two of the teachers were trained to incorporate referential questions into their teaching while two were not. Each of the teachers taught the same lesson to six of the non-native speakers and the lessons were recorded, transcribed, and analyzed. Brock found that the two teachers who had not been trained to ask referential questions asked a total of 141 questions, only twenty-four of which were referential. The teachers who were trained to ask referential questions asked a total of 194 questions, 173 of which were referential. Learners to whom referential questions were directed gave significantly longer and more syntactically complex responses to those questions.

In addition to quantification, researchers have also used qualitative and interpretative analyses of question-answer sequences. Extract 14 provides an example of a brief classroom extract along with the researcher's interpretive gloss. (A more detailed example of this type of analysis is given in the sample study that ends this chapter.)

Responding to student errors is considered to be a fundamental aspect of a teacher's work. You will notice that we said "responding to" instead of "correcting errors." This choice is deliberate because as teachers we often talk about error correction, but, in fact, only the learners can correct their errors by reconstructing their internalized interlanguage grammar systems and lexicons, so researchers tend to talk about *error treatment*—attempts to get learners to correct their errors. In conversational analysis, these attempts are often referred to as *repairs:*

> Conversational repair . . . has been found to consist of three components: the *trouble source* or *repairable*; the *repair initiation*, which is the indication that there is trouble to be repaired; and the *outcome*, which is either the success or the failure of the repair attempt. (Liebscher & Dailey-O'Cain, 2003, p. 376)

Leibscher and Dailey-O'Cain underscore the fact that the overall category is called "*repair* rather than *correction*, the latter being the particular subtype of repair that occurs when a notable language error is corrected" (ibid.).

Some of the questions that researchers have addressed in relation to error treatment include the following: (1) When should errors be treated? (2) How should they be treated? (3) Who should treat errors? (4) How effective is self- and peer-correction? (5) What errors should be treated? (6) To what extent do learners take up teachers' responses to their errors (i.e., how effective is teacher treatment of learners' errors)?

REFLECTION

Choose one of the questions listed above. What sort of study could you design to address the question of your choice?

Despite the importance attributed to error correction, the effectiveness of such feedback is by no means clear. Although it is somewhat dated now, a very comprehensive review of research on language teacher questions is found in Chaudron's (1988) chapter on teacher and student interaction. He states that

from the learners' point of view, the use of feedback in repairing their utterances, and involvement in repairing their interlocutors' utterances may constitute the most potent source of improvement in both target language development and other subject matter knowledge. Yet the degree to which this information in fact aids learners' progress in target language development (or in subject matter control) is still unknown. (p. 133)

How teachers, other learners, and the learners' themselves respond to students' errors is a fascinating topic with many practical implications. Even though it was one of the earliest foci of language classroom research, it is still a fruitful topic for investigation.

Student-Student Interaction

The other major area of interest naturally enough is that of student talk. As you might imagine, the range of research issues and questions is enormous although most seek to establish some type of relationship between input or environmental factors and learner acquisition. For example, researchers have asked, "What is the relationship between input and uptake?" That is, do items made available for learning subsequently appear in learner output? (This is one of the questions addressed by the sample study in the next section.) Other key questions include (1) What is the relationship between participation structures (group size and composition, etc.) and learner output? (2) What is the relationship between task type and learner language? and (3) What patterns of interaction typify student talk in language classrooms?

REFLECTION

The following datum is taken from a piece of classroom-based research. Two students are trying to classify vocabulary cards. Which of the above questions do you think was being investigated?

Extract 15:

A: *Statistic* and *diagram*—they go together. You know *diagram?*

B: Yeah.

A: *Diagram* and *statistic* . . . but maybe, I think, *statistic* and *diagram*—you think we can put in *science?* Or maybe . . .

B: *Science, astronomy,* [yeah] and, er, can be *agriculture.*

A: Agriculture's not a science.

B: Yes, it's similar.

A: No. . . . And, er, maybe *Darwin* and *science* . . .

B: What's the *Darwin?*

A: Darwin is a man.

B: No [doesn't fit], it's one of place in Australia.

A: Yes, but it's a man who discover something, yes, I'm sure.

B: Okay.

A: And maybe, look, yes, *picture, newspaper, magazine, cartoon, book, illustration* [yeah]. Maybe we can put *lazy* and *English* together. (Nunan, 1991c, p. 53)

In early classroom research, real-time coding systems tended to focus on teachers' speech. Learners' speech was sometimes categorized as being in the target language or the first language, on-task or off-task, and so on. These gross categorizations have been overshadowed by the advent of portable tape- and video-recording devices that allow researchers to record learners' speech and nonverbal behavior with some degree of accuracy.

Much has been written about the role of teacher-student and student-student interaction, particularly since communicative language teaching and task-based learning have become widespread. Much classroom research has analyzed the way learners negotiate for meaning when faced with a communicative task because, in the negotiation for meaning, the input to the learners gets simplified, or pitched, appropriately to the learners' level. (See, e.g., work by Gass, 1997; Long, 1996; and Pica, 1994.) To summarize (and perhaps oversimplify) the findings of a great deal of interactionist research, people learn the elements of languages by interacting, not by learning the components of language and then putting them together in interaction.

In recent years the interactionist perspective has been supplemented (some might say supplanted) by viewpoints derived largely from sociolcultural theory (Vygotsky, 1978; 1986). In this approach to understanding human development, "interaction in context is examined to find out how proficiency is collaboratively constructed or appropriated within and through practical activity" (van Lier, 2001, p. 163). Much has been written about sociocultural theory and language learning (see, e.g., the collection edited by Lantolf, 2000). Here we will focus only on a small portion of this literature that is directly related to analyzing learner language.

A key concept in sociocultural theory is the *zone of proximal development*, or ZPD. This concept is a metaphor (not a physical apparatus in the brain) that is defined as "the difference between what a person can achieve when acting alone and what the same person can accomplish when acting with support from someone else and/or cultural artifacts" (Lantolf, 2000, p. 17). Some researchers feel that the "someone else" referred to here must be more knowledgeable than the learner (e.g., a teacher or parent). But recent investigations into learner language suggest that language learners can facilitate one another's learning.

One way that learning takes place is through *scaffolding*. This term represents another metaphor, which you can understand if you picture a scaffold—normally a wooden or metal or bamboo structure built around a building that is under construction or being repaired or painted. It is never intended that the scaffold will be a permanent feature of the edifice: It will be removed as soon as its job is done.

Scaffolding in language teaching and learning is defined as "the support given to language learners to enable them to perform tasks and construct communications which are at the time beyond their capability" (Carter and Nunan, 2001, p. 226). Such assistance is "gradually pulled away when the learner no longer needs it" (Oxford, 2001, p. 167). Instances of scaffolding can be found in some of the transcripts of learner language reproduced in this chapter:

Look back at Extracts 11 and 15. In each one, find an example of a learner scaffolding another learner. Compare your ideas with a classmate or colleague.

Classroom research using a sociocultural perspective has documented and analyzed interaction among learners of Japanese (Donato, 2000; Ohta, 2000), French (Donato, 2000; Swain, 2000), Spanish (Donato, 2000; Roebuck, 2000), and English (Donato, 2000; Kramsch, 2000; Sullivan, 2000; Swain, 2000; and van Lier, 2000).

QUALITY CONTROL ISSUES

There are at least five key quality control issues to keep in mind when analyzing classroom interaction. The first and foremost recalls earlier chapters of this book. That is, it is essential to plan your study carefully to ensure that you collect the data you need to answer your research question, and—as we have seen in earlier chapters—collecting classroom interaction data is not an easy task. For instance, if you are working in the naturalistic inquiry tradition and observing ongoing classes (your own or another teacher's), you will observe and record what happens—which may or may not be what you expected would happen. There is ample evidence that lessons don't always go according to plan (see, e.g., Bailey, 1996; K. E. Johnson, 1992a; 1992b; Nunan, 1996).

Secondly, you can only analyze interactional data to answer your research questions if you have collected it in such a way as to make the analysis possible. If you wish to analyze turn distribution you need to collect and transcribe videotaped data since turn bids are often accomplished through nonverbal signals. You may even need to produce a fine-grained transcript for conversational analysis in which you document in-breaths and vocalized fillers signaling turn bids. If you wish to analyze teacher feedback following learners' errors and only collect tape-recorded data, you will miss the facial expressions and gestures that are sometimes used to indicate the presence and place of errors.

Third, if you are coding data, whether you use categories of your own devising or concepts borrowed from your review of the literature, it is important to operationally define your terms and to make sure that the category system can be used by other analysts. To demonstrate that the category system works well, you need to calculate inter-coder agreement (e.g., by dividing the number of instances two raters coded the data identically by the total number of instances coded).

Fourth, it is important to do a *member check* (Maxwell, 2005). This step is especially valuable if you are recording data in a classroom where you do not know all the students individually. It involves asking the members of the group under study (e.g., the teachers and the students you are observing) to make sure you have correctly interpreted and labeled the data. For instance, if you are transcribing full-class interaction, you should make sure you have identified the speakers correctly.

Fifth, if you are doing an interpretive analysis of your data, you need to provide ample descriptions and sufficient examples to convey your ideas clearly to your readers. This step can be quite challenging because of length restrictions if you try to publish your report in a professional journal. The sample study described below provides a good example of this effort.

A SAMPLE STUDY

For the sample study in this chapter, we have selected a report about some teacher research. Storch (2002) carried out an investigation into patterns of interaction in pair work. Her classroom-based study was conducted in a one-semester, credit-bearing ESL course offered at a university in Australia. The purpose of the course was "to develop learners' academic listening, reading, speaking and writing skills" (p. 123). Storch collected her data in the writing classes, which included a focus on grammatical accuracy. In this particular report, she addressed the following research questions:

1. What patterns of dyadic interaction can be found in an ESL university-level class?
2. Does task or passage of time affect the pattern of dyadic interaction?
3. Do differences in the nature of the dyadic interaction result in different outcomes in terms of second language development? (p.123)

Here, due to space constraints, we will only summarize her work on the first research question above.

ACTION
Think about Storch's first research question. How would you go about collecting data to address this question? List the specific steps you would take.

There were thirty-three students in the study. Storch (ibid.) describes them as follows:

The students came from a range of language backgrounds, although they were mostly Asian. The participating students ranged in age from 19 to 42 years, with the majority (76%) being in the age range 20 to 30. Most of the students were international students (70%), some coming on exchange programs for the duration of one semester, others to complete their entire degree in Australia. Their length of residence in Australia (for both international and resident students) ranged from one month to nine years at the time data were collected. In terms of ESL proficiency, given that all were students accepted by the university, they had met the required ESL threshold. However, their scores on writing and reading on the university's in-house ESL placement tests had demonstrated that they needed further work on their academic language skills, particularly writing and grammatical accuracy. Thus they were considered intermediate in this context. (p. 124)

From the complete data set, Storch (ibid.) selected the interactions of ten student pairs for a detailed analysis because the data for these pairs were complete and these pairs "were also fairly representative of the entire group of participants in terms of age, language background, length of residence, and residential status" (p. 124). She also had gender balance since four of the pairs consisted of two male students, three pairs were mixed (a male and female students in each), and the remaining three pairs involved two female students. Storch (ibid.) used three tasks to collect her data:

1. A short composition based on a given diagram showing differences in language fluency between two groups of migrants before and after arrival to Australia.

2. An editing task, where students were presented with a text of approximately 160 words in length containing a number of errors typical of these students: errors in verb tense, articles, word forms.

3. A text reconstruction task (Storch, 1998), in which students were presented with content words and had to insert function words (e.g., prepositions, articles) and change word forms (e.g., for tense morphology) to produce a meaningful and grammatically correct text. (p. 125)

She points out that all these tasks "were related to the course syllabus and formed part of the regular class work" (p. 14). The students did three versions of each task at one-week intervals—two in pairs and one alone. The interactions of the pairs were tape-recorded. The data that Storch analyzed in this study were the recordings from the second week, when students had gotten familiar with the tasks.

Storch (ibid.) also collected other data including a student attitude survey about group work and pair work. She used "an editing task administered at the beginning and end of the study to function as a pre- and post-test" (p. 125). Storch also made observational notes, both while the students did the pair work and right after the lessons. Of these notes and the interactions they documented, she says,

Given the large number of pairs working simultaneously, observation notes were fairly brief and were of the most salient behavioral features. These features were then noted when transcribing the pair talk. The transcription of the pair talk attempted to reflect the interactive nature of the talk and to represent the talk as it occurred. Thus special symbols were used . . . to indicate aspects such as overlapping talk and emphasis applied by the speaker to certain words or phrases. (pp. 125–126)

The author describes two stages in her data analysis. First, she analyzed the transcripts for "the pattern of dyadic interaction and the salient traits that characterize these patterns" (p. 126). Secondly, the transcripts and the tasks were analyzed "to trace the effect, if any, resolutions reached during pair interaction had on the subsequent individual performance" (ibid.).

Storch (ibid.) found four patterns of interaction based on the roles taken by the two members of the dyad: collaborative, dominant/dominant, dominant/passive, and expert/novice. Her analysis was influenced by Damon and Phelps (1989), who defined two variables—equality and mutuality. In their work, Storch (2002) says, *equality* is "the degree of control or authority over the task. Equality describes more than merely an equal distribution of turns of equal contributions but an equal degree of control over the direction of a task (van Lier, 1996b)" (p. 127). Interactions displayed a high degree of equality if "both participants take directions from each other" (ibid., p. 127). The second variable, *mutuality*, "refers to the levels of engagement with each other's contribution. High mutuality describes interactions that are rich in reciprocal feedback and a sharing of ideas (Damon & Phelps, 1989)" (ibid.). Storch's model, reprinted here as **Figure 12.1,** depicts these ideas.

The following extract from Storch's data and the commentary that follows illustrate one type of classroom analysis. It is discursive in style. In other words, rather than assigning speaking turns to analytical categories in a coding process, the researcher engages in a close, line-by-line description and interpretation of the interaction. Based on the framework shown in Figure 12.1 and her interpretation of this transcript, Storch says Excerpt 16 is an example of collaborative interaction. Storch uses the pseudonyms *Charley* and *Mai* to represent a Thai

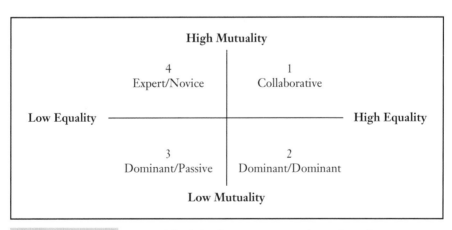

FIGURE 12.1 A model of dyadic interaction (from Storch, 2002, p. 128)

male and a Vietnamese female, respectively. She notes that they "contribute jointly to the composition and engage with each other's contribution" p. 130). A transcript from this pair is reprinted here as Extract 16:

Extract 16:
1 C: this (reads instructions) . . . what is this?
2 M: from the chart
3 C: this chart about
             [
4 M: the data
5 C: with percentage and eh . . .
6 M: describe describe the percentage of
7 C: English language fluency
       [   ]
8 M: English language fluency between two countries yeah?
9 Vietnam and Laos
10 C: yes and the compare before they came here and now
11 M: yes . . .
12 C: you can separate it here
13 M: yeah . . . first we . . . mm the
14 C: perhaps you should write
15 M: yeah I write yeah from the information of the chart yeah
16 . . . ((writing)) information of the chart
17 C: no from figure 3
             [
18 M: ah figure . . . figure 3? From figure 3 . . .
                        figure 3 ah
19 C: show the information
20: M: show the information . . . it it's
21: C: yeah it's ok it shows
22: M: it shows the . . . the data or the percentage?
23: C: should be the percentage (Storch, 2002, p. 131)

According to Storch (ibid.), this transcript

contains elements of cohesion as well as unpredictability. Cohesion is created as the participants incorporate or repeat each other's utterances and extend on them (e.g., lines 2–3, 5–6), or simply complete each other's utterances (e.g., lines 6–8, 8–10). The participants engage with each other's suggestions: there is negative or corrective feedback in the form of explicit peer repair (e.g., line 17) or recasting (e.g., line 6) as well as positive feedback in the form of confirmations (e.g., lines 10, 11). There are many requests (e.g., lines 1, 8, 22) and provision of information (e.g., line 23). (p. 131)

Storch notes that resolutions to problems are often attained "via a process of pooling resources. For example, in line 20 Mai notes a problem with subject-verb agreement and Charley suggests the appropriate correction. Thus, the talk shows a pattern of interaction that is high on equality and mutuality" (ibid.).

Storch (ibid.) provides additional extracts that show dominant/dominant, dominant/passive, and expert/novice patterns. The study concluded that the collaborative interaction pattern was the most common in the pair work data. She notes that the patterns of interaction were "fairly stable. Once they were established early in the semester . . . they remained so regardless of the passage of time" (pp. 144–145). Although not all the students worked collaboratively, the collaborative pattern was the most common and one dyad became more collaborative as time went by. She concluded that the learners did indeed scaffold one another's learning, and that that scaffolding was more likely in the collaborative or expert/novice pairs.

We find this report to be intriguing for a number of reasons. First, the research was conducted by a teacher in her own class. The data collection procedures were based on activities normally used during lessons. The literature review is current and wide-ranging, and the analysis of the interactions is clear and convincing. Storch also reports that 33% of the data were analyzed by a second researcher using the four descriptive categories, and that this process yielded 90% agreement.

PAYOFFS AND PITFALLS

The ways of analyzing interaction during lessons have evolved over the years— partly because technological developments have improved our ability to record and transcribe and partly because advances in discourse analysis have enhanced the possible means of investigating classroom interaction. Transcribing and analyzing classroom interaction are powerful tools in understanding how talk during lessons promotes (or impedes) language learning.

Still there are some pitfalls associated with these kinds of analyses. As noted in earlier chapters, using electronic recording devices can be a bit disruptive. You will probably need to record classroom interactions often enough that the learners grow accustomed to having a digital recorder or a video camera operating during lessons.

If you do make tape- or video-recordings, you must decide whether the research question demands that you transcribe the data. In some instances, it may be possible to code data directly from the recordings, but for many research questions with a linguistic focus, you will need to transcribe all or part of the data. For instance, if you are analyzing the way that teachers give learners instructions about doing group work, you may only need to transcribe the instruction-giving episodes. But if you wish to determine how clear (or unclear) those instructions are, you will also need to transcribe evidence of the groups' success in carrying them out.

A major concern in analyzing classroom discourse is the time involved to transcribe and interpret the data. Analyzing the data for R. L. Allwright's (1980) report on turns, topics, and tasks took up to twenty hours of transcribing for one hour of classroom data (Allwright and Bailey, 1991). As noted above, one issue that lends to the complexity of transcription is the level of analysis involved. If you are doing a fine-grained conversational analysis or creating a detailed phonetic transcript, the task will be much more time-consuming than if you are creating an orthographic transcript.

Transcripts of classroom interaction have served as data on their own and also in combination with other types of data. For instance, transcripts have been used in stimulated recall studies to help teachers recall what was happening during a lesson (see, e.g., Bailey, 1996; K. E. Johnson, 1992a; 1992b; Nunan, 1996).

The payoffs of analyzing interactional data are so numerous that classroom researchers forge ahead in spite of the challenges. Such data have given us a great deal of information about what various teaching activities accomplish—what sorts of talk result from the tasks that we pose to our learners.

CONCLUSION

This chapter focused on analyzing classroom interaction. We have discussed coding of classroom data and talked about various transcription systems that have been used to analyze teacher speech and learning language. We briefly considered conversational analysis and some of the substantive issues that classroom researchers have investigated. We close this chapter with some questions and tasks you can use to assess and reinforce your learning, as well as suggestions for further reading.

QUESTIONS AND TASKS

1. Think of a research question that interests you. What role might be played in answering that question by any of the approaches to analyzing classroom interaction that were described in this chapter?

2. Use the four basic discourse modes identified by McCarthy and Walsh (2003)—managerial mode, materials mode, skills and systems mode, and classroom context mode—to analyze the transcript in Extract 11 above.

3. Use the coding categories from Bowers (1980) in Figure 12.1 to analyze the data in Extract 10 above.

4. Using the four categories of interaction type described by Storch (2002) and depicted in Figure 12.1 above, analyze the data in Extract 11. That is, what pattern of interaction do these learners use?

5. Transcribe a recording of a piece of classroom interaction—five minutes worth of data should be sufficient. What problems do you encounter as you transcribe? What benefits are gained by the transcription process?

6. Now try to transcribe that same piece of data at the fine-grained microanalytic level demanded by conversational analysis. What additional challenges do you encounter working at this level of detail? What additional insights arise?

7. For any piece of classroom data involving error treatment, locate (1) the *trouble source* or *repairable*; (2) the *repair initiation*; and (3) the *outcome* (Liebscher & Dailey-O'Cain, 2003).

8. Using a transcript provided in this chapter or with one you yourself have developed, analyze the data with a coding system that interests you. If you are working with a classmate or colleague, it would be worthwhile to compute inter-coder agreement.

9. Next, try counting some instance of a particular phenomenon, such as errors made by learners and treatment moves by teachers or other learners. What terms must you operationally define in order to carry out this analysis?

10. Now using that same transcript, try some more interpretive analysis, such as the one undertaken by Johnson (see the notes following Extract 10) or Tsui (see Extract 14). Do you have sufficient data to have confidence in your interpretation? If not, what further data would you need to collect?

SUGGESTIONS FOR FURTHER READING

Tsui (1995) provides an introduction to classroom interaction. Walsh's (2006) book *Investigating Classroom Discourse* provides an overview of current approaches to analyzing classroom discourse and presents tools and techniques for analyzing classroom interaction.

Ellis and Barkhuizen (2005) give a comprehensive overview of methods of analyzing learner language. If you would like to read about group dynamics in the language classroom, see Dörnyei and Murphey (2003).

For a detailed discussion of transcription and coding in discourse analysis, see the collection edited by Edwards and Lampert (1993).

Markee (2000; 2003; 2005) and Lazaraton (2004) provide helpful information about conversational analysis, along with clear examples.

13

Quantitative Data Analysis

All science requires mathematics. The knowledge of mathematical things is almost innate in us. This is the easiest of sciences, a fact which is obvious in that no one's brain rejects it; for laymen and people who are utterly illiterate know how to count and reckon. (Roger Bacon, as cited in Andrews, 1993, p. 568).

INTRODUCTION AND OVERVIEW

You may dispute Bacon's claim that mathematics is "the easiest of sciences," but there is no denying that people through the ages have counted and measured things that mattered to them—from the stars in the sky to grains of rice. This chapter focuses on analyzing quantitative data—those data that have been generated through processes of counting or measuring, no matter what classroom research tradition you may use.

If mathematics is not your strong suit, don't worry: Just take your time in reading this material. If you can interpret decimal points and can add, subtract, multiply, divide, square numbers, and find square roots—all using a calculator—you can do the procedures described here. Keep in mind the analogy from Chapter 4 that learning about research is like entering a new culture. This chapter will teach you more of the vocabulary and values of quantitative data analysis.

In Chapter 4, we examined experimental research. We noted that it typically employs quantified data. However, in recent years, some experimental researchers have employed "mixed methods"—that is, qualitative data collection and analysis methods have been used along with quantitative methods. In addition, quantitative data have been used in classroom studies in both the action research and naturalistic inquiry approaches to research.

Quantitative data can be analyzed and displayed in many different ways. Some familiar ways of reporting numerical data include percentages and proportions. Such data can also be provided in helpful graphic displays such as bar graphs and pie charts. For example, Scales, Wennerstrom, Richard, and Wu (2006) used a pie chart to show the percentages of English language learners in their sample who correctly identified an American English accent. Twenty-nine percent of the listeners correctly attributed a speaker's accent to the United States, but the pie chart clearly demonstrates the remaining percent of listeners who attributed the accent to eleven other countries or regions. These same authors use bar graphs to good advantage to display other comparisons in their data.

In language classroom research, authors often use statistics to express their findings. What do we mean by *statistics*? The term has at least three meanings. First, it is the label given to a group of procedures by which researchers make decisions about accepting or rejecting hypotheses in the experimental approach. Secondly, *statistics* can refer to the actual mathematical formulae by which those procedures are carried out. Third, *statistics* refers to the results of those mathematical procedures—the numerical findings of a study. These ideas may sound very esoteric, but our purposes in this chapter are twofold: We want to help you understand both how to interpret some of the statistics that are commonly used in language classroom research and also how to use some of them with your own data.

To accomplish those goals, we will first discuss descriptive statistics and then discuss the specialized meaning of *significant* (as in *significant differences* or *significant correlations*) as the term relates to probability. We will also explore the notion of degrees of freedom and explore one commonly used statistic (the chi-squared test) in some detail before reading about other inferential statistics, including some tests of significant differences and some correlation procedures. Finally, we will briefly consider some technological advances for working with quantitative data.

You will recall from Chapter 4 that when we think about representing a group of people through quantitative data, we can use the measures of central tendency (the mean, mode, and median) and the measures of dispersion about the mean (range, standard deviation, and variance). These measures are called *descriptive statistics* because they describe the group in terms of the variables that have been measured or counted.

There is also an important group of statistical procedures called *inferential statistics*—so named because they help us make inferences about the population based on what is known about the sample. In general, inferential statistics are used to reach conclusions about significant differences between or among groups, or about significant relationships between variables. We will consider both types in turn after we first explore descriptive statistics.

DESCRIPTIVE STATISTICS

In Chapter 4, we learned about *frequency polygons*. You will recall that these are figures that depict the measurement of the trait being investigated on the horizontal axis (also called the *abscissa*) and the frequency on the vertical axis (sometimes referred to as the *ordinate*). (Look back at Figure 4.8 for a reminder.) In language classroom research, the measurement on the horizontal axis often involves a range of possible scores (for instance, on a language test). The frequency on the vertical axis often represents the number of people who received each particular score in the possible score distribution (see Figures 4.7, 4.8, and 4.9).

When we have a large number of scores or measurements represented in a data set, the shape of the frequency polygon may resemble a bell. This image is referred to as the *normal distribution* or the *bell-shaped curve* (or just the *bell curve*). Keep this visual image in mind as you read about measures of central tendency and measures of dispersion. *Central tendency* is the propensity of scores to group around the middle of a data set. The effects of central tendency are visible in the large central hump of the bell-shaped curve. *Dispersion* refers to the propensity of scores to spread out away from the mean. This tendency is reflected in the tapering tails of the bell curve. (See Figures 4.8 and 4.9 for a visual image of these ideas.)

Measures of Central Tendency

There are three main measures of central tendency in the descriptive statistics: the mean, the median, and the mode. As noted above, the *mean* is the mathematical average. The *median* is the middle score in a data set. The *mode* is the most frequently obtained score in a data set. These three statistics provide some useful information about a group (or groups) of measurements.

To illustrate, let's revisit the post-test scores from the students in the control and experimental groups in a study about innovative listening materials. These data were presented in Table 4.1 above and are reprinted here as **Table 13.1**.

In Table 13.1, the means for the two groups have been provided for you. These are the mathematical averages of the two sets of data. To find the mean, you simply add the scores in the group and divide by the number of people who contributed those scores. The actual formula looks like this:

$$\overline{X} = \Sigma X / n$$

The capital X with the line above it (X-bar) stands for the mean, the mathematical average. The capital Greek letter sigma (Σ) means "sum up the following" and the capital X represents "score(s)." The slash (/) indicates division. So, this formula says that to get the mean, we sum the scores and divide by the number (n).

To find the mode, you simply arrange the scores from highest to lowest and look to see which score was obtained most often. So, for example, the control

TABLE 13.1 EFL students' scores on a listening comprehension
test (n = 20)

Control Group		Experimental Group	
Student ID	Scores	Student ID	Scores
C-1	80	E-1	85
C-2	82	E-2	87
C-3	78	E-3	83
C-4	77	E-4	82
C-5	83	E-5	88
C-6	80	E-6	85
C-7	76	E-7	81
C-8	84	E-8	89
C-9	75	E-9	84
C-10	85	E-10	86
Mean	**80**		**85**

group obtained the following scores: 85, 84, 83, 82, 80, 80, 78, 77, 76, and 75. We can see that the score of 80 points was obtained by two students in the control group, and every other score was obtained just once. Therefore, in this small data set, the mode is 80.

REFLECTION

What is the mode for the experimental group data in Table 13.1?

It is not unusual to find two modes in a data set. When that happens, it is called a *bimodal distribution*. Sometimes there is no mode in a data set because no particular score is obtained by more people than any other score. This situation often occurs with small data sets.

The *median* is "the score which is at the center of the distribution" (Hatch and Lazaraton, 1991, p. 161). (Think of the median strip that divides a highway.) Another way to understand the median is to say that "50% of the scores fall at or below [the median] and 50% of the scores fall above that value" (Jaeger, 1993, p. 37).

If you have an odd number of scores in your data set, the median will be the score that is right in the middle. If you have an even number of scores in the data set, the median is the "midpoint between the two middle scores" (ibid.).

Look at the control group data in Table 13.1 for a moment. There are ten people in the control group. Therefore, the median score is found between the fifth and sixth scores (the two middle scores): 85, 84, 83, 82, **80, 80**, 78, 77, 76, and 75. We add the two middle scores and divide by two (80 + 80 = 160/2 = 80). In this case, the two middle scores happen to be identical.

If this had been a slightly bigger data set— say, 88, 86, 85, 84, 83, 82, 80, 80, 78, 77, 76, and 75—what would the median be? Find the two middle scores. They are 82 and 80. Add them together and divide by 2 to find the midpoint. In this case, 81 is the median.

REFLECTION

What is the median for the scores of the experimental group in Table 13.1? Here are the ten scores arranged in order from the highest to the lowest score.

89, 88, 87, 86, 85, 85, 84, 83, 82, and 81

What is the median for this slightly larger data set?

89, 88, 87, 86, 85, 85, 84, 83, 82, 81, 80, and 79

The median "is often used as the measure of central tendency when the number of scores is small and/or when the data are obtained by ordinal measurement" (Hatch and Farhady, 1982, p. 4). The median is sometimes used to divide a group into two groups through a procedure called the *median split*. Imagine, for instance, that you want to investigate the effects of a particular teaching method on students who have a high or a low aptitude for language learning. You might operationally define high and low aptitude by administering a language learning aptitude test at the beginning of the experiment, finding the median score, and using that point to divide the subjects into two equal (or very nearly equal) groups. This would be an application of the median split.

REFLECTION

Can you think of any possible problems with the median split as a technique for defining groups?

Imagine two cases where a researcher used the median split technique to operationally define high and low aptitude students in an experiment. On a language aptitude test with a possible score of 100 points, the mean is 63 and the median is 60.

Scenario 1: The highest student in the low aptitude group scores 55. The lowest student in the high aptitude group scores 65.

Scenario 2: The highest student in the low aptitude group scores 59. The lowest student in the high aptitude group scores 61.

Measures of Dispersion

Measures of central tendency are very important, but they present only part of the picture in descriptive statistics. The other necessary element is to know how the measurements in a data set differ from one another. The amount of variability in a data set gives us additional information that the measures of central tendency do not provide. The three key measures of dispersion are the range, the standard deviation, and variance.

The difference between the highest score and the lowest score in a data set is called the *range*. It can be reported in two ways. If we look at the scores in Table 13.1, we can see that the lowest score in the control group is 75 and the highest is 85. We can say that the range is from 75 to 85, or that the range is 10. Two related concepts are *exclusive range* and *inclusive range* of the scores in a group. The *exclusive range* is what we get when we subtract the lowest measurement from the highest measurement (in this case $85 - 75 = 10$). The inclusive range is found by subtracting the lowest score from the highest score and adding one. In the control group data shown in Table 13.1, the inclusive range is computed as follows: $85 - 75 = 10 + 1 = 11$.

Here is a practical way to remember the difference between exclusive range and inclusive range. Imagine you have borrowed a book from the library and you wish to photocopy the chapter that appears on pages 22 to 32. How many pages will you photocopy? If you said ten pages, you have used the exclusive range (simple subtraction). But if you wish to have a copy of every page in the chapter, you will need to copy eleven pages (pages 22, 23, 24, 25, 26, 27, 28, 29, 30, 31, and 32). In other words, you will need to use the inclusive range.

ACTION

Determine the inclusive range and the exclusive range for the experimental group data in Table 13.1.

The range is useful, but it is strongly influenced by two single measurements—the highest and the lowest score. For instance, if student C-9 had scored 70 instead of 76, the exclusive range for the control group would be 15 instead of 10. For this reason, a more useful statistic is the standard deviation.

Once you understand the concepts of the average and range, you are well on your way to understanding the notion of *standard deviation* because it is a measure of the average difference among the scores in a particular data set. Standard deviation is the most commonly reported measure of dispersion because it is so informative.

To make sure you understand this concept, we will compute the standard deviation for the scores of the control group in Table 13.1 above. We will begin by providing part of the formula for computing standard deviation and then adding to it. The symbols below tell us to perform a certain set of operations in a certain sequence. You already know about Σ, X and X-bar. So what does this part of the equation say? (Remember our language learning analogy: The issue of mathematical sequencing of operations is like learning word-order rules in a new language.)

$$\frac{\Sigma(X - \overline{X})^2}{N - 1}$$

Start your calculations from within the parentheses. (This starting point is a mathematical convention.) The X-minus-X-bar component inside the parentheses is telling us that we subtract the mean from each individual score. We do this step to find the distance between each individual score and the mean of that group of scores.

The superscript (^{2}) to the right of the parentheses tells us to square each of the differences we find by subtracting. The purpose of squaring is to get rid of the minus signs that will appear when we subtract the mean from each individual score. We do this step because minus signs are inconvenient to work with—especially if you are doing calculations by hand. (There will always be minus signs in this step because, logically, some scores are higher than the mean and some are lower than the mean.)

After we have done all the subtraction and the squaring, the capital sigma (Σ) in the numerator of the standard deviation formula tells us to sum those amounts. So the numerator in this equation says, "First, subtract the mean from each score. Square those results and add them all up." The denominator tells us to subtract one from the number of data points (the scores here) that contributed to the mean.

So far, so good. But remember that we squared all the differences to get rid of the minus signs. So now we must undo that step by finding the square root of the results. When we include the square root sign we have the complete formula:

$$\sqrt{\frac{\Sigma(X - \overline{X})^2}{N - 1}}$$

To apply this formula to any data set (e.g., the data for the control group in Table 13.1), it is convenient to create a table with column headings that represent the steps in the equation. When we do so, we get the set-up shown in **Table 13.2.**

The last step is to sum the values in the right column. When we do that we get 108 as the value in the numerator of the equation. We then divide it by $N - 1$, which is 9 in this case (10 − 1 = 9):

$$108/9 = 12$$

TABLE 13.2 Computing standard deviation for the control group

Student ID	Scores	$(X - \bar{X})$	$(X - \bar{X})^2$
C-1	80	0	0
C-2	82	2	4
C-3	78	−2	4
C-4	77	−3	9
C-5	83	3	9
C-6	80	0	0
C-7	76	−4	16
C-8	84	4	16
C-9	75	−5	25
C-10	85	5	25

Finally we take the square root of that result:

$$\sqrt{12} = 3.46$$

This amount is our standard deviation. What does it mean? It is telling us that the average distance from the mean of 80 in the control group's scores was about 3.5 points. When you look at the raw data, you will see that this result makes sense.

ACTION

Compute the standard deviation for the experimental group data in Table 13.1.

A concept related to the standard deviation is *variance*, which is defined as the standard deviation squared. This idea is very important in language assessment and also in a statistical procedure called Analysis of Variance, which we will consider shortly. When we square 3.46 (the value of the standard deviation we found for the control group data in Table 13.1), we find that the variance for the control group is 11.97.

REFLECTION

If the square root of 12 is reported as 3.46, why is 3.46 squared reported as 11.97? Share your ideas with a classmate or colleague.

Degrees of Freedom

Notice that the denominator of the standard deviation formula says $N - 1$. Why is 1 subtracted from the N in this formula? The answer is based on a concept called *degrees of freedom*. This is an abstract notion that is easier to illustrate than to define. Think about a simple algebraic equation, like this:

$$3 + 4 + X = 12$$

You can determine that X in this formula represents the whole number 5. You do this by adding $3 + 4$, which gives you 7. You then subtract 7 from 12 and get 5. There is nothing else that X can be in this formula. In other words, once we know that the sum of the three values in the equation is 12, and that two of the values are 3 and 4, then the other value must be 5. That one particular value is not free to vary. It is predetermined by the other values in the formula. So, once you know all but one of the values, the last one is accounted for. The mathematical way of saying this is $N - 1$.

Here's another way to think about this concept. Imagine that you are teaching a class with twenty students. There are twenty desks in the room. Seventeen students are present and there are three empty chairs when the lesson begins. A student enters the room and selects one of the three desks, so two remain empty. Another student enters the room and chooses one of the remaining chairs. When the twentieth student enters the room, how many chairs are available? How many choices does he have?

If you said one chair, you are correct. But we hope you also said that he had no choice! Since only one desk remained, he had no choice but to sit there (unless he wished to sit on the floor, which takes him outside of the equation). The point is that when all the quantities except one of the quantities are known and the total is known, then the last quantity can have only one particular value, and that value is not free to vary. Many statistical formulae include "$N - 1$" to account for this fact.

In summary, we have seen that the three main measures of dispersion are the range, the standard deviation, and the variance, while the three main measures of central tendency are the mean, the mode, and the median. These descriptive statistics are extremely important in language classroom research. They are regularly used in experimental research, but they are frequently provided in reports of action research and naturalistic inquiry as well. In addition, the descriptive statistics underpin the inferential statistics and the concept of statistical significance—the topic of our next section.

THE SIGNIFICANCE OF "SIGNIFICANCE"

In the discussion that follows, we will repeatedly use the term *significant*, and you will see it used in many research reports that employ quantitative analyses. What does this mean? Very briefly, a significant difference or a significant relationship is one that is too substantial to have occurred by chance. By convention, in our field the outcomes of statistical analyses are typically considered to be significant if there are fewer than five chances out of a hundred that the results have occurred by chance. (In some instances, the standard is set more stringently—for instance, at one chance out of a hundred.) This standard is set at the beginning of a study, and it is called *alpha*—the first letter of the Greek alphabet, which is in fact the symbol that is used (α). You may see this symbol, which looks like a fat little fish swimming to the left, in research reports—it is part of the "code" of quantitative analyses.

When we do quantitative analyses in studies seeking either significant differences or significant relationships, we check for *statistical significance*—the confidence you can have that the finding is stable or trustworthy. In reading a research report, you may come across a note that says "$p < .05$." Here the lower-case "p" stands for *probability*. It represents the likelihood, or probability, that the findings are erroneous or fluky or atypical. The little carat lying on its side ($<$) means "is less than." (When it faces the opposite direction [$>$], it means "is greater than".) So, if a value is given and the probability is represented as "$p < .05$," it means that if we repeated the study 100 times, we would only get substantially different results fewer than 5 times out of 100. In other words, if "$p < .05$," it is likely that the result is very stable.

Statistics books include tables called the *critical values tables*. These days, the information in those tables is also contained in statistical software packages. Over the ages, statisticians have determined what the critical values are for the various statistical procedures. These tables help us decide whether the results of our own quantitative analyses are likely to have occurred by chance. The outcomes of the inferential statistics formulae that you use with your own data are called the *observed values*. In general, if the observed value from your data equals or exceeds the predetermined *critical value* printed in the table, then you can say that your results are statistically significant.

INFERENTIAL STATISTICS: SIGNIFICANT DIFFERENCES

In experimental studies, the researcher frequently wants to determine the possible effect of the treatment(s) (one or more levels of the independent variable). The question is often whether the treatment(s) caused a difference in the performance of the group(s) that got the treatment(s) in comparison with the control group, which did not. This situation occurs in both of the true experimental designs (the post-test only control group design and the pre-test post-test control group design).

Researchers also look for significant differences in scores and measurements in studies that employ the criterion groups design. You will recall from Chapter 4 that this is a design in the ex post facto class that compares groups on the basis of preexisting conditions (such as gender, first language, country of origin, handedness, and so on).

Inferential statistics are used to test for significant differences in some of the weaker research designs as well, such as the intact groups design. In this design, data are compared from two or more groups that were not randomly selected from the population or randomly assigned to groups. Rather, groups that were established for some other purpose are used in the research. Still, at least one group gets the treatment and at least one group does not, so that we can compare the groups' results. This situation is very common in classroom research because learners may have been assigned to particular classes on the basis of placement test scores, teacher recommendations, or parental requests rather than through random sampling procedures.

Another situation in which researchers look for significant differences is the one-group pre-test post-test design. In this context, a single group of learners is tested or measured on some variable at the outset of the study. Then some sort of treatment is administered to them. In classroom research, this treatment often takes the form of an instructional unit, a particular teaching method, or a set of materials. A statistical procedure is used that checks for significant differences between the pre-test scores (the measurement *before* the treatment) and the post-test scores of the students in the group.

Many different inferential statistics are used to determine significant differences between or among groups. Here we will discuss just a few that are widely used in language classroom research. In general, the choice of the statistic is determined, first and foremost, by the type of hypothesis being tested or research question being posed. Secondly, the choice of statistic to use is largely a function of (1) the types of data (interval, ordinal, or nominal); (2) the number of groups in the comparison; (3) the sample size; and (4) whether or not there are any moderator variables included in the design.

Comparing Frequency Data: The One-Way Chi-Square Test

We will begin our exploration of these procedures by examining in some detail a statistic called the *chi-square test*. (Here *chi* rhymes with *eye* rather than with *key*, and the letters *ch-* make the /k/ sound.) We focus on the chi-square test for three reasons. First, it is often used in language classroom research. Secondly, the way it functions demonstrates statistical reasoning with the least technical jargon of the various inferential statistics. And third, its procedures are intuitively plausible; the reasoning underlying the chi-square test is less abstract than is that of some other procedures.

This statistic is represented by the Greek symbol *chi* (χ) with the superscript ^{2} to indicate the mathematical operation of squaring (χ^2). The chi-square test is often used in educational research when the dependent variable consists of frequency counts rather than measurements.

The chi-square test is used when we want to learn whether an observed pattern of occurrence is significantly different from what we would expect by chance. (Another way of thinking about the issue is whether there is a relationship among the variables being investigated, but we will save that wording for our discussion of correlation studies below.) Here is an example. Suppose we wonder if students in a British secondary school choose to study any particular foreign language more often than others. Let's imagine that a certain school has 600 students and that they all must enroll in a foreign language course, but they can choose whether to enroll in French, Spanish, or German. If there are no systematic differences among the languages in terms of students' preferences, we would expect something like the enrollment pattern shown in **Table 13.3:**

TABLE 13.3 Hypothetical enrollment data in three foreign languages

French	Spanish	German
200 Ss	200 Ss	200 Ss

However, this much symmetry rarely occurs in real life! We are more likely to get different numbers in the various language groups, but at what point could we say that there is a significant difference in the number of students who chose French, Spanish, or German? The data set shown in **Table 13.4** would probably not suggest a remarkable difference in the students' choices:

TABLE 13.4 More hypothetical enrollment data in three foreign languages

French	Spanish	German
205 Ss	200 Ss	195 Ss

But what about the data shown in **Table 13.5**?

TABLE 13.5 Somewhat more diverse hypothetical enrollment data in three foreign languages

French	Spanish	German
250 Ss	200 Ss	150 Ss

And what about the data in **Table 13.6**? When are the differences in group size big enough for us to say that they are statistically significant?

TABLE 13.6 Very diverse hypothetical enrollment data in three foreign languages

French	Spanish	German
300 Ss	200 Ss	100 Ss

At what point can we safely conclude that among these particular students, French is significantly more popular than Spanish, which, in turn, is significantly more popular than German? It is the chi-square test that lets us determine when an observed pattern in nominal frequency data differs significantly from what we would expect by chance. Here's how it works. In this case, we are comparing the students in terms of just one variable—their choice of which language to study—so we will use what is called a *one-way chi-square test*. It is a statistical procedure that can be done by hand with a calculator or with a statistical software package. Here is the formula, and while it may look intimidating, it is actually rather straightforward once you understand the symbols:

$$\chi^2 = \Sigma_{(\text{Observed} - \text{Expected})^2}/\text{Expected}$$

As we saw earlier, the capital Greek letter sigma (Σ) simply means "sum up the following," and the slash (/) is just a convenient way to indicate division. (A horizontal line separating the numerator and the denominator in a division equation is another way of indicating that division is needed, as shown in **Table 13.7**.)

Let's look at the last of the three data sets presented in Table 13.6 and set up a table that will let us use this equation easily. Here are the steps:

1. First, create a column where you can label your variables (the three languages).

2. Then add a column for the observed frequencies (the data that actually occurred).

3. The third column is for the expected frequencies (what we would find by straightforward division of the total N into three equal groups).

4. Create another column for the difference between these two values (found by subtraction).

5. Add a fifth column where we can square the differences we find between the observed and the expected frequencies.

6. In the sixth column the values in the fifth column are divided by the expected frequencies.

Once again, the purpose of squaring is to get rid of the negative numbers that have arisen in finding the difference between the observed and the expected frequencies. The calculations are shown in Table 13.7:

TABLE 13.7 Chi-square computations table for enrollment data in three language courses

Language Chosen	Observed Frequency	Expected Frequency	Observed Minus Expected $(O - E)$	$(O - E)^2$	$\dfrac{(O - E)^2}{E}$
French	300 Ss	200 Ss	100	10,000	50
Spanish	200 Ss	200 Ss	0	0	0
German	100 Ss	200 Ss	−100	10,000	50

After you have created these columns and entered your data, there are just a few more steps to determine whether the observed pattern is statistically significantly different from what we would expect by chance. First, we add the values in the last column (50 + 0 + 50). This sum is the value of our chi-square observed, so in this case, $\chi^2_{observed} = 100$ (because 50 + 0 + 50 = 100).

Finally, we must compare the value of $\chi^2_{observed}$ to the value of $\chi^2_{critical}$. If you are doing the computations by hand, you can find that value in statistics books in a table called the "Table of Critical Values for Chi-Square." (See, e.g., J. D. Brown [1988] and Hatch and Lazaraton [1991].) As noted above, if you are working with a statistics software package, the critical values are usually built into the package and the computer will typically do the comparison for you.

To use the table of critical values, you must know how to compute the degrees of freedom. In working with a one-way chi-square test, the degrees of freedom are defined as the number of groups being compared minus one. Here we are comparing students' choices to enroll in each of three languages, so $3 - 1 = 2$ (which is typically written as "df = 2").

When you locate the table of critical values for chi-square in a statistics book (usually in the appendices near the end of the book), you will see that it is set up something like **Table 13.8**:

TABLE 13.8 Partial table of critical values of chi-square (adapted from Hatch and Lazaraton, 1991, p. 603)

Probability	.10	.05	.025	.01	.001
df					
1	2.706	3.841	5.024	6.635	10.828
2	4.605	5.991	7.378	9.210	13.816
3	6.251	7.815	9.348	11.345	16.266
4	7.779	9.488	11.143	13.277	18.467
5	9.236	11.070	12.832	15.086	20.515

(The actual chi-square critical values table is much longer. It usually goes all the way to df = 100. Here we have just reproduced a small portion of the table.)

To determine whether our $\chi^2_{observed}$ value is statistically significant, we compare it to the $\chi^2_{critical}$ value in the appropriate row (in this case, where df = 2) and under the probability level selected at the beginning of the study (in this case, .05). If the observed value is equal to or greater than the critical value at that point, we can say that the results are statistically significant.

ACTION

Use Table 13.8 to determine whether the results of our chi-square analysis are statistically significant. All the information you need is given above.

We can see that the value of $\chi^2_{observed} = 100$ in our language enrollment data is much greater than the critical value (5.991). As a result, we can conclude that in this case the differences in the numbers of students who have enrolled in the three different languages are too great to have happened by chance. In other words, the differences students' language preferences are statistically significant.

REFLECTION

What do you notice as you read down each column of numbers in the table of values of chi-square critical (Table 13.8)?

For example, in the column headed by .10 (meaning the 10% probability level), the critical values are 2.706, 4.605, 6.251, 7.779, and 9.236.

Does the same pattern hold in the remaining columns in the table? What does this mean, in practical terms, about the results needed in your $\chi^2_{observed}$ in order to get statistically significant results?

You will recall that *probability* is the likelihood that our results are due to chance. By convention in our field, we usually set that level (called the *alpha level* because it is determined at the beginning of an investigation) at .05—meaning that we are only willing to be wrong five times out of 100.

REFLECTION

Look back at the row labeled *Probability* in Table 13.8.

What do you notice as you read across a row in the portion of the chi-square critical values tables reprinted above? For example, here are the critical values for χ^2 in the row for df = 1:

2.706   3.841   5.024   6.635   10.828

Skim the remaining rows. Does the same pattern hold true? What does this mean, in practical terms, about the $\chi^2_{observed}$ you need to find in order to get statistically significant results?

Comparing Frequency Data: The Two-Way Chi-Square Test

The chi-squared test can be used whether or not there is a moderator variable in the study. If there is a moderator variable, we use what is called a *two-way chi-square test* because two variables are included in one analysis. For the sake of illustration, let us use students' gender as a moderator variable. The question now becomes whether there is a significant difference between the propensity of male and female students to enroll in French, Spanish, or German. **Table 13.9** presents the data from Table 13.6 with the frequency counts for male and female students added:

TABLE 13.9 Hypothetical enrollment data of male and female students in three language courses

Gender/Language	French	Spanish	German	Totals
Male	100 Ss	100 Ss	75 Ss	275 Ss
Female	200 Ss	100 Ss	25 Ss	325 Ss
Totals	300 Ss	200 Ss	100 Ss	600 Ss

Once again, we can analyze these data to see if there are significant differences in this enrollment pattern from what we would expect purely by chance— that is, if there were no connection between students' gender and their tendency to choose French, Spanish, or German as the foreign language they would study. We can see from the data above that there are 325 female students and 275 male students. Their choices of what language to study constitute the observed frequencies in this data set. The first step in calculating chi-square then is to determine what the expected frequencies would be if there were no particular difference between male and female students in their choice of what language to study. The row and column totals in Table 13.9 help us to do this. Here's how.

The values in the row and the column labeled "Totals" are called the *marginal frequencies*, or just the *marginals*, because they appear in the margins of the table. (Note that the cell in the lower right-hand corner of this table should show a number equal to the total number of students in the study. We get that value— 600 in this case—by adding up the numbers in the "Totals" column. We should get the same number when we add the figures in the "Totals" row as well.)

We use the marginal frequencies to get the expected frequencies with the following formula:

$$E_{ij} = \frac{n_i n_j}{N}$$

What does this mean? Well, the E just represents the expected frequency—the thing we need to determine before we can calculate the chi-square value. The upper case N represents the number in the study—the one in the lower right corner of the table (in this case, 600). The lower-case n just represents the smaller numbers in each cell and the subscripts i and j are mathematical symbols that refer to "whatever row and whatever column" in the table, where i represents row data and j represents column data.

Let's look at an example. The first cell in Table 13.9 tells us that 100 males registered for French. If we read down that column, we will see that the column total is 300 Ss. If we read to the far right of that row, we see that the row total is 275 Ss. The numerator in the equation for calculating expected frequencies in a two-way chi-square study tells us to multiply the value for the row total (n_i) times the value for the column total (n_j). In this case, we would multiply 300 times 275, which gives us 82,500.

The next step in calculating the expected frequency for this particular cell is to divide 82,500 by the N—that large number that represents all the students in the study and that appeared in the lower-right corner cell of Table 13.8 above. In this case, that value was 600. When we divide 82,500 by 600 we get 137.5—a value representing the number of male students we would expect to enroll in French courses if there were no significant differences between the boys' and the girls' choices of language to study.

We continue calculating the expected frequency for every cell in the table. Some of those frequencies have been calculated for you in **Table 13.10** below:

TABLE 13.10 Partially completed expected frequencies for enrollment of male and female students in three language courses

Gender/Language	French	Spanish	German
Male	137.50	91.67	
Female	162.50		

ACTION

Using the data from Table 13.9 and the examples in Table 13.10 above, calculate the expected frequencies for the number of male students studying German and the number of female students studying Spanish and German.

Given the observed and expected frequencies, we can now do the subtraction to calculate the difference between the observed frequencies in the data set and the expected frequencies (O − E), just as we did in the one-way chi square calculations above. Once again, this process will yield some negative numbers, so for convenience, the statistic tells us to square those values so we can get rid of the minus signs. We then divide the resulting values by the value

---

ACTION

Complete **Table 13.11** by calculating the observed minus the expected frequencies for the empty cells, and then squaring the results, and then dividing each one by the expected frequency for that particular row. The last step is to add the values in the far-right column to get the value of chi-square observed.

TABLE 13.11 Partial calculation of a two-way chi-square analysis

Language Chosen by Gender of Ss	Observed Frequency	Expected Frequency	Observed Minus Expected (O − E)	$(O − E)^2$	$\dfrac{(O − E)^2}{E}$
French by Males	100	137.5	−37.5	1,406.25	10.23
French by Females	200	162.5	37.5	1,406.25	8.65
Spanish by Males	100	91.67	8.33	69.39	0.76
Spanish by Females	100	75.0			
German By Males	75	45.80			
German by Females	25	37.5			

$\chi^2_{observed} = $ ___

of E (the expected frequencies). Finally, we sum those values to get our chi-square observed. Each of these steps is represented in the column headings of Table 13.11.

In order to determine whether the value of this chi-square observed is statistically significant, we go back to the table of critical values (Table 13.8 above). To use the table, we need to know the degrees of freedom. In a two-way chi-square analysis, the degrees of freedom is equal to the number of columns minus one times the number of rows minus one. In our enrollment data, we were working with three columns (enrollment in French or Spanish or German) and two rows (male and female students). So we calculate degrees of freedom like this:

$$(3 − 1)(2 − 1) = 2 \times 1 = 2.$$

ACTION

Compare the value of chi-square observed (which you got when you totaled the last column in Table 13.11) with the values of chi-square critical given in Table 13.8. Assume that alpha was set at .05. Are your findings statistically significant? How do you interpret the result?

What does all this calculating have to do with classroom research issues that concern teachers and students? Let's revisit the sample study that was summarized at the end of Chapter 3. This was the investigation by Sato (1982)—the ESL teacher who wanted to investigate the perception that Asian students did not participate as much in ESL classes as non-Asian students. Sato used the one-way chi-square statistic to investigate this issue. Here is a summary of her findings:

1. The 19 Asian students took 107 (36.4%) of the turns. The 12 non-Asian students took 186 (63.5%) of the turns. Sato reported that the chi-square observed for these data was 75.78, df = 1, p < .001. (p. 17)
2. The 19 Asian students self-selected for turns 52 times (33.99% of the time) while the 12 non-Asian students self-selected 101 times (66.01% of the time). The reported chi-square observed was 48.89, df = 1, p < .001. (p. 18)
3. The two teachers (including the researcher—an Asian-American herself) allocated 37 turns to the 19 Asian students (39.66% of the turns) and 57 turns (60.44%) to the 12 non-Asian students. The reported chi-square observed was 19.04, df = 1, p < .001. (p. 18)

REFLECTION

Given what you now know about the chi-square statistic, how do you interpret Sato's findings? What do these results say to us as language teachers?

Comparing Two Means: Using t-Tests

The chi-square test works with frequency counts of nominal data, but often the dependent variable in a study is some form of measurement involving interval data, such as test scores. When that is the case, we often look for differences between the means of two or more groups or for differences between pre-test and post-test scores.

One widely used statistic for determining significant differences between two means is the t-test (always written with a lowercase *t*). The t-test is only used if the measurements consist of interval data (such as scores). Also, t-tests are always used to compare only two sets of data. (You can remember this rule if you think of the title of the old song, "Tea for Two.")

Another characteristic of the t-test is that it is designed to work well with small data sets. It can even be applied when there are thirty or fewer subjects in a sample. (It can also be used when there are more, but the noteworthy point is that t-tests work well with small data sets, while some other statistical procedures don't.) Since language classroom research often involves small data sets, the t-test is frequently used in our field.

When there are two different groups contributing data, the *independent samples t-test* is used. The word *independent* here is a technical term that means that the scores or measurements from one group are not influenced by (i.e., are independent of) the scores of the other group. Let's look at an example.

Suppose a secondary school principle is pleased to see that the ESL students enrolled in a sheltered social studies course seemed to do just as well on a standardized achievement test of social studies knowledge as did the native English speaking students who were enrolled in a regular (i.e., not sheltered) course. She has the test results from fifteen ESL students in the sheltered class and twelve students in the regular social studies class. She wants to determine whether the test scores of these two groups are significantly different. (Her hypothesis is that the test scores of the two groups will *not* be significantly different.)

The principal knows that there are just two groups and that the test scores consist of interval data. She also knows that the scores of the two groups are independent of one another. So, she enters the test scores of the two groups into the spreadsheet program on her laptop computer and runs an independent samples t-test. (She could also determine whether the differences are significant by using a hand calculator and computing the mean and the standard deviation for each group and then entering those data into the formula for the independent samples t-test.)

Just for your information, here is the formula for the independent samples t-test:

$$t_{obs} = \sqrt{\frac{\overline{X}_1 - \overline{X}_2}{SD_{(\overline{X}_1 - \overline{X}_2)}}}$$

In this formula, the subscripts *1* and *2* refer to the first and second group. The subscripts *e* and *c* are also used sometimes—referring to the experimental and control groups in an experiment.

ACTION

Based on what you know already, interpret the formula above. What steps are done and in what sequence? Talk through the steps with a classmate or colleague.

When there is just one group contributing two sets of data, as in the one-group pre-test post-test design, the post-test scores cannot be said to be independent of the pre-test scores since the same individuals are providing both sets of data. In that case, we use a slightly different formula for the t-test, which is called the *dependent samples t-test*. (You may also see the labels *matched-pairs t-test* or *correlated t-test*, but we will not use those terms here as they are not so common in our field.)

The dependent samples t-test is also used in another context. That is when there are two groups, but the members of the two groups are intentionally matched on some criterion. For example, adults in an experiment might be matched in terms of their scores on a language learning aptitude test administered at the beginning of the study. This step would allow us to check that the experimental group and the control group were equivalent prior to the administration of the treatment. This situation is not very common in language classroom research since in our field we seldom have the power to set up this kind of matched design as we form groups for a study.

REFLECTION

Which statistic would you choose in each of the following situations—the independent samples t-test or the dependent samples t-test?

1. A Spanish teacher has two classes of beginning students. It seems that the afternoon class members are less motivated and study less than those in the morning class. The teacher wishes to compare the midterm examination scores of the sixteen students in the afternoon class with the twelve students in the morning class to see if the differences are significant.

2. A community college composition teacher wants to determine whether there is a significant difference in the knowledge of the native English-speaking students and the non-native English-speaking students in her classes. She wants to compare their scores on a 100-point test (of grammar, usage, vocabulary, punctuation, and mechanics), which was taken by all the students in her classes.

3. A teacher in Australia is investigating the use of authentic reading materials with secondary school ESL students. She sets up a post-test only control group design in which she is able to randomly select and randomly assign students to groups. One group will read authentic materials and the other will read prepared ESL textbook materials. The teacher wonders if the writing system of the students' first language may influence their outcomes on a standardized test of English reading proficiency, so she makes sure that for every Chinese speaker in the control group, there is a Chinese speaker in the experimental group, and so on. The two groups are composed of matched pairs of students whose native languages are Arabic, Spanish, Korean, Turkish, Tagalog, Yoruba, Japanese, and Russian.

Here is an example from a study that two teachers conducted (Bailey and Saunders, 1998). The data are from university students who were lower-intermediate EFL learners in Hong Kong. Over the course of an academic year, the two teachers taught six different sections of a speaking and listening course. They wanted to know if their students had made substantial improvement in their listening skills, so they used a dependent samples t-test to see if there were significant differences in the students' scores on a video-based listening test before and after the fifteen-week course. The pre-test and post-test data are displayed in **Table 13.12**.

TABLE 13.12 EFL Students' pre-test and post-test means and standard deviations on a listening test (n = 129)

	Pre-Test	Post-Test
Mean	66.23	76.94
Standard Deviation	8.87	6.89

REFLECTION

What do the means in Table 13.12 tell you about the students' pre-test scores and their post-test scores? What do the two standard deviations say? Compare your interpretations with those of a classmate or colleague.

These teachers used a software package called SPSS, the Statistical Package for the Social Sciences, to calculate the dependent samples t-test in order to compare the pre-test and post-test means. The results showed that that the students' mean post-test scores were indeed statistically significantly higher than their mean pre-test scores ($p < .001$).

REFLECTION

How do you interpret the finding that the difference between the pre-test and post-test means was statistically significant ($p < .001$)?

There are a few things to keep in mind here. First of all, as these authors noted in their report, this was a one-group pre-test post-test design (see Chapter 4). There was no control group for comparison. So, the teachers cannot claim for certain that the English course was what made the difference in the students' listening test scores. Secondly, there was only one form of the listening test available, so the results might have been influenced by the practice effect. (Fortunately, the students didn't know at the beginning of the course that they'd be retested with the same instrument at the end of the semester.) Also, because the t-test compares the means of two sets of scores, we cannot infer that every single student made significant progress. We can only conclude that—overall—the students' post-test scores were significantly higher than their pre-test scores.

Comparing Two or More Means: One-Way Analysis of Variance (ANOVA)

The independent and dependent samples t-tests allow us to compare two means. However, there are many instances in which researchers wish to compare more than two means. In such cases, the t-test is not appropriate. One statistic that is appropriate for comparing the mean scores of two or more groups to test for significant differences is called *ANOVA*—the acronym for *analysis of variance*. The ANOVA procedure uses interval data.

In a nutshell, the ANOVA procedure asks if the differences *between* groups are greater than the differences *within* those groups. Here's why. At the beginning of experimental studies, any differences within groups can be assumed to be the result of the sampling techniques by which people were selected from the population and assigned to groups. Any differences between groups at the end of the study are assumed to be the result of the treatment(s) to which the groups are exposed (providing the researchers have controlled for possible confounding variables). So, the statistical family called ANOVA is one that calculates a ratio of the measured differences within groups and the measured differences between groups. This statistic is called the *F ratio*, after the person who invented it (a Mr. Fisher).

The ANOVA procedure can be used when there are two or more groups whose characteristics or performances are measured on interval scales. Let's take an example. Imagine that the school principal described above wanted to compare the social studies achievement test scores of three classes rather than two. The three classes she wished to compare are (1) the fifteen ESL students in the sheltered class, (2) the twelve students in the regular social studies class, and (3) ten additional students enrolled in the Advanced Placement (AP) honors class. (Advanced Placement is a system whereby secondary school students can get college credit by successfully completing a particular advanced curriculum.) The principal wants to determine whether the test scores of these three groups are significantly different.

The principal knows she cannot use the t-test because she is now planning to compare the mean scores for more than two groups, so she works with ANOVA. In particular, since there is no moderator variable in this study, she will use the *one-way ANOVA*—a name derived from the fact that the different groups are being compared in terms of scores on one variable (which social studies class they took). A visual image of this design is presented in **Figure 13.1**:

Sheltered Social Studies Course	Regular Social Studies Course	Advanced Placement Course
n = 15	n = 12	n = 10

FIGURE 13.1 A research design comparing three social studies courses

In studies that use the one-way ANOVA to compare three or more group, the authors will sometimes report on what are called *post hoc comparisons*. These are statistics that systematically calculate all the possible comparisons of the group means in the design. For example, if the one-way ANOVA used in this study detected one or more statistically significant differences in the performance of these three groups on the test, we would want to know where those statistically significant differences were located. Was it the difference between the sheltered course students' scores and those of the students in the regular social studies course? Or between the students in the regular course and the AP course? Or was it the difference between the students in the sheltered course and those in the AP course that was significant? Different post hoc procedures can be used to compare the means of the specific groups within the one-way ANOVA.

Comparing Two or More Means in Factorial Studies: Two-Way ANOVA

Another important use of ANOVA is in *factorial studies*—that is, in situations where there is an independent variable and one or more moderator variables. To illustrate, imagine that the principal noticed when she examined the social studies test scores that often the girls seemed to get higher scores than the boys. This pattern seemed to hold true in the sheltered course for non-native English-speaking students and the regular course for native speakers, as well as the advanced placement course. So, she decided to add the students' gender as a moderator variable. That is, she wanted to analyze the possible effect of gender as well as the effect of the independent variable (the sheltered course versus the regular course versus the AP class). This design is depicted in **Figure 13.2:**

	Sheltered Social Studies Course (n = 15)	Regular Social Studies Course (n = 12)	AP Social Studies Course (n = 10)
Female Students	n = 6	n = 7	n = 6
Male Students	n = 9	n = 5	n = 4

FIGURE 13.2 A research design comparing three social studies courses with gender as a moderator variable

The principal knows she cannot use a t-test because of the moderator variable as well as the three levels of the independent variable. So, she uses an adaptation of the ANOVA for factorial studies. This procedure is called a *two-way ANOVA* because the different groups are being compared in terms of two variables (the particular social studies course they took and their gender). And in cases where one or more statistically significant differences are detected by the two-way ANOVA, a post-hoc comparison can be used to pinpoint those differences.

Using the two-way ANOVA with factorial designs not only allows us to test for significant differences in the levels of the independent variable (here, the type of social studies course), as well as in the levels of the moderator variable (here, the students' gender). It also lets us determine if one group or another is favored by the various levels of the treatment. In other words, we can ask whether male or female students did particularly well (or badly) in the sheltered, the regular, or the AP social studies course.

The possibility that the moderator variable may somehow interact with the independent variable is called the *interaction effect*. Being able to detect an interaction effect is one of the benefits of using a two-way ANOVA. The comparisons between or among the levels of the independent variable are called *the main effects for A* and the comparisons between or among the levels of the moderator variable are called *the main effects for B*. These possible comparisons are depicted in **Figure 13.3:**

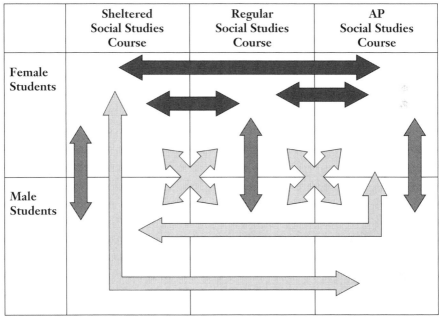

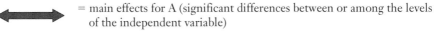 = main effects for A (significant differences between or among the levels of the independent variable)

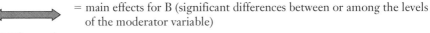 = main effects for B (significant differences between or among the levels of the moderator variable)

 = interaction effects (A × B)

FIGURE 13.3 Possible comparisons in a three-by-two ANOVA study

When you read a research report that uses two-way ANOVA, there will often be a table that shows the "main effects for A" and the "main effects for B" and any possible interaction effects that may have been found. Being able to test for possible interaction effects using the two-way ANOVA is important because we may wish to know if some materials or teaching methods or computer programs or types of curricula are advantageous (or disadvantageous) for certain types of students.

INFERENTIAL STATISTICS: SIGNIFICANT RELATIONSHIPS BETWEEN VARIABLES

Heretofore we have considered statistics that allow us to compare groups or sets of scores. Another important set of statistical procedures is used to determine whether two or more variables are related in a way that is too strong to be due to chance. The technical term for such a relationship is a *correlation*. As we saw in Chapter 4, *correlation* is the name of a research design in the ex post facto class, but it is also the name of a family of statistical procedures that are used to determine whether the relationship between two variables is significant. There are three main correlation statistics that are used in language classroom research and we will examine each in turn.

Pearson's Correlation Coefficient

The most common and most important correlation statistic is called *Pearson's product-moment correlation coefficient*, or *Pearson's correlation coefficient*, or just *Pearson's r*. (We can think of *r* as representing "relationship.") This procedure is used when the two variables under consideration are both measured on interval scales.

Imagine you want to determine the relationship between your college ESL students' knowledge of English grammar and their ability to understand academic lectures. You administer a twenty-five-point grammar test and then a listening comprehension task based on video-taped lectures filmed during the first week in two of their required introductory courses: psychology and biology. Each listening comprehension task has ten points possible, for a total of twenty points. After you score the thirty students' performance, you can mark their scores on a figure called a *scatterplot* (or *scattergram*) in which the two axes represent the two measures. For each student, a dot or an *X* is placed on the scatterplot at the point where his two scores intersect, as shown in **Figure 13.4.**

As you can see from Figure 13.4, as the students' scores on the listening task increase, so do their scores on the grammar test. This pattern is called a *positive correlation*.

When the data points in the scatterplot cluster tightly along the diagonal line, the correlation is said to be strong. As the points spread out further and the dots are not so tightly clustered around the diagonal line, the correlation is less strong. Also, sometimes there is a clear pattern but a few data points that don't quite fit. For instance, look at the asterisk in Figure 13.4 that represents the person who got eighteen points on the grammar test but only four points on the listening task. This person is apparently good at grammar but doesn't have strong listening skills (according to these two tests). A person whose data fall outside the observed correlation pattern like this is called an *outlier*.

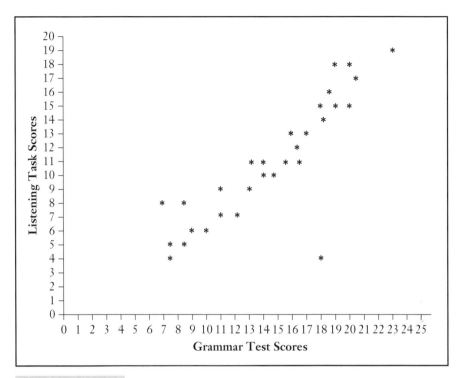

FIGURE 13.4 A scatterplot of hypothetical grammar scores and hypothetical listening task scores

There can also be *negative correlations*. In that case, as scores on one variable increase, the scores on the other variable decrease. Suppose you noticed that your language students who had broad vocabulary knowledge always seemed to finish in-class readings faster than students whose vocabulary knowledge wasn't quite as strong. You decide to investigate this phenomenon, so you correlate the relationship between your students' scores on a 100-point vocabulary test and the speed with which they can read a passage in the target language. The scatterplot for a group of thirty-five students might look like the one in **Figure 13.5**.

In Figures 13.4 and 13.5, the relationship between two variables under consideration is depicted by the points on the scatterplot. However, we often need a more concise way of representing this relationship. When the two variables are both measured on interval scales, we use the Pearson's correlation statistic to calculate a numerical index that represents the relationship. The outcome of that statistic is called the correlation coefficient. It is obtained by using this formula (the *raw score formula*) with our data:

$$\frac{N(\Sigma XY) - (\Sigma X)(\Sigma Y)}{\sqrt{[N\Sigma X^2 - (\Sigma X)^2][N\Sigma Y^2 - (\Sigma Y)^2]}}$$

This formula may seem like a monster, but if you look closely, you'll see that you have the knowledge to figure it out. You already know that *N* stands for

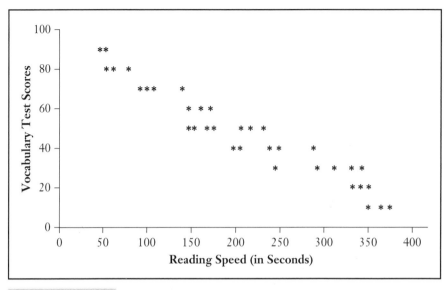

FIGURE 13.5 A hypothetical scatterplot of vocabulary knowledge and hypothetical reading speed

number and Σ tells us to sum what follows. Here X represents the score on the X-variable and Y stands for the score on the Y-variable. Remember that parentheses tell you where to start. The square brackets work like parentheses.

In order to solve this formula by hand, it is convenient to set up a table, just as we did for the chi-square test, which shows us the steps. We will use the following (hypothetical) data to illustrate the process.

X Variable: Vocabulary test scores out of 30 points possible

Y Variable: Reading speed in seconds

Table 13.13 shows the column headings and uses a small data set to illustrate:

TABLE 13.13 Steps in calculating the raw score formula for Pearson's r

ID Number	X Variable	X-squared	Y Variable	Y-squared	X times Y
1	25	625	30	900	750
2	20	400	40	1,600	800
3	12	144	50	2,500	600
4	10	100	60	3,600	600
5	8	64	70	4,900	560
Totals	75	1,333	250	13,500	3,310

When we complete the multiplication and addition we get the following setup:

$$\frac{5(3,310) - (75)(250)}{\sqrt{[5(1,333) - (75)^2][5(13,500) - (250)^2]}}$$

And continuing with the calculations, we get the following values:

$$\frac{16,550 - 18,750}{\sqrt{[6,665 - 5,625][67,500 - 62,500]}} = \frac{-2,200}{\sqrt{[1,040][5,000]}}$$

$$= \frac{-2,200}{\sqrt{5,200,000}} = \frac{-2,200}{2,280.35} = -96.65 = r$$

So our correlation coefficient is -96.65—but what does it mean? The minus sign indicates that we have a negative correlation, and the magnitude (96.65) indicates that it is a very strong correlation. When we check a table of critical values for Pearson's correlation coefficient (e.g., J. D. Brown, 1988), we see that when alpha is set at .05 and $n = 5$, the $r_{critical}$ is .8783, so we can say that this $r_{observed}$ is statistically significant. In other words, we can have confidence ($p < .05$) that our findings are stable. As vocabulary scores increase, reading speed decreases.

Spearman's Rank Order Correlation Coefficient

The second common form of correlation is called *Spearman's rank order correlation coefficient*, or *Spearman's rho*, or just *Spearman's r*. It is symbolized by the Greek symbol rho (ρ), or by the word *rho*, or sometimes by an *r* with the subscript $_s$ for Spearman's (r_s). Spearman's rank order correlation coefficient, as the name implies, is used when one or both of the variables under investigation consists of ordinal data. If one of the variables has been measured on an interval scale, those data can be rank-ordered and thus converted to ordinal data before the statistic is used.

Suppose that some of your EFL students were finalists in a regional speech contest, and that two judges ranked-ordered the finalists. You might want to know the extent to which the two judges agreed with one another in their ranking of the finalists. In this situation, you would use the formula for Spearman's r.

Likewise, if a teacher rank-ordered her students in terms of her impressions of their speaking fluency and wanted to see if there was a correlation between their speaking fluency and their TOEFL scores, she could use Spearman's r to do this. She would first rank-order the students' TOEFL scores to create ordinal data and then correlate their TOEFL ranks with their fluency ranks.

Point-Biserial Correlation Coefficient

The third main type of correlation statistic is called the *point-biserial correlation*. It is used under some circumstances when one variable is interval data and the other is *dichotomous nominal data*. This term refers to categorical (nominal) variables that have only two levels, such as right/wrong, yes/no, present/absent, and so on. The word *point* in the name of the statistic refers to which of the two nominal categories is entered in the data set, and the term *serial* refers to the series in the interval data set. The symbol that is usually used to represent this statistic is r with the subscript$_{pbi}$ (r_{pbi}). This statistic is very important in language assessment and test development, but it is not used very often in language classroom research.

Interpreting Correlation Coefficients

No matter which correlation formula you use, the correlation coefficient (the numerical index you get when you use a particular formula with your data) is interpreted in the same way. There are three main concepts represented in any correlation coefficient. These are the magnitude, statistical significance, and directionality.

The *magnitude* of a correlation coefficient is its size, which represents the strength of the association between the two variables. The *r* value is read as a decimal approaching the absolute value of the whole number 1. (Hence, a correlation coefficient of .99 is "stronger than" one of .75) A correlation coefficient of r = 1.00 would be a "perfect" correlation and the dots in the scatterplot would line up perfectly on the diagonal line.

As was the case in the discussion of significant difference studies, we want to know whether the findings of a correlation study are consistent and trustworthy. We want to guard against the possibility that the outcome may be in error. So, as we did before, we check to see if the correlation coefficient we obtain is statistically significant. We do this either by checking the value of $r_{observed}$ against the value of $r_{critical}$ in the table of critical values, or—if we are using a software package to compute the statistic for us—by checking the value of p (probability) that the computer program produces.

Correlation coefficients also have direction. *Directionality* refers to the fact that correlations can be either positive or negative, as we saw in Figures 13.4 and 13.5, respectively. If a correlation coefficient is negative, that fact is indicated by a minus sign in front of the r value, as in "r = $-.76$, p < 0.05." If a correlation is positive, no minus sign is used (e.g., "r = .76, p < .05").

REFLECTION

How do you interpret the following statements?

1. "... and we found that r = .92, p < 0.001. ..."
2. "... but in this case, r = $-.84$, p < 0.01. ..."
3. "... and it revealed that r = .24, p > .05. ..."

Due to space constraints, we will not present the formulae for the Spearman's rank order correlation or the point-biserial correlation statistics here. However, you can find them in many books in our field (see, e.g., Bailey, 1998b; J. D. Brown, 1988; 2005; Brown and Rodgers, 2002; and Hatch and Lazaraton, 1991).

REFLECTION

What do you think it means if a researcher reports that for a particular correlation coefficient "$p < .01$"?

USING TECHNOLOGICAL TOOLS TO ANALYZE QUANTITATIVE DATA

Computer technology has greatly eased the burden and increased the speed of doing quantitative analyses. For example, the search function in word-processing programs can help you do frequency counts for key words if you are looking for patterns in field notes, or for particular linguistic forms in transcripts. Spreadsheet programs, such as Excel in the Microsoft Office program, will compute the descriptive statistics and many of the most commonly used inferential statistics for you. There are also several Web sites that offer you free access to tools for computing the most frequently used statistical formulae.

Of course, learning to use these procedures takes time and a certain amount of effort. Why should we bother to learn to use these technological tools? First, computer analyses greatly increase the speed of our computations—especially if you are working with a complicated formula, like ANOVA, or with large data sets. Secondly, the use of computer programs to calculate a formula greatly increases the accuracy of your computations. The likelihood of making an error on a hand calculator, for instance, is greatly reduced by the computer's systematic programming.

Likewise, computer programs make it easy to check a data set, either in a printout or on screen, before you run the formula. Using a computer is more convenient than using a calculator to add new data if cases are added to the data set and easier to correct data if errors are detected. In addition, it is convenient to do new analyses with the same data set as new variables of interest emerge or as you receive feedback and suggestions about how to improve your analyses. Various computer programs are also helpful in creating professional looking tables, graphs, and figures to represent your data.

Finally, there are the practical factors of storage and transportation. Computer technology makes it relatively convenient to store records and back-up sets of data. Once they have been stored, those data are easily transportable, whether physically or electronically. In the form of e-mail attachments, quantitative data can easily be "shipped" to a colleague in a spreadsheet just as qualitative data can easily be sent as Word documents.

QUALITY CONTROL ISSUES IN QUANTITATIVE ANALYSES

There are several issues to keep in mind as we calculate and interpret quantitative analyses. The concern that is first and foremost is whether the right statistical procedure has been chosen. **Table 13.14** below provides a summary of the issues that influence a decision about what sort of statistic to use when you are looking for significant differences between or among groups. For instance, having posed a hypothesis or research question about significant differences, the next concern is what type of data is being compared. We have simplified this initial presentation to involve just interval-scale measurements and frequency counts. (There are other statistics that determine, for instance, significant differences between groups where the dependent variable is based on ordinal data.)

These are just a few of the most basic statistical tests of significant differences. A good statistics course will teach you much more about how to analyze quantitative data to test various kinds of hypotheses and answer research questions. However, the procedures discussed here are often used in language classroom research and you are likely to come across them in your reading of the research literature in our field.

The choice of the right statistic to use is just as important in correlation studies. The characteristics of the three correlation statistics we have studied are summarized in **Table 13.15**. Once again, the choice of formula depends on the type of data involved.

TABLE 13.14 Commonly used statistical tests of significant differences

Type of Data	Number of Groups	Moderator Variable	Sample Size	Matched Scores	Statistical Test
Interval Measure	2	No	Small	No	Independent Samples t-Test
Interval Measure	2	No	Small	Yes	Dependent Samples t-Test
Interval Measure	2 or more	No	Large	No	One-Way ANOVA
Interval Measure	4 or more	Yes	Large	No	Two-Way ANOVA
Frequency Data	2 or more	No		No	One-Way Chi-Square
Frequency Data	4 or more	Yes		No	Two-Way Chi-Square

TABLE 13.15 Types of data involved in three major correlation coefficients

Correlation Procedure	Symbol(s)	Types of Data Involved
Pearson's product-moment correlation coefficient	r	Two sets of interval data
Spearman's rank order correlation coefficient	ρ or r_s or *rho*	Two sets of ordinal data (or one set of interval data and one set of ordinal data)
Point-biserial correlation coefficient	r_{pbi}	One set of interval data and one set of dichotomous nominal data

REFLECTION

For each of the following situations, decide which correlation statistic is called for: Pearson's r, Spearman's r, or the point-biserial correlation coefficient.

1. A group of secondary school French students are finalists in an essay contest, and the winner will receive a scholarship. Two judges independently rank-order the students' essays. Their combined rankings will determine who wins the scholarship. The students' teachers wish to determine whether there is a clear relationship between the two judges' rankings.

2. A secondary school French teacher wishes to see if there is a significant relationship between her intermediate students' scores on a 100-point French vocabulary test she designed and on a standardized French reading test.

3. A researcher is investigating American university students' tolerance for the accentedness of non-native speaking content-area professors. She has the students rate tape-recorded samples of several non-native speaking professors reading the instructions for an assignment. The students rate the speech samples on a scale of 1 to 30, using scale descriptors. The students also must say *yes* or *no* in response to the question, "Should this professor be hired to teach introductory courses in his or her field at this university?" The researcher wants to determine the relationship between the ratings on the thirty-point interval scale and the *yes/no* votes for employment.

This chapter has described just a few of the inferential statistics that are commonly used in language classroom research, and for even these few, we have just presented introductory concepts. If you would like to do some substantial quantitative analyses, we recommend that you take an introductory course, but there are also several good books that you can consult to help you make the right choices. (See the Suggestions for Further Reading at the end of this chapter.)

A SAMPLE STUDY

In Israel, an EFL context, a researcher named Bejarano (1987) wanted to see which of three different instructional methods would be most effective. The three methods were called (1) discussion groups, (2) student teams, and (3) the whole-class method. (In her paper, Bejarano operationally defines these terms.) We will use some information from this study to reinforce the concepts introduced in this chapter.

There were eighteen teachers and a total of 665 third-year secondary school students involved in this study. The teachers were randomly assigned to use one of the three teaching methods. This was a process-product study in the sense that it included an observational component: "Three trained observers visited every class twice during the experimental period" (ibid., p. 491).

The dependent variable in the study was a test that was given twice—once as a pre-test and once as a post-test. Bejarano wanted to know whether the difference in the means of the control group (the whole-class group) and the two experimental groups (the discussion groups and the student teams) was a big enough difference to conclude that one or both of the treatments had been effective. **Table 13.16** shows some results of the main descriptive statistics in Bejarano's research project:

TABLE 13.16   Descriptive statistics for pre-test and post-test scores (total test) of students in three teaching situations (adapted from Bejarano, 1987, p. 492)

	Discussion Groups (n = 229)		Student Teams (n = 198)		Whole Class (n = 238)	
	Pre-Test	Post-Test	Pre-Test	Post-Test	Pre-Test	Post-Test
Mean	50.52	57.28	53.94	61.39	57.58	62.45
Standard Deviation	19.59	20.87	19.94	21.35	17.49	18.31

As you can see from Table 13.16, all three groups improved between the pre-test and the post-test. (Unfortunately, the researcher did not report how many points there were on the total test, so we cannot tell what these mean scores indicate in any absolute sense—only what they suggest in comparison to one another.)

We can see from the descriptive statistics in Table 13.16 that the students in the whole-class group started out the highest (their mean pre-test scores) and ended up the highest (their mean post-test scores). But did they make the most progress? Answering that question shows the benefit of a pre-test post-test design like the one Bejarano used. Having pre- and post-test data allows us to calculate the groups' *gain scores*—the difference between their performances on the pre-test and the post-test.

Use the data in Table 13.16 to answer the following questions:

1. Looking just at the pre-test means, which group started out with the lowest scores? Which group started out with the highest scores?
2. Looking just at the post-test means, which group ended up with the lowest scores? Which group ended up with the highest scores?
3. Compare the standard deviations for the three groups. Which group showed the least variation in its pre-test scores? Which group showed the least variation in its post-test scores?

Gain scores can be interpreted as a measure of students' progress between the pre-test and the post-test. But keep in mind that sometimes students' scores actually decrease over time. When that happens, we say that the gain scores are negative. The gain scores for the three groups in Bejarano's study are presented in **Table 13.17.**

Use the data in Table 13.17 to answer the following questions:

1. Which group or groups improved the most? (Compare the gain scores for the three groups.)
2. Are the differences between the pre- and post-test scores big enough to say that all three groups made substantial progress?

Bejarano's report also provided some data about how well the students did on the various subtests. One set of data that is particularly interesting consists of the three groups' listening subtest scores. These are shown in **Table 13.18.** (The researcher reports that there was a range of 0 to 57 points in these scores, but she does not tell us the range for each group or the total points possible.)

TABLE 13.17 Gain scores of students in three teaching situations (adapted from Bejarano, 1987, p. 492)

	Discussion Groups (n = 229)		Student Teams (n = 198)		Whole Class (n = 238)	
	Pre-Test	Post-Test	Pre-Test	Post-Test	Pre-Test	Post-Test
Mean	50.52	57.28	53.94	61.39	57.58	62.45
Gain Score	6.76		7.45		4.87	

TABLE 13.18 Descriptive statistics for pre-test and post-test scores (listening subtest) of students in three teaching situations (adapted from Bejarano, 1987, p. 492)

	Discussion Groups		Student Teams		Whole Class	
	Pre-Test	Post-Test	Pre-Test	Post-Test	Pre-Test	Post-Test
Mean	31.51	36.00	34.46	38.80	36.74	38.97
Standard Deviation	11.78	12.91	11.83	13.02	10.47	11.15
Gain Scores						

REFLECTION

Use the data in Table 13.18 to answer the following questions:

1. Looking just at the pre-test means, which group started out the lowest scores? Which group started out with the highest scores?
2. Looking just at the post-test means, which group ended up with the lowest scores? Which group ended up with the highest scores?

ACTION

Now calculate the gain scores on the listening subtest for these three groups. Fill in the blanks in the row labeled "Gain Scores" in Table 13.18. Which group(s) made the greatest improvement?

Bejarano (1987, p. 492) reported the following findings regarding the data presented in Table 13.16 and Table 13.18, respectively:

Pupils in the discussion group had greater gains than those in the whole-class situation on the total test: $F (1, 465) = 4.23$ ($p < .05$).

Pupils in the discussion group classes had greater gains than those in the whole-class situation on the listening subtest: $F (1, 465) = 11.99$ ($p < .001$).

If you were reading Bejarano's report, how would you interpret these statements? They are written in a kind of code or shorthand that is familiar to people who have studied statistics but can be quite daunting to people who have not. Let's crack the code.

First of all, what does F represent in these claims? As noted above, F stands for the F Ratio—the ratio we get when we divide the difference between the groups by the difference within the groups. The F value reported here is the $F_{observed}$—that is, the value of the statistic that Bejarano obtained when she put her data into the computer program that calculates Analysis of Variance. (Computing ANOVA is a very long and complicated process. People almost always do it with a computer instead of by hand because there are so many chances for error if you use a calculator.) According to the two statements above, the F values Bejarano obtained were 4.23 for the difference on the whole test and 11.99 for the difference on the listening subtest. But what do these F values mean? In a nutshell, if the value of F greatly exceeds the whole number 1, the differences between groups were greater than the differences within the groups.

Once again, to determine the statistical significance of the F ratio, we will compare the observed value of the statistic with the critical values printed in a particular statistical table (and embedded in the computer's statistical program). But when you consult the table of critical values for Analysis of Variance, you need to have two different values in mind for degrees of freedom in order to locate $F_{critical}$. The two statements above both include the parenthetic statement (1, 465)—and, as you may have guessed, these values represent degrees of freedom. What do they mean? The 1 comes from the fact that two groups were being compared (the discussion group context and the whole-class format). The 1 in the parentheses is the number of groups in the comparison, minus one. This term is often represented by K − 1, where K = the number of groups.

What about the other value reported in these findings, that is, 465? It represents the number of subjects minus the number of groups (N − K, where N = the number of subjects). When we check Bejarano's report, we see that there were 229 students in the discussion group format and 238 in whole class format. When we add these two numbers we get 467—the value of N in this case. And when we subtract N − K, we get 465.

ACTION

Interpret this paraphrase of one result from Bejarano's report (1987):

Pupils in the student teams group had greater gains than those in the whole-class situation on the total test: $F(1, 434) = 6.27$ ($p < .05$).

Look inside the parentheses. Where did the number "1" come from? Where did the number "434" come from? (Hint: There were 198 students in the student teams format and 238 students in the whole class format.) (p. 492)

Once again, in this statement, the *1* in the phrase "F (1, 434)" tells us that the $F_{observed}$ here is based on a comparison of two groups—the student teams group and the whole class group (2 − 1 = 1). The number 434 tells us that scores from 436 students were involved in these two groups, because 2 (the number of groups) added to 434 in the phrase above is 436. Knowing the degrees of freedom for the number of groups and the number of subjects enables us to check the critical values table or interpret a computer printout. Since the $F_{observed}$ was much greater than the $F_{critical}$, Bejarano was able to conclude that her findings were statistically significant (p < .05).

We have only reported a few of Bejarano's findings here in order to illustrate some of the concepts associated with descriptive statistics and with the inferential statistic called ANOVA. We recommend you read the full article and we hope that you feel empowered to interpret many statistical findings in this and other research reports. But please keep in mind that we have only provided an introduction to some of the statistical procedures that are commonly used in language classroom research. There are many others to learn about.

PAYOFFS AND PITFALLS

There are several payoffs associated with analyzing quantitative data. The first is that this approach to investigation is widely used around the world and is understood by researchers trained in the psychometric tradition. Once you are familiar with the various statistics and how to interpret them, you will find that you can understand (well-written) quantitative research articles in professional books and journals.

The second is that, for better or for worse, people often find statistical results convincing. (This fact is unfortunate because statistics can be misused. Newspaper reports are notorious for providing partial data and/or the results of inappropriate statistical procedures. They can get away with such shoddy practices because interpreting statistical evidence is so foreign to most people.)

Another benefit of quantitative analyses is that they are compact. Reporting the mean and the standard deviation for a group of learners speaks volumes to those who can interpret descriptive statistics, so a great deal of information can be conveyed in a small space—an important economical fact for the publishers of books and print-based journals. For example, look back at the sample study in Chapter 9, where the authors (Lynch and Maclean, 2000) characterized two students, Alicia and Daniela, very succinctly in terms of their scores on the TOEFL, the IELTS, and a dictation.

In addition, regardless of the approach you choose—psychometric, naturalistic, or action research—numerical results are informative. We will return to this concept in Chapter 15, where we consider *mixed methods studies*—those that involve both quantitative and qualitative data analyses.

As usual, the pitfalls are related to the payoffs. The first is that while people trained in interpreting statistics can understand quantitative analyses, people who lack this kind of experience and training may find statistical results confusing, or even uninterpretable. No matter what statistically significant differences or statistically significant correlations you may have found, it is important to report your findings in clear prose, with ample explication, so that readers unfamiliar with statistical procedures and the logic of hypothesis testing can still benefit from your findings.

Also, while statistical results often seem impressive and convincing, they can be easily misused. For example, what does it mean if a serious person in a white lab coat in a TV advertisement says, "No toothpaste has been found to be more effective than Shiny-White toothpaste"? This statement can be interpreted in at least three ways:

1. Research has been conducted that found no other toothpaste was more effective than Shiny-White, because Shiny-White performed the same as the other brands.

2. In the research that was conducted, Shiny-White scored lower than the others but the difference was not statistically significantly different.

3. No research has been conducted comparing Shiny-White to other brands of toothpaste—hence, no other toothpaste has been shown to be more effective.

It is this kind of multiplicity and ambiguity of interpretation that makes many people mistrust statistics.

REFLECTION

Watch for examples in the popular press where statistics are used to support a certain point of view. Do you find the examples credible? Why or why not?

Another issue is that almost all of the inferential statistics are based on assumptions about the data—assumptions that may not be met in language classroom research. For example, as we noted above, the independent samples t-test can only be used to compare the means of two groups on an interval scale when the two groups' scores are independent of (not influenced by) each other. Another example is found with the chi-square test. In cases where df = 1 (as in Sato's [1982] data), a variation of the chi-square statistic called *Yates' correction for continuity*, or *Yates' correction factor*, must be used, though some researchers have skipped this step. Likewise, in working with Pearson's correlation coefficient, the measures on the two variables being correlated must meet the following assumptions (Hatch and Lazaraton, 1991, pp. 549–550):

1. The two data sets being correlated are interval in nature.

2. The measures have equal reliability (i.e., they have been shown to be consistent).

3. The two data sets being correlated are independent.

4. Using data from a restricted range of scores (e.g., using data from just intermediate learners without including data from beginners or advanced students) may mask a correlation (Jaeger, 1993, p. 69).

Given these assumptions, we must proceed with caution in using and interpreting such analyses. We recommend that you read further and take a good basic course in statistics.

Finally, let us return to the metaphor we used at the beginning of this chapter. Don't let yourself get overwhelmed by all this mathematical terminology! Learning to interpret and to compute statistics is very much like learning a new language when you enter a new culture. There is a great deal of vocabulary to be learned, and there are ordering rules to follow (just like syntax) as you calculate the formulae. There are also cultural values associated with statistical logic. We have only scratched the surface of this complex and fascinating new culture, but we hope the ideas presented here will help you be a more confident consumer of quantitative analyses and encourage you to try some quantitative procedures (as appropriate) with your own data.

QUESTIONS AND TASKS

1. Read a research report on a topic that interests you that uses quantitative data. Does it incorporate any of the procedures discussed in this chapter? If so, check your ability to interpret the information provided about critical values, observed values, the degrees of freedom, and the probability levels.

2. In the study you read, check to see if the author(s) used the appropriate statistic. Identify (1) the hypothesis being tested, (2) the type of data collected, (3) the number of groups, (4) the presence or absence of a moderator variable, and so on.

3. Look at the data in Table 13.5 about the enrollment patterns (French = 250, Spanish = 200 Ss, and German = 150 Ss). Using the layout in Table 13.7, calculate the value of chi-square observed.

4. Compare your results to the critical values given in Table 13.8. Are the results statistically significant? How do you interpret your findings?

5. Draw a scatterplot of the data in Table 13.13.

6. Here is another statement from Bejarano's report. How would you interpret it—particularly the mathematical parts?

> Pupils in the student teams group had greater gains than those in the whole-class situation on the listening subtest: $F(1, 434) = 8.60$ $(p < .005)$.

SUGGESTIONS FOR FURTHER READING

There are many excellent statistics books and books that introduce novice researchers to reading quantitative analyses. For instance, we recommend the second edition of Jaeger's (1993) *Statistics: A Spectator Sport*, though his examples are from general education rather than language teaching. J. D. Brown (1988) and Perry (2005) also provide good introductions to people who want to learn about interpreting statistics. Their examples come from the field of language teaching and applied linguistics.

To learn to actually calculate the various statistics, we recommend Shavelson (1981; 1996) and Hatch and Lazaraton (1991). For guidelines on using SPSS with data from applied linguistics studies, see Dörnyei (2007). J. D. Brown (2005) gives clear guidance on computing basic statistics using Excel with data from language tests.

Qualitative Data Analysis

I have a rule of thumb for judging the value of a piece of art. Does it give me energy, or take energy away? When I staggered out of United 93, *this rule had lost traction. I realised I had spent most of the screening crouching forward half out of my seat, with my hand clamped around my jaw. Something in me had been violently shifted off centre. . . . I'm [left with] the same old haunting question: why do stories matter so terribly to us that we will offer ourselves up to, and later be grateful for an experience that we know is going to fill us with grief and despair?*
(Garner, 2006, p. 62)

INTRODUCTION AND OVERVIEW

In this chapter, we look at techniques for qualitative data analysis. Whereas quantitative data have to do with measuring, qualitative data have to do with meanings. Qualitative data have an immediacy and ways of touching us that quantitative data typically do not, as the reaction by Helen Garner to the dramatized documentary *United 93* so vividly attests. We begin the chapter by defining qualitative data. We then look at specific techniques for finding patterns through meaning condensation and grounded analysis. We then briefly compare discourse analysis, conversational analysis, and interaction analysis before considering the use of technology in qualitative data analysis. We examine some quality control issues in doing qualitative analyses. As usual, the chapter ends with the summary of a sample study and a discussion of the pitfalls and payoffs of this approach to analyzing data.

What Is/Are Qualitative Data?

Both quantitative and qualitative data are important in language classroom research, but when it comes to making sense of research, qualitative data come first. In saying this, we mean that while qualitative data can be quantified, all quantitative research must ultimately be referenced against the qualitative sources that gave rise to them in the first place. For example, a researcher investigating the 'good language learner' might collect test scores from a sample of secondary school language learners. 'Good learners' might be operationally defined as those students who scored better than two standard deviations above the mean of the sample as a whole. In order for the study to have any value, the researcher would then need to identify what it was that gave rise to the superior scores in the first place. (Did these students devote more time to language study? Did they attempt to activate their language out of class? Did they use a greater range of learning strategies?) Answers to these questions can only be determined through the analysis of qualitative data: learner diaries, focused interviews, responses to open-ended items on questionnaires, and so on.

In the subheading to this section of the chapter, we use both the singular and plural form of the verb *to be* separated by a backslash. We do so to reflect a useful distinction drawn by Holliday (2002), who suggests that quantitative research consists of counting occurrences across large populations:

> Data [therefore] are essentially plural—the number of Ford or Peugot cars sold, a number of questionnaire responses, or the number of times a teacher asks a question in class. Qualitative data is conceived very differently. It is what happens in a particular social setting—in a particular place or amongst a particular group of people. I use the word 'data' as an uncountable noun—e.g. 'data is' instead of 'data are'. The uncountable singular form is in popular use but considered less correct by many qualitative as well as quantitative researchers. I use the uncountable form because to me it signifies a *body of experience*. This is a conceptual break from quantitative research which sees data as a number of items. (p. 69)

Qualitative data in second language classroom research can take many forms, including the following:

- Narrative accounts of a typical school day by a teacher or a student
- Observers' notes about lessons
- Maps showing the position(s) of the participants and furniture
- Transcripts of lessons
- Lesson plans and teachers' notes
- Open-ended questionnaire responses
- Video or audio recordings of classroom interaction
- Stimulated recall responses from students or teachers based on viewing video recordings of lessons

- Focused interview protocols
- Entries in teachers' or learners' diaries
- Copies of students' work

There is also a type of information called archival data—existing (i.e., archived) records that may shed light on an investigation. In language classroom research, these can include enrollment data, course syllabi and descriptions, school policy statements, memos to parents, and so on.

The basis of all these data sources is language. As Freeman (1996b) notes in his coda to a collection of research studies into teacher education:

> Language provides the pivotal link in data collection between the unseen mental worlds of the participants and the public world of the research process. In the study of teacher knowledge and the cognitive processes that are part of teaching, this issue is a central one since language is always used to express—and to represent—thought. Thus, the ways in which language data come about in a particular study are intimately connected to the purposes of the study; there is a crucial link between means and ends. (p. 367)

Table 14.1 provides Freeman's useful synthesis of issues in data collection and analysis.

Although it is not exhaustive, Table 14.1 illustrates the richness and diversity of qualitative data sources and forms of analysis. The data can be recorded in written, tape-recorded, or videotaped form. They can provide insider (emic) or outsider (etic) perspectives, and interpretation can be bottom-up (grounded) or top-down (guided).

All qualitative data can be quantified in some way. In other words, things can be counted in qualitative data. In fact, there is almost no limit to the things that can be counted in qualitative data sets. Consider a lesson transcript. Here is a nonexhaustive list of some of the things that can be quantified:

- The number of display questions versus the number of referential questions
- The number of times errors are corrected
- The amount of time spent focusing on form versus the amount of time spent focusing on meaning
- The number of positive evaluations by the teacher versus the number of negative evaluations
- The amount of time the target language is used during a lesson
- The amount of time spent 'on task' versus the amount of time spent 'off task'
- The length of 'wait time' a teacher allows between asking a question and requiring a response
- The amount of time spent on drill and reproductive language work versus the amount of time spent on communicative and creative language work

TABLE 14.1 Summary of research methodology in the study of teacher learning (adapted from Freeman, 1996b, p. 368)

| How are the data gathered? | | How are the data analyzed? | | |
Data source	Gathering	Analysis stance	Analysis process	Analysis categories
Observation/ field notes Interviews	Time "real" versus ex post facto collection	What is the researcher's relationship to the study?	How are data linked to analysis?	How is the interpretation of the data arrived at and by whom?
Documentary analysis	Relation of researcher to data	Participatory	Linear/ Iterative	Emic
Stimulated recall (videotape)	Emic			Grounded
Classroom discourse language data (audiotape)	Self-generated Collaborative Documentary	Collaborative		Negotiated Guided
Survey data / questionnaire	Etic	Declaratory		A priori Etic

- The percentage of time spent on listening, speaking, reading, and/or writing
- Whether (and if so when) the teacher responds to the code or to the message in a student's utterance
- Whether students' responses are extended or restricted to a single word, clause, or sentence
- The number of opportunities that students take to initiate the discourse

REFLECTION

What are some of the things that could be counted in the following data sets? Why might a researcher want to count those particular things?

- A narrative account of a typical school day by a teacher or a student
- Observers' notes on a lesson
- Lesson plans and teachers' notes

- Open-ended questionnaire responses
- Stimulated recall responses from students or teachers based on viewing a video of a lesson
- Focused interview protocols
- Teachers' or learners' diaries
- Copies of students' work

WORKING WITH QUALITATIVE DATA

Analyzing qualitative data is an iterative process of reading, thinking, rereading, posing questions, searching through the records, and trying to find patterns. Some authors have described the process as *sifting* or *combing* or *searching*. It is somewhat intuitive and involves a number of mental processes that are rather difficult to explain. In this section, we will describe ways that we and other researchers have worked with qualitative data from language classrooms.

Finding Patterns in the Data

When people write about analyzing qualitative data, they often say that they look for patterns. But how does a researcher find patterns in a data set?

One way is to look for repeated themes or *key words*. In this procedure, the data are scanned for words or phrases that appear to be significant. These are highlighted. Related concepts are then grouped together, given a superordinate heading, and then tabulated. Here is an example from an unpublished language learning diary by one of the authors.

> I tried **creating little dialogs** from the phrases I was trying to learn in order to give them some context, but didn't get very far. I don't even know how to say 'yes'. From what I know of other Asian languages, I guess there won't be a single word as there is in English. (Nunan's diary entry, December 5, 2002)
>
> Trying the **'creative construction'** technique, I come up with the following question form for 'what is this?' 'matyeh hei ni?' I bet it's wrong. I'll check with a native speaker before I try to learn it. (Nunan's diary entry, November 11, 2002)
>
> Superordinate heading: Independent learning strategy
> dialog creation
> creative construction

Another way to find patterns is to look for parallel or connected comments. For example, in her analysis of eleven diary studies, Bailey (1983b) noticed that comments related to competitiveness often appeared with remarks about anxiety.

After combing through a great deal of qualitative data, she posited a relationship between competitiveness and anxiety among adult second language learners. Looking for metaphoric uses of language can also help you find patterns in qualitative data. In Bailey's (1983b) study of competitiveness and anxiety, she found language associated with racing imagery. Phrases such as *falling behind* and *can't keep up the pace* were associated with anxiety-inducing episodes in the diary data.

Sometimes there are natural divisions or stages in longitudinal data. For example, in a diary study about learning Spanish at a language school in Mexico, Campbell (1996) provides journal excerpts identified by the particular week in the two-month course. In Schmidt and Frota's (1986) diary study of Schmidt's learning Portuguese, there were three periods that emerged in the data, which were kept over a period of twenty-two weeks. When Schmidt first went to Brazil, he was not taking a Portuguese class and he had no interaction in Portuguese in the environment. Then there was a period of time when he was taking a Portuguese course as well as interacting with Portuguese speakers outside of class. Later the class ended and he continued learning only through interaction with native speakers.

Qualitative researchers also look for turning points and highly salient events that seem important but that may not be part of a pattern. For instance, Bailey (1981) describes a heated discussion after a French test that the students were very angry about and how that argument seemed to clear the mounting tension in the class. Similarly, in his study of anxiety among sixteen- and seventeen-year-old ESL students in residential school in Singapore, Hilleson (1996) used a range of qualitative data to track the students' experiences and feelings. He notes an important turning point:

> Students at all proficiency levels reported an almost magical transformation when they commenced the second term (about four months after beginning the course). Many had been away on holiday, some in a non-English-speaking environment, but they all remarked on the difference in their attitude after the break. They felt as if a barrier had been lifted and suddenly their confidence had returned. . . . Students were more relaxed after the break because the demands they were making on themselves were more realistic. (pp. 273–274)

It is also important to look for contrasts, inconsistencies and/or unanswered questions. For example, Bailey (1984) conducted a study of the classroom communication problems of international teaching assistants (TAs) who were teaching math and science courses at a U. S. university in English—their second language. She made audio recordings and handwritten field notes while she observed twelve native speaking and twelve non-native speaking TAs over the course of a ten-week semester. Through a series of qualitative analytical procedures, Bailey was able to identify five types of teaching styles exhibited by twenty-one of these TAs: (1) inspiring cheerleaders, (2) entertaining allies, (3) knowledgeable helpers and casual friends, (4) mechanical problem solvers, and (5) active but unintelligible TAs. But there were three TAs who did not quite fit among the types. For example, one of the native-speaking math TAs was a casual friend but not a knowledgeable helper to his students since he himself was unable to do their math homework problems. Such anomalies help to clarify strengths and problems in categorization systems.

Another way to organize your data analysis procedures is to contrast the viewpoints of various constituencies in the culture you are studying. For instance, Block (1996) contrasted students' interpretations of EFL lessons in Spain with the teacher's intended purposes. Harrison (1996) provides extensive quotes from both regional inspectors and EFL teachers in the Sultanate of Oman in analyzing the outcomes of a curriculum renewal project.

Meaning Condensation

Working with qualitative data is a different matter from using the kinds of quantitative analytical procedures described in Chapter 14. When we are analyzing numerical data, we can use mathematical procedures to calculate the mean, the standard deviation, and the other descriptive statistics that concisely characterize the sample in a study. The parallel activity in analyzing qualitative data is a major challenge: reducing large amounts of text (whether spoken, written, or graphic) to manageable proportions that allow for patterns in the data to emerge.

One way to accomplish this data reduction is through a technique known as *meaning condensation*, which involves abridging free-form questionnaire responses, interview transcripts, observers' field notes, and so on into shorter formulations. Long statements are compressed into briefer statements in which the main sense of what is said is rephrased in a few words. Meaning condensation thus involves a reduction of large quantities of text into briefer, more succinct formulations. This process results in condensed statements that are then subjected to further analysis.

Here is an example of a condensed narrative. It was constructed from a life-history interview with a second language learner called 'Gloria' (a pseudonym). In this study, Gloria was identified as a "good language learner" because she had received a grade of A on the Use of English exam at the end of high school. Her retrospective story was part of an investigation into the lifelong language learning experiences of fifty language learners (Nunan, 2007b). The interview ran to thousands of words. The condensed narrative is just over a thousand words.

A Condensed Narrative: The Case of Gloria

I first encountered English in kindergarten. I really don't remember if I ever heard it before then. I remember that the first thing we learned was the alphabet—A, B, C, A is for apple, that kind of thing. It was nothing special, just one more subject. But I didn't think it was a very important subject.

I don't remember whether my primary school was supposed to be Chinese- or English-medium. I don't think it was ever said. All subjects were taught in Chinese, even English. The main focus of the lessons was vocabulary and simple conversations. *Hello, I'm Gloria. Who are you?*—that sort of thing. I remember that it was pretty boring. We had a book, and had to follow along as the teacher read. Now and then, he'd ask us to spell words. Most of the time in primary school was spent copying stuff out. It didn't matter what the subject was. In English class, the teacher would give you a sentence and tell you to write it out several times.

I had no contact with English at all out of class, unless you consider doing English homework as contact. Extra-curricular activities after school were mainly sports. There was nothing in English.

When I got to years 5 and 6, I still didn't think that English was very important. We prepared for the Academic Aptitude Test, but the emphasis was on Chinese and mathematics. We didn't have any special preparation for English or extra homework, so I didn't think that it was important. I remember that the focus in class was on grammar—memorizing tenses and that sort of thing.

After primary school, I went to an English-medium secondary school. In the beginning, what that meant was that for many subjects the textbook was in English. In class, the teachers spoke Chinese because their job was to make sure we understood, and the best way to do that was through Chinese.

Although we had a School English Society, my friends and I never thought of joining it on our own initiative. We thought more about what sports we would play when we joined the Sports Club. English wasn't an activity that you could use or have fun with, it was a subject that you had to study and learn.

When I started in high school, I had more contact with English because it was an English-medium school and the teacher more-or-less had to speak English. Then my view of English began to change. I began to see that in addition to being a subject to be studied, it could also be used as a tool to study other subjects. For example, I studied history, and classes were conducted in English, so English became more important. In most classes the teachers used a mixture of Cantonese and English—probably fifty-fifty. There was a lot of switching between languages. Some people say this is bad, but the main thing is that the teachers use language that we can understand. What's the point of teaching a perfect lesson in English if we can't understand? So Chinese played an important part, even in English class.

In senior high school, the most important influences were the public examinations and preparing for them. English was now more important than other subjects because I needed it to learn the other subjects. Also, the English exams were different. In the past, you only had to know grammar and vocabulary, but now you needed a much deeper understanding because you were tested on listening and speaking. The public exams completely dominated my life because my future depended on getting good results, and getting good results required good English. Everything we did was based on the exams. What it tested, we learned!

But I also started to see the importance of English out of class. I realized that I needed the language if I wanted to communicate with other people. When I was young, it never occurred to me that I would talk with a foreigner in English. The teacher also stressed the importance of using English out of class. She encouraged us to watch English television and subscribe to English language newspapers. But I hardly ever did these things, I was too lazy. I couldn't see how they would help me pass the public examination. English was important because of the exams. Sometimes I would read a newspaper if it was required for an assignment, but that's all.

Then in form seven, I had an experience that changed my attitude. I took a summer job at Philips and because it was on Hong Kong Island, I came into contact with a lot of foreigners. I was the only one in the store who could speak much English at all, and it made me feel superior. But speaking with foreigners made me realize my deficiencies. I sometimes had to get them to repeat three or four times before I could understand. And I noticed that the English that foreigners spoke was different from the English that Chinese people spoke. This experience made me realize that I really did need to learn English more wholeheartedly, that I would have a need to communicate with other people one day, and that English is really very important.

Now that I'm at university, I think of English in a very different way from when I was in school. I don't have the pressure of an English exam hanging over me, and I use English, not because I have to take an exam, but because it's the medium of communication. Many of my lecturers are foreigners, so if I talk to them I have to use English. You have to write, speak and think in English. It's part of daily life. Also, if you're good at English you feel superior, and other people look at you as though you're superior. One of the differences between English and other subjects, such as geography, is that I don't look at people who are good at geography as that smart, necessarily, but I think of someone who is fluent in English as very smart.

REFLECTION

What patterns/insights occur to you as you read the condensed narrative account of Gloria's English learning history?

Insights that came to Nunan (2007b) as he created and reflected on the condensed narratives included the following: 'Good' language learners such as Gloria (1) reflect on their experiences as language users and use these reflections as the basis for further learning; (2) see language as a tool for communicating rather than as a body of content to be memorized; and (3) integrate inside-the-classroom learning opportunities with outside-the-classroom opportunities to activate their language. Nunan also noted that (4) language learning and attitudes towards language learning are unstable and change over time. In addition, (5) collecting data from informants about events that occurred over a prolonged period revealed that as learners accumulated experiences and developed their proficiency, their beliefs and attitudes changed. Finally, from looking at many such life histories, (6) it is clear that learner difference is a complex construct that cannot be reduced to the influence of isolated variables.

Through the process of meaning condensation, an interview that was over 6,000 words long was condensed to a 1,000-word narrative and subsequently woven into the six-point summary above, based on data from all the informants. Meaning condensation enables insights to emerge that may not have been readily apparent in the original data. The danger, of course, is that these insights may in some ways be the result of the meaning condensation process. In the process of condensing the data and eliminating hesitations, false starts, repetitions, and other infelicities of natural speech in the original interview, the researcher may have highlighted some issues that are not particularly salient in the original data, while overlooking or downplaying others. As a safeguard against this problem, Gloria and the other participants in the study were each asked to review the condensed versions of their stories to verify that the summary was accurate and complete.

A 'Grounded' Approach to Data Analysis

Lincoln and Guba (1985) called their pioneering approach to qualitative research *grounded* because the analytical categories emerge from the data rather than being imposed on them. Analysts working within this tradition use inductive reasoning processes, in contrast with deductive approaches. Deductive reasoning begins with a theory and looks for data to confirm or disconfirm that theory (as in experimental research). In contrast, inductive reasoning begins with data and ends up with a theory:

> [In the] grounded theory approach, the researcher begins with the data and through analysis (searching for salient themes or categories and arranging these to form explanatory patterns) arrives at an understanding of the phenomenon under investigation. These themes and patterns do not simply jump out at the researcher—discovering them requires a systematic approach to analysis based on familiarity with related literature and research experience. (Ellis and Barkhuizen, 2005, pp. 254–255)

Ellis and Barkhuizen go on to point out that inductive and deductive approaches should be seen as either end of a continuum, rather than as a pair of binary opposites. Qualitative research (or any other kind of research, for that matter) cannot be entirely based on one or the other.

ACTION

The following statements are some data David Nunan collected in a workshop he ran for English teachers in Hong Kong. (The teachers were asked to describe three beliefs they have about language development that influence the way they teach.) Do a key word analysis and assign the data to categories. (Hint: In the original study, these statements were organized into six categories.)

Spoken language should be mastered before written.

Children need to be immersed in all types of writing/reading literature.

Children learn by using the language.

Children need to be a part of a rich language environment.

All children benefit from immersion of [*sic*] the written print.

Children's language develops through experiences so in order for the children to gain the most out of any given lesson, many experiences should be given.

[Language] occurs across the curriculum and therefore should not be seen as a separate subject.

I believe grammar, spelling and reading are the basis for language development.

Language develops through all curriculum areas.

A child needs to be aware of basic grammatical structures.

There is a strong relationship between oral language development and expression and the ability to express oneself in writing.

Children learn best when there is a positive encouraging environment.

Here is the categorization of these comments from the original study (Nunan, 1993):

IMMERSION

Children need to be immersed in all types of writing/reading literature.

All children benefit from immersion of [*sic*] the written print.

LEARNING BY DOING/EXPERIENTIAL LEARNING

Children's language develops through experiences so in order for the children to gain the most out of any given lesson, many experiences should be given.

Children learn by using the language.

LANGUAGE ACROSS THE CURRICULUM

It occurs across the curriculum and therefore should not be seen as a separate subject.

Language develops through all curriculum areas.

GRAMMAR, STRUCTURE, CORRECTNESS

A child needs to be aware of basic grammatical structures.

I believe grammar, spelling and reading are the basis for language development.

ORAL/WRITTEN LANGUAGE RELATIONSHIPS

Spoken language should be mastered before written.

There is a strong relationship between oral language development and expression and the ability to express oneself in writing.

CREATION OF RICH, POSITIVE ENVIRONMENT

Children need to be a part of a rich language environment.
Children learn best when there is a positive encouraging environment.

REFLECTION

Compare the categories you developed with those listed above. How similar were they? Did they overlap or diverge? In cases where there was divergence, what explains the differences? If you are working with classmates or colleagues, compare your categories to theirs.

Discourse Analysis, Conversational Analysis, and Interaction Analysis

Discourse analysis is a very broad term that covers a range of methods, techniques, and approaches. In a recent book on language, it is defined as "the systematic study of language in context" (Nunan, 2007a, p. 208). Discourse analysis is sometimes contrasted with text analysis, which focuses on analyzing the formal properties of language.

Conversation and interaction analysis are closely related to discourse analysis. In fact, some linguists see them as part of discourse analysis although there are differences of emphasis. Discourse and interaction analysts work with both elicited and naturalistic data, while conversation analysts work with naturalistic data. Discourse analysts work with either spoken or written language, while conversation and interaction analysts only work with spoken data. Discourse analysts very often use categorical schemes in their analysis, while conversation and interaction analysts carry out detailed interpretive analyses—sometimes of quite limited samples of language.

Developing Themes in Qualitative Data

One of the most straightforward ways of analyzing condensed statements was developed by Lieblich, Tuval-Mashiach, and Zilber (1998). While their research focused on the analysis of life-history data, the procedure itself can be used to identify patterns in any qualitative data. The procedure has five steps as follows:

1. Read the material several times until a pattern emerges. . . . There are aspects of the life story to which you might wish to pay special attention, but their significance depends on the entire story and its contents. Such aspects are, for example, the opening of the story, or evaluations . . . of the parts of the story that appear in the text.

2. Put your initial and global impressions of the case into writing.

3. Decide on special foci of content or themes that you want to follow in the story as it evolves from beginning to end.

4. Using colored markers . . . mark the various themes in the story, reading separately and repeatedly for each one.

5. Follow each theme throughout the story and note your conclusion. Be aware of where a theme appears for the first and last times, the transitions between the themes, the context for each one, and their relative salience in the text. (ibid., pp. 62–63)

An illustration of this procedure is found in a study by a teacher who wished to support her teaching decisions with data (O'Farrell, 2003). O'Farrell was teaching an English listening comprehension course to international scholars studying nuclear nonproliferation. Her students had to listen to videotaped lectures by experts on this topic. The teacher transcribed the lectures and then used two procedures to analyze the language used. First, she identified frequently used grammatical structures so she could include those structures in her lessons. Secondly, she used the color-highlighting function of her word-processing system to identify and code the speech acts the lecturers used. As a result, she could easily see in the data the various speech acts that were most important in the lectures her students would have to understand.

The Card Sort Technique

A similar procedure is the *card sort technique* initially developed by Lincoln and Guba (1985). (See also Strauss, 1988.) This procedure has five steps.

1. Place each individual statement on an index card and place the cards in a pile.

2. Select the first card in the pile, read it and note its contents. The first card represents the first entry in the yet-to-be-named category. Place it to one side.

3. Select the second card, read it and note its contents. Make a determination on tacit or intuitive grounds whether this second card is a "look-alike" or "feel-alike" with Card 1, that is, whether its contents are "essentially" similar. If so, place the second card with the first and proceed to the third card; if not, the second card represents the first entry in the second yet-to-be-named category.

4. Continue with successive cards. For each card, decide whether it is a "look/feel alike" of cards that have already been placed in some provisional category or whether it represents a new category. Proceed accordingly.

5. After some cards have been processed, the analyst may feel that a new card neither fits any of the provisionally established categories nor seems to form a new category. Other cards may also be recognized as possibly irrelevant to the developing set. These cards should be placed into a miscellaneous pile; they should *not* be discarded at this point, but should be retained for later review. (adapted from Lincoln and Guba, 1985, pp. 347–348)

From this process of creating categories, you can then write descriptors of each category. These category definitions should be specific enough that someone unfamiliar with your data set could use them to sort the cards and come up with the same groupings you generated.

REFLECTION

Think about a research question that has interested you as you think about conducting your own classroom-based or classroom-oriented studies. How might you use the card sort technique to work with the data in that investigation?

USING TECHNOLOGY FOR QUALITATIVE DATA ANALYSIS

Technology has become ubiquitous. In research, it is extremely valuable. It is difficult to imagine doing research without word processors, statistical packages, spreadsheets, and so on. Technology is indispensable for collecting, recording, and analyzing large sets of data. In the electronic classroom, where learners interact with texts and with each other through their keyboards, computers are able to capture, record, and analyze large amounts of data:

> [C]omputers can collect information about the user's actions at the keyboard, such as by recording each single keystroke in real time. These can be played back by the researcher to see, for example, successive drafts in the writing process and use (and abuse) of tools such as spelling and grammar checkers and templates. (Beatty, 2003, p. 178)

In this section we will look briefly at some techniques that exploit technology for data analysis. The two main techniques that we will consider in this section are data tagging and concordancing. We give more space to concordancing than tagging because it is a technique that is relatively easy to use. Tagging requires either programming skills or expensive software. What they share is the capability of revealing patterns, regularities and relationships in large sets of data, called *corpora*. (Some corpora currently being assembled in Europe contain several hundred thousand words.) Because of the amount of data involved, patterns are not immediately apparent without the aid of technology.

Data Tagging

Data tagging is a procedure in which information about a piece of text is tagged and embedded into the text. When the text is analyzed, the computer can be instructed to find and extract items of interest. For example, particular grammatical features can be tagged. This process could be useful in investigating patterns of learner errors in large samples of classroom data, student writing samples, and so on.

In a study into the errors made by French-speaking learners of English, Dagneaux, Denness, and Granger (1998) worked with a database of 150,000 words. The database was tagged for errors using the following comprehensive error tagging and classification system. In terms of the major categories, *FG* represented formal grammatical problems. *X* stood for lexico-grammatical issues, *R* for register problems, and *S* for Style issues. The tag *W* represented a missing word, redundant word, or a word order problem. These major categories also contained subcategories:

> For the grammatical category, for instance, the first subcode refers to the word category: **GV** for verbs, **GN** for nouns, **GA** for articles. This code is in turn followed by any number of subcodes. For instance, the **GV** category is further broken down into **GVV** (voice errors) etc. The system is flexible: analysts can add or delete subcodes to fit their data. (ibid., p. 166)

These tags are inserted into the text to be analyzed. Here is an example of a tagged text. The dollar signs indicate the correct version of the item.

There was a forest with dark green dense foliage and pastures where a herd of tiny **(FS)** braun $brown$ cows was grazing quietly **(XVPR)** watching at $watching$ the toy train going past (ibid.).

The tags can then be retrieved using a similar procedure to that used in concordancing (see below). This lists all of the errors bearing a certain code and then lists these along with the immediate linguistic environment in which they appear. Here are some lines from the output of a search for errors bearing the code XNPR.

---

1. complemented by other **(XNPR)** approaches of $approaches to$ the subject. The written
2. are concerned. Yet the **(XNPR)** aspiration to $aspiration for$ a more equitable society
3. can walk without paying **(XNPR)** attention of $attention to$ the **(LSF)** circulation $traffic$

One of the most widely used pieces of tagging software is a program called NUD•IST. The name stands for Non-Numerical Unstructured Data Indexing, Learning and Theorizing (Weitzman and Miles, 1995). This program was developed for analyzing texts in research into the social sciences in general, rather than in applied linguistics or language teaching. Unfortunately, the program is expensive and is difficult to use without extensive training. However, it is both powerful and flexible. In some ways, it is the electronic equivalent of the card sort technique discussed above. Once the data are tagged, the program can pull out, rearrange, and cluster pieces of text that are thematically related. It is therefore much more flexible and time saving than the use of the card sort technique, in which the researcher has to go through the relatively tedious and time-consuming process of transferring data on to cards, losing the context in the process.

Concordancing

As we have already seen, *concordancing* is a procedure used in *corpus linguistics* (the study of extremely large sets of language data) to extract and show in context a single linguistic item. It can reveal patterns that are not immediately apparent from a casual inspection of the data. This process is illustrated by a search for the word *got* (Carter, Goddard, Reah, Sanger, and Bowering, 2001, p. 161):

1. He couldn't turn the water on. And he	got	badly burned. It happened in Mar
2. anyone in the neighborhood who	got	broken into recently? I know
3. any extra precautions since the car	got	broken into last time? Er well, I
4. he jilted her at the altar. So she	got	brought up by her grandmother
5. she's been a bit nervous ever since we	got	burgled and dark nights
6. you know of? They got burgled. They	got	burgled once. Yeah. That was a while
7. by crime that you know of. They they	got	burgled. They got burgled once.
8. done that so I suppose I could have	got	caned. Yeah. And as you've gone
9. fool for being honest. You know he	got	called an idiot for being honest

Searching for naturally occurring instances of a word in context can yield interesting insights. For example, Nunan (2007a) points out that from this database

> we find that people tend to use *get* as a passive voice rather than active voice construction to describe things that happened to them personally rather than to describe what is done to impersonal things—the only inanimate object in the above sample is the car in line 3. . . . Another feature of the data is that *get* appears to be associated with emotionally charged, even violent, actions and events—*burned, broken, burgled, caned, deported.* (p. 53).

Concordancing programs reveal patterns like this one quickly and easily. The technology makes locating such patterns much faster and easier.

In second language research, concordancing has been used to investigate error patterns in large samples of learner data. In his review of the computer-based analyses of learner corpora, Barlow (2005) makes the point that storing data digitally greatly facilitates error classification, form-function mappings, and other forms of linguistic analysis. It is simple to extract particular lexical items and grammatical patterns along with their accompanying linguistic context.

QUALITY CONTROL ISSUES IN ANALYZING QUALITATIVE DATA

As we have noted in the chapters about collecting data qualitatively, there are concerns about reliability and validity in naturalistic inquiry and action research, just as there are in the psychometric approach. Writing about the life history method in qualitative inquiry, Plummer (1983) makes this contrast:

> Reliability is primarily concerned with technique and consistency— with ensuring that if the study was conducted by someone else similar findings would be obtained; while validity is concerned with making sure that the technique is actually studying what it is supposed to. A clock that was consistently ten minutes fast would hence be reliable but invalid since it did not tell the correct time. In general, reliability is the preoccupation of 'hard' methodologists getting the attitude scale or the questionnaire design as technically replicable as possible through standardization, measurement, and control—while validity receives relatively short shrift. (p. 101)

He notes that reliability can be achieved more easily than validity, which becomes harder to demonstrate as we investigate more complex phenomena. Still, there are some widely used procedures for demonstrating reliability and validity in qualitative analyses and we will discuss some of them here.

Coder Agreement Indices

One concern about analyzing qualitative data that relates to reliability is the issue of subjectivity. How much of what we find has come out of the data and how much of the interpretation has been inserted by the researcher? Would different researchers find the same thing in a data set? One way to sort out this problem is to determine *intercoder agreement*—an index of the consistency with which different people categorize the same data. (This construct is analogous to interrater reliability in quantitative research.) A simple percentage is calculated by dividing the number of items upon which coders agree by the total number of items that were coded. The general rule of thumb is that intercoder agreement should be at least 85% for readers to have confidence in the reported findings (Allwright and Bailey, 1991).

A parallel issue is *intracoder agreement*—the extent to which a single person codes or categorizes the same set of data consistently over time. The same mathematical steps are used, and again, a minimum of 85% consistency is expected. If you are working with a team of researchers or can find a colleague to help you code your data, you should use the usual intercoder agreement procedure. If you are conducting classroom research alone and do not have someone to help you with the coding, you should compute intracoder agreement.

The following quote details the procedures used to determine intercoder agreement by researchers at the University of Hawaii in coding transcripts of classroom data:

> Four pages of two transcripts were coded according to the guidelines by three coders who reached consensus on the codes. Three- to four-page segments of four additional transcripts were coded separately by two of these coders until 90% agreement was reached, and the remaining differences were used to establish modifications and clarifications of the guidelines and a standard set of codes for the entire set of training transcripts. The first two transcripts were then discussed in a group with all the coders to assure understanding of the guidelines. (Chaudron, 1988, p. 24)

Using these steps to establish indices of coder agreement can help you locate holes or ambiguities in your coding categories. In addition, acceptably high inter- or intracoder agreement indices can give your readers confidence in the categories you use to analyze your data.

You can use the card sort technique as a quality control mechanism. When you have used the card sort technique to establish categories, you can have a colleague sort the same cards and see if the same categories emerge. As a different way of using the card sort to check your categories, you can provide your colleague with the descriptors for the categories you wish to use and have that person distribute all the cards into those categories. Where there are cards that do not fit well in an existing category, discuss these items with your colleague. You may find that you need to adjust the descriptors and/or add new ones.

Member Validation

One procedure for checking the validity of qualitative data analyses is called *member validation* or *member checking*. It is used to determine whether qualitative data are convincing as evidence. (Some researchers [e.g., Dörnyei, 2007] also use the terms *respondent feedback* or *respondent checking*.) This step involves asking people (the members) in the culture under investigation (whether it is a school, a department, or a classroom) to review the data and the interpretation thereof to provide the researcher with feedback. So, for example, when Nunan (1993) had Gloria and the other good language learners in his study verify his condensations of their lengthy narratives, he was using a member checking strategy. According to Richards, such validation "involves more than simply asking members to confirm what we have written about them: as participants in the research process, they have a wider call on our attention and it may be worthwhile to involve them in other ways" (p. 264).

Dörnyei (2007) states that participants should comment on the conclusions of a study: "They can, for example, read an early draft of the research report or listen to a presentation of some tentative results or themes, and can then express their views in what is called a 'validation interview'" (pp. 60–61). If the researchers and the participants agree on the findings, then the researchers can have confidence in the validity of their results.

What happens in cases where the researchers and the participants disagree on the interpretation of the data? Dörnyei points out that "even though the participants are clearly the 'insiders,' there is no reason to assume that they can interpret their own experiences or circumstances correctly" (ibid., p. 61). As an example, he notes that in heated situations, such as family arguments, "insiders often have conflicting views about the same phenomenon" (ibid.).

Qualities of Qualitative Analyses

Working with ideas from Coffey and Atkinson (1996), Richards describes seven important characteristics of qualitative analyses. These are reprinted as **Table 14.2.**

A SAMPLE STUDY

As mentioned above, Bailey (1982) investigated the classroom communication problems of non-native speaking teaching assistants in a U. S. university—the University of California at Los Angeles (UCLA). The study had both a quantitatively oriented language assessment component and a qualitative component, but here we will focus on just the qualitative data analysis.

The research question was, "What are the classroom communication problems of non-native speaking teaching assistants?" This question arose from a highly politicized situation in which many undergraduate American students had complained (to parents, administrators, and legislators) that their TAs didn't speak English well enough to be teaching at UCLA. (The legislators were involved because UCLA is a publicly funded university—its budget is derived from public taxes.)

To determine what the communication problems were, Bailey observed physics and math courses over a ten-week term. Physics and math were chosen because these two disciplines had numerous international teaching assistants and many of the complaints lodged by the undergraduates had been about courses in these departments. Since men far outnumbered women among the international graduate students who received teaching assistantships in math and physics, all the TAs observed were men.

TABLE 14.2 Essential qualities of qualitative analysis

Quality	Explanation
Artful	Successful analysis is founded on good technique, but this in itself is not enough and there is always more to be learnt.
Imaginative	Analysis is not mechanistic. In order to penetrate beneath the surface of things, the researcher must make time to stand back and find different ways of seeing the data.
Flexible	Where necessary, the researcher must be prepared to find alternative approaches to organizational and interpretive challenges, which means not adhering too rigidly to any one approach.
Reflexive	In order to make the best of opportunities to advance the process of discovery, the researcher should keep in review the continually evolving interrelationship between data, analysis, and interpretation.
Methodical	Although feeling and instinct may play an important part in all of the above, the researcher must decide on appropriate analytical methods and continue to reflect on these as they are applied.
Scholarly	Analysis should take place in the context of a wider understanding of the relevant literature, whether relating to analytical or interpretive issues.
Intellectually Rigorous	The researcher must be prepared to make available the workings of the analytical process and take account of all the available evidence, including discrepant cases. This also means that the researcher has to resist the temptation to reduce everything to a single explanation.

REFLECTION

Answer the following questions about this study, based on what you know so far:

1. What is the design of the study? (This is a trick question. Even though the data were qualitatively collected and analyzed, the investigation used one of the research designs from the psychometric approach.)
2. What is the independent variable and how many levels did it have?
3. What are some control variables in this study?
4. Based on your reading and your own experiences as a teacher and a student, what do you think the NNS TAs' communication problems might have been?

TABLE 14.3   Sampling decisions in comparing NNS and NS teaching assistants

Department/Course		NNS TAs	NS TAs
Math	Basic	1	1
Math		1	1
Math		1	1
Math		1	1
Math		1	1
Math	Advanced	1	1
Math Totals		**6**	**6**
Physics	Basic	1	1
Physics		1	1
Physics		1	1
Physics		1	1
Physics		1	1
Physics	Advanced	1	1
Physics Totals		**6**	**6**

For comparison purposes, the observations were conducted in classes taught by non-native speaking TAs (NNSs) and also native English speaking TAs (NSs), in a range of basic to advanced classes. Each NNS TA in the sample was paired, in the analysis, with a NS TA who taught the same course during the same semester. These pairings are shown in **Table 14.3**.

Time sampling involves decisions about when you collect data in a qualitative study. Bailey observed each teaching assistant three times—once at the beginning, once at the middle, and once at the end of the ten-week term. The handwritten field notes she took during the classes were fleshed out as soon as possible afterwards. That is, abbreviations were spelled out, examples were added, and ambiguities were clarified. Then the field notes were rewritten in a format that put the prose data on the right two-thirds of the page while the left third of the page remained blank, as space for coding, inserting questions, and so on.

The analytic procedure that finally enabled Bailey to capture meaningful interpretations of the data involved a form of meaning condensation to discover the themes. First, each set of field notes was summarized. Bailey forced herself to distill the copious and detailed lesson descriptions into a two-page summary. (Two colleagues helped her with these summaries, as a check on the data condensation process.) Then the summaries about each TA were combined and reworked to generate a prose profile of that TA. This process is summarized in **Figure 14.1:**

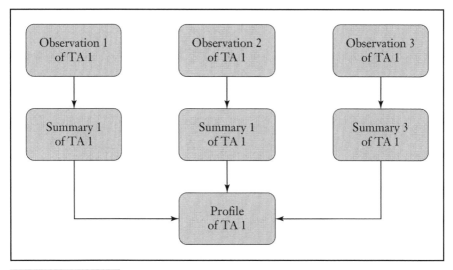

FIGURE 14.1 Summarizing lengthy field notes to create prose profiles of TAs (adapted from Bailey, 2006, p. 111)

When the twenty-four TA profiles were available for comparison, types of teacher styles quickly emerged from the data. In a process analogous to the card sort technique, Bailey compared and contrasted the twenty-four summaries to discover types or categories of teaching styles, as depicted in **Figure 14.2**:

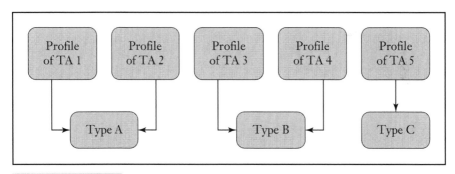

FIGURE 14.2 Deriving a TA typology from prose profiles of TAs (adapted from Bailey, 2006, p. 111)

In the process, five clear types of teaching styles emerged among these twenty-four teaching assistants. As mentioned above, these were the (1) inspiring cheerleaders, (2) entertaining allies, (3) knowledgeable helpers and casual friends, (4) mechanical problem solvers, and (5) active but unintelligible TAs. In the research report, each type is described and then illustrated by a profile of one of the TAs who represented that type. This process of condensation and comparison allowed Bailey to interpret the field notes and make claims about the types of TAs that were more and less successful in the eyes of their undergraduate students.

REFLECTION

Based on the five category labels above, which types of TAs do you predict would be seen as successful and which would be seen as less successful in the opinion of the undergraduate students whom these TAs taught?

PAYOFFS AND PITFALLS

As noted at the outset of this chapter, qualitative data are powerful. They are more accessible to readers without statistical training than are the kinds of sophisticated quantitative analyses that appear in many published journal articles. They can be used to explain important concepts to teachers, administrators, journalists, and parents in human terms, while quantitative data sometimes seem too abstract and detached or—conversely—too concrete and impersonal.

There are many pitfalls in choosing to collect and then in analyzing qualitative data. The first, especially for novice researchers, is the possibility of getting overwhelmed by the sheer volume of data. Detailed field notes about an hour-long lesson can run to thousands of words.

If you are generating handwritten observational field notes during a lesson, you may choose to word process the data before you analyze it. (We recommend that you do so.) While word processing is initially time-consuming, having the data stored electronically can save you time in the long run and will make the analysis easier.

The length of qualitative data sometimes creates problems when researchers try to publish their findings. Most journals and many anthologies impose page restrictions on manuscripts submitted for publication. It is very difficult to provide a convincing analysis of reams and reams of data in a short article. Sometimes researchers choose to focus on very particular issues in reporting their findings. In some cases, lengthy studies have been published as journal articles or book chapters. For example, Schmidt and Frota's (1986) analysis of Schmidt's learning of Portuguese in Brazil is eighty-nine pages long.

Sometimes qualitative data analyses don't pan out. For example, Bailey originally coded her observational field notes on math and science teaching assistants' lessons using a category system designed to analyze classroom discourse (Sinclair and Coulthard, 1975). The categories had seemed promising in terms of addressing the research question, but they did not really reveal the core issues separating the successful and less successful TAs. It was not until she tried the summarizing process described above that Bailey was able to arrive at a satisfying explanation of the communication problems experienced by the non-native speaking TAs.

As noted above, transcription is an important tool in classroom research, but it is a tedious and time-consuming process. Allwright and Bailey (1991) described the data collection procedure used by R. L. Allwright (1980), which involved suspending stereo audio microphones from a wire above the students' desks. The stereo function allowed the researchers to tune out some of the extraneous noise as they were trying to transcribe the data, and having the microphones suspended (rather than sitting on the desks) minimized some of the bumps and scrapes, as people moved chairs, opened books, and so on. Researchers working with children have sometimes used wireless recording microphones clipped to the students' clothing to get better quality audio recordings. Doing so is helpful in making transcription easier, but it is also costly.

In sum, time and the propensity to drown in the data are the biggest problems associated with doing qualitative analyses. Yet, it is partly the element of extensive time spent with the data that gives qualitative research its power to illustrate, to illuminate, and to convince readers. So, if you are considering doing a study that involves qualitative data collection and analysis, plan to spend ample time in working with the data.

QUESTIONS AND TASKS

1. Read a published article on classroom research that utilized qualitative data. How were the data analyzed? What difficulties did the researcher(s) report? Can you think of other difficulties that might have occurred but that were not discussed by the author(s)?

2. In the article you read, what were the benefits of the qualitative analyses undertaken by the author(s)?

3. Think about a study you would like to conduct. Focus on the research question(s). What kinds of qualitative data would you want to collect? How would you want to analyze those data? Sketch out your ideas and share them with a classmate or colleague.

4. Ask a language learner you know to tape-record or write his or her language learning history. Then create a condensed narrative from that narrative.

5. Analyze some of your own qualitative data using the card sort technique. If possible, compare your results with another reader. What similarities and differences are there between the two analyses?

6. If you are teaching or taking a language class, try to write a report of a typical day. (For an example, turn to Chapter 7 for van Lier's [1996a] description of a typical day in a bilingual school in Peru.) As you do so, be aware of the mental processes you use in deciding what information to include and what to exclude.

7. Go to a concordancing program on the Internet (the one below is free) and complete a search for a word, idiom, or grammatical item that interests you. What insights can you derive from the data? (The aim of this task is to give you an experience of using a concordancing program rather than analyzing learner data.) If you are teaching a language class, how could you use these data in developing a unit or lesson plan?

British National Corpus Sample Queries:

http://sara.natcorp.ox.ac.uk/lookup.html

SUGGESTIONS FOR FURTHER READING

We recommend K. Richards' (2003) book *Qualitative Inquiry in TESOL*. It contains clear explanations and many helpful examples.

We also suggest that you consult Holliday's (2002) *Doing and Writing Qualitative Research*. While this book is written by an applied linguist, it provides a general introduction to planning, organizing, and writing up qualitative research. Although many of the examples are taken from disciplines outside of applied linguistics such as sociology, management, and health care, the principles and techniques introduced in the book can be readily applied to applied linguistics and language education.

Dörnyei (2007) has a very fine treatment of issues related to analyzing qualitative data.

Another helpful resource is the special issue of *TESOL Quarterly* edited by Davis and Lazaraton (1995), entitled *Qualitative Research in TESOL*.

If you would like to learn more about concordancing as a research tool, see Biber, Conrad, and Reppen's (1998) *Corpus Linguistics: Investigating Language Structure and Use*. See also Barlow (2005).

Weitzman and Miles (1995) explain many computer software programs for analyzing qualitative data. They discuss the various programs in the categories of text retrievers, text-base managers, programs for coding and retrieving, code-based theory builders, and conceptual network builders.

15

Putting It All Together

What we learn in the university is not scientific theory and certainly not a theory of how to do science. We are exposed to practices: the practices of our teachers in the classroom and laboratory and the practices they admire, which we read about in the articles they assign to us. The theory of how science should be done is almost never taught. And even the theory that explains the practices and articles to which we are exposed and that gives the discipline some coherence is constructed after the fact. It is not always taught directly, is always incomplete, and is often internally contradictory. (Piore, 2006, pp. 143–144)

INTRODUCTION AND OVERVIEW

In this concluding chapter, we build upon some of the main themes that have been presented earlier in the book. Looking back, you will recall that after providing an overview of language classroom research in Chapters 1, 2, and 3, we turned to issues related to planning and implementing research (Chapters 4 through 8). The focus then shifted to data collection (in Chapters 9, 10, and 11) and data analysis (Chapters 12, 13, and 14). We realize that we have covered quite a bit of material in the foregoing pages, so the intent in this chapter is to help you put it all together.

To that end, in this chapter we review some issues raised earlier and discuss ways of combining qualitative and quantitative procedures in your own proposals and subsequent investigations. We also look at the practicalities of doing research and suggest some steps that you can take to make the enterprise more successful and more satisfying. Finally, we address issues related to reporting on your research findings, whether in formal or informal contexts, both in writing and in oral presentations.

Research as it is presented in scholarly books, journal articles, and formal monographs is in many ways a misrepresentation. These publications seem to suggest that research is neat and tidy, and that it flows logically and irrevocably from abstract to conclusion. But such reports are products. Some of the processes by which the products were arrived at are reported, but some can only be inferred. The missteps, blind alleys, false starts, and frustrations that the researchers encountered in the process of arriving at the final products are rarely discussed (see Gass and Schachter, 1996). Dingwall (1984) contrasts the messiness of the research process with the resulting product (be it a book, paper, or conference presentation) as follows:

> It may be too strong to suggest that there is a 'conspiracy of silence' among academics about the problems, the possibilities, the limitations, and the pressures of research practice; but certainly for most graduate researchers working in comparative isolation, it is painful to discover the extent of compromise and ambiguity inherent in their work. (p. 1)

Neophyte researchers who are unaware of these ambiguities often experience a sense of demoralization—if not outright distress—at what they perceive to be their own inadequacies and shortcomings when they come to conducting and writing up their own research.

ACTION

Skim through two or three articles about language classroom research. What problems, if any, do the authors report? Share your findings with a classmate or colleague.

The messiness of the research process is mirrored in the history of scientific inquiry. Just as individual research projects do not grow neatly from conception through gestation to birth, neither does the advancement of scientific knowledge. Rather it is marked by both incremental changes and seismic intellectual earthquakes and paradigm shifts (Kuhn, 1996). The broadening out of approaches to doing language classroom research is one such shift. The field has now moved from a rather narrow early focus on the psychometric approach and experimental attempts to control variables, to the methodological eclecticism of naturalistic inquiry, and on to the legitimization of action research. Thus, language classroom research has seen substantial changes in the ways that data are collected and analyzed as well as in the types of issues that are investigated.

The way research methods texts talk about doing research has changed too. Kuhn (1996) writes about *reconstructed logic* and *logic in use*. The former term refers to the articulated, codified procedures that science uses and replicates, while the latter refers to those judgment calls, hunches, and ideas we try out as we go about the tricky and sometimes frustrating business of conducting research.

In fact, although we have emphasized planning, systematicity, and careful decision making based (in part) on reviewing the available literature, we acknowledge that intuition, judgment, insight, and inspiration also have a role to play in research. This claim may be especially apt in language classroom research, where real students and real teachers come together to grapple with the challenges of language teaching and learning.

In this book, we have tried to go a bit beyond the often-described procedures of experimental science to develop discussions of case studies, ethnographies, surveys, classroom observation techniques, diary studies, and other introspective processes for gathering and analyzing data. We close with a brief discussion of the melding of approaches in what has come to be called mixed methods research.

COMBINING QUANTITATIVE AND QUALITATIVE APPROACHES

Throughout this book, we have argued that the qualitative/quantitative divide is unnecessary and unhelpful. Neither approach is inherently superior to the other, and referring to research as either quantitative or qualitative is, in most cases, an oversimplification. The types of data that are collected and the types of analyses that are performed on those data should be driven by the research questions that are posed as the study unfolds, not by some preconceived notion of one approach being automatically superior to another.

Some studies, particularly those seeking causal relationships or correlations between variables, will lead the researcher towards an experimental research design that is likely to involve quantitatively collected data and quantitative analyses. Other studies, which focus more on description and portrayal rather than on determining causal or correlational relationships, will incorporate data that are qualitatively collected and qualitatively analyzed. Still others will involve a *mixed methods* or *hybrid* design that combines qualitative and quantitative data collection and analysis procedures. Dörnyei (2007) defines a mixed methods study as one that "involves the collection or analysis of both qualitative and quantitative data in a single study with some attempts to integrate the two approaches at one or more stages of the research process" (p. 163).

REFLECTION

Are you familiar with any mixed methods studies? If so, think about one that interests you. What combination of qualitative and quantitative procedures did it involve?

Some studies that are predominantly naturalistic in their approach have nevertheless used quantified data to support the authors' claims and provide information about the participants. For example, in the sample study by Lynch and

Maclean (2000) described in Chapter 9, the English proficiency of two students was characterized as follows: Alicia had a 4.0 on the IELTS and a 400 on the TOEFL, and had scored only 5% on a dictation administered at the start of the course. Daniela had a score of 7.0 on the IELTS and a 600 on the TOEFL. Her dictation score was 97% at the beginning of the course. Even if we know nothing about the dictation, the IELTS, or the TOEFL, the contrast between the two learners is striking, and the quantitative characterization helps us to imagine their English proficiency.

Other predominantly qualitative studies have included quantitative data as part of the findings. For example, van Lier's (1996a) ethnography of the Spanish-Quechua bilingual program in the Peruvian highlands (summarized at the end of Chapter 7) included percentage data on the teachers' language use (Spanish, Quechua, or both), as well as test results on the children's knowledge of colors, numbers, and body parts in both languages. These quantitative data allowed van Lier to state that "as the students were learning Spanish, they were *unlearning* Quechua. In other words, a process of *subtractive bilingualism* was underway" (p. 382).

Still other studies interweave qualitative and quantitative procedures as key parts of the analyses. As an example, let us return to Bailey's research on the classroom communication problems of non-native speaking (NNS) teaching assistants, described in Chapter 14 (Bailey, 1982; 1984). Her original proposal had called for the coding of observational field notes using a modification of Sinclair and Coulthard's (1975) category system for analyzing classroom interaction, but although that analysis was done, it failed to reveal any meaningful outcomes. Additional quantitative data were collected and further analyses were conducted that involved both quantitative and qualitative procedures, as shown in **Table 15.1**.

After many false starts and problems applying coding categories to her data, Bailey ended up reducing the voluminous observational field notes in a sequential meaning condensation process that involved summarizing, comparing, and profiling (see Table 15.1 and Figures 14.1 and 14.2). Through these procedures, Bailey produced a typology of teaching assistants. In this grounded theory approach, the categories arose from the data rather than being imposed upon them.

TABLE 15.1   An example of a mixed methods study

	Data Collection	Data Analysis
Qualitative	Field notes written during and after observations in the regularly scheduled classes of 24 TAs (12 NSs and 12 NNSs)	Field notes summarized and profiles generated for each TA; 24 profiles compared in order to identify types of TAs
Quantitative	Students' end-of-course evaluations of the TAs collected using the university's regular numerical rating scales	Mean scores computed for each TA type; testing for statistically significant differences across the ratings of the various types of TAs

The five clear TA types that emerged among this cohort were labeled with metaphors that described their behavior and apparent attitudes toward their students. These labels were (1) the inspiring cheerleaders, (2) the entertaining allies, (3) the knowledgeable helpers and casual friends, (4) the mechanical problem solvers, and (5) the active but unintelligible TAs. Twenty-one of the twenty-four TAs could be categorized using these labels, but three could not. Those three did not quite fit the categories for a variety of reasons. For example, one math TA (a native speaker of English) was a "casual friend" to his students but couldn't be considered a "knowledgeable helper" since he was unable to solve the students' homework problems, and they left his classes frustrated and confused.

In fact, after rereading the field notes many times, Bailey realized that during the classes she had observed, the students had responded differently to the TAs who adopted these various teaching styles. So, she turned to the students' numerical ratings of these TAs and matched the quantitative data to the TA typology. The university's regular end-of-course evaluation system included categories for evaluating TAs' overall effectiveness and their helpfulness to the students outside of class. The mean ratings reported in **Table 15.2** are based on a scale in which the average is 50 and the standard deviation is 10. (Higher numbers indicate more positive ratings.)

REFLECTION

What pattern do you notice in Table 15.2 when you examine the mean scores from the students' evaluations across the five TA groups in terms of their overall effectiveness and outside helpfulness?

The stable pattern of change across the mean scores in the student evaluation data shows that the students did indeed evaluate teaching assistants who used some teaching styles in the typology more favorably than they did others. That is, the inspiring cheerleaders were rated more highly than the entertaining

TABLE 15.2 Mean ratings on overall effectiveness and outside helpfulness of five TA types (adapted from Bailey, 1982, p. 140)

TA Type	N	X̄ Overall Effectiveness	X̄ Outside Helpfulness
Inspiring Cheerleaders	2	62.7	59.7
Entertaining Allies	2	59.0	57.2
Knowledgeable Helpers & Casual Friends	8	55.0	53.2
Mechanical Problem Solvers	6	42.7	46.5
Active Unintelligible TAs	3	36.8	36.1

allies, who in turn were rated more highly than the knowledgeable helpers and casual friends, and so on.

Bailey did not set out to find these five types, or styles, among the teaching assistants. As noted in the sample study in Chapter 14, her original research question was, "What are the classroom communication problems of non-native speaking teaching assistants?" In the proposal stage, she and her advisory committee envisioned a discussion of the linguistic elements (e.g., pronunciation, vocabulary, syntax, morphology, etc.) that influenced the NNS TAs' abilities to communicate with their students. While these linguistic issues did in fact play an important role, the differences among the students' mean ratings of the TAs representing these five types suggest that how the TAs related to their students was part of the communication problem, in addition to the language competence of the TAs. (See Rounds, 1987, for further discussion of this typology in her own classroom research.)

Since the early 1980s, it has become more common to incorporate both quantitative and qualitative data collection and analysis procedures in the same investigation (see Chaudron, 1986). In recent years, researchers have employed hybrid designs that involve both qualitative and quantitative data collection and interpretation. As Nunan (2005) points out, "Classroom researchers appear to be increasingly reluctant to restrict themselves to a single data collection techniques, or even to a single research paradigm" (p. 237). Although the qualitative-quantitative debate introduced at the beginning of this book is still alive and well, the issue has lost a great deal of the heat that it had some years ago.

We will now return to issues covered earlier in order to synthesize the concepts presented in recent chapters. Our hope is to help you integrate ideas about quantitative and qualitative data collection and analysis in your own research projects.

DEVELOPING AND CARRYING OUT A RESEARCH PLAN

If you are completing a master's degree or doctoral studies, you will probably have to create a research plan for your proposed study and get it approved by a committee or your research supervisor before you proceed. If you are a researcher seeking either internal or external funding, you will have to convince the funding agency that you have a clear plan as well as the knowledge and skills to carry it out. Even if you are working completely independently and do not need approval from any other individual or group to carry out your investigation, we encourage you to develop a research plan before you begin. Doing so will save you time and trouble later.

A formal plan for research is called a *proposal* because the author proposes the study to a group or an advisor by submitting a document that clearly articulates the plan. In graduate programs, the proposal must typically be approved by a faculty committee before the researcher begins the study. In other contexts, researchers present proposals to funding agencies in hopes of getting grants to support the research.

Although there is variation in the format required of proposals in different contexts, a research proposal normally consists of some predictable, standard sections. The introduction usually includes a literature review, including identifying the research gap (Cooley & Lewkowicz, 2003), which helps provide the motivation for the new study (see Chapter 2 above). The research questions and/or hypotheses are clearly articulated and key terms are operationally defined. The next section may be called "Procedures" or "Methods." It includes a description of who will participate in the study, the steps to be taken to collect and analyze the data, and a description of the instruments to be used. If a study involves a questionnaire or a structured interview, copies of these tools will typically be included in an appendix to the proposal. The likely outcomes and the potential value of the study are also discussed.

Steps in the Research Process

You will recall from Chapters 2 and 3 that the research process begins with an area of interest or concern. This focus can come from reading theory or learning about what others have set out to explore or establish. More often than not, in the case of language classroom research, it comes from our own teaching experience. Some of us are interested in the effects of our own actions and practices (such as the kinds of questions we ask or the classroom climate we set up) on classroom dynamics and learning outcomes. Others wish to focus on aspects of student behavior (such as preferred learning styles and strategies, task types, and student-student interaction). For others, the experience of being a language learner provides a stimulus for research. (See, for example, Campbell's [1996] diary study based on her experiences as a student of Spanish in Mexico.)

After establishing an area of interest, the crucial next step is to frame that interest as a research question. Pinning down what is initially a vague prospect into a specific question can be extraordinarily difficult. We have been involved in projects, either as researchers or research supervisors, in which it has taken weeks, and sometimes even months, to get the question right.

Framing a research question properly will force you to be precise. Imagine, for instance, that your area of interest is learning styles and strategies. This is a huge general area that has spawned an enormous number of research questions, including the following:

- Do effective language learners share a particular set of learning strategies?
- Is there a relationship between cultural background and learning style?
- Is there a relationship between previous learning experiences and learning strategy preferences?
- What are the preferred classroom learning strategies of learners who have been identified has having particular learning styles?
- What effect on students' language learning does deliberate teaching of learning strategies have?

Having established a research question, the hard work of planning a research design begins. Is the study to be an exploratory one or one that confirms or contests prior research? Is it going to test the strength of relationships between two or more variables or is it to be more open-ended and descriptive? Is it going to involve the collection of one large set of data at a single point in time or is it to be an iterative process in which multiple data sets are collected over a period of time?

Considering questions such as those posed above may lead you to adopt one of the two 'pure' research paradigms discussed in Chapters 1, 4, 7, and 10 (Grotjahn, 1987). One of these, you may recall, is the analytical-nomological paradigm, which involves an experimental or quasi-experimental design, quantitatively collected data, and statistical analyses. The other 'pure' paradigm is the exploratory-interpretive kind, in which selection and intervention are eschewed in favor of naturalistic inquiry. This research paradigm entails a nonexperimental design, qualitatively collected data, and interpretive analyses.

Returning to the theme of mixed methods research, it is quite possible that you will adopt a 'hybrid' design involving both qualitative and quantitative data collection and analysis. For example, an investigation into learning styles and strategies might involve the administration of a questionnaire that would yield quantitative data that could be analyzed statistically. You could combine those results with a series of follow-up interviews that would provide qualitatively collected data to be interpreted qualitatively.

In Chapter 1 we introduced Grotjahn's two 'pure' research designs—the psychometric approach (experimental design, quantitative data, statistical analysis) and the naturalistic approach (non-experimental design, qualitative data, interpretive analysis). The remaining mixed forms of Grotjahn's classification system are listed in **Table 15.3.**

Some studies involve more than one paradigm in a single investigation. As Dörnyei (2007) has noted, "mixed methods research offers researchers the advantage of being able to choose from the full repertoire of methodological options, producing as a result many different kinds of creative mixes" (p. 168).

TABLE 15.3 The mixed methods paradigms in Grotjahn's research classification (adapted from Grotjahn, 1987, pp. 59–60)

Paradigm Number and Label	Research Design	Data Collection	Data Analysis
1. Analytical-nomological	Experimental	Quantitative	Statistical
2. Exploratory-interpretive	Nonexperimental	Qualitative	Interpretive
3. Experimental-qualitative-interpretive	Experimental or quasi-experimental	Qualitative	Interpretive
4. Experimental-qualitative-statistical	Experimental or quasi-experimental	Qualitative	Statistical
5. Exploratory-qualitative-statistical	Nonexperimental design	Qualitative	Statistical
6. Exploratory-quantitative-statistical	Nonexperimental design	Quantitative	Statistical
7. Exploratory-quantitative-interpretive	Nonexperimental design	Quantitative	Interpretive
8. Experimental-quantitative-interpretive	Experimental or quasi-experimental	Quantitative	Interpretive

Having decided on the research question(s), the design, the type(s) of data to be collected, and the type(s) of analysis to be done, the next step is to identify the informants for the study. These people are often called the *subjects* in experimental research, the *cohort* in naturalistic inquiry, the *respondents* when surveys or interviews are involved, and the *participants* in action research.

Sometimes a very well-constructed project with a well-articulated research question never gets beyond the planning stage because appropriate subjects cannot be located. Or it may be that the subjects are available, but the conditions cannot be arranged that will enable you to carry out the study to your satisfaction. This problem arises, for instance, in classroom-based experiments requiring the assignment of subjects to experimental and control groups. In many school contexts, the randomization required of the true experimental designs is simply not feasible. In fact, "in our experience, in the world of real schools, real teachers, and real students, this almost never happens" (Spada, Ranta, and Lightbown, 1996, p. 38).

Another important preliminary step is to define and operationalize the key constructs underlying the study. Imagine, for instance, that motivation emerges as a problem in your teaching situation. You may feel that the motivation of your students is declining over the course of the academic year, and you would like to carry out a study to determine whether there is any evidence to support your perception. Having reviewed the literature, you might decide on a definition of language learning motivation along the lines of "the internal drive to persist in language learning over a protracted period of time."

The process of operationalizing the construct involves creating procedures and tools that will enable you to collect data on the construct. For instance, you might decide that motivated students are those who take steps to improve their language outside of the formal classroom environment. You therefore decide to keep a record of the frequency and duration of their visits to the school's self-access language center. Your operational definition of motivation has thus become "the frequency and duration of visits to the self-access language center." This operationalization could be problematic in terms of internal validity, however, because it is possible to posit alternative reasons for the students' actions. Some may visit the center because it is a comfortable and quiet place to check e-mails, chat with friends, read magazines, watch videos, etc.—activities that might have little to do with the students' motivation for language learning.

In Chapter 2, we discussed the importance of doing a literature review. One function of the literature review is to help the researcher operationally define the constructs under investigation. In many cases, it perfectly acceptable (in fact, often desirable) to operationalize your constructs in the same way that other researchers have done. Under some circumstances, you may choose to adapt others' operational definitions somewhat to suit your study. Either way, you need to cite your sources accurately and appropriately.

One type of print-medium resource that can be particularly helpful for people getting started on a research project is the genre known as the *handbook*. This type of book is a compendium of key information, usually written by established, credible authors with recognized expertise on the topic. For example, Hinkle (2005) has edited the thousand-plus-page *Handbook of Research in Second Language Teaching and Learning*—a collection of short explanations of key topics in the field. The equally voluminous *Handbook of Qualitative Research* (Denzin and Lincoln, 2000) is not solely about language learning, but it is helpful for language classroom researchers. Burns and Richards (in press) have edited the *Cambridge Guide to Language Teacher Education*, while Long and Doughty (in press) have produced a collection called the *Handbook of Second and Foreign Language Teaching*. Two other books, which were not designed specifically for research purposes but will be helpful nonetheless, are Carter and Nunan's (2001) *The Cambridge Guide to Teaching English to Speakers of Other Languages* and Nunan's (2003) *Practical English Language Teaching*. The chapters in all these handbooks are typically written to be concise and clear. They identify key issues on the topics and can be helpful sources of definitions and of bibliographic information as well.

ACTION

Locate one of the handbooks described above. Skim through it to see which operational definitions provided by the authors might be helpful in research projects that you would be interested in conducting.

Deciding on how your data are going to be analyzed is the next step in the process. Qualitative data, as we saw in Chapter 14, are usually voluminous and often must be condensed, sorted, and categorized before patterns emerge. If the study involves quantification, you need to determine what statistical tools are appropriate for working with the data in question. Are you looking at significant differences in mean scores? Correlations between different data sets? Differences in the frequency with which various events occur? All of these require different statistical procedures, as we discussed in Chapter 13.

Ethical Concerns in Doing Language Classroom Research

In addition to articulating all the procedures involved in planning a study, we must also be concerned about ethical issues. These include being honest and fair with the participants in research projects and meeting professional standards for how the study will be carried out.

Before you actually begin collecting any data, you need to address such ethical considerations. Most universities these days have ethics committees (also called *human subjects committees*) that are required to vet and approve all research proposals before a study begins. The procedures usually require researchers to inform potential subjects about the study and obtain formal written approval from them prior to any data being collected. This process is normally called *obtaining informed consent*. If you are observing or interviewing children, you must typically get the informed consent of their parents or guardians.

ACTION

In the context where you would like to conduct research, find out if there is a policy about involving people in research. If there is, what steps must you take with regard to informing the potential participants in your study?

Some journals require contributing authors to comply with informed consent procedures. For instance, the *TESOL Quarterly* has two ways that potential authors can meet the informed consent guidelines. Contributors can either document that they have followed the human subjects review procedures of their home institutions or that they have complied with a list of conditions for informing the people in the study. These steps can be found in the last few pages of the *TESOL Quarterly*, along with guidelines about publishing data from students' work.

Obtaining informed consent can be problematic in the case of investigations into language learning and use. Telling the subjects what we are looking for may prompt them to change their behavior, thus invalidating our results. As Labov (1972) pointed out through his concept of the observer's paradox, the purpose of much language-related research is to document how people use language when they are not being observed, but the main way to collect such data is through observation, which may influence how they use language.

Another interesting ethical challenge for researchers wishing to conduct investigations in second language contexts is to make sure that the informed consent process is understood by the participants in the study. That is, written documents that explain the study must either be translated into the subjects' first language or written at a level that will be clear to them, so they will fully understand what they are agreeing to do.

ACTION

Think of a study that you would like to conduct. Draft the statement about the research that you would give potential participants in order to obtain their informed consent to be involved in the study.

Evaluating the Research Plan

At all stages in doing research, it is important to keep the research plan and the data collection and analysis procedures constantly under review. Here is a nonexhaustive list of questions that can help guide the planning and implementation of your research. This list has been developed from a set originally proposed by Nunan (1992). You can use these questions to reflect on your study and self-evaluate your work as the investigation evolves. These questions can also guide a peer review process. As shown in **Figures 15.1, 15.2,** and **15.3,** some questions are most logically posed before the study, others during the investigation, and some as you are concluding the research.

We wish to stress again the importance of addressing these issues before you begin collecting your data. More time spent planning will pay off in time saved later. Remember the carpenter's rule: Measure twice, cut once.

Not all the problems that may occur can be identified in advance, however. Figure 15.2 lists six key questions to ask during the investigation.

Finally, as your research project is coming to a close, there are many issues to consider as you interpret the data. These issues will influence how and where you report on your study. Questions about the results and how to present them are listed in Figure 15.3.

Although we have separated these questions into those that are posed at the beginning of a project, during the data collection and analysis, and after the study has been conducted, it is actually a good practice to anticipate all these questions at the outset. Doing so will help you save time and minimize frustrations.

Getting Support and Going Public

As noted in Chapter 1, we believe there is value in 'going public' with the results of your study. If you do decide to share your research findings (and we hope you will), a good way to start is by presenting your findings to a supportive audience. We typically have our research students present both their initial plans and then later their findings to groups of their peers.

Research Questions

Are the research questions worth investigating?

Are the questions feasible, given available resources?

Do the research questions imply a strong causal or correlational relationship between two or more variables?

What are the constructs underlying the questions?

How are these constructs to be operationalized?

Subjects

Will it be possible to obtain the requisite number of relevant subjects?

What sampling strategies, if any, will be used to obtain subjects?

Does the research design require random assignment of subjects to different conditions? If so, will the required randomization be feasible?

If the study entails longitudinal data collection, will subjects be available for a sufficiently long period of time?

Data Collection Method

What data collection methods can be used for investigating the questions?

Which of these are feasible, given available resources and expertise?

Is it possible and/or desirable to utilize more than one data collection method?

Given the chosen data collection method(s), what threats are there to the internal reliability of the study?

Given the chosen data collection method(s), what threats are there to the external reliability of the study?

Given the chosen data collection method(s), what threats are there to the internal validity of the study?

Given the chosen data collection method(s), what threats are there to the external validity of the study?

How will the data collection tools and procedures be field tested prior to the actual data collection?

Data Analysis Procedures

Does the research entail statistical analyses, interpretive analyses, or both?

Given the research questions and the type(s) of data, what statistical and/or analytical tools are appropriate?

Is it necessary or desirable to quantify qualitative data? If so, how will this quantification be done?

Do you, as a researcher, have the necessary skills to carry out the statistical analysis? If not, is consulting help available?

FIGURE 15.1 Questions to pose before the study formally begins (adapted from Nunan, 1992, p. 227)

What practical problems are emerging as the research proceeds?

What solutions to these problems are available?

In what way(s) is the research changing and evolving during the course of the data collection process?

Are alternative questions or issues emerging as the data are collected?

Is the nature of the research changing as the research proceeds?

Are additional data or data collection procedures required?

FIGURE 15.2   Questions to pose during the study (adapted from Nunan, 1992)

Results

What are the actual outcomes of the research?

Does the investigation answer the research question(s) originally posed?

Does it answer other questions as well (or instead)?

Are the results consistent with the findings of similar studies?

Are there any contradictory findings? If so, how can these be accounted for?

What are the implications of the findings for practice?

What additional questions and suggestions or further research are prompted by the research?

Presentation

How can the research best be presented?

Who is/are the appropriate audience(s) for this study?

What form(s) will the research report take—monograph, thesis, journal article, conference presentation?

FIGURE 15.3   Questions to pose after conducting the study (adapted from Nunan, 1992)

Our research students have found it useful to get evaluative feedback from fellow students at different stages in the research process. Peer feedback can be extremely valuable, particularly if it is from students who are a stage or two ahead in the research process. In their guide to writing qualitative research proposals, Marshall and Rossman (1995) state,

> The experiences of our graduate students suggest that the support of peers is crucial for the personal and emotional sustenance that students find so valuable in negotiating among faculty whose requests and demands may be in conflict with one another. Graduate seminars or advanced courses in qualitative methods provide excellent structures for formal discussions as students deal with issues arising from role

management to grounded theory-building in their dissertations. Student support groups also build in a commitment to others. . . . By establishing deadlines and commitments to one another, students become more efficient and productive. (p. 136)

They add that "these groups bridge the 'existential aloneness' of the conduct of dissertation research" (ibid.).

Collaborative feedback can also be provided in round-table discussions among students who are at the same stage in their research. In addition to providing substantive feedback from people who are 'in the same boat' as it were, round-table discussions can reduce the sense of isolation that research students often experience. The questions listed in Figures 15.1 through 15.3 above can be adapted for peer evaluations and round-table discussions as well as for reflective self-evaluation.

For those who are ready to 'go public,' we often encourage our research students to give presentations at professional conferences. Depending on the culture of the professional organization you choose, you will find that most people who attend such conferences do so because they are interested and wish to learn. In addition, if you are presenting in a concurrent session (i.e., in a time slot when there are several different presentations scheduled), conference goers can choose the session that most appeals to them. As a result, the people who attend your talk are likely to be motivated and interested audience members, As such, they can be quite supportive of research students and teachers reporting on their original investigations.

REFLECTION

What are the possible advantages and disadvantages of giving a public presentation about your research? Brainstorm a list with a colleague or classmate.

How does one get to give a presentation at a conference? Normally, conference organizers require potential presenters to submit an abstract—a concise, informative summary that will appear in the program booklet so that attendees can decide which session will be most beneficial for them to attend. Sometimes a longer text (e.g., 200 words) is reviewed by a selection committee and a very short version (40 or 50 words) appears in the printed program. These summaries are usually subjected to a *blind review process*—which means that the referees who review proposals don't know who has written them and the authors don't know who reads them. The blind review procedure is used to promote fairness and impartiality in selecting the papers to be presented at the conference.

Conference presentations can take the form of workshops, demonstrations, or formal papers that are read aloud. One format that we have found particularly useful for novice researchers is the poster presentation. In this context, the presenter creates a poster representing his or her project. Such posters can include the research question(s), a list of the data collection and analysis procedures used, flowcharts of how the study proceeded, tables or graphs depicting the findings, and a list of recommendations based on the results. At the conference, instead of reading a paper aloud to an audience, the presenter stands by the poster for a period of time and explains the information to interested people who come to view the poster. In this way, novice presenters get the opportunity to talk to individuals or small groups in an interactive fashion. In addition, presenting the ideas more than once can build confidence and help the speaker anticipate the kinds of questions that will arise.

Some Practicalities of Doing Research

We close this section by summarizing some of the practical advice that has been offered throughout this volume. Specifically, we will discuss anticipating problems, making sure the project is feasible, letting the questions lead the way, and knowing where to go to get help.

First, if you can anticipate problems, they can often be forestalled. In Chapter 2 we listed the following problems identified in a survey of graduate students and teachers involved in action research (Nunan, 1992). However, these issues can be problems in undertaking a study using any research method:

1. Lack of time (a particular problem for those who are working full time)
2. Lack of expertise, particularly with critical phases of the research, such as formulating the research question and determining the appropriate research design and statistical tools
3. Difficulty in identifying research subjects
4. Problems in negotiating access to research sites
5. Issues of confidentiality
6. Ethical questions relating to collecting data
7. Problems flowing from the growth of the project after its initiation
8. Sensitivity of reporting negative findings, particularly if these relate to worksites or individuals with whom one is associated
9. Preparation of a written report of the research. (p. 219)

Of these, lack of time was seen as the most important.

The time issue is, of course, related to whether or not the project is feasible. Some of the most exciting research ideas founder because of practical impediments. These are many and various. They can include lack of time or expertise on the part of the researcher, ethical considerations, cost factors, or the inability to find sufficient numbers of appropriate subjects. It is therefore important to develop a detailed and carefully considered plan before launching into the project proper. A plan that is detailed, well considered and—if possible—reviewed by someone who has research experience will reveal pitfalls that may not be immediately apparent to less experienced researchers.

It is also important to let the questions lead the way. One point we have made a number of times in this book is that no research tradition or method is inherently superior to any other. The procedures that you adopt should be determined by the research questions you pose. The research questions are the lynchpins of the entire investigative enterprise, which is why they are so important. This is not to say that the questions should be set in stone. They may very well evolve as you begin to collect and interrogate your data, particularly in naturalistic inquiry and action research.

This point is vividly illustrated by Freeman (1992). In this classroom-based study, the researcher set out to investigate issues of teacher discipline and control in secondary school French-as-a-foreign-language classrooms in the United States. However, as the research proceeded, he discovered that teacher discipline was less of an issue than student self-discipline and self-control. In the course of his investigation, he found an intriguing connection between control over the target language and self-discipline on the part of the students.

Finally, throughout the life of an investigation, knowing where to get help when it is needed is important. Sources of help include information available in books, journals, and on the Internet; other researchers; and peers. If the research is part of a formal degree, the research supervisor has an important role to play in reviewing and evaluating the research. As Marshall and Rossman (1995) state,

> In planning qualitative dissertation research, support from university faculty to make judgments about the adequacy of the proposal is crucial. At least one committee member, preferably the chair, should have had experience conducting qualitative studies. Such experience should also help in making decisions about how to allocate time realistically to various tasks, given that all-important idea that qualitative research often takes much more time than one might predict. Faculty support and encouragement are critical for developing research proposals that are substantial, elegant, and doable, and for advocacy in the larger university community to legitimize this particular study and qualitative research generally. (pp. 135–136)

QUALITY CONTROL ISSUES

The quality control issues in mixed methods studies are an amalgam of those related to quantitative research (e.g., trying to ensure both internal and external reliability as well as internal and external validity) and those related to more qualitative research. Rather than repeat what we said in Chapters 13 and 14 on these points, let us just suggest a metaphor here. That is, doing a mixed methods study is rather like a balancing act. There are strengths and weaknesses to both approaches, and it is generally felt that using procedures from both may help to address the weaknesses.

Sometimes researchers, especially novice researchers, can get bogged down in the sheer volume of data that emerges in a mixed methods study. A technique we have found helpful is to take a conceptual step back and try to review the big picture. Is your study primarily quantitative in nature, with the qualitative data (observational field notes, interview transcripts, etc.) meant to explicate the numerical outcomes? Or is it, like van Lier's (1996a) study of bilingual education in Peru, primarily qualitative in design with some quantified data that can be used to illustrate and substantiate patterns observed in and interpretations suggested by the qualitative data?

Sometimes the qualitatively and quantitatively collected data share equal weight in the research equation. To mix our metaphors just a bit, in this situation it is almost as if the two sorts of data are dance partners, but the lead changes continuously. As illustrated in Bailey's struggle with the international TA data, sometimes the qualitative data point the way, and then the quantitative data take over and point you in a different direction. Being able to cope with this sort of ambiguity and being open to the nudges from the data are useful characteristics for mixed methods researchers.

One practical technique is to create a chart for each research question you are addressing, which lists the quantitative data collection procedures on one axis and the qualitative data collection procedures on the other. By filling in the cells in the chart, you can keep track of what information is emerging and what remains elusive. Sometimes the quantitatively and qualitatively collected data dovetail nicely, and other times they diverge. In either case, you will need to explain the patterns that emerge.

SAMPLE STUDY

As our final sample study, we will summarize research by Katz (1996). We chose this mixed methods study because it uses both quantitative and qualitative data collection methods as well as qualitative and quantitative analyses. It also illustrates some interesting problems in operationalizing classroom constructs.

Katz (ibid.) studied the teaching styles of four teachers who all taught different sections of the same ESL composition course at a large university in the United States. The course assignments were intended "to prepare students for the academic writing in their university content courses" (p. 59). The students in these classes represented forty-three different first-language backgrounds. The report "describes the interaction between teachers and university students as students are engaged in learning how to improve their writing skills in a second language" (p. 57). The four instructors involved in the study were selected because of (1) their interest in participating in the project, (2) their recognized excellence as teachers, and (3) their teaching style.

Katz particularly wished to investigate this last construct—*teaching style*. Initially she defined this concept as "the manner in which the teacher interprets his or her role within the context of the classroom in creating the culture of the classroom" (p. 58). She notes, however, that teaching style "is a slippery construct" since it involves both teachers' behaviors (which are observable) and their beliefs (which may not be directly observable) (p. 61).

This study employed multiple data collection procedures. Katz tape-recorded two interviews with each of the four teachers—one at the beginning and one at the end of the semester. In addition, she observed their regularly scheduled classes throughout the semester: "two weeks at the beginning of the semester, one in the middle, and one at the end, averaging eleven hours per teacher" (p. 60). During the observations, she made both written field notes and audio recordings. Katz also kept notes in her researcher's journal throughout the project.

To compare these four teachers, Katz examined teaching activities and transcripts of the teachers' talk. She contrasted classroom events in the four teachers' lessons across the dimensions of class openings, taking roll, the teachers' use of space, the dominant structures of talk during lessons, turn selection, use of narratives, use of rhetorical questions, and the teachers' policies on students arriving late. She examined these data in order to discover

> the similarities and differences across teachers as they engage in shaping their writing classrooms. The portraits that follow combine an analysis of these behaviors with excerpts from teacher interviews as we talked about their goals and beliefs about writing and teaching, discussing specific aspects of what occurred in their classrooms (p. 61).

Using these procedures, Katz selected metaphors to identify four styles among the teachers she observed. Meg was characterized as the Choreographer, Sarah as the Earth Mother, Ron as the Entertainer, and Karen as the Professor. The qualitative analyses yielded a prose profile of each. Katz also used quantitative data to help explain the differences among these four styles, as show in **Table 15.4**.

Katz (ibid.) used these (and other) quantitative data to help characterize the four teachers and explain how they used their lesson time. But the quantitative data alone do not fully convey the stable style differences that emerged. For example, if we compare the percent of teacher-to-class interaction across the four teachers, we find that Meg, the Choreographer, and Karen, the Professor, appear to be quite similar, with 79.1% and 79.7% of their class time, respectively, given over to the teacher addressing the entire class. Katz points out that Karen's and Meg's classrooms "actually differ dramatically in terms of how each teacher plays

TABLE 15.4 Percent of class time various interactional groupings were used by four teachers (adapted from Katz, 1996, p. 67)

	Meg (Choreographer)	Sarah (Earth Mother)	Ron (Entertainer)	Karen (Professor)
Teacher-to-class	79.1	64.0	65.3	79.7
Individual work	11.4	2.2	6.0	6.5
Group	9.5	28.7	9.0	13.8
Student-to-student (brief)		5.1	3.3	
Student-to-student (extended)			16.4	

out her lessons during these frames of teacher-to-class interaction" (p. 82). As shown in numerous transcripts, Meg's talk time consisted largely of "carefully shaped question and answer sequences," while Karen "delivered the lesson content by means of extensive lectures" (ibid.). It would not have been possible to make this important contrast confidently without the qualitatively collected data (the transcripts and observation field notes).

Here we have summarized just a small portion of Katz's study of teacher style, but we hope these excerpts give you the flavor of how one classroom researcher was able to combine quantitative and qualitative data collection and analysis procedures to produce a rich picture of classroom interaction. In a standard experimental design, these four teachers might have been considered to be quite similar: They all taught from the same curriculum in the same program with students drawn from the same population. Yet the teaching styles they adopted and the ways they enacted that curriculum differed markedly, as shown by the rich data sources Katz employed in this mixed methods study.

REFLECTION

Katz (1996) warns against the problem that a metaphor might "shape perceptions rather than clarifying them" (p. 62). Look back at the sample study described at the end of Chapter 4. That process-product study involved Bailey and some colleagues as observers in low-level language classes at a U. S. military installation. Consider this anecdote:

> There was one teacher whom Bailey and the other observers privately thought of as the "Gestapo" because her error treatment strategies were so intense. The teacher would interrupt students and emphatically model the correct form if they mispronounced words or made grammar or vocabulary errors during lessons. She sometimes belittled students about their errors. However, one day after an observation, a student who had just been the object of the teacher's scathing error treatment made the unsolicited comment to the observer that he really liked this teacher because she prepared him and his classmates so well for the exams they would have to take. Since those exams emphasized accuracy, he appreciated her consistent emphasis on the learners being correct.

What metaphor do you think this student would have used to characterize this teacher?

PAYOFFS AND PITFALLS

It has been said that "books that deal with classroom research do little to help researchers and future researchers understand the complexities and the problems of conducting classroom-based research" (Schachter and Gass, 1996, p. viii). We hope that this book has proven to be an exception to this claim (with which we generally agree). The difficulty with being candid is that we don't want to discourage anyone from getting started on classroom research. With that caveat in mind, let us turn to the last set of "payoffs and pitfalls" in this book, starting with potential problems.

The first pitfall associated with undertaking a mixed methods study has to do with data. It is easy to get overwhelmed with masses of information any time you are working with qualitatively collected data, and this problem can be compounded by having quantitative data added to the study. We would suggest that you develop techniques for managing the data in your particular research project that will enable you to see clearly what has been done and what needs to be done next. It is essential that you label all data with the date, time, and place of collection, and that you make back-up files immediately of any information you cannot afford to lose.

Another issue related to managing copious qualitative and quantitative data sets is connected to the ethical issues discussed above. If you have promised that your data will be treated confidentially, then you must lock them away—either electronically or physically—and shield the identities of the participants. If you have promised the participants anonymity, you must provide pseudonyms that neither give hints as to their identities nor obscure relevant information. You need to develop a written key about the actual names and the pseudonyms you use for your participants in any written reports or oral presentations. Keep that list hidden and safe and only use the pseudonyms any time you discuss your project.

Yet another major pitfall associated with mixed methods studies is the problem of time. Many of our research students over the years have eschewed statistical research because they were nervous about mathematical analyses or didn't want to spend the time needed to learn about statistical procedures. This choice is ironic since, in our experience, nice, neat quantitative analyses usually take much less time than does the laborious process of analyzing qualitative data or working back and forth between qualitative and quantitative data sets in the same study.

One reason why mixed methods studies can be so time-consuming is that different sorts of data may suggest different interpretations of the results. For instance, if there is no significant difference between the pre-test and post-test scores of a group of learners we have observed in a study, does this finding indicate that no learning has occurred? If we have observational field notes and transcripts of audio recordings we have made in a language class, we may be able to look at those data and find evidence that what the students learned was not addressed in the test, but doing so is very time-consuming.

This last point, of course, provides us with a segue into the payoffs. Combining quantitative and qualitative data collection and analysis procedures, as Katz (1996) and van Lier (1996a) did, can help us understand anomalies in our results. The qualitative findings often shed light on the statistical outcomes, but at the same time, numerical information can flesh out patterns observed in qualitative data.

An advantage of using quantitative data is that, for better or for worse, policy makers, legislators, and administrators are often impressed by "hard data"—statistical results showing significant gains or differences or relationships. An advantage of using the results of qualitative data is that they are often more memorable and more intelligible to laypersons or to teachers who may lack formal statistical training.

We predict that as technological tools for collecting and analyzing data continue to increase in number and improve, there will be more mixed methods language classroom studies in the future. If you would like to try your hand at a project that involves both quantitative and qualitative data collection and analyses, we suggest you start small. Investigate an issue in a class you are teaching or taking that can utilize the existing or naturally occurring data sets. For instance, if you are a teacher and you wish to document the development of your secondary school language students' confidence and their writing skills over time, photocopy the homework and in-class writing assignments they submit to you. These data are naturally collected as part of the work you must do anyway, and they can provide a rich source of information about the students' emerging syntactic, morphological, lexical, and discourse development. Combined with test scores or questionnaire data, they could help you determine whether the learners' writing skill and confidence have increased in the course of a school year.

CONCLUSION

In this final chapter, we have revisited some of the themes, issues, and concerns that run through this book. We have considered combining quantitative and qualitative data collection and data analysis procedures to produce mixed methods studies. We have suggested a sequence of steps to take in developing a research plan and reviewed the steps involved in planning and conducting language classroom research. Our hope is that this chapter has both introduced new ideas and reminded you of concepts introduced earlier in order to help you put it all together in designing and carrying out your own language classroom research.

QUESTIONS AND TASKS

1. Both Bailey (1982; 1984) and Katz (1996) used metaphors to describe different teaching styles. Following the work of Miles and Huberman (1984), Katz notes that using metaphors helps to reduce massive amounts of qualitative information by turning particularities into generalizations and thereby creating patterns. She also notes, however, that using metaphors runs the risk of "shaping perceptions rather than clarifying them" (p. 62). What do you think? Can you envision a study in which you would want to characterize participants in some way that employed metaphor?

2. Think of teachers that you have observed. Based on your experience, can you recall a teacher who could be characterized as an "Entertainer" or a "Choreographer" or an "Earth Mother" or a "Professor"? These labels are from Katz's (1996) research (see Table 15.4). We can ask the same question about the metaphors Bailey (1982; 1984) used to describe the teaching assistants in her study. In other words, do these metaphors seem trustworthy or broadly applicable based on your own experience (as an observer, a student, a researcher, or a teacher)?

3. Prepare a detailed research plan for a project of your choice. Include information on the following aspects of the research. (The following list is adapted from Nunan, 1992, pp. 227–228.)

I. Background

General area

Title

The problem or issue

Purpose of the study

Likely importance of the study

Background to the study

The aims and justification of the study

Limitations of the study

What the study proposes to do

II. Literature review

A plan for the literature review including headings and subheadings

Resources (books, journals, Web sites, etc.) to be consulted

III. Research design

The research questions or hypotheses

Definitions of terms

Sampling strategies

Subjects, participants, or informants

Data collection methods

Data analysis procedures

IV. Presentation and dissemination

Statement on how the results will be presented

Suggestions as to which conferences and/or publications would be appropriate

4. Grotjahn's (1987) two 'pure paradigms' were introduced in Chapter 1 and discussed further in Chapters 7, 4, and 10. In this final chapter, we have introduced the other combinations of the variables in his framework. Given the study you sketched out in the task above, which of Grotjahn's research paradigms would you use? Think about (a) the research involved, (b) the types of data to be collected, and (c) the types of analyses to be done.

5. Review and evaluate your plan. What problems or difficulties do you anticipate? How might these be dealt with?

6. Share your plan with a classmate or colleague for feedback and discuss any issues that may arise.

7. Visit the Web sites of at least three professional organizations that interest you. Find out when their upcoming conferences are scheduled and what you must do in order to propose presentations that you could offer at those conferences.

8. From the Web sites you visit, choose the conference that appeals to y u most. Draft an abstract for a presentation you would like to make follo ing the organization's guidelines. Share your abstract with a classmate or colleague for feedback.

9. Visit the Web sites of some organizations that fund research in our field. We suggest these three:

   A. The Spencer Foundation:

   www.spencer.org

   B. The Social Sciences and Humanities Research Council of Canada:

   http://sshrc.ca

   C. The International Research Foundation for English Language Education (TIRF):

   www.tirfonline.org

   Find out what kinds of research they support and what their applicatio processes involve.

10. Compare the submission guidelines for at least three professional journals that interest you. (The kinds of journals that accept language classroom research reports include the *TESOL Quarterly, Modern Language Journal, Prospect—A Journal of Australian TESOL, The ELT Journal, Language Teaching Research, Asian Journal of English Language Teaching*, and so on.) How do their submission requirements differ? Which journal might be the best for you to consider if you would like to submit a research article for publication?

11. Here is a 200-word summary that could be submitted to a conference adjudicating committee. Space in conference program booklets is usually quite limited, however, and often all that appears there is a forty- or fifty-word abstract. Imagine that you are the author of this study. Using the information below, compose an interesting and informative fifty-word abstract which would encourage conference attendees to come to your presentation.

Summary: This paper reports on the results of a yearlong investigation of ESL courses at community colleges in the United States. The study addressed the issue of how teachers using content-based instruction shift the focus of the lesson from content foci to language foci. *Content-based instruction* (CBI) is defined as an approach to language curriculum design that entails "the integration of content learning with language teaching aims" (Brinton, Snow, & Wesche, 2003, p. ix). Also, "the form and sequence of language presentation are dictated by content material" (Brinton et al., 2003, p. ix). Thus, the research question posed in this language classroom research was what strategies do teachers use to teach language in content-based English as a second language classes? The researcher observed classes in Arizona, California, Hawaii, Florida, Illinois, and Texas, taking running field notes to document the activities involved. In some cases, teachers were interviewed. The refined field notes were sent to the teachers for member checking. This presentation will concentrate on the patterns observed in the lessons of six teachers whose classes were the most clearly content-based. A question-and-answer period will follow the presentation and participants will be given Internet access to a lengthy reference list on content-based instruction.

Reference: Brinton, D.M., Snow, M.A., & Wesche, M. (2003). *Content-based second language instruction.* Ann Arbor: University of Michigan Press.

12. If you were a member of the conference selection committee that reviews such summaries for the conference program, what questions or comments would you have for the author of the summary above? What suggestions would you have for improving the summary?

SUGGESTIONS FOR FURTHER READING

In an earlier chapter, we suggested you read the book *Second Language Classroom Research: Issues and Opportunities*, edited by Schachter and Gass (1996). We remind you of that book here because the authors in that volume intentionally discussed the problems they encountered in their studies in hopes that other researchers would benefit from a candid discussion of the sorts of difficulties that arise. In particular, the chapters by Markee (1996) and Polio (1996) are useful.

For helpful advice on writing research proposals and reports, we recommend Dörnyei (2007), Galvan (1999), and Hatch and Lazaraton (1991). For guidance on planning qualitative research, see Marshall and Rossman (1995; 1999; and 2006).

Some ethical considerations in proposing and conducting language classroom research are discussed by McKay (2006).

For an interesting and influential discussion about the qualitative/ quantitative debate, see Smith and Heshusius (1986).

In recent years, teacher research has become more widely accepted. The volume edited by Beaumont and O'Brien (2000) provides many examples of teacher research in our field, as does the one edited by Edge and Richards (1993). Some teacher research has been motivated by Allwright's work. Several authors contributed to *Understanding the Language Classroom* (Gieve & Miller, 2006)—a book inspired by his ideas. See also Burnaford, Fischer, and Hobson (1996), Nunan (1997a, 1997b), and Stewart (2006). In general education, Kincheloe (1991) and Lankshear and Knobel (2004) are good resources.

For two 'user-friendly' books see K. E. Johnson's (1998) *Teachers Understanding Teaching* and (1999) and *Understanding Language Teaching: Reasoning in Action* (1999). For research on language teachers' decision making, see Woods (1996).

In addition, the TESOL organization has published a series of edited research volumes that focus on studies conducted by teachers in various parts of the world, including Asia (Farrell, 2006), Europe (Borg and Farrell, 2007), the Americas (McGarrell, 2007), the Middle East (Coombe and Barlow, 2007), and Australia and New Zealand (Burton and Burns, 2008). We recommend these volumes because they provide numerous interesting examples of research done by teachers in their own professional contexts.

REFERENCES

Acheson, K. A., & Gall, M. D. (1997). *Techniques in the clinical supervision of teachers: Preservice and inservice applications* (4th ed.). New York: Longman.

Adelman, C., Jenkins, D., & Kemmis, S. (1976). Rethinking case study: Notes from the second Cambridge conference. *Cambridge Journal of Education, 6(3),* 139–150.

Aljaafreh, A., & Lantolf, J. P. (1994). Negative feedback as regulation and second language learning in the zone of proximal development. *Modern Language Journal, 78,* 465–483.

Allen, P. J., Fröhlich, M., & Spada, N. (1984). The communicative orientation of second language teaching. In J. Handscombe, R. Orem, & B. Taylor (Eds.), *On TESOL '83: The question of control* (pp. 231–252). Washington, DC: TESOL.

Allison, D. (1998). Investigating learners' course diaries as explorations of language. *Language Teaching Research, 2(4),* 24–47.

Allwright, D. (1983). Classroom-centered research on language teaching and learning: A brief historical overview. *TESOL Quarterly, 17(2),* 191–204.

Allwright, D. (1988). *Observation in the language classroom.* New York: Longman.

Allwright, D. (1997). Quality and sustainability in teacher-research. *TESOL Quarterly, 31(2),* 368–370.

Allwright, D. (2001). Three major processes of teacher development and the appropriate design criteria for developing and using them. In B. Johnston & S. Irujo (Eds.), *Research*
and practice in language teacher education: Voices from the field (pp. 115–133). Minneapolis, MN: Center for Advanced Research on Language Acquisition.

Allwright, D. (2003). Exploratory practice: Rethinking practitioner research in language teaching. *Language Teaching Research, 7,* 113–141.

Allwright, D. (2005). Developing principles for practitioner research: The case of exploratory practice. *Modern Language Journal, 89(3),* 353–363.

Allwright, D., & Bailey, K. M. (1991). *Focus on the classroom: An introduction to classroom research for language teachers.* Cambridge: Cambridge University Press.

Allwright, D., & Lenzuen, R. (1997). Exploring practice: Work at the Cultura Inglesa, Rio de Janeiro, Brazil. *Language Teaching Research, 1(1),* 71–79.

Allwright, R. L. (1980). Turns, topics, and tasks: Patterns of participation in language learning and teaching. In D. Larsen-Freeman (Ed.), *Discourse analyses in second language research* (pp. 165–187). Rowley, MA: Newbury House.

Alreck, P., & Settle, R. (1985). *The survey research handbook.* Homewood, IL: Irwin.

Amanpour, C. (2005). Commentary on National Pubic Radio.

Andrews, R. (Ed.). (1993). *The Columbia dictionary of quotations.* New York: Columbia University Press.

Appel, J. (1995). *Diary of a language teacher.* Oxford: Heinemann English Language Teaching.

Applewhite, A., Evans III, W., & Frothingham, A. (2003). *And I quote: The definitive collection of quotes, sayings, and jokes for the contemporary speechmaker.* New York: Thomas Dunne Books.

Asher, J. J., Kusudo, J. A., & de la Torre, R. (1993). Learning a second language through commands: The second field test. In J. W. Oller, Jr. (Ed.), *Methods that work: Ideas for literacy and language teachers* (2nd ed., pp. 13–21). Boston: Heinle & Heinle.

Auerbach, E. (1994). Participatory action research. In A. Cumming, Alternatives in TESOL research: Descriptive, interpretive and ideological orientations. *TESOL Quarterly, 28(4),* 673–703.

Bachman, L. F., & Palmer, A. S. (1996). *Language testing in practice: Designing and developing useful language tests.* Oxford: Oxford University Press.

Bailey, K. M. (1981). An introspective analysis of an individual's language learning experience. In S. Krashen & R. Scarcella (Eds.), *Issues in second language acquisition: Selected papers of the Los Angeles Second Language Research Forum* (pp. 58–65). Rowley, MA: Newbury House.

Bailey, K. M. (1982). Teaching in a second language: The communicative competence of non-native speaking teaching assistants. Ph.D. dissertation in Applied Linguistics, University of California, Los Angeles.

Bailey, K. M. (1983a). Some illustrations of Murphy's Law from classroom centered research on language use. *TESOL Newsletter, 17(4),* August. (Reprinted in *Selected articles from the TESOL Newsletter, 1966–1983,* pp. 81–85, by J. F. Haskell, Ed., Washington, DC: TESOL).

Bailey, K. M. (1983b). Competitiveness and anxiety in adult second language learning: Looking *at* and *through* the diary studies. In H.W. Seliger & M. H. Long (Eds.), *Classroom oriented research in second language acquisition* (pp. 67–102). Rowley, MA: Newbury House.

Bailey, K. M. (1984). A typology of teaching assistants. In K. M. Bailey, F. Pialorsi, & J. Zukowski/Faust (Eds.), *Foreign teaching assistants in U.S. universities* (pp. 110–125). Washington, DC: NAFSA.

Bailey, K. M. (1990). The use of diary studies in teacher education programs. In J. C. Richards & D. Nunan (Eds.), *Second language teacher education* (pp. 215–226). Cambridge: Cambridge University Press.

Bailey, K. M. (1991). Diary studies of classroom language learning: The doubting game and the believing game. In E. Sadtono (Ed.), *Language acquisition and the second/foreign language classroom* (Anthology Series 28), (pp. 60–102). Singapore: SEAMEO Regional Language Center.

Bailey, K. M. (1992). The processes of innovation in language teacher development: What, why and how teachers change. In J. Flowerdew, M. Brock, & S. Hsia (Eds.), *Perspectives on second language teacher education* (pp. 253–282). Hong Kong: City Polytechnic of Hong Kong.

Bailey, K. M. (1996). The best laid plans: Teachers' in-class decisions to depart from their lesson plans. In K. M. Bailey & D. Nunan (Eds.), *Voices from the language classroom: Qualitative research on language education* (pp. 15–40). New York: Cambridge University Press.

Bailey, K. M. (1998a). Approaches to empirical research in instructional language settings. In H. Byrnes (Ed.), *Learning foreign and second languages: Perspectives in research and scholarship* (pp. 75–104). New York: Modern Language Association of America.

Bailey, K. M. (1998b). *Learning about language assessment: Dilemmas, decisions and directions.* Boston: Heinle & Heinle.

Bailey, K. M. (2001a). Action research, teacher research, and classroom research in language teaching. In M. Celce-Murcia (Ed.), *Teaching English as a second or foreign language* (3rd ed., pp. 489–498). Boston: Heinle & Heinle.

Bailey, K. M. (2001b). What my EFL students taught me. *The PAC Journal, 1*, 7–31.

Bailey, K. M. (2005). Looking back down the road: A recent history of language classroom research. *Review of Applied Linguistics in China: Issues in Language Learning and Teaching, 1*, 6–47.

Bailey, K. M. (2006). *Language teacher supervision: A case-based approach.* New York: Cambridge University Press.

Bailey, K. M., Bergthold, B., Braunstein, B., Fleischman, N. J., Holbrook, M. P., Tuman, J., Waissbluth, X., & Zambo, L. (1996). The language learner's autobiography: Examining the "apprenticeship of observation." In D. Freeman & J .C. Richards (Eds.), *Teacher learning in language teaching* (pp. 11–29). New York: Cambridge University Press.

Bailey, K. M., Curtis, A., & Nunan, D. (2001). *Pursuing professional development: The self as source.* Boston: Heinle & Heinle.

Bailey, K. M., & Nunan, D. (Eds.) (1996). *Voices from the language classroom: Qualitative research on language education.* New York: Cambridge University Press.

Bailey, K. M., & Ochsner, R. (1983). A methodological review of the diary studies: Windmill tilting or social science? In K. M. Bailey, M. H. Long, & S. Peck (Eds.), *Second language acquisition studies* (pp. 188–198). Rowley, MA: Newbury House.

Bailey, K. M., & Saunders, S. (1998, March). Relationships among course objectives, self-assessment, and achievement in a learning strategies course. Paper presented at the Language Testing Research Colloquium, Monterey, California.

Barlow, M. (2005). Computer-based analyses of learner language. In R. Ellis & G. Barkhuizen, *Analyzing learner language* (pp. 335–357). Oxford: Oxford University Press.

Bateson, G. (1972). *Steps to an ecology of mind.* New York: Ballantine.

Beatty, K. (2003). *Teaching and researching computer-assisted language learning.* London: Longman.

Beaumont, M., & O'Brien, T. (2000). *Collaborative research in second language education.* Stoke on Kent, England: Trentham Books.

Bejarano, Y. (1987). A cooperative small-group methodology in the language classroom. *TESOL Quarterly, 21(3),* 483–504.

Bell, J. (1987). *Doing your research project.* Milton Keynes, England: Open University Press.

Benson, P., & Nunan, D. (2005). *Learners' stories: Difference and diversity in language learning.* New York: Cambridge University Press.

Biber, D., Conrad, S., & Reppen, R. (1998). *Corpus linguistics: Investigating language structure and use.* Cambridge: Cambridge University Press.

Birch, G. J. (1992). Language learning case study approach to second language teacher education. In J. Flowerdew, M. N. Brock, & S. Hsia (Eds.), *Perspectives on second language teacher education* (pp. 283–294). Hong Kong: City Polytechnic of Hong Kong.

Bley-Vroman, R., & Chaudron, C. (1994). Elicited imitation as a measure of second-language competence. In E. E. Tarone, S. M. Gass, & A. D. Cohen (Eds.), *Research methodology in second-language acquisition* (pp. 245–262). Hillsdale, NJ: Lawrence Erlbaum Associates.

Block, D. (1996). A window on the classroom: Classroom events viewed from different angles. In K. M. Bailey & D. Nunan (Eds.), *Voices from the language classroom: Qualitative research on language education* (pp. 168–194). New York: Cambridge University Press.

Block, D. (1998). Tale of a language learner. *Language Teaching Research, 2(2)*, 148–176.

Borg, S., & Farrell, T. S. C. (Eds.). (2007). *Language teacher research in Europe.* Alexandria, VA: TESOL.

Bowers, R. (1980). Verbal behaviour in the language teaching classroom. Unpublished doctoral dissertation, University of Reading, England.

Braine, G. (1994). Comments on A. Suresh Canagarajah's "Critical ethnography of a Sri Lankan classroom." *TESOL Quarterly, 28(3)*, 609–623.

Brinton, D., & Holten, C. (1989). What novice teachers focus on: The practicum in TESL. *TESOL Quarterly, 23*, 343–350.

Brinton, D. M., Snow, M. A., & Wesche, M. (2003). *Content-based second language instruction.* Ann Arbor: University of Michigan Press.

Brock, C. (1986). The effect of referential questions on ESL classroom discourse. *TESOL Quarterly, 20(1)*, 47–58.

Brock, M. N., Yu, B., & Wong, M. (1992). 'Journaling' together: Collaborative diary-keeping and teacher development. In J. Flowerdew, M. N. Brock, & S. Hsia (Eds.), *Perspectives on second language teacher development* (pp. 295–307). Hong Kong: City University of Hong Kong.

Brown, C. (1985a). Two windows on the classroom world: Diary studies and participant observation differences. In P. Larson, E. L. Judd, & D. S. Messerschmitt (Eds.), *On TESOL '94: Brave new world for TESOL* (pp. 121–134). Washington, DC: TESOL.

Brown, C. (1985b). Requests for specific language input: Differences between older and younger adult language learners. In S. Gass & C. Madden (Eds.), *Input in second language acquisition* (pp. 272–284). Rowley, MA: Newbury House.

Brown, H. D. (2004). *Language assessment: Principles and classroom practices.* White Plains, NY: Longman.

Brown, J. D. (1988). *Understanding research in second language learning: A teacher's guide to statistics and research design.* Cambridge: Cambridge University Press.

Brown, J. D. (2001). *Using surveys in language programs.* Cambridge: Cambridge University Press.

Brown, J. D. (2005). *Testing in language programs: A comprehensive guide to English language assessment.* New York: McGraw-Hill.

Brown, J. D., & Rodgers, T. S. (2002). *Doing second language research.* Oxford: Oxford University Press.

Brown, R. (1973). *A first language: The early stages.* London: Allen and Unwin.

Brumfit, C., & Mitchell, R. (1990a). The language classroom as a focus for research. In C. Brumfit & R. Mitchell (Eds.), *Research in the language classroom: ELT Documents, 133* (pp. 3–15). London: Modern English Publications and British Council.

Brumfit, C., & Mitchell, R. (Eds.). (1990b). *Research in the language classroom: ELT Documents, 133.* London: Modern English Publications and British Council.

Bruner, J. (1983). *Child's talk: Learning to use language.* New York: Norton.

Burling, R. (1978). Language development of a Garo and English-speaking child. In E. M. Hatch (Ed.), *Second language acquisition: A book of readings* (pp. 54–75). Rowley, MA: Newbury House.

Burnaford, G., Fischer, J., & Hobson, D. (1996). *Teachers doing research: Practical possibilities*. Mahwah, NJ: Lawrence Erlbaum Associates.

Burns, A. (1995). Teacher-researchers: Perspectives on teacher action research and curriculum renewal. In A. Burns & S. Hood (Eds.), *Teachers voices: Exploring course design in a changing curriculum* (pp. 3–29). Sydney: NCELTR, Macquarie University.

Burns, A. (1997). Valuing diversity: Action researching disparate learner groups. *TESOL Journal, 7(1)*, 6–9.

Burns, A. (1999). *Collaborative action research for English language teachers*. Cambridge: Cambridge University Press.

Burns, A. (2000). Facilitating collaborative action research: Some insights from the AMEP. *Prospect: A Journal of Australian TESOL, 15(3)*, 23–34.

Burns, A. (2004). Action research. In E. Hinkel (Ed.), *Handbook of research in second language teaching and learning* (pp. 241–256). Mahwah, NJ: Lawrence Erlbaum Associates.

Burns, A., & Burton, J. (Eds.). (2008). *Language teacher research in Australia and New Zealand*. Alexandria, VA: TESOL.

Burns, A., de Silva Joyce, H., & Hood, S. (Eds.). (1995). *Exploring course design in a changing curriculum: Teachers' voices 1*. Sydney: National Centre for English Language Teaching and Research, Macquarie University.

Burns, A, de Silva Joyce, H., & Hood, S. (Eds.). (1997). *Teaching disparate learner groups: Teachers' voices 2*. Sydney: National Centre for English Language Teaching and Research, Macquarie University.

Burns, A., de Silva Joyce, H., & Hood, S. (Eds.). (1999a). *Teaching critical literacies: Teachers' voices 3*. Sydney:

National Centre for English Language Teaching and Research, Macquarie University.

Burns, A., de Silva Joyce, H., & Hood, S. (Eds.). (1999b). *Staying learner-centred in a competency-based curriculum: Teachers' voices 4*. Sydney: National Centre for English Language Teaching and Research, Macquarie University.

Burns, A., de Silva Joyce, H., & Hood, S. (Eds.). (1999c). *Teaching casual conversation: Teachers' voices 6*. Sydney: National Centre for English Language Teaching and Research, Macquarie University.

Burns, A., de Silva Joyce, H., & Hood, S. (Eds.). (2000). *A new look at reading practices: Teachers' voices 5*. Sydney: National Centre for English Language Teaching and Research, Macquarie University.

Burns, A., & Richards, J. C. (in press). *Cambridge guide to language teacher education*. Cambridge: Cambridge University Press.

Burton, J., & Burns, A. (Eds.). (2008). *Language teacher research in Australia and New Zealand*. Alexandria, VA: TESOL.

Busch, M. (1993). Using Likert scales in L2 research. *TESOL Quarterly, 24(4)*, 733–736.

Campbell, C. C. (1996). Socializing with the teachers and prior language learning experience: A diary study. In K. M. Bailey & D. Nunan (Eds.), *Voices from the language classroom: Qualitative research on language education* (pp. 201–223). New York: Cambridge University Press.

Campbell, D. T., & Stanley, J. C. (1963). *Experimental and non-experimental designs for research*. Washington, DC: American Educational Research Association.

Canagarajah, A. S. (1993). Critical ethnography of a Sri Lankan classroom: Ambiguities in student opposition to reproduction through ESOL. *TESOL Quarterly, 27(4),* 601–625.

Carless, D. (1999). Catering for individual learner differences: Primary school teachers' voices. *Hong Kong Journal of Applied Linguistics, 4(2),* 15–40.

Carr, W., & Kemmis, S. (1986). *Becoming critical: Education, knowledge and action research.* London: Falmer.

Carrasco, R. L. (1981). Expanded awareness of student performance: A case study in applied ethnographic monitoring of a bilingual classroom. In H. T. Trueba, G. P. Guthrie, & H. P. Au (Eds.), *Culture and the bilingual classroom: Studies in classroom ethnography* (pp. 153–177). Rowley, MA: Newbury House.

Carroll, M. (1994). Journal writing as a learning and research tool in the adult classroom. *TESOL Journal, 4,* 19–22.

Carson, J. G., & Longhini, A. (2002). Focusing on learning styles and strategies: A diary study in an immersion setting. *Language Learning, 52(2),* 401–438.

Carter, R., Goddard, A., Reah, D., Sanger, K., & Bowering, M. (2001). *Working with texts: A core introduction to language analysis* (2nd ed.). London: Routledge.

Carter, R., & Nunan, D. (Eds.). (2001). *The Cambridge guide to teaching English to speakers of other languages.* Cambridge: Cambridge University Press.

Celce-Murcia, M. (1978). The simultaneous acquisition of English and French in a two-year-old child. In E. M. Hatch (Ed.), *Second language acquisition: A book of readings* (pp. 38–53). Rowley, MA: Newbury House.

Chamot, A. U. (1995). The teacher's voice: Research in your classroom. *ERIC/CLL News Bulletin, 19(2),* 1, 5.

Chan, Y. H. (1996). Action research as professional development for ELT practitioners. *Working Papers in ELT and Applied Linguistics, 2(1),* 17–28. Hong Kong: Hong Kong Polytechnic University.

Chaudron, C. (1986). The interaction of quantitative and qualitative approaches to research: A view of the second language classroom. *TESOL Quarterly, 20(4),* 709–717.

Chaudron, C. (1988). *Second language classrooms: Research on teaching and learning.* Cambridge: Cambridge University Press.

Choi, J. (2006). A narrative analysis of second language acquisition and identity formation. Unpublished master's of science dissertation, Anaheim University, Anaheim, California.

Christison, M. A. (2003). Learning styles and strategies. In D. Nunan (Ed.), *Practical English language teaching* (pp. 267–288). New York: McGraw-Hill.

Christison, M. A., & Bassano, S. (1995). Action research: Techniques for collecting data through surveys and interviews. *The CATESOL Journal, 8(1),* 89–103.

Christison, M. A., & Nunan, D. (2001, March). Pedagogical functions in synchronous e-learning interaction: The online conversation class. Paper presented at the international TESOL Convention, St. Louis, Missouri.

Clark, J. L. D. (1969). The Pennsylvania Project and the audiolingual vs. traditional question. *Modern Language Journal, 53,* 388–396.

Clarke, M. A. (1995, March). Ideology, method, style: The importance of particularizability. Paper presented at the international TESOL Convention, Long Beach, California.

Cleghorn, A., & Genesee, F. (1984). Languages in contact: An ethnographic study of interaction in an immersion school. *TESOL Quarterly, 18(4),* 595–625.

Coffey, A., & Atkinson, P. (1996). *Making sense of qualitative data.* Thousand Oaks, CA: Sage.

Cohen, A. D., & Hosenfeld, C. (1981). Some uses of mentalistic data in second language research. *Language Learning, 31(2),* 285–313.

Cohen, J. M., & Cohen, M. J. (1980). *The Penguin dictionary of modern quotations* (2nd ed.). London: Penguin.

Cohen, L., & Manion, L. (1985). *Research methods in education.* London: Croom Helm.

Cole, R., Raffier, L. M., Rogan, P., & Schleicher, L. (1998). Interactive group journals: Learning as a dialogue among learners. *TESOL Quarterly, 32(3),* 556–568.

Cooley, L., & Lewkowicz, J. (2003). *Dissertation writing in practice: Turning ideas into text.* Hong Kong: Hong Kong University Press.

Coombe, C., & Barlow, L. (Eds.). (2007). *Language teacher research in the Middle East.* Alexandria, VA: TESOL.

Crago, M. B. (1992). Communicative interaction and second language acquisition: An Inuit example. *TESOL Quarterly, 26(3),* 487–505.

Crookes, G. (1993). Action research for second language teaching: Going beyond teacher research. *Applied Linguistics, 14,* 130–142.

Crookes, G. (1998). On the relationship between second and foreign language teachers and research. *TESOL Journal, 7(3),* 6–11.

Crookes, G. (2005). Resources for incorporating action research as critique into applied linguistics graduate education. *Modern Language Journal, 89(3),* 467–475.

Curtis, A. (1998). Action research: What, how, and why. *The English Connection, 3(1),* 12–14.

Curtis, A. (1999). Use of action research in exploring the use of spoken English in Hong Kong classrooms. In Y. M. Cheah & S. M. Ng (Eds.), *IDAC Monograph: Language instructional issues in the Asian classroom* (pp. 78–88). Newark, DE: International Reading Association.

Curtis, A., & Bailey, K. M. (In press). Diary studies. *On CUE Journal.*

Dagneaux, E., Denness, S., & Granger, S. (1998). Computer-aided error analysis. *System, 26,* 163–174.

Damon, W., & Phelps, E. (1989). Critical distinctions among three approaches to peer education. *International Journal of Educational Research, 58,* 9–19.

Danielson, D. (1981, March). Views of language learning from an "older learner" (Part II). *CATESOL Newsletter, 12(5),* 6 and 16.

Davidson, F. (1998). The ordinal-interval distinction reconsidered. *Language Testing Update, 23,* 56–64.

Davis, K. A., & Lazaraton, A. (Eds.). (1995). Qualitative research in ESOL. *TESOL Quarterly, 29(3).*

Delaney, A. E., & Bailey, K. M. (2000, March). Teaching journals: Writing for professional development. *ESL Magazine,* 16–18.

Denzin, N. K. (1978). *The research act: A theoretical introduction to sociological methods* (2nd ed.). New York: McGraw-Hill.

Denzin, N. K., & Lincoln, Y. S. (Eds.). (2000). *Handbook of qualitative research* (2nd ed.). Thousand Oaks, CA: Sage Publications.

Dingwall, S. (1984). Critical self-reflection and decisions in doing research: The case of a questionnaire survey of EFL teachers. In S. Dingwall & S. Mann (Eds.), *Methods and problems in doing research* (pp. 3–30). Lancaster, England: Department of Linguistics and Modern English Language, University of Lancaster.

Donato, R. (2000). Sociocultural contributions to understanding the foreign and second language classroom. In J. P. Lantolf (Ed.), *Sociocultural theory and second language learning* (pp. 27–50). Oxford: Oxford University Press.

Donato, R., & Adair-Hauck, B. (1992). Discourse perspectives on formal instruction. *Language Awareness, 1(2)*, 73–89.

Donato, R., Antonek, J. L., & Tucker, G. R. (1994). A multiple perspectives analysis of a Japanese FLES program. *Foreign Language Annals, 27(3)*, 365–378.

Dörnyei, Z. (2003). *Questionnaires in second language research: Construction, administration, and processing.* Mahwah, NJ: Lawrence Erlbaum Associates.

Dörnyei, Z. (2007). *Research methods in applied linguistics.* Oxford: Oxford University Press.

Dörnyei, Z., & Murphey, T. (2003). *Group dynamics in the language classroom.* Cambridge: Cambridge University Press.

Doughty, C., & Pica, T. (1986). "Information gap" tasks: Do they facilitate second language acquisition? *TESOL Quarterly, 20(2)*, 305–325.

Dowsett, G. (1986). Interaction in the semi-structured interview. In M. Emery (Ed.), *Qualitative research* (pp. 50–56). Canberra: Australian Association of Adult Education.

Duff, P. A. (1990). Developments in the case study approach to SLA research. In T. Hayes & K. Yoshioka (Eds.), *Proceedings of the 1st Conference on Second Language Acquisition and Teaching* (pp. 34–87). Tokyo: International University of Japan.

Duff, P. A. (1991a). Innovations in foreign language education: An evaluation of three Hungarian-English dual-language programs. *Journal of Multilingual and Multicultural Development, 12*, 459–476.

Duff, P. A. (1991b). *The efficacy of dual-language education in Hungary: An investigation of three Hungarian-English programs.* (Final Report for Year-Two [1990–91] of the project). Los Angeles, CA: University of California, Los Angeles, The Language Resource Program.

Duff, P. A. (1995). An ethnography of communication in immersion classrooms in Hungary. *TESOL Quarterly, 29(3)*, 505–537.

Duff, P. A. (1996). Different languages, different practices: Socialization of discourse competence in dual-language school classrooms in Hungary. In K. M. Bailey & D. Nunan (Eds.), *Voices from the language classroom: Qualitative research on language education* (pp. 407–443). New York: Cambridge University Press.

Duff, P. A. (2008). *Case study research in applied linguistics.* New York: Lawrence Erlbaum Associates/Taylor & Francis.

Dulay, H., & Burt, M. (1973). Should we teach children syntax? *Language Learning, 23*, 245–258.

Duterte, A. (2000). A teacher's investigation of her own teaching. *Applied Language Learning, 11(1)*, 99–122.

Edge, J. (Ed.). (2001). *Action research.* Alexandria, VA: TESOL.

Edge, J., & Richards, K. (Eds.). (1993). *Teachers develop teachers research: Papers on classroom research and teacher development.* Oxford: Heinemann International.

Edwards, J. A., & Lampert, M. D. (Eds.). (1993). *Talking data: Transcription and coding in discourse research.* Hillsdale, NJ: Lawrence Erlbaum Associates.

Ehlich, K. (1993). HIAT: A transcription system for discourse data. In J. A. Edwards & M. D. Lampert (Eds.), *Talking data: Transcription and coding in discourse research* (pp. 123–148). Hillsdale, NJ: Lawrence Erlbaum Associates.

Ellis, R. (1984). *Second language classroom development*. Oxford: Pergamon.

Ellis, R. (1985). *Understanding second language acquisition*. Oxford: Oxford University Press.

Ellis, R. (1988). *Classroom second language development*. London: Prentice Hall.

Ellis, R. (1989). Classroom learning styles and their effect on second language acquisition: A study of two learners. *System, 17*, 249–262.

Ellis, R. (1990a). Researching classroom language learning. In C. Brumfit & R. Mitchell (Eds.), *Research in the language classroom* (pp. 54–70). London: Modern English Publications.

Ellis, R. (1990b). *Instructed second language acquisition: Learning in the classroom*. Oxford: Basil Blackwell.

Ellis, R., & Barkhuizen, G. (2005). *Analysing learner language*. Oxford: Oxford University Press.

Ericcson, K. A., & Simon, H. A. (1984). *Protocol analysis: Verbal reports as data*. Cambridge, MA: MIT Press.

Ericcson, K. A., & Simon, H. A. (1987). Verbal reports on thinking. In C. Færch & G. Kasper (Eds.), *Introspection in second language research* (pp. 24–53). Clevedon, England: Multilingual Matters.

Ericcson, K. A., & Simon, H. A. (1993). *Protocol analysis: Verbal reports as data* (Rev. ed.). Cambridge, MA: MIT Press.

Færch, C., & Kasper, G. (Eds.). (1987). *Introspection in second language research*. Clevedon, England: Multilingual Matters.

Fanselow, J. F. (1977). Beyond Rashomon—conceptualizing and describing the teaching act. *TESOL Quarterly, 11(1)*, 17–39.

Fanselow, J. F. (1987). *Breaking rules—generating and exploring alternatives in language teaching*. White Plains, NY: Longman.

Fanselow, J. F., & Barnard, R. (2006). Take 1, take 2, take 3: A suggested three-stage approach to exploratory practice. In S. Gieve & I. K. Miller (Eds.), *Understanding the language classroom* (pp. 175–199). Basingstoke, Hampshire, England: Palgrave Macmillan.

Farrell, T. S. C. (Ed.). (2006). *Language teacher research in Asia*. Alexandria, VA: TESOL.

Fetterman, D. M. (1989). *Ethnography: Step by step*. Newbury Park, CA: Sage.

Flanders, N. (1970). *Analyzing teaching behavior*. Reading, MA: Addison-Wesley.

Flick, U. (1998). *An introduction to qualitative research*. London: Sage.

Fowler, F. (1988). *Survey research methods*. Newbury Park, CA: Sage.

Fox, K. (2004). *Watching the English: The hidden rules of English behaviour*. London: Hodder and Stoughton.

Fraser, B., Rintell, E., & Walters, J. (1980). An approach to conducting research on the acquisition of pragmatic competence in a second language. In D. Larsen-Freeman (Ed.), *Discourse analyses in second language research* (pp. 75–91). Rowley, MA: Newbury House.

Freeman, D. (1989). Teacher training, development, and decision making: A model of teaching and related strategies for language teacher education. *TESOL Quarterly, 23(1)*, 27–45.

Freeman, D. (1992). Collaboration: Constructing shared understandings in a second language classroom. In D. Nunan (Ed.), *Collaborative language learning and teaching* (pp. 56–80). Cambridge: Cambridge University Press.

Freeman, D. (1996a). Redefining the relationship between research and what teachers know. In K. M. Bailey & D. Nunan (Eds.), *Voices from the language classroom: Qualitative research* on *language education* (pp. 88–115). New York: Cambridge University Press.

Freeman, D. (1996b). The "unstudied problem": Research on teacher learning in language teaching. In D. Freeman & J. C. Richards (Eds.), *Teacher learning in language teaching* (pp. 351–378). Cambridge: Cambridge University Press.

Freeman, D. (1998). *Doing teacher research: From inquiry to understanding*. Boston: Heinle & Heinle.

Fry, J. (1988). Diary studies in classroom SLA research: Problems and prospects. *JALT Journal, 9*, 158–167.

Gaies, S. J. (1980, July). Classroom centered research: Some consumer guidelines. Paper presented at the TESOL Summer Meeting, Albuquerque, NM.

Gaies, S. J. (1983). The investigation of language classroom processes. *TESOL Quarterly, 17(2)*, 205–217.

Galda, D. (in press). "My words is big problem": The life and learning experiences of three elderly Eastern European refugees studying ESL at a community college. In K. M. Bailey & M. G. Santos (Eds.), *Research on English as a second language in U.S. community colleges: People, programs and potential*. Ann Arbor, MI: University of Michigan Press.

Galvan, J. L. (1999). *Writing literature reviews: A guide for students of the social and behavioral sciences*. Los Angeles: Pyrczak Publishing.

Garner, H. (2006). The rules of engagement: Paul Greengrass's United 93. *The Monthly Online.* Retrieved January 25, 2008, from http://www.themonthly.com.au/tm/node/271

Gass, S. M. (1997). *Input, interaction, and the second language learner*. Mahwah, NJ: Lawrence Erlbaum Associates.

Gass, S. M., & Mackey, A. (2000). *Stimulated recall methodology in second language research*. Mahwah, NJ: Lawrence Erlbaum Associates.

Gass, S. M., & Mackey, A. (2007). *Data elicitation for second and foreign language research*. Mahwah, NJ: Lawrence Erlbaum Associates.

Gass, S. M., & Schachter, J. (Eds.). (1996). *Second language classroom research: Issues and opportunities*. Mahwah, NJ: Lawrence Erlbaum Associates.

Gieve, S., & Miller, I. K. (Eds.). (2006). *Understanding the language classroom*. Basingstoke, Hampshire, England: Palgrave Macmillan.

Giroux, H. (1983). *Theory and resistance in education: A pedagogy for the opposition*. South Hadley, MA: Bergin and Garvey.

Gliksman, L., Gardner, R. C., & Smythe, P. C. (1982). The role of the integrative motive on students' participation in the French classroom. *Canadian Modern Language Review, 38*, 625–647.

Grandcolas, B., & Soulé-Susbielles, N. (1986). The analysis of the foreign language classroom. *Studies in Second Language Acquisition, 8*, 293–308.

Green, J., & Wallat, C. (Eds.). (1981). *Ethnography and language in educational settings*. Norwood, NJ: Ablex Publishing Corporation.

Grotjahn, R. (1987). On the methodological basis of introspective methods. In C. Færch & G. Kasper (Eds.), *Introspection in second language research* (pp. 54–81). Clevedon, England: Multilingual Matters.

Gu, P. Y., & Wen, Q. (2005). How often is often? Reference ambiguities of the Likert scale in language learning strategy research. *Review of Applied Linguistics in China: Issues in Language Learning and Teaching, 1*, 61–80.

Halbach, A. (2000). Finding out about students' learning strategies by looking at their diaries: A case study. *System, 28*, 85–96.

Halliday, M. A. K. (1975). *Learning how to mean: Explorations in the development of language*. London: Edward Arnold.

Hammersley, M., & Atkinson, P. (1983). *Ethnography: Principles in practice.* London: Tavistock Publications.

Harklau, L. (1994). ESL versus mainstream classes: Contrasting L2 learning environments. *TESOL Quarterly, 28(2),* 241–272.

Harklau, L. (2000). From the "good kids" to the "worst": Representations of English language learners across educational settings. *TESOL Quarterly, 34(1),* 35–67.

Harrison, I. (1996). Looks who's talking now: Listening to voices in curriculum renewal. In K. M. Bailey & D. Nunan, (Eds.), *Voices from the language classroom: Qualitative research on second language education* (pp. 283–303). New York: Cambridge University Press.

Hatch, E. M. (Ed.). (1978). *Second language acquisition: A book of readings.* Rowley, MA: Newbury House.

Hatch, E. M., & Farhady, H. (1982). *Research design and statistics for applied linguistics.* Rowley, MA: Newbury House.

Hatch, E. M., & Lazaraton, A. (1991). *The research manual: Design and statistics for applied linguistics.* New York: Newbury House.

Heath, S. B. (1983). *Ways with words.* Cambridge: Cambridge University Press.

Henze, R. C. (1995). Guides for the novice qualitative researcher. *TESOL Quarterly, 29(3),* 595–599.

Hilleson, M. (1996). "I want to talk to them but I don't want them to hear": An introspective study of second-language anxiety in an English-medium school. In K. M. Bailey & D. Nunan (Eds.), *Voices from the language classroom: Qualitative research in second language education* (pp. 248–275). Cambridge: Cambridge University Press.

Hinkel, E. (Ed.). (2005). *Handbook of research in second language teaching and learning.* Mahwah, NJ: Lawrence Erlbaum Associates.

Ho, B., & Richards, J. (1993). Reflective thinking through teacher journal writing: Myths and realities. *Prospect: A Journal of Australian TESOL, 8(3),* 7–24.

Holliday, A. (2002). *Doing and writing qualitative research.* London: Sage.

Holmes, O. W. (1906). *The professor at the breakfast table.* London: J. M. Dent & Co.

Hornberger, N. (1988). *Bilingual education and language maintenance: A Southern Peruvian case study.* Dordrecht: Foris Publications.

Huang, J. (2005). A diary study of difficulties and constraints in EFL learning. *System, 33,* 609–621.

Hughes, A. (1989). *Testing for language teachers.* Cambridge: Cambridge University Press.

Hunt, K. W. (1970). *Syntactic maturity in school children and adults.* Chicago, IL: University of Chicago Press.

Jaeger, R. (1988). Survey research methods in education. In R. M. Jaeger (Ed.), *Complementary methods for research in education* (pp. 303–338). Washington, DC: American Educational Research Association.

Jaeger, R. M. (1993). *Statistics—a spectator sport* (2nd ed.). Newbury Park, CA: Sage.

Jarvis, J. (1992). Using diaries for reflection on in-service courses. *English Language Teaching Journal, 46(2),* 133–143.

Jepson, K. (2005). Conversations—and negotiated interaction—in text and voice chat rooms. *Language Learning and Technology, 9(3),* 79–98.

Johnson, D. (1992). *Approaches to research in second language learning.* White Plains, NY: Longman.

Johnson, K. E. (1992a). Learning to teach: Instructional actions and decisions of preservice ESL teachers. *TESOL Quarterly, 26(3),* 507–535.

Johnson, K. E. (1992b). The instructional decisions of pre-service English as a second language teachers: New directions for teacher preparation programs. In J. Flowerdew, M. Brock, & S. Hsia (Eds.), *Perspectives on second language teacher development* (pp. 115–134). Hong Kong: City University of Hong Kong.

Johnson, K. E. (1995). *Understanding communication in second language classrooms.* Cambridge: Cambridge University Press.

Johnson, K. E. (1996). The vision versus the reality: The tensions of the TESOL practicum. In D. Freeman & J. C. Richards (Eds.), *Teacher learning in language teaching* (pp. 30–49). Cambridge: Cambridge University Press.

Johnson, K. E. (1998). *Teachers understanding teaching.* Boston: Heinle & Heinle.

Johnson, K. E. (1999). *Understanding language teaching: Reasoning in action.* Boston: Heinle & Heinle.

Jones, F. R. (1994). The lone language learner: A diary study. *System, 22(4),* 441–454.

Jones, F. R. (1995). Learning an alien lexicon: A teach-yourself case study. *Second Language Research, 11(2),* 95–111.

Jourdenais, R. (2001). Cognition, instruction, and protocol analysis. In P. Robinson (Ed.), *Cognition and second language learning* (pp. 354–375). Cambridge: Cambridge University Press.

Katz, A. (1996). Teaching style: A way to understand instruction in language classrooms. In K. M. Bailey & D. Nunan (Eds.), *Voices from the language classroom: Qualitative research on language education* (pp. 57–87). New York: Cambridge University Press.

Kebir, C. (1994). An action research look at the communication strategies of adult learners. *TESOL Journal, 4(1),* 28–31.

Kemmis, S., & Henry, C. (1989). Action research. *IATEFL Newsletter, 102,* 2–3.

Kemmis, S., & McTaggart, R. (1982). *The action research planner.* Victoria: Deakin University.

Kemmis, S., & McTaggart, R. (1988). *The action research planner* (3rd ed.). Victoria: Deakin University.

Kennedy, M. (1990). *Policy issues in teacher education.* East Lansing, MI: National Center for Research on Teaching.

Kincheloe, J. L. (1991). *Teachers as researchers: Qualitative inquiry as a path to empowerment.* London: The Falmer Press.

Knezedvoc, B. (2001). Action research. *IATEFL Teacher Development SIG Newsletter, 1(1),* 10–12.

Knowles, T. (1990). Action research: A way to make our ideas matter. *The Language Teacher, 14(7).*

Kramsch, C. (2000). Social discursive constructions of self in L2 learning. In J. P. Lantolf (Ed.), *Sociocultural theory and second language learning* (pp. 133–153). Oxford: Oxford University Press.

Krishnan, L. A., & Hoon, L. H. (2002). Diaries: Listening to 'voices' from the multicultural classroom. *English Language Teaching Journal, 56(3),* 227–239.

Kuhn, T. (1996). *The structure of scientific revolutions* (3rd ed.). Chicago: University of Chicago Press.

Kumaravadivelu, B. (1994). The post-method condition: (E)merging strategies for second/foreign language teaching. *TESOL Quarterly, 28(1),* 28–49.

Kumaravadivelu, B. (2003). *Beyond methods: Macrostrategies for language teaching.* New Haven, CT: Yale University Press.

Kwan, T. Y. L. (1993). Contexts for action research development: The case for Hong Kong. *Curriculum Forum, 3(3)*, 11–23.

Labov, W. (1972). Some principles of linguistics methodology. *Language in Society, 1*, 97–120.

Lankshear, C., & Knobel, M. (2004). *A handbook for teacher research: From design to implementation.* New York: Open University Press.

Lantolf, J. P. (Ed). (2000). *Sociocultural theory and second language learning.* Oxford: Oxford University Press.

Larimer, R. E., & Schleicher L. (Eds.). (1999). *New ways in using authentic materials in the classroom.* Alexandria, Virginia: TESOL.

Larsen-Freeman, D. (1996). The changing nature of second language classroom research. In J. Schachter & S. Gass (Eds.), *Second language classroom research: Issues and opportunities* (pp. 157–170). Mahwah, NJ: Lawrence Erlbaum Associates.

Law, B., & Eckes, M. (1995). *Assessment and ESL: A handbook for K-12 educators.* Winnipeg: Peguis Publishers.

Lazaraton, A. (2004). Gesture and speech in the vocabulary explanations of one ESL teacher: A microanalytic inquiry. *Language Learning, 54*, 79–118.

LeCompte, M., & Goetz, J. (1982). Problems of reliability and validity in ethnographic research. *Review of Educational Research, 52(1)*, 31–60.

Lee, E., & Lew, L. (2001). Diary studies: The voices of nonnative English speakers in a master of arts program in teaching English to speakers of other languages. *CATESOL Journal, 13(1)*, 135–149.

Legutke, M. (2000, December). Redesigning the foreign language classroom: A critical perspective on information technology (IT) and educational change. Plenary presentation at the International Language in Education Conference, University of Hong Kong, Hong Kong.

Leopold, W. F. (1978). A child's learning of two languages. In E. M. Hatch (Ed.), *Second language acquisition: A book of readings* (pp. 23–32). Rowley, MA: Newbury House.

Levine, H., Gallimore, R., Weisner, T. S., & Turner, J. L. (1980). Teaching participant observation research methods: A skills-building approach. *Anthropology and Education Quarterly, 11(1)*, 38–45.

Lewin, K. (1946). Action research and minority problems. *Journal of Social Issues, 2*, 34–46.

Lewin, L. (1948). *Resolving social conflicts.* New York: Harper and Row.

Lieblich, A., Tuval-Mashiach, R., & Zilber, T. (1998). *Narrative research: Reading, analysis, and interpretation.* Thousand Oaks, CA: Sage.

Liebscher, G., & Dailey-O'Cain, J. (2003). Conversational repair as a role-defining mechanism in classroom interaction. *Modern Language Journal, 87(3)*, 375–390.

Likert, R. (1932). A technique for the measurement of attitude scales. *Archives of Psychology, 140*, 1–55.

Lin, A. M. Y. (1999). Doing-English-lessons in the reproduction or transformation of social worlds? *TESOL Quarterly, 33(3)*, 393–412.

Lin, Y., & Hedgcock, J. (1996). Negative feedback incorporation among high-proficiency and low-proficiency Chinese-speaking learners of Spanish. *Language Learning, 46*, 567–611.

Lincoln, Y. S., & Guba, E. G. (1985). *Naturalistic inquiry.* Newbury Park, CA: Sage.

Long, M. H. (1980). Inside the 'black box': Methodological issues in research on language teaching and learning. *Language Learning, 30(1)*, 1–42. (Reprinted in *Classroom oriented research in second language acquisition,* pp. 3–35, by H. W. Seliger and M. H. Long, Eds., 1983, Rowley, MA: Newbury House).

Long, M. H. (1983a). Does second language instruction make a difference? *TESOL Quarterly, 17(3)*, 359–382.

Long, M. H. (1983b). Linguistic and conversational adjustments to nonnative speakers. *Studies in Second Language Acquisition, 5*, 177–193.

Long, M. H. (1984). Process and product in ESL program evaluation. *TESOL Quarterly, 18(3)*, 409–425.

Long, M. H. (1985). A role for instruction in second language acquisition: Task-based language training. In K. Hyltenstam & M. Pienemann (Eds.), *Modelling and assessing second language acquisition* (pp. 77–100). Clevedon, England: Multilingual Matters.

Long, M. H. (1996). The role of the linguistic environment in second language acquisition. In W. Ritchie & T. Bhatia (Eds.), *Handbook of research on second language acquisition* (pp. 413–469). New York: Academic Press.

Long, M. H., & Doughty, C. J. (Eds.). (in press). *Handbook of second and foreign language teaching*. Oxford: Blackwell.

Lowe, T. (1987). An experiment in role reversal: Teachers as language learners. *English Language Teaching Journal, 4(2)*, 89–96.

Lozanov, G. (1979). *Suggestology and outlines of Suggsestopedia*. New York: Gordon and Breach Science Publishers, Inc.

Lozanov, G. (1982). Suggestology and Suggestopedia. In R. W. Blair (Ed.), *Innovative approaches to language teaching* (pp. 146–159). Rowley, MA: Newbury House.

Lynch, T., & Maclean, J. (2000). Exploring the benefits of task repetition and recycling for classroom language learning. *Language Teaching Research, 4(3)*, 221–250.

Mackey, A., & Gass, S. M. (2005). *Second language research: Methodology and design*. Mahwah, NJ: Lawrence Erlbaum Associates.

Markee, N. (1996). Making second language classroom research work. In J. Schachter & S. Gass (Eds.), *Second language classroom research: Issues and opportunities* (pp. 117–155). Mahwah, NJ: Lawrence Erlbaum Associates.

Markee, N. (2000). *Conversational analysis*. Mahwah, NJ: Lawrence Erlbaum Associates.

Markee, N. (2003). Qualitative research guidelines (conversational analysis). *TESOL Quarterly, 37*, 169–172.

Markee, N. (2005). Conversational analysis for second language acquisition. In E. Hinkel (Ed.), *Handbook of research in second language teaching and learning* (pp. 355–374). Mahwah, NJ: Lawrence Erlbaum Associates.

Marshall, C., & Rossman, G. B. (1995). *Designing qualitative research* (2nd ed.). Thousand Oaks, CA: Sage.

Marshall, C., & Rossman, G. B. (1999). *Designing qualitative research* (3rd ed.). Thousand Oaks, CA: Sage.

Marshall, C., & Rossman, G. B. (2006). *Designing qualitative research* (4th ed.). Thousand Oaks, CA: Sage.

Martyn, E. (1996). The influence of task-type on the negotiation of meaning in small group work. Paper presented at the Annual Pacific Second Language Research Forum, Auckland, New Zealand.

Martyn, E. (2001). The effects of task type on negotiation of meaning in small group work. Unpublished doctoral dissertation, University of Hong Kong, Hong Kong.

Mason, J. (1996). *Qualitative researching*. London: Sage.

Matsuda, A., & Matsuda, P. (2001). Autonomy and collaboration in teacher education: Journal sharing among native and nonnative

English-speaking teachers. *CATESOL Journal, 13(1),* 109–121.

Matsumoto, K. (1987). Diary studies of second language acquisition: A critical overview. *JALT Journal, 9,* 17–34.

Matsumoto, K. (1989). An analysis of a Japanese ESL learner's diary: Factors involved in the L2 learning process. *JALT Journal, 11,* 167–192.

Maxwell, J. A. (2005). *Qualitative research design: An interactive approach* (2nd ed.). Thousand Oaks, CA: Sage.

McCarthy, M., & Walsh, S. (2003). Discourse. In D. Nunan (Ed.), *Practical English language teaching* (pp. 173–195). New York: McGraw-Hill.

McKay, S. L. (2006). *Researching second language classrooms.* Mahwah, NJ: Lawrence Erlbaum Associates.

McDonough, J. (1994). A teacher looks at teachers' diaries. *English Language Teaching Journal, 48(1),* 57–65.

McGarrell, H. M. (Ed.). (2007). *Language teacher research in the Americas.* Alexandria, VA: TESOL.

McPherson, P. (1997). Action research: Exploring learner diversity. *Prospect: A Journal of Australian TESOL, 12(1),* 50–62.

Merriam, S. B. (1988). *Case study research in education: A qualitative approach.* San Francisco: Jossey-Bass.

Merriam, S. B. (1998). *Qualitative research and case study applications in education.* (2nd ed.). San Francisco: Jossey-Bass.

Michonska-Stadnik, A., & Szulc-Kurpaska, M. (Eds.). (1997). Action research in the lower Silesia cluster colleges: Developing learner independence. *Orbis Linguarum, 2.* Legnica, Poland: Nauczycielskie Kolegium Jezkw Obcych and the British Council.

Miles, M. B., & Huberman, A. (1984). *Qualitative data analysis: A sourcebook of new methods.* Beverly Hills, CA: Sage.

Miles, M. B., & Huberman, A. (1994). *Qualitative data analysis: An expanded sourcebook.* Thousand Oaks, CA: Sage.

Mingucci, M. (1999). Action research in ESL staff development. *TESOL Matters, 9(2),* 16.

Mitchell, M., & Jolley, J. (1988). *Research design explained.* New York: Holt Rinehart Winston.

Mok, A. (1997). Student empowerment in an English language enrichment programme: An action research project in Hong Kong. *Educational Action Research, 5(2),* 305–320.

Moore, T. (1977). An experimental language handicap: Personal account. *Bulletin of the British Psychological Society, 30,* 107–110.

Morgan, D. (1997). *Focus groups as qualitative research* (2nd ed.). Thousand Oaks, CA: Sage.

Moskowitz, G. (1968). The effects of training foreign language teachers in Interaction Analysis. *Foreign Language Annals, 1(3),* 218–235.

Moskowitz, G. (1971). Interaction Analysis—a new modern language for supervisors. *Foreign Language Annals, 5,* 211–221.

Moskowitz, G. (1976). The classroom interaction of outstanding foreign language teachers. *Foreign Language Annals, 9,* 125–143 and 146–157.

Nassaji, H., & Cumming, A. (2000). What's in a ZPD? A case study of a young ESL student and teacher interacting through dialogue journals. *Language Teaching Research, 4(2),* 95–121.

Nisbett, R., & Wilson, T. (1977). Telling more than we can know: Verbal reports on mental process. *Psychological Review, 84,* 231–259.

Numrich, C. (1996). On becoming a language teacher: Insights from diary studies. *TESOL Quarterly, 30(1),* 131–151.

Nunan, D. (1988). *The learner-centred curriculum: A study in second language teaching*. Cambridge: Cambridge University Press.

Nunan, D. (1989). *Understanding language classrooms: A guide for teacher-initiated action*. New York: Prentice Hall.

Nunan, D. (1990). Action research in the language classroom. In J. C. Richards & D. Nunan (Eds.), *Second language teacher education* (pp. 62–81). Cambridge: Cambridge University Press.

Nunan, D. (1991a). Methods in second language classroom-oriented research: A critical review. *Studies in Second Language Acquisition, 13(2)*, 249–274.

Nunan, D. (1991b). Second language acquisition research in the language classroom. In E. Sadtono (Ed.), *Language acquisition and the second/foreign language classroom* (Anthology Series 28, pp. 1–24). Singapore: SEAMEO Regional Language Center.

Nunan, D. (1991c). *Language teaching methodology*. London: Prentice Hall.

Nunan, D. (1992). *Research methods in language learning*. Cambridge: Cambridge University Press.

Nunan, D. (1993a). Action research in language education. In J. Edge & K. Richards (Eds.), *Teachers develop teachers research: Papers on classroom research and teacher development* (pp. 39–50). Oxford: Heinemann International.

Nunan, D. (1993b). *Teachers' interactive decision-making*. Sydney: National Centre for English Language Teaching and Research.

Nunan, D. (1996). Hidden voices: Insiders' perspectives on classroom interaction. In K. M. Bailey & D. Nunan (Eds.), *Voices from the language classroom: Qualitative research on language education* (pp. 41–56). New York: Cambridge University Press.

Nunan, D. (1997a). Developing standards for teacher-research in TESOL. *TESOL Quarterly, 31(2)*, 365–367.

Nunan, D. (1997b). Research, the teacher and classrooms of tomorrow. In G. M. Jacobs (Ed.), *Language classrooms of tomorrow: Issues and responses* (pp. 183–194). Singapore: SEAMEO Regional Language Center.

Nunan, D. (1999). *Second language teaching and learning*. Boston: Heinle & Heinle.

Nunan, D. (Ed.). (2003). *Practical English language teaching*. New York: McGraw-Hill.

Nunan, D. (2004). *Task-based language teaching*. Cambridge: Cambridge University Press.

Nunan, D. (2005). Classroom research. In E. Hinkel (Ed.), *Handbook of research in second language teaching and learning* (pp. 225–240). Mahwah, NJ: Lawrence Erlbaum Associates.

Nunan, D. (2007a). *What is this thing called language?* London: Palgrave Macmillan.

Nunan, D. (2007b, September). Diverse voices: What we can learn from listening to our learners? Plenary presentation at the English Australia Conference, Sydney, Australia.

Nunan, D., & Lamb, C. (1996). *The self-directed teacher: Managing the learning process*. Cambridge: Cambridge University Press.

Nunan, D., & Wong, L. (2003, December). Learning styles and strategies: An empirical investigation. Paper presented at the Chulalongkorn University Language Institute International Conference, Bangkok, Thailand.

Nunan, D., & Wong, L. (2006). The good language learner: An empirical investigation. Unpublished manuscript, University of Hong Kong, The English Centre.

O'Farrell, A. (2003). The language of nonproliferation studies. Unpublished manuscript, Monterey Institute of International Studies, Monterey, California.

Ohta, A. S. (2000). Rethinking interaction in SLA: Developmentally appropriate assistance in the zone of proximal development and the acquisition of L2 grammar. In J. P. Lantolf (Ed.), *Sociocultural theory and second language learning* (pp. 51–78). Oxford: Oxford University Press.

Otto, F. M. (1969). The teacher in the Pennsylvania project. *Modern Language Journal, 53,* 411–420.

Oxford, R. (2001). Language learning strategies. In R. Carter & D. Nunan (Eds.), *The Cambridge guide to teaching English to speakers of other languages* (pp. 166–172). Cambridge: Cambridge University Press.

Oxford, R. (2002). Language learning styles and strategies. In M. Celce-Murcia (Ed.), *Teaching English as a second or foreign language* (3rd ed., pp. 359–383). Boston: Heinle & Heinle.

Palmer, C. H. (1992). Diaries for self-assessment and INSET programme evaluation. *European Journal of Teacher Education, 15(3),* 227–238.

Palmer, G. M. (1992). The practical feasibility of diary studies for INSET. *European Journal of Teacher Education, 15(3),* 239–254.

Parkinson, B., & Howell-Richardson, C. (1990). Learner diaries. In C. Brumfit & R. Mitchell (Eds.), *Research in the language classroom: ELT Documents, 133* (pp. 128–140). London: English Publications and the British Council.

Peck, S. (1980). Language play in child second language acquisition. In D. Larsen-Freeman (Ed.), *Discourse analysis in second language research* (pp. 154–164). Rowley, MA: Newbury House.

Peck, S. (1996). Language learning diaries as mirrors of students' cultural sensitivity. In K. M. Bailey & D. Nunan (Eds.), *Voices from the language classroom: Qualitative research in second language education* (pp. 236–247). Cambridge: Cambridge University Press.

Pennington, M. C., & Richards, J. C. (1997). Reorienting the teaching universe: The experience of five first-year English teachers in Hong Kong. *Language Teaching Research, 1(2),* 149–178.

Perecman, E., & Curran, S. (2006). *A handbook for social science field research.* Thousand Oaks, CA: Sage.

Perry, F. L. (2005). *Research in applied linguistics: Becoming a discerning consumer.* Mahwah, NJ. Lawrence Erlbaum Associates.

Peyton, J. K. (1990). Beginning at the beginning: First-grade ESL students learning to write. In A. Padilla, H. H. Fairchild, & C. M. Valadez (Eds.), *Bilingual education: Issues and strategies* (pp. 195–218). Newbury Park, CA: Sage.

Pica, T. (1994). Research on negotiation: What does it reveal about second language learning conditions, processes and outcomes. *Language Learning, 44,* 493–527.

Pica, T. (1997). Second language teaching and research relationships: A North American view. *Language Teaching Research, 1(1),* 48–72.

Pica, T., & Doughty, C. (1985a). The role of group work in classroom second language acquisition. *Studies in Second Language Acquisition, 7(2),* 233–248.

Pica, T., & Doughty, C. (1985b). Input and interaction in the communicative language classroom: A comparison of teacher-fronted and group activities. In S. Gass & C. Madden (Eds.), *Input in second language acquisition* (pp. 115–132). Rowley, MA: Newbury House.

Pike, K. L. (1964). *Language in relation to a unified theory of structures of human behavior.* The Hague: Mouton.

Piore, M. (2006). Combining qualitative and quantitative tools: Qualitative research—does it fit in economics? In E. Perecmann & S. Curan (Eds.), *A handbook for social science field research* (pp. 143–157). London: Sage.

Plummer, K. (1983). *Documents of life: An introduction to the problems and literature of a humanistic method.* London: George Allen and Unwin.

Polio, C. (1996). Issues and problems in reporting classroom research. In J. Schachter & S. Gass (Eds.), *Second language classroom research: Issues and opportunities* (pp. 61–79). Mahwah, NJ: Lawrence Erlbaum Associates.

Polio, C., & Wilson-Duffy, C. (1998). Teaching ESL in an unfamiliar context: International students in a North American TESOL practicum. *TESOL Journal, 7(4),* 24–29.

Popper, K. (1968). *The logic of scientific discovery.* London: Hutchinson.

Popper, K. (1972). *Objective knowledge.* Oxford: Oxford University Press.

Porter, P. A., Goldstein, L. M., Leatherman, J., & Conrad, S. (1990). An ongoing dialogue: Learner logs for teacher preparation. In J. C. Richards & D. Nunan (Eds.), *Second language teacher education* (pp. 227–240). Cambridge: Cambridge University Press.

Porto, M. (2007). Learning diaries in the English as a foreign language classroom: A tool for accessing learners' perceptions of lessons and developing learner autonomy and reflection. *Foreign Language Annals, 40(4),* 672–696.

Quirke, P. (2001). Hearing voices: A robust and flexible framework for gathering and using student feedback.

In J. Edge (Ed.), *Action research* (pp. 81–91). Alexandria, VA: TESOL.

Radecki, W. (2002). Student and teacher preferences in the high-tech classroom Unpublished manuscript, Zayed University, Dubai, United Arab Emirates.

Reid, J. (1990). The dirty laundry of ESL survey research. *TESOL Quarterly, 24(2),* 323–338.

Richards, J. C., & Lockhart, C. (1994). *Reflective teaching in second language classrooms.* Cambridge: Cambridge University Press.

Richards, K. (1992). Pepys into a TEFL course. *English Language Teaching Journal, 46(2),* 144–152.

Richards, K. (2003). *Qualitative inquiry in TESOL.* Houndsmill, UK: Palgrave, Macmillan.

Rivers, W. (1979). Learning a sixth language: An adult learner's diary. *Canadian Modern Language Review, 36(1),* 67–82.

Rivers, W. (1983). *Communicating naturally in a second language: Theory and practice in language teaching.* Cambridge: Cambridge University Press.

Roebuck, R. (2000). Subjects speak out: How learners position themselves in a psycholinguistic task. In J. P. Lantolf (Ed.), *Sociocultural theory and second language learning* (pp. 79–95). Oxford: Oxford University Press.

Rounds, P. L. (1987). Characterizing successful classroom discourse for NNS teaching assistant training. *TESOL Quarterly, 21(4),* 643–671.

Rounds, P. L., & Schachter, J. (1996). The balancing act: Theoretical, acquisitional and pedagogical issues in second language research. In J. Schachter & S. Gass (Eds.), *Second language classroom research: Issues and opportunities* (pp. 99–116). Mahwah, NJ: Lawrence Erlbaum Associates.

Rowntree, D. (1981). *Statistics without tears: A primer for non-mathematicians.* London: Longman.

Rowsell, L. V., & Libben, G. (1994). The sound of one hand clapping: How to succeed in independent language learning. *Canadian Modern Language Review, 50(4),* 668–687.

Rubin, J., & Henze, R. (1981, February). The foreign language requirement: A suggestion to enhance its educational role in teacher training. *TESOL Newsletter,* 15, 17, 19, 24.

Ruiz de Gauna, P., Diaz, C., Gonzalez, V., & Garaizar, I. (1995). Teachers' professional development as a process of critical action research. *Educational Action Research, 3(2),* 183–194.

Ruso, N. (2007). The influence of task based learning on EFL classrooms. *Asian EFL Journal, 18.* Retrieved July 11, 2007, from http://www. asian-efl-journal.com/pta_February_ 2007_nr.php

Santana-Williamson, E. (2001). Early reflections: Journaling a way into teaching. In J. Edge (Ed.), *Action research* (pp. 33–44). Alexandria, VA: TESOL.

Sato, C. (1982). Ethnic styles in classroom discourse. In M. Hines & W. Rutherford (Eds.), *On TESOL '81* (pp. 11–24). Washington, DC: TESOL.

Scales, J., Wennerstrom, A., Richard, D., & Wu, S. H. (2006). Language learners' perceptions of accent. *TESOL Quarterly, 4(4),* 715–737.

Schachter, J., & Gass, S. (Eds.). (1996). *Second language classroom research: Issues and opportunities.* Mahwah, NJ: Lawrence Erlbaum Associates.

Scherer, G. A. C., & Wertheimer, M. (1964). *A psycholinguistic experiment in foreign language teaching.* New York: McGraw-Hill.

Schmidt, R. W. (1983). Interaction, acculturation, and the acquisition of communicative competence: A case study of an adult. In N. Wolfson & E. Judd (Eds.), *Sociolinguistics and language acquisition* (pp. 137–174). Rowley, MA: Newbury House.

Schmidt, R. W. (1984). The strengths and limitations of acquisition: A case study of an untutored language learner. *Language Learning and Communication, 3(1),* 1–16.

Schmidt, R. W., & Frota, S. N. (1986). Developing basic conversational ability in a second language: A case study of an adult learner of Portuguese. In R. R. Day (Ed.), *Talking to learn: Conversation in second language acquisition* (pp. 237–326). Rowley, MA: Newbury House.

Schrank, A. (2006). Bringing it all back home: Personal reflections on friends, findings and fieldwork. In E. Perecman & S. Curran (Eds.), *A handbook for social science field research* (pp. 217–225). Thousand Oaks, CA: Sage.

Schumann, F. (1980). Diary of a language learner: A further analysis. In S. Krashen & R. Scarcella (Eds.), *Research in second language acquisition: Selected papers of the Los Angeles Second Language Research Forum* (pp. 51–57). Rowley, MA: Newbury House.

Schumann, F. E., & Schumann, J. H. (1977). Diary of a language learner: An introspective study of second language learning. In H. D. Brown, R. H. Crymes, & C. A. Yorio (Eds.), *On TESOL '77: Teaching and learning English as a second language—trends in research and practice* (pp. 241–249). Washington, DC: TESOL.

Schumann, J. (1978a). *The Pidginization Hypothesis: A model for second language acquisition.* Rowley, MA: Newbury House.

Schumann, J. (1978b). Second language acquisition: The Pidginization Hypothesis. In E. M. Hatch (Ed.), *Second language acquisition: A book of readings* (pp. 256–271). Rowley, MA: Newbury House.

Seliger, H., & Shohamy, E. (1989). *Second language research methods*. Oxford: Oxford University Press.

Seliger, H. W. (1977). Does practice make perfect? A study of interaction patterns and L2 competence. *Language Learning, 27*, 263–278.

Seliger, H. W. (1983a). Classroom-centered research in language teaching: Two articles on the state of the art. *TESOL Quarterly, 17(2)*, 189–190.

Seliger, H. W. (1983b). The language learner as linguist: Of metaphors and realities. *Applied Linguistics, 4*, 179–191.

Shamim, F. (1996). In or out of the action zone: Location as a feature of interaction in large ESL classes in Pakistan. In K. M. Bailey & D. Nunan (Eds.), *Voices from the language classroom: Qualitative research on language education* (pp. 123–144). New York: Cambridge University Press.

Shavelson, R. J. (1981). *Statistical reasoning for the behavioral sciences*. Boston: Allyn and Bacon.

Shavelson, R. J. (1996). *Statistical reasoning for the behavioral sciences* (3rd ed.). Boston: Allyn and Bacon.

Shaw, P. A. (1983). A sociolinguistic analysis of spoken discourse in undergraduate engineering classes. Unpublished doctoral dissertation, University of Southern California, Los Angeles.

Shaw, P. A. (1996). Voices for improved learning: The ethnographer as co-agent of pedagogic change. In K. M. Bailey & D. Nunan (Eds.), *Voices from the language classroom: Qualitative research on language education* (pp. 318–337). New York: Cambridge University Press.

Shaw, P. A. (1997). With one stone: Models of instruction and their curricular implications in an advanced content-based foreign language program. In S. B. Stryker & B. L. Leaver (Eds.), *Content-based instruction in foreign language education: Models and methods* (pp. 259–281). Washington, DC: Georgetown University Press.

Shuy, R. W. (1993). Using language functions to discover a teacher's implicit theory of communicating with students. In J. K. Peyton & J. Staton (Eds.), *Dialogue journals in the multilingual classroom: Building language fluency and writing skills through written interaction* (pp. 127–154). Norwood, NJ: Ablex.

Simard, D. (2004). Using diaries to promote metalinguistic reflection among elementary school students. *Language Awareness, 13(1)*, 34–48.

Sinclair, J., & Coulthard, M. (1975). *Toward an analysis of discourse*. London: Oxford University Press.

Smith, L. M., & Geoffrey, W. (1968). *The complexities of an urban classroom: An analysis toward a general theory of teaching*. New York: Holt, Rinehart and Winston.

Smith, J. K., & Heshusius, L. (1986). Closing down the conversation: The end of the quantitative-qualitative debate among educational inquirers. *Educational Researcher, 15(1)*, 4–12.

Smith, P. D. (1970). *A comparison of the cognitive and audiolingual approaches to foreign language instruction: The Pennsylvania foreign language project*. Philadelphia: Center for Curriculum Development.

Snow, M. A., Hyland, J., Kamhi-Stein, L., & Yu, J. H. (1996). U.S. language minority students: Voices from the junior high classroom. In K. M. Bailey & D. Nunan (Eds.), *Voices from the language classroom: Qualitative research on language education* (pp. 304–317). New York: Cambridge University Press.

Spada, N. (1990). Observing classroom behaviours and learning outcomes in different second language classrooms. In J. C. Richards & D. Nunan (Eds.), *Second language teacher education* (pp. 293–310). Cambridge: Cambridge University Press.

Spada, N., & Fröhlich., M. (1995). *Communicative Orientation of Language Teaching observation scheme: Coding conventions and applications.* Sydney: NCELTR Macquarie University.

Spada, N., Ranta, L., & Lightbown, P. M. (1996). Working with teachers in second language acquisition research. In J. Schachter & S. Gass (Eds.), *Second language classroom research: Issues and opportunities* (pp. 61–79). Mahwah, NJ: Lawrence Erlbaum Associates.

Spradley, J. P. (1979). *The ethnographic interview.* New York: Holt, Rinehart and Winston.

Spradley, J. P. (1980). *Participant observation.* New York: Holt, Rinehart and Winston.

Springer, S. E. (2003). Contingent language use and scaffolding in a project-based ESL course. Unpublished manuscript, Monterey Institute of International Studies, Monterey, California.

Springer, S. E., & Bailey, K. M. (2006, April). Diversity in reflective teaching practices: International survey results. Paper presented at the CATESOL State Conference, San Francisco, California.

Sreedharan, N. (2006). *Sura's quotations of wit and wisdom.* Chennai, India: Sura Books.

Stake, R. E. (1988). Case study methods in educational research: Seeking sweet water. In R. M. Jaeger (Ed.), *Complementary methods for research in education* (pp. 253–266). Washington, DC: American Educational Research Association.

Stake, R. E. (1995). *The art of case research.* Newburg Park, CA: Sage.

Stenhouse, L. (1983). Case study in educational research and evaluation. In L. Bartlett, S. Kemmis, & G. Gillard (Eds.), *Case study: An overview* (pp. 11–54). Geelong, Australia: Deakin University Press.

Stewart, D., & Shamdasani, P. (1990). *Focus groups: Theory and practice.* Newbury Park, CA: Sage.

Stewart, T. (2006). Teacher-researcher collaboration or teachers' research? *TESOL Quarterly, 40(2),* 421–430.

Storch, N. (2002). Patterns of interaction in ESL pair work. *Language Learning, 52(1),* 119–158.

Strauss, A. (1988). Teaching qualitative research methods: A conversation with Andrew Strauss. *Qualitative Studies in Education, 1(1),* 91–99.

Strong, M. (1986). Teachers' language to limited English speakers and submersion classes. In R. R. Day (Ed.), *Talking to learn: Conversation in second language acquisition* (pp. 53–63). Rowley, MA: Newbury House.

Sullivan, P. N. (2000). Playfulness as mediation in communicative language teaching in a Vietnamese classroom. In J. P. Lantolf (Ed.), *Sociocultural theory and second language learning* (pp. 115–131). Oxford: Oxford University Press.

Swaffar, J., Arens, K., & Morgan, M. (1982). Teacher classroom practices: Redefining method as task hierarchy. *Modern Language Journal, 66(1),* 24–33.

Swain, M. (2000). The output hypothesis and beyond: Mediating acquisition through collaborative dialogue. In J. P. Lantolf (Ed.), *Sociocultural theory and second language learning* (pp. 97–114). Oxford: Oxford University Press.

Szostek, C. (1994). Assessing the effects of cooperative learning in an honors foreign language classroom. *Foreign Language Annals, 27,* 252–261.

Thorpe, J. (2004). Coal miners, dirty sponges, and the search for Santa: Exploring options in teaching listening comprehension through TV news broadcasts. Unpublished manuscript, Monterey Institute of International Studies, Monterey, California.

Tinker Sachs, G. (2000). Teacher and researcher autonomy in action research.

Prospect: A Journal of Australian TESOL, 15(3), 35–51.

Tinker Sachs, G. (2002). Learning Cantonese: Reflections of an EFL teacher educator. In D. C. S. Li (Ed.), *Discourses in search of members: In honor of Ron Scollon* (pp. 509–540). Lanham, MD: University Press of America.

Trueba, G., Guthrie, P., & Au, K. H. P. (Eds.). (1981). *Culture and the bilingual classroom: Studies in classroom ethnography*. Rowley, MA: Newbury House.

Tsang, W. K. (2003). Journaling from internship to practice teaching. *Reflective Practice, 4(2)*, 221–240.

Tsui, A. B. M. (1995). *An introduction to classroom interaction*. London: Penguin.

Tsui, A. B. M. (1996). Reticence and anxiety in second language learning. In K. M. Bailey & D. Nunan (Eds.), *Voices from the language classroom: Qualitative research on language education* (pp. 145–167). New York: Cambridge University Press.

Tsui, A. B. M. (2003). *Understanding expertise in teaching: Case studies of second language teachers*. Cambridge: Cambridge University Press.

Tuckman, B. (1999). *Conducting educational research* (5th ed.). Ft. Worth, TX: Harcourt Brace College Publishers.

Turner, J. (1993). Another researcher comments. *TESOL Quarterly, 24(4)*, 736–739.

Tyacke, M., & Mendelsohn, D. (1986). Student needs: Cognitive as well as communicative. *TESL Canada Journal* (Special Issue 1), 171–183.

Ulichny, P. (1996). Performed conversations in an ESL classroom. *TESOL Quarterly, 30(4)*, 739–764.

van Lier, L. (1988). *The classroom and the language learner: Ethnography and second language classroom research*. London: Longman.

van Lier, L. (1989). Reeling, writhing, fainting and stretching in coils: Oral proficiency interviews as conversation. *TESOL Quarterly, 23(3)*, 489–508.

van Lier, L. (1990a). Ethnography: Bandaid, bandwagon, or contraband? In C. Brumfit & R. Mitchell (Eds.), *Research in the language classroom: ELT Documents, 133* (pp. 33–53). London: Modern English Publications and British Council.

van Lier, L. (1990b). Classroom research in second language acquisition. *Annual Review of Applied Linguistics, 10*, 73–186.

van Lier, L. (1992). Not the nine o'clock linguistics class: Investigating contingency grammar. *Language Awareness, 1(2)*, 91–108.

van Lier, L. (1994a). Action research. *Sintagma, 6*, 31–37.

van Lier, L. (1994b). Some features of a theory of practice. *TESOL Journal, 4(1)*, 6–10.

van Lier, L. (1996a). Conflicting voices: Language, classrooms, and bilingual education in Puno. In K. M. Bailey & D. Nunan (Eds.), *Voices from the language classroom: Qualitative research on language education* (pp. 363–387). New York: Cambridge University Press.

van Lier, L. (1996b). *Interaction in the language curriculum: Awareness, autonomy, and authenticity*. New York: Longman.

van Lier, L. (1998). Constraints and resources in classroom talk: Issues of equality and symmetry. In H. Byrnes (Ed.), *Learning foreign and second languages: Perspectives in research and scholarship* (pp. 157–182). New York: Modern Language Association of America.

van Lier, L. (2000). From input to affordance: Social-interactive learning from an ecological perspective. In J. P. Lantolf (Ed), *Sociocultural theory and second language* (pp. 245–259). Oxford: Oxford University Press.

van Lier, L. (2001). Language awareness. In R. Carter & D. Nunan (Eds.),

The Cambridge guide to teaching English to speakers of other languages (pp. 160–165). Cambridge: Cambridge University Press.

van Lier, L. (2005). Case study. In E. Hinkel (Ed.), Handbook of research in second language teaching and learning (pp. 195–208). Mahwah, N.J.: Lawrence Erlbaum Associates.

Verity, D. P. (2000). Side affects: The strategic development of professional satisfaction. In J. P. Lantolf (Ed.), Sociocultural theory and second language learning (pp. 179–197). Oxford: Oxford University Press.

Vygotsky, L. S. (1978). Mind in society. Cambridge, MA: Harvard University Press.

Vygotsky, L. S. (1986). Thought and language. Cambridge, MA: Massachusetts Institute of Technology.

Wajnryb, R. (1992). Classroom observation tasks: A resource book for language teachers and trainers. Cambridge: Cambridge University Press.

Wallace, M. J. (1998). Action research for language teachers. Cambridge: Cambridge University Press.

Walsh, S. (2006). Investigating classroom discourse. London: Routledge Taylor Francis Group.

Wang, J. (2003). Students' needs and teachers' dilemmas: A case of one university. Hong Kong Journal of Applied Linguistics, 8(1), 33–50.

Warden, M., Swain, M., Lapkin, S., & Hart, D. (1995). Adolescent language learners on a three-month exchange: Insights from their diaries. Foreign Language Annals, 28(4), 537–550.

Watson-Gegeo, K. A. (1988). Ethnography in ESL: Defining the essentials. TESOL Quarterly, 22(4), 575–592.

Weitzman, E. A., & Miles, M. B. (1995). A software sourcebook: Computer programs for qualitative data analysis. Thousand Oaks, CA: Sage.

Wesche, M. B. (1983). Communicative testing in a second language. Modern Language Journal, 67(1), 41–55.

Whyte, W. F. (1981). Street corner society: The social structure of an Italian slum (3rd ed.). Chicago: University of Chicago Press.

Wiersma, W. (1986). Research methods in education. Boston: Allyn and Bacon.

Willing, K. (1988). Learning styles in adult migrant education. Sydney: National Centre for English Language Teaching and Research.

Willing, K. (1990). Teaching how to learn. Sydney: National Centre for English Language Teaching and Research.

Winer, L. (1992). "Spinach to chocolate": Changing awareness and attitudes in ESL writing teachers. TESOL Quarterly, 26(1), 57–79.

Woodfield, H., & Lazarus, E. (1998). Diaries: A reflective tool on an INSET language course. English Language Teaching Journal, 52(4), 315–322.

Woods, D. (1989). Studying ESL teachers' decision-making: Rationale, methodological issues and initial results. Carleton Papers in Applied Language Studies, 6, 107–123.

Woods, D. (1996). Teacher cognition in language teaching: Beliefs, decision-making and classroom practice. Cambridge: Cambridge University Press.

Yahya, N. (2000). Keeping a critical eye on one's own teaching practice. EFL teachers' use of reflective teaching journals. Asian Journal of English Language Teaching, 10, 1–18.

Yin, R. (1984). Case study research: Design and methods. Beverly Hills, CA: Sage.

Yin, R. (2003). Case study research: Design and methods (3rd ed.). Thousand Oaks, CA: Sage Publishing.

Youngman, M. B. (1986). Analyzing questionnaires. Nottingham, UK: University of Nottingham, School of Education.

INDEX

Numrich, C. 296
Nunan, D. 9, 16–17, 21, 25, 27, 66, 79, 124, 148, 150, 152, 154, 161, 194, 197, 199, 201, 204, 206, 228, 231, 250, 253, 264, 269, 276, 282, 289, 291, 297, 308, 326, 328, 332–333, 342–343, 348, 361–363, 369, 416, 418, 420–423, 427, 429, 442, 444, 446, 448–450, 452, 459, 462
O'Brien, T. 462
Observation 3–4, 7, 10–11, 14–15, 33, 35, 49, 50, 57, 76–77, 87–88, 102, 161, 163, 165, 170, 173–174, 182, 186–187, 189–199, 201, 205, 211–213, 221–223, 228, 234, 255, 257– 261, 263–264, 266–270, 272–273, 275–279, 281–283, 289, 297–299, 305, 321, 325, 332–334, 365, 415, 432–434, 439–440, 447, 453, 455–457
Observation schedule (or scheme or system) 4, 11, 15, 87, 164, 212, 234, 255, 258–261, 264, 266–268, 270, 279, 339
Observer's paradox (reactivity) 196, 205, 216, 280–281, 306, 212, 234, 258, 447
O'Farrell, A. 424
Ochsner, R. 292
Ohta, A. S. 363
One-group pre-test post-test design 90, 92, 94, 100, 365, 381, 392
One-shot case study 90, 92, 94, 100–102, 158, 183, 229
Open-ended items 136–137, 140–141, 153, 155, 413, 416, 444
Operational definitions 2, 36, 41–42, 56, 63, 120, 326, 358, 363, 370, 375, 404, 413, 443, 445–446, 449, 454
Ordinal data 38–39, 108, 136, 156, 375, 381, 399, 402–403
Ordinary conversation 353
Organizing 264–265, 341, 343
Otto, F. M. 25
Outcome 7, 13–15, 19, 45–46, 56, 58, 60–62, 66, 68–69, 85, 88, 94–95, 97, 103, 117, 119–120, 158, 167, 171, 186, 203–206, 227–229, 231, 242, 247–250, 275, 279, 281, 302, 323, 359, 364, 370, 380, 391, 397, 400, 418, 440, 443, 450, 454, 457
Oxford, R. 243, 362
Palmer, A. S. 325, 335
Palmer, C. H. 295
Palmer, G. M. 295
Paradigm 11, 12, 81, 83, 170, 207, 211, 228, 292, 349–350, 438, 442, 444–445, 460
Paraphrase 22, 43, 407
Parkinson, B. 294
Participant bias factor 85

Participant observer 165, 193–195, 197, 203, 213, 219, 223–224, 259, 279
Particularization 171–172
Peck, S. 168, 294
Pennington, M. C. 296
Pennsylvania Project 25
Perecman, E. 334
Perry, F. L. 411
Peyton, J. K. 175
Phelps, E. 366
Pica, T. 24, 327, 362
Pike, K. L. 197
Piloting 87, 124, 140–141, 145
Piore, M. 437
Plummer, K. 297, 428
Polio, C. 295, 296, 461
Popper, K. 57, 174
Population 2, 44, 46–48, 53, 63–67, 70–71, 83–84, 86, 88–89, 92, 94, 98, 104–106, 110, 113–115, 124–125, 127–129, 144–145, 150, 152–153, 158, 170–172, 183, 196, 199, 207, 372, 381, 393, 413, 456
Porter, P. A. 296
Porto, 294
Post-test only control group design 98–99, 100, 380, 391
Practice effect 85, 87, 123, 192
Pre-experimental designs 100
Presenting 265, 341
Pre-test post-test control group design 99–100, 103, 380
Probability 372, 380, 384–385, 400, 410
Process studies 1, 13–14, 117, 257, 275
Production tasks 256, 312, 321, 326–327, 333
Process-product studies 1, 14, 117, 172, 257, 275, 404, 456
Product studies 1, 14, 117, 172, 257, 275, 281
Profiles 10, 432–433, 440, 455
Prompt 140, 179–180, 263, 290, 321–323, 325, 330, 345
Proof 57, 67
Proposal 18, 130, 225, 249, 338, 437, 440, 432–443, 447, 450–451, 453, 461
Prospect–a Journal of Australian TESOL 11, 119, 460
Psychometric research 6, 7, 11, 23, 46, 67, 73, 202, 230, 408, 428, 431, 438, 444
Publishing 11, 13, 16, 27, 33, 53, 75, 120, 227, 337, 364, 434–435, 447–452, 459–460
Qualitative data analysis 10–11, 19, 153, 156, 164, 179, 190, 198–199, 249, 292–293, 304, 330, 337, 359, 408, 412–436, 442, 444, 447, 456–458

Text Credits

Ch. 2: P. 31, 35, From William Wiersma & Stephen G. Jurs, *Research Methods in Education: An Introduction*, 9/e Published by Allyn and Bacon, Boston, MA. Copyright (c) 2009 by Pearson Education.

Ch. 3: P. 75, adapted from Nunan, D. 1992. *Research Methods in Language Learning*. Cambridge University Press. Reprinted with permission.

Ch. 5: P. 142, from Pamela Alrech and Robert Settle, *The Survey Research Handbook*. McGraw Hill. Copyright 1985. Reprinted with permission. P. 137–138, James Dean Brown, *Using Surveys in Language Programs*. Copyright 2001. Reprinted with the permission of Cambridge University Press.

Ch. 7: P. 190, 204, 206, adapted from Nunan, D. 1992. *Research Methods in Language Learning*. Cambridge University Press. Reprinted with permission. P. 213, adapted from Springer, S. E. (2003). Contingent language use and scaffolding in a project-based ESL course. Unpublished manuscript, Monterey Institute of International Studies, Monterey, California. Reprinted with permission.

Ch. 8: P. 88, adapted from Quirke, P. (2001). Hearing voices: A robust and flexible framework for gathering and using student feedback. In J. Edge (Ed.), *Action research* (pp. 81–91). Alexandria, VA: TESOL. Reprinted with permission. P. 75, adapted from Nunan, D. 1992. *Research Methods in Language Learning*. Cambridge University Press. Reprinted with permission. P. 231, adapted from Quirke, P. (2001). Hearing voices: A robust and flexible framework for gathering and using student feedback. In J. Edge (Ed.), *Action research* (pp. 81–91). Alexandria, VA: TESOL. Reprinted with Permission. P. 238–240, adapted from Thorpe, J. (2004). Coal miners, dirty sponges, and the search for Santa: Exploring options in teaching listening comprehension through TV news broadcasts. Unpublished manuscript, Monterey Institute of International Studies, Monterey, California. Reprinted with permission.

Ch. 9: P. 258, 273, adapted from Bailey, K. M. (2006). *Language teacher supervision: A case-based approach*. Cambridge University Press. P. 111. Reprinted with permission. P. 269, 276, adapted from Nunan, D. 1992. *Research Methods in Language Learning*. Cambridge University Press. Reprinted with permission.

Ch. 10: P. 291, adapted from Nunan, D. (1996). Hidden voices: Insiders' perspectives on classroom interaction. In K. M. Bailey & D. Nunan (Eds.), *Voices from the language classroom: Qualitative research on language education*. Cambridge University Press, p. 51. Reprinted with permission.

Ch. 11: P. 328, adapted from Martyn, E. (2001). The effects of task type on negotiation of meaning in small group work. Unpublished doctoral dissertation, University of Hong Kong, Hong Kong. Reprinted with permission. P. 328–329, 330–332, adapted from Snow, M. A., Hyland, J., Kamhi-Stein, L., & Yu, J. H. (1996). U.S. language minority students: Voices from the junior high classroom. In K. M. Bailey & D. Nunan (Eds.), *Voices from the language classroom: Qualitative research on language education* (pp. 304–317). Cambridge University Press. Reprinted with permission.

Ch. 12: P. 344–346, From McCarthy, M., and Walsh, S. Discourse. In D. Nunan *Practical English language teaching*. Copyright 2003. McGraw Hill. Reprinted by permission. P. 347–348, adapted from Nunan and Lamb 1996. *The Self-Directed Teacher*. Cambridge University Press. Reprinted with permission.

Ch.13: P. 404–406, adapted from Bejarano, Y. (1987). A cooperative small-group methodology in the language classroom. *TESOL Quarterly*, 21, 483–504. P. 492. Reprinted with Permission.

Ch. 14: P. 431, adapted from Richards, K., *Qualitative inquiry in TESOL*, 2003, Palgrave Macmillan. Reproduced with permission of Palgrave Macmillan.

Ch. 15: P. 445, adapted from On the methodological basis of introspective methods. From C. Færch & G. Kasper (Eds.), *Introspection in second language research*, 1987, Multilingual Matters/Channel View Publications. Reprinted with permission. P. 449, 459, 450, 452, adapted from Nunan, D. 1992. *Research Methods in Language Learning*. Cambridge University Press. Reprinted with permission. P. 455, adapted from Katz, A. (1996). Teaching style: A way to understand instruction in language classrooms. In K. M. Bailey & D. Nunan (Eds.), *Voices from the language classroom: Qualitative research on language education* (pp. 57–87). Cambridge University Press p. 67. Reprinted with permission.

Every effort has been made to contact holders of copyright material that appears in this book. If there are any oversights or omissions, please contact the publishers, and these will be rectified.

Heinle International Contact Information

United States
Heinle
20 Channel Center Street
Boston, MA 02210
United States
Tel: 617-289-7700
Fax: 617-289-7844

Australia / New Zealand
Tel: 61-(0)3-9685-4111
Fax: 61-(0)3-9685-4199

Brazil
Tel: (55 11) 36659931
Fax: (55 11) 36659901

Canada
Tel: 416-752-9448
Fax: 416-750-8102

China
Tel: 86-10-8286-2095
Fax: 86-10-8286-2089

Japan
Tel: 81-3-3511-4390
Fax: 81-3-3511-4391

Korea
Tel: 82-2-322-4926
Fax: 82-2-322-4927

Latin America
Tel: (52 55) 1500-6000
Fax: (52 55) 1500-6019
Toll Free: 01-800-800-3768

Singapore - Regional Headquarters
Tel: 65-6410-1200
Fax: 65-6410-1208

Taiwan
Tel: 886-2-2558-0569
Fax: 886-2-2558-0360

UK / Europe/Middle East / Africa
Tel: 44-20-7067-2667
Fax: 44-20-7067-2600

Made in the USA
San Bernardino, CA
30 January 2017